Rick Steves' ®
EASY
ACCESS
EUROPE

Rick Steves & Ken Plattner

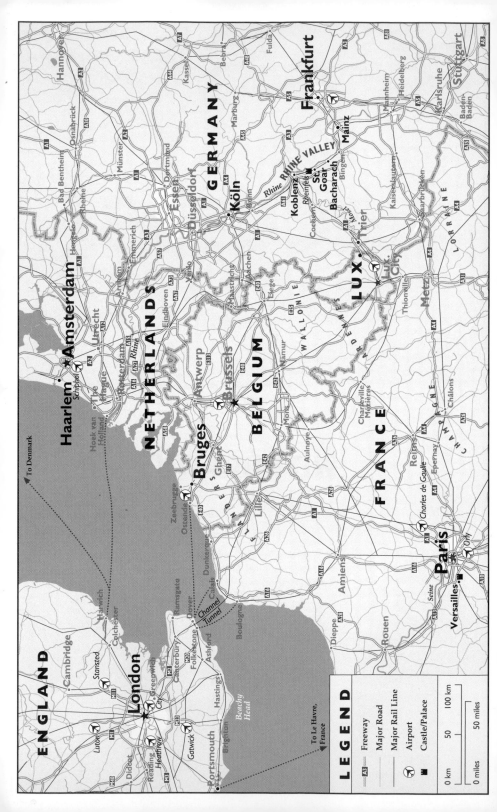

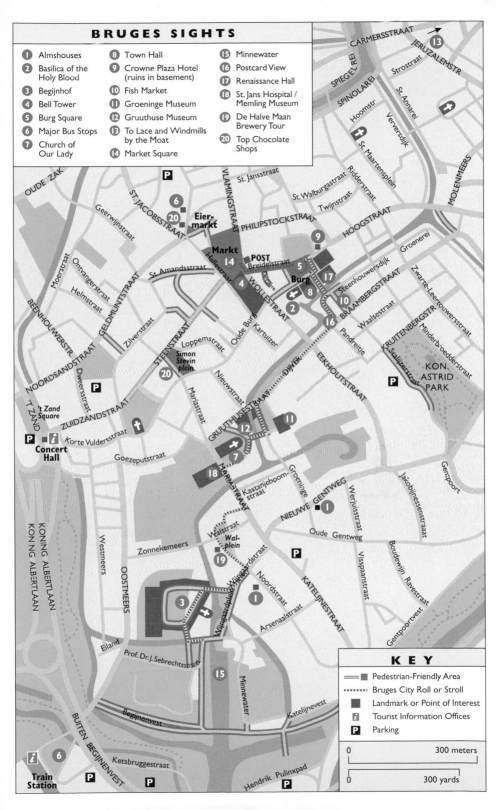

BRUGES SIGHTS

1. Almshouses
2. Basilica of the Holy Blood
3. Begijnhof
4. Bell Tower
5. Burg Square
6. Major Bus Stops
7. Church of Our Lady
8. Town Hall
9. Crowne Plaza Hotel (ruins in basement)
10. Fish Market
11. Groeninge Museum
12. Gruuthuse Museum
13. To Lace and Windmills by the Moat
14. Market Square
15. Minnewater
16. Postcard View
17. Renaissance Hall
18. St. Jans Hospital / Memling Museum
19. De Halve Maan Brewery Tour
20. Top Chocolate Shops

KEY

═══ Pedestrian-Friendly Area
········· Bruges City Roll or Stroll
■ Landmark or Point of Interest
ⓘ Tourist Information Offices
🅿 Parking

0 ——————— 300 meters

0 ——————— 300 yards

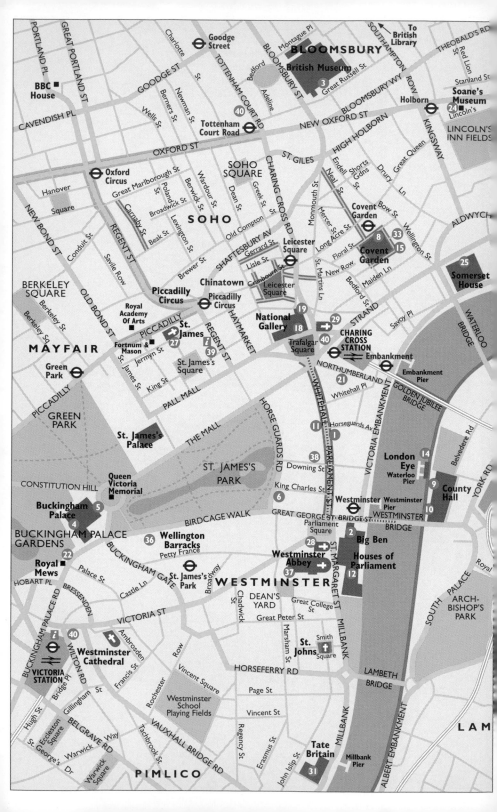

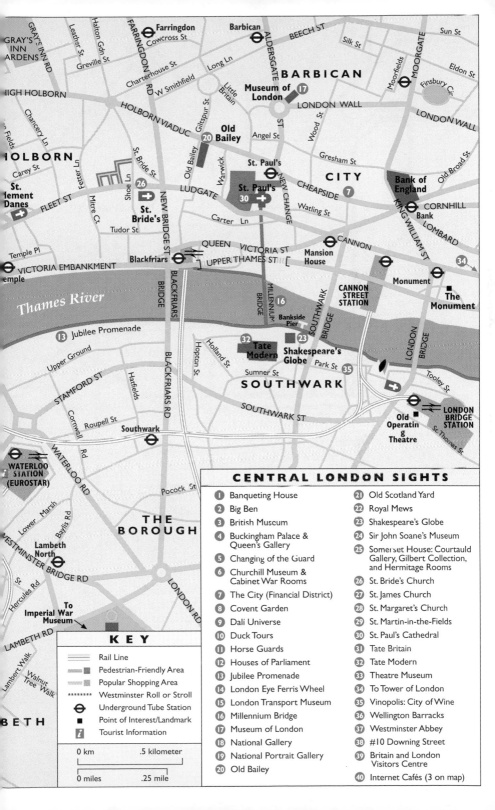

CENTRAL LONDON SIGHTS

1 Banqueting House
2 Big Ben
3 British Museum
4 Buckingham Palace & Queen's Gallery
5 Changing of the Guard
6 Churchill Museum & Cabinet War Rooms
7 The City (Financial District)
8 Covent Garden
9 Dalí Universe
10 Duck Tours
11 Horse Guards
12 Houses of Parliament
13 Jubilee Promenade
14 London Eye Ferris Wheel
15 London Transport Museum
16 Millennium Bridge
17 Museum of London
18 National Gallery
19 National Portrait Gallery
20 Old Bailey

21 Old Scotland Yard
22 Royal Mews
23 Shakespeare's Globe
24 Sir John Soane's Museum
25 Somerset House: Courtauld Gallery, Gilbert Collection, and Hermitage Rooms
26 St. Bride's Church
27 St. James Church
28 St. Margaret's Church
29 St. Martin-in-the-Fields
30 St. Paul's Cathedral
31 Tate Britain
32 Tate Modern
33 Theatre Museum
34 To Tower of London
35 Vinopolis: City of Wine
36 Wellington Barracks
37 Westminster Abbey
38 #10 Downing Street
39 Britain and London Visitors Centre
40 Internet Cafés (3 on map)

KEY

Rail Line
Pedestrian-Friendly Area
Popular Shopping Area
Westminster Roll or Stroll
Underground Tube Station
Point of Interest/Landmark
Tourist Information

0 km   .5 kilometer
0 miles   .25 mile

†Chesham
Chalfont &
Latimer
Amersham
Chorleywood
Rickmansworth
Watford
Croxley
Moor Park
Northwood
Northwood Hills
Pinner
North Harrow
West Ruislip
Hillingdon
Ruislip
Ruislip Manor
Eastcote
Harrow-
on-the-Hill
Harrow &
Wealdstone
Stanmore
Canons Park
Edgware
Burnt Oak
Colindale
Hendon Central
Uxbridge†
Ickenham
Ruislip Gardens
South Ruislip
Northolt
Rayners Lane
West Harrow
South Harrow
North Wembley
Wembley Central
Stonebridge Park
Harlesden
Northwick
Park
South Kenton
Preston
Road
Kenton
Wembley Park
Kingsbury
Queensbury
Brent Cross
Golders Green
Hampstead
Belsize Park
Chalk Farm
†Camden Town
Greenford
Perivale
Hanger Lane
Sudbury Hill
Sudbury Town
Alperton
Willesden Junction
Queen's Park
Kilburn Park
Neasden
Dollis Hill
Willesden Green
Kilburn
West
Hampstead
Finchley Road
Swiss Cottage
St. John's Wood
Kensal Green
Maida Vale
Warwick Avenue
Royal Oak
Westbourne Park
Paddington
Edgware
Road
Marylebone
Baker Street
Mornington
Crescent
Great
Portland
Street
Euston
Warren Street
Park Royal
North Ealing
Ealing Broadway
North
Acton
West
Acton
East
Acton
White
City
Ladbroke Grove
Latimer Road
Holland
Park
Bayswater
Shepherd's
Bush
Notting
Hill Gate
Lancaster
Gate
Marble
Arch
Bond
Street
Oxford
Circus
Regent's
Park
Goodge
Street
Tottenham
Court Road
Leicester
Square
Ealing Common
Acton
Town
Shepherd's
Bush
Goldhawk Road
Kensington
(Olympia)†
High Street
Kensington
Hyde Park Corner
Green
Park
Piccadilly
Circus
South Ealing
Northfields
Boston Manor
Osterley
Hounslow East
Hounslow Central
Hounslow West
Gunnersbury
Chiswick
Park
Turnham
Green▲
Stamford
Brook
Ravenscourt
Park
Hammersmith
Barons
Court
West
Kensington
Earl's
Court
Gloucester
Road
South
Kensington
Knightsbridge
Sloane
Square
St. James's
Park
Victoria
Westminster
Charing
Cross
Waterloo
Heathrow
Terminals
1, 2, 3
Hatton Cross
for Heathrow Terminal 4
Heathrow
Terminal 4†
Kew Gardens
Richmond
West Brompton
Fulham Broadway
Parsons Green
Putney Bridge
East Putney
Southfields
Wimbledon Park
Pimlico
Vauxhall
River Thames
†Kennington
Oval
Stockwell
Clapham North
Clapham Common
Clapham South
Balham
Tooting Bec
Tooting Broadway
Colliers Wood
South Wimbledon
Morden
Brixton
Wimbledon

Improvement work to tracks and stations may
affect your journey, particularly at weekends.
For help planning your journey look for
publicity at stations, call 020 7222 1234
or visit www.tfl.gov.uk

Key to symbols

🦽 A wheelchair symbol means you **can** use this
station without using stairs or escalators

🚫 Access facilities under construction

➡ An arrow means you can use this station
without using stairs or escalators **only** if you
want to catch a train going in the same
direction as the arrow is pointing

○ An empty blue circle means you might be
able to **change** trains without using stairs or
escalators (check overleaf). You will **not** be
able to get in or out of the station without
using stairs or escalators

⬤ A filled blue circle means you **cannot** catch
a train or change trains at this station **or** by
these lines without using stairs or
escalators

A pale blue station name means you **cannot** catch
a train or change trains at this station
without using stairs or escalators

≋ Accessible National Rail connection

✈ Accessible airport connection

🚋 Accessible Tramlink connection

▲ Served by Piccadilly line trains early morning
and late evening

Key to lines †Points to remember

<table>
<tr><td>Bakerloo</td><td>Special fares apply for printed single and return tickets to and from Harrow & Wealdstone</td></tr>
<tr><td>Central</td><td>No service Woodford - Hainault after 2000 daily. Queensway station will be closed for modernisation works until May 2006.</td></tr>
<tr><td>Circle</td><td>Cannon Street open until 2100 Mondays to Fridays. Open Saturdays 0730 to 1930. Closed Sundays. Due to track replacement work there will be no Circle line trains on selected weekends. Please see local publicity.</td></tr>
</table>

LONDON

District	Cannon Street open until 2100 Mondays to Fridays. Open Saturdays 0730 to 1930. Closed Sundays. Earl's Court - Kensington (Olympia) 0700 to 2345 Mondays to Saturdays, 0800 to 2345 Sundays. Due to track replacement work parts of the District line will be closed on selected weekends. Please see local publicity.
East London	Shoreditch station opens 0700 to 1030 and 1530 to 2030 Mondays to Fridays. Closed Saturdays. Open from 0700 to 1500 Sundays.

Hammersmith & City	No service Whitechapel - Barking early morning or late evening Mondays to Saturdays or all day Sundays.
Jubilee Metropolitan	Due to station improvement works at Wembley Park there will be disruptions to the service. For more information see local publicity. For Chesham change at Chalfont & Latimer on most trains.
Northern	At off-peak times most trains run to/from Morden via the Bank branch. To travel to/from the Charing Cross branch please change at Kennington. On Sundays between 1300 and 1730, Camden Town is open for interchange and exit only.

Piccadilly	No service Uxbridge - Rayners Lane in the early mornings. Heathrow Terminal 4 Underground station closed until September 2006. Replacement bus services run from Hatton Cross.
Victoria	
Waterloo & City	0615 to 2130 Mondays to Fridays. 0800 to 1830 Saturdays. Closed Sundays.
DLR	Certain stations are closed on public holidays.
≋ National Rail	

Index to Tube station access and connections

D2 ○ Acton Town (C) (A)
Connection only: District line eastbound and Piccadilly line eastbound. District line westbound and Piccadilly line westbound

D6 ○ Aldgate (B) (B)
Connection only: Circle line and terminating Metropolitan line

C7 ○ Aldgate East (A) (A)
Connection only: District line eastbound and Hammersmith & City line eastbound. District line westbound and Hammersmith & City line westbound

D7 ♿ All Saints (A) 🛗

A1 ➡ Amersham (B) ≋ (P)
Metropolitan line and National Rail southbound only

B5 ○ Archway (B)
Connection only between terminating and continuing northbound trains

C4 ○ Baker Street (B) (B)
Connection only: Bakerloo line northbound and Jubilee line northbound. Bakerloo line southbound and Jubilee line southbound

D6 ♿ Bank (A) 🛗
Docklands Light Railway only, lift located in King William Street

C9 ♿ Barking (C) EB (B) WB (C) 🛗 ≋ 🚌

B9 ⬆ Barkingside (A) (P)
Eastbound Central line only

D3 ○ Barons Court (C) (B) 🛗
Connection only: District line eastbound and Piccadilly line eastbound. District line westbound and Piccadilly line westbound

D9 ♿ Beckton (A)

D9 ♿ Beckton Park (A) 🛗

D6 ♿ Bermondsey (A) 🛗

C7 ○ Bethnal Green (B)
Connection only for reverse direction travel to Mile End for eastbound Central, District and Hammersmith & City lines

D5 ○ Blackfriars (B) (B)
Connection only: District line eastbound and Circle line eastbound. District line westbound and Circle line westbound

D8 ♿ Blackwall (A) 🛗

E5 ⬆ Borough (B) 🛗
Northern line northbound only

C8 ♿ Bow Church (A) 🛗 small

F5 ♿ Brixton (B) 🛗

B6 ♿ Caledonian Road (B) 🛗

B5 ○ Camden Town (B)
Connection only: Northern line northbound (Barnet/Mill Hill East services) and Northern line northbound (Edgware branch service)

D7 ♿ Canada Water (A) (A) 🛗 🚌

D8 ♿ Canary Wharf (A) (A) 🛗 WC (ticket hall)
200 metres between Jubilee line and DLR

D8 ○ Canning Town (A) (A) 🛗 🚌 ✈ (via bus)

A3 ○ Canons Park (B)
Connection only between terminating and continuing northbound trains

A1 ♿ Chalfont & Latimer (C) ≋ (P)

A1 ♿ Chesham (B) (P)

A1 ♿ Chorleywood (B) SB (C) NB (P)

F5 ○ Clapham North (B)
Connection only for reverse direction Northern line travel to Borough from London Bridge

E8 ♿ Crossharbour & London Arena (A) 🛗 small

D8 ♿ Custom House (A) 🛗

E8 ♿ Cutty Sark (A) 🛗

D9 ♿ Cyprus (A) 🛗

B9 ○ Dagenham East (B)
Connection only between terminating and continuing eastbound trains

B9 ♿ Dagenham Heathway (C)

A8 ⬆ Debden (A) (P)
Central line eastbound only, connection between terminating and continuing eastbound trains

E8 ♿ Deptford Bridge (A) 🛗

D8 ♿ Devons Road (A) 🛗 small

C1 ○ Ealing Broadway
(C) Platform 9 (B) Platforms 7&8 ≋
Connection only between Central and District lines and National Rail eastbound (for Paddington)

D2 ○ Ealing Common (A) (C)
Connection only: District line eastbound and Piccadilly line eastbound. District line westbound and Piccadilly line westbound

D3 ♿ Earl's Court (B) (B) 🛗
District and Piccadilly lines accessible

C8 ♿ East Ham (C) (C) 🛗

D8 ♿ East India (A) 🛗

C4 ○ Edgware Road (B) (B)
Connection only: Circle line eastbound and Hammersmith & City line eastbound. Circle line westbound and Hammersmith & City line westbound

B9 ♿ Elm Park (C)

E8 ♿ Elverson Road (A)

D5 ○ Embankment (B) (B)
Connection only: Circle line eastbound and District line eastbound. Circle line westbound and District line westbound

A8 ♿ Epping (A)
Full accessibility to platform 2 only

C5 ○ Euston (B) (B)
Connection only: Victoria line northbound and Northern line (Bank Branch) northbound. Victoria line southbound and Northern line (Bank Branch) southbound

A5 ○ Finchley Central (B) (P)
Connection only between Northern line (Barnet service) northbound and Northern line (Mill Hill East service) northbound

B4 ○ **Finchley Road** Ⓑ EB Ⓐ WB Ⓒ
Connection only: Metropolitan line northbound and Jubilee line northbound. Metropolitan line southbound and Jubilee line southbound

B6 ○ **Finsbury Park** Ⓑ Ⓑ
Connection only: Victoria line northbound and Piccadilly line northbound. Victoria line southbound and Piccadilly line southbound

E3 🚋 **Fulham Broadway** Ⓒ EB Ⓐ WB ⬆

D9 🚋 **Gallions Reach** Ⓐ ⬆

D3 ○ **Gloucester Road** Ⓑ Ⓑ
Connection only between District line eastbound and Circle line

B1 ○ **Greenford** ⇌

E8 🚋 **Greenwich** Ⓐ ⇌ ⬆

D4 ○ **Green Park** Ⓑ Ⓑ ⬆
Connection only between Piccadilly and Jubilee lines. Long walkway between lifts

A9 ○ **Hainault** Ⓒ 🅿
Connection only between terminating eastbound or starting westbound (certain trains only)

D3 ○ **Hammersmith** Ⓑ EB Ⓒ WB 🄱 Ⓒ ⬆ 🄸 🔄
WC (shopping mall)
Long distance between District and Piccadilly lines and Hammersmith & City line via street

A3 🚋 **Harrow & Wealdstone** Ⓒ ⇌ ⬆

B2 🚋 **Harrow-on-the-Hill** Ⓑ 🅿
Connection only between fast, semi-fast and 'all stations' Metropolitan line services

E1 🚋 **Heathrow Terminals 1, 2, 3** Ⓑ ⬆ ✈ 🄸 🔄
WC (airport)
Lift on request. Long subway or travalator between terminals and booking hall

E1 🚋 **Heathrow Terminal 4** Ⓑ ⬆ ✈ 🄸
WC (airport)
Closed until September 2006

D8 🚋 **Heron Quays** Ⓐ ⬆

B6 ○ **Highbury & Islington** Ⓑ ⇌
Connection only: Victoria line northbound and National Rail (WAGN) northbound. Victoria line southbound and National Rail southbound

A1 🚋 **Hillingdon** Ⓒ Ⓐ ⬆ 🅿

D1 🚋 **Hounslow East** Ⓐ
Piccadilly line westbound only

E1 🚋 **Hounslow West** Ⓑ

E8 🚋 **Island Gardens** Ⓐ ⬆

E5 ○ **Kennington** Ⓑ
Connection only between terminating and continuing southbound trains

D3 🚋 **Kensington (Olympia)** Ⓑ ⇌
Open 0700 to 2345 Mondays to Saturdays and 0800 to 2345 Sundays

E2 🚋 **Kew Gardens** Ⓒ EB Ⓑ WB ⇌

B4 🚋 **Kilburn** Ⓐ NB Ⓑ SB

C5 ○ **King's Cross St. Pancras** Ⓑ Ⓑ Ⓑ
Connection only between Hammersmith & City, Circle and Metropolitan lines

E8 🚋 **Lewisham** Ⓐ ⬆ ⇌ 🔄

B8 ○ **Leytonstone** Ⓐ
Connection only from Central line eastbound Epping branch to trains via Hainault (for Barkingside)

D7 🚋 **Limehouse** Ⓐ ⬆ small

C6 ➔ **Liverpool Street** Ⓑ Ⓑ Ⓑ ⇌ ⬆ 🄸
WC (National Rail concourse)
Accessible Circle, Metropolitan and Hammersmith & City lines eastbound only. Long distance to National Rail via lift. Connection only between westbound Circle, Metropolitan and Hammersmith & City lines

D6 🚋 **London Bridge** Ⓐ Ⓑ ⇌ ⬆ 🔄
WC (National Rail concourse)
Long distances between Northern line, Jubilee line and National Rail via street

A8 ○ **Loughton** Ⓑ
Connection only between terminating and continuing eastbound trains

D5 ○ **Mansion House** Ⓑ Ⓑ
Connection only: Circle line eastbound and District line eastbound (non-terminating). Circle line westbound and District line westbound

C7 ○ **Mile End** Ⓑ Ⓑ Ⓑ
Connection only: District line, Hammersmith & City line and Central line eastbound. District line, Hammersmith & City line and Central line westbound

D6 ○ **Monument** Ⓑ Ⓑ
Connection only: Circle line eastbound and District line eastbound. Circle line westbound and District line westbound

C6 ○ **Moorgate** Ⓑ Ⓑ Ⓑ
Connection only: Hammersmith & City line eastbound, Circle line eastbound and Metropolitan line eastbound. Hammersmith & City line westbound, Circle line westbound and Metropolitan line westbound

E8 🚋 **Mudchute** Ⓐ

B3 ○ **Neasden** Ⓒ
Connection only for reverse direction travel to Wembley Park from Stanmore for northbound Metropolitan line. Also connection between terminating and continuing northbound trains

E7 ➔ **New Cross** Ⓒ ⇌
East London line and southbound National Rail only

C2 ○ **North Acton** Ⓒ
Connection only between terminating and continuing westbound trains

D1 ○ **Northfields** Ⓑ
Connection only between terminating and continuing westbound trains

D8 🚋 **North Greenwich** Ⓐ ⬆ WC (ticket hall)

B3 ○ **Northwick Park** Ⓑ
Connection only for reverse direction travel between Amersham, Chesham and Uxbridge

Index to Tube station access and connections

C3 ◯ **White City** Ⓑ
Connection only between terminating and
continuing westbound trains

B3 ◯ **Willesden Green** ⦿Ⓑ
Connection only between terminating and
continuing northbound trains

B3 ⊖ **Willesden Junction** Ⓒ⇌🛗
F3 ⊖ **Wimbledon** Ⓑ⇌🛗🚋⊖Ⓟ
A8 ⊖ **Woodford** Ⓐ Ⓟ
A5 ⊖ **Woodside Park** ⊕SB ⒶNB Ⓟ

Key to index

Platform to train step
Colour of circle indicates line

Ⓐ Level to 100mm (4 inches)

Ⓑ 100 to 200mm (4 to 8 inches)

Ⓒ 200 to 300mm (8 to 12 inches)

⁻Ⓐ Minus figures indicate a step down
into the train

NB Platform to train measurements indicate
the step height only. There may also
be a significant gap. See 'Access to the
Underground' for more detail

Abbreviations

EB Eastbound   WB Westbound
NB Northbound   SB Southbound

Explanation of symbols

⊖ Step-free access to platforms

⊘ Access facilities under construction

⊖ Step-free access to platforms in one
direction only

◯ Some step-free access between connections.
Entry and exit not accessible. Always check
the index for details

🛗 Access via lift(s). Limited capacity
(8 to 12 persons) indicated by 'small'

⇌ Accessible National Rail connections

🚌 Accessible station with major bus connections

🚋 Accessible connection to Tramlink

✈ Accessible airport connection

Ⓟ Accessible station with car park

WC Accessible station with toilet on site
or nearby (you must have a valid ticket to
use toilets in a Compulsory Ticket Area)

ℹ Accessible station with Transport for London
Travel Information Centre

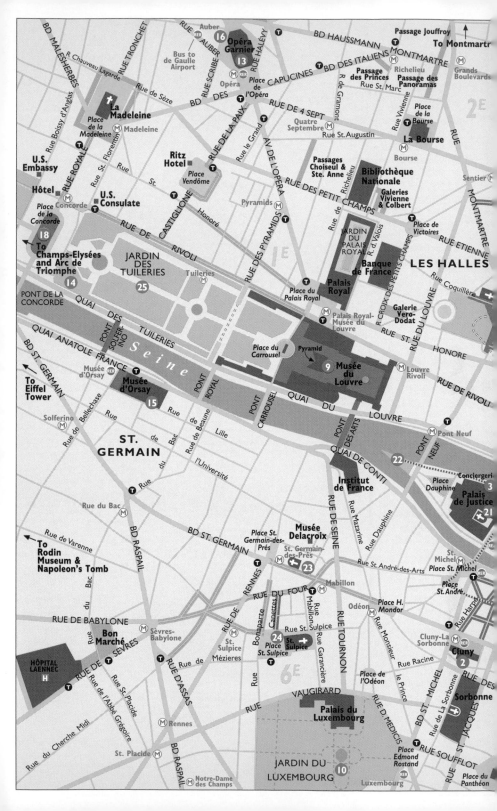

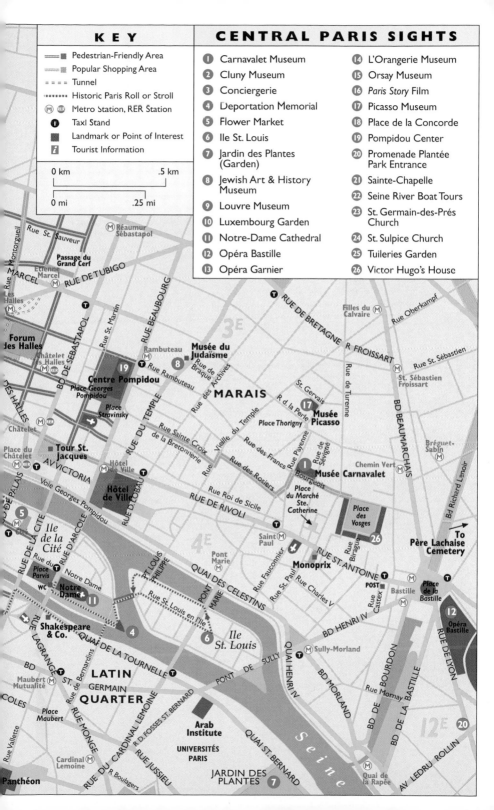

K E Y

- ▬▬■ Pedestrian-Friendly Area
- ▬▬■ Popular Shopping Area
- = = = = Tunnel
- •••••• Historic Paris Roll or Stroll
- Ⓜ ⓇⒺⓇ Metro Station, RER Station
- ❶ Taxi Stand
- ■ Landmark or Point of Interest
- 🅸 Tourist Information

0 km — .5 km

0 mi — .25 mi

CENTRAL PARIS SIGHTS

- ❶ Carnavalet Museum
- ❷ Cluny Museum
- ❸ Conciergerie
- ❹ Deportation Memorial
- ❺ Flower Market
- ❻ Ile St. Louis
- ❼ Jardin des Plantes (Garden)
- ❽ Jewish Art & History Museum
- ❾ Louvre Museum
- ❿ Luxembourg Garden
- ⓫ Notre-Dame Cathedral
- ⓬ Opéra Bastille
- ⓭ Opéra Garnier
- ⓮ L'Orangerie Museum
- ⓯ Orsay Museum
- ⓰ *Paris Story* Film
- ⓱ Picasso Museum
- ⓲ Place de la Concorde
- ⓳ Pompidou Center
- ⓴ Promenade Plantée Park Entrance
- ㉑ Sainte-Chapelle
- ㉒ Seine River Boat Tours
- ㉓ St. Germain-des-Prés Church
- ㉔ St. Sulpice Church
- ㉕ Tuileries Garden
- ㉖ Victor Hugo's House

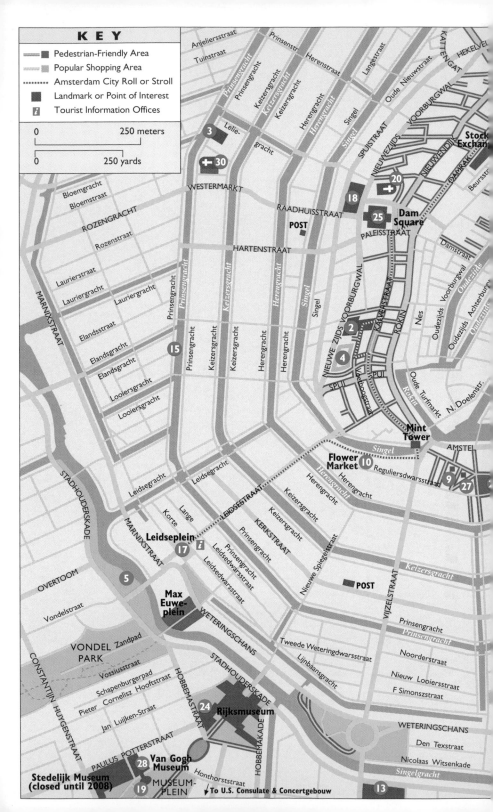

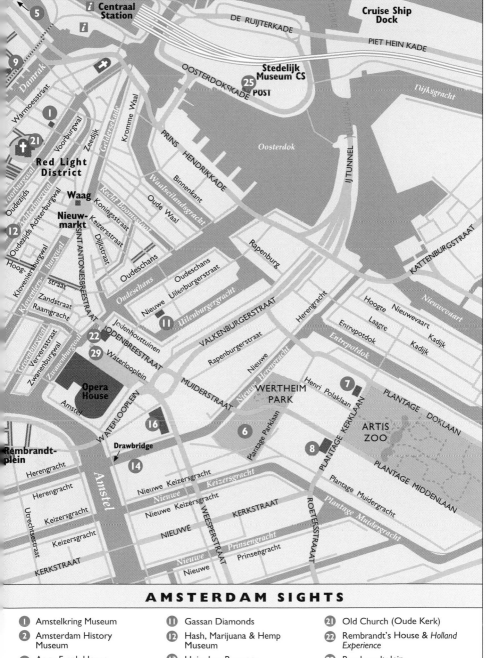

AMSTERDAM SIGHTS

Rick Steves'
EASY ACCESS EUROPE

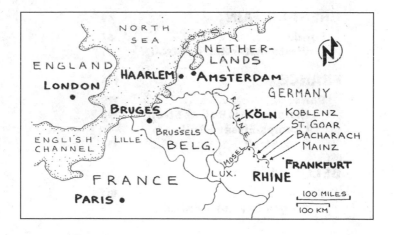

AVALON
TRAVEL

CONTENTS

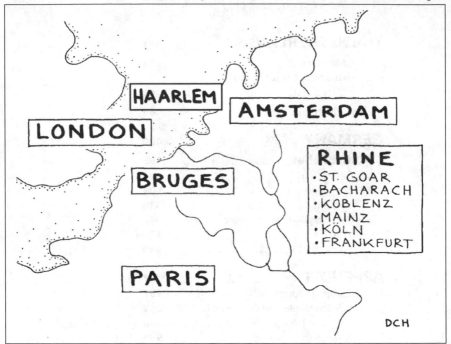

FOREWORD
By Susan Sygall, Executive Director of Mobility International USA

In my 30 years of international travel, I have found there are few things in life as exhilarating as visiting and exploring another culture. I've been traveling the Rick Steves way since 1973, and being a wheelchair rider has not held me back one bit. I was thrilled to be asked to write this foreword, since my most enriching experiences abroad have often been off the beaten path. As a person with a disability, you are almost guaranteed one thing: You will never have an ordinary day.

I cherish my memories of traveling in Europe. I spent a month traveling with no plans or reservations throughout Italy, hopping on different trains and staying in both accessible and inaccessible hotels. I spoke to strangers in my makeshift Italian and flew down a hill in my wheelchair in Tuscany—to the surprise of whizzing cars—while inhaling the fragrant smells of the vineyards and cows.

I was welcomed and befriended by strangers. I was also thrown out of restaurants and left in the rain with flat tires in the middle of a big city. I volunteered for a community service project with 15 other folks from across Europe, sleeping on the floor in a sleeping bag and cooking our dinner of simple boiled potatoes while discussing international politics. I skied using adaptive equipment with other disabled people, and I bicycled and camped for several weeks in Holland and France using an adapted bicycle—with my wheelchair (and camping gear) in tow.

Europe is an enchanting place to visit. Where else can you be surrounded by some of the world's most spectacular art and architecture? Where better to dine on fabulous food and experience a slower pace, where sitting for hours at an outdoor café with a cappuccino and rich chocolate dessert is a way of life? I love the excitement of large cities, where you can see an original painting by van Gogh or Chagall. But I'm often drawn to the smaller villages and towns, where pungent cheese and fresh bread from the local bakery, or a picnic lunch surrounded by farmland and snowcapped mountains, make memories that continue to refresh and renew me long after I have returned home to my busy life. This book gives you the detailed information to make those life-changing experiences possible, and perhaps a bit easier.

As more people with disabilities enjoy the *real* Europe, they'll also be drawn to other non-traditional travel. Mobility International USA (www.miusa.org) and our National Clearinghouse on Disability and Exchange (NCDE) promote international exchange opportunities for people with disabilities, including study, volunteer, teaching, and internships abroad. An opportunity to live and learn alongside European people may significantly increase the value of your trip, and may also make it more affordable. (For more information, see page 32.)

As more civil rights legislation emerges in Europe and throughout the world, people with disabilities can look forward to a future of greater accessibility wherever we travel. We will undoubtedly be frustrated at times by the lack of access, but it is important that we do not internalize those feelings. Our frustration should be placed on the fact that people with disabilities have not yet achieved our human right to full access. Your travel experiences can become a positive force for changing the world, for fellow travelers as well as the people with disabilities who live in the countries that you explore—who also want access to hotels, restaurants, historical landmarks, theaters, and campgrounds.

I know that you will enjoy this rich, well-researched book, which offers a rare combination of detailed information on accessibility with true local flavor. In the future, when all guidebooks include accessibility information as a standard feature, *Easy Access Europe* will be a welcome supplement.

Whether you travel alone, in a group of friends or family, or with a personal assistant, this book will assist you in exploring your European dreams. It is up to you to choose your own travel style, how much accessibility you require, and the type of experience you want to have. Use this book as a guide, but don't stop yourself from pursuing whatever wild idea you have. Be safe, be smart, have fun—and through your travels, make this world a better place for all people.

INTRODUCTION

Until now, wheelchair users and slow walkers have not had a resource—designed just for them—to guide them through Europe's highlights. The creaky, cobblestoned Old World has long had a reputation for poor accessibility. But in recent years, Europe has been making impressive advances toward opening its doors to everybody, including travelers with limited mobility. Maybe you're a wheelchair user with an adventurous spirit. Or perhaps you're traveling with a loved one who has limited mobility. Or you simply don't get around as well as you used to, but your sense of wanderlust refuses that rocking chair. This book is written for you.

Easy Access Europe

Since writing my first guidebook in 1980, my mission has been to make Europe accessible. Until now, my books have focused on *economic* accessibility—travel needn't be a rich person's hobby. With this book, I broaden that passion to include *physical* accessibility.

I've teamed up with a committed band of researchers—led by Ken Plattner—who care about those who face extra physical challenges. Ken, a therapist, has a long and impressive track record of reaching out to people with disabilities. Together, we've written this book to help guide slow walkers and wheelchair users through Europe.

I picked a handful of Europe's best and most accessible destinations: London, Paris, Bruges, Amsterdam, and Germany's Rhine River Valley. Using core material from my existing guidebooks (the most carefully updated books available), Ken and his helpers researched everything one more time for accessibility.

Ken, our researchers, and I do not have disabilities. Even so, whenever possible, a person using a wheelchair accompanied the research team to help us make a completely accurate assessment of accessibility. This also allowed us to experience firsthand the way wheelchair users are treated at each place.

Like an additional fermentation turns a good wine into fine champagne, this second research trip was designed to bring our Easy Access travelers a smooth and bubbly experience.

For simplicity, from this point on, all of us who worked on this book will shed our respective egos and become "I."

ACCESSIBILITY IN EUROPE

Let's face it: Compared to the U.S., Europe is not very accessible. It's the very charm of Europe—old, well-preserved, diverse, and very different from home—that often adds to the barriers. Many merchants, museum curators, hoteliers, and restaurateurs don't care about accessibility. My challenge is to find and describe the places that are welcoming and properly equipped.

This sounds pessimistic. But I'm inspired by the fact that, wherever I go in Europe, I see locals who have disabilities. The days of "hiding disability" are over: On the streets, in the museums, in the restaurants, and on the trains, you'll see people using wheelchairs, scooters, walkers, canes, and walking umbrellas to get around. If they can live rich and full lives in Europe, then you can certainly have an enjoyable and worthwhile vacation there. It's a new world out there, and anyone with adventure in their soul can take advantage of all Europe has to offer.

I know levels of personal mobility vary tremendously from person to person. You need to consider your own situation very thoughtfully in choosing which attractions to visit, which hotels to sleep at, which restaurants to dine at...and which things you might want to avoid. I'm not here to tell you what you can and can't do. Instead, I'll give you a thorough description of each sight, hotel, and restaurant to help you make informed decisions for yourself.

I've come up with various ways of letting you know what accessibility features you can expect at each building. Most important are

Accessibility Levels and Accessibility Codes.

Adapted vs. Suitable

Throughout this book, I use two very different terms to describe buildings and facilities that can be used by wheelchair riders: *adapted* and *suitable*.

An **adapted** building has been designed or retrofitted specifically for the use of people who use wheelchairs. For example, an adapted bathroom has wide doors, a roll-in shower, a specially adapted sink that can easily be accessed by a wheelchair user, and grab bars to facilitate toilet transfers.

A **suitable** building has not been specifically designed for wheelchair users, but it can still be used by people with limited mobility—that is, wheelchair users who have a greater degree of mobility (can make transfers or walk a few steps without assistance), or wheelchair users with a lesser degree of mobility who have assistance. For example, a suitable bathroom has wide enough doors for a person in a wheelchair to enter, and enough space inside to negotiate the wheelchair—but it does *not* have specially adapted toilets, sinks, or showers (for instance, no grab bars to help with transfers).

In Europe, most buildings are suitable, rather than adapted.

Accessibility Levels

This book rates sights, hotels, and restaurants using four levels, each one representing a different degree of accessibility. Determine which of these levels matches your own level of personal mobility, then use the levels as a shortcut for deciding which buildings are accessible to you.

Level 1—Fully Accessible: A Level 1 building is completely barrier-free. Entryways, elevators, and other facilities are specifically adapted to accommodate a person using a wheelchair. If there's a bathroom, it has wide doors and an adapted toilet and sink. Where applicable, the bathing facilities are also fully adapted (including such features as bath boards, grab bars, or a roll-in, no-rim shower). Fully adapted hotel rooms often have an alarm system with pull cords for emergencies. Level 1 properties are rare in Europe.

Level 2—Moderately Accessible: A Level 2 building is suitable for, but not specifically adapted to accommodate, a person using a wheelchair. This level will generally work for a wheelchair user who can make transfers and take a few steps. A person who is permanently in a wheelchair may require some assistance here (either from a companion or from staff).

Accessibility Codes

To provide more specific information on exactly what accessibility features each building has, I use a series of easy-to-understand symbols. These accessibility codes are intended to give you a quick overview of what to expect. If applicable, more specific details about the facility (e.g., exact number and height of steps, special instructions for gaining entry) are also explained in the listing.

Code	Meaning	Explanation
AE	Accessible Entryway	A level entryway with no steps or barriers and a door wide enough for an independent wheelchair user.
AE+A	Accessible Entry with Assistance	An entryway with one or two small steps and a door wide enough for a wheelchair user.
AI	Accessible Interior	A flat, spacious, barrier-free interior with enough room to comfortably negotiate a wheelchair.
AI+A	Accessible Interior with Assistance	An interior that has enough room to negotiate a wheelchair, but is not barrier-free (e.g., a few steps, narrow doors, tight aisles, and so on).
AT	Accessible Toilet	The toilet is at an appropriate height and has grab bars to allow the wheelchair user to transfer without assistance.
AT+A	Accessible Toilet with Assistance	A toilet that is suitable for a wheelchair user, but is not specifically adapted. Wheelchair users will likely need assistance.
AL	Accessible Lift (elevator)	An elevator big enough to be used by an independent wheelchair user.
AL+A	Accessible Lift with Assistance	An elevator that is small or presents other barriers to the wheelchair user, who will require assistance.
AR	Accessible Room	A hotel room big enough for a wheelchair to move around freely. There are

		no barriers to impede independent wheelchair users.
AR+A	Accessible Room with Assistance	A hotel room that is cramped and not barrier-free, but suitable for a wheelchair user who has assistance.
AB	Accessible Bathroom	A hotel bathroom specially adapted for wheelchair users, with wide entry doors, grab bars throughout, raised toilet, adapted sink, and adapted bathtub or roll-in shower.
AB+A	Accessible Bathroom with Assistance	The door is wide enough for wheelchair entry, but the wheelchair user will require some assistance to transfer to the tub or toilet (no grab bars).
♥	Heart	An establishment that has a positive, helpful attitude toward travelers with limited mobility.

Note that to receive a ♥ rating, a business must be welcoming to our wheelchair-using researcher upon arrival, and demonstrate a willingness to accommodate the wheelchair user's needs. One caveat about this rating: I assume that if one representative of the business treated our researcher well, others will also—but it's possible that you may have a different experience. (If this is the case, please send me an e-mail at rick@ricksteves.com. Thanks.)

So, for example, imagine a restaurant with one 8" entry step, a spacious and fully accessible interior, toilets that are down a narrow winding stairway of ten 6" steps, and a staff that is warm and welcoming. This place would be coded as: **AE+A, AI, ♥,** Level 2—Moderately Accessible.

Now imagine a hotel that is fully accessible, with no barriers at the entry or inside; a wheelchair-accessible elevator; and a specially adapted room and bathroom designed for wheelchair users. That hotel would be coded as: **AE, AI, AL, AR, AB,** Level 1—Fully Accessible.

Level 3—Minimally Accessible: A Level 3 building is satisfactory for people who have minimal mobility difficulties (that is, people who usually do not use a wheelchair, but take more time to do things than a non-disabled person). This building may have some steps and a few other barriers—but not too many. Level 3 buildings are best suited to slow walkers; wheelchair users will require substantial assistance here.

Level 4—Not Accessible: Unfortunately, some places in this book are simply not accessible to people with limited mobility. This means that barriers such as staircases, tight interiors and facilities (elevators, bathrooms, etc.), or other impediments interfere with passage for travelers with disabilities. Buildings in this category might include a church tower that is reachable only by climbing several flights of steep stairs, or a museum interior that has many levels with lots of steps and no elevator. I've included a few Level 4 buildings in this book, either because they are important to know about, or because the information might be useful to a non-disabled companion or to readers with limited mobility, but an adventurous spirit (such as slow walkers who can climb several flights of stairs, if given enough time, to reach a worthwhile sight).

Just because a building is Minimally Accessible or Not Accessible doesn't necessarily mean it's completely off-limits to a traveler with limited mobility. Many buildings in Europe are constrained by centuries-old construction, so Europeans have come to excel at finding ways to help you get past barriers. If you ask for assistance, a merchant or friendly passer-by will, more than likely, eagerly help you turn "Not Accessible" into "Definitely Possible."

ABOUT THIS BOOK

The **Accessibility Resources and Tips** chapter includes an array of disability organizations, books, and other resources to help you plan a smooth trip, and contains tips from experienced travelers with limited mobility.

The **Country Introductions** give you a snapshot of each country's culture and include country-specific resources for accessible travel.

Each destination in this book is covered as a mini-vacation on its own, filled with exciting sights and homey, accessible, and affordable places to stay. Using the levels and codes described above, this book provides detailed information on accessibility for sights, restaurants, hotels, tourist offices, public transportation, and so on. In the following chapters, you'll find these elements:

Accessibility gives you an overview of what kind of access concerns you can expect.

Orientation includes tourist information, city transportation, and an easy-to-read map designed to make the text clear and your arrival smooth.

Sights are rated: ▲▲▲—Don't miss; ▲▲—Try hard to see; ▲—Worthwhile if you can make it; no rating—Worth knowing about.

Sleeping and **Eating** include descriptions (including accessibility details, addresses, and phone numbers) of my favorite hotels and restaurants.

Transportation Connections covers how to reach nearby destinations by train, bus, or taxi, with a focus on only the most accessible options.

Roll or Stroll chapters offer self-guided tours of Europe's most interesting neighborhoods, while thoroughly describing each destination's accessibility and top sights.

The **Appendix** is a traveler's tool kit, with a list of national tourist offices and U.S. embassies, telephone tips, and a climate chart.

Browse through this book, choose your favorite destinations, and link them up. Then have a great trip! You'll travel like a temporary local, getting the absolute most out of every mile, minute, and dollar. As you travel the route I know and love, I'm happy you'll be meeting some of my favorite Europeans.

PLANNING

Trip Costs

Five components make up your trip cost: airfare, surface transportation, room and board, sightseeing/entertainment, and shopping/miscellany.

Airfare: Don't try to sort through the mess yourself. Get and use a good travel agent. A basic round-trip U.S.A.-to-Europe flight should cost $500 to $1,100 (even cheaper in winter), depending on where you fly from and when. Always consider saving time and money in Europe by flying "open-jaw" (flying into one city and out of another, such as flying into London and out of Frankfurt).

Surface Transportation: Your best mode depends upon accessibility concerns, the time you have, and the scope of your trip.

Trains are often—but not always—moderately accessible or better, and conveniently connect the big cities in this book (especially London and Paris, just 2.75 hours apart by Eurostar train). If you go by train, consider a Eurail Selectpass (see page 21). Train passes are normally available only outside of Europe. You may save money by simply buying tickets as you go.

Renting a **car** has its advantages. Most major car-rental agencies have specially adapted vehicles. Though struggling with traffic and parking can be stressful—especially in the big cities covered in this book—having your own adapted rental car means that you don't have to rely on public transportation. Drivers can figure $300 per person per week (based on 2 people splitting the cost of the car, tolls, gas, and insurance). Car rental is cheapest to arrange from the United States. Leasing, for trips longer than three weeks, is even cheaper.

When it comes to mobility, **taxis** are the great equalizer. Budget a little extra to get around in cities by taxi.

Room and Board: You can manage just fine in Europe on an average of $100 a day per person for room and board (more for cities, less for towns). A $100-per-day budget allows $10 for lunch, $15 for dinner, $5 for snacks, and $70 for lodging (based on 2 people splitting a $140 double room that includes breakfast). Note that London is a bit more expensive than the other destinations in this book (allow $120 per day in London).

Sightseeing and Entertainment: In big cities, figure $6 to $12 per major sight, $2 to $5 for minor ones, and $30 for splurge experiences (e.g., bus tours, concerts, and plays). If you use a wheelchair, you (or your travel partner) will get in free at many attractions—I've listed which ones in this book. An overall average of $15 a day works for most. Don't skimp here. After all, this category directly powers most of the experiences all the other expenses are designed to make possible.

Shopping and Miscellany: Figure $1 per postcard and $2 per coffee, beer, and ice-cream cone. Shopping can vary in cost from nearly nothing to a small fortune. Good budget travelers find that this category has little to do with assembling a trip full of lifelong and wonderful memories.

When to Go

May, June, September, and October are the best travel months. Peak season (July and August) offers the sunniest weather and the most exciting slate of activities, but the worst crowds. Because it's also the most physically grueling time to travel, many travelers with limited mobility prefer to visit outside of summer.

Off-season, October through April, expect generally shorter hours at attractions, more lunchtime breaks, fewer activities, and fewer guided tours in English. If you're traveling off-season, be careful to confirm opening times. In winter, I like to set up for a full week in a big city

Sightseeing Priorities

This book covers northern Europe's top destinations, which could be lined up for a quick one-week getaway or a full-blown three-week vacation. Combining London and Paris with the speedy Eurostar train offers perhaps the most exciting 10 days of big-city thrills Europe has to offer.

Of course, you should arrange your itinerary according to your own level of mobility—building in as much rest as you need. But for a relatively fast-paced tour of the destinations in this book, consider this plan:

Day	Plan	Sleep in
1	Arrive in London	London
2	London	London
3	London	London
4	London	London
5	Eurostar to Paris	Paris
6	Paris	Paris
7	Paris	Paris
8	Paris	Paris
9	To Bruges	Bruges
10	Bruges	Bruges
11	Bruges	Bruges
12	To Amsterdam	Amsterdam
13	Amsterdam	Amsterdam
14	Amsterdam	Amsterdam
15	To Köln, then Rhine	Rhine
16	Rhine	Rhine
17	To Frankfurt	Frankfurt
18	Fly home	

(like Paris or London) to take advantage of fewer crowds and a cultural calendar in full swing.

As a general rule of thumb any time of year, the climate north of the Alps is mild (like Seattle), and south of the Alps, it's like Arizona. For specifics, check the climate chart in the appendix.

Travel Smart

Your trip to Europe is like a complex play—easier to follow and really appreciate on a second viewing. While no one does the same trip twice to gain that advantage, reading this book before your trip accomplishes much the same thing.

Design an itinerary that enables you to hit the museums on the right days. As you read through this book, note special days (such as festivals and colorful market days). Anticipate problem days: Mondays are bad in Bruges, Tuesdays are bad in Paris. Anywhere in Europe, Saturday morning feels like any bustling weekday morning, but at lunchtime, many shops close down. Sundays have pros and cons, as they do for travelers in the U.S. (special events, limited hours, shops and banks closed, limited public transportation, no rush hours). Popular places are even more popular on weekends. Museums and sights, especially large ones, usually stop admitting people 30 to 60 minutes before closing time.

Plan ahead for laundry, Internet stops, and picnics. To maximize rootedness, minimize one-night stands. Mix intense and relaxed periods. Every trip (and every traveler) needs at least a few slack days. Pace yourself. Assume you will return.

Reread entire chapters as you travel, and visit local tourist information offices. Upon arrival in a new town, lay the groundwork for a smooth departure. Buy a phone card and use it for reservations and confirmations. Enjoy the friendliness of the local people. Ask questions. Most locals are eager to point you in their idea of the right direction. Wear your money belt, pack along a pocket-size notebook to organize your thoughts, and practice the virtue of simplicity. Those who expect to travel smart, do.

RESOURCES

Tourist Information Offices
In the U.S.
Each country has a national tourist office in the U.S. These offices are a wealth of information (see the appendix for addresses). Before your trip, you can ask for the free general-information packet and for specific information (such as city maps and schedules of upcoming festivals). Most offices also have information for travelers with limited mobility.

In Europe
The tourist information office is your best first stop in any new town or city. In this book, I'll refer to a tourist information office as a **TI**. Have a list of questions and a proposed sightseeing plan to confirm. If you're arriving late, telephone ahead (and try to get a map for your next destination from a TI in the town you're leaving). Throughout Europe, you'll find TIs are usually well-organized and English-speaking.

As national budgets tighten, many TIs have been privatized. This means they become sales agents for big tours and hotels, and their "information" becomes unavoidably colored. While TIs are eager to book you a room, you should use their room-finding service only as a last resort. TIs can as easily book you a bad room as a good one—they are not allowed to promote one place over another. Go direct, using the listings in this book.

Rick Steves' Guidebooks, Public Television Show, and Radio Show

While my other guidebooks are written for a general audience—and are not mobility-specific—they may be helpful in your travels.

Rick Steves' Europe Through the Back Door gives you budget-travel skills, such as minimizing jet lag, packing light, planning your itinerary, traveling by car or train, finding rooms, changing money, avoiding rip-offs, buying a mobile phone, hurdling the language barrier, staying healthy, taking great photographs, using a bidet, and much more. The book also includes chapters on 38 of my favorite "Back Doors."

Country Guides: These annually updated books offer you the latest on the top sights and destinations, with tips on how to make your trip efficient and fun:

Rick Steves' Best of Europe	*Rick Steves' Great Britain*
Rick Steves' Best of Eastern Europe	*Rick Steves' Ireland*
Rick Steves' Croatia & Slovenia	*Rick Steves' Italy*
(new in 2007)	*Rick Steves' Portugal*
Rick Steves' England	*Rick Steves' Scandinavia*
Rick Steves' France	*Rick Steves' Spain*
Rick Steves' Germany & Austria	*Rick Steves' Switzerland*

City and Regional Guides: Updated every year, these focus on Europe's most compelling destinations. Along with specifics on sights, restaurants, hotels, and nightlife, you'll get self-guided, illustrated tours of the outstanding museums and most characteristic neighborhoods:

Rick Steves' Amsterdam,	*Rick Steves' Prague &*
Bruges & Brussels	*the Czech Republic*
Rick Steves' Florence & Tuscany	*Rick Steves' Provence &*
Rick Steves' Istanbul (new in 2007)	*the French Riviera*
Rick Steves' London	*Rick Steves' Rome*
Rick Steves' Paris	*Rick Steves' Venice*

Begin Your Trip at www.ricksteves.com

At www.ricksteves.com, you'll find a wealth of **free information** on destinations covered in this book, including fresh European travel and tour news every month and helpful "Graffiti Wall" tips from thousands of fellow travelers.

While you're visiting the site, the **online Travel Store** is a great place to save money on travel bags and accessories designed by Rick Steves to help you travel smarter and lighter, plus a wide selection of guidebooks, planning maps, and DVDs.

Traveling through Europe by rail is a breeze, but choosing the right railpass for your trip—amidst hundreds of options—can drive you nutty. At www.ricksteves.com, you'll find **Rick Steves' Annual Guide to European Railpasses**—your best way to convert chaos into pure travel energy. Buy your railpass from Rick, and you'll get a bunch of free extras to boot.

Rick Steves' Phrase Books: In much of Europe, a phrase book is as fun as it is useful. This practical and budget-oriented series covers French, Italian, German, Spanish, Portuguese, and French/Italian/German. You'll be able to make hotel reservations over the phone, chat with your cabbie, and bargain at street markets.

And More Books: *Rick Steves' Europe 101: History and Art for the Traveler* (with Gene Openshaw) gives you the story of Europe's people, history, and art. Written for smart people who slept through their history and art classes before they knew they were going to Europe, *101* helps Europe's sights come alive.

Rick Steves' Postcards from Europe, my autobiographical book, packs 25 years of travel anecdotes and insights into the ultimate 2,000-mile European adventure.

Rick Steves' European Christmas covers the joys, history, and quirky traditions of the holiday season in seven European countries.

Public Television Show: My series, *Rick Steves' Europe,* keeps churning out shows (60 at last count), including several featuring the sights in this book.

Radio Show: My weekly radio show, which combines call-in questions (à la *Car Talk*) and interviews with travel experts, airs on public radio stations. For a schedule of upcoming topics and an archive of past programs (just click on a topic of your choice to listen), see www.ricksteves.com/radio.

Other Guidebooks

You may want some supplemental information, especially if you'll be traveling beyond my recommended destinations. When you consider the improvements they'll make in your $3,000 vacation, $25 or $35 for extra maps and books is money well spent. Especially for several people traveling by car, the weight and expense are negligible.

There are a handful of useful books for travelers with limited mobility. Candy Harrington has written a pair of good books: *Barrier-Free Travel: A Nuts and Bolts Guide for Wheelers and Slow Walkers* and *There Is Room at the Inn: Inns and B&Bs for Wheelers and Slow Walkers*. For travel in London and Paris, we also highly recommend *Access in London* and *Access in Paris* (by Gordon Couch et al.; Access Project, 39 Bradley Gardens, West Ealing, London W13 8HE, www.accessproject-phsp .org, gordon.couch@virgin.net).

Patrick Simpson's *Wheelchair Around the World* (www.wheelbooks .com) includes an extensive bibliography with resources to assist people who have physical disabilities to plan their own trip. The *Around the World Resource Guide*, published by Access for Disabled Americans (www.accessfordisabled.com), is an easy-to-use bibliography of services and resources for disabled people.

For more resources, see the next chapter.

Maps

The black-and-white maps in this book, drawn by Dave Hoerlein, are concise and simple. Dave, who is well-traveled in Europe, has designed the maps to help you locate recommended places and get to the tourist information offices, where you can pick up a more in-depth map (usually free) of the city or region.

European bookstores, especially in tourist areas, have good selections of maps. For drivers, I'd recommend a 1:200,000- or 1:300,000-scale map for each country. Train travelers can usually manage fine with the freebies they get with their train pass and at local tourist offices.

PRACTICALITIES

Red Tape: Americans need a passport, but no visa and no shots, to travel throughout Europe. Crossing borders is easy. Sometimes you won't even realize it's happened. When you do change countries, however, you change phone cards, postage stamps, gas prices, ways to flush a toilet, words for "hello," figurehead monarchs, and breakfast breads. Plan ahead for these changes: Brush up on the new language, and use up stamps, phone cards, and—when you're going between Britain and the Continent—any spare coins (spend them on candy, souvenirs, gas, or a telephone call home).

Time: In Europe—and in this book—you'll be using the 24-hour clock. After 12:00 noon, keep going—13:00, 14:00, and so on. For anything over 12, subtract 12 and add p.m. (14:00 is 2 p.m.). Continental European time is six/nine hours ahead of the East/West Coasts of the U.S., though Great Britain is only five/eight hours ahead.

Discounts: While discounts for sights and transportation are not listed in this book, seniors (60 and over), students (with International Student Identity Cards), and youths (under 18) may snare discounts—but only by asking. Some discounts (particularly for sights) are granted only to European residents. Most attractions and events have special discounts for wheelchair users (many are free to you, as well as your companion). A traveler with limited mobility generally may go to the head of the line for attractions and events. Don't be shy. Europe may not have as many ramps and elevators as the United States, but it's socially aware.

Watt's Up? If you're bringing electrical gear, you'll need an adapter plug (two round prongs for the continent, three flat ones for Britain) and a converter. Travel appliances often have convenient, built-in converters; look for a voltage switch marked 120V (U.S.) and 240V (Europe).

News: Americans keep in touch in Europe with the *International Herald Tribune* (published almost daily via satellite). Every Tuesday, the European editions of *Time* and *Newsweek* hit the stands with articles of particular interest to travelers in Europe. Sports addicts can get their fix from *USA Today*. Good Web sites include www.europeantimes.com and http://news.bbc.co.uk.

MONEY

Banking

Bring plastic (ATM, debit, or credit cards) along with several hundred dollars in hard cash as an emergency backup. Traveler's checks are a waste of time and money.

Before you go, verify with your bank that your card will work, inquire about fees (can be up to $5 per transaction), and alert them that you'll be making withdrawals in Europe; otherwise, the bank may not approve transactions if it perceives unusual spending patterns. Bring an extra card in case one gets demagnetized or gobbled up by a machine.

The best and easiest way to get cash is to use the readily available, easy-to-use, 24-hour ATMs (with English instructions, low fees). You'll

Exchange Rates

Throughout this book, prices are listed in the local currency. You'll use pounds sterling in Britain and euros everywhere else.

1 British pound sterling (£) = about $1.80

The British pound (£), also called a "quid," is broken into 100 pence (p). Pence means "cents." You'll find coins ranging from 1p to £2 and bills from £5 to £50. Some travelers try to kid themselves that pounds are dollars. But when they get home, that £1,000 Visa bill isn't asking for $1,000—it wants $1,800. To avoid this shock, double British prices to estimate dollars. By overshooting it, you'll spend less...maybe even less than you budgeted (good luck).

1 euro (€) = about $1.20

One euro (€) is broken down into 100 cents. You'll find coins ranging from one cent to two euros, and bills from five euros to 500 euros. To convert prices in euros to dollars, add 20 percent: €20 = about $24, €45 = about $54.

need a PIN code—numbers only, no letters—to use with your Visa or MasterCard.

Just like at home, credit or debit cards work easily at larger hotels, restaurants, and shops. Visa and MasterCard are more commonly accepted than American Express. Smart travelers function with plastic and cash. Smaller businesses prefer—and sometimes require—payment in hard cash, rather than plastic. If you have lots of large bills, break them for free at a bank, especially if you like shopping at mom-and-pop places; they rarely have huge amounts of change.

Bring some $20 American bills along for those times when you need just a little more local cash (e.g., if you're just passing through or about to leave a country).

Keep your credit and debit cards and most of your money hidden away in a money belt (a cloth pouch worn around your waist and tucked under your clothes). Thieves target tourists. A money belt provides peace of mind and allows you to carry lots of cash safely. Don't be petty about getting money. Withdraw a week's worth of money, stuff it in your money belt, and travel!

Damage Control for Lost or Stolen Cards

If you lose your credit, debit, or ATM card, you can stop people from using your card by reporting the loss immediately to the respective global customer-assistance centers. Call these 24-hour U.S. numbers collect: Visa (tel. 410/581-9994), MasterCard (tel. 636/722-7111), and American Express (tel. 336/393-1111).

Have, at a minimum, the following information ready: the name of the financial institution that issued you the card, along with the type of card (classic, platinum, or whatever). Ideally, plan ahead and pack photocopies of your cards—front and back—to expedite their replacement. Providing the following information will allow for a quicker cancellation of your missing card: full card number, whether you are the primary or secondary cardholder, the cardholder's name exactly as printed on the card, billing address, home phone number, circumstances of the loss or theft, and identification verification (your birthdate, your mother's maiden name, or your Social Security number—memorize this, don't carry a copy). If you are the secondary cardholder, you'll also need to provide the primary cardholder's identification verification details. You can generally receive a temporary card within two or three business days in Europe.

If you promptly report your card lost or stolen, you typically won't be responsible for any unauthorized transactions on your account, although many banks charge a liability fee of $50.

Tips on Tipping

Tipping in Europe isn't as automatic and generous as it is in the U.S.—but for special service, tips are appreciated, if not expected. As in the U.S., the proper amount depends on your resources, tipping philosophy, and the circumstance, but some general guidelines apply.

Restaurants: Tipping is an issue only at restaurants that have waiters and waitresses. If you order your food at a counter, don't tip.

At a pub or restaurant with wait staff, the service charge (10–15 percent) is usually listed on the menu and included in your bill. When the service is included, there's no need to tip beyond that, but if you like to tip and you're pleased with the service, you can round up the bill (but not more than 5 percent).

If the service is not included, tip up to 10 percent by rounding up or leaving the change from your bill. Leave the tip on the table or hand it to your server. It's best to tip in cash even if you pay with your credit card. Otherwise the tip may never reach your server.

Taxis: To tip the cabbie, round up. For a typical ride, round up to the next euro on the fare (to pay a €13 fare, give €14); for a long ride, to the nearest 10 (for a €75 fare, give €80). If the cabbie hauls your bags and zips you to the airport to help you catch your flight, you might want to toss in a little more. But if you feel like you're being driven in circles or otherwise ripped off, skip the tip.

Hotels: I don't tip at hotels, but if you do, give the porter a euro for carrying bags and leave a couple of euros in your room at the end of your stay for the maid if the room was kept clean.

Special Services: Tour guides at public sites sometimes hold out their hands for tips after they give their spiel; if I've already paid for the tour, I don't tip extra, though some tourists do give a euro or two, particularly for a job well done. In general, if someone in the service industry does a super job for you, a tip of a couple of euros is appropriate...but not required.

When in doubt, ask. If you're not sure whether (or how much) to tip for a service, ask your hotelier or the tourist information office; they'll fill you in on how it's done on their turf.

VAT Refunds for Shoppers

Wrapped into the purchase price of your souvenirs is a Value Added Tax (VAT) that's generally around 20 percent. If you make a purchase of more than a certain amount at a store that participates in the VAT refund scheme, you're entitled to get most of that tax back (see sidebar for VAT rates and minimum-purchase requirements). Personally, I've never felt that VAT refunds are worth the hassle, but if you do, here's the scoop.

If you're lucky, the merchant will subtract the tax when you make your purchase (this is more likely to occur if the store ships the goods to your home). Otherwise, you'll need to do all this:

Get the paperwork: Have the merchant completely fill out the necessary refund document, called a "cheque." You'll have to present your passport at the store.

Get your stamp at the border or airport: Process your cheque(s) at your last stop in the EU with the customs agent who deals with VAT refunds. It's best to keep your purchases in your carry-on for viewing, but if they're too large or dangerous (such as knives) to carry on, then track down the proper customs agent to inspect them before you check your

VAT Rates and Minimum Purchases Required to Qualify for Refunds

Country of Purchase	VAT rate*	Minimum in Local Currency	Minimum in U.S. dollars**
Belgium	21%	€125	$152
France	19.6%	€175	$213
Germany	16%	€25	$30
Great Britain	17.5%	£20	$36
Netherlands	19%	€137	$167

*The VAT Standard Rate is charged on the original value of the item, not on the purchase price. Refund percentages will therefore be slightly less than the above rate and may also be subject to commission fees.
**Exchange rate as of January 9, 2006
Source: HOTREC (Hotels, Restaurants & Cafés in Europe). Please note that figures are subject to change. For more information, visit www.hotrec.org or www.globalrefund.com.

bag. You're not supposed to use your purchased goods before you leave. If you show up at customs wearing your new lederhosen, officials might look the other way—or deny you a refund.

Collect your refund: You'll need to return your stamped documents to the retailer or its representative. Many merchants work with services such as Global Refund or Premier Tax Free, with offices at major airports, ports, or border crossings. These services, which extract a 4 percent fee, can refund your money immediately in your currency of choice or credit your card (within 2 billing cycles). If you have to deal directly with the retailer, mail the store your stamped documents and then wait. It could take months.

Customs Regulations

You can take home $800 in souvenirs per person duty-free. The next $1,000 is taxed at a flat 3 percent. After that, you pay the individual item's duty rate. You can also bring in duty-free a liter of alcohol (slightly more than a standard-size bottle of wine), a carton of cigarettes, and up to 100 cigars. As for food, anything in cans or sealed jars is acceptable. Skip dried meat, cheeses, and fresh fruits and veggies. To check customs rules and duty rates, visit www.customs.gov.

TRANSPORTATION

By Car or by Train?

Each has pros and cons. Cars are an expensive headache in big cities, but are fully accessible. Groups of three or more go cheaper by car. If you're packing heavy, go by car. Trains are best for city-to-city travel and give you the convenience of doing long stretches overnight. By train, you'll arrive relaxed and well-rested—not so by car. Note that most of Europe's large train stations are fully accessible, but many others are not.

If visiting only the destinations covered in this book, you're probably best off simply buying train tickets. A car is worthless in the cities, where taxis and public transit make more sense. Connecting London and Paris is clearly easiest via the fully accessible Eurostar train. And train connections for Bruges, Amsterdam, and the Rhine are convenient, with good access.

Traveling by Train

A major mistake Americans make in Europe is relating public transportation in Europe to the pathetic public transportation they're used to at home. By rail, you'll have Europe by the tail. To study train schedules in advance on the Web, look up http://bahn.hafas.de/english.html.

While you can buy tickets as you go ("point-to-point"), you can save money by getting a railpass if you plan to travel beyond the destinations in this book.

If you want to travel first-class between the destinations in this book, a Eurail Selectpass for five or six days of travel in France, Benelux, and Germany is convenient and worthwhile (starts at $325 per person for 2 or more traveling together, 5 days within a 2-month travel period). If you plan to travel beyond these destinations, the pass can actually save you money, particularly for long rides in Germany or France. However, if you're happy in second class, or if you can take advantage of discounts for wheelchair users, then point-to-point tickets are cheaper for this route. Note that a Eurostar ticket from London to the continent is not covered by any railpass, but railpass-holders and wheelchair users get discounts.

For a summary of railpass deals and point-to-point ticket options (available in the U.S. and in Europe), check out www.ricksteves.com/rail.

Car Rental

It's cheaper to arrange European car rentals in the United States, so check rates with your travel agent or directly with the companies. Most

Driving: Distance and Time

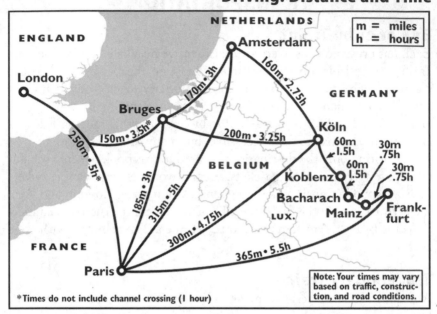

car-rental agencies offer cars that are adapted for drivers who have disabilities. Rent by the week with unlimited mileage. If you'll be renting for three weeks or more, ask your agent about leasing, which is a scheme to save on insurance and taxes. I normally rent the smallest, least expensive model. Explore your drop-off options and costs. Drop-off in another country can be very expensive.

For peace of mind, I spring for the Collision Damage Waiver insurance (CDW, about $15–25 per day), which limits my financial responsibility in case of an accident. Unfortunately, CDW now has a high deductible, hovering around $1,200. When you pick up your car, many car-rental companies will try to sell you "super CDW" at an additional cost of $7–15 per day to lower the deductible to zero.

Some credit cards offer CDW-type coverage for no charge to their customers. Quiz your credit-card company on the worst-case scenario. You have to choose either the coverage offered by your car-rental company or by your credit-card company. This means that if you go with the credit-card coverage, you'll have to decline the CDW offered by the car-rental company. In this situation, some car-rental companies put a hold on your credit card for the amount of the full deductible (which can equal the value of the car). This is bad news if your credit limit is low—particularly if you plan on using that card for other purchases during your trip.

Another alternative is buying CDW insurance from Travel Guard for $9 a day (tel. 800-826-4919, www.travelguard.com). It's valid throughout Europe, but some car-rental companies refuse to honor it, especially in Italy and the Republic of Ireland. Oddly, residents of some states (including Washington) are not allowed to buy this coverage.

In sum, buying CDW—and the supplemental insurance to buy down the deductible, if you choose—is the easiest but priciest option. Using the coverage that comes with your credit card is cheaper, but can involve more hassle. If you're taking a short trip, an easy solution is to buy Travel Guard's very affordable CDW.

Driving

For much of Europe, all you need is your valid U.S. driver's license and a car. Confirm with your rental company if an international license is required in the countries you plan to visit. You probably won't need it for the destinations in this book, other than Germany. If you're traveling farther, you'd also need it for Austria, Italy, Portugal, Spain, and Eastern Europe (at your local AAA office—$10 plus the cost of two passport-type photos).

While gas is expensive, if you keep an eye on the big picture, paying $4 per gallon is more a psychological trauma than a financial one. I use the freeways whenever possible. They are free in the Netherlands and Germany. The French autoroutes are punctuated by tollbooths (charging about $1 for every 10 minutes). The alternative to these expressways often is being marooned in rural traffic. The autoroute usually saves enough time, gas, and nausea to justify its expense. Mix scenic country-road rambling with high-speed autobahning, but don't forget that in Europe, the shortest distance between two points is the autobahn.

Get used to metric. A liter is about a quart, four to a gallon; a kilometer is 0.6 mile. Convert

STOP AND LEARN THESE ROAD SIGNS

Speed Limit (km/hr) — Yield — No Passing — End of No Passing Zone

One Way — Intersection — Main Road — Freeway

Danger — No Entry — No Entry for cars — All Vehicles Prohibited

Parking — No Parking — Customs — Peace

kilometers to miles by cutting them in half and adding back 10 percent of the original (120 km: 60 + 12 = 72 miles).

Parking: Parking is a costly headache in big cities. You'll pay about $20 a day to park safely. Ask at your hotel for advice. I keep a pile of coins in my ashtray for parking meters, public phones, launderettes, and wishing wells.

Transportation at Your Destination

The most accessible way to get around town is usually by taxi (though often you'll have to transfer into the car and have the driver fold your wheelchair to put it in the trunk). Some cities have some fully accessible buses and subway routes. Other cities' transportation systems—like Paris' Métro—have very poor accessibility. I've explained your options for each destination and recommended what works best.

COMMUNICATING

Telephones

Smart travelers learn the phone system and use it daily to reserve or reconfirm rooms, get tourist information, reserve restaurants, confirm tour times, or phone home.

Types of Phones

You'll encounter various kinds of phones in Europe.

Public pay phones are on every corner. On the Continent, a few coin-operated phones still exist, but most only accept phone cards. In Great Britain, coin-operated phones are still the norm. For details on both types of payment, see below.

Hotel room phones are fairly cheap for local calls, but pricey for international calls—unless you use an international phone card (see below).

American mobile phones work in Europe if they're GSM-enabled, tri-band (or quad-band), and on a calling plan that includes international calls. With a T-Mobile phone, you can roam using your home number, and pay $1-2 per minute for making or receiving calls.

Some travelers buy a **European mobile phone** in Europe. For about $125, you can get a phone that will work in most countries once you pick up the necessary chip (about $30) per country. Or you can buy a cheaper, "locked" phone that only works in the country where you purchased it (about $100, includes $20 worth of calls). If you're interested, stop by any European shop that sells mobile phones; you'll see prominent store window displays. You aren't required to (and shouldn't) buy a monthly contract—buy prepaid calling time instead (as you use it up, buy additional minutes at newsstands or mobile-phone shops). If you're on a budget, skip mobile phones and use phone cards instead.

Paying for Calls

You can spend a fortune making phone calls in Europe...but why would you? Here's the skinny on different ways to pay, including the best deals.

European **phone cards** come in two types: phone cards that you insert into a pay phone (best for local calls or quick international calls), and phone cards that come with a dial-up code and can be used from virtually any phone (best for international calls; note that these are not a good value when used from German public pay phones—see below).

• **Insertable phone cards,** which are widely used on the Continent, but not in Britain, are a convenient way to pay for calls from public pay phones. Buy these cards at TIs, tobacco shops, post offices, and train stations. The price of the call (local or international) is automatically deducted while you talk. They are sold in several denominations starting at about €5. Calling the U.S. with one of these phone cards is reasonable (about 2–3 min per euro), but more expensive than using an international phone card. Each European country has its own insertable phone card—so your German card won't work in a Dutch phone.

• **International phone cards,** which are sold throughout Europe (including Britain), can be used from virtually any phone. These are not inserted into the phone. Instead, you dial the toll-free number listed on the card, reaching an automated operator. When prompted, you dial in a code number, also written on the card. A voice tells you how much is left in your account. Then dial your number. Usually you can select English, but if the prompts are in another language, experiment: dial your code, followed by the pound sign (#) then the number, then pound again, and so on, until it works. Since you don't insert the card in the phone, you can use these to make inexpensive calls from most phones, including the one in your hotel room, avoiding pricey hotel rates. Remember that you don't need the actual card to use a card account, so you can write down the access and code numbers in your notebook and share it with friends.

Calls to the U.S. are very cheap (about 20–25 min per euro). You can use the cards to make local and domestic long-distance calls as well. Buy cards at small newsstand kiosks and hole-in-the-wall long-distance phone shops. Because there are so many brand names, simply ask for an international telephone card and tell the vendor where you'll be making most calls ("to America"), and he'll select the brand with the best deal. Some international calling cards work in multiple countries—try to buy a card that will work in all of your destinations. Because cards are occasionally duds, avoid the high denominations.

These international phone cards are such a good deal that the irritated German phone company is making them less cost-effective. In Germany, the cards are only cheap if you use them from a fixed line, like a hotel-room phone. From a pay phone, you'll get far fewer minutes for your money (for example, 10 minutes instead of 100 on a €5 card).

Some public pay phones—including all phones in Britain—are **coin-operated**. The British coin-operated phones clearly list which coins they'll take (usually from 10p to £1, with a minimum toll of 30p; some new phones even accept euro coins), and a display shows how your money supply's doing. Only completely unused coins will be returned, so put in biggies with caution. (If money's left over, push the "make another call" button, rather than hanging up.)

British phones also work with a **major credit card**. Just insert the card into the phone and dial away (minimum charge for a credit-card call is 50p). This is a handy way to make quick calls, but the rates are high, so avoid long chats.

Dialing direct from your hotel room without using an international calling card is usually quite expensive for international calls. (I always ask first how much I'll be charged.) Keep in mind that you might have to pay for local and occasionally even toll-free calls.

Receiving calls in your hotel room is often the cheapest way to keep in touch with the folks back home—especially if your family has an inexpensive way to call you (for example, a good deal on their long-distance plan, a prepaid calling card with good rates to Europe, or access to an Internet phone service, such as Skype—www.skype.com). Give them a list of your hotels' phone numbers before you go. As you travel, send your family an e-mail or make a quick pay-phone call to set up a time for them to call you, and then wait for the ring.

U.S. calling cards (such as the ones offered by AT&T, MCI, or Sprint) are the worst option. You'll nearly always save a lot of money by paying with a phone card instead.

How to Dial

Calling from the U.S. to Europe, or vice versa, is simple—once you break the code. The European calling chart on page 560 will explain the procedure. Remember that Continental European time is six/nine hours ahead of the East/West Coasts of the U.S. (and British time is five/eight hours ahead).

Making Calls within a European Country: About half of all European countries use area codes; the other half use a direct-dial system without area codes.

In countries that use area codes (such as Britain, Germany, the Netherlands, Austria, Croatia, Hungary, Ireland, Poland, Slovakia, and Slovenia), you dial the local number when calling within a city, and you add the area code if calling long distance within the same country. For example, London's area code is 020, and the number of one of my recommended London hotels is 7282-5500. To call the hotel within London, dial 7282-5500. To call it from elsewhere in Britain, dial 020/7282-5500.

To make calls within a country that uses a direct-dial system (such as France, Belgium, the Czech Republic, Denmark, Italy, Spain, and Switzerland), you dial the same number whether you're calling across the country or across the street.

Making International Calls: You always start with the international access code (011 if you're calling from the U.S. or Canada, or 00 from Europe). If you see a phone number that begins with +, you have to replace the + with the international access code.

Once you've dialed the international access code, dial the country code of the country you're calling (see chart in appendix).

What you dial next depends on the phone system of the country you're calling. If the country uses area codes, drop the initial zero of the area code, then dial the rest of the number. To call the London hotel from Paris, dial 00, 44 (Britain's country code), 20/7282-5500 (omitting the initial zero in the area code).

Countries that use direct-dial systems (no area codes) vary in how they're accessed internationally by phone. For instance, if you're making an international call to the Czech Republic, Denmark, Estonia, Italy, Norway, Portugal, or Spain, simply dial the international access code, country code, and phone number. But if you're calling France, Belgium, or Switzerland, drop the initial 0 of the phone number.

To call my office from Europe, I dial 00 (Europe's international access code), 1 (U.S.A.'s country code), 425 (Edmonds' area code), and 771-8303.

Don't be surprised that in some countries, local phone numbers have different numbers of digits within the same city, or even the same hotel (e.g., a hotel can have a 6-digit phone number, a 7-digit mobile phone number, and an 8-digit fax number).

E-mail and Mail

E-mail: Internet cafés are available at just about every destination in this book, giving you reasonably inexpensive and easy Internet access. Your hotelier can direct you to the nearest place. Many hotels have Internet terminals in their lobbies for guests, and some offer Wi-Fi wireless connections for travelers with laptop computers.

Mail: While you can arrange for mail delivery to your hotel (allow 10 days for a letter to arrive), phoning and e-mailing are so easy that I've dispensed with mail stops altogether.

SLEEPING

In the interest of smart use of your time, I favor hotels and restaurants handy to your sightseeing activities. Rather than list hotels scattered throughout a city, I describe two or three favorite neighborhoods and recommend the best accommodations values in each.

This book lists accommodations of various accessibility levels. I've listed several cheaper, small hotel options. But because truly accessible rooms are at a premium in some destinations, I've also listed some expensive—but plush and fully adapted—splurges.

Rooms with private bathrooms are often bigger, more recently renovated, and more likely to be accessible, while the cheaper rooms without bathrooms often will be on the top floor or not yet refurbished—and usually not accessible. Any room without a bathroom has access to a bathroom in the corridor (free, unless otherwise noted). Rooms with tubs often cost more than rooms with showers. All rooms have a sink.

Before accepting a room, confirm your understanding of the complete price. The only tip our recommended hotels would like is a friendly, easygoing guest. I appreciate feedback on your hotel experiences.

Hotels

While most hotels listed in this book cluster around $70 to $100 per double, they can be as much as $200-plus (maximum plumbing and more) per double. The cost is higher in big cities and heavily touristed cities and lower off the beaten track. Three or four people can save money by requesting one big room. Traveling alone can get expensive: A single room is often only 20 percent cheaper than a double. If you'll accept a room with twin beds and you ask for a double, you may be turned away. Ask for "a room for two people" if you'll take a twin or a double.

Rooms are generally safe, but don't leave valuables lying around. More (or different) pillows and blankets are usually in the closet or available on

---

Sleep Code

To give maximum information with a minimum of space, I use the following code to describe accommodations listed in this book. Prices are listed per room, not per person. When a range of prices is listed for a room, the price fluctuates with room size or season. You can assume a hotel takes credit cards unless you see "cash only" in the listing. Hotel clerks speak at least some English unless otherwise noted.

S = Single room (or price for one person in a double).

D = Double or Twin. Double beds are usually big enough for non-romantic couples.

T = Triple (often a double bed with a single bed moved in).

Q = Quad (an extra child's bed is usually cheaper).

b = Private bathroom with toilet and shower or tub.

s = Private shower or tub only (the toilet is down the hall).

According to this code, a couple staying at a "Db-€90" hotel would pay a total of 90 euros (about $110) for a double room with a private bathroom. The hotel accepts credit cards or cash in payment.

---

request. Remember, in Europe, towels and linen aren't always replaced every day. Drip-dry and conserve.

Unless I note otherwise, the cost of a room includes a breakfast (sometimes continental, but usually buffet).

Pay your bill the evening before you leave to avoid the time-wasting crowd at the reception desk in the morning.

Hostels

Consider taking advantage of Europe's impressive network of youth hostels. Of course, these vary widely in accessibility—but many are modern and likely to have at least moderately accessible facilities.

Hostels are open to all ages (except in Bavaria, where a maximum age of 26 is strictly enforced at official hostels, though not at independent hostels). They usually cost $10–20 per night (cheaper for those under 27) and serve good, cheap meals and/or provide kitchen facilities. Generally, travelers without a membership card ($28 per year, sold at hostels in most U.S. cities or online at www.hiusa.org, tel. 202/783-6161) are admitted for an extra $5. If you plan to stay in hostels, bring your own sheet (or pay $4 extra to rent one). While many hostels have a few doubles or family rooms available upon request for a little extra money, plan on gender-segregated dorms with 4–20 beds per room. Hostels can be idyllic and peaceful, but school groups can raise the rafters. School groups are most common on summer weekends and on school-year weekdays. I like small hostels best. While many hostels may say over the telephone that they're full, most hold a few beds for people who drop in, or they can direct you to budget accommodations nearby.

Making Reservations

It's possible to travel at any time of year without reservations, but given the high stakes, erratic accommodations values, and the quality of the gems I've found for this book, I'd highly recommend calling for rooms at least several days in advance as you travel (and book well in advance for festivals).

If tourist crowds are minimal, you might make a habit of calling between 9:00 and 10:00 on the day you plan to arrive, when the hotel knows who'll be checking out and just which rooms will be available. I've taken great pains to list telephone numbers with long-distance instructions (see "Telephones," page 24; also see the appendix). Use the telephone and the convenient telephone cards. Most hotels listed are accustomed to English-only speakers. A hotel receptionist will trust you and hold a room until 16:00 without a deposit, though some will ask for a credit-card number. Honor (or cancel by phone) your reservations. Long distance is cheap and easy from public phone booths. *Trusting people to show up is a hugely stressful issue and a financial risk for B&B owners. Don't let these people down—I promised you'd call and cancel if for some reason you can't show up.* Don't needlessly confirm rooms through the tourist offices; they'll take a commission.

If you know exactly which dates you need and really want a particular place, reserve a room long before you leave home. To reserve from home, call, e-mail, or fax the hotel. E-mail is free, phone and fax costs are reasonable, and simple English is usually fine. To fax, use the form in the appendix (online at www.ricksteves.com/reservation). A two-night stay in August would be "2 nights, 16/8/06 to 18/8/06." (Europeans write the date day/month/year, and European hotel jargon uses your day of departure.) Hotels often require one night's deposit to hold a room. Usually a credit-card number and expiration date will be accepted as the deposit. Faxing your card number (rather than e-mailing it) keeps it private, safer, and out of cyberspace. If you do reserve with a credit card, you can pay with your card or cash when you arrive; if you don't show up, you'll be billed for the night.

Hotels in larger cities sometimes have strict cancellation policies (you might lose, say, a deposit if you cancel within 2 weeks of your reserved stay, or you might be billed for the entire visit if you leave early); ask about cancellation policies before you book.

On the road, reconfirm your reservations a day or two in advance for safety (or you may be bumped—really). Also, don't just assume you can extend. Take the time to consider in advance how long you'll stay.

EATING

Europeans are masters at the art of fine living. That means eating long and well. Two-hour lunches, three-hour dinners, and endless hours sitting in outdoor cafés are the norm. Americans eat on their way to an evening event and complain if the check is slow in coming. For Europeans, the meal is an end in itself, and only rude waiters rush you.

Even those of us who liked dorm food will find that the local cafés, cuisine, and wines become a highlight of our European adventure. This is sightseeing for your palate, and even if the rest of you is sleeping in cheap hotels, your taste buds will want an occasional first-class splurge. You can eat well without going broke. But be careful: You're just as likely to blow a small fortune on a mediocre meal as you are to dine wonderfully for $15.

Restaurants
To conserve your time and energy, I've focused on restaurants in the neighborhood close to your hotel or handy to your sightseeing. For each one, I've indicated the specific accessibility features you can expect to find.

If restaurant-hunting on your own, choose a place filled with locals, not the place with the big neon signs boasting, "We Speak English and Accept Credit Cards." Look for menus posted outside; if you don't see one, move along.

When you're in the mood for something halfway between a restaurant and a picnic meal, look for take-out food stands, bakeries (with sandwiches and small pizzas to go), delis, a department-store cafeteria, or simple little eateries for fast and easy restaurant food.

Picnics
To be able to afford the occasional splurge in a nice restaurant, I like to picnic. In addition to the savings, picnicking is a great way to sample local specialties. And, in the process of assembling your meal, you get to plunge into local markets like a European.

Gather supplies early. Many shops close for a lunch break. While

---

Send Me an E-mail, Drop Me a Line

If you enjoy a successful trip with the help of this book and would like to share your discoveries, please fill out the survey at www.ricksteves .com/feedback. I personally read and value all feedback.

---

it's fun to visit the small specialty shops, a *supermarché* gives you more efficiency with less color for less cost.

When driving, I organize a backseat pantry in a cardboard box: plastic cups, paper towels, a water bottle (the standard disposable European half-liter plastic mineral water bottle works fine), a damp cloth in a Ziploc baggie, a Swiss Army knife, and a petite tablecloth. To take care of juice once and for all, stow a rack of liter boxes of orange juice in the trunk. (Look for "100%" on the label, or you'll get a sickly sweet orange drink.)

Picnics (especially French ones) can be an adventure in high cuisine. Be daring: Try the smelly cheeses, midget pickles, ugly pâtés, and minuscule yogurts. Local shopkeepers sell small quantities of produce and even slice and stuff a sandwich for you.

A typical picnic for two might be fresh bread (half loaves on request), two tomatoes, three carrots, 100 grams of cheese (about a quarter-pound), 100 grams of meat, two apples, a liter box of orange juice, and yogurt. Total cost for two: about $10.

TRAVELING AS A TEMPORARY LOCAL

We travel all the way to Europe to enjoy differences—to become temporary locals. You'll experience frustrations. Certain truths that we find "God-given" or "self-evident," such as cold beer, ice in drinks, bottomless cups of coffee, and bigger being better, are suddenly not so true. One of the benefits of travel is the eye-opening realization that there are logical, civil, and even better alternatives. A willingness to go local ensures that you'll enjoy a full dose of European hospitality.

If there is a negative aspect to the image Europeans have of Americans, it is that we are big, aggressive, impolite, rich, loud, and a bit naive. Americans tend to be noisy in public places, such as restaurants and trains. Our raised voices can demolish Europe's reserved ambience. Talk softly. While Europeans look bemusedly at some of our Yankee excesses—and worriedly at others—they nearly always afford us individual travelers all the warmth we deserve.

Judging from all the happy postcards I receive from travelers who have used this book, it's safe to assume you'll enjoy a great, affordable vacation—with the finesse of an independent, experienced traveler. Thanks, and happy travels!

BACK DOOR TRAVEL PHILOSOPHY
From *Rick Steves' Europe Through the Back Door*

Travel is intensified living—maximum thrills per minute and one of the last great sources of legal adventure. Travel is freedom. It's recess, and we need it.

Experiencing the real Europe requires catching it by surprise, going casual..."Through the Back Door."

Affording travel is a matter of priorities. (Make do with the old car.) You can travel—simply, safely, and comfortably—almost anywhere in Europe for $100 a day plus transportation costs (allow more for London). In many ways, spending more money only builds a thicker wall between you and what you came to see. Europe is a cultural carnival, and, time after time, you'll find that its best acts are free and the best seats are the cheap ones.

A tight budget forces you to travel close to the ground, meeting and communicating with the people, not relying on service with a purchased smile. Never sacrifice sleep, nutrition, safety, or cleanliness in the name of budget. Simply enjoy the local-style alternatives to expensive hotels and restaurants.

Extroverts have more fun. If your trip is low on magic moments, kick yourself and make things happen. If you don't enjoy a place, maybe you don't know enough about it. Seek the truth. Recognize tourist traps. Give a culture the benefit of your open mind. See things as different but not better or worse. Any culture has much to share.

Of course, travel, like the world, is a series of hills and valleys. Be fanatically positive and militantly optimistic. If something's not to your liking, change your liking. Travel is addictive. It can make you a happier American, as well as a citizen of the world. Our Earth is home to six billion equally important people. It's humbling to travel and find that people don't envy Americans. They like us, but, with all due respect, they wouldn't trade passports.

Globe-trotting destroys ethnocentricity. It helps you understand and appreciate different cultures. Regrettably, there are forces in our society that want you dumbed down for their convenience. Don't let it happen. Thoughtful travel engages you with the world—more important than ever these days. Travel changes people. It broadens perspectives and teaches new ways to measure quality of life. Many travelers toss aside their hometown blinders. Their prized souvenirs are the strands of different cultures they decide to knit into their own character. The world is a cultural yarn shop. And Back Door travelers are weaving the ultimate tapestry. Come on, join in!

ACCESSIBILITY RESOURCES AND TIPS

European countries, at various speeds, are doing what they can to open their doors and make their cobbled streets negotiable for more visitors. It's smart to do some advance groundwork. Here are useful resources to help you plan ahead. The tips come from a variety of sources, including Susan Sygall, the Executive Director of Mobility International USA (MIUSA) and writer of this book's Foreword; the National Clearinghouse on Disabilities and Exchange (run by MIUSA); and my readers.

For more advice on the ups and downs of Europe via walker or wheelchair, visit the Graffiti Wall at www.ricksteves.com.

PLANNING YOUR TRIP

Organizations

These organizations can help you plan an accessible, enjoyable journey.

Mobility International USA (MIUSA) is a nonprofit organization whose mission is to empower people with disabilities around the world through international exchange and international development to achieve their human rights. MIUSA periodically sponsors international exchange programs for people with disabilities. They also sell helpful resources, such as the book *Survival Strategies for Going Abroad: A Guide* *for People with Disabilities,* in which more than 20 experienced travelers with disabilities share stories, tips, and resources related to participating in international programs. This easy-to-use guide addresses the disability-related aspects of participating in international exchange programs, including choosing a program, applying, preparing to travel, adjusting to life in a new country, and returning home (www.miusa.org, tel./TTY 541/343-1284, info@miusa.org).

The **National Clearinghouse on Disability and Exchange (NCDE)** provides information about work, study, volunteer, and research opportunities abroad for people with disabilities. The NCDE offers many resources, including a Peer-to-Peer Network connecting people with disabilities who have been abroad with those planning to go abroad; an online database with information about exchanges and disability organizations worldwide; the free publication *Preparing for an International Career: Pathways for People with Disabilities*; Web resources for parents and youth; and the free journal *A World Awaits You,* with tips and stories about a wide range of exchange opportunities. NCDE is a project sponsored by the Bureau of Educational and Cultural Affairs of the U.S. State Department and administered by MIUSA (same contact as above; www.miusa.org/ncde).

Access-Able Travel Source sponsors a useful Web site (www.access-able.com) that has access information and resources for travelers with disabilities, and offers a free e-mail newsletter. They have information about guidebooks, accessible transportation, wheelchair travel, scooter rental, disabled-travel forums, accessible transportation, and more (P.O. Box 1796, Wheat Ridge, CO 80034, tel. 303/232-2979, carol@access-able.com, Bill and Carol Randall).

The **Society for Accessible Travel and Hospitality (SATH),** an educational nonprofit membership organization, publishes a travel magazine *(Open World)* and offers travel advice ($45 membership, $30 for students and seniors, includes magazine; $13 for magazine subscription only; tel. 212/447-7284, fax 212/725-8253, www.sath.org, info@sath.org).

Several organizations specialize in **health** issues: The **International Association for Medical Assistance to Travelers (IAMAT)** provides a directory of English-speaking doctors in 500 cities in 120 countries who charge affordable, standardized fees for medical visits (membership free but donation requested, 417 Center Street, Lewiston, NY 14092, tel. 716/754-4883, www.iamat.org, info@iamat.org). The **Centers for Disease Control and Prevention (CDC)** maintain health-related information online, including travel preparation and health information for travel worldwide (www.cdc.gov/travel). **PersonalMD.com** provides information on a wide variety of health topics. The main feature is the PersonalMD Emergency Card, a free service that allows users to enter their medical information into a secure database that can be accessed anywhere in the world via the Internet, in case of an emergency. **Shoreland's Travel Health Online** offers health tips, a planning guide, and country information (www.tripprep.com).

Susan Sygall, the Executive Director of Mobility International USA, suggests the following: "I always get information about disability groups where I am going. They have the best access information, and many times they will become your new traveling partners and friends. Remember that you are part of a global family of disabled people. It can also be helpful to contact tourism offices and local transit providers before you travel. Some even include information about accessibility for people with disabilities on their Web sites." (See the appendix for a list of tourist information offices and their Web sites.)

Web Sites

In addition to the organizations listed above, you can find helpful resources and links pages on the Web sites for **Emerging Horizons** (www.emerginghorizons.com), **Gimp on the Go** (www.gimponthego .com), **Disabled Peoples' International** (www.dpi.org), and **MossRehab ResourceNet** (www.mossresourcenet.org/travel.htm). **AARP**'s Web site features articles written for seniors and slow walkers (www.aarp.org /destinations). **Access Abroad** is a good resource for students with disabilities planning to study abroad (www.umabroad.umn.edu/access). **Wheelchair Accessible Europe** lists hotels throughout Europe offering accessible rooms (www.wheelchairaccessibleeurope.com).

GETTING THERE

Here are some resources and tips for getting to Europe, whether on your own or with a tour.

Air Travel

The **U.S. Department of Transportation**'s "New Horizons" guide provides information for air travelers with disabilities, including navigating security, getting on and off aircraft, and handling seating assignments (available online at http://airconsumer.ost.dot.gov/publications/horizons .htm).

Thanks to the National Clearinghouse on Disabilities and Exchange, run by Mobility International USA (www.miusa.org), for the following helpful information:

Though many transatlantic air carriers try to accommodate disabled travelers, airline policies are inconsistent. They change often and can vary from company to company and terminal to terminal.

Regardless of the inconsistencies, be aware that the Air Carrier Access Act of 1986 prohibits airlines from discriminating on the basis of disability (see www.faa.gov/acr/dat.htm). Airlines can no longer require that passengers with disabilities travel with attendants, carry medical certificates, or agree to assume liability for the damage of mobility equipment.

Be Assertive: If you have a disability, traveling by plane can be an exercise in relinquishing control. You temporarily surrender autonomy in exchange for necessary assistance and compliance with policies. Be flexible and ready to deal with frustrating situations.

It is important to know the policies of an airline before arriving at the airport. Unfortunately, it is not uncommon for a passenger with a disability to be assured over the phone that his or her needs can be accommodated, only to find that employees at the gate have a different understanding of policies and procedures. Be assertive about your needs and insist upon the services necessary to complete a flight.

If you feel you've been discriminated against because of your disability, document your experience. Complaints should first go to an airline's Complaint Resolution Officer (CRO) on-site. Later, try the airline's community relations department. If these approaches are not successful, file a complaint with the U.S. Department of Transportation's Aviation Consumer Protection Division (tel. 202/366-2220, http://airconsumer .ost.dot.gov, airconsumer@ost.dot.gov) or the Disability Rights Education and Defense Fund (voice telephone & TTY: 800-466-4232, www .dredf.org).

You can also call a toll-free hotline at 800-778-4838 or TTY 800-455-9880, seven days a week (answered 7:00–23:00 EST), run by the U.S. Department of Transportation. They can provide immediate and pre-travel assistance in resolving disability-related air-travel problems by suggesting and facilitating alternative solutions for you and the airline.

Choosing an Airline: Organizations that advocate for disabled air travelers are reluctant to recommend a specific air company, because even the "good" ones are inconsistent. Having a positive air travel experience depends to a great extent on the needs of the individual, the departure and destination cities, and the particular staff on duty.

Air carriers abroad have significantly different policies regarding people with disabilities than U.S. air carriers. Some European airlines have excellent reputations for being very helpful to customers with disabilities. Other companies may have virtually no experience with disabled passengers.

Some foreign airlines may require a doctor's certificate for all independent air travel. Other foreign airlines may require that a person with a disability travel with a personal assistant. Advance research and comparison-shopping are crucial to having a successful trip.

Fortunately, the European Commission recently drafted legislation—that will go into effect in 2006—to force airlines to meet the needs of people with disabilities.

Planning Ahead: Whenever possible, plan and book flights well in advance. It is important to inform the travel agent and airline representative of the following information:

- Your type of disability and equipment aids used for locomotion, such as a cane, crutches, manual wheelchair, or electric wheelchair.
- Your special dietary requirements or need for assistance at meals (airline personnel are not required to help with eating, but should assist with preparing to eat).
- Whether another person will accompany you.

It is essential to call the airline directly to make sure all disability-related needs will be met. Always ask for the name and position of each airline employee and record this information with the time, day, and content of the call. It can be helpful to work with an airline special-services representative who can assist with facilitating arrangements.

Think carefully about flight length. You may find long flights uncomfortable if you can't use cramped airline toilets. Shorter connecting flights can be a good alternative. It's a good idea to schedule at least two hours between flights in case of delays or boarding and de-boarding problems—especially if you want your wheelchair, scooter, or other mobility equipment delivered to the gate at each stop (see below). Be sure your wheelchair is marked with your name and contact information, including those parts that can become separated.

Most airplanes lack accessible bathrooms. Either work out alternative systems for dealing with this issue (such as limiting fluids immediately before a flight) or book flights on planes with accessible bathrooms.

At the Airport: On the day of departure, consider arriving at least an hour earlier than the normal flight check-in time.

You'll probably need local accessible transportation for going to or from airports. Many major transportation companies, like airport shuttles, offer accessible vans with advance reservations.

If you don't own a wheelchair, but need to use one at the airport, request a wheelchair and assistance from the airline. On the plane, canes or crutches can be kept under the seat, provided that the equipment does not block the aisles.

If you can't walk onto the plane, you'll be transported to your seat on an aisle chair (a narrow chair on wheels) by airline personnel. Be prepared to instruct the staff on the best transfer method and to assist with the boarding process.

If you have your own manual wheelchair, you'll generally be allowed to use it until you reach the door of the airplane. Your wheelchair will then be stowed with luggage in the baggage compartment or placed in an onboard storage space. Insist that your wheelchair be brought to the *gate* upon landing, rather than to the baggage claim area. Request this arrangement between flights and at the final destination.

More Air Travel Tips

My readers offer these suggestions for people with limited mobility traveling by air:

"If possible, speak to the ramp/baggage personnel who will be loading your chair (especially important for power chairs). Let them know how to take it out of gear, how to push it, and anything else of importance. Be sure you know what kind of battery you have. If your battery is a sealed, gel-cell type, it will have to be disconnected from your chair and boxed up—and you generally won't get help at the other end to put it back together. If your chair has removable leg rests, armrests, and the like, bring a separate bag to hold them. Ask the baggage handlers about the size of the opening to the baggage compartment and make any adjustments necessary to your chair yourself, such as reclining a high backrest."

"Power chairs and scooters can easily be damaged on airplanes. Having damage-proof packaging for your scooter or wheelchair can provide big relief."

"When making ticket reservations, request a bulkhead aisle seat, and take a plane that is nonstop."

"If you wear a catheter leg bag onto a plane, make sure it is connected tight and TAPED. Otherwise you will have a big wet mess (I learned this one from experience)."

"Know your rights. Demand (politely at first) your rights. Know that every U.S.-based airline is obligated to follow the laws as set forth in the ACAA (Air Carrier Access Act). If you run into a problem, ask immediately for the Complaints Resolution Officer. Every U.S.-based airline is required to have a CRO on duty, and they have the authority to make sure your rights are respected."

"Make sure to inform the airline you have a disability. I used to not do so, until one time a flight attendant noticed and, in a firm but friendly way, counseled me not to board an airplane without making my disability known to the crew. As she put it: Otherwise, in case of an emergency, 'We're going to be asking ourselves, why is he not running?' Remember that we as disabled travelers have a responsibility to inform others about our situation."

"A word of caution about European 'no-frills' airlines: While mainstream airlines employ their own customer-service assistants to help wheelchair passengers from check-in to boarding, no-frills airlines use a pool of people employed by the airport for a variety of duties. If you're flying a no-frills airline and you have asked for wheelchair assistance, you are not by any means guaranteed to receive that service. As a wheelchair passenger flying no-frills, it's a good idea to check in as early as possible, since smaller airports (the kind cheap airlines fly out of) often use old mobile steps to board the aircraft or require passengers to take a bus to the aircraft. Both methods obviously have implications for wheelchair passengers, who may need to be carried."

Tours

If you'd rather not go it alone, you'll find a selection of groups that run accessible tours to Europe, including **Accessible Journeys** (wheelchair trips to Britain, France, and Holland, 35 West Sellers Avenue, Ridley Park, PA 19078, tel. 800-846-4537, www.disabilitytravel.com, sales@disabilitytravel.com), **Flying Wheels Travel** (escorted tours to Great Britain and France, plus custom itineraries, P.O. Box 382, Owatonna, MN 55060, tel. 507/451-5005, www.flyingwheelstravel.com, thq@ll.net), and **Nautilus Tours and Cruises** (tours to France, Belgium, and the Netherlands, plus cruises to other destinations, 22567 Ventura Boulevard, Woodland Hills, CA 91364, tel. outside California 800-797-6004, in California 818/591-3159, www.nautilustours.com).

Access/Abilities offers information and custom searches on accessible-travel opportunities (tel. 415/388-3250). **Accessible Europe** is a collection of European travel agents and tour operators who specialize in disabled travel (www.accessibleurope.com). **Accessible City Breaks,** based in Britain, runs trips to all the cities covered in this book and has a Web site with travel tips and some destination information (www.accessiblecitybreaks.co.uk).

In Case of Discrimination: Under the Americans with Disabilities Act, if you feel you have been discriminated against (such as not being allowed on a U.S. tour company's tour of Europe), contact the U.S. Department of Justice ADA Information Line at 800-514-0301 or the Disability Rights Education and Defense Fund at voice telephone & TTY: 800-466-4232 (www.dredf.org).

ON THE ROAD

These resources and tips will help keep your on-the-road experiences smooth and fun.

Accommodations

A growing number of hotels have elevators and rooms with accessible bathrooms. But hotels aren't your only option.

Hostelling International provides a guide to hostels around the world that indicates which hostels are accessible. Fortunately, most newly built hostels are accessible (tel. 202/783-6161, www.hiayh.org).

The Sweden-based **Independent Living Institute**'s Accessible Vacation Home Exchange Web site can put you in touch with disabled Europeans looking to swap homes or help you find an assistant overseas (www.independentliving.org).

Candy Harrington's new book, *There Is Room at the Inn: Inns and B&Bs for Wheelers and Slow Walkers* provides helpful advice on finding accessible accommodations without sacrificing charm.

Here are some more tips about accommodations from my readers:

"I strongly suggest that you confirm all 'accessible' rooms by phone prior to booking. It is worth it to do this and make absolutely sure that there are no unhappy surprises when you show up!"

"Do your research. The Internet is a wonderful resource, but be sure you talk to people on the phone or by e-mail to ask specific questions, especially about accommodations. Get dimensions of doorways and elevators especially. Elevators in Europe tend to be quite small, which can really be a problem if you are in a power chair. Ask, ask, ask."

"Always plan a minimum of two nights at a destination. This cuts down on the physical hassle of moving from place to place, and gives you a chance to rest on alternate days. Be sure that the hotel is accessible by giving them all your specific requirements (door widths included) before you reserve."

"The most difficult part of planning a trip is being sure that the hotels have both an elevator and a room available with a step-in or roll-in shower. (We e-mail each hotel directly to confirm their ability to meet our specific needs and to request that they save the room we need.) I carry a small rolled-up rubber shower mat in case the shower is slippery."

Parking
Parking spaces reserved for people with disabilities are commonly available throughout Europe. If you have a permit to use these spaces in the U.S., it is also valid in Europe. For more information on parking in Europe, see www.oecd.org/cem/topics/handicaps/parking.htm.

Wheelchairs
Some museums (listed in this book) offer free loaner wheelchairs for mobility-impaired visitors. Be prepared to leave a photo ID as a deposit.
Here are some tips for Europe-bound wheelchair users:

"Electric wheelchairs must be recharged every one to two days, depending on use. Compare the voltage requirements (120V in the United States and 220V in Europe) and be sure you have the proper voltage transformer and type of adapter plug: three flat prongs for Britain, two round prongs for the Continent." *(From NCDE)*

"Repairs for electric or 'power' wheelchairs are more expensive than for manual wheelchairs. Electric-wheelchair parts may be difficult to find when traveling abroad. Assembling an emergency kit of basic tools and frequently broken, hard-to-get parts for power wheelchair users is a smart idea." *(From NCDE)*

"I use a lightweight manual wheelchair with pop-off tires. I take a backpack that fits on the back of my chair and store my daypack underneath my chair in a net bag. Since I usually travel alone, if I can't carry it myself, I don't take it. I keep a bungee cord with me for the times I can't get my chair into a car and need to strap it in the trunk or when I need to secure it on a train." *(From Susan Sygall)*

"If the weather turns poor and you're traveling with a power chair or scooter, get a poncho that covers the occupant and the batteries to stay dry." *(From a reader)*

"Bring information about your wheelchair equipment and repair shop with you. Find out if the manufacturers sell equipment in Europe and get their contact information." *(From a reader)*

"Low-slung backs are great when the wheelchair users push on their own. In cases where they may need assistance, it would be great to be able to attach some higher handles for assistants to use as pushing and leverage points." *(From NCDE)*

"When traveling anywhere with rough terrain or cobblestones, I would highly recommend using Frog Legs shock absorbers on the front of your chair (www.froglegsinc.com), and also use the larger front wheels. The Frog Legs help prevent you from getting stuck in holes and will 'jump' obstacles that can stop you dead in your tracks with regular front wheels and stems. My daughter uses Frogs Legs and we have climbed the Rockies and the hills of Tuscany and have never gotten stuck, nor have I ever dumped her or flipped her and her chair forward." *(From a reader)*

"If using a wheelchair, it is important to measure the outside width of the wheels because some of the doors, elevators, and London cabs are not as wide as ours here in the U.S." *(From a reader)*

"We often discovered that doorways into restaurants or funiculars were too narrow, but, upon looking again, we found that there were second narrow doors next to the main door that can open up if unlocked, therefore creating a wider entrance." *(From NCDE)*

"When using a wheelchair and traveling outside the major cities by car, don't be afraid to drive around a lot to find the accessible entrances and parking areas before you park the car. Otherwise you may find yourself wheeling down busy streets dodging potholes to get to the accessible entrance." *(From a reader)*

Restrooms

"Bathrooms are often a hassle, so I have learned to use creative ways to transfer into narrow spaces. To be blatantly honest, when there are no accessible bathrooms in sight I have found ways to pee discreetly just about anywhere (outside the Eiffel Tower or on a glacier in a national park). Bring along an extra pair of pants and a great sense of humor." *(From Susan Sygall)*

"There are plenty of accessible restrooms in Paris and London. The restrooms are usually locked with entrance limited to people who really need them. At the Eiffel Tower, there is an elevator to the restroom, which is below ground. You must ask the matron, who will then 'beam you down.' WCs in Europe tend to be smaller than those in the United States (probably because we tend to have more girth in general), so if you use a chair larger than 29 inches total width, you may want to bring a smaller one for your trip. Cambered wheels usually make the difference." *(From a reader)*

"When you are out and about and find an accessible toilet, use it! (Or, in other words: Go when you can, not when you have to.) Some 'modernized' tourist facilities offer adapted toilets, but off the beaten path they are rare." *(From a reader)*

Overcoming Challenges

For anyone, challenges are a part of travel. Here are some pointers on traveling well.

"If a museum lacks elevators for visitors, be sure to ask about freight elevators. Almost all have them somewhere, and that can be your ticket to seeing a world-class treasure." *(From Susan Sygall)*

"Bring non-disabled friends. Having more helping hands with you if you need a quick lift up a curb, or if you have trouble handling your luggage, is always good. Also, when things go wrong, having a support group cuts down on panic and increases the number of ideas for solving problems." *(From a reader)*

"Consider making your first trip to a country where you know someone. Visiting friends is great, and having a local to check things out for you before you come is very helpful. They also know you and know the local sources of help if you get in trouble." *(From a reader)*

"Don't confuse being flexible and having a positive attitude with settling for less than your rights. I expect equal access and constantly let people know about the possibility of providing access through ramps or other modifications. When I believe my rights have been violated, I do whatever is necessary to remedy the situation, so the next traveler, or disabled people in that country, won't have the same frustrations." *(From Susan Sygall)*

"Bring a camera with a zoom lens. It allows you to 'get closer' to things without physically moving (and you don't necessarily have to take a picture of everything you look at)." *(From a reader)*

"Note that Europeans, who walk more than the average American, have a different concept of 'not far.' We were once given directions to a hotel that was 'only three streets away.' Yes, but the streets were about three kilometers apart—a long walk for my parents! You may want to ask, 'How many minutes to walk?' instead of, 'How many blocks?' (Or just take a cab if there's any doubt at all.)" *(From a reader)*

"If you get in trouble or need supplies, ask for help. Being shy is a real liability in traveling to a foreign place. Most people are very friendly and helpful. If someone isn't, shrug it off and keep asking. In many cases, you will not need to ask people will jump to your aid." *(From a reader)*

"Asking for help and smiling a lot gets you all kinds of assistance. The staff at the Belgian railway were wonderful. At one point, two employees helped us change trains, carried luggage, took us to hidden freight elevators, and insisted on staying with us until we were safely on the second train. When we tried to tip them after they spent nearly 30 minutes helping us and waiting with us, they refused to accept the tip and insisted it was their job to make our trip pleasant. When we arrived at our destination, we discovered that they had called ahead and had a wheelchair and another smiling attendant waiting at the exit of our rail car!" *(From a reader)*

"Choose your travel wardrobe carefully and fit it into one small piece of luggage. People will be more likely to help you cheerfully if there isn't a lot of hauling involved. (My daughter says, 'Gee, Mom, you meet all the cute, athletic young guys.' But I bet they wouldn't be so helpful if I had a mountain of luggage!)" *(From a reader)*

"Plan short days with time for breaks, and be satisfied with seeing what you can and not regretting what you can't get to. I found that because we moved more slowly, I experienced things that I had missed on earlier trips. Smell the roses, talk with the children, smell the bakeries, and so on." *(From a reader)*

"Be cheerful about your limitations. Sitting in the garden while your companions tour a steep-staired medieval castle is not all bad. You might actually meet and chat with some of the locals." *(From a reader)*

"Keep in mind that accessibility can mean different things in different countries. In some countries, people rely more on human support systems than on physical or technological solutions. People may tell you their building is accessible because they're willing to lift you and your wheelchair over the steps at the entryway. Be open to trying new ways of doing things, but also ask questions to make sure you are comfortable with the access provided." *(From Susan Sygall)*

"I always try to learn some of the language of the country I'm in, because it cuts through the barriers when people stare at you (and they will), and also comes in handy when you need assistance in going up a curb or a flight of steps. Don't accept other people's notions of what is possible—I have climbed Masada in Israel and made it to the top of the Acropolis in Greece." *(From Susan Sygall)*

GREAT BRITAIN

GREAT BRITAIN

Regardless of the revolution we had 200 years ago, many American travelers feel that they "go home" to Britain. This most popular tourist destination has a strange influence and power over us.

Geographically, the isle of Britain is small—600 miles long, and 300 miles across at its widest point. Its highest mountain is 4,400 feet, a foothill by our standards. The population is a fifth of the United States'. At its peak in the mid-1800s, Britain owned one-fifth of the world and accounted for more than half of the planet's industrial output. Today, the empire has been reduced to the isle of Britain itself, a troubled province in Northern Ireland, and small, distant outposts like Gibraltar and the Falklands.

Economically, Great Britain's industrial production is about 5 percent of the world's total. For the first time in history, Ireland has a higher per capita income than Britain. Still, the economy is healthy, and inflation, unemployment, and interest rates are all low.

Culturally, Britain is still a world leader. Her heritage, her culture, and her people cannot be measured in traditional units of power. London is a major exporter of actors, movies, and theater, rock and classical music, and writers, painters, and sculptors.

British television is so good—and so British—that it deserves a mention as a special sightseeing treat. After a hard day of sightseeing, watch the telly over tea in the living room of your B&B. England has five channels. BBC-1 and BBC-2 are government-regulated, commercial-free, and traditionally highbrow. Channels 3, 4, and 5 are private and a little more Yankee, and they have commercials—but those commercials are

How Big, How Many, How Much

- 95,000 square miles (about the size of Oregon or Michigan)
- 60 million people (nearly the same as California)
- 1 British pound sterling (£1) = about $1.80

Great Britain

clever and sophisticated and provide a fun look at England. Broadcasting is funded by a £126-per-year, per-household tax. Hmmm, 60 cents per day to escape commercials and public television pledge drives.

Oscar Wilde said, "The English have everything in common with the Americans—except, of course, language." Traveling through England is an adventure in accents and idioms. Every day, you'll see babies in prams, sucking dummies as their mothers change wet nappies. Soon the kids can trade in their nappies for smalls and spend a penny on their own. "Spend a penny" is British for a visit to the loo (bathroom). In England, chips are fries and crisps are potato chips. A hamburger is a beefburger on a toasted bap. One of the beauties of touring the British Isles is the illusion of hearing a foreign language and actually understanding it—most of the time.

People of leisure punctuate their afternoon with a "cream tea" at a tearoom. You'll get a pot of tea, small finger foods (like cucumber sandwiches), homemade scones, jam, and thick clotted cream. For maximum pinkie-waving taste per calorie, slice your scone thin like a miniature loaf of bread. Tearooms, which often serve appealing light meals, are usually open for lunch and close around 17:00, just before dinner.

My chocoholic readers are enthusiastic about English chocolates. Their favorites include Cadbury Wispa Gold bars (filled with liquid caramel), Cadbury Crunchie bars, Nestle's Lion bars, Cadbury's Boost bars (a shortcake biscuit with caramel in milk chocolate), and Galaxy chocolate bars (especially the ones with hazelnuts). Thornton shops (in larger train stations) sell a box of sweets called the Continental Assortment, which comes with a tasting guide. The highlight is the mocha white-chocolate truffle. British M&Ms (Smarties) are better than American ones. For a few extra pence, adorn your ice cream cone with a "flake"—a chocolate bar stuck right into the middle.

ACCESSIBILITY IN GREAT BRITAIN

Great Britain is one of the world's more accessible countries in terms of attractions, accommodations, and transportation. London, easily the best destination for a first-time visitor, is the epicenter of all things British—one of Europe's most accessible and most enjoyable cities.

The **British Tourist Authority** provides information to help people with disabilities plan a visit to the United Kingdom (551 Fifth Ave. #701, New York, NY 10176, tel. 800-462-2748, fax 212/986-1188, www.visitbritain.com, travelinfo@visitbritain.org).

Transportation

Great Britain provides some helpful resources for people with disabilities: For example, London Taxi International's "black cabs" are wheelchair-accessible. Eurostar, which runs the "Chunnel" train to Paris or Brussels, offers special fares for wheelchair users and their companions (see www .ricksteves.com/eurostar). If traveling by rail within Britain, wheelchair users and one companion can automatically receive a 34 percent discount on point-to-point tickets or 50 percent off same-day round-trips.

Transport for London Access & Mobility provides maps, station guides, and information on access to the London Underground, buses, and river services for people with disabilities. Recent improvements include better wheelchair accessibility and the introduction of audio and visual cues to announce stops on the Tube. This organization will help keep you up-to-date on all the changes (42/50 Victoria Street, London SW1H 0TL, tel. 020/7941-4600, fax 020/7941-4605, www.tfl.gov.uk, access&mobility@tfl.gov.uk). For more details on available resources, see page 69.

Wheelchair Travel rents adapted, lift-equipped vans (with or without driver) that can accommodate up to three wheelchairs. They also rent cars with hand controls and "Chairman" cars (1 Johnston Green, Guildford, Surrey, GU2 6XS, near London, tel. 01483/233 640, fax 01483/237 772, www.wheelchairtravel.co.uk, info@wheelchairtravel.co.uk).

Organizations

Great Britain has numerous organizations designed to support the needs of disabled travelers.

British Council of Organizations of Disabled People (BCODP) provides information to those with disabilities (Litchurch Plaza, Litchurch Lane, Derby DE24 8AA, tel. 01332/295-551, TTY 01332/295-581, www.bcodp.org.uk, general@bcodp.org.uk). Also consider the **Disability Rights Commission** (www.drc-gb.org).

National Association of Disablement Information and Advice Lines (DIAL) can direct you to local groups in the United Kingdom that offer free information and advice on all aspects of disability (www .dialuk.info).

Greater London Action on Disability (GLAD) is a voluntary organization that provides valuable information for disabled visitors and residents. It publishes the biweekly *Disability Update* (relevant excerpts from national newspapers), the monthly *London Disability News,* and the bimonthly *Boadicea* for disabled women (London Bridge 1, London SE1 9BG, tel. 020/7022-1890, www.glad.org.uk).

Government Codes for Accessible Lodging

In London, accommodations are coded for accessibility using a four-tiered National Accessible Scheme (NAS):

M1   Typically suitable for a person who can climb a flight of stairs, but who also might benefit from grab bars.

M2   Typically suitable for a person with restricted walking ability and those who occasionally use a wheelchair or a scooter.

M3   Typically suitable for a person who depends on the use of a wheelchair, and who transfers unaided to and from the wheelchair.

M4   Typically suitable for person who depends on a wheelchair and needs help in transferring from a caregiver, assistant, or a hoist.

Notice that this scheme—while helpful—is upside-down from the Accessibility Levels used in this book (where Level 1 is the most accessible, and Level 4 is the least accessible). If you see an M4 lodging in London, know that it is the same as my "Level 1" designation.

RADAR (Royal Association for Disability and Rehabilitation) provides information and referral to resources for people with disabilities in the United Kingdom. They operate a National Key Scheme (NKS), allowing people with disabilities to get a map and key for 5,000 accessible toilets throughout the UK (£8, tel. 020/7250-3222, fax 020/7250-0212, TTY 020/7250-4119, www.radar.org.uk, radar@radar.org.uk). RADAR also offers a search engine for finding accessible accommodations (www .directenquiries.com).

Holiday Care Services is an advisory service with free listings of accessible accommodations. They also have a good Web site on the travel industry for people with disabilities, and they offer phone support (tel. 01293/774-535 or 01293/784-647, UK info line 0845/124-9971, www .holidaycare.org.uk).

These London companies specialize in travel for people with disabilities: **Can Be Done** (tel. 020/8907-2400, www.canbedone.co.uk, holidays @canbedone.co.uk) and **Access Travel** (www.access-travel.co.uk).

Artsline has information on disabled access to arts and entertainment events in London and on adapted facilities in cinemas, art galleries, restaurants, and theaters (Mon–Fri 9:30–17:30, 54 Chalton St, London NW1 1HS, tel. 030/7388-2227, www.artsline.org.uk).

Web Sites

Undiscovered Britain, run by Ann Litt, is an excellent resource when planning a trip to Britain (www.undiscoveredbritain.com/access).

Tourism For All offers access guides and disability information (www.tourismforall.org.uk).

DisabledGo, funded largely by Marks & Spencer, covers hotels, restaurants, shopping, and attractions in Britain (www.disabledgo.info).

The Irish Wheelchair Association's Web site is a service provider for wheelchair travel in the UK (www.iwa.ie).

Disability Action provides education, advice, and access for travelers with limited mobility (www.disabilityaction.org).

You're Able offers disability-related information, news, chat rooms, and other resources (www.youreable.com).

Guidebooks and Publications

This guidebook should fulfill your needs for a visit to London. But here are a few other guides to consider, especially if you're lingering in London or venturing further into the British Isles.

The Greater London Association for Disabled People publishes a free *London Disability Guide,* available by mail (336 Brixton Road, London SW9 7AA, tel. 020/7346-5800).

London Disability Arts Forum (LDAF) produces a 32-page monthly magazine—*Disability Arts in London,* or *DAIL*—with listings, reviews, and articles on disabled artists (£10/yr or £30/yr for overseas subscribers, www.ldaf.org).

Access in London, written by Gordon Couch, William Forrester, and David McGaughey, and published by Pauline Hephaistos Survey Projects, provides detailed information on London accessibility for people with disabilities (Access Project, 39 Bradley Gardens, West Ealing, London W13 8HE, www.accessproject-phsp.org, gordon.couch@virgin.net). The same team also produces the book *Access in Paris.*

Holidays in Britain and Ireland: A Guide for Disabled People, which features more than 1,400 places to stay in the UK and Ireland, is published by the Royal Association for Disability and Rehabilitation (see below for more on RADAR; book costs £15, tel. 020/7250-322, fax 020/7250-0212, TTY 020/7250-4119, www.radar.org.uk, radar@radar.org.uk). You can also search RADAR's Web site for accessible accommodations (www.radarsearch.org).

The National Trust Disability Office annually publishes the booklet *Information for Visitors with Disabilities,* which contains useful information on the accessibility of National Trust properties available in standard or large print and on audiocassette; National Trust Disability Office, 36 Queen Anne's Gate, London SW1H 9AS, tel. 020/7447-6742, accessforall@ntrust.org.uk).

Comments from Readers

These thoughts on traveling in Britain were submitted by my readers, mostly through my "Graffiti Wall" Web site (www.ricksteves.com).

"Always ask for special discounts when traveling in London if you have a disability (these discounts are called 'concessions')."

"At the Tower of London, we were approached by a Beefeater guard who took us on a private tour and assisted by pushing the chair over the rough terrain. Every place we visited in London was terrific with the assistance and the accessibility. The Londoners came to us everywhere we went; we never needed to ask for help. America could learn some lessons!"

"The Tube was a good option, and we used the Westminster, South Kensington, and Olympia routes at least three times to get around the city. (Lifts always were in good working order when we were there.) But had I not had an able-bodied companion to jump the 'gap,' I don't think I would have used it. My wheelie skills are not that good!"

"My companion and I used London city buses, the Tube, the railway, black cabs, and a Thames riverboat, as well as renting a car and driving in and around Somerset and Yorkshire. A few standout memories include the 45 minutes it took for the National Express coach driver (and several other coach staff) to figure out how to operate the beautiful brand-new wheelchair lift on the coach from Heathrow to Bath—with teamwork, it finally got figured out and the commuters on the coach were quite understanding about the delay...and we got to Bath!"

"Living and working in London, I use black cabs every day with my electric wheelchair. To get an idea of how the ramp works, the cab manufacturers have videos on their site: www.lti.co.uk."

LONDON

London is more than 600 square miles of urban jungle. With nine million people—who don't all speak English—it's a world in itself and a barrage on all the senses. On my first visit, I felt very, very small.

London is more than its museums and landmarks. It's a living, breathing, thriving organism...a coral reef of humanity. The city has changed dramatically in recent years, and many visitors are surprised to find how "un-English" it is. Whites are now a minority in major parts of the city that once symbolized white imperialism. Arabs have nearly bought out the area north of Hyde Park. Chinese take-outs outnumber fish-and-chips shops. Many hotels are run by people with foreign accents (who hire English chambermaids), while outlying suburbs are home to huge communities of Indians and Pakistanis. With the English Channel Tunnel in place and union with the rest of Europe inevitable, many locals see even more holes in their bastion of Britishness. London is learning—sometimes fitfully—to live as a microcosm of its formerly vast empire.

With just a few days here, you'll get no more than a quick splash in this teeming human tidal pool. But with a good orientation, you'll find London manageable and fun. You'll get a sampling of the city's top sights, history, and cultural entertainment, and a good look at its ever changing human face.

Blow through the city on the open deck of a double-decker orientation tour bus and take a pinch-me-I'm-in-London roll or stroll through the West End. Ogle the crown jewels at the Tower of London, hear the chimes of Big Ben, and see the Houses of Parliament in action. Cruise the Thames River and take a spin on the London Eye Ferris Wheel. Hobnob with the tombstones in Westminster Abbey, enjoy Shakespeare in a replica of the Globe Theatre, and gawk in awe at the original Magna Carta at the British Library. Visit with Leonardo, Botticelli, and Rembrandt in the National Gallery. Rummage through our civilization's attic at the British Museum. And sip your tea with your pinky raised and clotted cream dribbling down your scone. Spend one evening at a theater and the others catching your breath.

Accessibility in London

A staggering 20 million people visit London every year, and many of them have disabilities. With recent improvements and a barrier-free mentality, the city makes a great first stop for your trip.

Mention accessibility, and hoteliers, restaurateurs, and civil servants snap to attention. Many venues and services are geared to people who use wheelchairs. The city tours help you taste the fabled history of this diverse and multicultural place. The central restaurants, pubs, and hotels put you in the midst of London's sights and attractions. The city's taxis are convenient, inexpensive, and fully accessible. The bus system has recently completed a transition to full accessibility, and many Tube stations are also possible for someone who uses a wheelchair. The airports are accessible, from customs to baggage claim to queuing for a taxi.

Most of London's big sights are Level 1—Fully Accessible: Churchill Museum and Cabinet War Rooms, National Gallery, National Portrait Gallery, Somerset House, London Transport Museum, Theatre Museum, British Museum, British Library, Wallace Collection, Madame Tussaud's Waxworks, Buckingham Palace, Royal Mews, Hyde Park and Speakers' Corner, Apsley House, Victoria and Albert Museum, Natural History Museum, Science Museum, St. Paul's Cathedral (main floor only), City Hall, London Eye Ferris Wheel, Imperial War Museum, Tate Britain, Tate Modern, Shakespeare's Globe, Bramah Tea and Coffee Museum, Vinopolis City of Wine, and Kew Gardens.

A few London sights will work for wheelchair users who have some assistance (Level 2—Moderately Accessible): Westminster Abbey, Houses of Parliament, St. Martin-in-the-Fields Church (except the crypt), Museum of London, and Dalí Universe.

Fortunately, not many of London's sights are Level 3—Minimally Accessible or Level 4—Not Accessible. Travelers with limited mobility will only have to skip one major attraction (the Tower of London, where only the crown jewels are accessible) and a few minor ones (such as the Banqueting House, Sir John Soane's Museum, Old Bailey, and the top of St. Paul's dome).

Accessibility Levels

This book rates sights, hotels, and restaurants using four levels:

Level 1—Fully Accessible: A Level 1 building is completely barrier-free. Entryways, elevators, and other facilities are specifically adapted to accommodate a person using a wheelchair. If there's a bathroom, it has wide doors and an adapted toilet and sink. Where applicable, the bathing facilities are also fully adapted (including such features as bath boards, grab bars, or a roll-in, no-rim shower). Fully adapted hotel rooms often have an alarm system with pull cords for emergencies.

Level 2—Moderately Accessible: A Level 2 building is suitable for, but not specifically adapted to accommodate, a person using a wheelchair. This level will generally work for a wheelchair user who can make transfers and take a few steps. A person who is permanently in a wheelchair may require some assistance here (either from a companion or from staff).

Level 3—Minimally Accessible: A Level 3 building is satisfactory for people who have minimal mobility difficulties (that is, people who usually do not use a wheelchair, but take more time to do things than a non-disabled person). This building may have some steps and a few other barriers—but not too many. Level 3 buildings are best suited to slow walkers; wheelchair users will require substantial assistance here.

Level 4—Not Accessible: Unfortunately, some places in this book are simply not accessible to people with limited mobility. This means that barriers such as staircases, tight interiors and facilities (elevators, bathrooms, etc.), or other impediments interfere with passage for travelers with disabilities. Buildings in this category might include a church tower that has several flights of steep stairs, or a museum interior that has many levels with lots of steps and no elevator.

For a complete listing of the Accessibility Codes used in this chapter, please see pages 6–7.

To help you prioritize and plan your time, note the ranking that accompanies each sight listing (ranging from ▲▲▲—a can't-miss sight—to zero, for a sight that is easily skippable).

ORIENTATION

(area code: 020)

To grasp London comfortably, see it as the old town in the city center without the modern, congested sprawl. The Thames River runs roughly west to east through the city, with most of the visitor's sights on the north bank. Mentally, maybe even physically, trim down your map to include only the area between the Tower of London (to the east), Hyde Park (west), Regent's Park (north), and the Thames (south). (This is roughly the area bordered by the Tube's Circle Line.) This three-mile stretch between the Tower and Hyde Park—looking like a milk bottle on its side (see map on the next page)—holds 80 percent of the sights mentioned in this chapter.

London is a collection of neighborhoods:

The City: Shakespeare's London was a walled town clustered around St. Paul's Cathedral. Today, it's the modern financial district.

Westminster: This neighborhood includes Big Ben, Parliament, Westminster Abbey, and Buckingham Palace—the grand government buildings from which Britain is ruled.

The West End: Lying between Westminster and The City (that is, at the "west end" of the original walled town), this is the center of London's cultural life. Trafalgar Square has major museums. Piccadilly Circus and Leicester Square host tourist traps, cinemas, and nighttime glitz. Soho and Covent Garden are thriving people zones that house theaters, restaurants, pubs, and boutiques.

The South Bank: Until recently, the entire south bank of the Thames River was a run-down, generally ignored area, but now it's the hottest real estate in town, with upscale restaurants, major new sightseeing attractions, and pedestrian bridges allowing convenient access from the rest of London.

Residential Neighborhoods to the West: Though they lack major tourist sights, Mayfair, South Kensington, Notting Hill, Chelsea, and Belgravia are home to London's wealthy and trendy, as well as many shopping streets and enticing restaurants.

With this focus and a good orientation, you'll find London manageable and even fun. You'll get a sampling of the city's top sights, history, and cultural entertainment, and a good look at its ever changing human face.

Tourist Information

The Britain and London Visitors Centre, just a block off Piccadilly Circus, is the best tourist information service in town (**AE, AI, AL+A, AT+A,** Level 2—Moderately Accessible, no adapted toilet, but small lift leads to suitable upper-level toilet; Mon–Fri 9:00–18:30, Sat–Sun 10:00–16:00, phone not answered after 17:00 Mon–Fri and not at all Sat–Sun, booking service, 1 Lower Regent Street, tel. 020/8846-9000, www.visitbritain.com, www.visitlondon.com). If you're traveling beyond

London's Neighborhoods

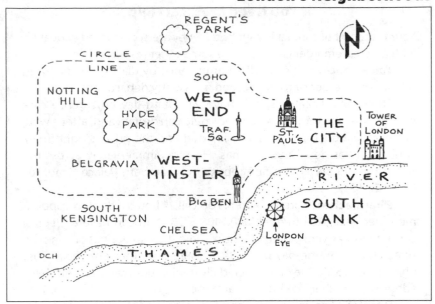

London, take advantage of the Centre's well-equipped England desk. Bring your itinerary and a checklist of questions. At the London desk, pick up these free publications: *London Map and Guide*, *London Planner* (a great free monthly that lists all the sights, events, and hours), walking-tour schedule fliers, a theater guide, *Central London Bus Guide*, and the Thames River Services brochure. If you'll be taking the Underground, pick up a free copy of the Accessible Tube Map. After you've grazed through the great leaflet racks, take the elevator upstairs to find inviting tables and Internet access (with disk-burning service).

The Britain and London Visitors Centre ("pink desk") sells long-distance bus tickets and passes, train tickets (convenient for reservations), and tickets to plays (20 percent booking fee). They also sell **Fast Track tickets** to some of London's attractions (at no extra cost), allowing you to skip the queue at the sights. These can be worthwhile for places that sometimes have long ticket lines, such as the Tower of London, London Eye Ferris Wheel, and Madame Tussaud's Wax Museum. (But remember that many of these sights allow wheelchair users and their companions to skip the line anyway.) While the Visitors Centre books rooms, you can avoid their £5 booking fee by calling hotels direct (see "Sleeping," page 132).

The **London Pass** provides free entrance to most of the city's sights, but since many museums are free, it's hard to justify the purchase.

If You Need Medical Help

Your first point of contact is your hotel. They are accustomed to dealing with medical emergencies. Here are some other resources:

Ambulance: You can call an ambulance by dialing 999 or 112. In Britain, an emergency room is called a "casualty department."

Hospitals: Local hospitals have 24-hour-a-day emergency care centers where any tourist who needs help can drop in and, after a wait, be seen by a doctor. The quality is good and the price is right (free). Your hotel has details. St. Thomas' Hospital, immediately across the river from Big Ben, has a fine reputation (Lambeth Palace Road, tel. 020/7928-9292).

Pharmacies: Pharma-Center is on call 24 hours a day (no appointment necessary, toll-free tel. 0808-108-5720). You can have a medical consultation at your hotel or visit a clinic (travel vaccinations, health screening, and same-day blood test results). Another pharmacy, Bliss Chemist, is at 5 Marble Arch (open daily until 24:00). Police stations have addresses for other late-night pharmacies.

Dentists: For dental emergencies, consider the 24-Hour Accident and Acute Dental Emergency Service (75 Glouster Road, opposite Glouster Road Tube station, tel. 020/7373-3744 or 020/7373-6708). Or call the Dental Emergency Care Service, an all-hours advisory service that can direct you where to go for dental emergencies (tel. 020/7935-4486).

Still, fervent sightseers can check the list of covered sights and do the arithmetic (£27/1 day, £42/2 days, £52/3 days, £72/6 days, includes 160-page guidebook, tel. 0870-242-9988 for purchase instructions, www .londonpass.com).

Nearby you'll find the **Scottish Tourist Centre** (**AE, AI,** Level 2—Moderately Accessible; Mon–Fri 8:00–20:00, Sat 9:00–17:30, Sun 10:00–16:00, Cockspur Street, tel. 0845-225-5121, www.visitscotland .com) and the slick **French National Tourist Office** (**AE, AI,** Level 2—Moderately Accessible; Mon–Fri 10:00–18:00, Sat until 17:00, closed Sun, 178 Piccadilly Street, tel. 0906-824-4123).

Unfortunately, **London's Tourist Information Centres** (which present themselves as TIs at major train and bus stations and airports) are now simply businesses selling advertising space to companies with fliers to distribute. For solid information, visit the Britain and London Visitors Centre, mentioned above.

Local bookstores sell London guides and maps; *Bensons Map Guide* is the best (£3, also sold at newsstands).

Arrival in London

By Train: London has eight train stations, all connected by the Tube (subway) and all with ATMs, exchange offices, and luggage storage. From any station, ride the Tube or taxi to your hotel.

By Bus: The bus ("coach") station is one block southwest of Victoria Station, which has a TI and Tube entrance.

By Plane: For detailed information on getting from London's airports to downtown London, see "Transportation Connections" (page 154).

Helpful Hints

Accessibility Resources: Call the Accessibility Officer of London if you need help with any accessibility issue (tel. 020/7332-1995 or tel. 020/7332-1933). The extremely helpful *Access in London* guidebook is a deal for £10 at Waterstone's and other good London bookstores (see "Travel Bookstores," below; see also www.accessproject-phsp.org).

Safety Crossing Streets: Cars drive on the left side of the road, so before crossing a street, 1 always look right, look left, then look right again just to be sure.

Theft Alert: The Artful Dodger is alive and well in London. Be on guard, particularly on public transportation and in places crowded with tourists. Tourists, considered naive and rich, are targeted. More than 7,500 handbags are stolen annually at Covent Garden alone.

U.S. Embassy: The embassy is fully accessible (**AE, AI, AL, AT,** Level 1; open Mon–Fri 8:30–17:30, closed Sat–Sun, 24 Grosvenor Square, Tube: Bond Street, tel. 020/7499-9000).

Changing Money: ATMs are the way to go (many accessible on-street ATMs charge no fees). Regular banks charge several pounds to change traveler's checks, but most American Express offices offer a fair rate and will change any brand of traveler's checks for no fee. A handy, fully accessible AmEx office is at Heathrow's Terminal 4 Tube station (daily 7:00–19:00). The always accessible Marks & Spencer stores give good rates with no fees.

Avoid changing money at exchange bureaus. Their latest scam: They advertise very good rates with a same-as-the-banks fee of 2 percent. But the fine print explains that the fee of 2 percent is for buying pounds. The fee for selling pounds is 9.5 percent. Ouch!

Internet Access: The **easyInternetcafé** chain offers up to 500 computers per store and is open long hours daily. Depending on the time of day, a £2 ticket buys anywhere from 80 minutes to six hours of computer time. The ticket is valid for four weeks and multiple visits at any of their branches. They also sell 24-hour, seven-day, and 30-day passes (www.easyinternetcafe.com). The locations—which have varying degrees of accessibility—include Trafalgar Square (456 Strand), Tottenham Court Road (#9–16), Oxford Street (#358, opposite Bond Street Tube station), and Kensington High Street (#160–166). The fully accessible (and appropriately named) **Access Printers,** across the street from Victoria Station (next to the Apollo Victoria Theatre), has plenty of terminals (£1/30 min, open long hours daily).

Travel Bookstores: Stanfords Travel Bookstore, in Covent Garden, is good and stocks current editions of my books (**AE, AI,** Level 2—Moderately Accessible; Mon–Fri 9:00–19:30, Sat 10:00–19:00, Sun 12:00–18:00, 12 Long Acre, tel. 020/7836-1321). Two impressive Waterstone's bookstores have the biggest collection of travel guides in town (both **AE, AI,** Level 2—Moderately Accessible): on Piccadilly (Mon–Sat 10:00–22:00, Sun 12:00–18:00, 203 Piccadilly, tel. 020/7851-2400) and on Trafalgar Square (Mon–Sat 9:30–21:00, Sun 12:00–18:00, next to Costa Café, tel. 020/7839-4411).

Left Luggage: As security concerns heighten, train stations have replaced their lockers with left-luggage counters. Each bag must go through a scanner (just like at the airport), so lines can be long. Expect a wait to pick up your bags, too (each item-£6/24 hrs, daily 7:00–24:00). You can also check bags at the airports (£5/day). If leaving London and returning later, you may be able to leave a box or bag at your hotel for free—assuming you'll be staying there again.

Getting Around London

To travel smart in a city this size, get comfortable with public transportation. London's excellent taxis, buses, and subway system make a private car unnecessary. In fact, the "congestion charge" of £8 levied on any private car entering the city center has been effective in cutting down traffic jam delays and bolstering London's public transit. The revenue raised subsidizes the buses, which are now cheaper, more frequent, and even more user-friendly than before. Today, the vast majority of vehicles in the city center are buses, taxis, and service trucks. (Drivers, for all the details on the congestion charge, see www.cclondon.com.)

Slow walkers and non-disabled travelers find the Tube and buses to be the cheapest and most efficient way to get around. If you're a wheelchair user, you'll be glad to know that all London buses are fully accessible, though the Tube networks still have several non-accessible

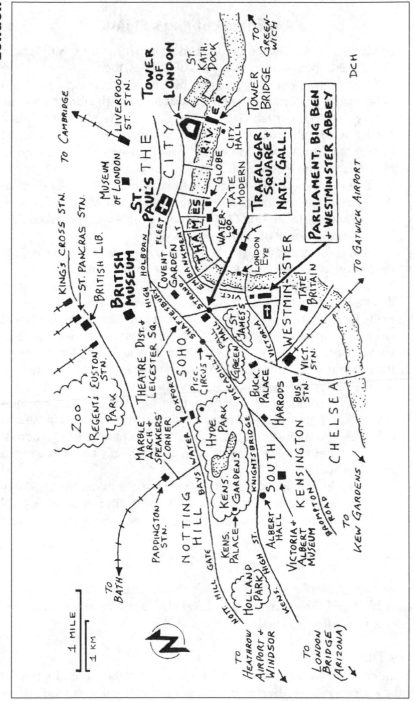

Affording London's Sights

London is, in many ways, Europe's most expensive city, with lots of pricey sights, but—fortunately—lots of freebies, too.

Many of the city's biggest and best museums won't cost you a dime. Free sights include the British Museum, British Library, National Gallery, National Portrait Gallery, Tate Britain, Tate Modern, Wallace Collection, Imperial War Museum, Victoria and Albert Museum, Natural History Museum, Science Museum, Sir John Soane's Museum, Theatre Museum, and the Museum of London.

Some museums, such as the British Museum, request a £2–3 donation, but whether you contribute or not is up to you. Many offer essential audioguides for around £3. If I spend the money on an audioguide, I don't feel bad about not donating otherwise.

Remember that if you use a wheelchair, you (or your companion) will get free or discounted entry to sights that normally charge admission.

Other freebies to consider: You can get into the Tower of London by attending the Ceremony of the Keys (which requires a reservation made long in advance—see page 115). You can view the legislature at work in the Houses of Parliament. There are plenty of free concerts, such as the lunch concerts at St. Martin-in-the-Fields. You can also enjoy the pageantry of Changing of the Guard and the wild people-watching scene at Covent Garden.

Smaller churches let worshippers in free (even tourist worshippers), having given up on asking for donations. The big sightseeing churches—Westminster Abbey and St. Paul's—charge £9–10 for admission, but offer free evensong services virtually daily and a free organ recital on Sunday.

When budgeting your sightseeing money, consider the £5.50 city walking tours as one of the best deals going. The hop-on, hop-off big-bus tours (£16–20), while expensive, provide a great overview, and

stops (see "Accessibility on London's Public Transportation" sidebar for details). Taxis, which are all fully accessible, are also very convenient for people who use wheelchairs.

By Taxi

London is the best taxi town in Europe. Big, black, carefully regulated cabs are everywhere. Best of all, every taxi in London is required to be wheelchair-accessible.

include boat tours as well as city walks, depending on the company you choose (see page 77). A one-hour Thames ride costs about £7, but generally comes with entertaining commentary (see page 81).

The queen charges big-time to open her palace to the public: Buckingham Palace (£14, open Aug–Sept only) and her art gallery and carriage museum (adjacent to the palace, about £7 each) are interesting but expensive.

Gimmicky private enterprises can charge sky-high prices, such as the London Dungeon (£14), the fun, popular, and overpriced Madame Tussaud's Waxworks (£23, but £14 after 17:00), and the Dalí Universe (£9), which capitalizes on its location next to the popular London Eye Ferris Wheel.

Big-ticket sights worth their admission fees are Kew Gardens (£8.50), Shakespeare's Globe Theatre (£9, includes a tour), and the Cabinet War Rooms, with its fine Churchill Exhibit (£10). The London Eye Ferris Wheel is an unforgettable experience (£12.50), and Vinopolis wine museum provides a classy way to get a buzz and call it museum-going (£12.50 entry includes 5 small glasses of wine).

Many classy smaller museums cost around £5. My favorites include the three Somerset House museums (Courtauld Gallery, Heritage Rooms, and the Gilbert Collection) and the Wellington Museum at Apsley House.

The freestanding "tkts" booth at Leicester Square offers discounted tickets to London's famous shows; unfortunately, it's not suited for people who use wheelchairs (see page 130).

These days, London doesn't come cheap. But with its many free museums and affordable plays, this cosmopolitan, cultured city offers days of sightseeing thrills without requiring you to pinch your pennies (or your pounds).

I've never met a crabby cabbie in London. They love to talk, and they know every nook and cranny in town. I ride in one each day just to get my London questions answered.

Access: AE, Level 1—Fully Accessible. All "Black Cabs" have ramps that pull down on the side of the car, so you can wheel right in. The older cabs carry a ramp in the trunk, which the driver will take out when needed. Cab drivers have sometimes been known to switch off their light when they see a wheelchair user on the road, but this is unusual. In fact, if a taxi driver is reported to be discourteous to a wheelchair user (or anyone else, for that matter), he can lose his license.

Cost and Procedure: Rides start at £2.20. Connecting downtown sights is quick and easy and will cost you about £5 (for example, St. Paul's to the Tower of London). For a short ride, three people in a cab travel at Tube prices. Groups of four or five should taxi everywhere. While telephoning a cab will get you one in a few minutes (try Radio Taxi, tel. 020/7272-0272; or DiAL+A-Cab, tel. 020/7253-5000; tell them if you're using a wheelchair), it's generally not necessary; hailing a cab is easy and costs less. If a cab's top light is on, just wave it down. (Drivers flash lights when they see you.) They have a tiny turning radius, so you can wave at cabs going in either direction. If waving doesn't work, ask someone where you can find a taxi stand.

Don't worry about meter cheating. British cab meters come with a sealed computer chip and clock that ensure you'll get the regular tariff #1 most of the time, tariff #2 during "unsociable hours" (18:00–6:00 and Sat–Sun), and tariff #3 only on holidays. (Rates only go up about 10 percent with each higher tariff.) All extra charges are explained in writing on the cab wall. The only way a cabbie can cheat you is to take a needlessly long route. Another pitfall is taking a cab when traffic is bad to a destination efficiently served by the Tube. On my last trip to London, I hopped in a taxi at South Kensington for Waterloo Station and hit bad traffic. Rather than spending 20 minutes and £2 on the tube, I spent 40 minutes and £16 in a taxi.

Tip a cabbie by rounding up (maximum 10 percent). If you overdrink and ride in a taxi, be warned: Taxis charge £40 for "soiling" (a.k.a. pub puke).

By Bus

Riding city buses doesn't come naturally to many travelers, but if you make a point to figure out the system, you'll swing like Tarzan through the urban jungle of London.

Access: Thanks to a recent initiative, all London buses are now Level 1—Fully Accessible. A mechanical ramp electronically lowers to the curb to allow wheelchair users to board the bus.

Taking the Bus: Pick up the free *Central London Bus Guide* at a transport office or TI for a fine map listing all the bus routes best for sightseeing. If you learn how to decipher bus stop signs, you can figure out on your own where to catch the bus to get to your destination. Find a bus stop and study the signs mounted on the pole next to the stop. You'll see a chart listing (alphabetically) the destinations served by buses

Accessibility on London's Public Transportation

London has one of the world's best public transportation networks—and making all of the trains, buses, and boats fully accessible to all visitors is a priority. There are gaps in the network, but they are gradually being filled. New Tube stations and buses are fully adapted, and old ones are continually being retrofitted to meet accessibility standards.

If you have specific questions about accessibility on London's public transportation, call **Transport for London** at tel. 020/7222-1234. There is also accessibility information on their Web site: www.tfl.gov .uk (click on "Travel info & planned works," then "Passenger help," then "Accessibility").

Transport for London offers several free resources for travelers with limited mobility, including a Tube map listing all accessible stations (see pages vi–vii, or online at www.thetube.com). Be warned that even when the Tube map says a station is "accessible," there's often a 4–10" step between the platform and the train. (That's why they say, "Mind the gap.") You can call Transport for London to request any of these materials (from the U.S., dial 011-44-20-7222-1234). Once in London, you can get the Accessible Tube Map at any Tube station. For the other materials, or for questions, visit a Travel Information Center (at various Tube stations around London, including Victoria Station, Victoria Coach Station, both Tube stations at Heathrow Airport, Piccadilly Circus, Liverpool Street, Euston, West Croydon, Bromley, and Camden Town Hall).

For a specific trip within London, Transport for London's online **Journey Planner** will figure out if you can get to your destination without encountering barriers (http://journeyplanner.tfl.gov.uk; click on "More Options" to specify your mobility level).

that pick up at this spot or nearby; the names of the buses; and alphabet letters that identify where the buses pick up. After locating your destination, remember or write down the bus name and bus stop letter. Next, refer to the neighborhood map (also on the pole) to find your bus stop. Just match your letter with a stop on the map. Make your way to that stop—you'll know it's yours because it will have the same letter on its

Key Bus Routes

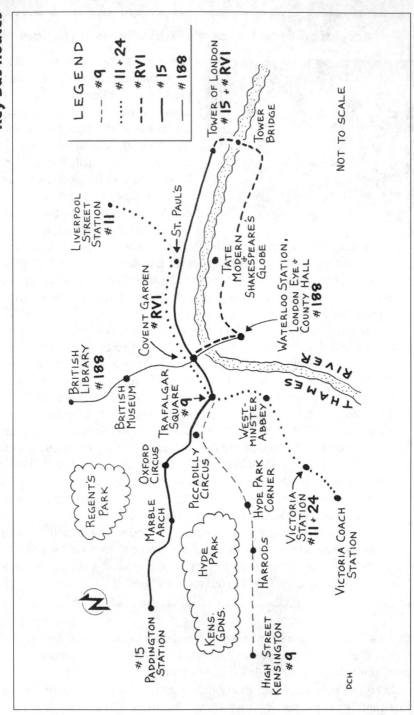

Handy Buses

London's great bus system is fully wheelchair-accessible. And, since the institution of London's "congestion charge" for cars, it's faster and easier than ever. Tube-oriented travelers need to make a point to get over their tunnel vision, learn the bus system, and get around quickly and easily.

Here are some of the most useful routes:

Route #9: Harrods to Hyde Park Corner to Piccadilly Circus to Trafalgar Square.

Routes #11 and #24: Victoria Station to Westminster Abbey to Trafalgar Square (#11 continues to St. Paul's).

Route #RV1: Tower of London to Tower Bridge to Tate Modern/Shakespeare's Globe to London Eye/ Waterloo Station/County Hall Travel Inn accommodations to Trafalgar Square to Covent Garden (a scenic joyride).

Route #15: Paddington Station to Oxford Circus to Regent Street/ TI to Piccadilly Circus to Trafalgar Square to Fleet Street to St. Paul's to Tower of London.

Route #188: Waterloo Station/London Eye to Trafalgar Square to Covent Garden to British Museum.

In addition, several buses (including #6, #12, #13, #15, #23, #139, and #159) make the corridor run from Trafalgar, Piccadilly Circus, and Oxford Circus to Marble Arch.

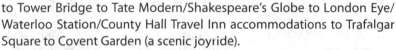

pole—and wait for the bus with the right name to arrive. Some fancy stops have electric boards indicating the minutes until the next bus arrives; but remember to check the name on the bus before you get on. Crack the code, and you're good to go.

On most buses, you'll pay at a machine at the bus stop (exact change only; bus rides covered by Travelcards or Oyster cards), then show your ticket as you board. If you're using an Oyster card (see below), don't forget to touch it to the electronic card reader as you board (there's no need to do so when you get off). On a few of the older double-decker buses (serving "Heritage" routes #9 and #15, not accessible), you still pay a conductor; he or she will come around and collect your fare. Any ride in downtown

London costs £1.50 for those paying cash. If you have an Oyster card, the trip costs 80p (except before 9:30, when it's £1). A ticket six-pack costs £6, and an all-day bus pass costs £3.50. If you're staying longer, consider the £13.50 all-week bus pass. The best views are upstairs on a double-decker.

If you have a Travelcard or Oyster card, get in the habit of using buses for quick little straight shots, even just to get to a Tube stop. During bump-and-grind rush hours (8:00–10:00 and 16:00–19:00), you'll go faster by Tube.

By Tube

London's subway system (called the Tube or Underground, but never "subway") is one of this planet's great people-movers and the fastest long-distance transport in town (runs Mon–Sat about 5:00–24:00, Sun about 7:00–23:00).

Access: Ranges from Level 4—Not Accessible to Level 1—Fully Accessible. The Accessible Tube Map (available at any Tube station, in the front of this book, or online at www.thetube.com) shows which Tube stops are accessible. It can be hit-or-miss downtown. The handy Jubilee line has accessible stations at several important downtown stops, including Westminster, Waterloo, Southwark, and London Bridge; several other outlying stops on other lines are also accessible (including both Heathrow Airport stops on the Piccadilly Line). Even at "accessible" stations, you will have to conquer the famous "gap" between the platform and the train, which can be as big as 10 inches.

Using the Tube: Survey a Tube map. At the front of this book, you'll find a complete Tube map with color-coded lines and names. You can also pick up a free Tube map at any station. Each line has a name (such as Circle, Northern, or Bakerloo) and two directions (indicated by the end-of-the-line stop). Find the line that will take you to your destination, and figure out roughly what direction (north, south, east, west) you'll need to go to get there.

In the Tube station, feed your paper ticket or pass into the turnstile, reclaim it, and hang onto it—you'll need it to get through the turnstile at the end of your journey. If you are using a plastic Oyster card (see below), make sure you touch the card to the yellow card reader when you enter and exit the station. Find your train by following signs to your line and the (general) direction it's headed (such as Central Line: east).

Since some tracks are shared by several lines, you'll need to double-check before boarding a train: First, make sure your destination is one of the stops listed on the sign at the platform. Also, check the electronic signboards that announce which train is next, and make sure the destination (the end-of-the-line stop) is the one you want. Some trains, particularly on the Circle and District lines, split off for other directions, but each train has its final destination marked above its windshield. When in doubt, ask a local or a blue-vested staff person for help.

Trains run roughly every three to 10 minutes. If one train is absolutely packed and you notice another to the same destination is coming in three minutes, you can wait and avoid the sardine experience. The system can be fraught with construction delays and breakdowns, so pay attention to signs and announcements explaining necessary detours. The Circle Line is notorious for problems. Rush hours (8:00–10:00 and 16:00–19:00) can be packed and sweaty. Bring something to do to make your waiting time productive. If you get confused, ask for advice at the information window located before the turnstile entry.

You can't leave the system without feeding your ticket to the turnstile or touching your Oyster card to a scanner. (The turnstile will either eat your now-expired single-trip ticket, or spit your still-valid pass back out.) Save time by choosing the best street exit—check the maps on the walls or ask any station personnel. "Subway" means "pedestrian underpass" in "English." For Tube and bus information, visit www.tfl.gov.uk (and check out the Journey Planner). And always...mind the gap.

Cost: Any ride in Zone 1 through 4 costs a steep £3 for adults paying cash. Riding out to Zones 5 or 6 (e.g., to Heathrow Airport) costs £4. The savings you get from any of the below passes or Oyster cards make paying cash each time an expensive ride. Tube tickets or Oyster cards are also valid on city buses and the Docklands Light Railway.

If you do buy a single Tube ticket, you can avoid ticket-window lines in stations by using the coin-op or credit-card machines; practice on the punchboard to see how the system works (hit "Adult Single" and your destination). These tickets are valid only on the day of purchase.

London Tube and Bus Passes: Consider using the following passes, valid on both the Tube and buses. Note that all passes can be purchased as easily as a normal ticket at any Tube station, get you a 30 percent discount on most Thames cruises (details online at www.tfl.gov.uk, look under "Tickets and Oyster"), and come in a pricier all-zone version.

If you take at least two rides in a day, a Travelcard is a good deal. The **One-Day Travelcard,** covering Zones 1 and 2, gives you unlimited travel for a day. The regular price is £6.20, but an "Off-Peak" version is only

London at a Glance

▲▲▲**Westminster Abbey** Britain's finest church and the site of royal coronations and burials since 1066. **Hours:** Mon–Fri 9:30–15:45, Wed also until 19:00, Sat 9:30–13:45, closed Sun to sightseers but open for services. **Access:** Level 2—Moderately Accessible.

▲▲▲**Churchill Museum and Cabinet War Rooms** Underground WWII headquarters of Churchill's war effort. **Hours:** Daily April–Sept 9:30-18:00, daily Oct–March 10:00–18:00. **Access:** Level 1—Fully Accessible.

▲▲▲**National Gallery** Remarkable collection of European paintings (1250–1900), including Leonardo, Botticelli, Velázquez, Rembrandt, Turner, van Gogh, and the Impressionists. **Hours:** Daily 10:00–18:00, Wed until 21:00. **Access:** Level 1—Fully Accessible.

▲▲▲**British Museum** The world's greatest collection of artifacts of Western civilization, including the Rosetta Stone and the Parthenon's Elgin Marbles. **Hours:** Daily 10:00–17:30, Thu–Fri until 20:30 but only a few galleries open after 17:30. **Access:** Level 1—Fully Accessible.

▲▲▲**British Library** Impressive collection of the most important literary treasures of the Western World, from the Magna Carta to Handel's *Messiah*. **Hours:** Mon–Fri 9:30–18:00, Tue until 20:00, Sat 9:30–17:00, Sun 11:00–17:00. **Access:** Level 1—Fully Accessible.

▲▲▲**St. Paul's Cathedral** The main cathedral of the Anglican Church, designed by Christopher Wren, with a climbable dome and daily evensong services. **Hours:** Mon–Sat 8:30–16:30, closed Sun except for worship. **Access:** Everything except the dome and American Memorial Chapel is Level 1—Fully Accessible.

▲▲▲**Tower of London** Historic castle, palace, and prison, today housing the crown jewels and a witty band of Beefeaters. **Hours:** March–Oct Tue–Sat 9:00–18:00, Sun–Mon 10:00–18:00; Nov–Feb Tue–Sat 9:00–17:00, Sun–Mon 10:00-17:00. **Access:** Level 3—Minimally Accessible. Only the crown jewels are fully accessible.

▲▲▲**London Eye Ferris Wheel** Enormous observation wheel, dominating—and offering commanding views over—London's skyline. **Hours:** April–mid-Sept daily 9:30–21:00, until 22:00 in July–Aug, mid-Sept–March daily 9:30-20:00, closed Jan. **Access:** Level 1—Fully Accessible.

▲▲▲**Tate Modern** Works by Monet, Matisse, Dalí, Picasso, and Warhol displayed in a converted powerhouse. **Hours:** Daily 10:00–18:00, Fri–Sat until 22:00. **Access:** Level 1—Fully Accessible.

▲▲**Houses of Parliament** London's famous neo-Gothic landmark, topped by Big Ben and occupied by the Houses of Lords and Commons. **Hours** (both houses): Generally Mon 14:30–22:30, Tue–Thu 11:30–19:30, Fri 9:30–15:00. **Access:** Level 2—Moderately Accessible.

▲▲**National Portrait Gallery** Who's Who of British history, featuring portraits of this nation's most important historical figures. **Hours:** Daily 10:00–18:00, Thu–Fri until 21:00. **Access:** Level 1—Fully Accessible.

▲▲**Buckingham Palace** Britain's royal residence, with the famous Changing of the Guard. **Hours:** Palace—Aug–Sept only, daily 9:30–17:00; Guard—almost daily in summer at 11:30, every other day all year long. **Access:** Level 1—Fully Accessible.

▲▲**Victoria and Albert Museum** The best collection of decorative arts anywhere. **Hours:** Daily 10:00–17:45, Wed and last Fri of the month until 22:00 except mid-Dec–mid-Jan. **Access:** Level 1—Fully Accessible.

▲▲**Shakespeare's Globe** Timbered, thatched-roofed reconstruction of the Bard's original wooden "O." **Hours:** Mid-May–Sept exhibition open daily 9:00–18:00, tours go on the half-hour from 9:30, generally until 12:30, until 11:30 on Sun, 17:30 on Mon; Oct–mid-May exhibition open daily 10:00–17:00 with 30-min tours on the half-hour. Plays are also held here; see page 130. **Access:** Level 1—Fully Accessible.

▲▲**Vinopolis: City of Wine** Offers a breezy history of wine, with plenty of tasting opportunities. **Hours:** Daily 12:00–18:00, Fri–Sat and Mon until 21:00. **Access:** Level 1—Fully Accessible.

▲▲**Tate Britain** Collection of British painting from the 16th century through modern times, including works by William Blake, the Pre-Raphaelites, and J.M.W. Turner. **Hours:** Daily 10:00–17:50. **Access:** Level 1—Fully Accessible.

London for Early Birds and Night Owls

Most sightseeing in London is restricted to between 10:00 and 18:00. Here are a few exceptions:

Sights Open Early

British Library: Mon–Sat at 9:30.
Buckingham Palace: Aug–Sept daily at 9:30.
Churchill Museum and Cabinet War Rooms: April–Sept daily at 9:30.
Houses of Parliament: Fri at 9:30.
Kew Gardens: Daily at 9:30.
London Eye Ferris Wheel: Daily at 9:30.
Madame Tussaud's Waxworks: Sat–Sun at 9:30.
Shakespeare's Globe: Mid-May–Sept exhibition opens at 9:00, tours start at 9:30.
St. Paul's Cathedral: Mon–Sat at 8:30.
Tower of London: Mon–Sat at 9:00 (Tue–Sat in winter).
Westminster Abbey: Mon–Sat at 9:30.

Sights Open Late

British Library: Tue until 20:00.
British Museum (some galleries): Thu–Fri until 20:30.
Houses of Parliament (when in session): Mon until 22:30, Tue–Thu until 19:30.
London Eye Ferris Wheel: Daily until 21:00 (22:00 in July–Aug, 20:00 in winter).
National Gallery: Wed until 21:00.
National Portrait Gallery: Thu–Fri until 21:00.
Sir John Soane's Museum: First Tue of month until 21:00.
Tate Modern: Fri–Sat until 22:00.
Victoria and Albert Museum: Wed and last Fri of month until 22:00.
Vinopolis: Mon and Fri–Sat until 21:00.

£4.90; it's good for travel starting after 9:30 on weekdays and anytime on weekends. A One-Day Travelcard for Zones 1 through 6, which includes Heathrow Airport, costs £12.40; the restricted "off-peak" version (good for travel after 9:30 on weekdays and all day on weekends and holidays) costs £6.30.

Families save with the "Kid for a Quid" promotion: Any adult with a Travelcard can buy an Off-Peak One-Day Travelcard for up to four kids age 15 or younger for only £1 ("quid") each.

The **Three-Day Travelcard,** covering Zones 1 and 2 for £15.40, costs 20 percent less than three One-Day "Peak" Travelcards and is also good any time of day. Most travelers staying three days will easily take enough Tube and bus rides to make this worthwhile. Buying three separate One-Day "Off-Peak" Travelcards will save you 70 pence, but you'll only be able to travel after 9:30 on weekdays. Three-Day Travelcards are not available in an "Off-Peak" version.

The **Seven-Day Travelcard** costs £22.20 and covers Zones 1 and 2. Those that cover travel beyond Zone 2 cost progressively more, up to £41. All Seven-Day Travelcards are now sold as plastic Oyster cards (no photo needed; see below).

Groups of 10 or more adults can travel all day on the Tube for £3.50 each (but not on buses). Kids 17 and younger pay £1 when part of a group of 10.

You'll likely see signs advertising the **Oyster card,** designed for commuters (but potentially useful for tourists staying more than a few days). These prepaid, rechargeable plastic "smart cards" are good for Tube, bus, and Docklands Light Railway trips, depending on what version you buy. There's a £10 minimum to get or add to a card, and you'll pay an additional £3 deposit, refundable at any Tube station ticket office when you return the card. You should also receive a cash refund of any remaining balance. Using an Oyster card slashes the cost of a Tube ride in half to £1.50 when traveling in Zone 1 (additional zones cost more), and the money on the card never expires. If you ride a lot in one day, the Oyster card will never deduct more than the price of a One-Day Travelcard. When it runs low, your Oyster card can be "topped up" at most Tube station ticket offices or self-serve machines, Victoria or Euston train stations, Heathrow Tube station, or at more than 2,000 participating convenience stores. For more details, visit www.tfl.gov.uk/oyster.

TOURS

▲▲▲**Hop-on, Hop-off Double-Decker Bus Tours**—Two competitive companies (Original and Big Bus) offer essentially the same tours with buses that have either live (English-only) guides or a tape-recorded, dial-a-language narration. This two-hour, once-over-lightly bus tour drives by all the famous sights, providing a stress-free way to get your bearings and at least see the biggies. You can sit back and enjoy the entire two-hour orientation tour (a good idea if you like the guide and the weather), or get on and get off at any of the nearly 30 stops and catch a later bus. Buses run about every 10–15 minutes in summer, every 20 minutes in winter. It's an inexpensive form of transport, as well as an informative tour. Buses operate daily (from about 9:00 until early evening in summer, until late afternoon in winter) and stop at Victoria Station, Marble Arch, Piccadilly Circus, Trafalgar Square, and elsewhere. These tours aren't fully accessible (specific details for each company described below), so if you use a wheelchair, you may prefer to get oriented by taxi or public bus instead.

Both Original and Big Bus offer a core two-hour overview tour, two other routes, and a narrated Thames boat tour covered by the same ticket (buy ticket from driver, credit cards accepted at major stops such as Victoria Station, ticket good for 24 hours, bring a sweater and a camera). Big Bus tours are a little better, but more expensive (£20), while Original tours are cheaper (£13.50 with this book) and nearly as good. Pick up a map from any flier rack or from one of the countless salespeople, and study the complex system. Note: If you start at Victoria Station at 9:00, you'll finish near Buckingham Palace in time to see the Changing of the Guard at 11:30; ask your driver for the best place to get off. Sunday morning—when traffic is light and many museums are closed—is a fine time for a tour. The last full loop leaves Victoria at 17:00. Both companies have entertaining as well as boring guides. The narration is important. If you don't like your guide, get off and find another. If you like your guide, settle in for the entire loop. Unless you're using the bus tour mainly for transportation, consider saving money with a night tour (described below).

Original London Sightseeing Bus Tour: Live-guided buses have a Union Jack flag and a yellow triangle on the front of the bus. If the front has many flags or a green or red triangle, it's a tape-recorded multilingual tour—avoid it, unless you have kids who'd enjoy the entertaining recorded kids' tour (£16, £2.50 discount with this book, limit 2 discounts per book, they'll rip off the corner of this page—raise bloody hell if they don't honor this discount, ticket good for 24 hours, tel. 020/8877-1722, www.theoriginaltour.com). Your ticket includes a 50-minute round-trip boat tour from Westminster Pier (departs hourly, tape-recorded narration) or a point-to-point boat trip from Embankment Pier to Greenwich, with stops in between (14 departures per day).

Access: AE+A Level 2—Moderately Accessible. The driver will assist a wheelchair user onto the bus. They have one space available per bus for a wheelchair. If you use a wheelchair, this company is your best bet for access.

Big Bus Hop-on, Hop-off London Tours: For £20 (£18 if you book online), you get the same basic tour plus coupons for several silly one-hour London walking tours and the scenic and usually entertainingly guided Thames boat ride (normally £5.60) between Westminster Pier and the Tower of London. The pass and extras are valid for 24 hours. Buses with live guides are marked in front with a picture of a red bus; buses with tape-recorded spiels display a picture of a blue bus and headphones. These pricier tours tend to have better, more dynamic guides than Original (daily 8:30–18:00, winter until 16:30, from Victoria Station, tel. 020/7233-9533, www.bigbus.co.uk).

Access: Level 3—Minimally Accessible. There are no wheelchair-accessible buses, so the wheelchair user will need to be able to climb on the bus.

At Night: The London by Night Sightseeing Tour runs basically the same circuit as the other companies, but after hours, with none of the extras (e.g., walking tours, boat tours) and for half the price. While the narration can be pretty weak, the views at twilight are grand (£9, pay driver or buy tickets at Victoria Station or Paddington Station TI, April–Sept only, 2-hour tour with live guide, normally departs 19:30–21:30 every half hour from Victoria Station, live guides at 19:30, 20:30, and 21:30, Taxi Road, at front of station near end of Wilton Road, tel. 020/8646-1747, www.london-by-night.net). Munch a scenic picnic dinner (from the top deck, if you are able to climb the stairs up) for a memorable and economical evening.

Access: Level 3—Minimally Accessible. There are no wheelchair-accessible buses; passengers need to be able to climb on the bus.

▲▲**Walking/Wheeling Tours**—Several times a day, top-notch local guides lead (often big) groups through specific slices of London's past. Wheelchair users are generally welcome to roll along on these tours—but call ahead to check with the individual companies to be sure that their tours are appropriate for your mobility level. Schedule fliers litter the desks of TIs, hotels, and pubs. *Time Out* lists many, but not all, scheduled walks. Simply show up at the announced location, pay £5.50, and enjoy two chatty hours of Dickens, the Plague, Shakespeare, Legal London, the Beatles, Jack the Ripper, or whatever is on the agenda. Original London Walks, the dominant company, lists its extensive daily schedule in a beefy, plain, black-and-white *The Original London Walks* brochure (walks offered

Daily Reminder

Sunday: Some sights don't open until noon. The Tower of London and British Museum are both especially crowded today. Hyde Park Speakers' Corner rants from early afternoon until early evening.

These places are closed: Banqueting House, Sir John Soane's Museum, and legal sights (Houses of Parliament, City Hall, and Old Bailey; the neighborhood called The City is dead). Evensong is at 15:00 at Westminster Abbey (plus free organ recital at 17:45) and 15:15 at St. Paul's (plus free organ recital at 17:00); both churches are open during the day for worship but closed to sightseers. Many stores are closed. There are no plays on Sunday as actors take a day off. Street markets flourish: Camden Lock, Spitalfields, Greenwich, and Petticoat Lane.

Monday: Virtually all sights are open except for Apsley House, the Theatre Museum, Sir John Soane's Museum, and a few others. The St. Martin-in-the-Fields church offers a free 13:00 concert. At Somerset House, the Courtauld Gallery is free until 14:00. Vinopolis is open until 21:00. Houses of Parliament are usually open until 22:30.

Tuesday: All sights are open; the British Library is open until 20:00. St. Martin-in-the-Fields has a free 13:00 concert. On the first Tuesday of the month, St. John Soane's Museum is also open 18:00–21:00.

year-round—even on Christmas, private tours for £95, tel. 020/7624-3978, for a recorded listing of today's walks call 020/7624-9255, www.walks .com). They also run minimally accessible **Explorer day trips,** a good option for those with limited time and transportation (different trip daily: Stonehenge/Salisbury, Oxford/Cotswolds, York, Bath, and so on).

Beatles: Fans of the still Fabulous Four can take one of the Beatles walks (Original London Walks, above, has 5/week; Big Bus, above, has a daily walk included with their bus tour). While these "walks" include wheelchair-using participants (Level 2—Moderately Accessible), the route ends with an inaccessible Tube ride to Abbey Road (skip this ending, or take a taxi to meet the group at your own expense).

Private Guides—Standard rates for London's registered guides are £100 for four hours, £159 for eight hours (tel. 020/7403-2962, wheelchair users can call tel. 020/7495-5504 to request a guide that suits your needs; www.touristguides.org.uk, www.blue-badge.org.uk). William Forrester,

Wednesday: All sights are open, plus evening hours at Westminster Abbey (until 19:00, but no evensong), the National Gallery (until 21:00), and Victoria and Albert Museum (until 22:00).

Thursday: All sights are open, British Museum until 20:30 (selected galleries), National Portrait Gallery until 21:00. St. Martin-in-the-Fields hosts a 19:30 evening concert (for a fee).

Friday: All sights are open, British Museum until 20:30 (selected galleries only), National Portrait Gallery until 21:00, Vinopolis until 21:00, Tate Modern until 22:00. Best street market: Spitalfields. St. Martin-in-the-Fields offers two concerts (13:00-free, 19:30-fee).

Saturday: Most sights are open except legal ones (Old Bailey, City Hall, Houses of Parliament—open summer Sat for tours only; skip The City). Vinopolis is open until 21:00, Tate Modern until 22:00. Best street markets: Portobello, Camden Lock, Greenwich. Evensong is at 15:00 at Westminster Abbey, 17:00 at St. Paul's. St. Martin-in-the-Fields hosts a concert at 19:30 (fee).

Notes: Evensong occurs daily at St. Paul's (Mon-Sat at 17:00 and Sun at 15:15) and daily except Wednesday at Westminster Abbey (Mon–Tue and Thu–Fri at 17:00, Sat–Sun at 15:00). London by Night Sightseeing Tour buses leave from Victoria Station every evening at 19:30 and 21:30. The London Eye Ferris Wheel spins nightly until 21:00, until 22:00 in summer, until 20:00 in winter (closed Jan).

one of the authors of *Access in London* and a wheelchair user himself, is a London Registered Guide. He offers tailor-made day tours, as well as group tours (early booking necessary, mobile 0148-357-5401). Robina Brown leads tours of small groups in her Toyota Previa. She has led tours for deaf, blind, and other travelers with disabilities, and wheelchair users are welcome—though they must be able to climb into her car (£220/half day, £320-400/day, tel. 020/7228-2238, www.driverguidetours.com, robina@driverguidetours.com).

▲▲**Cruises**—Boat tours with entertaining commentaries sail regularly from many points along the Thames.

Access: All passenger boats on the Thames (including all listed below, except on Regent's Canal) are legally required to be wheelchair-accessible (Level 1). Boats are accessed via ramps (no steps or other barriers), but the steepness of the ramp depends on the level of the water. At the lowest tide, the ramp is much steeper than at high tide—so some wheelchair users might require assistance. While some boats have accessible toilets, not all do. If finding a boat with an adapted toilet is important to you, or if you want to check on when the ramp will be the least steep, call the individual companies (listed below). The most modern fleet is City Cruises, and Thames River Services also has newer boats with good access. They cost the same. For general questions, contact London River Services at 020/7941-2400.

Options: It's confusing, since there are several companies offering essentially the same thing. Your basic options are downstream (to the

Tower and Greenwich), upstream (to Kew Gardens), and round-trip scenic tour cruises. Most people depart from the Westminster Pier (**AE, AI, AT,** dock area and boat ramp are Level 1—Fully Accessible; at the base of Westminster Bridge under Big Ben). You can catch most of the same boats (with less waiting) from Waterloo Pier at the London Eye Ferris Wheel across the river (Level 1—Fully Accessible dock area and boat ramp). For pleasure and efficiency, consider combining a one-way cruise (to Kew, Greenwich, or wherever) with a Tube ride back. While Tube and bus tickets don't work on the boats, a Travelcard can snare you a 33 percent discount on most cruises (just show the card when you pay for the cruise). Children and seniors get discounts. You can purchase drinks and scant, pricey snacks on board. Buy boat tickets at the small ticket offices on the docks. Clever budget travelers pack a small picnic and munch while they cruise.

Here are some of the most popular cruise options:

To the Tower of London: City Cruises boats sail 30 minutes to the Tower from Westminster Pier (£5.60 one-way, £6.80 round-trip, one-way included with Big Bus London tour; covered by £9 "River Red Rover" ticket that includes Greenwich—see next paragraph; 3/hr during June–Aug daily 9:40–20:40, 2/hr and shorter hours rest of year).

To Greenwich: Two companies head to Greenwich from Westminster Pier. Choose between **City Cruises** (£6.80 one-way, £8.60 round-trip; or get their £9 all-day, hop-on, hop-off "River Red Rover" ticket to have option of getting off at London Eye and Tower of London; June–Aug daily 10:00–17:00, less off-season, every 40 min, 70 min to Greenwich, usually narrated only downstream—to Greenwich, tel. 020/7740-0400, www.citycruises.com) and **Thames River Services** (£6.80 one-way, £8.60

Thames Boat Piers

While Westminster Pier is the most popular, it's not the only dock in town. Consider all the options:

Westminster Pier, at the base of Big Ben, offers round-trip sight-seeing cruises and lots of departures in both directions. Because it adjoins the accessible Westminster Tube station, it's convenient and offers excellent access: adapted toilets, fully accessible boats, and wide ramps that are easy to navigate and have a mild grade. City Cruises and Thames River Services—which both have modern fleets offering good access—both use this dock.

Waterloo Pier, at the base of London Eye Ferris Wheel, is a good, less crowded alternative to Westminster, with many of the same cruise options.

Embankment Pier is near Covent Garden, Trafalgar Square, and Cleopatra's Needle (the obelisk on the Thames). You can take a round-trip cruise from here, or catch a boat to the Tower of London and Greenwich.

Tower Millennium Pier is at the Tower of London. Boats sail west to Westminster Pier or east to Greenwich.

Bankside Pier (near Tate Modern and Shakespeare's Globe) and **Millbank Pier** (near Tate Britain) are connected to each other by the "Tate to Tate" ferry service.

round-trip, April–Oct daily 10:00–16:00, July–Aug until 17:00, has shorter hours and runs every 40 min rest of year, 2/hr, 50 min, usually narrated only to Greenwich, tel. 020/7930-4097, www.westminsterpier.co.uk).

To Kew Gardens: Westminster Passenger Services Association leaves for Kew Gardens from Westminster Pier (£11 one-way, £17 round-trip, 4/day, generally departing 10:30–14:00, 90 min, narrated for 45 min, tel. 020/7930-2062, www.wpsa.co.uk). Some boats continue on to Hampton Court Palace for an additional £3 (and 90 min). Because of the river current, you'll save 30 minutes cruising from Hampton Court back into town.

Round-Trip Cruises: Fifty-minute round-trip cruises of the Thames go hourly from Westminster Pier to the Tower of London (£8, included with Original London Bus tour—listed above, tape-recorded narration, Catamaran Circular Cruises, tel. 020/7987-1185). The London Eye Ferris Wheel operates its own "River Cruise Experience," offering a similar

40-minute live-guided circular tour from Waterloo Pier (£10, £21 with Ferris Wheel, reservations recommended, departures generally :45 past hour, tel. 0870-443-9185, www.ba-londoneye.com).

From Tate to Tate: This boat service for art-lovers connects the Tate Modern and Tate Britain in 18 scenic minutes, stopping at the London Eye Ferris Wheel en route (£4 one-way or £7 for a day ticket; with a Travelcard, it's £2.70-one-way/£4.50-day ticket; buy ticket at gallery desk or on board, departing every 40 min 10:00–17:00, tel. 020/7887-8008).

On Regent's Canal: Consider exploring London's canals by taking a cruise on historic Regent's Canal in north London. The good ship *Jenny Wren* (**AE+A,** Level 2—Moderately Accessible) offers 90-minute guided canal boat cruises from Walker's Quay in Camden Town through scenic Regent's Park to Little Venice (£7, March–Oct daily 12:30 and 14:30, Sat–Sun also at 16:30, Walker's Quay, 250 Camden High Street, near Tube: Camden Town, tel. 020/7485-6210, www.walkersquay.com). While in Camden Town, stop by the popular, punky Camden Lock Market to browse through trendy arts and crafts (daily 10:00–18:00, busiest on weekends, a block from Walker's Quay).

London Duck Tours—A bright-yellow amphibious WWII-vintage vehicle (the model that landed troops on Normandy's beaches on D-Day) takes a gang of 30 tourists past some famous sights on land—Big Ben, Trafalgar Square, Piccadilly Circus—then splashes into the Thames for a cruise (Level 3—Minimally Accessible, 5 steps to enter; £18, 2/hr, daily 10:00–17:30, 75 min—45 min on land and 30 min in the river, these book up in advance, departs from Chicheley Street—you'll see the big ugly vehicle parked 100 yards behind London Eye Ferris Wheel, Tube: Waterloo or Westminster, tel. 020/7928-3132, www.londonducktours .co.uk). All in all, it's good fun at a rather steep price; the live guide works hard, and it's kid-friendly to the point of goofiness.

SIGHTS

From Westminster Abbey to Trafalgar Square

These sights are linked by the Westminster Roll or Stroll chapter on page 161.

▲▲▲**Westminster Abbey**—As the greatest church in the English-speaking world, Westminster Abbey has been the place where England's kings and queens have been crowned and buried since 1066. A thousand years of English history—3,000 tombs, the remains of 29 kings and queens, and hundreds of memorials—lie within its walls and under its stone slabs. Like a stony refugee camp huddled outside St. Peter's Pearly Gates, this

Westminster Abbey to Trafalgar Square

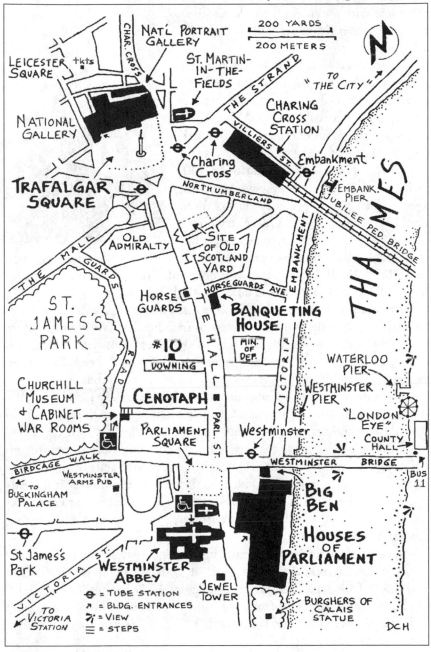

place has a story to tell and the best way to enjoy it is with a tour (audioguide-£3, live-£4; many prefer the audioguide because it's self-paced).

Access: AE, AI, Level 2—Moderately Accessible. Most of the museum is wheelchair-accessible. There are loaner wheelchairs, but no accessible toilets. Wheelchair riders use the main entrance on the north (Big Ben) side of the museum.

Cost, Hours, Information: £10, includes cloisters and Abbey Museum; abbey open Mon–Fri 9:30–15:45, Wed until 19:00, Sat 9:30–13:45, last entry 1 hour before closing, closed Sun to sightseers but open for services; cloisters open daily 8:00–18:00: Abbey Museum open daily 10:30–16:00. Photography is prohibited. (Tube: Westminster or St. James's Park, call for tour schedule, tel. 020/7222-7110.)

The main entrance, on the Parliament Square side, often has a sizable line; visit early or late to avoid tourist hordes. Midmornings are most crowded. On weekdays after 15:00 it's less crowded; come then and stay for the 17:00 evensong (except Wed). Since the church is often closed to the public for special services, it's wise to call first.

Museums: Three tiny **museums** (all **AE, AI, AT,** Level 1—Fully Accessible) ring the cloisters: the Chapter House (where the monks held their daily meetings, notable for its fine architecture and well-described but faded medieval art), the Pyx Chamber (containing an exhibit on the king's treasury), and the Abbey Museum (which tells of the abbey's history, royal coronations, and burials). Look into the impressively realistic eyes of Henry VII's funeral effigy (one of a fascinating series of wax-and-wood statues that, for three centuries, graced royal coffins during funeral processions).

Music: Experience an **evensong** service—awesome in a nearly empty church (weekdays except Wed at 17:00, Sat–Sun at 15:00). The 40-minute **free organ recital** on Sunday at 17:45 is another highlight. Organ concerts (different from the Sunday recital) held here are great and inexpensive; look for signs with schedule details (or visit www .westminster-abbey.org).

▲▲**Houses of Parliament (Palace of Westminster)**—This neo-Gothic icon of London, the royal residence from 1042 to 1547, is now the meeting place of the legislative branch of government. Tourists are welcome to view debates in either the bickering House of Commons or the genteel House of Lords (in session when a flag flies atop the Victoria Tower). While the actual debates are generally extremely dull, it is a thrill to be inside and see the British government in action (for details, see below).

Just past security to the left, study the big dark **Westminster Hall,** which survived the 1834 fire. The hall was built in the 11th century and its famous self-supporting hammer-beam roof was added in 1397. The Houses of Parliament are located in what was once the Palace of Westminster, long the palace of England's medieval kings, until it was largely destroyed by fire in 1834. The palace was rebuilt in the Victorian Gothic style (a move away from neoclassicism back to England's Christian and medieval heritage, true to the Romantic Age). It was completed in 1860.

The **Jewel Tower** is the only other part of the old Palace of Westminster to survive (besides Westminster Hall). It contains a fine little exhibit on Parliament (1st floor—history, 2nd floor—Parliament today) with a 25-minute video and lonely, picnic-friendly benches (£2, April–Sept daily 10:00–17:00, across street from St. Stephen's Gate, tel. 020/7222-2219).

Big Ben, the clock tower (315 feet high), is named for its 13-ton bell, Ben. The light above the clock is lit when the House of Commons is sitting. The face of the clock is huge—you can actually see the minute hand moving. For a good view of it, cross halfway over Westminster Bridge.

Access: AE+A, Al, AT, AL+A, Level 2—Moderately Accessible. To enter either House of Parliament, you need to alert the main entrance guards to your presence. You will be escorted to a separate entry and guided to your choice of house. Security is very tight and body searches should be expected, especially if the House of Commons is in session.

Cost, Hours, Location: Free. Both houses usually open Mon 14:30–22:30, Tue–Thu 11:30–19:30, Fri 9:30–15:00, closed Sat–Sun, generally less action and no lines after 18:00, use St. Stephen's entrance, Tube: Westminster, tel. 020/7219-4272 for schedule, www.parliament.uk. The House of Lords has more pageantry, shorter lines, and less interesting debates (tel. 020/7219-3107 for schedule, and visit www.parliamentlive .tv for a preview).

How to Visit: If there's only one line outside, it's for the House of Commons. Wheelchair users can go to the head of the line (see above). Slow walkers and non-disabled travelers can go to the gate and tell the guard you want the Lords (that's the 2nd "line," with no people in it; it just takes a few minutes and both are worth seeing). You may pop right in—that is, after you've cleared the security gauntlet. Once you've seen the Lords (hide your HOL flier), you can often slip directly over to the

House of Commons and join the gang waiting in the lobby. Inside the lobby, you'll find an announcement board with the day's lineup for both houses.

Tours: Houses of Parliament tours are offered in August and September (£7, 75 min; roughly Mon, Tue, Fri, and Sat 9:15–16:30; Wed and Thu 13:15–16:30; to avoid waits, book in advance through First Call, tel. 0870-906-3773, www.firstcalltickets.com, no booking fee). Meet your Blue Badge guide (at the Sovereign's Entrance—far south end) for a behind-the-scenes peek at the royal chambers and both houses.

▲▲▲Churchill Museum and Cabinet War Rooms—This is a fascinating trip through the underground headquarters of the British government's fight against the Nazis in the darkest days of the Battle for Britain. The 27-room nerve center of the British war effort was used from 1939 to 1945. Churchill's room, the map room, and other rooms are just as they were in 1945. For details on all the blood, sweat, toil, and tears, pick up the excellent and included audioguide at the  entry and follow the 60-minute tour; be patient—it's well worth it. Don't bypass the new Churchill Museum (entrance is a half dozen rooms into the exhibit), giving a human look at the man behind the famous cigar, bowler hat, and V-for-victory sign. It shows his wit, irascibility, work ethic, American ties, writing talents, and drinking habits. A long touch-the-screen timeline lets you zero in on events in his life, from his birth (November 30, 1874) to his election as Prime Minister in 1940. It's all the more amazing considering that, in the 1930s, the man who became my vote for greatest statesman of the 20th century was considered a washed-up loony ranting about the growing threat of fascism. The shop is great for anyone nostalgic for the 1940s.

Access: AE, AI, AT, AL, ♥, Level 1—Fully Accessible. The accessible entrance is on Horse Guards Road (to get there, go up Great George Street opposite the Westminster Bridge and turn right on Horse Guards Road; if you try to enter from Whitehall via King Charles Street, you'll run into a steep flight of stairs). Once inside, the accessible toilet is nearby, as is an accessible elevator to the underground headquarters. Loaner wheelchairs are available.

Cost, Hours, Location: £11, daily 9:30–18:00, last entry 60 min before closing, on King Charles Street, 200 yards off Whitehall, follow the signs, Tube: Westminster, tel. 020/7930-6961, www.iwm.org.uk.

Eating Nearby: If you're hungry, get your rations at the museum's fully accessible Switch Room café. Or, for a nearby pub lunch, try the Westminster Arms (**AE, AI**, Level 2—Moderately Accessible) on Storeys Gate a couple of blocks south of the War Rooms (food served outside on patio, downstairs, or on the accessible ground floor; no accessible toilet, but you can use the one nearby at Westminster Tube station).

Horse Guards—The Horse Guards change daily at 11:00 (10:00 on Sun), and there's a colorful dismounting ceremony daily at 16:00. The rest of the day, they just stand there—terrible for camcorders (on Whitehall, between Trafalgar Square and #10 Downing Street, Tube: Westminster). While Buckingham Palace pageantry is canceled when it rains, the horse guards change regardless of the weather.

▲**Banqueting House**—England's first Renaissance building was designed by Inigo Jones around 1620. It's one of the few London landmarks spared by the 1698 fire and the only surviving part of the original Palace of Whitehall. Don't miss its Rubens ceiling, which, at Charles I's request, drove home the doctrine of the legitimacy of the divine right of kings. In 1649—divine right ignored—Charles I was beheaded on the balcony of this building by a Cromwellian Parliament. Admission includes a restful 20-minute audiovisual history, which shows the place in banqueting action; a 30-minute audio tour—interesting only to history buffs; and a look at the exquisite banqueting hall.

Access: AE+A, Level 4—Not Accessible. There is one 4" step to enter the lobby. From then on, the building is divided into upper and lower levels with no lifts or ramps.

Cost, Hours, Location: £4, Mon–Sat 10:00–17:00, closed Sun, last entry at 16:30, subject to closure for government functions, aristocratic WC, immediately across Whitehall from the Horse Guards, Tube: Westminster, tel. 020/7930-4179.

Just up the street is Trafalgar Square.

Trafalgar Square

▲▲**Trafalgar Square**—London's recently renovated central square, the climax of most marches and demonstrations, is a thrilling place to simply hang out. Lord Nelson stands atop his 185-foot-tall fluted granite column, gazing out to Trafalgar, where he lost his life but defeated the French fleet. Part of this 1842 memorial was made from his victims' melted-down cannons. He's surrounded by giant lions, hordes of people, and—until recently—even more pigeons. London's mayor, Ken Livingstone, nicknamed "Red Ken" for his passion for an activist government, decided that London's "flying rats" were a public nuisance and evicted the venerable seed salesmen (Tube: Charing Cross).

▲▲▲**National Gallery**—Displaying Britain's top collection of European paintings from 1250 to 1900—including works by Leonardo, Botticelli,

Velázquez, Rembrandt, Turner, van Gogh, and the Impressionists—this is one of Europe's great galleries. While the collection is huge, following the route suggested on the map on page 90 will give you my best quick visit. The audioguide tours (suggested £4 donation) are the best I've used in Europe. On the first floor, the "Art Start" computer room lets you study any artist, style, or topic in the museum, and print out a tailor-made tour map.

In 2006, the new main entrance opened, offering visitors a grand first impression of Britain's greatest collection of paintings.

Access: AE, AI, AL, AT, Level 1—Fully Accessible. Loaner wheelchairs are available.

Cost, Hours, Information: Free, daily 10:00–18:00, Wed until 21:00, free 1-hour overview tours daily at 11:30 and 14:30, plus Wed at 18:00 and 18:30. Photography is prohibited. It's on Trafalgar Square (Tube: Charing Cross or Leicester Square, tel. 020/7839-3321, www .nationalgallery.org.uk).

▲▲**National Portrait Gallery**—Put off by halls of 19th-century characters who meant nothing to me, I used to call this "as interesting as someone else's yearbook." But a selective wander through this 500-year-long *Who's Who* of British history is quick and free and puts faces on the story of England. A bonus is the chance to admire some great art by painters such as Holbein, Van Dyck, Hogarth, Reynolds, and Gainsborough. The collection is well described, not huge, and in historical sequence, from the 16th century on the second floor to today's royal family on the ground floor.

Some highlights: Henry VIII and wives; several fascinating portraits of the "Virgin Queen" Elizabeth I, Sir Francis Drake, and Sir Walter Raleigh; the only real-life portrait of William Shakespeare; Oliver Cromwell and Charles I, with his head on; self portraits and other portraits by Gainsborough and Reynolds; the Romantics (Blake, Byron, Wordsworth, and company); Queen Victoria and her era; and the present royal family, including the late Princess Diana.

The excellent audioguide tours (free, but £2 donation requested) describe each room (or era in British history) and more than 300 paintings. You'll learn more about British history than art and actually hear interviews with 20th-century subjects as you stare at their faces.

Access: AE, AI, AL, AT, Level 1—Fully Accessible. Loaner wheelchairs are available.

Cost, Hours, Information: Free, daily 10:00–18:00, Thu–Fri until 21:00. It's 100 yards off Trafalgar Square (around corner from National Gallery, opposite Church of St. Martin-in-the-Fields, Tube: Charing Cross or Leicester Square, tel. 020/7306-0055, www.npg.org.uk).

Eating Nearby: The elegant Portrait Restaurant on the top floor comes with views and high prices; the cheaper Portrait Café is in the basement. Both are Level 1—Fully Accessible.

▲**St. Martin-in-the-Fields**—This church, built in the 1720s with a Gothic spire atop a Greek-type temple, is an oasis of peace on the wild and noisy Trafalgar Square. St. Martin cared for the poor. "In the fields" was where the first church stood on this spot (in the 13th century), between Westminster and The City. Going inside, you still feel a compassion for the needs of the people in this community. A free flier provides a brief yet worthwhile self-guided tour. The church is famous for its concerts. Consider a free lunchtime concert (Mon, Tue, and Fri at 13:00) or an evening concert (£8–18, at 19:30 Thu–Sat and on some Tue and Wed, box office tel. 020/7839-8362, church tel. 020/7766-1100). Downstairs (and not accessible for wheelchair users) is a ticket office for concerts, a gift shop, a brass-rubbing center, and a fine support-the-church cafeteria.

Access: The main floor is **AE, AI, ♥,** Level 2—Moderately Accessible. A ramp on the north side of the building takes wheelchair users directly into the sanctuary/concert hall. Fourteen steps lead downstairs (Level 4—Not Accessible) to the café, bookstore, exhibit hall, and brass-rubbing center. The toilets are clean and free, but not accessible.

Cost, Hours, Location: Free, donations welcome, open daily, Tube: Charing Cross, www.smitf.com.

National Gallery Highlights

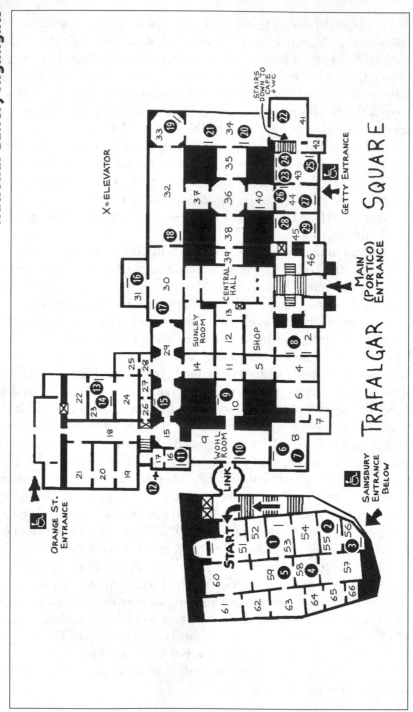

MEDIEVAL & EARLY RENAISSANCE
❶ Wilton Diptych
❷ UCCELLO – Battle of San Romano
❸ VAN EYCK – The Arnolfini Marriage

ITALIAN RENAISSANCE
❹ BOTTICELLI – Venus and Mars
❺ CRIVELLI – The Annunciation with St. Emidius

HIGH RENAISSANCE
❻ MICHELANGELO – Entombment
❼ RAPHAEL – Pope Julius II
❽ LEONARDO DA VINCI – The Virgin of the Rocks; Virgin and Child with St. John the Baptist and St. Anne

VENETIAN RENAISSANCE
❾ TITIAN – Bacchus and Ariadne
❿ TINTORETTO – The Origin of the Milky Way

NORTHERN PROTESTANT ART
⓫ VERMEER – A Young Woman
⓬ "A PEEPSHOW"
⓭ REMBRANDT – Belshazzar's Feast
⓮ REMBRANDT – Self-Portrait

BAROQUE & ROCOCO
⓯ RUBENS – The Judgment of Paris
⓰ VAN DYCK – Charles I on Horseback
⓱ VELÁZQUEZ – The Rokeby Venus
⓲ CARAVAGGIO – The Supper at Emmaus
⓳ BOUCHER – Pan and Syrinx

BRITISH
⓴ CONSTABLE – The Hay Wain
㉑ TURNER – The Fighting Téméraire
㉒ DELAROCHE – The Execution of Lady Jane Grey

IMPRESSIONISM & BEYOND
㉓ MONET – Gare St. Lazare
㉔ MONET – The Water-Lily Pond
㉕ MANET – The Waitress (Corner of a Café-Concert)
㉖ RENOIR – Boating on the Seine
㉗ SEURAT – Bathers at Asnières
㉘ VAN GOGH – Sunflowers
㉙ CEZANNE – Bathers

More Top Squares: Piccadilly, Soho, and Covent Garden

▲▲**Piccadilly Circus**—London's most touristy square got its name from the fancy ruffled shirts—*picadils*—made in the neighborhood long ago. Today, the square, while pretty grotty, is surrounded by fascinating streets swimming with youth on the rampage. For overstimulation, drop by the extremely trashy **Pepsi Trocadero Center's** (**AE, AI+A, AL,** Level 2—Moderately Accessible) "theme park of the future" for its Segaworld virtual reality games, nine-screen cinema, and thundering IMAX theater (admission to Trocadero is free; individual attractions cost £2–8; before paying full price for IMAX, look for a discount ticket on brochure racks at the TI or hotels; located between Coventry and Shaftesbury, just off Piccadilly, Tube: Piccadilly Circus). Chinatown, to the east, has swollen since the British colony of Hong Kong was returned to China in 1997. Nearby Shaftesbury Avenue and Leicester Square teem with fun-seekers, theaters, Chinese restaurants, and street singers.

Soho—North of Piccadilly, seedy Soho is becoming trendy and is well worth a gawk. Most sidewalk corners have curb cuts, and the sidewalks are very negotiable. Some of the streets have been made into pedestrian malls, so the sidewalk and the road are all on one level.

Soho is London's red light district, where "friendly models" wait in tiny rooms up dreary stairways and voluptuous con artists sell strip shows. While venturing into a building to check out a model is interesting, anyone who goes into any one of the shows will be ripped off. Every time. Even a £5 show in a "licensed bar" comes with a £100 cover or minimum (as it's printed on the drink menu) and a "security man." You may accidentally buy a £200 bottle of bubbly. And suddenly, the door has no handle.

Telephone sex is hard to avoid these days in London. Phone booths are littered with racy fliers of busty ladies "new in town." Some travelers gather six or eight phone booths' worth of fliers and take them home for kinky wallpaper.

▲▲**Covent Garden**—This boutique-ish shopping district is a people-watcher's delight, with cigarette eaters, Punch and Judy acts, food that's good for you (but not your wallet), trendy crafts, sweet whiffs of marijuana, two-tone hair (neither color natural), and faces that could set off a metal detector

London's Top Squares

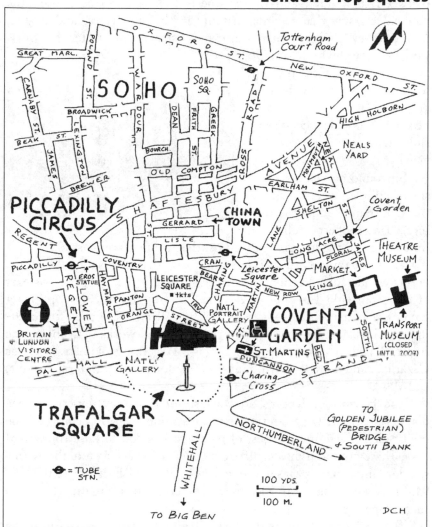

(Tube: Covent Garden). The sidewalks have curb cuts, but are quite narrow—so you may have to negotiate around other pedestrians. But the area is predominately accessible. For better Covent Garden lunch deals, get a block or two away from the eye of this touristic hurricane (check out the places north of the Tube station along Endell and Neal Streets).

Museums near Covent Garden

▲▲**Somerset House**—This grand 18th-century civic palace offers a marvelous public space, three fine art collections, and a riverside terrace (between the Strand and the Thames). The palace once housed the national registry that records Britain's births, marriages, and deaths, "...where they hatch 'em, match 'em, and dispatch 'em." Enter the court-

yard to enjoy the fountain. Go ahead...roll or stroll through it. The 55 jets get playful twice an hour. (In the winter, this becomes a popular ice-skating rink, with a toasty café for viewing.)

Surrounding you are three small and sumptuous sights: the Courtauld Gallery (paint-ings), the Gilbert Collection (fine arts), and the Hermitage Rooms (the art of czarist Russia).

The **Courtauld Gallery** is less impressive than the National Gallery, but its wonderful collection of paintings is still a joy. The gallery is part of the Courtauld Institute of Art, and the thoughtful description of each piece of art reminds visitors that the gallery is still used for teach-ing. You'll see medieval European paintings and works by Rubens, the Impressionists (Manet, Monet, Degas), Post-Impressionists (such as Cézanne), and more (free Mon until 14:00, downstairs cafeteria, lockers, and WC).

The **Hermitage Rooms** offer a taste of Romanov imperial splen-dor. As Russia struggles and tourists are staying away, someone had the bright idea of sending the best of its art to London to raise some hard cash. These five rooms host a different collection every six months, with a standard intro to the czar's winter palace in St. Petersburg (tel. 020/7420-9410). To see what's on, visit www.somerset-house.org.uk/attractions/hermitage.

The **Gilbert Collection** displays 800 pieces of the finest in European decorative arts, from diamond-studded gold snuffboxes to intricate Italian mosaics. Maybe you've seen Raphael paintings and Botticelli frescoes... but this lush collection is refreshingly different (includes free audioguide with a highlights tour and a helpful loaner magnifying glass).

Access: AE, AI, AL, AT, Level 1: All of the Somerset House gal-leries are fully accessible. The west door provides accessible entry to the complex, and you can take the lift to the accessible toilet in the basement. Accessible parking and loaner wheelchairs are also available.

Cost, Hours, Location: £5 per sight, £8 for any two sights, £12 for all three. All three are open the same hours (daily 10:00–18:00, last entry

17:15). Somerset House is located between the Strand and the Thames, off Waterloo Bridge. Coming from Trafalgar Square, catch bus #6, #9, #11, #13, #15, or #23. Tube: Temple (closer) or Covent Garden. Info: tel. 020/7848-2526 or 020/7845-4600, www.somerset house.org.uk. The Web site lists a busy schedule of tours, kids' events, and concerts. The riverside terrace is picnic-friendly (deli inside lobby).

▲**London Transport Museum**—This wonderful museum (closed until early 2007) is a delight for kids. Whether you're cursing or marveling at the buses and Tube, the growth of Europe's biggest city has been made possible by its public transit system.

Access: AE, AI, AL, AT, Level 1—Fully Accessible. Loaner wheelchairs are available.

Cost, Hours, and Location: £6, kids under 16 free, Sat–Thu 10:00–18:00, Fri 11:00–18:00, in southeast corner of Covent Garden courtyard, Tube: Covent Garden, tel. 020/7379-6344 or recorded info 020/7565-7299, www.ltmuseum.co.uk.

Theatre Museum—This earnest museum traces British theater from Shakespeare to today.

Access: AE, AI, AL, AT, ♥, Level 1—Fully Accessible. Loaner wheelchairs are available.

Cost, Hours, Location: Free, Tue–Sun 10:00–18:00, closed Mon, free guided tours at 12:00 and 14:00, a block east of Covent Garden's marketplace down Russell Street, Tube: Covent Garden, tel. 020/7943-4700, www.theatremuseum.org.uk.

North London

▲▲▲**British Museum, Great Court, and Reading Room**—Simply put, this is the greatest chronicle of civilization...anywhere. A visit here is like taking a long journey through Encyclopedia Britannica National Park. Entering on Great Russell Street, you'll find yourself in the Great Court, the glass-domed hub of a two-acre cultural complex, containing restaurants, shops, and lecture halls plus the Round Reading Room.

Access: AE, AI, AT, AL, Level 1—Fully Accessible: The museum and the Great Court, as well as the top-floor restaurant, are all fully accessible. The main entry on Great Russell Street and the entry on Montague Place are both fully accessible.

Cost, Hours, Location: The British Museum is free (£3 donation requested, daily 10:00–17:30, plus Thu–Fri until 20:30—but from 17:30, only selected galleries and the Reading Room are open, least crowded weekday late afternoons, Great Russell Street, Tube: Tottenham Court Road, tel. 020/7323-8000, recorded info tel. 020/7388-2227,

North London

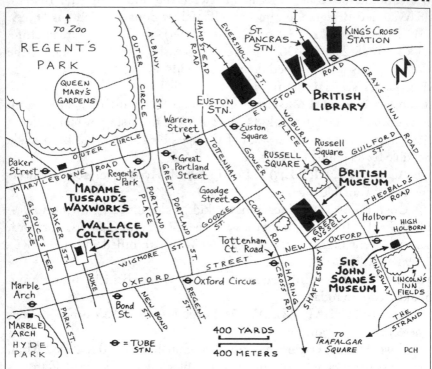

www.thebritishmuseum.ac.uk). The Reading Room is free and open daily 10:00–17:30 (Thu–Fri until 20:30). Computer terminals within the Reading Room offer COMPASS, a database of information about selected museum items (also available on their Web site, listed above). The Great Court has longer opening hours than the museum (daily 9:00–18:00, Thu–Sat until 23:00).

Tours: The various Eye-Opener tours are free (nearly hourly 11:00–15:30, 50 min); each one is different, focusing on one particular subject within the museum. The Highlights tours are expensive but meaty (£8, 90 min, at 10:30, 13:00, and 15:00). There are also several different audioguide tours (£3.50, requires leaving photo ID), including Top 50 Highlights (90 min), the Parthenon Sculptures (60 min), and Family Tours (length varies).

❍ Self-Guided Tour: The most popular sections of the museum fill the ground floor: Egyptian, Mesopotamian, and ancient Greek—with the famous Elgin Marbles from the Athenian Parthenon. Huge winged lions (which guarded Assyrian palaces 800 years before Christ) guard these great ancient galleries. For a brief tour, connect these ancient dots:

British Museum Overview

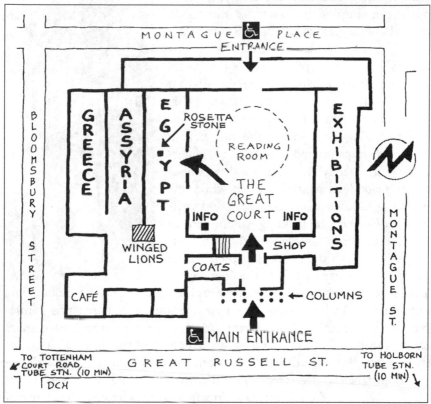

Start with the **Egyptian.** Wander from the Rosetta Stone past the many statues. Make your way to Room 7 (back at the winged lions) and explore the dark, violent, and mysterious **Assyrian** rooms. The Nimrud Gallery is lined with royal propaganda reliefs and wounded lions.

The most modern of the ancient art fills the **Greek** section. Find Room 11 behind the winged lions and start your tour through Greek art history with the simple and primitive Cycladic fertility figures. Later, painted vases show a culture really into partying. The finale is the Elgin Marbles. The much-wrangled-over bits of the Athenian Parthenon (from 450 B.C.) are even more impressive than they look. To best appreciate these ancient carvings, take the audioguide tour (available in this gallery).

Be sure to venture to the upper level to see artifacts from **Roman Britain** (Room 50) that surpass anything you'll see at Hadrian's Wall or elsewhere in Britain. Nearby, the Dark Age Britain exhibits offer a worthwhile peek at that bleak era; look for the Sutton Hoo Burial Ship artifacts from a 7th-century royal burial on the east coast of England

(Room 41). If you want more Egypt, check out the mummies in Rooms 62 and 63. A rare Michelangelo cartoon is in Room 90.

The **Great Court** is Europe's largest covered square—bigger than a football field. This people-friendly court—delightfully out of the London rain—was for 150 years one of London's great lost spaces...closed off and gathering dust. While the vast British Museum wraps around the court, its center-piece is the stately **Reading Room**—famous as the place Karl Marx hung out while formulating his ideas on communism and writing *Das Kapital*. The Reading Room—one of the fine cast-iron buildings of the 19th century—is open to the public, but there's little to see that you can't see from the doorway.

▲▲▲**British Library**—The British Empire built its greatest monuments out of paper. And it's in literature that England made her lasting contribution to civilization and the arts. Britain's national archives has more than 12 million books, 180 miles of shelving, and the deepest basement in London. But everything that matters for your visit is in one delightful room labeled "The Treasures." This room is filled with literary and

historical documents that changed the course of history. You'll trace the evolution of European maps over 800 years. Follow the course of the bible—from the earliest known gospels (written on scraps of papyrus) to the first complete bible to the original King James version and the Gutenberg Bible. You'll see Leonardo's doodles, the Magna Carta, Shakespeare's First Folio, the original *Alice in Wonderland* in Lewis Carroll's handwriting, and manuscripts by Beethoven, Mozart, Lennon, and McCartney. Finish in the fascinating *Turning the Pages* exhibit, which lets you actually browse through virtual manuscripts of a few of these treasures on a computer.

Access: AE, AI, AT, AL, ❤, Level 1—Fully Accessible.

Cost, Hours, Location: Free, Mon–Fri 9:30–18:00, Tue until 20:00, Sat 9:30–17:00, Sun 11:00–17:00; 60-min tours for £6 usually offered Mon, Wed, and Fri–Sun at 15:00, Sat 10:30, and Sun 11:30; call 020/7412-7332 to confirm schedule and reserve; for £3.50 audioguide,

British Library

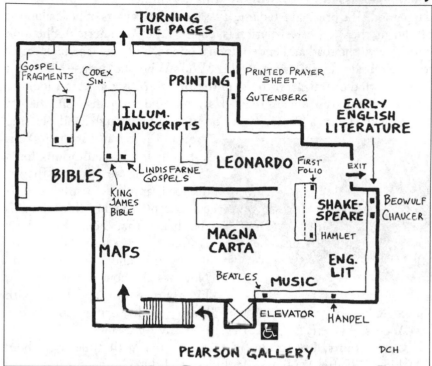

leave photo ID or 20 deposit; Tube: King's Cross, turn right out of station and go a block to 96 Euston Road, library tel. 020/7412-7000, www.bl.uk. The ground-floor café is next to a vast and fun pull-out stamp collection, and the cafeteria upstairs serves good hot meals; both eateries are Level 1—Fully Accessible.

▲**Wallace Collection**—Sir Richard Wallace's fine collection of 17th-century Dutch Masters, 18th-century French Rococo, medieval armor, and assorted aristocratic fancies fills the sumptuously furnished Hertford House on Manchester Square. From the rough and intimate Dutch lif-escapes of Jan Steen to the pink-cheeked Rococo fantasies of Boucher, a wander through this little-visited mansion makes you nostalgic for the days of empire.

Access: AE, AI, AT, Level 1—Fully Accessible.

Cost, Hours, Location: Free, Mon–Sat 10:00–17:00, Sun 12:00–17:00, audioguide-£3, just north of Oxford Street on Manchester Square, Tube: Bond Street, tel. 020/7563-9500, www.wallacecollection.org. The museum has an upscale, fully accessible restaurant, Café Bagatelle (tel. 020/7563-9500).

▲**Madame Tussaud's Waxworks**—This is gimmicky and expensive, but dang good. The original Madame Tussaud did wax casts of heads lopped off during the French Revolution (such as Marie Antoinette's). She took her show on the road and ended up in London, and now it's much easier to be featured. The gallery is one big Who's Who photo-op—a huge hit with the kind of travelers who skip the British Museum. After looking a hundred famous people in their glassy eyes and surviving a silly hall of horror, you'll board a Disney-type ride and cruise through a kid-pleasing

"Spirit of London" time trip. Your last stop is the auditorium for a 15-minute stage show. They've dumped anything really historical (except for what they claim is the blade that beheaded Marie Antoinette) because "There's no money in it, and we're a business." Now, it's all about squeezing Brad Pitt's bum, wining and dining with George Clooney, and partying with Beyoncé, Kylie, Britney, and Posh.

Access: AE, AI, AT, AL, Level 1—Fully Accessible.

Cost, Hours, Location: Admission varies with time, but about £23, kids-£19; after 17:00, it's £14, kids-£9; children under 5 always free; Mon–Fri 10:00–18:30, Sat–Sun 9:30–18:30, last entry 60 min before closing, Marylebone Road, Tube: Baker Street.

Crowd-Beating Tips: The Waxworks are popular—and crowded. Unlike at some other sights, a wheelchair user cannot skip to the head of the line here. Avoid the wait by either booking ahead to get a ticket with an entry time (tel. 0870-400-3000, online at www.madame-tussauds .com for a £2 fee, or at no extra cost at the Britain and London Visitors Centre or the TIs at Victoria and Waterloo train stations) or arriving at 17:00 (avoiding any lines and saving £9 on admission—90 minutes is plenty of time for the exhibit).

Sir John Soane's Museum—Architects and fans of eclectic knickknacks love this quirky place, as do Martha Stewart types and lovers of Back Door sights. Tour this furnished home on a bird-chirping square and see 19th-century chairs, lamps, and carpets, wood-paneled nooks and crannies, and stained-glass skylights. The townhouse is cluttered with Soane's (and his wife's) collection of ancient relics, curios, and famous paintings, including Hogarth's series on *The Rake's Progress* (read the fun plot) and several excellent Canalettos. In 1833, just before his death, Soane established his house as a museum, stipulating that it be kept as nearly as possible in the state he left it. If he visited today, he'd be entirely satisfied. You'll leave wishing you'd known the man.

Access: Level 3—Minimally Accessible. The entrance has eight steps up, and the ground floor is 80 percent on one level. The other two levels require a trip up or down narrow flights of stairs, and the doors are also narrow. Once inside, a narrow loaner wheelchair is available. Full accessibility is planned to be complete by 2007.

Cost, Hours, Location: Free, Tue–Sat 10:00–17:00, first Tue of the month also 18:00–21:00, closed Sun–Mon, good £1 brochure, £3 guided tours Sat at 14:30, quarter mile southeast of British Museum, Tube: Holborn, 13 Lincoln's Inn Fields, tel. 020/7405-2107.

Buckingham Palace

▲Buckingham Palace—This lavish home has been Britain's royal residence since 1837. When the queen's at home, the royal standard flies (a red, yellow, and blue flag); otherwise the Union Jack flaps in the wind. Recently, the queen has opened her palace to the public—but only in August and September, when she's out of town.

Access: AE, AI, AL, AT, Level 1—Fully Accessible.

Cost, Hours, Location: £14 for state apartments and throne room, Aug–Sept daily 9:30–18:50, only 8,000 visitors a day—come early to get an entry time, or for £1 extra you can book ahead by phone or online, Tube: Victoria, tel. 020/7766-7300, www.royalcollection.org.uk.

▲Queen's Gallery at Buckingham Palace—Queen Elizabeth's 7,000 paintings make up the finest private art collection in the world. It's actually a collection of collections, built on by each successive monarch since the 16th century, and rivaling Europe's biggest national art galleries. She rotates her paintings, enjoying some privately in her many palatial residences while sharing others with her subjects in public galleries in Edinburgh and London. Small, thoughtfully presented, and always exquisite displays fill the handful of rooms open to the public in a wing of Buckingham Palace. As you're in "the most important building in London," security is tight. You'll see a temporary exhibit and the permanent "treasures"—which come with a room full of "antique and personal jewelry." Compared to the crown jewels at the Tower, it may be Her Majesty's bottom drawer—but it's still a dazzling pile of diamonds. Temporary exhibits change about twice a year and are always lovingly

Buckingham Palace Area

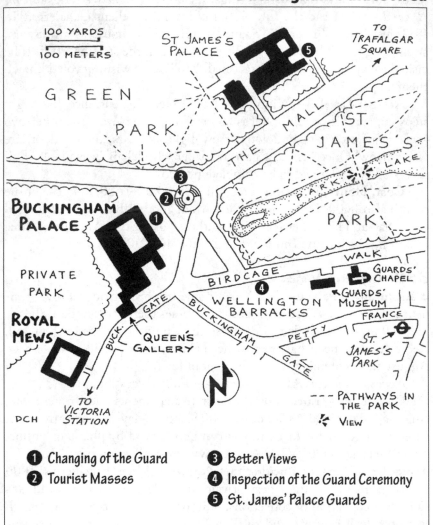

100 YARDS

100 METERS

St James's Palace

TO TRAFALGAR SQUARE

GREEN

PARK

THE MALL

ST. JAMES'S

LAKE

PARK

BUCKINGHAM PALACE

PARK

PRIVATE PARK

WALK

BIRDCAGE

GUARDS' CHAPEL

GUARDS' MUSEUM

WELLINGTON BARRACKS

FRANCE

ROYAL MEWS

BUCK. GATE

QUEEN'S GALLERY

BUCKINGHAM

GATE

PETTY

ST. JAMES'S PARK

TO VICTORIA STATION

DCH

PATHWAYS IN THE PARK

VIEW

❶ Changing of the Guard

❷ Tourist Masses

❸ Better Views

❹ Inspection of the Guard Ceremony

❺ St. James' Palace Guards

described with the included audioguides. While the admissions come with an entry time, this is only enforced during rare days when crowds are a problem.

Access: AE, AI, AL, AT, Level 1—Fully Accessible.

Cost, Hours, Location: £7.50, £11.50 with Royal Mews, daily 10:00–17:30, last entry 60 min before closing, Tube: Victoria, tel. 020/7766-7301 (but Her Majesty rarely answers). Men shouldn't miss the mahogany-trimmed urinals.

Royal Mews—The queen's working stables, the "mews," are open to visitors. The visit is likely to be disappointing (you'll see 2 horses out of the queen's 30, a fancy car, and a bunch of old carriages) unless you follow the included guided tour, in which case it's thoroughly entertaining—especially if you're interested in horses and/or royalty. The 45-minute tours go twice an hour and finish with the Gold State Coach (c. 1760, 4 tons, 4 mpg). Queen Victoria said absolutely no cars. When she died in 1901, the mews got its first Daimler. Today, along with the hay-eating transport, the stable is home to five Rolls-Royce Phantoms.

Access: AE, AI, Level 1—Fully Accessible.

Cost, Hours, Location: £6, Aug–Sept Sat–Thu 10:00–17:00, March–July and Oct Sat–Thu 11:00–16:00, closed Fri, closed Nov–Feb, Buckingham Palace Road, Tube: Victoria, tel. 020/7766-7302.

▲▲**Changing of the Guard at Buckingham Palace**—The guards change with much fanfare at around 11:30 almost daily in the summer and, at a minimum, every other day all year long (no band when it's rainy). Each month, it's either daily or on odd or even days. Call 020/7321-2233 for the day's plan or check www.royalresidences.com. Wave down a big black taxi and say, "Buck House, please" (a.k.a. Buckingham Palace).

Most tourists just mob the palace gates for a peek at the Changing of the Guard, but those who know the drill will enjoy the event more.

Here's the lowdown on what goes down: It's just after 11:00, and the on-duty guards, actually working at nearby St. James's Palace, are ready to finish their shift. At 11:15, these tired guards, along with the band, head out to the Mall, and then take a right turn for Buckingham Palace. Meanwhile, their replacement guards—fresh for the day—gather at 11:00 at their Wellington Barracks, 500 yards east of the palace (on Birdcage Walk), for a review and inspection. At 11:30, they also head for Buckingham Palace. As both the tired and fresh guards converge on the palace, the Horse Guard  enters the fray, marching down the Mall from the Horse Guard Barracks on Whitehall. At 11:45, it's a perfect storm of Red Coat pageantry, as all three groups converge. Everyone parades around, the guard changes (passing the regimental flag, or "color") with much shouting, the band

Harry Potter's London

Harry Potter's story is set in a magical Britain, and all of the places mentioned in the books except London are fictional, but you can visit many real film locations. Many of the locations are closed to visitors, though, or are an unmagical disappointment in person, unless you're a huge fan. For those diehard fans, here's a list.

Spoiler Warning: Information in this sidebar will ruin surprises for those who haven't yet read the Harry Potter *series or seen the movies.*

Harry's story begins in suburban London, in the fictional town of Little Whinging. In the first film, the gentle giant Hagrid touches down at #4 Privet Drive on his flying motorcycle. He leaves baby Harry—who was orphaned by the murder of his wizard parents—on the doorstep to be raised by an anti-magic aunt and uncle. The scene was shot in the town of **Bracknell** (pop. 50,000, 10 miles west of Heathrow) on a street of generic brick rowhouses called Picket Close. Later, 10-year-old Harry first realizes his wizard powers when talking with a boa constrictor, filmed at the **London Zoo's Reptile House** in Regent's Park (Tube: Great Portland Street). Harry soon gets invited to Hogwarts School of Witchcraft and Wizardry, where he'll learn the magical skills he'll need to eventually confront his parents' murderer, Lord Voldemort.

Big Ben and **Parliament,** along the Thames, welcome Harry to the modern city inhabited by Muggles (non-magic folk). London bustles along, oblivious to the parallel universe of wizards. Hagrid takes Harry shopping for school supplies. They enter the glass-roofed **Leadenhall Market** (Tube: Bank), and approach a **storefront** in Bull's Head Passage—the entrance to the Leaky Cauldron pub (which, in the books, is placed among the bookshops of Charing Cross Road). The pub's back wall parts, opening onto the magical Diagon Alley (filmed on a set at Leavesden Studios, north of London), where Harry shops for wands, cauldrons, and wizard textbooks. He pays for it with gold Galleons from goblin-run Gringotts Bank, filmed in the marble-floored

plays a happy little concert, and then they march out. A few minutes later, fresh guards set up at St. James's Palace, the tired ones dress down at the barracks, and the tourists disperse.

If you are able, stake out the high ground on the circular Victoria Monument for the best overall view. Or start early either at St. James's Palace or the Wellington Barracks (the inspection is in full view of the street) and come in with the band. The marching troops and bands are colorful and even stirring, but the actual Changing of the Guard is a and chandeliered Exhibition Hall of **Australia House** (Tube: Temple), home of the Australian Embassy.

Harry catches the train to Hogwarts at **King's Cross Station**. (The fanciful exterior shot from film #2 is actually of nearby **St. Pancras Station.**) Inside the glass-roofed train station, on a **pedestrian sky bridge** over the tracks, Hagrid gives Harry a train ticket. Harry heads to platform 9 3/4, actually filmed at **platform 4.** Harry and his new buddy Ron magically push their luggage carts through a brick pillar between the platforms, emerging onto a hidden platform. (For a fun photo op, find the *Platform 9 3/4* sign and the luggage cart that appears to be disappearing into the wall.)

A red steam train—the *Hogwarts Express*—speeds them through the (Scottish) countryside to Hogwarts, where Harry will spend the next seven years. Harry is taught how to wave his wand by tiny Professor Flitwick in a wood-paneled classroom filmed at **Harrow School** in Harrow on the Hill, eight miles northwest of London (Tube: Harrow on the Hill).

In film #3, Harry careens through London's lamplit streets on a purple three-decker bus that dumps him at the Leaky Cauldron. In this film, the pub's exterior was shot on rough-looking Stoney Street at the southeast edge of **Borough Street Market,** by the Market Porter Pub, with trains rumbling overhead (Tube: London Bridge).

Other scenes from the books are set in London—Sirius Black and the Order reside at "Twelve Grimmauld Place" and Harry plumbs the depths of the "Ministry of Magic"—but these places are fictional.

Finally, cinema buffs can visit Leicester Square (Tube: Leicester Square), where Daniel Radcliffe and other stars strolled past paparazzi and down red carpets to the Odeon Theater to watch the movies' premieres.

nonevent. It is interesting, however, to see nearly every tourist in London gathered in one place at the same time. Afterwards, stroll or roll through nearby St. James's Park (Tube: Victoria, St. James's Park, or Green Park).

West London

▲**Hyde Park and Speakers' Corner**—London's "Central Park," originally Henry VIII's hunting grounds, has more than 600 acres of lush greenery, a huge man-made lake, the royal Kensington Palace, and the

West London

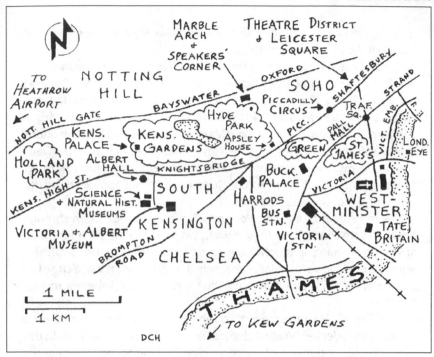

ornate neo-Gothic Albert Memorial across from the Royal Albert Hall. Early afternoons on Sunday (until early evening), Speakers' Corner offers

soapbox oratory at its best (Tube: Marble Arch). This "grass roots of democracy" is actually a holdover from when the gallows stood here, and the criminal was allowed to say just about anything he wanted before he swung. I dare you to raise your voice and gather a crowd—it's easy to do.

The Princess Diana Memorial Fountain opened in 2004 in honor of the "People's Princess," who once lived in nearby Kensington Palace. The low-key circular stream is in the eastern part of the park, near the Serpentine Gallery. (Don't be confused by signs to the Diana Princess of Wales Children's Playground, also found within the park.)

Access: Level 1—Fully Accessible.

▲**Apsley House (Wellington Museum)**—Having beaten Napoleon at Waterloo, the Duke of Wellington was once the most famous man in Europe. He was given London's ultimate address, #1 London. His newly refurbished mansion offers one of London's best palace experiences. An 11-foot-tall marble statue (by Canova) of Napoleon, clad only in a fig leaf, greets you. Downstairs is a small gallery of Wellington memorabilia (including a pair of Wellington boots). The lavish upstairs shows off the duke's fine collection of paintings, including works by Velázquez and Steen.

Access: AE, AI, AT, Level 1—Fully Accessible.

Cost, Hours, Location: £4.50, Tue–Sun 10:00–17:00, until 16:00 in winter, closed Mon, well-described by included audioguide, 20 yards from Hyde Park Corner Tube station, tel. 020/7152-6156, www.english -heritage.org.uk. Hyde Park's pleasant and picnic-wonderful rose garden is nearby.

▲▲**Victoria and Albert Museum**—The world's top collection of decorative arts (vases, stained glass, fine furniture, clothing, jewelry, carpets, and more) is a surprisingly interesting assortment of crafts from the West as well as Asian and Islamic cultures.

The V&A grew out of the Great Exhibition of 1851—the ultimate festival celebrating the greatness of Britain. After much support from Queen Victoria and Prince Albert, it was renamed after the royal couple.

Many visitors start with the **British Galleries** (upstairs)—a one-way tour stretching through 400 years of British lifestyles, almost a museum in itself.

In Room 46 are the plaster casts of **Trajan's Column,** a copy of Rome's 140-foot spiral relief telling the story of the conquest of Romania. (The V&A's casts are copies made for the benefit of 19th-century art students who couldn't afford a rail-pass.) Plaster casts of **Renaissance sculptures** (Room 46B) let you compare Michelangelo's monumental *David* with Donatello's girlish *David;* see also Ghiberti's bronze Baptistery doors, which inspired the Florentine Renaissance.

In Room 48A are **Raphael's "cartoons,"** seven huge watercolor designs by the Renaissance master for tapestries meant for the Sistine

Chapel. The cartoons were sent to Brussels, cut into strips (see the lines), and placed on the looms. Notice that the scenes, the Acts of Peter and Paul, are the reverse of the final product (lots of left-handed saints).

Access: AE, AI, AT, AL, Level 1—Fully Accessible. There are two accessible entrances to the museum. An accessibility information sheet and loaner wheelchairs are available.

Cost, Hours, Location: Free, £3 donation requested, possible fee for special exhibits (reduced for wheelchair users), daily 10:00–17:45, open every Wed and last Fri of the month until 22:00 except mid-Dec–mid-Jan. (Tube: South Kensington, a long tunnel leads directly from the Tube station to the museum, tel. 020/7942-2000, www.vam.ac.uk).

Tours: The museum has 150 rooms and over 12 miles of corridors. While just wandering works well here, consider catching one of the free 60-minute orientation tours (daily, on the half-hour from 10:30–15:30, also daily at 13:00, Wed at 16:30, and a half-hour version at 18:30) or buying the fine £5 *Hundred Highlights* guidebook, or the handy £1 *What to See at the V&A* brochure (outlines 5 self-guided tours).

▲**Natural History Museum**—Across the street from Victoria and Albert, this mammoth museum is housed in a giant and wonderful Victorian, neo-Romanesque building. Built in the 1870s specifically for this huge collection (50 million specimens), it has two halves: the Life Galleries (creepy-crawlies, human biology, the origin of species, "our place in evolution," and awesome dinosaurs) and the Earth Galleries (meteors, volcanoes, earthquakes, and so on). Exhibits are wonderfully explained, with lots of creative interactive displays. Pop in, if only for the wild collection of dinosaurs and the roaring *Tyrannosaurus rex.*

Access: AE, AI, AT, AL, Level 1—Fully Accessible. There are multiple entrances to the museum, and all are accessible. Loaner wheelchairs and brochures about museum access are available.

Cost, Hours, Location: Free, possible fee for special exhibits, Mon–Sat 10:00–18:00, Sun 11:00–18:00, last entrance 17:30, a long tunnel leads directly from South Kensington Tube station to museum, tel. 020/7942-5000, exhibit info and reservations tel. 020/7942-5011, www.nhm.ac.uk. Free 45-minute highlights tours occur daily about every hour from 11:00 to 16:00.

▲**Science Museum**—Next door to the Natural History Museum, this sprawling wonderland for curious minds is kid-perfect. It offers hands-on fun, from moon walks to deep-sea exploration, with trendy technology exhibits, an IMAX theater (£7–10 tickets for grownups, kids less), cool rotating themed exhibits, and a kids' zone in the basement.

Access: AE, AI, AT, AL, Level 1—Fully Accessible.

The City

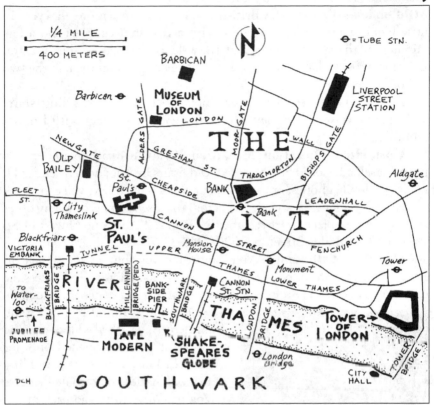

Cost, Hours, Location: Free, daily 10:00–18:00, Exhibition Road, Tube: South Kensington, tel. 0870-870-4868, www.sciencemuseum.org .uk. The museum features the kid-friendly Deep Blue Café, plus several other small, fully accessible eateries. A picnic terrace is on the lower level.

East London: The City

▲▲**The City of London**—When Londoners say "The City," they mean the one-square-mile business, banking, and journalism center that 2,000 years ago was Roman Londinium. The outline of the Roman city walls can still be seen in the arc of roads from Blackfriars Bridge to Tower Bridge. Within The City are 23 churches designed by Sir Christopher Wren, mostly just ornamentation around St. Paul's Cathedral. Today, while home to only 5,000 residents, The City thrives, with over 500,000 office workers coming and going daily. It's a fascinating district to wander on weekdays, but since almost nobody actually lives there, it's dull in the evenings and on Saturday and Sunday.

▲**Old Bailey**—To view the British legal system in action—lawyers in little blond wigs speaking legalese with a British accent—spend a few minutes in the visitors' gallery at the Old Bailey, called the "Central Criminal Court." Don't enter under the dome; signs point you to the two visitors' entrances.

Access: Level 4—Not Accessible. With lots of winding stairs and many levels, Old Bailey will challenge any traveler with limited mobility.

Cost, Hours, Location: Free, Mon–Fri about 10:30–16:30 depending on caseload, closed Sat–Sun, reduced hours in Aug; no kids under 14; no bags, mobile phones, or cameras, but small purses OK; you can check your bag at Bailey's Sandwich Bar across the street for £2 or at any other entrepreneurial place nearby; Tube: St. Paul's, 2 blocks northwest of St. Paul's on Old Bailey Street, tel. 020/7248-3277.

▲▲▲**St. Paul's Cathedral**—Wren's most famous church is the great St. Paul's, its elaborate interior capped by a 365-foot dome. The accessible crypt (included with admission) is a world of historic bones and memori-

als, including Admiral Nelson's tomb and interesting cathedral models. The great West Door is opened only for great occasions, such as the wedding of Prince Charles and the late Princess Diana in 1981. Go to the back of the church and imagine how Diana felt before making the hike to the altar with the world watching. Sit under the second-largest dome in the world and eavesdrop on guided tours.

Since World War II, St. Paul's has been Britain's symbol of resistance. Despite 57 nights of bombing, the Nazis failed to destroy the cathedral, thanks to the St. Paul's volunteer fire watch, who stayed on the dome. Non-disabled travelers can climb the dome for a great city view and some fun in the Whispering Gallery—where the precisely designed barrel of the dome lets sweet nothings circle audibly around to the opposite side.

Access: Everything except the dome and American Memorial Chapel is **AE, AI, AL, AT,** Level 1—Fully Accessible. The temporary accessible entrance is to the left of the main entrance, halfway down the

St. Paul's

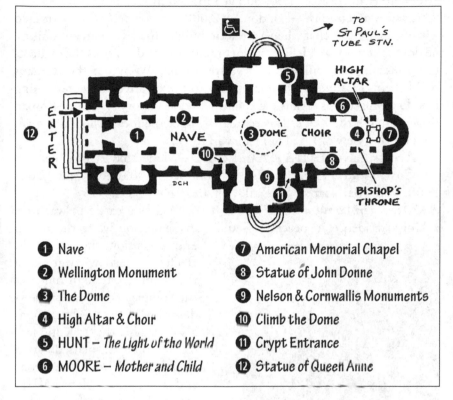

1. Nave
2. Wellington Monument
3. The Dome
4. High Altar & Choir
5. HUNT – *The Light of the World*
6. MOORE – *Mother and Child*
7. American Memorial Chapel
8. Statue of John Donne
9. Nelson & Cornwallis Monuments
10. Climb the Dome
11. Crypt Entrance
12. Statue of Queen Anne

length of the cathedral. This entrance is scheduled to move back to the south side of the cathedral in spring 2007. The main floor and crypt (both fully accessible) can be reached by lift. Follow signs to the accessible toilet. The dome and Whispering Gallery (Level 4—Not Accessible) can be reached only by climbing many flights of stairs.

Cost, Hours, Information: £9, includes church entry and dome climb, Mon–Sat 8:30–16:30, last entry 16:00, last dome entry 16:15, closed Sun except for worship. No photography is allowed. Ninety-minute "Super Tours" of the cathedral and crypt cost £3 (Mon–Sat at 11:00, 11:30, 13:30, and 14:00—confirm schedule at church or call tel. 020/7246-8350 Mon–Fri 9:00–17:00 or 020/7236-4128 for recorded info; £3.50 for 1-hour audioguide which covers 17 stops, available Mon–Sat 9:00–15:30). There's a cheery café in the crypt of the cathedral (Tube: St. Paul's, tel. 020/7236-4128, www.stpauls.co.uk).

Services: Sunday services are at 8:00, 10:15, 11:30 (sung Eucharist), 15:15 (evensong), and 18:00, with a **free organ recital** at 17:00. The **evensong** services are free, but nonpaying visitors are not allowed to linger afterward (Mon–Sat at 17:00, Sun at 15:15, 40 min).

▲**Museum of London**—London, a 2,000-year-old city, is so littered with Roman ruins that when a London builder finds Roman antiquities, he doesn't stop work. He simply documents the finds, moves the artifacts to a museum, and builds on. If you're asking, "Why did the Romans build their cities underground?", a trip to the creative and entertaining London Museum is a must. Explore London history from pre-Roman times through the 1920s. This regular stop for the local schoolkids gives the best overview of London history in town.

Access: AE+A, AI, AT, AL, Level 2—Moderately Accessible.

Cost, Hours, Location: Free, Mon–Sat 10:00–18:00, Sun 12:00–18:00, Tube: Barbican or St. Paul's, tel. 0870-444-3852.

▲▲▲**Tower of London**—The Tower has served as a castle in wartime, a king's residence in peacetime, and, most notoriously, as the prison

and execution site of rebels. Beefeaters lead witty tours of the premises (though much of the complex is not accessible—described below). Attractions also include the executioner's block that dispensed with troublesome heirs to the throne and a couple of Henry VIII's wives. The crown jewels, dating from the Restoration, are the best on Earth—and come with hour-long lines for most of the day. To avoid the crowds, arrive when the Tower opens and go straight for the jewels, then (if you are able) do the Beefeater tour and White Tower later. If you want to go later in the day, the jewels are less crowded from about 16:30.

Access: AE, AT, AL, Level 3—Minimally Accessible. The Tower of London is a mixed bag for accessibility. The entry and toilet are fully accessible, as are the crown jewels. But beyond that, many steps make further access challenging. For more accessibility details, call 0870-751-5191.

Cost, Hours, Information: £14.50, or £8.75 for a person with a disability (companion enters free), family-£42, March–Oct Tue–Sat 9:00–18:00, Sun–Mon 10:00–18:00; Nov–Feb Tue–Sat 9:00–17:00, Sun–Mon 10:00–17:00; last entry 60 min before closing. No photography is allowed of the jewels or in chapels. Tube: Tower Hill, tel. 0870-751-5177, recorded info tel. 0870-756-6060, booking tel. 0870-756-7070.

Crowd-Beating Tips: The long but fast-moving ticket line is worst on Sunday. You can avoid the line entirely by picking up your ticket at any London TI or the Tower Hill Tube station ticket office.

Ceremony of the Keys: Every night at precisely 21:30, with pageantry-filled ceremony, the Tower of London is locked up (as it has been for the last 700 years). To attend this free 30-minute event, you need to request an invitation at least two months before your visit. Write to Ceremony of the Keys, H.M. Tower of London, London EC3N 4AB. Include your name; the addresses, names, and ages of all people attending (up to 6 people, nontransferable, no kids under 8 allowed); requested date; alternative dates; and two international reply coupons (buy at U.S. post office—if your post office doesn't have the $1.75 coupons in stock, they can order them; the turnaround time is a few days).

South London, on the South Bank

The long, cool, smooth, fully accessible riverside path along the South Bank is a thriving arts and cultural center. This popular, pub-crawling people zone—called the Jubilee Promenade—stretches from Tower Bridge past Westminster Bridge, where it offers grand views of the Houses of Parliament. (The promenade hugs the river except just east of London Bridge, where it cuts inland for a couple of blocks.)

City Hall—Opened in 2002, the glassy, egg-shaped building near the south end of Tower Bridge is London's City Hall, designed by Lord Norman Foster, the architect who worked on London's Millennium Bridge and Berlin's Reichstag. An interior spiral ramp allows visitors to watch and hear the action below in the Assembly Chamber; ride the lift to the second floor (the highest visitors can go) and spiral down. The Visitors Centre on the lower ground floor has a handy cafeteria. A top-floor observation deck known as "London's Living Room" is open for tours, usually on Monday morning (phone-in reservation required), and on occasional weekends 10:00–16:30.

The South Bank

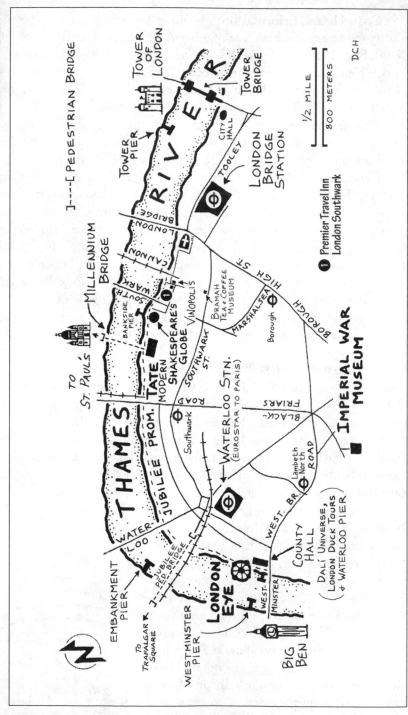

Access: AE, AI, AT, AL, Level 1—Fully Accessible.

Cost, Hours, Location: Free, Visitors Centre open Mon–Fri 8:00–20:00, closed Sat–Sun, between the London Bridge and Tower Hill Tube stations. The Hall occasionally opens up for public tours—call or check Web site to confirm tour times and opening hours, tel. 020/7983-4100, www.london.gov.uk.

▲▲▲**London Eye Ferris Wheel**—Built by British Airways, the wheel towers above London opposite Big Ben. This is the world's highest observational wheel, giving you a chance to fly British Airways without leaving London. Designed like a giant bicycle wheel, it's a pan-European undertaking: British steel and Dutch engineering, with Czech, German, French, and Italian mechanical parts. It's also very "green," running extremely efficiently and virtually silently. Twenty-five people ride in each of its 32 air-conditioned  capsules for the 30-minute rotation (each capsule has a bench, but most people stand). From the top of this 450-foot-high wheel—the highest public viewpoint in the city—Big Ben looks small. You go around only once; save a shot on top for the glass capsule next to yours. Its original five-year lease has been extended to 25 years, and it looks like this will become a permanent fixture on the London skyline. Thames boats come and go from here using the Waterloo Pier at the foot of the wheel (fully accessible dock area and ramp—see page 81).

Access: AE, AI, AT, AL, Level 1—Fully Accessible. People with limited mobility can call 0870-990-8885 to reserve a free "Fast Track" service that allows them to skip the line.

Cost, Hours, Location: £12.50, £2 discount for a wheelchair user and free ticket for a companion if you book in advance by calling 0870-990-8885. April–mid-Sept daily 9:30–21:00, until 22:00 in July-Aug, mid-Sept–March 9:30–20:00, often closed Jan for maintenance, Tube: Waterloo or Westminster, www.ba-londoneye.com (10 percent discount for booking online).

Crowd-Beating Tips: Visitors face two lines: one to get your ticket, and the other to board. You can generally just buy your ticket at the wheel (never more than a 30-min wait, worst on weekends and school holidays). If you want to book a ticket (with an assigned time) in advance, call 0870-500-0600 or book online at www.ba-londoneye.com (and save

10 percent). Upon arrival, you either pick up your pre-booked ticket (if you reserved ahead; use the ATM-type machines to save time—just type in your confirmation number) or wait in the line inside to buy tickets. Then you join the ticket-holders' line at the wheel (starting 10 min before your assigned half-hour time slot).

Dalí Universe—Cleverly located next to the hugely popular London Eye Ferris Wheel, this exhibit features 500 works of mind-bending art by Salvador Dalí. While pricey, it's entertaining if you like Surrealism and want to learn about Dalí.

Access: AE, AI, AL, AT, Level 2—Moderately Accessible. Wheelchair users should call ahead to let them know you are coming. When you arrive, go to the box office, where you will be assisted.

Cost, Hours, Location: £9, audioguide-£2.50, daily 10:00–18:30, generally summer evenings until 20:00, last entry 1 hour before closing, Tube: Waterloo or Westminster, tel. 020/7620-2720.

▲▲Imperial War Museum—This impressive museum covers the wars of the last century, from heavy weaponry to love notes and Varga Girls, from Monty's Africa campaign tank to Schwarzkopf's Desert Storm uniform. You can trace the development of the machine gun, watch footage of the first tank battles, see one of over a thousand V2 rockets Hitler rained on Britain in 1944 (each with over a ton of explosives), hold your breath through the gruesome WWI trench experience, and buy WWII-era toys in the fun museum shop. The "Secret War" section gives a fascinating peek into the intrigues of espionage in World Wars I and II. The section on the Holocaust is one of the best on the subject anywhere. Rather than glorify war, the museum does its best to shine a light on the powerful human side of one of mankind's most persistent traits.

The museum is housed in what was the Royal Bethlam Hospital. Also known as "the Bedlam asylum," the place was so wild it gave the world a new word for chaos: "bedlam." Back in Victorian times, locals—without trash-talk shows and cable TV—came here for their entertainment. The asylum was actually open to the paying public on weekends.

Access: AE, AI, AT, AL, Level 1—Fully Accessible. Loaner wheelchairs are available.

Cost, Hours, Location: Free, daily 10:00–18:00, 2 hours is enough time for most visitors, Tube: Lambeth North or bus #12 from Westminster, tel. 020/7416-5000, www.iwm.org.uk.

▲▲▲Tate Modern—Dedicated in the spring of 2000, this striking museum across the river from St. Paul's opened the new century with art from the old one. Its powerhouse collection of Monet, Matisse, Dalí, Picasso, Warhol, and much more is displayed in a converted powerhouse.

Each year, the main hall features a different monumental installation by a prominent artist.

Access: AE, AI, AT, AL, Level 1—Fully Accessible.

Cost, Hours, Location: Free, fee for special exhibitions, Sun–Thu 10:00–18:00, Fri–Sat 10:00–22:00, Fri–Sat evenings a good time to visit, audioguide-£2, multimedia handheld device-£3.50, call to confirm schedule, view café on top floor; cross the Millennium Bridge from St. Paul's, or Tube: Southwark plus a half-mile roll or stroll; or connect by fully accessible Tate Boat ferry from Tate Britain for £4—see specifics on page 84; tel. 020/7887-8008, www.tate.org.uk.

▲**Millennium Bridge**—This pedestrian bridge—London's first new bridge in a century—links St. Paul's Cathedral and the Tate Modern

across the Thames. When it first opened, the $25 million bridge wiggled when people walked on it, so it promptly closed for a $7 million stabilization; now it's stable and open again (free). Nicknamed "a blade of light" for its sleek minimalist design—370 yards long, four yards wide, stainless steel with teak planks—it includes clever aerodynamic handrails to deflect wind over the heads of pedestrians.

Access: AE, AI, Level 1—Fully Accessible.

▲▲**Shakespeare's Globe**—The original Globe Theater has been rebuilt, half-timbered and thatched, as it was in Shakespeare's time. (This is the

first thatched roof in London since they were outlawed after the Great Fire of 1666.) The Globe originally accommodated 2,000 seated and another 1,000 standing. (Today, slightly smaller and leaving space for reasonable aisles, the theater holds 900 seated guests and 600 groundlings.) Its promoters brag that the theater melds "the three

A's"—actors, audience, and architecture—with each contributing to the play. Open as a museum and a working theater, it hosts authentic old-time performances of Shakespeare's plays. The Globe's exhibition on Shakespeare is the world's largest, with interactive displays and film presentations, a sound lab, a script factory, and costumes. The theater can be toured when there are no plays going on—it's worth planning ahead for these excellent tours. For details on seeing a play, see page 130. The Globe Café is open daily (10:00–18:00, tel. 020/7902-1433).

Access: AE, AI, AT, AL, ♥, Level 1—Fully Accessible. You can download an "Access Guide" at www.shakespeares-globe.org. For specific accessibility questions, call the Access Information Line at 020/7902-1409.

Cost, Hours, Information: £9 includes exhibition and actor-led guided tour; mid-May–Sept exhibition open daily 9:00–18:00, tours go on the half-hour from 9:30, generally until 12:30, until 11:30 on Sun, 17:30 on Mon; Oct–mid-May exhibition open daily 10:00–17:00 with 30-min tours on the half-hour as above. It's on the South Bank directly across the Thames over Southwark Bridge from St. Paul's (Tube: London Bridge, plus a roll or stroll). Info: tel. 020/7902-1500, www.shakespeares-globe.org.

Bramah Tea and Coffee Museum—Aficionados of tea or coffee will find this small museum fascinating. It tells the story of each drink almost passionately. The owner, Mr. Bramah, comes from a big tea family and wants the world to know how the advent of commercial television, with breaks not long enough to brew a proper pot of tea, required a faster hot drink. In came the horrible English instant coffee. Tea countered with finely chopped leaves in tea bags, and it's all gone downhill ever since. The museum café, which serves more kinds of coffees and teas than cakes, is open to the public (same hours as museum).

Access: AE, AI, AT, Level 1—Fully Accessible.

Cost, Hours, Location: £4, daily 10:00–18:00, 40 Southwark Street, Tube: London Bridge plus a quarter-mile roll or stroll. Info: tel. 020/7403-5650, www.bramahmuseum.co.uk. The #RV1 bus zips you to the museum easily and scenically from Covent Garden.

▲▲Vinopolis: City of Wine—While it seems illogical to have a huge wine museum in London, Vinopolis makes a good case. Built over a Roman wine store and filling the massive vaults of an old wine warehouse, the museum offers an excellent audioguide with a light yet earnest history of wine. Sipping various reds and whites, ports, and champagnes—immersed in your audioguide as you explore—you learn about the libation from its

Georgian origins to Chile, including a Vespa ride through Chianti country in Tuscany. Allow some time, as the included audioguide takes 90 minutes—and the sipping can slow things down wonderfully.

Access: AE, AI, AT, ♥, Level 1—Fully Accessible. This place is wheelchair-friendly, all on one level, fun, and hospitable.

Cost, Hours, Location: £12.50 with 5 tastes, only £11 Tue–Thu; don't worry...for £3, you can buy 5 more tastes inside; £15 gets you a premium service with a couple of especially fine wines and a tasting lesson, daily 12:00–18:00, Mon and Fri–Sat until 21:00, last entry 2 hrs before closing, between the Globe and Southwark Cathedral at 1 Bank End, Tube: London Bridge, tel. 0870-241-4040 or 020/7940-8322, www .vinopolis.co.uk.

South London, on the North Bank

▲▲Tate Britain—One of Europe's great art houses, Tate Britain specializes in British painting from the 16th century through modern times. The museum has a good representation of William Blake's religious sketches, the Pre-Raphaelites' realistic art, and J. M. W. Turner's swirling works.

Access: AE, AI, AL, AT, Level 1—Fully Accessible, but there is a limit of six wheelchairs at one time.

Cost, Hours, Location: Free, £2 donation requested, daily 10:00–17:50, last entry at 17:00.

Tours and Information: The museum offers a fine, free, and necessary audioguide, plus free tours (normally Mon–Fri at 11:00—16th, 17th, and 18th centuries; at noon—19th century; at 14:00—Turner; at 15:00—20th century; Sat–Sun at noon and 15:00—highlights; call to confirm schedule, tel. 020/7887-8000, recorded info tel. 020/7887-8008, www.tate.org.uk). No photography is allowed. Tube: Pimlico, then a quarter-mile roll or stroll; or arrive directly at museum by taking bus #88 from Oxford Circus or #77A from National Gallery, or more fun, the fully accessible £4 Tate Boat ferry from Tate Modern—see specifics on page 84.

Greater London

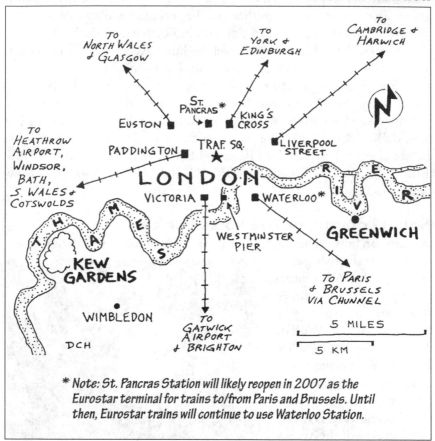

TO
NORTH WALES
& GLASGOW

TO
YORK &
EDINBURGH

TO
CAMBRIDGE &
HARWICH

N

ST.
PANCRAS *

EUSTON

KING'S
CROSS

TO
HEATHROW
AIRPORT,
WINDSOR,
BATH,
S. WALES &
COTSWOLDS

PADDINGTON

TRAF. SQ.

LIVERPOOL
STREET

R I V E R

LONDON

VICTORIA

WATERLOO *

GREENWICH

WESTMINSTER
PIER

T H A M E S

KEW
GARDENS

WIMBLEDON

TO
GATWICK
AIRPORT
& BRIGHTON

TO PARIS
& BRUSSELS
VIA CHUNNEL

5 MILES

5 KM

DCH

* Note: St. Pancras Station will likely reopen in 2007 as the
Eurostar terminal for trains to/from Paris and Brussels. Until
then, Eurostar trains will continue to use Waterloo Station.

Greater London

▲**Kew Gardens**—For a fine riverside park and a palatial greenhouse

jungle to swing through, take the Tube or the boat to every botanist's favorite escape, Kew Gardens. While for most visitors, the Royal Botanic Gardens of Kew are simply a delightful opportunity to wander among 33,000 different types of plants, to the hardworking organization that runs the gardens, it's a way to promote understanding and preservation of the botanical diversity of our planet. The Kew Tube station drops you in a little herbal business community two blocks from Victoria Gate (the main garden entrance). Pick up a map brochure and check at the gate for a monthly listing of best blooms.

Garden-lovers could spend days exploring Kew's 300 acres. For a quick visit, spend a fragrant hour wandering through three buildings: the Palm House, a humid Victorian world of iron, glass, and tropical plants built in 1844; a Waterlily House that Monet would swim for; and the Princess of Wales Conservatory, a modern greenhouse with many different climate zones growing countless cacti, bug-munching carnivorous plants, and more.

Access: AE, AI, AT, Level 1—Fully Accessible. Imagine peaceful, flat, gorgeous, and green (with only occasional areas of inaccessibility). For the most part, you can roll wherever you please—and there are accessible toilets, too. Loaner wheelchairs are available.

Cost, Hours, Location: £8.50, £6 at 15:00 or later, Mon–Fri 9:30–18:30, Sat–Sun 9:30–19:30, until 16:30 or sunset off-season, galleries and conservatories close at 17:30, a £3.50 narrated floral 35-minute joyride on an accessible little train departs on the hour until 16:00 from Victoria Gate, Tube: Kew Gardens, boats run between Kew Gardens and Westminster Pier—see page 83, tel. 020/8332-5000, www.rbgkew.org .uk. For a sun-dappled lunch, roll or stroll from the Palm House to the fully accessible Orangery (£6 hot meals, daily 10:00–17:30).

Disappointments of London

On the South Bank, the London Dungeon, a much visited but amateurish attraction, is just a highly advertised, overpriced haunted house—certainly not worth the £20 admission, much less your valuable London time. It comes with long and rude lines. Wait for Halloween and see one in your hometown to support a better cause. "Winston Churchill's Britain at War Experience" (next to the London Dungeon) also wastes your time and money (especially considering the wonderful new Churchill Museum in the Cabinet War Rooms; see page 88). The Jack the Ripper walking tours (by any of several companies) are big sellers, but don't offer much. Anything actually related to the notorious serial killer was torn down a century ago, and all that's left are a few small sights and lots of bloody stories.

SHOPPING

Marks & Spencer—No one in London is doing a better job with confronting accessibility issues than Marks & Spencer shops and department stores, even sponsoring an annual contest where major hotels compete for accessible designs. Their stores are sprinkled throughout London, and each one has an accessible food and wine section for gathering your picnic goodies (main store in South Kensington, store finder at www .marksandspencer.com/stores).

Access: AE, AI, AL, AT, ♥, Level 1—Fully Accessible.

Harrods—Harrods is London's most famous and touristy department store. With a million square feet of retail space on seven floors, it's a place where some shoppers could spend all day. (To me, it's a department store.) Big yet classy, Harrods has everything from elephants to toothbrushes.

Access: AE, AI, AT, AL, ♥, Level 1—Fully Accessible. All floors are accessible by elevator, and the toilets are easily accessible.

Hours and Location: Mon–Sat 10:00–19:00, closed Sun, mandatory storage for big backpacks-£2.50, on Brompton Road, Tube: Knightsbridge, tel. 020/7730-1234, www.harrods.com.

◑ Self-Guided Tour: Sightseers should pick up the free *Store Guide* at any info post. Here's what I enjoyed: On the Ground and Lower Ground Floors, find the Food Halls, with their Edwardian tiled walls, creative and exuberant displays, and staff in period costumes—not quite like your local supermarket back home.

Descend to the Lower Ground Floor and follow signs to the Egyptian Escalator—lined with pharaoh-headed sconces, papyrus-plant lamps, and hieroglyphic balconies (Harrods' owner is from Egypt). Here you'll find a memorial to Dodi Fayed and Princess Diana. The huge (and slightly creepy) bronze statue was commissioned by Dodi Fayed's father, Mohamed al Fayed, who owns Harrods. Photos and flowers honor the late Princess and her lover, who both died in a car crash in Paris in 1997. See the wineglass still dirty from their last dinner, and the engagement ring that Dodi purchased the day before they died.

Ascend to the Fourth Floor, and go to the far corner of the store (toys) to find child-sized luxury cars that actually work. A junior Jaguar or Mercedes will set you back about $13,000. The child's Hummer ($30,000) is as big as my car.

Also on the Fourth Floor is the fully accessible Georgian Restaurant. Enjoy a fancy tea under a skylight as a pianist tickles the keys of a Bösendorfer, the world's most expensive piano (tea-£19, includes finger sandwiches and pastries, served after 15:45).

Many of my readers report that Harrods is overpriced, snooty, and teeming with American and Japanese tourists. Still, it's the palace of department stores. The nearby Beauchamp Place is lined with classy and fascinating shops.

Harvey Nichols—Once Princess Diana's favorite, "Harvey Nick's" remains the department store du jour. Want to pick up a little £20 scarf for the wife? You won't do it here, where they're more like £200. The store's fifth floor is a veritable food fest, with a gourmet grocery store, a fancy (but smoky) restaurant, a Yo! Sushi bar, and a lively café. Consider a take-away tray of sushi to eat in the Hyde Park rose garden two blocks away.

Access: AE, AI, AT+A, AL, Level 1—Fully Accessible, including all of the eateries.

Hours and Location: Mon–Tue and Sat 10:00–19:00, Wed–Fri until 20:00, Sun 12:00–18:00, near Harrods, Tube: Knightsbridge, 109 Knightsbridge, www.harveynichols.com.

Toys—The biggest toy store in Britain is **Hamleys,** with seven floors buzzing with 28,000 toys, managed by a staff of 200. At the "Bear Factory," kids can get a made-to-order teddy bear by picking out a "bear skin," and watch while it's stuffed and sewn.

Access: AE, AI, AL, AT, Level 1—Fully Accessible. The accessible toilet is on the fourth floor.

Hours and Location: Mon–Sat 9:00–20:00, Thu until 21:00, Sun 12:00–18:00, 188 Regent Street, tel. 0870-333-2455, www.hamleys.com.

Carnaby Street—This pedestrian mall has big, flat cobblestones and no break between the sidewalk and street area. Most stores have a flat entry (or 1 step of less than 6"), and all corners have curb cuts. It's a short distance from here to Regent Street, where the sidewalks are wide and interesting shops abound.

Street Markets—Antique buffs, people-watchers, and folks who brake for garage sales love to haggle at London's street markets. While some nooks and crannies may be difficult for wheelchair users to reach, the markets generally have decent accessibility. There's good early-morning market activity somewhere any day of the week. The best are **Portobello Road** (Mon–Wed and Fri–Sat 8:00–18:30, closes at 13:00 on Thu, closed Sun, Tube: Notting Hill Gate, near recommended B&Bs, tel. 020/7229-8354) and **Camden Lock Market** (daily 10:00–18:00, Tube: Camden Town, tel. 020/7284-2084, www.camdenlock.net). The TI has a complete, up-to-date list. Warning: Markets attract two kinds of people—tourists and pickpockets.

ENTERTAINMENT

Theater (a.k.a. "Theatre")

London's theater rivals Broadway's in quality and beats it in price. Choose from Shakespeare, musicals, comedies, thrillers, sex farces, cutting-edge fringe shows, revivals starring movie celebs, and more. London does it all well. I prefer big, glitzy—even bombastic—musicals over serious chamber dramas, simply because London can deliver the lights, sound, dancers, and multimedia spectacle I rarely get back home.

Most theaters, marked on tourist maps, are found in the West End between Piccadilly and Covent Garden. The majority of big venues are accessible and wheelchair-friendly (you'll find accessibility details for the most popular venues in the "What's On in the West End" sidebar on page 128); you can also find accessibility information for specific theaters online at www.officiallondontheatre.co.uk or www.theatremonkey.com.

Box offices, hotels, and TIs offer a handy, free *Theatre Guide* (also at www.londontheatre.co.uk). Performances are nightly except Sunday, usually with one or two matinees a week (Shakespeare's Globe is the rare theater that does offer performances on Sunday, mid-May–Sept). Tickets range from about £8 to £40. Matinees are generally cheaper and rarely sell out.

To book a ticket, simply call the theater box office directly, ask about prices and available dates, and purchase with your credit card. You can call from the U.S. as easily as from England (check www.officiallondontheatre.co.uk, the American magazine *Variety*, or photocopy your hometown library's London newspaper theater section). Arrive about 30 minutes before the show starts to pick up your ticket and avoid lines.

For a booking fee, you can reserve online (www.ticketmaster.co.uk or www.firstcalltickets.com) or call Keith Prowse Ticketing, formerly Global Tickets (U.S. tel. 800-223-6108). While booking through an agency is quick and easy, prices are inflated by a standard 25 percent fee. Ticket agencies (whether in the United States, at London's TIs, or scattered throughout the city) are scalpers with an address. If you're

London's Major Theaters

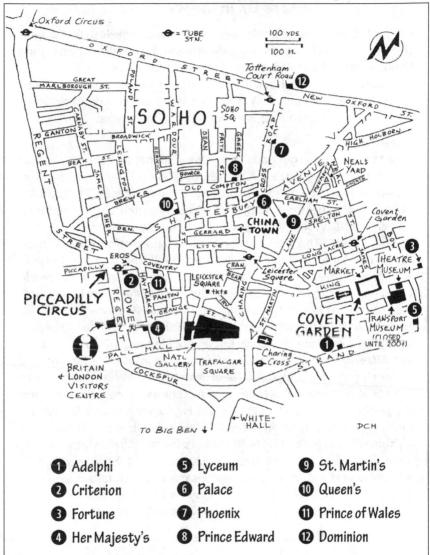

1 Adelphi

2 Criterion

3 Fortune

4 Her Majesty's

5 Lyceum

6 Palace

7 Phoenix

8 Prince Edward

9 St. Martin's

10 Queen's

11 Prince of Wales

12 Dominion

buying from an agency, look at the ticket carefully (your price should be no more than 30 percent over the printed face value; the 17.5 percent VAT is already included in the face value) and understand where you're sitting according to the floor plan (if your view is restricted, it will state this on the ticket; for floor plans of the various theaters, see www .theatremonkey.com). Agencies are worthwhile only if a show you've just got to see is sold out at the box office. They scarf up hot tickets, planning

What's On in the West End

Here are some of the perennial favorites that you're likely to find among the West End's evening offerings. If spending the time and money for a London play, I like a full-fledged, high-energy musical.

Generally, you can book tickets for free at the box office or for a £2 fee by telephone or online. Wheelchair users and their companions are often eligible for discounts; ask when you buy your ticket.

Musicals

Chicago—A chorus girl gone bad forms a nightclub act with another murderess to bring in the bucks (**AE, AI, AT,** Level 1—Fully Accessible; £15–42.50, Mon–Thu and Sat 20:00, Fri 20:30, matinees Fri 17:00 and Sat 15:00, Adelphi Theatre, Strand, Tube: Covent Garden or Charing Cross, booking tel. 020/7344-0055, www.chicagothemusical.com).

Mamma Mia!—This high-energy spandex-and-platform-boots musical weaves together 20 or 30 ABBA hits to tell the story of a bride in search of her real dad as her promiscuous mom plans her Greek Isle wedding. The production has the audience dancing by its happy ending (**AE, AI, AT,** Level 1—Fully Accessible; £25–49, Mon–Thu and Sat 19:30, Fri 20:30, matinees Fri 17:00 and Sat 15:00, Prince of Wales Theatre, Coventry Street, Tube: Piccadilly Circus, booking tel. 0870-850-0393).

Les Misérables—Claude-Michel Schönberg's musical adaptation of Victor Hugo's epic follows the life of Jean Valjean as he struggles with the social and political realities of 19th-century France. This inspiring mega-hit takes you back to the days of France's struggle for a just and modern society (**AE, AI, AT,** Level 1—Fully Accessible; £10–45, Mon–Sat 19:30, matinees Wed and Sat 14:30, Queen's Theatre, Shaftesbury Avenue, Tube: Piccadilly Circus, box office tel. 020/7494-5040, www.lesmis.com).

Phantom of the Opera—A mysterious masked man falls in love with a singer in this haunting Andrew Lloyd Webber musical about life beneath the stage of the Paris Opera (**AE, AI,** Level 2—Moderately

to make a killing after the show is sold out. U.S. booking agencies get their tickets from another agency, adding even more to your expense by involving yet another middleman. Many tickets sold on the street are forgeries. Although some theaters have booking agencies handle their advance sales, you'll stand a good chance of saving money and avoiding the middleman by simply calling the box office directly to book your tickets (international phone calls are cheap, and credit cards make booking a snap).

Accessible; £15–45, Mon–Sat 19:30, matinees Tue and Sat 14:30, Her Majesty's Theatre, Haymarket, Tube: Piccadilly Circus, booking tel. 0870-890-1106, www.thephantomoftheopera.com).

The Lion King—In this Disney extravaganza featuring music by Elton John, Simba the lion learns about the delicately balanced circle of life on the savanna (**AE, AI, AT,** Level 1—Fully Accessible; £17.50–40, Tue–Sat 19:30, matinees Wed and Sat 14:00 and Sun 15:00, Lyceum Theatre, Wellington Street, Tube: Charing Cross or Covent Garden, booking tel. 0870-243-9000 or 020/7344-4444, theater info tel. 020/7420-8112, www.thelionking.co.uk).

We Will Rock You—Whether or not you're a fan of Queen, this musical tribute—more to the band than to Freddie Mercury—is an understandably popular celebration of their work (**AE, AI, AT,** Level 1—Fully Accessible; £23.50–55, Mon–Fri at 19:30, matinees Wed and Sat at 14:30, Dominion Theatre, Tottenham Court Road, Tube: Tottenham Court Road, Ticketmaster tel. 0870-169-0116, www.queenonline.com/wewillrockyou).

Thrillers

The Mousetrap—Agatha Christie's whodunit about a murder in a country house continues to stump audiences after 50 years (**AE, AI+A, AT,** Level 2—Moderately Accessible; £11.50–30, Mon–Sat 20:00, matinees Tue 14:45 and Sat 17:00, St. Martin's Theatre, West Street, Tube: Leicester Square, box office tel. 0870-162-8787).

The Woman in Black—The chilling tale of a solicitor who is haunted by what he learns when he closes a reclusive woman's affairs (Level 3—Minimally Accessible; £12.50–32.50, Mon–Sat 20:00, matinees Tue 15:00 and Sat 16:00, Fortune Theatre, Russell Street, Tube: Covent Garden, box office tel. 020/7369-1737, www.thewomaninblack.com).

Theater Lingo: Stalls (ground floor), dress circle (first balcony), upper circle (second balcony), balcony (sky-high third balcony), slips (cheap seats on the fringes). Many cheap seats have a restricted view (behind a pillar).

Cheap Theater Tricks: Most theaters offer cheap returned tickets, standing-room, matinee, and senior or student standby deals. These "concessions" are indicated with a "conc" or "s" in the listings. Picking up a late return can get you a great seat at a cheap-seat price. If a show is "sold out," there's usually a way to get a seat. Call the theater box office and ask how.

Many theaters are so small that there's hardly a bad seat. After the lights go down, scooting up is less than a capital offense. Shakespeare did it.

Half-Price "tkts" Booth: This famous but minimally accessible (steps and no ramp) ticket booth at **Leicester Square** sells discounted tickets for top-price seats to shows on the push list the day of the show only (£2.50 service charge per ticket, Mon–Sat 10:00–19:00, Sun 12:00–15:30, matinee tickets from noon, lines often form early, list of shows available online, www.tkts.co.uk). Most tickets are half-price; other shows are discounted 25 percent.

Here are some sample prices: A top-notch seat to *Chicago* costs £40 bought directly from the theater, but only £22.50 at Leicester (LESSter) Square. The cheapest balcony seat (bought from the theater) is £15. Half-price tickets can be a good deal, unless you want the cheapest seats or the hottest shows. But check the board; occasionally they sell cheap tickets to good shows. For example, a first-class seat to the long-running *Les Misérables* (which rarely sells out) costs £45 when bought from the theater ticket office, but you'll save 25 percent and pay £36.50 at the tkts booth. Note that the real half-price booth (marked *tkts*) is a freestanding kiosk at the edge of the garden in Leicester Square. Several dishonest outfits nearby advertise "official half-price tickets"; avoid these.

West End Theaters: The commercial (non-subsidized) theaters cluster around Soho (especially along Shaftesbury Avenue) and Covent Garden. With a centuries-old tradition of pleasing the masses, these present London theater at its glitziest. See the "What's On in the West End" sidebar.

Royal Shakespeare Company: If you'll ever enjoy Shakespeare, it'll be in Britain. The RSC performs at various theaters around London and in Stratford year-round. To get a schedule and accessibility information for each venue, contact the RSC (Royal Shakespeare Theatre, Stratford-upon-Avon, tel. 01789/403-444, www.rsc.org.uk).

Shakespeare's Globe: To see Shakespeare in a replica of the theater for which he wrote his plays, attend a play at the Globe. This round, thatch-roofed, open-air theater performs the plays much as Shakespeare intended (with no amplification). The play's the thing from mid-May through September (usually Tue–Sat 14:00 and 19:30, Sun at either 13:00 and 18:30 or 16:00 only, Mon at 19:30, tickets can be sold out months in advance). You'll pay £13–29 for a seat (usually on a backless bench; only a few rows and the pricier Gentlemen's Rooms have seats with backs; £2 cushions are considered a good investment by many). Or pay £5 to stand (or sit in your wheelchair) in the "groundling" pit; these tickets—while the only ones open to rain—are most fun. Scurry in early to stake out a spot on the stage's edge leaning rail, where the most interaction with the actors occurs. You're a crude peasant. You can lean your elbows on the stage, munch a picnic dinner, or wander around. I've never enjoyed Shakespeare as much as here, performed as it was meant to be in the "wooden O." Plays can be long. Many groundlings leave before the end. If you like, hang out an hour before the finish and beg or buy a ticket from someone leaving early (groundlings are allowed to come and go).

Access: AE, AI, AT, AL, ♥, Level 1—Fully Accessible. Wheelchair users have two options at Shakespeare's Globe: fancy "Gentlemen's Rooms" seating for a discounted £20 (same discount for companion, book in advance), or in special elevated groundling pit spaces (though the view of the stage may still be partially obstructed). The staff will gladly assist if necessary. The theater runs a Disabled Access Information line (tel. 020/7902-1409), and you can download an "Access Guide" from their Web site (www.shakespeares-globe.org).

Information and Contact: For information on plays or £9 tours (see page 119), contact the theater at tel. 020/7902-1500 (or see www.shakespeares-globe.org). To reserve tickets for plays, call or drop by the box office (Mon–Sat 10:00–18:00, until 20:00 on day of show, at Shakespeare's Globe at New Globe Walk entrance, tel. 020/7401-9919). If you reserve online (www.wayahead.com/shakespeares-globe), be warned: Your ticket price will have an added booking fee.

The theater is on the South Bank, directly across the Thames over the Millennium Bridge from St. Paul's Cathedral (Tube: Mansion House or London Bridge). The Globe is inconvenient for public transport, but during theater season, there's a regular supply of black cabs outside the main foyer on New Globe Walk.

Fringe Theatre: London's rougher evening entertainment scene is thriving, filling pages in *Time Out.* Choose from a wide range of fringe theater and comedy acts (generally £5).

Classical Music

For easy, cheap, or free concerts in historic churches, check the TIs' listings for **lunch concerts,** especially:

- **Wren's St. Bride's Church,** with free lunch concerts Mon–Fri at 13:15 (**AE, AI,** Level 2—Moderately Accessible, no accessible toilet; church tel. 020/7427-0133, www.stbrides.com).

- **St. James at Piccadilly,** with concerts on Mon, Wed, and Fri at 13:10 (**AE, AI+A, AT+A,** Level 2—Moderately Accessible, 2 ramps lead from Piccadilly to the church, then a few steps inside; suggested donation-£3, info tel. 020/7381-0441, www.st-james-piccadilly.org).
- **St. Martin-in-the-Fields,** offering free concerts on Mon, Tue, and Fri at 13:00 (**AE, AI, ♥,** Level 2—Moderately Accessible; concerts are accessible but toilet and box office are not, so call ahead for tickets, box office tel. 020/7839-8362, church tel. 020/7766-1100, www .smitf.com).

St. Martin-in-the-Fields also hosts fine **evening concerts** by candlelight (see accessibility information above; £8–18, Thu–Sat at 19:30, sometimes also on Tue or Wed, box office tel. 020/7839-8362).

At St. Paul's Cathedral (**AE, AI, AL, AT,** Level 1—Fully Accessible, except for dome), **evensong** is held Monday through Saturday at 17:00 and on Sunday at 15:15. At Westminster Abbey (**AE, AI,** Level 2—Moderately Accessible, loaner wheelchairs), it's sung weekdays at 17:00 (but not on Wed) and Saturday and Sunday at 15:00. Free **organ recitals** are held on Sunday at Westminster Abbey (17:45, 30 min, tel. 020/7222-7110) and at St. Paul's (17:00, 30 min, tel. 020/7236-4128).

For a fun **classical event** (mid-July–early Sept), attend a "Prom Concert" (shortened from "Promenade Concert") during the annual festival at the Royal Albert Hall (**AE, AI, AL, AT,** Level 1—Fully Accessible, loaner wheelchairs). Nightly concerts are offered at give-a-peasant-some-culture prices to "Promenaders"—those willing to stand throughout the performance (£4 standing-room spots sold at the door, £7 restricted-view seats, most £22 but depends on performance, Tube: South Kensington, tel. 020/7589-8212, www.royalalberthall.com).

Some of the world's best **opera** is belted out at the prestigious Royal Opera House, near Covent Garden (**AE, AI, AT, AL,** Level 1—Fully Accessible, call ahead to reserve wheelchair space, use accessible Bow Street entrance; box office tel. 020/7304-4000, www.royalopera.org), and at the less-formal Sadler's Wells Theatre (**AE, AI, AT, AL,** Level 1—Fully Accessible, call ahead to reserve wheelchair space; Rosebery Avenue, Islington, Tube: Angel, info tel. 020/7863-8198, box office tel. 0870-737-7737, www.sadlerswells.com).

SLEEPING

London is expensive. Cheaper rooms are relatively dumpy. Don't expect £90 cheeriness in a £60 room. For £70 ($125), you'll get a double with breakfast in a safe, cramped, and dreary place with minimal service and

---

Sleep Code

(£1 = about $1.80, country code: 44, area code: 020)
S = Single, **D** = Double/Twin, **T** = Triple, **Q** = Quad, **b** = bathroom,
s = shower only. Unless otherwise noted, credit cards are accepted, and
prices include a generous breakfast and all taxes.

---

difficult accessibility. For £90 ($160), you'll get a basic, clean, reasonably cheery double in a usually cramped, cracked-plaster building with a private bath, or a soulless but comfortable room without breakfast in a huge, mostly accessible Motel 6–type place. My London splurges, at £100–150 ($180–270), are spacious, thoughtfully appointed, and fully accessible. Competition softens prices, especially for multi-night stays. Hearty English or generous buffet breakfasts are included unless otherwise noted, and TVs are standard in rooms.

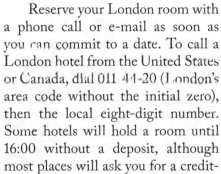

Reserve your London room with a phone call or e-mail as soon as you can commit to a date. To call a London hotel from the United States or Canada, dial 011 44-20 (London's area code without the initial zero), then the local eight-digit number. Some hotels will hold a room until 16:00 without a deposit, although most places will ask you for a credit-card number. The pricier ones have expensive cancellation policies (such as no refund if you cancel with less than 2 weeks' notice). Some fancy £120 rooms rent for a third off if you arrive late on a slow day and ask for a deal.

For more options, check out *Access in London*, with information on accessible accommodations, pubs, and toilets in London (£10, by Gordon Couch, William Forrester, and Justin Irwin; www.accessproject-phsp .org).

Big, Cheap, Modern Hotels

These places—popular with budget tour groups—are well-run and offer elevators and all the modern comforts in a no-frills, practical package. Though not quaint, these hotels offer the best (and cheapest) accessibility in London. Some of the more forward-thinking hotel chains (such as

London's Hotel Neighborhoods

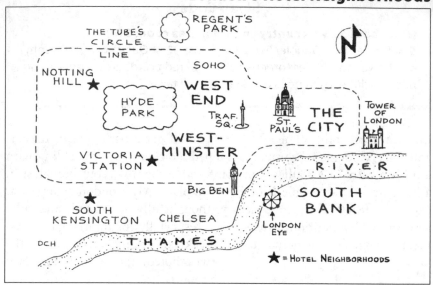

Ibis, Travel Inn, Holiday Inn Express, Comfort Inn, Thistle, and Forte Travelodge) have made it corporate policy to provide adapted facilities for persons with limited mobility.

With the notable exception of the Premier Travel Inn London County Hall, the following listings are often located on busy streets in dreary train-station neighborhoods, so use common sense after dark and wear your money belt. The doubles for £75–100 are a great value for London. Mid-week prices are generally higher than weekend rates. Online bookings are often the easiest way to make reservations, and will get you a discount if you're staying at a Jurys or a Travelodge.

Level 1—Fully Accessible

Premier Travel Inn London County Hall (AE, AI, AL, AR, AB), literally down the hall from a $400-a-night Marriott Hotel, fills one end of London's massive former County Hall building. This place is wonderfully located near the base of the London Eye Ferris Wheel and across the Thames from Big Ben. Its 300 slick rooms come with all the necessary comforts (Db-£87–90 for 2 adults and up to 2 kids under age 15, couples can request a bigger family room—same price, breakfast extra, book in advance, no-show rooms are released at 15:00, elevator, non-smoking rooms, 500 yards from Westminster Tube stop and Waterloo Station, Belvedere Road, you can call central reservations at 0870-242-8000 or 0870-238-3300, you can fax 020/7902-1619 but you might not get a response, it's easiest to book online at www.premiertravelinn.com). There is a special accessible entrance and lift at the rear of the hotel, and there are 16 specially adapted rooms for travelers who use wheelchairs.

Other Premier Travel Inns: These other locations in London are less central, but have at least one room per hotel that is fully adapted (**AE, AI, AL, AR, AB**; figure £75–85 per room, breakfast extra): **Premier Travel Inn King's Cross** (276 large rooms, 14 of which are accessible; non-smoking rooms, 24-hour reception, elevator, just east of King's Cross station at 26–30 York Way, tel. 0870-990-6414, fax 0870-990-6415); **London Euston** (big, blue, Lego-type building on handy but noisy street and packed with families on vacation, 141 Euston Road, Tube: Euston, tel. 0870-238-3301); **London Kensington** (11 Knaresboro Place, Tube: Earl's Court or Gloucester Road, tel. 0870-238-3304); and **London Putney Bridge** (farther out, 3 Putney Bridge Approach, Tube: Putney Bridge, tel. 0870-238-3302). Avoid the **Tower Bridge** location, which is an inconvenient half-mile roll or stroll from the nearest Tube stop. For any of these, call 0870-242-8000, fax 0870-241-9000, or best, book online at www.premiertravelinn.com.

Jurys Inn Islington (**AE, AI, AL, AR, AB**) rents 200 compact, comfy rooms near King's Cross station (Db/Th-£100, some discounted rooms available online, 2 adults and 2 kids—under age 12—can share 1 room, breakfast extra, non-smoking floors, 60 Pentonville Road, Tube: Angel, tel. 020/7282-5500, fax 020/7282-5511, www.jurysdoyle.com). Built less than 10 years ago, this hotel has 20 fully adapted rooms. The main entrance is also fully accessible.

Hotel Ibis London Euston (**AE, AI, AL, AR, AB**), which feels a bit classier than a Premier Travel Inn, is located on a quiet street a block behind and west of Euston Station (380 rooms, Db-£70–80, breakfast extra, no family rooms, non-smoking floor, 3 Cardington Street, tel. 020/7388-7777, fax 020/7388-0001, www.ibishotel.com, h0921@accor -hotels.com). The hotel has eight accessible rooms (4 twins and 4 doubles). The main entrance on Cardington Street is fully accessible.

Travelodge London Islington (**AE, AI, AL, AR, AB**) is another typical chain hotel with lots of cookie-cutter rooms, two of which are accessible and on the ground floor (Db-£60–80, some £26 rooms available online only for scattered dates, breakfast extra, family rooms, non-smoking rooms, just south of King's Cross Station at 100 King's Cross Road, tel. 0870-191-1773, fax 020/7833-8261, www.travelodge .co.uk). Other Travelodge London locations are at **King's Cross, Covent Garden, Liverpool Street,** and **Farringdon.** For all the details on each, see www.travelodge.co.uk.

Thistle Hotels: This chain operates elegant hotels in London with wonderful amenities for travelers who use wheelchairs (**AE, AI, AL, AR, AB**). The beautifully located **Thistle Royal Horseguards** in Westminster has an accessible restaurant and two adapted rooms that include roll-in showers—call ahead to reserve (Db-£184, much cheaper off-season, 2 Whitehall Court, Tube: Westminster, tel. 0870-333-9122, www.thistlehotels.com). **Thistle Charing Cross** combines Old World elegance with reasonable prices (and 2 fully adapted rooms—book ahead) in a great location connected to Charing Cross Station (Db-£163, much cheaper off-season, on the Strand, Tube: Charing Cross, tel. 0870-333-9105, www.thistlehotels.com).

Level 2—Moderately Accessible
Premier Travel Inn London Southwark (**AE, AI, AL, AR, AB+A,** ♥), with 55 rooms, is near Shakespeare's Globe on the South Bank (Db for up to 2 adults and 2 kids-£83–85, Bankside, 34 Park Street, tel. 0870-990-6402, www.premiertravelinn.com). This surprising little gem offers good accessibility except for the bathrooms, which are suitable, but not adapted.

Victoria Station Neighborhood (Belgravia)
The streets behind Victoria Station teem with budget B&Bs. It's a safe, surprisingly tidy, and decent area without a hint of the trashy, touristy glitz of the streets in front of the station. West of the tracks is Belgravia, where the prices are a bit higher and your neighbors include Andrew Lloyd Webber and Margaret Thatcher (her policeman stands outside 73 Chester Square). East of the tracks is Pimlico—cheaper and just as handy, but the rooms can be a bit dowdier. Decent eateries abound (see "Eating," page 141).

All the recommended hotels are near the Victoria Tube, bus, and train stations. On hot summer nights, request a quiet back room. Near the station are two places to get online that are accessible (**AE, AI**) but lack accessible toilets (though you can use the one inside the station): **Access Internet** (9–13 Wilton Road, tel. 020/7976-5943) and **Victoria Village Webspot Café** (across from Victoria Station at 164 Victoria Street, tel. 020/7168-8841).

Level 1—Fully Accessible
Victoria Park Plaza (**AE, AI, AL, AR, AB**) is ideally situated 50 yards from Victoria Station. While on the higher side for room expense (call and check for "bargain rates"), the hotel is excellent for wheelchair users

Victoria Station Neighborhood

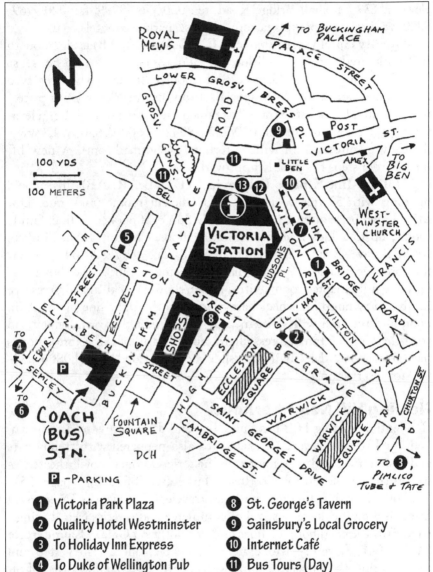

1. Victoria Park Plaza
2. Quality Hotel Westminster
3. To Holiday Inn Express
4. To Duke of Wellington Pub
5. Jenny Lo's Tea House
6. To La Poule au Pot Rest.
7. The Willow Walk
8. St. George's Tavern
9. Sainsbury's Local Grocery
10. Internet Café
11. Bus Tours (Day)
12. Bus Tours (Night)
13. TI, Tube, Taxis, City Buses

who need fully adapted rooms (Sb-£119, Db-£200, apartments available, elevator, 239 Vauxhall Bridge Road, tel. 020/7769-9999, fax 020/7769-9820, www.victoriaparkplaza.com, vppres@parkplazahotels.co.uk).

Quality Hotel Westminster (AE, AI, AL, AR, AB) is big, modern (but with tired carpets), well-located, and a good bet for no-nonsense "chain" comfort (Db-£145, accessible room costs £90 when reserved ahead, check for various Web specials, drop-ins can ask for "saver prices" on slow days, breakfast extra or bargained in, non-smoking floor, elevator, 82 Eccleston Square, tel. 020/7834-8042, fax 020/7630-8942, www.hotels-westminster.com, winchesterhotel17@hotmail.com). A new lift on the front steps has greatly improved access.

Holiday Inn Express Belgravia (AE, AI, AR, AB) fills an old building with 52 fresh, modern, and efficient rooms (rack rate: Db-£114, actual price often £80—especially Sun or if booked online; family rooms, up to 2 kids free, non-smoking floor, elevator, Tube: Pimlico, 106 Belgrave Road, tel. 020/7630-8888, fax 020/7828-0441, www.hiexpressvictoria.co.uk, info@hiexpressvictoria.co.uk). The hotel has only one fully adapted room (with a roll-in shower)—call ahead to reserve it. The entry ramp for wheelchair users is to the right side of the main door, and the staff will assist in your arrival. For those who enjoy and trust the Holiday Inn Express chain, note that all of the Express hotels have at least one wheelchair-accessible room (in London, call 0800-434-040 for reservations).

Notting Hill Neighborhood

Residential Notting Hill has quick bus and Tube access to downtown, and, for London, is very "homely." It's also peppered with trendy bars and restaurants, and is home to the historic Coronet movie theater, as well as the famous Portobello Road Market (see "Shopping," page 125).

Popular with young international travelers, Bayswater's Queensway Street is a multicultural festival of commerce and eateries (see "Eating," page 150). The neighborhood does its dirty clothes at **Galaxy Launderette (AE, AI+A,** Level 2—Moderately Accessible, one 2" entry step and tight interior; £4 self-serve, £8 full-serve, daily 8:00–20:00, corner of St. Petersburgh Place and Moscow Road at 65 Moscow Road, tel. 020/7229-7771). For Internet, **En Crypt (AE, AI,** Level 2—Moderately Accessible) has 70 terminals with reasonable prices in the back of a newsstand (123 Queensway Street, tel. 020/7727-6122).

Notting Hill Neighborhood

1. Westland Hotel
2. Somerset Bayswater Hotel
3. Ramada Hyde Park
4. Maggie Jones Restaurant
5. The Churchill Arms Pub & Thai Kitchens
6. The Prince Edward Pub
7. The Champion Pub
8. Black & Blue Restaurant
9. Mamounia Lounge
10. La Scala Rest.
11. Patisserie Francaise & Internet Café
12. Whiteleys Mall Food Court
13. Launderette

Level 1—Fully Accessible

Somerset Bayswater Hotel (AE, AI, AL, AR, AB) is elegantly modern, with five fully adapted rooms, a special lift for wheelchair users, and an adapted toilet in the lobby (Db-£75–125, 42 Prince's Square, Tube: Bayswater, tel. 020/7985-1188, fax 020/7985-1189). The parent company, Citadines, runs apartment hotels all over Europe with fully accessible rooms (www.citadines.com).

Ramada Hyde Park (AE, AI, AL, AR, AB) is a tidy, efficient American-style hotel with 80 rooms, of which five are fully accessible (roll-in showers). It's conveniently located across from the beautiful Kensington Gardens (Db-£178, much cheaper off-season, £10 more for breakfast, 150 Bayswater Road, Tube: Bayswater, tel. 020/7229-1212, fax 020/7229-2623, www.ramadajarvis.co.uk). Ramada hotels are located all over the U.K., and all have fully accessible rooms.

Level 2—Moderately Accessible

Westland Hotel (AE+A, AI, AL, AR, AB+A) is comfortable, convenient, and hotelesque, with a fine lounge and spacious rooms. Rooms are recently refurbished and quite plush. Their £105 doubles (less your 10 percent discount—see below) are the best value (Sb-£88–99, Db-£105, deluxe Db-£121, cavernous deluxe Db-£138, sprawling Tb-£132–154, gargantuan Qb-£150–175, Quint/b-£165–187, 10 percent discount with this book if claimed upon arrival; elevator, free garage with 6 spaces; between Notting Hill Gate and Queensway Tube stations; 154 Bayswater Road, tel. 020/7229-9191, fax 020/7727-1054, www.westlandhotel.co.uk, reservations@westlandhotel.co.uk). They can cover the three 6" steps with a removable ramp. Past wheelchair users have stayed on the ground floor, where there is one suitable room. Call ahead to alert the staff of your needs.

Other Neighborhoods

Level 1—Fully Accessible

In South Kensington: **Jurys Kensington Hotel (AE, AI, AL, AR, AB)** is big, stately, and impersonal, with a greedy pricing scheme—but it offers decent accessibility (Sb/Db/Tb-£100–220 depending on "availability," ask for a deal, breakfast extra, piano lounge, non-smoking floor, elevator, Queen's Gate, tel. 020/7589-6300, fax 020/7581-1492, www.jurysdoyle.com, kensington@jurysdoyle.com). Some travelers have reported having difficulty with the access here, as many accessibilty features have been retrofitted.

Near London Zoo and Regent's Park: **Swiss Cottage Holiday Inn Express (AE, AI, AT, AB, AR, ♥)** is a contemporary hotel built in 2004. Four of its 230 rooms are fully adapted, including roll-in showers, pull cords, and adapted toilets and sinks (Db £89.50, cheaper with 14-day advance booking, 152–156 Finchley Road, directly across from Finchley Road Tube station, 10 minutes by bus or train to central London, tel. 020/7433-6666, fax 020/7433-6667, www.expressbyholidayinnsc.com, reservations@expressbyholidayinnsc.com).

Near Gatwick Airport: **London Gatwick Airport Premier Travel Inn (AE, AI, AL, AR, AB)**, at the airport, rents cheap rooms, eight of which are accessible (Db-£58, £2.50 accessible shuttle bus from airport, tel. 0870-238-3305, www.premiertravelinn.com). **Gatwick Travelodge (AE, AI, AL, AR, AB)**, two miles from the airport, has budget rooms, five of which are accessible (Db-£50, £3 accessible shuttle from airport, breakfast extra, Church Road, Lowfield Heath, Crawley, tel. 0870-191-1531, www.travelodge.co.uk). **Thistle London Gatwick (AE, AI, AL, AR, AB)**, once a Tudor coaching inn, is within easy reach of the Surrey and Sussex countryside, yet convenient to Gatwick Airport (Db-£117, much cheaper off-season, Brighton Road, Tube: Gatwick, tel. 0870-333-9134, www.thistlehotels.com).

Near Heathrow Airport: It's so easy to get to Heathrow from central London, I see no reason to sleep there. But for budget beds near the airport, consider **Heathrow Ibis (AE, AI, AL, AR, AB;** Db-£68, Db-£45 on Fri–Sun nights, breakfast extra, £3 shuttle bus to/from terminals except T-4, look for G23 "Hopabus" run by National Express, 112 Bath Road, tel. 020/8759-4888 or 0870-540-0400, fax 020/8564-7894, www.ibishotel.com, h0794@accor-hotels.com).

EATING

If you want to dine (as opposed to eat), check out the extensive listings in the weekly entertainment guides sold at London newsstands (or catch a train to Paris). The thought of a £40 meal in Britain generally ruins my appetite, so my London dining is limited mostly to easygoing, fun, but inexpensive alternatives. I've listed places by neighborhood—handy to your sightseeing or hotel—and provided accessibility information for each place.

Important: Unless otherwise noted (by **AT** or **AT+A**), these restaurants do *not* have accessible toilets. Even if they're otherwise fully accessible, if they don't have an adapted toilet, I consider them Level 2—Moderately Accessible.

Ethnic restaurants—especially Indian and Chinese—are popular, plentiful, and cheap. Most large museums (and many churches) have inexpensive, cheery cafeterias. Of course, picnicking is the fastest and cheapest way to go. Good grocery stores and sandwich shops, fine park benches, and polite pigeons abound in Britain's most expensive city.

Tipping

Tipping is an issue only at restaurants and fancy pubs that have waiters and waitresses. If you order your food at a counter, don't tip.

If the menu states that service is included, there's no need to tip beyond that. If service isn't included, tip about 10 percent by rounding up. Leave the tip on the table, or hand it to your server with your payment for the meal and say, "Keep the rest, please."

Pubs

Pubs are a basic part of the British social scene, and, whether you're a teetotaler or a beer guzzler, they should be a part of your travel here. "Pub" is short for "public house." It's an extended living room where, if you don't mind the stickiness, you can feel the pulse of London. Smart travelers use the pubs to eat, drink, get out of the rain, watch the latest sporting event, and make new friends.

Pub hours vary. The strict wartime hours (designed to keep the wartime working force sober and productive) ended in 1988, and now pubs generally serve beer Mon–Sat 11:00–23:00 and Sun 12:00–22:30 (though pubs can be open later, particularly on Fri–Sat). As it nears closing time, you'll hear shouts of "Last orders." Then comes the 10-minute warning bell. Finally, they'll call "Time!" to pick up your glass, finished or not, when the pub closes.

Children are served food and soft drinks in pubs, but you must be 18 to order a beer. Smoky pubs are becoming a rarity. Many pubs already prohibit smoking, and there's serious talk of requiring any place serving food (pub or restaurant) to be smoke-free by 2008.

A cup of darts is free for the asking. People go to a public house to be social. They want to talk. Get vocal with a local. This is easiest at the bar, where people assume you're in the mood to talk (rather than at a table, where you're allowed a bit of privacy). The pub is the next best thing to having relatives in town. Cheers!

Pub Grub

Pub grub gets better each year. It's London's best eating value. For £6–8, you'll get a basic, budget, hot lunch or dinner in friendly surroundings. The *Good Pub Guide,* published annually by the British Consumers Union, is excellent. Pubs attached to restaurants often have fresher food and a chef who knows how to cook.

Pubs generally serve traditional dishes, like fish and chips, vegetables, "bangers and mash" (sausages and mashed potatoes), roast beef with Yorkshire pudding (batter-baked in the oven), and assorted meat pies, such as steak-and-kidney pie or shepherd's pie (stewed lamb topped with mashed potatoes). Side dishes include salads (sometimes even a nice self-serve salad bar), vegetables, and—invariably—"chips" (French fries). "Crisps" are potato chips. A "jacket potato" (baked potato stuffed with fillings of your choice) can almost be a meal in itself. A "ploughman's lunch" is a modern "traditional English meal" of bread, cheese, and sweet pickles that nearly every tourist tries...once. These days, you'll likely find more Italian pasta, curried dishes, and quiche on the menu than "traditional" fare.

Meals are usually served from 12:00 to 14:00 and from 18:00 to 20:00, not throughout the day. There's usually no table service. Order at the bar, then take a seat and they'll bring the food when it's ready (or sometimes you pick it up at the bar). Pay at the bar (sometimes when you order, sometimes after you eat). Again, don't tip unless it's a place with full table service. Servings are hearty, service is quick, and you'll rarely spend more than £8. A beer or cider adds another couple of pounds. (Free tap water is always available.) Pubs that advertise their food and are crowded with locals are less likely to be the kinds that serve only lousy microwaved snacks. Because pubs make more money selling drinks than food, many stop cooking fairly early.

Beer

The British take great pride in their beer. Many Brits think that drinking beer cold and carbonated, as Americans do, ruins the taste. Most pubs will have **lagers** (cold, refreshing, American-style beer), **ales** (amber-colored, cellar-temperature beer), **bitters** (hop-flavored ale, perhaps the most typical British beer), and **stouts** (dark and somewhat bitter, like Guinness). At pubs, long-handled pulls are used to pull the traditional, rich-flavored "real ales" up from the cellar. These are the connoisseur's favorites: fermented naturally, varying from sweet to bitter, often with a hoppy or nutty flavor. Notice the fun names. Short-handled pulls at the bar mean colder, fizzier, mass-produced, and less interesting keg beers. Mild beers are sweeter, with a creamy malt flavoring. Irish cream ale is a smooth, sweet experience. Try the draft cider (sweet or dry)...carefully.

Order your beer at the bar and pay as you go, with no need to tip. An average beer costs £2.50. Part of the experience is standing before a line of "hand pulls," or taps, and wondering which beer to choose.

Drinks are served by the pint (20-ounce imperial size) or the half-pint. (It's almost feminine for a man to order just a half; I order mine with quiche.) Proper English ladies like a half-beer and half-lemonade **shandy.**

Besides beer, many pubs actually have a good selection of wines by the glass, a fully stocked bar for the gentleman's "G and T" (gin and tonic), and the increasingly popular bottles of alcohol-plus-sugar (such as Bacardi Breezers) for the younger, working-class set. **Pimm's** is a refreshing and fruity summer cocktail, traditionally popular during Wimbledon. It's an upper-class drink...a rough bloke might insult a pub by claiming it sells more Pimm's than beer. Teetotalers can order from a wide variety of soft drinks.

Near Trafalgar Square

These two places are within about 100 yards of Trafalgar Square (see the map on page 147).

Crivelli's Garden Restaurant (AE, AI, AT, AL, Level 1—Fully Accessible), serving a classy lunch in the National Gallery, is a good place to treat your palate to pricey, light Mediterranean cuisine (£15 lunches, daily 10:00–17:00, first floor of Sainsbury Wing).

The Lord Moon of the Mall Pub (AE+A, AI, AT, ♥, Level 2—Moderately Accessible) fills a great old former Barclays Bank building a block down Whitehall from Trafalgar Square. They have real ales on tap and good, cheap pub grub, including a two-meals-for-the-price-of-one deal (£7.50, offer valid Mon–Fri 14:00–21:30, all day Sat–Sun). The pub is kid-friendly and smoke-free throughout (daily 10:00–23:00, 18 Whitehall, tel. 020/7839-7701). The staff will assist your entry; after that, they promise "no worries."

Cheap Eating near Piccadilly

Hungry and broke in the theater district? Head for Panton Street (off Haymarket, 2 blocks southeast of Piccadilly Circus) where several hardworking little places compete.

The palatial **Criterion Brasserie** (AE, AI, AT, Level 1—Fully Accessible) serves a special £15 two-course "Anglo-French" menu (or £18 for 3 courses) under gilded tiles and chandeliers in a dreamy Byzantine church setting from 1880. It's right on Piccadilly Circus but a world away from the punk junk. The house wine is great and so is the food (specials available Mon–Sat 12:00–14:30 & 17:30–19:00, closed Sun, tel. 020/7930-0488). After 19:00, the menu becomes really expensive. Anyone can drop in for coffee or a drink.

Strada (AE, AI, AT, Level 1—Fully Accessible) offers designer pizza and retro Italian at restrained prices (£3–12 plates, £8.95 beforetheater fixed-price *menu*, Mon–Sat 12:00 23:00, Sun 12:00–22:00, 39 Panton Street, tel. 020/7930-8535).

Pizza Express (AE, AI, AT, Level 1—Fully Accessible) combines modern, glassy bistro atmosphere with a fresh, creative menu and reasonable prices (£4–10 pizzas, Mon–Sat 11:30–24:00, Sun 12:00–34:00, 26 Panton Street, tel. 020/7930-8044).

Wagamama Noodle Bar (AE, AI, AT, Level 1—Fully Accessible) is a noisy, pan-Asian, organic slurpathon. As you enter, check out the kitchen and listen to the roar, as benches rock with happy eaters. Everybody sucks. Feel the energy of all this "positive eating" (£12 meals, daily 12:00–23:00, crowded after 20:00, non-smoking, between Haymarket and Regent at 8 Norris Street). Other fully accessible locations are 14 Irving Street (Tube: Leicester Square), 101-A Wigmore Street (Tube: Bond Street), 1 Tavistock Street (Tube: Covent Garden), just west of the Tower of London (Tube: Tower Hill), 26 Kensington High Street (Tube: High Street Kensington), and opposite Vinopolis at 1 Clink Street (Tube: London Bridge). Other central branches are located in basements with no elevator (and are therefore Level 4—Not Accessible), including 10-A Lexington Street in Soho and 4-A Streatham Street near the British Museum.

Hip Eating from Covent Garden to Soho

London has a trendy, Generation-X scene that most Beefeater-seekers miss entirely. These restaurants are scattered throughout the hipster, gay, and girlie bar district, teeming each evening with fun-seekers and theater-goers. Even if you plan to have dinner elsewhere, it's a treat to just wander around this lively area. Beware of the extremely welcoming girls that stand outside the strip bars. But if you're curious, head down Great Windmill Street and stop by the door at each of the three bars. Enjoy the sales pitch, but only fools enter—like a fish attracted to a fancy, well-polished lure, you hardly see the hook. Naive guys bite for the "£5 drink and show" and go inside...and then can't get out without emptying their wallets.

Belgo Centraal (AE, AI, AL, AT, ♥, Level 1—Fully Accessible) serves hearty Belgian specialties. It's a seafood, chips, and beer emporium dressed up as a mod-monastic refectory—with noisy acoustics and waiters garbed as Trappist monks. The classy restaurant section is more comfortable and less rowdy, but usually requires reservations. It's often more fun to just grab a spot in the boisterous beer hall, with its tight, communal benches (no reservations accepted). The same menu and specials work on both sides. Belgians claim they eat as well as the French and as heartily as the Germans. Specialties include mussels, great fries, and a stunning array of dark, blond, and fruity Belgian beers. Belgo actually makes Belgian things trendy—a formidable feat (£10–14 meals; open daily until 23:00; Mon–Fri 17:00–18:30 "beat the clock" meal specials for £5–6.30—the time you order is the price you pay—and you get mussels, fries, and beer; no meal-splitting after 18:30, and you must buy food with beer; daily £6 lunch special 12:00–17:00; 2 kids eat free for each parent ordering a regular entrée; 1 block north of Covent Garden Tube station at intersection of Neal and Shelton streets, 50 Earlham Street, tel. 020/7813-2233). People with limited mobility are given priority seating and service.

Yo! Sushi (AE, AI, AL, Level 2—Moderately Accessible) is a futuristic Japanese-food-extravaganza experience. It's not cheap, but it's sure to be memorable, complete with thumping rock music, Japanese cable TV, a 195-foot-long conveyor belt—the world's longest sushi bar—and automated sushi machines. For £1 each, you get unlimited tea or water (from spigot at bar, with or without carbonation). Snag a bar stool and grab dishes as they rattle by (priced by color of dish; check the chart: £1.50–5 per dish, £1.50 for miso soup, daily 12:00–24:00, 2 blocks south of Oxford Street, where Lexington Street becomes Poland Street, 52 Poland Street, tel. 020/7287-0443). If you like Yo!, there are several

Central London Hotels and Restaurants

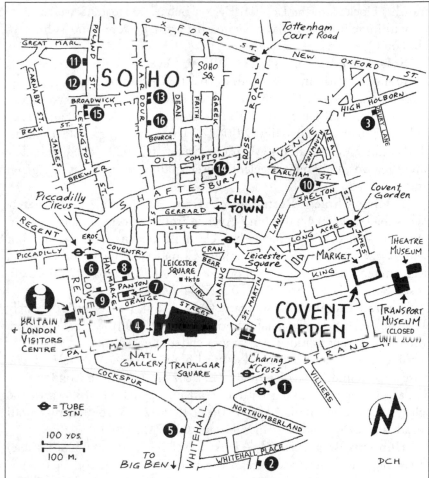

1. Thistle Hotel Charing Cross
2. Thistle Hotel Royal Horseguards
3. Travelodge Covent Garden
4. Crivelli's Garden Restaurant
5. The Lord Moon of the Mall Pub
6. Criterion Brasserie
7. Strada Restaurant
8. Pizza Express
9. Wagamama Noodle Bar
10. Belgo Centraal
11. Yo! Sushi
12. Polka Restaurant
13. Soho Spice Indian & The Ship Pub
14. Y Ming Chinese Restaurant
15. Andrew Edmunds & Pret a Manger
16. Hummus Bros

locations around town—but most of them are not accessible. There's a branch a block from the London Eye on Belvedere Road, as well as outlets within Selfridges, Harvey Nichols department stores, and Whiteleys Mall on Queensway—see below.

Soho Spice Indian (AE, AI, AT, ♥, Level 1—Fully Accessible) is where modern Britain meets Indian tradition—fine cuisine in a trendy, jewel-tone ambience. Unlike many Indian restaurants, when you order an entrée here (£10), it comes with side dishes—nan, dal, rice, and vegetables (£7 lunch special, daily 12:00–22:30, non-smoking, 5 blocks north of Piccadilly Circus at 124 Wardour Street, tel. 020/7434-0808). For safety reasons, only one wheelchair user is allowed inside at any given time.

Y Ming Chinese Restaurant (AE+A, AI, Level 2—Moderately Accessible)—across Shaftesbury Avenue from the ornate gates, clatter, and dim sum of Chinatown—has clean European decor, serious but helpful service, and authentic Northern Chinese cooking (good £10 meal deal offered 12:00–18:00—last order at 18:00, Mon–Sat 12:00–23:30, closed Sun, 35 Greek Street, tel. 020/7734-2721).

Andrew Edmunds Restaurant (AE, AI, ♥, Level 2—Moderately Accessible, ask for accessible ground-floor table) is a tiny, candlelit place where you'll want to hide your camera and guidebook and act as local as possible. This great little place—with a jealous and loyal clientele—is the closest I've found to Parisian quality in a cozy restaurant in London. The modern European cooking with a creative seasonal menu is worth the splurge (£25 meals, daily 12:30–15:00 & 18:00-22:45, come early or call ahead, 46 Lexington Street in Soho, tel. 020/7437-5708).

Hummus Bros (AE, AI, AT+A, Level 2—Moderately Accessible) serves hummus with fresh, creative toppings from tall copper tureens in a no-nonsense, squeaky-clean setting with communal tables (£1.50–4.50 plates, Mon–Sat 11:00–23:00, closed Sun, 88 Wardour Street, tel. 020/7734-1311).

The Ship (AE, AI, Level 2—Moderately Accessible) is a classic pub setting deep in the heart of Soho. Hang out with young locals and enjoy your fish and chips or other pub grub (£5–12 plates, Mon–Sat 12:00–23:00, closed Sun, 116 Wardour Street, tel. 020/7437-8446).

Polka (AE, AI, AT, Level 1—Fully Accessible) is a slick, glassy bistro serving creative nouvelle cuisine with English-Scottish flair (£3–13 dishes, Mon–Sat 12:00–24:00, closed Sun, 58–59 Poland Street, tel. 020/7287-7500).

Pret a Manger (AE, AI, Level 2—Moderately Accessible) is a rollthrough deli offering fresh, soup, salads, sandwiches, and bakery items.

They also roast their own coffee (indoor and outdoor tables, Mon–Fri 7:30–17:00, closed Sat–Sun, 35 Broadwick Street, tel. 020/7932-5274).

The Soho "Food is Fun" Three-Course Dinner Crawl: For a multicultural, movable feast, consider eating (or splitting) one course and enjoying a drink at each of these places. Start around 18:00 to avoid lines, get in on early specials, and find waiters willing to let you split a meal. Prices, while reasonable by London standards, add up. Servings are large enough to share. All are open nightly. Arrive before 18:00 at **Belgo Centraal** and split the early-bird dinner special: a kilo of mussels, fries, and dark Belgian beer. At **Yo! Sushi,** have beer or sake and a few dishes. Slurp your last course at **Wagamama Noodle Bar** (the most accessible location in this neighborhood is near Piccadilly Circus at 8 Norris Street, described above). Then, for dessert, people-watch at Leicester Square, where the serf's always up.

Near Recommended Victoria Station Accommodations

Here are places a couple of blocks southwest of Victoria Station where I've enjoyed eating (see map on page 137).

The Duke of Wellington pub (AE, AI, AT+A, Level 2—Moderately Accessible) is good, if somewhat smoky, and dominated by local drinkers. It's the neighborhood place for dinner, with woody sidewalk seating and an inviting interior (£6–7 meals, daily specials, Mon–Sat 11:00–15:00 & 18:00–21:00, closed Sun, 63 Eaton Terrace, at intersection with Chester Row, tel. 020/7730-1782). The staff is welcoming and regularly serves local residents who use wheelchairs.

Jenny Lo's Tea House (AE+A, AI, AT, Level 2— Moderately Accessible, one 3" entry step, large entry door) is a simple, budget place serving up reliably tasty £5–8 eclectic Chinese-style meals to locals in the know. While the menu is small, everything is high quality. Jenny clearly learned from her father, Ken Lo, one of the most famous Cantonese chefs in Britain, whose fancy place is just around the corner (Mon–Fri 11:30–15:00 & 18:00–22:00, Sat 18:00-22:00, closed Sun, cash only, 14 Eccleston Street, tel. 020/7259-0399).

La Poule au Pot (AE+A, AI, Level 2—Moderately Accessible, friendly staff will assist with the 8" entry step), ideal for a romantic splurge, offers a classy, candlelit ambience with well-dressed patrons and expensive but fine country-style French cuisine (£15 lunch, £25 dinners, daily 12:30–14:30 & 18:45–23:00, Sun until 22:00, leafy patio dining, reservations smart, end of Ebury at intersection with Pimlico, 231 Ebury Street, tel. 020/7730-7763).

The Willow Walk (AE, AI, AT, Level 1—Fully Accessible) prides itself on prices that are half those of other nearby establishments—not a bad deal, if you're looking for a British Denny's offering a little bit of everything in a modern setting across from Victoria Station (£3-7 meals, daily 9:00–23:00, 25 Wilton Road, tel. 020/7828-2953).

St. George's Tavern (AE, AI, AT, Level 1—Fully Accessible) is a neighborhood hangout right behind Victoria Station, with traditional pub grub in a relaxed, friendly atmosphere (£3–9 plates, Mon–Sat 11:00–23:00, Sun 12:00–22:30, 14 Belgrave Road, tel. 020/7592-9911).

Food Court: If you miss America, there's a mall-type, fully accessible **food court** at Victoria Place, upstairs in Victoria Station; **Café Rouge** seems to be the most popular here (£8–11 dinners, daily 9:30-22:30).

Groceries in and near Victoria Station: A large and fully accessible grocery, **Sainsbury's Local,** is on Victoria Street in front of the station, just past the buses (daily 6:00–24:00). In the station you'll find another, smaller Sainsbury's (at rear entrance, on Eccleston Street) and a couple other late-hours mini-markets.

Notting Hill Neighborhood

Queensway Street is a multiethnic food circus, lined with lively and inexpensive eateries. See the map on page 139.

Maggie Jones (AE+A, AI, AT+A, Level 2—Moderately Accessible, staff will assist your entry up one 6" step; suitable toilet up 3 small steps), exuberantly rustic and very English, serves my favorite £30 London dinner. You'll get fun-loving if brash service, and solid English cuisine, including huge plates of crunchy vegetables—by candlelight. Avoid the stuffy basement on hot summer nights, and request upstairs seating for the noisy but less cramped section. If you eat well once in London, eat here—and do it quick, before it burns down (daily 12:30–14:30 & 18:30-23:00, less expensive lunch menu, reservations recommended, friendly staff, 6 Old Court Place, just east of Kensington Church Street, near High Street Kensington Tube stop, tel. 020/7937-6462).

The Churchill Arms pub and **Thai Kitchens** is a local hangout (both **AE, AI,** Level 2—Moderately Accessible, enter on Compden Street rather than at corner), with good beer and old-English ambience in front and hearty £6 Thai plates in an enclosed patio in the back. You can eat the Thai food in this tropical hideaway or in the smoky but wonderfully atmospheric pub section. Arrive by 18:00 to avoid a line. During busy times, diners are limited to an hour at the table (daily 12:00–21:30, 119 Kensington Church Street, tel. 020/7792-1246). Local wheelchair users like this welcoming place.

The Prince Edward pub (AE, AI, ♥, Level 2—Moderately Accessible) serves good pub grub in a quintessential pub setting (£8–10 meals, daily 12:00–15:00 & 18:00–22:00, closed Sun evenings, plush-pubby indoor seating or sidewalk tables, 2 blocks north of Bayswater Road at the corner of Dawson Place and Hereford Road, 73 Prince's Square, tel. 020/7727-2221).

The Champion (AE, AI, AT, Level 1—Fully Accessible) is a gay-friendly pub with a tantalizing menu. On Sundays, you can get a traditional English roast dinner here. They also serve afternoon tea with scones and fruit (daily 12:00–23:00, on Bayswater Road at the northwest corner of Kensington Gardens, 1 Wellington Terrace, tel. 020/7243-9531).

Black and Blue (AE, AI, AT, Level 1—Fully Accessible) is a trendy bistro serving steaks and burgers to local hipsters. Follow the crowds to the gas torches and patio seating (£10–12 meals, daily 12:00–23:00, 215 Kensington Church Street, tel. 020/7727-0004).

Whiteleys Mall Food Court (AE, AI, AT, AL, Level 1—Fully Accessible) offers a fun selection of 10 ethnic and fast-food eateries among Corinthian columns in a delightful mall (open daily long hours; options include Yo! Sushi, good salads at Café Rouge, pizza, Starbucks, an Internet café, and a Marks & Spencer for picnics; second floor, corner of Porchester Gardens and Queensway).

Mamounia Lounge (AE, AI, Level 2—Moderately Accessible) is a Middle Eastern tea room with cakes, water pipes, and free wireless Internet access (daily 12:00–23:00, 8 Queensway Street, tel. 020/7221-0202).

La Scala (AE, AI, Level 2—Moderately Accessible), Mamounia Lounge's sister restaurant, serves English breakfast and light snacks (£3–6) in a casual lingering atmosphere (daily 12:00–11:00, free Wi-Fi, 27 Queensway Street, tel. 020/7221-8045).

Patisserie Francaise (AE, AI, AT, Level 1—Fully Accessible) is a charming tearoom with exquisite pastry and light lunch in a refined atmosphere (£2–6 dishes, Mon–Wed 7:00–19:00, Thu 7:00–20:00, Sun 8:00–19:00, closed Fri–Sat, 127 Queensway Street, tel. 07958-416-691).

South Kensington

Popular eateries line Old Brompton Road and Thurloe Street (Tube: South Kensington). See the map on page 153. The fully accessible **Tesco Express** grocery store (**AE, AI**) is handy for picnics (daily 7:00-24:00, 54 Old Brompton Road).

The Zetland Arms (AE, AI, AT, Level 1—Fully Accessible) serves good pub meals with a classic pub ambience on the ground floor and a fancier olde English restaurant atmosphere upstairs (same menu throughout, £6–10 meals, hearty £9 specials, table service, Mon–Fri 12:00–22:00, Sat–Sun 13:00–22:30, 2 Bute Street, tel. 020/7589-3813).

La Bouchee Bistro Café (AE+A, AI, ♥, Level 2—Moderately Accessible, staff will assist with one-step entry) is a classy, hole-in-the-wall touch of France—candlelit and woody—serving early-bird, two-course £10 meals daily until 19:00 and £15 *plats du jour* all *jour* (daily 12:00–15:00 & 17:30–23:00, 56 Old Brompton Road, tel. 020/7589-1929).

The Khyber Pass Tandoori Restaurant (AE, AI, Level 2—Moderately Accessible) is handy, serving tasty Indian cuisine. Locals in the know travel to eat here (£12 dinners, daily 12:00–14:30 & 18:00–23:30, 21 Bute Street, tel. 020/7589-7311).

Moti Mahal Indian Restaurant (AE+A, AI, Level 2—Moderately Accessible) is a new favorite for value, offering Khyber Pass some competition. You'll find minimalist-yet-classy, mod ambience and attentive service (daily 12:00–23:00, 3 Glendower Place, tel. 020/7584-8428).

Oddono's Gelati Italiani (AE, AI, Level 2—Moderately Accessible) has a reputation for serving the best gelato in London. They use all-natural ingredients—the real deal, just like in Italy (Mon–Thu 11:00–23:00, Sat–Sun 11:00–24:00, closed Fri, 14 Bute Street, just around the corner from South Kensington Tube station, tel. 020/7052-0732).

Aubaine (AE, AI, AT, Level 1—Fully Accessible) offers a fine French café menu that includes quiches, pastries, salads, and an extensive breakfast menu. Sit inside, or outside on a tree-lined boulevard (£1–9 items, Mon–Sat 8:00–23:00, Sun 9:00–22:00, 260-262 Brompton Road, tel. 020/7052-0100).

Al Bustan (AE, AI, Level 2—Moderately Accessible) is a great place for Lebanese tapas, offering reasonably priced ethnic cuisine wrapped in simple elegance (£5–15 dishes, daily 12:00–22:00, 68 Old Brompton Road, tel. 020/7584-5805).

Bibendum Coffee Bar (AE, AI, Level 2—Moderately Accessible)—named for the "tire man" Michelin mascot—features an exotic selection of flowers, fresh seafood, sandwiches, and soups, plus a coffee bar. It's housed the ornate Art Deco tiled-and-wrought-iron original Michelin Tyre store (£3–12 items, Mon–Fri 12:00–14:30 & 19:00–23:30, Sat–Sun 12:30–15:00 & 19:00–22:30, coffee bar open Mon–Fri 8:00–17:00, Sat–Sun 9:00–12:00, 81 Fulham Road, tel. 020/7581-5817).

South Kensington Neighborhood

KENSINGTON GARDENS
ALBERT MEMORIAL
HYDE PARK
KENSINGTON ROAD
Knights-bridge →
HARRODS
ALBERT HALL
QUEEN'S GATE
EXHIBITION ROAD
VICTORIA & ALBERT MUSEUM
SCIENCE MUSEUM
NATURAL HISTORY MUSEUM
BROMPTON ROAD
STREET
WALTON
CROM-WELL ROAD
TO ❷
← Gloucester Road
GLOUCESTER
HARR. RD.
THUR. PL.
CROM. PL.
THUR. ST.
❹
❺
← South Kens.
❼
SLOANE AVE.
SUMNER PLACE
❶
❸
❻
POST
ONSLOW SQ.
ROAD
❽
BROMPTON
OLD ROAD
FULHAM
SYDNEY ST.

⊖ - SUBWAY
¼ MILE
400 METERS

DCH

❶ Jurys Kensington Hotel

❷ To Premier Travel Inn Kensington

❸ La Brioche Deli, Tesco Express, La Bouchee Bistro Café & Al Bustan Restaurant

❹ The Khyber Pass Tandoori Rest.

❺ Moti Mahal Indian Rest.

❻ The Zetland Arms Pub & Oddono's Gelati Italiani

❼ Aubaine Café

❽ Bibendum Coffee Bar

La Brioche (AE+A, AI, ♥, Level 2—Moderately Accessible) is a deli serving made-from-scratch cuisine that will knock your knickers off (£3–8 for a little of this and that, Mon–Sat 9:00–19:00, closed Sun, 40 Old Brompton Road). The staff will come out and help you make your choice or assist you over the entry step, then they'll package your order up for you to take away.

Elsewhere in London

Between St. Paul's and the Tower: **The Counting House** (AE, AI, AL, AT, ♥, Level 1—Fully Accessible), formerly an elegant old bank, offers great £7 meals, nice homemade meat pies, fish, and fresh vegetables (Mon–Fri 12:00–21:00, closed Sat–Sun, gets really busy with the buttoned-down 9-to-5 crowd after 12:15, near Mansion House in The City, 50 Cornhill, tel. 020/7283-7123).

TRANSPORTATION CONNECTIONS

Heathrow Airport

Heathrow Airport is the world's fourth busiest. Think about it: 63 million passengers a year on 425,000 flights from 170 destinations riding 90 airlines, like some kind of global maypole dance. While many complain about Heathrow, I think it's a great and user-friendly airport. Read signs, ask questions. Most of the airport is Level 1—Fully Accessible.

For Heathrow's airport, flight, and transfers information, call the switchboard at 0870-000-0123 (www.baa.com). It has four terminals: T-1 (mostly domestic flights, with some European), T-2 (mainly European flights), T-3 (mostly flights from the United States), and T-4 (British Air transatlantic flights and BA flights to Paris, Amsterdam, and Athens). Taxis know which terminal you'll need.

Each terminal has an airport information desk, car-rental agencies, exchange bureaus, ATMs, a pharmacy, a **VAT refund desk** (tel. 020/8910-3682; you must present the VAT claim form from the retailer here to get your tax rebate on items purchased in Britain, see page 19 for details), and a **baggage-check desk** (£6/day, daily 6:00–23:00 at each terminal). Get online 24 hours a day at Heathrow's **Internet cafés** (T-4, mezzanine level) and at wireless "hotspots" in its departure lounges (T-1, T-3, and T-4). There are **post offices** in T-2 and T-4. Each terminal has cheap **eateries** (such as the cheery Food Village self-service cafeteria in T-3). The **American Express** desk, in the Tube station at Terminal 4 (daily 7:00–19:00), has rates similar to the exchange bureaus upstairs, but doesn't charge a commission (typically 1.5 percent) for cashing any type of traveler's check.

Heathrow's small **TI,** even though it's a for-profit business, is worth a visit to pick up free information: a simple map, the *London Planner,* and brochures (daily 8:30–18:00, near T-3 in Tube station, follow signs to Underground; bypass queue for transit info to reach window for London questions).

If you're taking the Tube into London, buy a one-day Travelcard pass to cover the ride (see below).

Getting to London from Heathrow Airport

By Taxi: This is the simplest door-to-door option for wheelchair users and other travelers with limited mobility (see "Getting around London," page 66). Taxis from the airport cost about £45. For four people traveling together, this can be a deal. Hotels can often line up a cab back to the airport for about £30. For the cheapest taxi to the airport, don't order one from your hotel. Simply flag down a few and ask them for their best "off-meter" rate.

By Airport Shuttle Bus: Hotelink (**AE+A, AI+A,** Level 2— Moderately Accessible) offers door-to-door service, but the passenger must be able to make transfers to get into the bus (Heathrow-£17 per person, Gatwick-£22 per person, book the day before departure, buy online and save £1–2, tel. 01293/532-244, www.hotelink.co.uk, reservations@hotelink.co.uk).

By Tube (Subway): For £3.80, the Tube takes you the 14 miles to downtown London in 50 minutes on the Piccadilly Line, with stops (among others) at South Kensington, Leicester Square, and King's Cross Station (6/hr; depending on your destination, may require a change). Even better, buy a One-Day Travelcard that covers your trip into London and all your Tube travel for the day (£12 covers peak times, £6 "off-peak" card starts at 9:30, less-expensive Travelcards cover the city center only—see page 73 for details). Buy it at the Tube station ticket window. You can generally hop on the Tube at any terminal, but for most of 2006, Terminal 4's Tube station will be closed for renovation. You can still catch the Tube by taking a shuttle bus (from stop D) to the nearest station (allow 15 extra min). While the Tube stations at the airport are fully accessible, most other stations on that line (Piccadilly) are not (though you can transfer to the accessible Jubilee line at the Green Park stop). Remember that even so-called "accessible" stations often have a 10" to 12" gap between the platform and the train—so a taxi might work better for someone using a wheelchair. The Accessible Tube Map, showing which stops are accessible, can be found in the front of this book, at the London TI, or online at www.thetube.com.

If taking the Tube to the airport, note that Piccadilly Line cars post which airlines are served by which terminals.

By Heathrow Express Train: This slick train service (**AE, AI, AT,** Level 1—Fully Accessible) zips you between Heathrow Airport and London's Paddington Station. These trains are wheelchair-accessible and equipped with adapted toilets. You will arrive at Paddington Station on tracks 6–8 (accessible toilet near track 1), and the Express Service Agents are available to assist you. At Paddington Station, you're close to the city center (handy for an accessible taxi ride) and in the thick of the Tube system (although, unfortunately, Paddington's Tube station is not accessible). It's only 15 minutes to downtown from Terminals 1, 2, and 3, and 20 minutes from Terminal 4 (at the airport, you can use the Express as a free transfer between terminals). Buy your ticket to London before you board, or pay a £2 surcharge to buy it on the train (£14, but ask about discount promos at Heathrow ticket desk, kids under 16 ride half-price, under 5 ride free, covered by BritRail pass, 4/hr, daily 5:10–23:30, tel. 0845-600-1515, www.heathrowexpress.co.uk). For one person on a budget, combining the Heathrow Express with a taxi ride (between your hotel and Paddington Station) is nearly as fast and half the cost of taking a cab directly to (or from) the airport. For groups of three or more, a taxi is faster and easier, as well as cheaper.

Gatwick Airport

More and more flights, especially charters, land at the fully accessible Gatwick Airport, halfway between London and the southern coast (recorded airport info tel. 0870-000-2468).

Getting to London: A fully accessible express train shuttles conveniently between Gatwick and London's Victoria Station (see below for accessibility information on Victoria Station; £13, £24 round-trip, 4/hr during day, 1–2/hr at night, 30 min, runs 5:00–24:00 daily, can purchase tickets on train at no extra charge, tel. 0845-850-1530, www.gatwickexpress.co.uk). If you're traveling with three others, buy your tickets at the station before boarding, and you'll travel for the price of two. The only restriction on this impressive deal is that you have to travel together. So, if you see another couple in line, get organized and save 50 percent.

Victoria Station (**AE, AI, AL, AT,** Level 2—Moderately Accessible) has an accessible lift, accessible snack shops, accessible toilet and showers, and a drop-in Medi Centre doctor's office. At the station, follow signs to the taxi queue and catch a taxi to your hotel. Victoria Station's Tube station is mostly suitable for wheelchair users, but not fully adapted.

London's Other Airports

London's other three major airports are fully accessible: **Stansted** (tel. 0870-0000-303, www.baa.co.uk/main/airports/stansted), **Luton** (tel. 01582/405-100, www.london-luton.com), and **London City Airport** (tel. 020/7646-0088, www.londoncityairport.com). Taking a taxi is the easiest way to get into the city from any airport.

Discounted Flights from London

Although bmi british midland has been around the longest, the other small airlines generally offer cheaper flights. A visit to www.skyscanner .net sorts the many options offered by the myriad discount airlines, enabling you to see the best schedules for your trip and come up with the best deal. For accessibility details for specific flights, contact each airline company.

With **bmi british midland,** you can fly inexpensively to destinations in the U.K. and beyond (fares start around £30 one-way to Edinburgh, Paris, Brussels, or Amsterdam; or around £50 one-way to Dublin; prices can be higher, but there can also be much cheaper Internet specials—check online). For the latest, call British tel. 0870-607-0555 or U.S. tel. 800-788-0555 (check www.flybmi.com and their subsidiary, bmi baby, at www.bmibaby.com). Book in advance. Although you can book right up until the flight departs, the cheap seats will have sold out long before, leaving the most expensive seats for latecomers.

With no frills and cheap fares, **easyJet** flies from Luton, Stansted, and Gatwick. Prices are based on demand, so the least popular routes make for the cheapest fares, especially if you book early (tel. 0905-821-0905 to book by phone, 65p per minute, or do it free online at www .easyjet.com).

Ryanair is a creative Irish airline that prides itself on offering the lowest fares. It flies from London (mostly Stansted airport) to often obscure airports in Dublin, Glasgow, Frankfurt, Stockholm, Oslo, Venice, Turin, and many others. Sample fares: London–Dublin—£60 round-trip (sometimes as low as £15), London–Frankfurt—£67 round-trip (Irish tel. 0818-303-030, British tel. 0871-246-0000, www.ryanair .com). Because they offer promotional deals any time of year, you can get great prices on short notice. Be aware of their stiff fees for extra baggage. You can carry on only a small daybag and check 15 kilograms—about 33 pounds—of baggage for free. You'll pay €7 per extra kilo. If you're packing an extra 10 kilos, a cheap €30 flight skyrockets to €100.

Virgin Express is a British-owned company with good rates (book by phone and pick up ticket at airport an hour before your flight, www .virgin-express.com). Virgin Express flies from London Heathrow and Brussels. From its hub in Brussels, you can connect cheaply to Barcelona, Madrid, Nice, Malaga, Copenhagen, Rome, or Milan (round-trip from Brussels to Rome for as little as £105). Their prices stay the same whether or not you book in advance.

Crossing the Channel by Eurostar Train

The fastest and most convenient way to get from the Eiffel Tower to Big Ben is by rail. Eurostar, a joint service of the Belgian, British, and French railways, is the speedy passenger train that zips you (and up to 800 others in 18 sleek cars) from downtown London to downtown Paris (12–15/day, 2.75 hrs) faster and easier than flying. The actual tunnel crossing is a 20-minute, black, silent, 100-mile-per-hour non-event. Your ears won't even pop. Eurostar trains also run directly from London to Disneyland Paris (1/day direct, more often with transfer at Lille).

In London, the Eurostar uses the fully accessible **Waterloo Station** (in 2007, the Eurostar terminal will likely change to London's St. Pancras Station, also fully accessible). Check in at least 30 minutes in advance for your Eurostar trip. It's very similar to an airport check-in: You pass through airport-like security, show your passport to customs officials, and find a TV monitor to locate your departure gate. There are a few airport-like shops, newsstands, horrible snack bars, and cafés (bring food for the trip from elsewhere), pay-Internet terminals, and a currency-exchange booth with rates about the same as you'll find on the other end.

Getting between London's Train Stations: London has several different train stations, and all of them are connected by the fully adapted Stationlink bus (**AE, AI,** Level 1—Fully Accessible, low-floor buses with ramps and wide aisles). There are two routes: #205 (Paddington, Marylebone, Euston, St. Pancras, King's Cross, Liverpool Street, and Whitechapel) and #905 (Paddington, Victoria Coach Station, Victoria, Waterloo, London Bridge, Fenchurch Street, and Liverpool Street). Each bus runs twice a day in each direction.

Access

All Eurostar terminals (**AE, AI, AL, AT,** Level 1—Fully Accessible) feature elevators with controls at wheelchair height, ramps with hand-rails and landings, ramps and wheelchairs for boarding and disembarking (upon request), accessible toilets, and wheelchair-accessible check-in booths.

Eurostar trains themselves are also fully accessible to wheelchair users (**AE, AI, AT,** Level 1). The wheelchair user (and a companion) pay for second ("standard") class, but ride in the accessible first-class cabin (cars 9 and 10 have spaces reserved for wheelchair users and their companions, and there is an adapted toilet between these two cars). To take seats in second class, you must be able to walk a minimum of 200 yards. Wheelchair users should arrive 45 minutes before departure, so the staff

Eurostar Routes

can assist with ramps and alert appropriate personnel. Eurostar provides a free assistance service for wheelchair users (arrange when you book ticket, must book at least 48 hours in advance: call French tel. 08 92 35 35 39, British toll-free tel. 0870-518-6186, or British tel. 1233/617-575).

Eurostar Fares

Channel fares (essentially the same between London and Paris or Brussels) are reasonable but complicated. Prices vary depending on when you travel, whether you can live with restrictions, and whether you're eligible for any discounts (youth, seniors, and railpass holders all qualify). Rates are lower for round trips and off-peak travel (midday, midweek, low-season, and low-interest). For specifics, visit www.ricksteves.com /rail/eurostar.htm.

Note that **wheelchair users** and their companions pay second-class fares, but ride in accessible first class (see "Access," above).

As with airfares, the most expensive and flexible option is a **full-fare ticket** with no restrictions on refunds (even refundable after the departure date; for a one-way trip, figure around $375 in first class, $255 second class). A first-class ticket comes with a meal (a dinner departure nets you more grub than breakfast)—but it's not worth the extra expense.

Also like the airlines, **cheaper tickets** come with more restrictions—and are limited in number (so they sell out more quickly; for second-class, one-way tickets, figure $90–200). Non-full-fare tickets have severe restrictions on refunds (best-case scenario: you'll get 25 percent back; but with the cheapest options, you'll get nothing). But several do allow you to change the specifics of your trip once before departure.

Those traveling with a railpass for Britain, France, or Belgium should look first at the **passholder** fare, an especially good value for one-way Eurostar trips (around $75). In Britain, passholder tickets can be issued only at the Eurostar office at the terminal (Waterloo Station in 2006, probably changing to St. Pancras from 2007 on) or the American Express office in Victoria Station—not at any other stations. You can also order them by phone (see below), then pick them up at the Eurostar terminal (see below).

Buying Eurostar Tickets

Refund and exchange restrictions are serious, so don't reserve until you're sure of your plans. If you're confident about the time and date of your crossing, order ahead from the U.S.. Only the most expensive ticket (full fare) is fully refundable, so if you want to have more flexibility, hold off—keeping in mind that the longer you wait, the more likely the cheapest tickets will sell out. (You might end up having to pay for first class.)

You can check and book fares by phone or online in the U.S. (order online at www.ricksteves.com/rail/eurostar.htm, prices listed in dollars; order by phone at U.S. tel. 800/EUROSTAR) or in Britain (British tel. 08705-186-186, www.eurostar.com, prices listed in pounds). While tickets are usually cheaper if purchased in the U.S., fares offered in Europe follow different discount rules—so it can be worth it to check www.eurostar.com before buying. If you buy from a U.S. company, you'll pay for ticket delivery in the United States. In Europe, you can buy your Eurostar ticket at any major train station in any country or at any travel agency that handles train tickets (expect a booking fee).

Remember that Britain's time zone is one hour earlier than France's. Times listed on tickets are local times (departure from London is British time, arrival in Paris in French time).

WESTMINSTER ROLL OR STROLL

From Big Ben to Trafalgar Square

London is the L.A., D.C., and N.Y.C. of Britain. This tour starts with London's "star" attraction, continues to its "Capitol," passes its "White House," and ends at its "Times Square"...all in about an hour.

Just about every visitor to London traverses the historic Whitehall Boulevard from Big Ben to Trafalgar Square. This quick eight-stop tour gives meaning to that touristy ramble. Under London's modern traffic and big-city bustle lie 2,000 fascinating years of history. You'll get a whirlwind tour, as well as a practical orientation to London.

Access: Westminster Bridge is wheelchair-accessible, and all of the sidewalks for the remainder of the tour have curb cutouts.

THE TOUR BEGINS

• *Start halfway across Westminster Bridge (Tube: Westminster; take the Westminster Pier exit).*

❶ On Westminster Bridge
Views of Big Ben and Parliament
• *First look upstream, toward the Parliament.*
Ding dong ding dong. Dong ding ding dong. Yes, indeed, you are in London. **Big Ben** is actually "not the clock, not the tower, but the bell that tolls the hour." However, since the 13-ton bell is not visible, everyone just calls the whole works Big Ben. Named for a fat bureaucrat, Ben is scarcely older than my great-grandmother, but it has quickly become the city's symbol. The tower is 320 feet high, and the clock faces are 23 feet

across. The 13-foot-long minute hand sweeps the length of your body every five minutes.

Big Ben is the north tower of a long building, the **Houses of Parliament (AE+A, AI, AT, AL+A,** Level 2—Moderately Accessible, see page 86), stretching along the Thames. Britain is ruled from this building, which for five centuries was the home of kings and queens. Then, as democracy was foisted on tyrants, a parliament of nobles was allowed to meet in some of the rooms. Soon, commoners were elected to office, the neighborhood was shot, and the royalty moved to Buckingham Palace. Although the current building looks medieval, with its prickly flamboyant spires, it was built in the 1800s after a fire gutted old Westminster Palace.

Today, the **House of Commons,** which is more powerful than the queen and prime minister combined, meets in one end of the building. The rubber-stamp **House of Lords** grumbles and snoozes in the other end of this 1,000-room complex, and provides a tempering effect on extreme governmental changes. The two houses are very much separate: Notice the riverside tea terraces with the color-coded awnings—royal red for lords, common green for commoners. If a flag is flying from the Victoria Tower, at the far south end of the building, Parliament is in session.

• *Now look north (downstream).*

Views of the London Eye Ferris Wheel, The City, and the Thames

Built in 2000 to celebrate the new millennium, the London Eye (**AE, AI, AT, AL,** Level 1—Fully Accessible)— known to some as "the London Eyesore"—stands 443 feet tall and slowly spins 32 capsules, each filled with 25 visitors, up to London's best viewpoint (up to 25 miles on a rare clear day). Aside from Big Ben, Parliament, St. Paul's Cathedral (not visible from here), and the wheel itself, London's skyline is not overwhelming; it's a city that wows from within.

Westminster Roll or Stroll

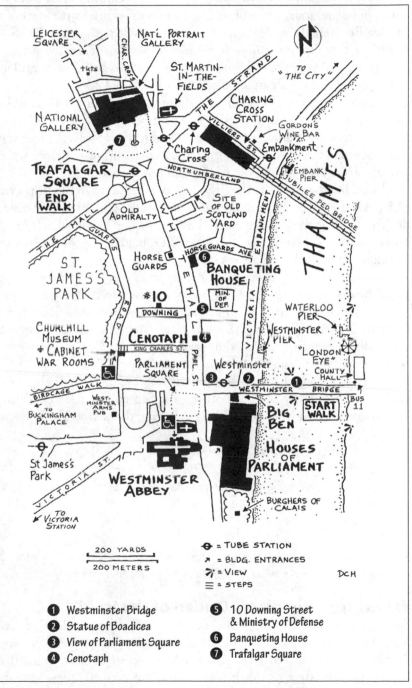

200 YARDS

200 METERS

⊖ = TUBE STATION
↗ = BLDG. ENTRANCES
7ι = VIEW
≡ = STEPS

DCH

❶ Westminster Bridge
❷ Statue of Boadicea
❸ View of Parliament Square
❹ Cenotaph

❺ 10 Downing Street
& Ministry of Defense
❻ Banqueting House
❼ Trafalgar Square

Next to the wheel sprawls the huge former **County Hall building,** now a hotel and tourist complex. The London Eye marks the start of the **Jubilee Promenade,** a pleasant one-hour riverside path along the "South Bank" of the Thames, through London's vibrant, gentrified arts-and-culture zone. Along the way, you have views across the river of St. Paul's stately dome and the financial district, called "The City."

London's history is tied to the **Thames,** the 210-mile river linking the interior of England with the North Sea. The city got its start in Roman times as a trade center along this watery highway. As recently as a century ago, large ships made their way upstream to the city center to unload. Today, the major port is 25 miles downstream.

Look for the piers on the Thames. A 50-minute round-trip **cruise** (**AE, AI,** Level 1—Fully Accessible, see page 81) geared for tourists departs from Waterloo Pier near the base of the Ferris wheel. On the other side of the river, at **Westminster Pier,** boats leave for the Tower of London, Greenwich, and Kew Gardens.

Lining the river, beneath the lampposts, are little green copper **lions' heads** with rings for tying up boats. Before the construction of the Thames Barrier in 1982 (the world's largest movable flood barrier, downstream near Greenwich), high tides from the nearby North Sea made floods a recurring London problem. The police kept an eye on these lions: "When the lions drink, the city's at risk."

Until 1750, only London Bridge crossed the Thames. Then a bridge was built here. Early in the morning on September 3, 1803, William Wordsworth stood where you are right now and described what he saw:

> *This city now doth like a garment wear*
> *The beauty of the morning; silent, bare,*
> *Ships, towers, domes, theaters, and temples lie*
> *Open unto the fields, and to the sky;*
> *All bright and glittering in the smokeless air.*

• *Go to Big Ben's side of the river. Near Westminster Pier is a big statue of a lady on a chariot (nicknamed "the first woman driver"...no reins).*

❷ Statue of Boadicea, Queen of the Iceni

Riding in her two-horse chariot, her daughters by her side, this Celtic Xena leads her people against Roman invaders. Julius Caesar had been the first Roman to cross the Channel, but even he was weirded out by the island's strange inhabitants, who worshipped trees, sacrificed virgins, and went to war painted blue. Later, Romans subdued and civilized them, building roads and making this spot on the Thames—"Londinium"—into a major urban center.

But Boadicea refused to be Romanized. In A.D. 60, after Roman soldiers raped her daughters, she rallied her people and "liberated" London, massacring its 70,000 Romanized citizens. However, the brief revolt was snuffed out, and she and her family took poison, rather than surrender.

• *There's an accessible public toilet down the stairs behind Boadicea. Continue past Big Ben one block inland to the busy intersection of Parliament Square.*

❸ View of Parliament Square

To your left is the orange-hued **Parliament.** If Parliament is in session, the entrance is lined with tourists, enlivened by political demonstrations, and staked out by camera crews interviewing Members of Parliament (MPs) for the evening news. Kitty-corner across the square, the two white towers of **Westminster Abbey (AE, AI,** Level 2—Moderately Accessible, loaner wheelchairs, see page 84) rise above the trees. The broad boulevard of Whitehall (here called Parliament Street) stretches to your right up to Trafalgar Square.

This is the heart of what was once a suburb of London—the medieval City of Westminster. Like Buda and Pest (later Budapest), London is two cities that grew into one. The City of London, centered near St.

Paul's Cathedral and the Tower of London, was the place to live. But King Edward the Confessor decided to build a church (minster) and monastery (abbey) here, west of the city walls—hence Westminster. And to oversee its construction, he moved his court to this spot and built a palace, which gradually evolved into a meeting place for debating public policy. To this day, the Houses of Parliament are known to Brits as the "Palace of Westminster."

Across from Parliament, the cute little church with the blue sundials, snuggling under the Abbey "like a baby lamb under a ewe," is **St. Margaret's Church.** Since 1480, this has been *the* place for politicians' weddings, including Churchill's.

Parliament Square, the small park between Westminster Abbey and Big Ben, is filled with statues of famous Brits. The statue of **Winston**

Churchill, the man who saved Britain from Hitler, shows him in the military overcoat he wore as he limped victoriously onto the beaches of Normandy after D-Day. According to tour guides, the statue has a current of electricity running through it to honor Churchill's wish that if a statue were made of him, his head shouldn't be soiled by pigeons.

In 1868, the world's first traffic light was installed on the corner where Whitehall now spills double-decker buses into the square. And speaking of lights, the little yellow lantern atop the concrete post on the street corner closest to Parliament says "Taxi." When an MP needs a taxi, this blinks to hail one.

• *Consider touring Westminster Abbey (see page 84). If you want to visit the Churchill Museum and Cabinet War Rooms, and you need an accessible route there (with no stairs), take Great George Street opposite the Westminster Bridge and turn right on Horse Guards Road to reach the museum. But if you want to skip this sight—or plan to continue this tour for now, then backtrack to the museum later—turn right (north), go away from the Houses of Parliament and the abbey, and continue up Parliament Street, which becomes Whitehall.*

❹ Rolling or Strolling Along Whitehall

Today, Whitehall is choked with traffic, but imagine the effect this broad street must have had on out-of-towners a century ago. In your horse-drawn carriage, you'd clop along a tree-lined boulevard past well-dressed lords and ladies, dodging street urchins. Gazing left, then right, you'd try to take it all in, your eyes dazzled by the bone-white walls of this man-made marble canyon.

Whitehall is now the most important street in Britain, lined with the ministries of finance, treasury, and so on. You may see limos and camera crews as an important dignitary enters or exits. Political demonstrators wave signs and chant slogans—sometimes about issues foreign to most Americans (Britain's former colonies still resent the empire's continuing influence), and sometimes about issues very familiar to us. (In recent years, the war in Iraq has been the catalyst for student walkouts and protest marches here.) Notice the security measures. Iron grates seal off the concrete ditches between the buildings and sidewalks for protection against explosives. The city has been on "orange alert" since long before September 2001, but Londoners refuse to be terrorized, as shown by their determination to continue with life as normal after the bombings of July 2005.

The black, ornamental arrowheads topping the iron fences were once colorfully painted. In 1861, Queen Victoria ordered them all painted black when her beloved Prince Albert ("the only one who called her Vickie") died. Possibly the world's most determined mourner, Victoria wore black for the standard two years of mourning—and tacked on 38 more.

• *Continue toward the tall, square, concrete monument in the middle of the road. On your right is a colorful pub, the Red Lion. Across the street, a 700-foot detour down King Charles Street (with a steep flight of stairs at the end) leads to the Churchill Museum and Cabinet War Rooms, the underground bunker of 21 rooms that was the nerve center of Britain's campaign against Hitler (AE, AI, AT, AL, ♥, Level 1—Fully Accessible, loaner wheelchairs; £10, daily 9:30–18:00; see page 88 for details). Note that the stairs at the end of King Charles Street are inaccessible. For an accessible route to the Churchill Museum, you'll backtrack to Parliament Square (this route is described above).*

❺ Cenotaph

This big white stone monument (in the middle of the boulevard) honors those who died in the two events that most shaped modern Britain— World Wars I and II. The monumental devastation of these wars helped turn a colonial superpower into a cultural colony of an American super-power.

The actual cenotaph is the slab that sits atop the pillar—a tomb. You'll notice no religious symbols on this memorial. The dead honored here came from many creeds and all corners of Britain's empire. It looks lost in a sea of noisy cars, but on each Remembrance Sunday (closest to November 11), Whitehall is closed off to traffic, the royal family fills the balcony overhead in the foreign ministry, and a memorial service is held around the cenotaph.

It's hard for an American to understand the impact of the Great War (WWI) on Europe. It's said that if all the WWI dead from the British Empire were to march four abreast past the cenotaph, the sad parade would last for seven days.

Eternally pondering the cenotaph is an equestrian statue up the street. Earl Haig, commander-in-chief of the British army from 1916 to 1918, was responsible for ordering so many brave and not-so-brave British boys out of the trenches and onto the killing fields of World War I.

• *Just past the cenotaph, on the other (west) side of Whitehall, is an iron security gate guarding the entrance to Downing Street.*

❻ #10 Downing Street and the Ministry of Defense

Britain's version of the White House is where the current prime minister and his family live, at #10 (in the black-brick building 300 feet down the

blocked-off street, on the right). It looks modest, but the entryway does open up into fairly impressive digs.

There's not much to see here unless a VIP happens to drive up. Then the bobbies (police officers) snap to and check credentials, the gates open, the traffic barrier midway down the street drops into its bat cave, the car drives in, and...the bobbies go back to mugging for the tourists.

The huge building across Whitehall from Downing Street is the **Ministry of Defense** (MOD), the "British Pentagon." This bleak place looks like a Ministry of Defense should. In front are statues of illustrious defenders of Britain. "Monty" is **Field Marshal Bernard Law Montgomery** of World War II, who beat the Nazis in North Africa (defeating Erwin "the Desert Fox" Rommel at El Alamein), giving the Allies a jumping-off point to retake Europe. Along with Churchill, Monty breathed confidence back into a demoralized British army, persuading them they could ultimately beat Hitler.

You may be enjoying the shade of London's **plane trees.** They do well in polluted London: roots that work well in clay, waxy leaves that self-clean in the rain, and bark that sheds and regenerates so the pollution doesn't get into their vascular systems.

• *At the equestrian statue, you'll be flanked by the Welsh and Scottish government offices. At the corner (same side as the Ministry of Defense), you'll find the Banqueting House.*

❼ Banqueting House

This two-story neoclassical building (**AE+A,** Level 4—Not Accessible, see page 89) is just about all that remains of what was once the biggest palace in Europe—Whitehall Palace, stretching from Trafalgar Square to Big Ben. Henry VIII started it when he moved out of the

Palace of Westminster (now the Parliament) and into the residence of the archbishop of York. Queen Elizabeth I and other monarchs added on as England's worldwide prestige grew. Finally, in 1698, a roaring fire destroyed everything at Whitehall except the name and the Banqueting House.

The kings held their parties and feasts in the Banqueting House's grand ballroom on the first floor. At 112 feet wide by 56 feet tall and 56 feet deep, the Banqueting House is a perfect double cube. Today, the exterior of Greek-style columns and pediments looks rather ho-hum, much like every other white, marble, neoclassical building in London. But in 1620, it was the first—a highly influential building by architect Inigo Jones that sparked London's distinct neoclassical look.

On January 27, 1649, a man dressed in black appeared at one of the Banqueting House's first-floor windows and looked out at a huge crowd that surrounded the building. He stepped out the window and onto a wooden platform. It was **King Charles I.** He gave a short speech to the crowd, framed by the magnificent backdrop of the Banqueting House. His final word was "Remember." Then he knelt and laid his neck on a block as another man in black approached. It was the executioner—who cut off the King's head.

Plop—the concept of divine monarchy in Britain was decapitated. But there would still be kings after **Oliver Cromwell,** the Protestant anti-monarchist who brought about Charles I's death and then became England's leader. Soon after, the royalty was restored, and Charles' son, **Charles II,** got his revenge here in the Banqueting Hall...by living well. His elaborate parties under the chandeliers celebrated the Restoration of the monarchy. But, from then on, every king knew that he ruled by the grace of Parliament.

Charles I is remembered today with a statue at one end of Whitehall (in Trafalgar Square at the base of the tall column), while his killer, Oliver Cromwell, is given equal time with a statue at the other end (at the Houses of Parliament).

• *Across the street on the left are the* **Horse Guards,** *dressed in Charge-of-the-Light-Brigade cavalry uniforms and swords. Until the Ministry of Defense was created, the Horse Guards was the headquarters of the British army. It's still the home of the queen's private guard. (Changing of the Guard Mon–Sat*

11:00, Sun at 10:00, dismounting ceremony daily at 16:00.)

*Continue up Whitehall, passing the **Old Admiralty,** headquarters of the British Navy that once ruled the waves. Across the street, behind the old Clarence Pub (**AE+A, AI, Level 2**—Moderately Accessible, no accessible toilet), stood the original Scotland Yard, headquarters of London's crack police force in the days of Sherlock Holmes. Finally, Whitehall opens up into the grand, noisy, traffic-filled...*

❽ Trafalgar Square

London's Times Square bustles around world's biggest Corinthian column, where **Admiral Horatio Nelson** stands 170 feet tall in the crow's nest. Nelson saved England at a time as dark as World War II. In 1805, Napoleon was poised on the other side of the Channel, threatening to invade England. Meanwhile, more than 900 miles away, the one-armed, one-eyed, and one-minded Lord Nelson attacked the French fleet off the coast of Spain at Trafalgar. The French were routed,

Britannia ruled the waves, and the once invincible French army was slowly worn down, then defeated at Waterloo. Nelson, while victorious, was shot by a sniper in the battle. He died, gasping, "Thank God, I have done my duty."

At the top of Trafalgar Square (north) sits the domed National Gallery (**AE, AI, AL, AT, Level 1**—Fully Accessible, loaner wheelchairs, see page 90) with its new grand staircase, and to the right, the steeple of **St. Martin-in-the-Fields,** built in 1722, inspiring the steeple-over-the-entrance style of many town churches in New England (main floor is **AE, AI, ❤, Level 2**—Moderately Accessible; for concert information, see page 91). In between is a small statue of America's **George Washington,** looking very much the English gentleman he was. Large statues of important nobodies on pedestals border the four corners of the square. The northwest pedestal remains empty, as Brits debate who should be honored.

Trafalgar Square

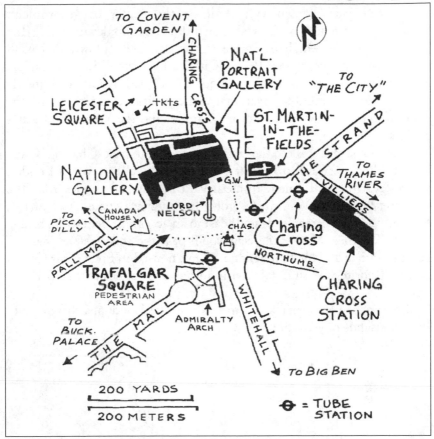

At the base of Nelson's column are bronze reliefs cast from melted-down enemy cannons, and four huggable lions dying to have their photo taken with you. In front of the column, Charles I sits on horseback with his head intact. In the pavement in front of the statue is a plaque marking

the center of London, from which all distances are measured.

Trafalgar Square is indeed the center of modern London, connecting Westminster, The City, and the West End. A recent remodeling of the square has rerouted some car traffic, helping reclaim the area for London's citizens. Spin clockwise 360 degrees and survey the city:

To the south (down Whitehall) is the center of government, Westminster. Looking southwest, down the broad boulevard called The Mall, you see Buckingham Palace in the distance. (Down Pall Mall is St. James' Palace, where Prince Charles lives when in London.) A few blocks northwest of Trafalgar Square is Piccadilly Circus. Directly north (2 blocks behind the National Gallery) sits Leicester Square, the jumping-off point for Soho, Covent Garden, and the West End theater district.

The boulevard called the Strand takes you past Charing Cross Station, then eastward to The City, the original walled town of London and today's financial center. In medieval times, when people from The City met with the Westminster government, it was here. And finally, Northumberland Street leads southeast to an accessible pedestrian bridge over the Thames. (Along the way, you'll pass the inaccessible Sherlock Holmes Pub at 10 Northumberland Street, housed in Sir Arthur Conan Doyle's favorite watering hole, with an upstairs replica of 221-B Baker Street.)

Soak it in. You're smack-dab in the center of London, a thriving city atop thousands of years of history.

FRANCE

FRANCE

France is Europe's most diverse, tasty, and, in many ways, exciting country to explore. It's a multifaceted cultural fondue.

France is nearly as big as Texas, with 60 million people and more than 500 different cheeses. *Diversité* is a French forte. From its Swiss-like Alps to its *molto Italiano* Riviera, and from the Spanish Pyrenees to *das* German Alsace, you can stay in France, feel like you've sampled much of Europe, and never be more than a quiche's throw from a good *vin rouge*.

The key political issues in France today are high unemployment (about 9 percent), a steadily increasing percentage of ethnic minorities, and the need to compete in a global marketplace. The challenge is to address these issues while maintaining the generous social benefits the French expect from their government. As a result, national policies seem to conflict with each other. For example, France supports the lean economic policies of the European Union, but recently reduced the French workweek to 35 hours—in pursuit of good living.

Imitate the French. Try to buy at least one of your picnics at a colorful open-air market street, like the rue Cler in Paris. Relax at a park while children sail toy boats in a pond. Enjoy the subtle pleasure of people-watching from a sun-dappled café. If you prefer to travel at a slower pace, you'll fit in fine in France. With five weeks' paid time off, the French can't comprehend why anyone would rush through a vacation.

If you make an effort to understand French culture, you'll have a richer experience. You've no doubt heard that the French are "mean and cold and refuse to speak English." This out-of-date preconception is left

---

How Big, How Many, How Much

- 210,000 square miles (like Texas)
- 60 million people (about 276 per square mile)
- 1 euro (€) = about $1.20

France

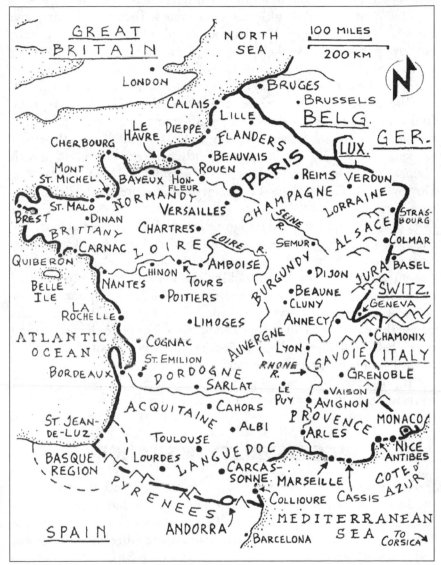

over from the de Gaulle days. The French are as sincere as any other people. Polite and formal, the French respect the fine points of culture and tradition. Recognize sincerity and look for kindness. Give them the benefit of the doubt. Parisians are no more disagreeable than New Yorkers. And, without any doubt, the French speak more English than Americans speak French. Be reasonable in your expectations: Waiters are paid to be efficient, not chatty. And Parisian postal clerks are every bit as speedy, cheery, and multilingual as ours are back home.

Communication difficulties are exaggerated. To hurdle the language barrier, bring a phrase book and a good supply of patience. If you learn only five phrases, choose these: *bonjour* (good day), *pardon* (pardon me), *s'il vous plaît* (please), *merci* (thank you), and *au revoir* (good-bye). For more, see the "French Survival Phrases" near the end of this book.

The French are language perfectionists—they take their language (and other languages) seriously. They often speak more English than they let on. This isn't a tourist-baiting tactic, but timidity on their part to speak another language less than fluently. Start any conversation with *"Bonjour, madame/monsieur. Parlez-vous anglais?"* ("Hello, madam/sir. Do you speak English?") and hope they speak more English than you speak French.

Diners around the world recognize French food as a work of art. The cuisine is sightseeing for your taste buds. Styles of cooking include *haute cuisine* (classic, elaborately prepared multi-course meals); *cuisine bourgeoise* (the finest quality home-cooking); *cuisine des provinces* (traditional dishes from specific regions, using the best ingredients); and *nouvelle cuisine* (the pricey "new style" from the 1970s, which breaks from tradition with a focus on small portions and close attention to the texture and color of the ingredients). Each region has its own specialties, and all of the influences come together in Paris.

If you make only one stop in France, make it Paris—the *pièce de résistance*. Paris is quintessential France, deservedly one of the world's most visited cities.

ACCESSIBILITY IN FRANCE

In France, special consideration is given to travelers with limited mobility. This thoughtfulness is obvious in public spaces and in such adaptations as special-access ramps, lifts, toilets, parking spaces, and telephone booths. However, some tourist attractions are not wheelchair-accessible, and some city streets do not feature sufficient curb cuts.

The **French Government Tourist Office** can help you plan your visit (444 Madison Ave., 16th floor, New York, NY 10022, fax 212/838-7855, www.franceguide.com, info.us@franceguide.com).

The **Paris Convention and Visitors Bureau** can also be a useful source of advice (toll tel. 08 92 68 30 00—€0.34/min, www.parisinfo.com).

You can also contact the **Comité National Français de Liaison pour la Réadaptation des Handicapés (CNRH).** Write to Service Publication, 236 Rue de Tolbiac, 7503 Paris (tel. 01 53 80 66 66).

Transportation

Rail is the most convenient form of travel for disabled travelers in France. Wheelchair compartments are available on all TGV services. Ask for the *Guide du voyageur à mobilité réduite* guidebook at train stations. SNCF, France's rail company, runs an accessibility hotline (French only, tel. 08 00 15 47 53). Taxi drivers are obliged to take passengers who use wheelchairs, and to assist you into and out of their vehicles.

The **Groupement pour l'Insertion des Handicapés Physiques** (**GIHP,** Group for the Inclusion of the Physically Handicapped) runs an accessible transport service in Paris; you'll need to book trips in advance (10 rue Georges de Porto-Riche, tel. 01 43 95 66 36, fax 01 45 40 40 26, gihp.nat@wanadoo.fr). Regional offshoots of this organization also provide transportation services elsewhere in France.

Organizations

The **Association des Paralysés de France** (**APF,** French Association for the Paralyzed) is an organization of and for people with mobility disabilities. With delegations across France, APF may be able to help find a personal attendant or other resources. Their Web site lists a number of links to other types of disability organizations (17 boulevard Auguste Blanqui, Paris, tel. 01 40 78 69 00, fax 01 45 89 40 57, www.apf.asso.fr, info@apf.asso.fr).

Guidebooks

Pick up a copy of *Paris-Ile-de-France for Everyone,* available at most TIs. It lists accessible sights, hotels, and restaurants in the City of Light.

Before You Go: An excellent resource is the guidebook *Access in Paris,* which has detailed information on accessible sights, hotels, and restaurants. The same team wrote *Access in London.* The book can be hard to find in Paris, so get it before you go (www.accessproject-phsp.org).

Comments from Readers

These thoughts on traveling in Paris were submitted by my readers, mainly from my Graffiti Wall Web site (www.ricksteves.com).

"I was very impressed in Paris that every street corner we crossed was wheelchair-accessible. We encountered no unexpected steps and were pleasantly surprised."

"Admission to the Louvre for wheelchair users is free, but its working elevators are few. When we were there, it was possible to see the

Winged Victory and the *Mona Lisa* (with a lot of pushing), but the elevator didn't go to the *Venus de Milo*. The Louvre is worth visiting, but call first to see if all (or even most) of the elevators are running."

"My 73-year-old mother can not get around well, so I took advantage of the free wheelchairs available at the Louvre and Musée d'Orsay in Paris. All I had to do was leave my passport at the counter—it was returned when I brought the wheelchair back."

"For Paris (and a few other French cities), there's a great guide where you can see maps detailing the location of accessible toilets and phones, the condition and width of sidewalks and roads, and so on. It's in French, but the legend shouldn't be too opaque with the help of a simple dictionary: www.mobile-en-ville.asso.fr, then click on 'Cartographie' (Maps), pick your city, *et voilà!*"

PARIS

The City of Light has been a beacon of culture for centuries. As a world capital of art, fashion, food, literature, and ideas, it stands as a symbol of all the fine things that human civilization can offer.

Paris serves up sweeping boulevards, chatty crêpe stands, chic boutiques, and world-class art galleries. Sip decaf with deconstructionists in a sidewalk café, then become part of an Impressionist painting in a tree-lined park. Cruise the Seine, ascend the Eiffel Tower, and roll or stroll down the avenue des Champs-Elysées. Master the Louvre and Orsay museums. Save some after-dark energy for one of the world's most romantic cities.

Some see the essentials and flee, overwhelmed. But with the proper approach and a good orientation, you'll fall head over heels for Europe's capital.

ACCESSIBILITY IN PARIS

Paris is more challenging than Belgium or London for people with disabilities. But if you can make a little extra effort and have a healthy sense of humor, you'll find the City of Light is worth it. The city has an information office for disabled people; unfortunately, most of their information is sketchy and limited (place Mazas 12e, tel. 01 43 47 76 60).

Public transportation in Paris can be difficult for wheelchair users. For example, you may need to wait a few extra minutes until a newer, accessible bus comes by. (Consider taking a taxi instead.) Paris' Métro is not accessible, but some RER (suburban subway) lines are. If traveling long distances by rail, you may want to book

Accessibility Levels

This book rates sights, hotels, and restaurants using four levels:

Level 1—Fully Accessible: A Level 1 building is completely barrier-free. Entryways, elevators, and other facilities are specifically adapted to accommodate a person using a wheelchair. If there's a bathroom, it has wide doors and an adapted toilet and sink. Where applicable, the bathing facilities are also fully adapted (including such features as bath boards, grab bars, or a roll-in, no-rim shower). Fully adapted hotel rooms often have an alarm system with pull cords for emergencies.

Level 2—Moderately Accessible: A Level 2 building is suitable for, but not specifically adapted to accommodate, a person using a wheelchair. This level will generally work for a wheelchair user who can make transfers and take a few steps. A person who is permanently in a wheelchair may require some assistance here (either from a companion or from staff).

Level 3—Minimally Accessible: A Level 3 building is satisfactory for people who have minimal mobility difficulties (that is, people who usually do not use a wheelchair, but take more time to do things than a non-disabled person). This building may have some steps and a few other barriers—but not too many. Level 3 buildings are best suited to slow walkers; wheelchair users will require substantial assistance here.

Level 4—Not Accessible: Unfortunately, some places in this book are simply not accessible to people with limited mobility. This means that barriers such as staircases, tight interiors and facilities (elevators, bathrooms, etc.), or other impediments interfere with passage for travelers with disabilities. Buildings in this category might include a church tower that has several flights of steep stairs, or a museum interior that has many levels with lots of steps and no elevator.

For a complete listing of the Accessibility Codes used in this chapter, please see pages 6–7.

---

the Thalys train (first class is wheelchair-accessible).

Many of Paris' top sights are fully accessible to wheelchair users (Level 1): the Louvre, the Palais Royal Courtyards, the Orsay, Eiffel Tower (up to the second level), Les Invalides (except crypt), Rodin Museum (ground floor only) and garden, the main floor of St. Sulpice Church, Luxembourg Garden, Montparnasse Tower, the Petit and Grand Palais, Grande Arche de La Défense, Victor Hugo House, Pompidou Center, Jewish Art and History Museum, Picasso Museum, and the Palace of Versailles.

Other sights will work for wheelchair users with some assistance (Level 2): Notre-Dame Cathedral interior (not the tower), Deportation Memorial, the lower level of Sainte-Chapelle, National Maritime Museum, St. Germain-des-Prés Church, Opéra Garnier (entry, but not tours), Jacquemart-André Museum, place des Vosges park, and the Erotic Art Museum in Montmartre.

Unfortunately, Paris also has a few sights that are best left to non-disabled travelers (or more adventurous slow walkers): Notre-Dame's tower, Paris Archaeological Crypt, Sainte-Chapelle upstairs chapel, Conciergerie, the top level of the Eiffel Tower, the upper level of the Rodin Museum, Cluny Museum, the Arc de Triomphe, the *Paris Story* film, Carnavalet Museum, Promenade Plantée Park, Père Lachaise Cemetery, and Sacré-Cœur Church.

ORIENTATION

Paris (population of city center: 2,150,000) is split in half by the Seine River, divided into 20 *arrondissements* (proud and independent governmental jurisdictions), circled by a ring-road freeway (the *périphérique*), and speckled with Métro stations. You'll find Paris easier to navigate if you know which side of the river you're on, which *arrondissement* you're in, and which Métro stop you're closest to. If you're north of the river (the top half of any city map), you're on the Right Bank (Rive Droite). If you're south of it, you're on the Left Bank (Rive Gauche). The bull's-eye of your Paris map is Notre-Dame, which sits on an island in the middle of the Seine. Most of your sightseeing will take place within five blocks of the river.

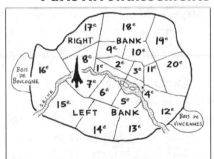

Paris *Arrondissements*

Arrondissements are numbered, starting at the Louvre and moving in a clockwise spiral out to the ring road. The last two digits in a Parisian zip code are the *arrondissement* number. The abbreviation for the Métro stop is "Mo." In Parisian jargon, Napoleon's Tomb is on *la Rive Gauche* (the Left Bank) in the *7ème* (7th *arrondissement*), zip code 75007, Mo: Invalides.

Paris Métro stops are used as a standard aid in giving directions, even for those not using the Métro. As you're tracking down addresses, these words and pronunciations will help: Métro (may-troh), *place* (plahs—square), *rue* (roo—road), *avenue* (ah-vuh-noo), *boulevard* (boo-luh-var), and *pont* (pohn—bridge).

Tourist Information

Paris TIs have long lines, offer little information, and charge for maps. This book, the *Pariscope* magazine (described below), and one of the freebie maps available at any hotel (or in the front of this book) are all you need. Paris' TIs share a single phone number: 08 92 68 30 00 (from the U.S., dial 011-33-8 92 68 30 00). For accessibility information, check out the "Tourisme & Handicap" section at www.parisinfo.com.

If you must visit a TI, there are several locations: **Grands Magasins** (**AE, AI,** Level 2—Moderately Accessible; Mon–Sat 9:00–18:30, closed Sun, near Opéra Garnier at 11 rue Scribe, accessible entry by American Express office), **Pyramides** (**AE, AI,** Level 2—Moderately Accessible, with an adapted desk to assist people who use wheelchairs; daily 9:00–19:00, at Pyramides Métro stop between the Louvre and Opéra), **Gare de Lyon** (**AE+A, AI,** Level 2—Moderately Accessible; Mon–Sat 8:00–18:00, closed Sun), **Montmartre** (**AE+A, AI,** Level 2—Moderately Accessible; daily 10:00–19:00, place du Tertre), and at the **Eiffel Tower** (**AE, AI,** Level 2—Moderately Accessible; May–Sept daily 11:00–18:42, closed Oct–April). Both **airports** have handy information offices (called ADP; **AE, AI,** Level 1—Fully Accessible, adapted toilet nearby) with long hours and short lines (see "Transportation Connections," page 277).

Pariscope: The weekly, €0.40 *Pariscope* magazine (or one of its clones, available at any newsstand) lists museum hours, art exhibits, concerts, festivals, plays, movies, and nightclubs. Smart tour guides and sightseers rely on this for the latest listings.

Other Publications: The American Church (see below) distributes a free, handy, and insightful monthly English-language newspaper called *Paris Voice*, which has useful reviews of concerts, plays, and current events (available at the American Church and about 200 locations throughout Paris, www.parisvoice.com). Also look for an advertisement paper called *France-U.S.A. Contacts*, with information on housing and employment for the community of 30,000 Americans living in Paris (free, pick it up at the American Church and elsewhere, www.fusac.fr). For a complete schedule of museum hours and English-language museum tours, get the free *Musées, Monuments Historiques, et Expositions* booklet from any museum.

Web Sites: Paris' TIs have an official Web site (www.parisinfo .com) offering practical information on hotels, special events, museums,

Daily Reminder

Monday: These sights are closed today—Orsay, Archaeological Crypt, Rodin, Carnavalet, Victor Hugo's House, and Versailles; the Louvre and Eiffel Tower are more crowded because of this. Napoleon's Tomb is closed the first Monday of each month (except July–Sept). Some small stores don't open until 14:00. Street markets, such as rue Cler and rue Mouffetard, are dead today. Some banks are closed. It's discount night at most cinemas.

Tuesday: Many museums are closed today, including the Louvre, Picasso, Cluny, Maritime, Pompidou, and Grand Palais. The Eiffel Tower, Orsay, and Versailles are particularly busy today.

Wednesday: All sights are open (Louvre until 21:45). The weekly *Pariscope* magazine comes out today. Most schools are closed, so many kids' sights are busy. Some cinemas offer discounts.

Thursday: All sights are open. The Orsay is open until 21:45. Department stores are open late.

Friday: All sights are open (Louvre until 21:45). Afternoon trains and roads leaving Paris are crowded; TGV train reservation fees are higher.

Saturday: All sights are open except the Jewish Art and History Museum. The fountains run at Versailles (July–Sept); otherwise, avoid weekend crowds at area châteaux and Impressionist sights. Department stores are jammed. The Jewish Quarter is quiet.

Sunday: Some museums are free the first Sunday of the month—and therefore more crowded (e.g., Louvre, Orsay, Rodin, Pompidou, Cluny, and Picasso). Several museums offer reduced prices every Sunday (Orsay, Cluny, and Rodin—other than first Sun of the month, when they're free). Napoleon's Tomb is open until 19:00 in summer. Versailles is more crowded than usual today, but the garden's fountains are running (early April–early Oct). Most of Paris' stores are closed on Sunday, but shoppers will find relief in the Marais neighborhood's lively Jewish Quarter and in Bercy Village, where many stores are open. Look for organ concerts at St. Sulpice and possibly other churches. The American Church often hosts a free evening concert at 17:00 or 18:00 (Sept–May only, but not every week). Many recommended restaurants in the rue Cler neighborhood are closed for dinner.

If You Need Medical Help

First, contact your hotelier, who is accustomed to dealing with emergencies.

Emergency rooms (called *Urgence*) are located in many Paris hospitals. To call an ambulance or paramedic (SAMU) anywhere in France, dial 15. To summon an ambulance in Paris, call 01 45 67 50 50. To reach the police, dial 17.

For the American Hospital, call 01 46 41 25 25 (63 boulevard Victor-Hugo, 92202 Neuilly, Mo: Porte Maillot, then bus #82). For SOS doctors, who charge affordable rates and will even come to your hotel, dial 01 47 07 77 77 or 01 48 28 40 04. Other useful numbers include the American Hospital Hotline (tel. 01 47 47 70 15), the English-language SOS Help crisis line (daily 15:00–23:00, tel. 01 47 23 80 80), and the emergency dental assistance hotline (tel. 01 43 37 51 00). You'll find listings for additional English-speaking doctors and dentists at www.paris-anglo.com (click on "Directory"). And for organizations offering counseling, check out www.pariswoman.com/paris/support_groups/counseling_health.htm.

A handy English-speaking pharmacy, Pharmacie les Champs, is open 24/7 (tel. 01 45 62 02 41, 84 avenue des Champs-Elysées, Mo: George V). The British and American Pharmacy is at 1 rue Auber (Mon–Fri 8:30–20:30, Sat 10:00–20:00, closed Sun, tel. 01 42 65 88 29).

children's activities, fashion, nightlife, and more. Two other Web sites that are entertaining and at times useful are www.bonjourparis.com (which claims to offer a virtual trip to Paris—featuring interactive French lessons, tips on wine and food, and news on the latest Parisian trends) and the similar www.paris-anglo.com (with informative stories on visiting Paris, plus a directory of over 2,500 English-speaking businesses).

American Church and Franco-American Center: This interdenominational church—in the rue Cler neighborhood, facing the river between the Eiffel Tower and Orsay Museum—is a nerve center for the American émigré community. The worship service at 11:00 on Sunday, the coffee hour after church, and the free Sunday concerts (generally Sept–May at 17:00 or 18:00—but not every week) are a great way to make some friends and get a taste of émigré life in Paris (Level 4—Not Accessible, fifteen 6" steps to enter; reception open Mon–Sat 9:30–13:00 & 14:00–22:30, Sun 9:00–14:00 & 15:00–19:00, 65 quai d'Orsay, Mo: Invalides, tel. 01 40 62 05 00, www.acparis.org). It's also a good place to pick up copies of *Paris Voice* and *France-U.S.A. Contacts* (described above).

Arrival in Paris

By Train: Paris has six train stations, all connected by taxi (the most accessible option if you can fold your wheelchair and place it in the trunk), bus (new ones are accessible), and Métro (dangerously poor access). All stations have ATMs, banks or change offices, information desks, telephones, cafés, newsstands, and clever pickpockets; most stations also have lockers *(consigne automatique)*. For details about each station, see "Transportation Connections" on page 277.

By Plane: For detailed information on getting from Paris' airports to downtown Paris (and vice versa), see "Transportation Connections" on page 284.

Helpful Hints

Heightened Security *(Plan Vigipirate)*: You may notice an abundance of police at monuments, on streets, and on the Métro, as well as security cameras everywhere. You'll go through quick and reassuring airport-like security checks at many major attractions. This is all part of Paris' anti-terror plan. The police are helpful, the security lines move quickly, and there are fewer pickpocket problems than usual on the Métro.

Theft Alert: Although the greater police presence has scared off some pickpockets, these troublesome thieves still thrive—particularly on Métro and RER lines that serve high-profile tourist sights. Wear a money belt, put your wallet in your front pocket, loop your day bag over your shoulders, and keep a tight grip on your purse or shopping bag. Muggings are rare, but do occur. If you're out late, avoid the dark riverfront embankments and any place where the lighting is dim and pedestrian activity is minimal.

Street Safety: Parisian drivers are notorious for ignoring pedestrians. Look both ways (many streets are one-way) and be careful of seemingly quiet bus/taxi lanes. Don't assume you have the right of way, even in a crosswalk. When crossing a street, keep your pace constant and don't stop suddenly. By law, drivers must miss pedestrians by one meter—a little more than three feet (1.5 meters in the countryside). Drivers carefully calculate your speed and won't hit you, provided you don't alter your route or pace.

Watch out for a lesser hazard: *merde.* Parisian dogs decorate the city's sidewalks with 16 tons of droppings per day. People get injured by slipping in it.

Paris Museum Pass: This worthwhile pass, covering most sights in Paris, is available at major Métro stations, TIs, and museums. For detailed information, see page 194.

Museum Strategy: When possible, visit key museums first thing (when your energy is best) and save other activities for the afternoon. Remember, most museums require you to check daypacks and coats, and important museums have metal detectors that will slow your entry. The Louvre, Orsay, and Pompidou are open on selected nights (see "Paris at a Glance," page 198), making for peaceful visits with fewer crowds.

Public WCs: Carry small change for pay toilets, or enter any sidewalk café like you own the place and find the toilet in the back. Restaurants with accessible toilets are noted under "Eating," page 258; you may want to seek out American chain restaurants, like McDonald's—more likely than the small, traditional places to have accessible toilets. The restrooms in museums are free and the best you'll find. Modern, sanitary, street-booth toilets provide both relief and a memory (coins required, don't leave small children inside unattended). Keep toilet paper or tissues with you, as some toilets are poorly supplied.

Bookstores: There are many English-language bookstores in Paris where you can pick up guidebooks (at nearly double their American prices). Most carry this book. My favorite is the friendly **Red Wheelbarrow Bookstore (AE+A, AI, ♥,** Level 2—Moderately Accessible) in the Marais neighborhood, run by charming Penelope and Abigail, who will come out to assist you if you need help with entry (daily 10:00–19:00, 22 rue St. Paul, Mo: St. Paul, tel. 01 42 77 42 17). Others include **Shakespeare and Company (AE, AI,** Level 2—Moderately Accessible; some used travel books, daily 12:00–24:00, 37 rue de la Bûcherie, across the river from Notre-Dame, Mo: St. Michel, tel. 01 43 26 96 50), **W.H. Smith (AE, AI,** Level 2—Moderately Accessible, no accessible toilet or elevator; Mon–Sat 10:00–19:00, closed Sun, 248 rue de Rivoli, Mo: Concorde, tel. 01 44 77 88 99), **Brentanos (AE, AI,** Level 2—Moderately Accessible, no accessible toilet or elevator; Mon–Sat 10:00–19:00, closed Sun, 37 avenue de l'Opéra, Mo: Opéra, tel. 01 42 61 52 50), and **Village Voice (AE+A, AI,** 3" entry step; near St. Sulpice Church at 6 rue Princesse, tel. 01 46 33 36 47).

Parking: Most of the time, drivers must pay to park curbside (buy parking card at tobacco shops), but not at night (19:00–9:00), all day Sunday, or anytime in August when most Parisians are on vacation. There are parking garages under Ecole Militaire, St. Sulpice Church, Les Invalides, the Bastille, and the Panthéon for about €20–25 per day (it's cheaper the longer you stay). Some hotels offer parking for less—ask.

Tobacco Stands *(Tabacs):* These little kiosks—usually just a counter inside a café—sell public transit tickets, cards for parking meters, postage stamps...and, oh yeah, cigarettes. To find one anywhere in Paris, just look for a *Tabac* sign and the red, cylinder-shaped symbol above some (but not all) cafés.

Getting Around Paris

Finding accessible transportation around Paris can be frustrating. Depending on your degree of personal mobility, your basic choices are Métro (in-city subway, generally not accessible), RER (suburban rail, tied into the Métro system, some stations with decent access), public bus (several accessible lines), and taxi (best access). For wheelchair users, taxis are the best option; if you prefer public transit, opt for the buses and skip the Métro. To save money on a trip to Versailles, it's worth considering the RER, though again, a taxi is easier.

By Taxi

Parisian taxis are reasonable, especially for couples and families. The meters are tamper-proof. Fares and supplements (described in English on the back windows) are straightforward. There's a €5.20 minimum. A 10-minute ride (e.g., Bastille to Eiffel Tower) costs about €10 (versus €1.07 to get anywhere in town using a *carnet* ticket on the Métro or bus).

Higher rates are charged at night (19:00–7:00), all day Sunday, and to either airport. There's a €1 charge for each piece of baggage and for train station pickups. To tip, round up to the next euro (minimum €0.50).

You can try waving down a taxi, but it's often easier to ask for the nearest taxi stand (*"Où est une station de taxi?"*; oo ay oon stah-see-ohn duh taxi). Taxi stands are indicated by a circled "T" on good city maps, and on many maps in this book. A taxi can fit three people comfortably, and cabbies are legally required to take up to four for a small extra fee (though some might resist). Groups of up to five can use a *grand taxi*, which must be booked in advance—ask your hotel to call. If a taxi is summoned by phone, the meter starts as soon as the call is received, adding €3–6 to the bill.

Taxis are tough to find when it's raining and on Friday and Saturday nights, especially after the Métro closes (around 24:30). If you need to catch a train or flight early in the morning, book a taxi the day before.

Paris

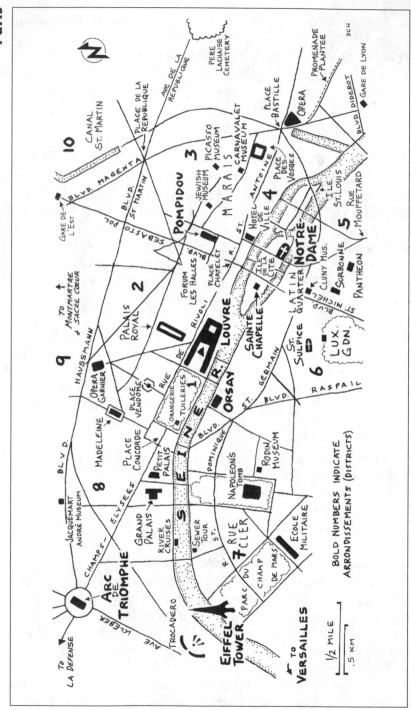

Access: Ranges from Level 2—Moderately Accessible to Level 1—Fully Accessible. For wheelchair users, taxis (**AE+A**) and minibuses (**AE+A**) are the way to go. Some minibuses (**AE**) even have ramps *(le gambade)*—call ahead to request one (tel. 06 07 49 58 92 or tel. 06 07 22 41 61 to get an accessible taxi or minivan on demand; figure €40-55 for a trip across central Paris). Most drivers are happy to assist persons using wheelchairs. Once you're in the taxi, the driver will fold up your wheelchair and place it in the trunk.

By City Bus

Paris' excellent bus system is worth figuring out. Remember, even though buses use the same tickets as the Métro and RER, you can't use a single ticket to transfer between the systems—or even to transfer from one bus to another. One ticket buys you a bus ride anywhere in central Paris—but if you leave the city center (shown as zone 1 on the diagram on board the bus) or transfer to another bus, you must validate a second ticket.

Buses don't seem as romantic as the famous Métro and are subject to traffic jams, but savvy travelers know that buses can have you swinging through the city like Tarzan in an urban jungle. They also offer superior accessibility to the Métro. Anywhere you are, you can generally see a bus stop, each one complete with all the information you need: a fine city bus map, route maps showing exactly where each bus that uses this stop goes, a frequency chart and schedule, a *plan du quartier* map of the immediate neighborhood, and a *soirées* map explaining night service, if available. While the Métro shuts down about 24:30, some buses continue running much later.

After entering the bus, punch your ticket in the machine behind the driver, or pay the higher cash fare. When you reach your destination, push the red button to signal you want a stop. Even if you're not certain you've figured out the system, do some joyriding (outside of rush hour: Mon–Fri 8:00–9:30 & 17:30–19:30). Handy bus-system maps *(plan des autobus)* are available in any Métro station (and in the €7 *Paris Pratique* map book sold at newsstands). Major stops are displayed on the side of each bus.

Access: All newer buses are wheelchair-accessible (**AE, AI,** Level 1—Fully Accessible, with low floors and hydraulic ramp, identified by the standard wheelchair symbol). The following bus lines are fully accessible: #20 (which runs in the Marais neighborhood), scenic #24, #26, #27, #30, #31, #38, #39, #43, #53, #60, #62, #63, #80, #81, #88, #91, #92, #94, #95, and #96. You can find specific details on each of these bus routes at http://infomobi.com/page4.php. Older buses (**AE+A,** Level 2—Moderately Accessible) have one 8" step to negotiate

Public Transit Tickets

The Métro, RER, and buses all work on the same tickets (note that you can transfer between the Métro and RER on a single ticket, but combining a Métro or RER trip with a bus ride takes two tickets). You can buy tickets and passes at a *tabac* (tobacco stand—described above) and at most Métro stations. While the majority of Métro stations have staffed ticket windows, smaller stations might discontinue this service as the Métro system converts to automated machines. A **single ticket** costs €1.40. To save 30 percent, buy a *carnet* (kar-nay) of 10 tickets for €10.70 (that's €1.07 per ticket—€0.33 cheaper than single tickets). It's less expensive for kids (ages 4–10 pay €5.35 for a *carnet*).

If you're staying in Paris for even just a few days, consider the **Carte Orange** (kart oh-RAHNZH), which pays for itself in 15 rides. For about €16, you get free run of the bus and Métro system for one week, starting Monday and ending Sunday. Ask for the Carte Orange *hebdomadaire* (ehb-doh-mah-dair) and supply a passport-size photo. Larger Métro stations have photo booths. The month-long version costs about €51—request a Carte Orange *mensuelle* (mahn-soo-ehl, good from the first day of the month to the last, also requires photo). These passes cover only central Paris. You can pay more for passes covering regional destinations (such as Versailles), but for most visitors, this is a bad value (instead, buy individual tickets for longer-distance destinations). Despite what some Métro agents say, Carte Orange passes are definitely not limited to residents; if you're refused, simply go to another station or a *tabac* to buy your pass.

The overpriced **Paris Visite** passes were designed for tourists and offer minor reductions at minor sights (1 day-€9, 2 days-€14, 3 days-€19, 5 days-€28), but you'll get a better value with a cheaper *carnet* of 10 tickets or a Carte Orange.

and an entry pole between the doors, making it a narrow opening. Some wheelchair users are able to board these buses with assistance.

By Métro

In Paris, you're never more than a quarter mile from a Métro station. Europe's best subway allows you to hop from sight to sight quickly and cheaply (runs daily 5:30–24:30). Learn to use it. Begin by studying the color Métro map at the beginning of this book.

Access: Level 3—Minimally Accessible. Slow walkers will find the

Métro challenging, but doable. For wheelchair users, the Métro is packed with barriers and very difficult to use, even with the help of a companion. Even though some of the newer trains are designed for accessible boarding, you'll have to negotiate lots of stairs and escalators (often broken)—usually without elevators—at most stations. As an alternative, wheelchair users who can make transfers and climb a few steps could find the RER useful for some trips (see "By RER," below).

Pickpockets: Thieves dig the Métro. Be on guard. For example, if your pocket is picked as you pass through a turnstile, you end up stuck on the wrong side (after the turnstile bar has closed behind you) while the thief gets away. Keep back from Métro doors to avoid being a target for a theft-and-run just before the doors close. Any jostling or commotion—especially when boarding or leaving trains—is likely the sign of a thief or a team of thieves in action. Make any fare inspector show proof of identity (ask locals for help if you're not certain). Never show anyone your wallet.

How the Métro Works: Remember, the Métro does work for slow walkers, but not for wheelchair users. To get to your destination, determine the closest "Mo" stop and which line or lines will get you there. The lines have numbers, but they're best known by their end-of-the-line stops. (For example, the La Défense/Château de Vincennes line, also known as line 1, runs between La Défense in the west and Vincennes in the east.) Once in the Métro station, you'll see blue-and-white signs directing you to the train going in your direction (e.g., "*direction:* La Défense"). Insert your ticket in the automatic turnstile, pass through, reclaim your ticket, and keep it until you exit the system. Fare inspectors regularly check for cheaters and accept absolutely no excuses.

Transfers are free and can be made wherever lines cross. When you transfer, look for the orange *correspondance* (connections) signs when you exit your first train, then follow the proper direction sign.

Even though the Métro whisks you quickly from one point to

another, be prepared to walk significant distances within stations to reach your platform (most noticeable when you transfer). Escalators are common, but they're often out of order. To limit excessive walking, avoid transferring at these sprawling stations: Montparnasse-Bienvenüe, Châtelet-Les Halles, Charles de Gaulle-Etoile, Gare du Nord, and Bastille.

Before taking the *sortie* (exit) to leave the Métro, check the helpful *plan du quartier* (map of the neighborhood) to get your bearings, locate your destination, and decide which *sortie* you want. At stops with several *sorties*, you can save lots of time and effort by choosing the best exit.

After you exit the system, toss or tear your used ticket so you don't confuse it with your unused ticket—they look virtually identical.

By RER

The RER (Réseau Express Régionale; air-ay-air) is the suburban arm of the Métro, serving destinations farther out of the center (such as Versailles, Disneyland Paris, and the airports). It also offers the disabled traveler more accessible stations than the Métro.

Access: The RER is cost-effective, but using it costs a lot of time and energy. The RER ranges from Level 3—Minimally Accessible to Level 2—Moderately Accessible. Only rarely will you find a completely flat, barrier-free surface throughout the duration of an RER trip (for example, 2" lips or steps are common). The RER is not ideal for wheelchair users as a primary means of getting around Paris, but it can work on certain journeys if you want to ride public transportation. Most stations on lines A and B are generally wheelchair-accessible, as is the trip on line C to Versailles. Even though the RER is designed to reach into the suburbs, it does make several stops in the city center—so you can use it (selectively) in town.

Using the RER: RER routes are indicated by thick lines on your subway map and identified by the letters A, B, C, and so on. Some suburban routes are operated by France's railroad (SNCF) and are called **Transilien**; they function the same way and use the same tickets as the RER. On Transilien trains (but not RER trains), railpasses are accepted; show your pass at a ticket window to get a free ticket to get through the turnstiles.

Within the city center, the RER works like the Métro, but can be speedier (if it serves your destination directly) because it makes fewer stops. Métro tickets are good on the RER when traveling in the city center. (You can transfer between the Métro and RER systems with the same ticket.) But to travel outside the city (to Versailles or the airport, for example), you'll need to buy a separate, more expensive ticket at the station window before boarding. Unlike in the Métro, you need to insert your ticket in a turnstile to exit the RER lines. Also unlike the Métro, not every train stops at every station along the way; check the sign over the platform to see if your destination is listed as a stop (*"toutes les gares"* means it makes all stops along the way), or confirm with a local before you board.

TOURS

Bus Tours

Non-Stop Bus Tours—Paris Vision (AE+A, Level 2—Moderately Accessible, must be able to step up into the bus) offers bus tours of Paris, day and night (advertised in hotel lobbies). I'd take a Paris Vision tour only at night (see "Nightlife," page 243); during the day, the hop-on, hop-off bus tours (listed immediately below) and the Batobus (see below)—which both provide transportation between sights, as well as commentary—are a better value.

Hop-on, Hop-off Bus Tours—Double-decker buses connect Paris' main sights while providing running commentary, allowing you to get on and off along the way. You get a disposable set of earplugs (dial English and listen to the narration). You can get off at any stop, tour a sight, then catch a later bus. These are ideal in good weather, if you can climb up to the top deck. There are two nearly equal companies: L'Open Tours and Les Cars Rouges; pick up their brochures showing routes and stops from any TI or on their buses. You can start either tour at just about any of the major sights, such as the Eiffel Tower (both companies stop on avenue Joseph Bouvard).

L'Open Tours (AE+A, ♥, Level 2—Moderately Accessible) uses bright yellow buses and provides more extensive coverage (and slightly better commentary) on four different routes, rolling by most of the important sights in Paris. You'll have to ascend three steps to get on the bus (attendants will assist and wheelchair must fold to go under bus). These people welcome travelers who have disabilities, and will do their best to find a way to get you onto the bus. Their Paris Grand Tour (the green route) offers the best introduction. The same ticket gets you on any of their routes within the validity period. Buy your tickets from the driver (1 day-€25, 2 days-€28, kids 4–11 pay €12 for 1 or 2 days, allow 2 hours per tour). Two or three buses depart hourly from about 10:00 to 18:00; expect to wait 10–20 minutes at each stop (stops can be tricky to find—look for yellow signs; tel. 01 42 66 56 56, www.paris-opentour.com).

Les Cars Rouges' (AE+A, Level 2—Moderately Accessible) bright red buses are slightly more accessible. You'll have to make it up one step into the bus (wide entry). Attendants can help lift the wheelchair onto the bus, but then you'll transfer to a seat and the driver will place your folded wheelchair under the bus. This is cheaper than L'Open, but they offer only one route and just nine stops (2 days: adult-€23, kids 4–12-€12, tel. 01 53 95 39 53, www.carsrouges.com).

The Paris Museum Pass

In Paris, there are two classes of sightseers—those with a Paris Museum Pass, and those who wait in line. Serious sightseers save time and money by getting this pass.

For slow walkers unable to stand for long periods of time, the biggest advantage of the Museum Pass is avoiding lines. If you use a wheelchair, the reasons to buy a Museum Pass are less convincing: wheelchair users—even without the pass—are often allowed to enter museums free and can sometimes (but not always) bypass the line.

Most of the sights listed in this chapter are covered by the pass (see list below). Notable exceptions are: the Eiffel Tower, Montparnasse Tower, Opéra Garnier, Notre-Dame treasury, Jacquemart-André Museum, Jewish Art and History Museum, Grand Palais, La Grande Arche de La Défense, *Paris Story* film, Museum of Erotic Art, and the ladies of Pigalle.

The pass pays for itself with three or four admissions and gets you into most sights with no lining up to buy tickets (2 consecutive days-€30, 4 consecutive days-€45, 6 consecutive days-€60, no youth or senior discount). It's sold at museums, main Métro stations (including Ecole Militaire and Bastille), and TIs (even at airports). Try to avoid buying the pass at a major museum (such as the Louvre), where supply can be spotty and lines long.

The pass isn't activated until the first time you use it (you write the starting date on the pass). Think and read ahead to make the most of your pass. You could spend a day or two at the beginning or end of your Paris visit seeing free sights (e.g., Carnavalet and Victor Hugo's House) and sights that don't accept the pass (e.g., Eiffel Tower). Validate your pass only when you're ready to tackle the covered sights on consecutive days. The free directory that comes with your pass lists the current hours of sights, phone numbers, and the price kids pay.

The pass isn't worth buying for children and teens, as most museums are free for those under 18 (teenagers may need to show proof of age). Of the museums that charge for children, some allow kids in free if their parent has a Museum Pass, while others charge admission, depending on age (the cutoff age varies from 5 to 18). If a sight is free for kids, they can skip the line with their passholder parents.

Included sights you're likely to visit (and admission prices without the pass): Louvre (€8.50), Orsay Museum (€7.50), Sainte-Chapelle

(€7), Arc de Triomphe (€8), Napoleon's Tomb/Army Museums (€7), Conciergerie (€7), Cluny Museum (€5.50), Pompidou Center (€7), Notre-Dame tower (€7), Paris Archaeological Crypt (€3.50), Picasso Museum (€5.50), Rodin Museum (€5), L'Orangerie Museum (when it reopens, about €7), Maritime Museum (€9). Outside Paris, the pass covers the Palace of Versailles (€7.50, plus its Trianon châteaux-€5), Château of Fontainebleau (€5.50), and Château of Chantilly (€8).

Tally up what you want to see—and remember, an advantage of the pass is that you skip to the front of most lines, which can save hours of waiting, especially in summer. Note that at a few sights (including the Louvre, Sainte-Chapelle, and Notre-Dame's tower), everyone has to move through the slow-moving baggage-check lines for security.

To use your pass at sights, boldly go to the front of the ticket line, hold up your pass, and ask the ticket-taker: *"Entrez, pass?"* (ahn-tray pahs). You'll either be allowed to enter at that point, or you'll be directed to a special entrance. For major sights, such as the Louvre, Orsay, and Versailles, we've identified passholder entrances on the maps in this book.

With the pass, you'll pop freely into sights that you're passing by (even for a few minutes) that otherwise might not be worth the expense (e.g., the Conciergerie or Archaeological Crypt).

Museum Tips: The Louvre and many other museums are closed on Tuesday. The Orsay, Rodin, Carnavalet, Archaeological Crypt, Petit Palais, Victor Hugo's House, and Versailles are closed Monday. Some museums offer reduced prices on Sunday. Most sights stop admitting people 30–60 minutes before closing time, and many begin shutting down rooms 45 minutes before.

For the fewest crowds, visit very early, at lunch, or very late. Most museums have slightly shorter hours October through March. French holidays (on Jan 1, May 1, July 14, Nov 1, Nov 11, and Dec 25) can really mess up your sightseeing plans.

The best Impressionist art museums are the Orsay (see page 205) and L'Orangerie (slated to reopen in spring 2006).

Many museums also host optional temporary exhibitions that are not covered by the Paris Museum Pass (generally €3–5 extra). You can find good information on many of Paris' sights on the French TI's official Web site: www.v1.paris.fr/EN/Visiting.

Boat Tours

Several companies offer one-hour boat cruises on the Seine (by far best at night).

Two companies are convenient to the rue Cler hotels: **Bateaux Parisiens** (AE, AI, ♥, Level 1—Fully Accessible) has smaller, covered boats with handheld audioguides and only one deck. The staff is very friendly to people with limited mobility (€9.50, kids age 4–11 pay €4.50, discounted half-price if you show a valid France or France-Switzerland railpass—does not use up a day of a flexipass, leaves from right in front of the Eiffel Tower, tel. 08 25 01 01 01). **Bateaux-Mouches** (AE, AI, Level 1—Fully Accessible) has the biggest open-top, double-decker boats and tour groups by the dozens (departs from pont de l'Alma's right bank, €7, kids 4–12 pay €4, daily 10:00–22:30, tel. 01 40 76 99 99). Both companies depart every 20–30 minutes (April–Oct daily 10:00–22:30; Nov–March there are fewer boats, and they stop running earlier).

The smaller, more intimate **Vedettes du Pont Neuf** (AE, AI, Level 1—Fully Accessible) are closer to the Marais area hotels. They depart only once an hour from the center of pont Neuf (2/hr after dark), but they come with a live guide giving explanations in French and English (€10, tip requested, kids 4–12 pay €5, tel. 01 46 33 98 38). To get to the river level, the wheelchair user goes one block upriver on the south side of the island to the ramp. This area has large, rough cobblestones to negotiate.

Walking/Wheeling Tours

Paris Walks—This company offers a variety of excellent two-hour tours, led by British or American guides. Their tours are thoughtfully prepared, relaxing, and humorous. Don't hesitate to get close to the guide to hear (range from Level 4—Not Accessible to Level 1—Fully Accessible; generally 2 tours per day, €10 each, private tours available, tel. 01 48 09 21 40 for recorded schedule in English, also posted at www.paris-walks.com, paris@paris-walks.com, run by Peter and Oriel Cane). Tours focus on the Marais (4/week), Montmartre (3/week), medieval Latin Quarter (Mon), Ile de la Cité/Notre-Dame (Mon), the "Two Islands" (Ile de la Cité and Ile St. Louis, Wed), *Da Vinci Code* tour (Wed), and Hemingway's Paris (Fri). Ask about their family-friendly tours. Call a day or two ahead to learn their schedule and starting point, and to find out which tour best fits your mobility level. These receptive, warm folks have welcomed wheelchair users on their tours in the past. Most tours don't require reservations, but specialty tours (such as the *Da Vinci Code* tour) require advance reservations and prepayment with a credit card (not refundable, even if you cancel months in advance).

Context Paris—This organization, already well-established in Rome, has recently expanded to the City of Light. Their "intellectual by design" walking tours are led by docents (historians, architects, and academics) and cover both museums and neighborhoods, often with a fascinating theme (explained on their Web site). They welcome travelers with limited mobility on their tours. (If there's an inaccessible stop on the tour, they'll compensate you with another, more accessible option.) Still, it's wise to call in advance and let them know your accessibility needs. Groups are small and can fill up (limited to 6 participants, generally 3 hours long and €50 per person plus admissions, tel. 06 13 09 67 11, www.contextparis.com, info@contextparis.com). While you're welcome on their group tours, they will happily design a private tour (for more money) tailored to your interests and level of personal mobility.

Private Guides—For many, Paris merits hiring a Parisian as a personal guide. **Arnaud Servignat** is an excellent licensed local guide (€150/half day, €250/full day, also does car tours of the countryside around Paris for a little more, tel. 06 68 80 29 05, www.arnaud-servignat.com, arnaud .servignat@noos.fr). **Elizabeth Van Hest** is another highly likeable and capable guide (€170 maximum/half day, €260/day, tel. 01 43 41 47 31, e.van.hest@noos.fr). These guides will take wheelchair users as long as they can transfer into a car or van. **Paris Walks** or **Context Paris** can also set you up with one of their guides; some Paris Walks guides are trained to work with families (both companies described above).

SIGHTS

Near the Tuileries Garden

Paris' grandest park, the Tuileries Garden, was once the private prop erty of kings and queens. Today, it links the museums of the Louvre, L'Orangerie, and the Orsay. And across from the Louvre are the tranquil, historic courtyards of the Palais Royal.

▲▲▲**Louvre**—This is Europe's oldest, biggest, greatest, and second-most-crowded museum (after the Vatican). Housed in a U-shaped, 16th-century palace (accentuated by a 20th-century glass pyramid), the Louvre is Paris' top museum and one of its key landmarks. It's home to *Mona Lisa*, *Venus de Milo*, and hall after hall of Greek and Roman masterpieces, medieval

Paris at a Glance

▲▲▲**Louvre** Europe's oldest and greatest museum, starring *Mona Lisa* and *Venus de Milo*. **Hours:** Wed–Mon 9:00–18:00, closed Tue. Most wings open Wed and Fri until 21:45. **Access:** Level 1—Fully Accessible.

▲▲▲**Orsay Museum** Nineteenth-century art, including Europe's greatest Impressionist collection. **Hours:** June 20–Sept 20 Tue–Sun 9:00–18:00; Sept 21–June 19 Tue–Sat 10:00–18:00, Sun 9:00–18:00; Thu until 21:45 year-round, always closed Mon. **Access:** Level 1—Fully Accessible.

▲▲▲**Sainte-Chapelle** Gothic cathedral with peerless stained glass. **Hours:** March–Oct daily 9:30–18:00, Nov–Feb daily 9:00–17:00. **Access:** Ground floor is Level 2—Moderately Accessible; upper chapel is Level 4—Not Accessible.

▲▲▲**Eiffel Tower** Paris' soaring exclamation point. **Hours:** Daily March–Sept 9:00–24:00, Oct–Feb 9:30-23:00. **Access:** Lower and middle floors are Level 1—Fully Accessible; top floor is Level 4—Not Accessible.

▲▲▲**Arc de Triomphe** Triumphal arch with viewpoint, marking start of Champs-Elysées. **Hours:** Outside always open; inside open April–Sept daily 10:00–23:00, Oct–March daily 10:00–22:00. **Access:** Level 4—Not Accessible.

▲▲▲**Versailles** The ultimate royal palace, with the Hall of Mirrors, vast gardens, a grand canal, and smaller palaces. **Hours:** April–Oct Tue–Sun 9:00–18:30, Nov–March Tue–Sun 9:00–17:30, closed Mon. Gardens open early (7:00, 8:00 in winter) and smaller palaces open late (12:00). **Access:** Level 1—Fully Accessible.

▲▲**Notre-Dame Cathedral** Paris' most beloved church, with towers and gargoyles. **Hours:** Church open daily 7:45–19:00; tower open July–Aug Mon–Fri 9:00–19:30, Sat–Sun 9:00–23:00, April–June and Sept daily 9:30–19:30, Oct–March daily 10:00–17:30; treasury open daily 9:30–17:30. **Access:** Level 2—Moderately Accessible.

▲▲**Deportation Memorial** Monument to Holocaust victims, near Notre-Dame. **Hours:** April-Sept daily 10:00–12:00 & 14:00–19:00, Oct–March 10:00–12:00 & 14:00–17:00. **Access:** Level 1—Fully Accessible.

▲▲**Napoleon's Tomb** The emperor's imposing tomb, flanked by army museums. **Hours:** April–Sept daily 10:00–18:00, summer Sun until 19:00, Oct–March daily 10:00–17:00, closed first Mon of month except July–Sept. **Access:** The attached museum is Level 1—Fully Accessible, but the tomb itself is Level 4—Not Accessible.

▲▲**Rodin Museum** Works by the greatest sculptor since Michelangelo. **Hours:** April–Sept Tue–Sun 9:30–17:45; Oct–March Tue–Sun 9:30–16:45, closed Mon. **Access:** Main floor is Level 1—Fully Accessible, but upper floor is Level 4—Not Accessible.

▲▲**Cluny Museum** Medieval art with unicorn tapestries. **Hours:** Wed–Mon 9:15–17:45, closed Tue. **Access:** Level 3—Minimally Accessible.

▲▲**Champs-Elysées** Paris' grand boulevard. **Hours:** Always open. **Access:** Level 2—Moderately Accessible.

▲▲**Jacquemart-André Museum** Art-strewn mansion. **Hours:** Daily 10:00–18:00. **Access:** Level 2—Moderately Accessible. Only the ground floor is accessible.

▲▲**Pompidou Center** Modern art in colorful building with city views. **Hours:** Wed–Mon 11:00–21:00, closed Tue. **Access:** Level 1—Fully Accessible.

▲▲**Jewish Art and History Museum** Displays history of Judaism in Europe. **Hours:** Mon–Fri 11:00–18:00, Sun 10:00–18:00, closed Sat. **Access:** Level 1—Fully Accessible.

▲▲**Picasso Museum** World's largest collection of Picasso's works. **Hours:** April–Sept Wed–Mon 9:30–18:00; Oct–March Wed–Mon 9:30–17:30, closed Tue. **Access:** Level 1—Fully Accessible.

▲▲**Carnavalet Museum** Paris' history wrapped up in a 16th-century mansion. **Hours:** Tue–Sun 10:00–18:00, closed Mon. **Access:** Level 4—Not Accessible.

▲▲**Sacré-Cœur** White basilica atop Montmartre, with spectacular views. **Hours:** Daily 7:00–23:00. **Access:** Level 4—Not Accessible.

jewels, Michelangelo statues, and paintings by the greatest artists from the Renaissance to the Romantics (mid-1800s).

Touring the Louvre can be overwhelming, so be selective. Consider taking a tour (see "Tours," below), or follow my self-guided tour at the end of this listing. Focus on the **Denon Wing** (south, along the river): Greek sculptures, Italian paintings (by the likes of Raphael and da Vinci), and—of course—French paintings (neoclassical and Romantic). For extra credit, tackle the **Richelieu Wing** (north, away from the river), with works from ancient Mesopotamia (today's Iraq), as well as French, Dutch, and Northern art; or the **Sully Wing** (connecting the other 2 wings), with Egyptian artifacts and more French paintings.

Access: AE, AI, AL, AT, Level 1—Fully Accessible. Loaner wheelchairs are available. The museum is fully accessible by elevator, including stores and restaurants on the lower level—though there are few elevators, and readers report that they are sometimes out of order. There are accessible toilets throughout the building. Like most of Europe's great museums, the Louvre is a modernized facility designed with the wheelchair user in mind. Still, the museum can be quite crowded, and there are sporadic obstacles that can make it difficult to maneuver a wheelchair.

Cost: Free for wheelchair user and companion, otherwise €8.50, €6 after 18:00 on Wed and Fri, free on first Sun of month, covered by Museum Pass. Optional additional charges apply for temporary exhibits. Tickets good all day; reentry allowed. The new self-serve ticket machines are faster than the ticket windows (they accept euro notes, coins, and Visa cards, but not MasterCard).

Hours: Wed–Mon 9:00–18:00, closed Tue. Most wings open Wed and Fri until 21:45. Evening visits are peaceful, and the pyramid glows after dark. Galleries start shutting down 30 minutes early. The last entry is 45 minutes before closing. Crowds are worst on Sun, Mon, Wed, and mornings.

Information: Pick up the free *Louvre Plan/Information* in English at the information desk under the pyramid as you enter. Tel. 01 40 20 53 17, recorded info: 01 40 20 51 51, www.louvre.fr.

Crowd-Beating Tips: Wheelchair users can skip to the front of the line; enter through the pyramid (elevator to the left on entry). If you're a slow walker, you have several options for avoiding the line. Museum Pass–holders can use the group entrance in the pedestrian passageway between the pyramid and rue de Rivoli (under the arches, a few steps north of the pyramid, find the uniformed guard at the entrance, with the escalator down). Otherwise, you can enter the Louvre from its (usually less crowded) underground entrance, accessed through the "Carrousel du

Paris Museums near the Tuileries Garden

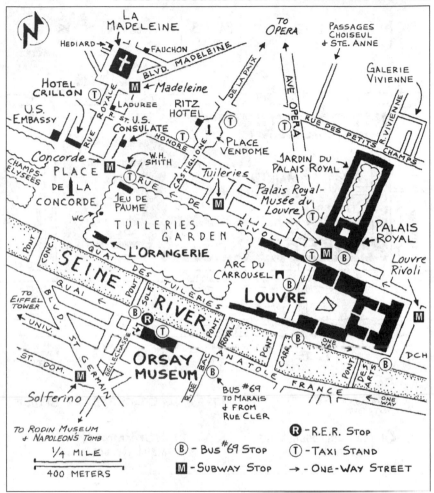

Louvre" shopping mall. Enter the mall at 99 rue de Rivoli (the door with the red awning, daily 8:30–23:00) or directly from the Métro stop Palais Royal-Musée du Louvre (stepping off the train, exit to the left, following signs to Carrousel du Louvre-Musée du Louvre). The taxi stand is across rue de Rivoli next to the Métro station.

Tours: The 90-minute English-language tours leave three times daily except Sun (wheelchair users and slow walkers welcome; normally at 11:00, 14:00, and 15:45, €5 plus your entry ticket, tour tel. 01 40 20 52 63). Sign up for tours at the *Acceuil des Groupes* area. Digital audioguides (available for €5 at entries to the 3 wings, at top of escalators) give you a directory of about 130 masterpieces, allowing you to dial a commentary

The Louvre

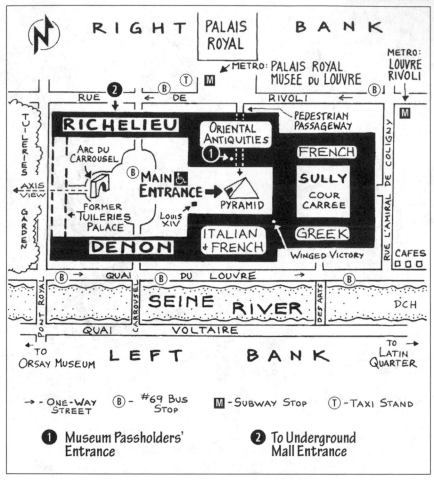

1 Museum Passholders'
Entrance

2 To Underground
Mall Entrance

on included works as you stumble upon them.

○ Self-Guided Tour: Start in the Denon wing and visit the highlights, in the following order (thanks to Gene Openshaw for his help with this).

Wander through the **ancient Greek and Roman works** to see the Parthenon frieze, Pompeii mosaics, Etruscan sarcophagi, and Roman portrait busts. You can't miss lovely *Venus de Milo (Aphrodite)*. This goddess of love (c. 100 B.C., from the Greek island of Melos) created a sensation when she was discovered in 1820. Most "Greek" statues are actually later Roman copies, but Venus is a rare Greek original. She, like Golden Age Greeks, epitomizes stability, beauty, and balance. Later Greek art was Hellenistic, adding motion and drama. For a good example, see the exciting *Winged Victory of Samothrace* (*Victoire de Samothrace,* on the landing). This statue of a woman with wings, poised on the prow of a ship, once stood on a hilltop to commemorate a great naval victory. This is the *Venus de Milo* gone Hellenistic.

The **Italian collection** is on the other side of *Winged Victory.* The key to Renaissance painting was realism, and for the Italians, "realism" was spelled "3-D." Painters were inspired by the realism and balanced beauty of Greek sculpture. Painting a 3-D world on a 2-D surface is tough, and after a millennium of Dark Ages, artists were rusty. Living in a religious age, they painted mostly altarpieces full of saints, angels, Madonnas-and-bambinos, and crucifixes floating in an ethereal gold-leaf heaven. Gradually, though, they brought these otherworldly scenes down to earth. The Italian collection—including the *Mona Lisa*—is scattered throughout rooms *(salles)* 3 and 4, in the long Grand Gallery, and in adjoining rooms. After several years and a €5 million renovation, *Mona* has returned to her permanent home in the Salle des Etats, standing alone behind glass on her own false wall.

Two masters of the Italian High Renaissance (1500–1600) were Raphael (see his *La Belle Jardinière,* showing the Madonna, Child, and John the Baptist) and Leonardo da Vinci. The Louvre has the greatest collection of Leonardos in the world—five of them, including the exquisite *Virgin, Child, and St. Anne,* the neighboring *Madonna of the Rocks,* and the androgynous *John the Baptist.* His most famous, of course, is the *Mona Lisa.*

Leonardo was already an old man when François I invited him to France. Determined to pack light, he took only a few paintings. One was a portrait of Lisa del Giocondo, the wife of a wealthy Florentine merchant. When Leonardo arrived, François I immediately fell in love with the painting and made it the centerpiece of the small collection of Italian masterpieces that would, in three centuries, become the Louvre museum. He called it *La Gioconda.* We know it as a contraction of the Italian for "my lady Lisa"—*Mona Lisa.* Warning: François I was impressed, but *Mona* may disappoint you. She's smaller and darker than you'd expect, located in a huge room, and behind a glaring pane of glass.

Mona's overall mood is one of balance and serenity, but there's also an element of mystery. Her smile and long-distance beauty are subtle and elusive, tempting but always just out of reach, like strands of a street singer's melody drifting through the Métro tunnel. *Mona* doesn't knock your socks off, but she winks at the patient viewer.

Now for something **neoclassical.** Notice the fine work, such as *The Coronation of Napoleon* by Jacques-Louis David, near *Mona* in the Salle

Daru. Neoclassicism, once the rage in France (1780–1850), usually features Greek subjects, patriotic sentiment, and a clean, simple style. After Napoleon quickly conquered most of Europe, he insisted on being made emperor (not merely king) of this "New Rome." He staged an elaborate coronation ceremony in Paris, and rather than let the pope crown him, he crowned himself. The setting is the Notre-Dame Cathedral, with Greek columns and Roman arches thrown in for effect. Napoleon's mom was also added, since she couldn't make it to the ceremony. A key on the frame describes who's who in the picture.

The **Romantic** collection, in an adjacent room (Salle Mollien), has works by Théodore Géricault *(The Raft of the Medusa)* and Eugène Delacroix *(Liberty Leading the People)*. Romanticism, with an emphasis on motion and emotion, is the complete flip side of neoclassicism, though they both flourished in the early 1800s. Delacroix's *Liberty*, commemorating the stirrings of democracy in France, is also a fitting tribute to the Louvre, the first museum opened to the common rabble of humanity. The good things in life don't belong only to a small wealthy part of society, but to all. The motto of France is *"Liberté, Egalité, Fraternité"*—liberty, equality, and brotherhood.

Exit the room at the far end (past the café) and and take the elevator down to find the large, twisting male nude who looks like he's just waking up after a thousand-year nap. The two *Slaves* (1513–1515) by Michelangelo are a fitting end to this museum—works that bridge the ancient and modern worlds. Michelangelo, like his fellow Renaissance artists, learned from the Greeks. The perfect anatomy, twisting poses, and idealized faces look like they could have been done 2,000 years earlier. Michelangelo said that his purpose was to carve away the marble to reveal the figures God put inside. The *Rebellious Slave,* fighting against his bondage, shows the agony of that process and the ecstasy of the result.

Palais Royal Courtyards—Directly north of the Louvre on rue de Rivoli are the pleasant courtyards of the stately Palais Royal. Although the palace is closed to the public, the courtyards are open and fully accessible. As you enter, you'll pass through a whimsical courtyard filled with stubby, striped columns and playful fountains (with fun, reflective metal balls) into another, curiously peaceful courtyard. This is where in-the-know Parisians come to take a quiet break, walk their poodle, or enjoy a rendezvous—surrounded by a serene arcade and a handful of historic restaurants.

Exiting the courtyard at the side facing away from the Seine brings you to the Galleries Colbert and Vivienne, good examples of shopping arcades from the early 1900s (courtyards free, always open).

Access: AE, AI, Level 1—Fully Accessible. The Jardins de Palais Royal are accessible via a ramp that enters from the rue de Rivoli/Palais Royal side (enter and exit using this same ramp).

▲**L'Orangerie Museum (Musée de l'Orangerie)**—This Impressionist museum, lovely as a water lily, was due to reopen in the spring of 2006. (For the latest, ask at any Paris TI.) If it's open, you can leave the tree-lined, sun-dappled Impressionist painting that is the Tuileries Garden, and enter L'Orangerie (loh-rahn-zheh-ree), a little *bijou* of select works by Utrillo, Cézanne, Renoir, Matisse, and Picasso. On the ground floor, you'll find a line of eight rooms dedicated to these artists. Downstairs is the finale: Monet's water lilies. The museum's collection is small enough to enjoy in a short visit, but complete enough to see the bridge from Impressionism to the Moderns. And it's all beautiful (likely €7, covered by Museum Pass, located in Tuileries Garden near place de la Concorde, Mo: Concorde). At press time, accessibility details were not yet available.

▲▲▲**Orsay Museum**—The Musée d'Orsay (mew-zay dor-say) houses French art of the 1800s (specifically, 1848 to 1914), picking up where the Louvre leaves off. For us, that means Impressionism. The Orsay houses the best general collection anywhere of Edouard Manet, Claude Monet, Pierre-Auguste Renoir, Edgar Degas, Vincent van Gogh, Paul Cézanne, and Paul Gauguin.

The museum shows art that is also both old and new, conservative and revolutionary. You'll start on the ground floor with the Conservatives and the early rebels who paved the way for the Impressionists, then head upstairs to see how a few visionary young artists bucked the system, revolutionized the art world, and paved the way for the 20th century.

Access: AE, AI, AL, AT, Level 1—Fully Accessible. The modern-ized Orsay building is designed to accommodate the wheelchair user. The *Museum Guide* has an overlay (available at information counter) that indicates accessible toilets, ramps, and elevators. Loaner wheelchairs are available.

Cost: €7.50; €5.50 after 16:15 and on Sun, free first Sun of month, covered by Museum Pass. Tickets are good all day. Museum Pass–holders and wheelchair users can enter quickly on the right side of the main

Orsay Museum—Ground Floor

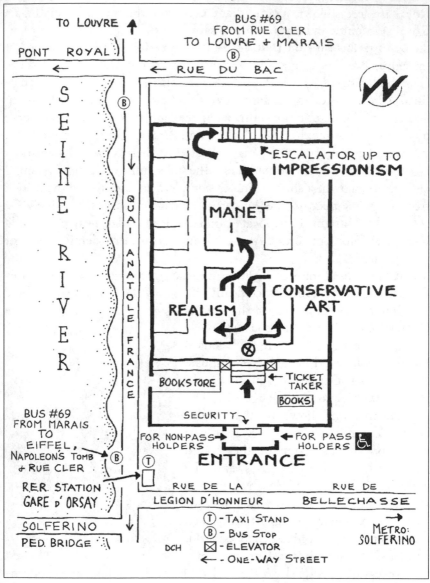

entrance; ticket-buyers enter along the left (river) side.

Free Entry near Closing: Right when the ticket booth stops selling tickets (17:00 on Tue–Wed and Fri–Sun, 20:45 on Thu), you're welcome to scoot in free of charge. (They won't let you in much after that, however.) For one hour, you'll have the art mostly to yourself before the museum closes. The Impressionism galleries on the upper level start shutting down first, so go there right away.

Hours: June 20–Sept 20 Tue–Sun 9:00–18:00, Sept 21–June 19 Tue–Sat 10:00–18:00, Sun 9:00–18:00, Thu until 21:45 year-round, always closed Mon. Last entry one hour before closing. The Impressionist galleries begin closing at 17:15, frustrating unwary visitors. Note that the Orsay is crowded on Tuesday, when the Louvre is closed.

Location: The Orsay sits above the RER-C stop called Musée d'Orsay. The nearest Métro stop is Solférino, three blocks south of the Orsay. Bus #69 from the Marais neighborhoods stops at the museum on the river side (quai Anatole France); from the rue Cler area, it stops behind the museum on the rue du Bac. A taxi stand is in front of the museum on quai Anatole France.

Information: The booth inside the entrance gives free floor plans in English. Tel. 01 40 49 48 41, www.musee-orsay.fr.

Tours: Audioguides are €5. Fully accessible English-language guided tours usually run daily (except Sun) at 11:30 (90-min tours-€6). Tours in English focusing on the Impressionists are offered Tuesdays at 14:30 (€6, sometimes also on other days).

Cuisine Art: There's a pricey but *très* elegant restaurant on the second floor, with affordable tea and coffee served 15:00–17:30. A simple fifth-floor café is sandwiched between the Impressionists; above it is an easy self-service place with sandwiches and drinks. All of these are rated **AE, AI, AT,** Level 1—Fully Accessible.

❺ Self-Guided Tour: For most visitors, the most important part of the museum is the Impressionist collection on the upper level. Here, you can study many pictures you've probably seen in books, such as Manet's *Luncheon on the Grass*, Renoir's *Dance at the Moulin de la Galette*, Monet's *Gare St. Lazare*, James Abbott McNeill Whistler's *Portrait of the Artist's Mother*, van Gogh's *The Church at Auvers-sur-Oise*, and Cézanne's *The Card Players*. As you approach these beautiful, easy-to-enjoy paintings, remember that there is more to this art than meets the eye.

Here's a primer on Impressionism: After the camera was invented, it threatened to make artists obsolete. A painter's original function was to record reality faithfully, like a journalist. Now a machine could capture a better likeness faster than you could say Etch-A-Sketch.

But true art is more than just painted reality. It gives us reality from the artist's point of view, putting a personal stamp on the work. It records not only a scene—a camera can do that—but the artist's impressions of that scene. Impressions are often fleeting, so the artist has to work quickly.

The Impressionist painters rejected camera-like detail for a quick style more suited to capturing the passing moment. Feeling stifled by the rigid rules and stuffy atmosphere of the Academy, the Impressionists took as their motto, "Out of the studio, into the open air." They grabbed their berets and scarves and took excursions to the country, where they set up their easels on riverbanks and hillsides, or sketched in cafés and dance halls. Gods, goddesses, nymphs, and fantasy scenes were out; common people and rural landscapes were in.

The quick style and simple subjects were ridiculed and called childish by the "experts." Rejected by the Salon, the Impressionists staged their own exhibition in 1874. They brashly took their name from an insult thrown at them by a critic, who laughed at one of Monet's impressions of a sunrise. During the next decade, they exhibited their own work independently. The public, opposed at first, was slowly drawn in by the simplicity, color, and vibrancy of Impressionist art.

Historic Core of Paris:
Notre-Dame, Sainte-Chapelle, and More

Many of these sights are covered in detail in the Historic Paris Roll or Stroll (plus map) on page 290. If a sight's covered in that tour, I've only listed its essentials here.

▲▲Notre-Dame Cathedral (Cathédrale Notre-Dame de Paris)—This 700-year-old cathedral is packed with history and tourists. With a pair of 200-foot-tall bell towers, a facade studded with ornate statuary, beautiful stained-glass rose windows, famous gargoyles, a picture-perfect Seine-side location, and textbook flying buttresses, there's a good reason that this cathedral of "Our Lady" (Notre-Dame) is France's most famous church (Mo: Cité, Hôtel de Ville, or St. Michel; clean toilets in front of church near Charlemagne's statue).

Check out the facade: Mary with the Baby Jesus (in rose window) above the 28 Kings of Judah (statues that were beheaded during the Revolution). Explore the interior, echoing with history. Then wander around the exterior, through a forest of frilly buttresses, watched over by a fleet of whimsical gargoyles. Finally, if you are able, climb the cathedral tower (400 steps, no elevator).

Cathedral Access: AE, AI+A, Level 2—Moderately Accessible. The entryway and three-fourths of the main floor are wheelchair-accessible. There are three 6" steps to enter the area of the Mass and the treasury.

Cathedral Cost and Hours: Free, daily 7:45–19:00; treasury-€2.50, not covered by Museum Pass, daily 9:30–17:30; ask about free English tours, normally Wed and Thu at 12:00, Sat at 14:30.

Tower Access: Level 4—Not Accessible (400 steps). Hardy slow walkers can climb to the top of the facade between the towers and then to the top of the south tower.

Tower Cost and Hours: €7, covered by Museum Pass, July–Aug Mon–Fri 9:00–19:30, Sat–Sun 9:00–23:00, April–June and Sept daily 9:30–19:30, Oct–March daily 10:00–17:30, last entry 45 min before closing, arrive early to avoid long lines.

Paris Archaeological Crypt—This is a worthwhile 15-minute stop with your Museum Pass. You'll visit Roman ruins, trace the street plan of the medieval village, and see diagrams of how early Paris grew, all thoughtfully explained in English.

The first few displays put the ruins in their historical context. Three models show the growth of Paris—from an uninhabited riverside plot; to the Roman town of Lutece; to an early-medieval city, with a church that preceded Notre-Dame. A fourth model shows the current Notre-Dame surrounded by buildings, along with the old, straight road—the rue Neuve de Notre-Dame—that led up to the church (and ran right down the center of the museum). The ruins in the middle of the museum are a confusing mix of foundations from all these time periods, including parts of the old rue Neuve de Notre-Dame.

Press the buttons on the display cases to light up a particular section, such as the medieval hospital (along the far side of the museum), a well-preserved Gallo-Roman paved room, and a Roman building with "hypocaustal" heating (narrow passages through which hot air was pumped to heat the room).

Access: Level 4—Not Accessible. There are fourteen 6" steps down to the entryway. The inside is mostly level.

Cost, Hours, Location: €3.50, covered by Museum Pass, Tue–Sun 10:00–18:00, closed Mon, enter 100 yards in front of cathedral.

▲▲**Deportation Memorial (Mémorial de la Déportation)**—This memorial commemorates the 200,000 French victims of the Nazi concentration camps. As Paris disappears above you, this monument draws you into the victims' experience. Once underground, you enter a one-way hallway—studded with tiny lights—commemorating the dead, leading you to an eternal flame.

Access: AE, AI, Level 2—Moderately Accessible. Use the accessible ramped entrance just past the steps. Once inside, the gardens are accessible, but the actual memorial chambers are not.

Cost, Hours, Location: Free, April–Sept daily 10:00–12:00 & 14:00–19:00, Oct–March daily 10:00–12:00 & 14:00–17:00. It's at the east tip of the island Ile de la Cité, behind Notre-Dame and near Ile St. Louis (Mo: Cité).

Ile St. Louis—The residential island behind Notre-Dame is known for its restaurants (see "Eating," page 275), great ice cream, and shops (along rue St. Louis-en-l'Ile).

Cité "Métropolitain" Stop and Flower Market—On place Louis Lépine, between Notre-Dame and Sainte-Chapelle, you'll find an early 19th-century subway entrance and a flower market (that chirps with a bird market on Sun).

▲▲▲**Sainte-Chapelle**—The interior of this 13th-century chapel is a triumph of Gothic church architecture. Built to house Jesus' Crown of Thorns, Sainte-Chapelle is jam-packed with stained-glass windows, bathed in colorful light, and slippery with the drool of awe-struck tourists. Ignore the humdrum exterior and climb the stairs into the sanctuary, where more than 1,100 Bible scenes—from the Creation to the Passion to Judgment Day—are illustrated by light and glass.

Access: Ground floor only—**AE, AI, AT+A,** Level 2—Moderately Accessible. Unfortunately, the upstairs chapel (with the stained-glass windows) can be reached only by climbing a narrow spiral staircase, is Level 4—Not Accessible, though slow walkers will find it's worth the climb). Wheelchair-accessible toilets are near the Palace of Justice entrance, with one 4" curb to negotiate and a long ramp with no railing.

Cost, Hours, Location: Free for wheelchair users, otherwise €7, €10.50 combo-ticket covers Conciergerie, both covered by Museum Pass. Open March-Oct daily 9:30–18:00, Nov–Feb 9:00–17:00. Mo: Cité.

▲**Conciergerie**—Marie-Antoinette was imprisoned here, as were Louis XVI, Robespierre, Marat, and many others on their way to the guillotine. Exhibits with good English descriptions trace the history of the building, and give some insight into prison life. You can also relive the drama in Marie-Antoinette's cell on the day of her execution—complete with dummies and period furniture.

Access: Level 4—Not Accessible. Visitors must negotiate a flight of stairs to get into the courtyard and lobby of the Conciergerie.

Cost, Hours, Location: €7, €10.50 combo-ticket covers Sainte-Chapelle, both covered by Museum Pass, April–Sept daily 9:30–18:00, Oct–March daily 10:00–17:00.

Southwest Paris: The Eiffel Tower to Les Invalides

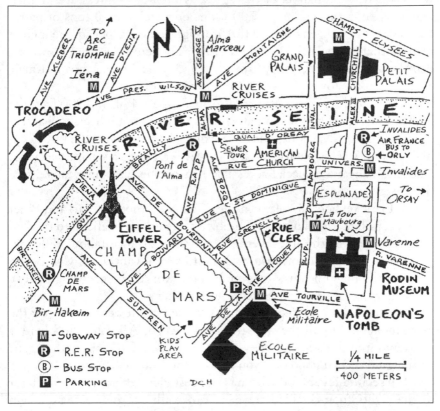

Southwest Paris: The Eiffel Tower Neighborhood

▲▲▲**Eiffel Tower (La Tour Eiffel)**—It's crowded and expensive, but this 1,000-foot-tall ornament is worth the trouble. Visitors to Paris may find *Mona Lisa* to be less than expected, but the Eiffel Tower rarely disappoints, even in an era of skyscrapers.

Built a hundred years after the French Revolution (and in the midst of an Industrial one), the tower served no function but to impress. Bridge-builder Gustave Eiffel won the contest for the 1889 Centennial World's Fair by beating out such rival proposals as a giant guillotine. To a generation hooked on technology,

the tower was the marvel of the age, a symbol of progress and human ingenuity. Indeed, despite its 7,000 tons of metal and 50 tons of paint, the tower is so well-engineered that it weighs no more per square inch at its base than a linebacker on tiptoes. Not all were impressed, however; many found it a monstrosity. The writer Guy de Maupassant routinely ate lunch in the tower just so he wouldn't have to look at it.

There are three observation platforms, at 200, 400, and 900 feet; the higher you go, the more you pay. The top level is not wheelchair-accessible (see "Access," below), but for anyone, the view from the 400-foot-high second level is plenty good. Each level requires a separate elevator (and line). There are special accessible lifts on the east and west sides of the tower.

A TI/ticket booth is between the Pilier Nord (north pillar) and Pilier Est (east pillar). The stairs (non-disabled travelers can walk up to the 2nd level) are next to the Jules Verne restaurant entrance (allow $300 per person for the restaurant, reserve 3 months in advance). As you ascend through the metal beams, imagine being a worker, perched high above nothing, riveting this giant erector set together.

The **top level** (900 feet) is tiny. And, because fewer visitors pay the extra money to go all the way, it's less crowded. All you'll find here is wind and grand, sweeping views. The city lies before you, with a panorama guide. On a good day, you can see for 40 miles.

The **second level** (400 feet) has the best views, because you're closer to the sights (non-disabled travelers can walk up the stairway to get above the netting). There's also a cafeteria and WCs (everything is fully accessible).

The **first level** (200 feet) has exhibits, a post office (daily 10:00–19:00, cancellation stamp will read Eiffel Tower), a snack bar, WCs, and souvenirs. Read the informative signs (in English) describing the major monuments, see the entertaining free movie on the history of the tower, and don't miss a century of fireworks—including the entire millennium blast—on video. Then consider a drink or a sandwich overlooking all of Paris at the fully accessible snack café outdoor tables in summer) or at the city's best view bar/restaurant, Altitude 95 (see page 268).

Access: Everything on the first and second levels is **AE, AI, AL, AT,** Level 1—Fully Accessible. This includes accessible toilets on both levels, restaurants, and shops. The top level is Level 4—Not Accessible to wheelchair users, but some slow walkers can make it up the narrow, steep steps from the elevator to the observation deck. If you have your heart set on a high-altitude panorama of Paris, ascend the accessible Montparnasse Tower instead (see "Sights—Southeast Paris," below).

Cost and Hours: It costs €4 to go to the first level, €7.50 to the second, and €11 to go to the top (not covered by Museum Pass). Open March–Sept daily 9:00–24:00, Oct–Feb daily 9:30–23:00, last entry 1 hour before closing, shorter lines at night, Mo: Bir-Hakeim or Trocadéro, RER: Champ de Mars-Tour Eiffel, tel. 01 44 11 23 23, www.tour -eiffel.fr.

Tips: Wheelchair users can go to the head of the line. To avoid most crowds, go early (by 8:45) or late in the day (after 18:00, after 20:00 in May–Aug, last entry 1 hour before closing); weekends are worst. Ideally, you'll arrive with some light and stay as it gets dark.

To pass the time in lines, pick up whatever free reading material is available at the tourist stands at ground level. I liked the *Eiffel Tower Gazette*, a free newspaper featuring a century of Eiffel Tower headlines.

Before or after your tower visit, you can catch the fully accessible Bateaux-Parisiens boat (near the base of the tower) for a Seine cruise (see page 196).

Best Views: The best place to view the tower is from **Trocadéro Square** to the north; it's a short roll or stroll across the river, a happening scene at night, and especially fun for kids. Consider arriving at the Trocadéro Métro stop for the view, then moving toward the tower. Another delightful viewpoint is the long, grassy field, **Le Parc du Champ de Mars**, to the south (great for dinner picnics). However impressive it may be by day, the tower is an awesome thing to see at twilight, when it becomes engorged with light, and virile Paris lies back and lets night be on top. When darkness fully envelops the city, the tower seems to climax at the top of each hour...for 10 minutes. (It's been doing this since the millennium festivities, when it was wired with thousands of special lights.)

National Maritime Museum (Musée National de la Marine)—This extensive museum houses an amazing collection of ship models, submarines, torpedoes, cannonballs, *beaucoup* bowsprits, and naval you-name-it—including a small boat made for Napoleon. You'll find some English information on the walls. The free audioguide is a godsend for *Master and Commander* types; kids like the museum either way.

Access: AE, AI, Level 2—Moderately Accessible.

Cost, Hours, Location: €9, kids-€7, covered by Museum Pass, Wed–Mon 10:00–18:00, closed Tue, on left side of Trocadéro Square with your back to Eiffel Tower, www.musee-marine.fr.

▲▲**Napoleon's Tomb and Army Museums (Les Invalides)**—The emperor lies majestically dead inside several coffins under a grand dome glittering with 26 pounds of gold—a goose-bumping pilgrimage for historians.

Napoleon is surrounded by the tombs of other French war heroes and fine military museums in Hôtel des Invalides. Non-disabled travelers can follow signs down the stairs to the crypt to find Roman Empire-style reliefs that list the accomplishments of Napoleon's administration. Check out the interesting World War II wing. The Army Museums' West Wing (with a focus on World War I) should reopen in 2006, while the East Wing (starring Napoleon) will likely close for renovation.

Access: Everything except the crypt is **AE, AI, AT,** Level 1—Fully Accessible. Loaner wheelchairs are available. Most of the museum is accessible for people using wheelchairs. The crypt itself, however, has an entryway of fifteen 4" steps and a 36" high solid railing around the tomb. Be aware of large areas of rough cobblestone.

Cost, Hours, Location: Free for wheelchair user and companion, otherwise €7, covered by Museum Pass, April–Sept daily 10:00–18:00, summer Sun until 19:00, Oct–March daily 10:00–17:00, closed the first Mon of every month except July–Sept; Mo: La Tour-Maubourg or Varenne, tel. 01 44 42 37 72, www.invalides.org.

▲▲**Rodin Museum (Musée Rodin)**—This user-friendly museum is filled with passionate works by the greatest sculptor since Michelangelo. Auguste Rodin (1840–1917) sculpted human figures on an epic scale, revealing through the body their deepest thoughts and feelings. Rodin's statues rise from the raw stone around them, driven by the life force. With missing limbs and scarred skin, these are prefab classics, making ugliness noble. Rodin's people are always moving restlessly. Even the famous *Thinker* is moving. Rodin worked with many materials—he chiseled marble (though not often), modeled clay, cast bronze, worked plaster, painted, and sketched. He often created different versions of the same subject in different media.

Rodin lived and worked in this mansion, renting rooms alongside Henri Matisse, the poet Rainer Maria Rilke (Rodin's secretary), and the dancer Isadora Duncan. Well-displayed exhibits trace Rodin's artistic development, explain how his bronze statues were cast, and show some of the studies he created to work up to his masterpiece (the unfinished *Gates of Hell*). Learn about Rodin's tumultuous relationship with his apprentice and lover, Camille Claudel. Mull over what makes his sculptures some of the most evocative since the Renaissance. For many, the gardens are the highlight of this museum. Here you'll find several of his greatest works, such as the *Thinker, Balzac,* the *Burghers of Calais,* and the *Gates of Hell.* The gardens are ideal for artistic reflection...or a picnic.

Access: Main floor only—**AE, AI, AT,** Level 1—Fully Accessible. Only the main floor of the museum is wheelchair-accessible (via an entry ramp); to get to the upper level, you'll have to be able to climb a flight of stairs (no elevator; Level 4—Not Accessible). The courtyard is made of rough cobblestone. The best part of the museum—the beautiful, sculpture-packed gardens—is fully accessible. Loaner wheelchairs are available.

Cost, Hours, Location: Free for wheelchair user and companion, otherwise €5, €3 on Sun, free first Sun of month, covered by Museum Pass. You'll pay €1 to get into the gardens only—which may be Paris' best deal, as many works are on display there. April–Sept Tue–Sun 9:30–17:45, closed Mon, gardens close 18:45; Oct–March Tue–Sun 9:30–16:45, closed Mon, gardens close 17:00. It's near Napoleon's Tomb (77 rue de Varenne, Mo: Varenne, tel. 01 44 18 61 10, www.musee-rodin.fr).

Southeast Paris: The Latin Quarter

This Left Bank neighborhood, just opposite Notre-Dame, is the Latin Quarter. (For more information and a self-guided tour, see the Historic Paris Roll or Stroll, page 290.)

▲▲**Cluny Museum (Musée National du Moyen Age)**—This treasure trove of Middle Age ("Moyen Age") art fills the old Roman baths, offering close-up looks at stained glass, Notre-Dame carvings, fine goldsmithing and jewelry, and rooms of tapestries. The star here is the exquisite "Lady and the Unicorn" tapestry: In five panels, a delicate-as-medieval-can-be noble lady introduces a delighted unicorn to the senses of taste, hearing, sight, smell, and touch.

Access: Level 3—Minimally Accessible. Large, rough cobblestones lead to the entrance, and the interior is even worse—multiple levels and lots of stairs without any elevators. The museum is not accessible for wheelchair users, but works for energetic, art-loving slow walkers.

Southeast Paris: The Latin Quarter

Cost, Hours, Location: €5.50, €4 on Sun, free first Sun of month, covered by Museum Pass, Wed–Mon 9:15–17:45, closed Tue, near corner of boulevards St. Michel and St. Germain; Mo: Cluny-La Sorbonne, St. Michel, or Odéon; tel. 01 53 73 78 16, www.musee-moyenage.fr.

St. Germain-des-Prés—A church was first built on this site in A.D. 452. The church you see today was constructed in 1163 and is all that's left of a once sprawling and influential monastery. The colorful interior reminds us that medieval churches were originally painted in bright colors. The surrounding area hops at night with venerable cafés, fire-eaters, mimes, and scads of artists.

Cost, Hours, Location: Free, daily 8:00–20:00, Mo: St. Germain-des-Prés.

Access: AE+A, AI, Level 2—Moderately Accessible. You'll have to climb four small steps to get inside.

▲**St. Sulpice Organ Concert**—Since it was featured in *The Da Vinci Code,* this grand church has become a trendy stop among the book's fans. But the real reason to visit is to see and hear its organ. For pipe-organ enthu-siasts, this is one of Europe's great musical treats. The Grand Orgue at St. Sulpice Church has a rich history, with a succession of 12 world-class organists (including Charles-Marie Widor and Marcel Dupré) going back 300 years. Widor started the tradition of opening the loft to visitors after the 10:30 service on Sundays. Daniel Roth continues to welcome guests in three languages while playing five keyboards at once. (See www.danielrothsaintsulpice .org for his exact dates and concert plans.) The 10:30 Sunday Mass is followed by a high-powered 25-minute recital at about 11:35. Then, just after noon, the small, unmarked door is opened (left of entry as you face the rear). Non-disabled visitors scamper like sixteenth notes up spiral stairs, past the 19th-century Stairmasters that five men once pumped to fill the bellows, into a world of 7,000 pipes. Here, they watch the master play during the next Mass. You'll generally have 30 minutes to kill (there's a plush lounge) before the organ plays; visitors can leave at any time. If late or rushed, show up around 12:30 and wait at the little door. As someone leaves, you can slip in, climb up, and catch the rest of the performance (church open daily 7:30–19:30, Mo: St. Sulpice or Mabillon).

Tempting boutiques surround the church (see "Shopping," below), and nearby is the Luxembourg Garden (described below).

Access: The main floor of the church is **AE, AI, AT,** Level 1—Fully Accessible. The upstairs organ loft, however, is accessed only by a tight staircase, and therefore Level 4—Not Accessible. To enter the main floor, use the ramp around the right side of building (as you face the church). To reach the accessible toilet, go to the right once you enter through this door (past the confessional and the sacristy to the Chapel of the Assumption).

▲**Luxembourg Garden (Jardin du Luxembourg)**—Paris' most beautiful, interesting, and enjoyable garden/park/recreational area is a great place to watch Parisians at rest and play (free, open daily until dusk, Mo: Odéon, RER: Luxembourg). It's ideal for families. These private gardens are property of the French Senate (housed in the château) and have special rules governing their use (e.g., where cards can be played, where dogs can be walked, where joggers can run, when and where music can be played). The brilliant flower beds are completely changed three times a year, and the boxed trees are brought out of the *orangerie* in May. Challenge the card and chess players to a game (near the tennis courts), rent a toy sailboat, or find a free chair near the main pond and take a breather. Notice any pigeons? The story goes that a poor Ernest Hemingway used to hand-hunt (read: strangle) them here.

The grand, neoclassical-domed Panthéon, now a mausoleum housing the tombs of several great Frenchmen, is a block away.

If you enjoy the Luxembourg Garden and want to see more, visit the nearby, colorful Jardin des Plantes (Mo: Jussieu or Gare d'Austerlitz, RER: Gare d'Austerlitz) and the more elegant Parc Monceau (Mo: Monceau).

Access: AE, AI, Level 1—Fully Accessible. The park has specific gated entrances that lead to paved or dirt paths.

Montparnasse Tower (La Tour Montparnasse)—This wheelchair-accessible 59-story superscraper is cheaper and easier to get to the top of than the Eiffel Tower, with the added bonus of offering one of Paris' best views—the Eiffel Tower is in sight, and the Montparnasse Tower isn't. If you couldn't go to the top of the Eiffel Tower to get your panoramic bearings, you can do it here instead, with easy access. Buy the €3 photo guide to the city, then go to the 56th floor and orient yourself. As you zip 56 floors in 38 seconds, watch the altitude meter above the door. Up top, scan the city, noticing the lush courtyards hiding behind grand street fronts.

Access: AE, AI, AL, AT, Level 1—Fully Accessible. The accessible elevator goes to the enclosed observation deck, panorama exhibit, and restaurant on the 56th floor of this 59-story building. The rooftop "panoramic terrace" is accessible only by stairs, but the views from the 56th floor are just as good. You'll find an accessible toilet in the shopping center below the tower.

Cost, Hours, Location: €8.50, discount for wheelchair users, not covered by Museum Pass, April–Sept daily 9:30–23:30, Oct–March 9:30-22:30, last entry 30 min before closing, disappointing after dark, entrance on rue de l'Arrivée, Mo: Montparnasse-Bienvenüe, www.tourmontparnasse56.com.

Northwest Paris: Champs-Elysées, Arc de Triomphe, and Beyond

▲▲**Place de la Concorde and the Champs-Elysées**—This famous boulevard is Paris' backbone and has the greatest concentration of traffic. All of France seems to converge on place de la Concorde, the city's

Northwest Paris:
Champs-Elysées, Arc de Triomphe, and Beyond

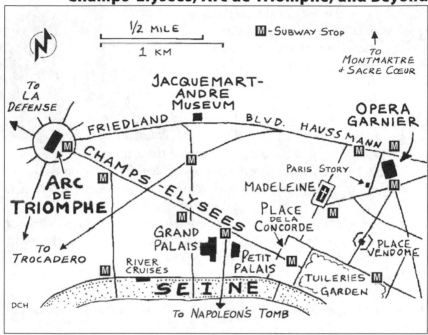

largest square. It was here that the guillotine took the lives of thousands—including King Louis XVI and Marie-Antoinette. Back then, it was called the place de la Revolution.

Catherine de' Medici wanted a place to drive her carriage, so she started draining the swamp that would become the Champs-Elysées. Napoleon put on the final touches, and it's been the place to be seen ever since. The Tour de France bicycle race ends here, as do all parades (French or foe) of any significance. While the boulevard has become a bit hamburgerized, a roll or stroll here is great fun. Still, this can be a challenging area for wheelchair users and slow walkers—with lots of traffic (Parisian drivers get the right-of-way) and stairs.

For a guided, accessible roll or stroll from the top to the bottom of the Champs-Elysées, see page 316.

▲▲▲ **Arc de Triomphe**—Napoleon had the magnificent Arc de Triomphe commissioned to commemorate his victory at the battle of Austerlitz. The foot of the arch is a stage on which the last two centuries of Parisian history has played out—from the funeral of Napoleon, to the goose-stepping arrival of the Nazis, to the triumphant return of Charles de Gaulle after the Allied liberation. Carvings on the pillars feature a mighty Napoleon and excitable Lady Liberty. Pay your respects at the Tomb of the Unknown Soldier. From the base of the arch, an elevator or a spiral staircase leads to a cute museum about the arch. From there, stairs (but no elevator) lead to a grand view at the top, even after dark.

Access: Level 4—Not Accessible. The arch is in the middle of one of Europe's busiest traffic circles. Adventurous slow walkers and non-disabled travelers can reach the base of the arch through an underground passage with stairs: twenty-five 6" steps down, then thirty 6" steps back up. The only way for a wheelchair user to reach the arch is to take a taxi to the center of the traffic circle and be dropped off at the base—which is both dangerous and illegal. Once at the arch, you can only take the elevator to the museum partway up (the rooftop viewpoint is accessed only by 46 stairs).

Cost, Hours, Location: The exterior is free to view. Admission to interior-€8, under 18 free, covered by Museum Pass, April-Sept daily 10:00–23:00, Oct–March daily 10:00–22:00. Mo: Charles de Gaulle-Etoile.

▲**Opéra Garnier**—This grand palace of the belle époque was built for Napoleon III and finished in 1875. From the grand avenue de l'Opéra, once lined with Paris' most fashionable haunts, the newly restored facade seems to say, "All power to the wealthy." And Apollo, holding his lyre high above the building, seems to declare, "This is a temple of the highest arts." While huge, the actual theater seats only 2,000. The real show was before and after, when the elite of Paris—out to see and be seen—strutted their elegant stuff in the extravagant lobbies.

Although the theater interior is mostly wheelchair-accessible for theatergoers, the in-depth walking tours of the Opéra are not. However you get inside, imagine the place filled with the beautiful people of the day. The massive foundations straddle an underground lake (creating the mysterious world of the *Phantom of the Opera*). The red velvet theater boasts a colorful ceiling by Marc Chagall (1964) playfully dancing around the eight-ton chandelier. Note the box seats next to the stage—the most expensive in the house, with an obstructed view of the stage...but just right if you're there only to be seen. The elitism of this place prompted President François Mitterand to have a people's opera house built in the 1980s (symbolically on place de la Bastille, where the French Revolution started in 1789). This left the Opéra Garnier home only to ballet and occasional concerts (usually no performances mid-July–mid-Sept). While the library/museum is of interest to opera buffs, non-disabled visitors will enjoy the second-floor grand foyer and Salon du Glacier, iced with decor typical of 1900.

Access: AE, AI, AL, Level 2—Moderately Accessible. There is a ramp entry on rue Scribe and special seats accessible by lift for wheelchair users. Friendly customer service agent Sandrine (tel. 01 40 01 18 50) can help you with accessibility arrangements and ticketing. Nondisabled travelers enter through the front, off place de l'Opéra.

Cost, Hours, Location: €7, not covered by Museum Pass, daily 10:00-17:00, July–Aug until 18:00, closed during performances, 8 rue Scribe, Mo: Opéra, www.opera-de-paris.fr.

Tours: There are English tours of the building on most afternoons. Unfortunately, they involve climbing stairs and are rated Level 4—Not Accessible (€10, includes entry, 90 min, call to confirm, tour ticket window at opposite end of entry from regular ticket booth).

Nearby: American Express, a TI, and the *Paris Story* film (see below) are on the left side of the Opéra, and the venerable Galeries Lafayette department store (**AE, AI, AL, AT,** Level 1—Fully Accessible; top-floor café with marvelous views) is just behind. Across the street, the illustrious **Café de la Paix** (**AE, AI, AT** in attached hotel, Level 1—Fully Accessible) has been a meeting spot for the local glitterati for generations. If you can afford the coffee, this offers a delightful break.

Paris Story **Film**—This entertaining film offers a good and painless overview of the city's turbulent and brilliant past, covering 2,000 years in 45 fast-moving minutes. The theater's wide-screen projection and cushy chairs provide an ideal break from bad weather and sore feet, and the movie's a fun activity with kids. It makes a good first-day orientation.

Access: Level 4—Not Accessible. Slow walkers must climb stairs to get to the theater (no elevator).

Cost, Hours, Location: Adults-€8, kids-€5, family of 4-€21, not covered by Museum Pass. Individuals get a 20 percent discount with this book in 2006 (no discount on family rate). The film shows on the hour daily 9:00–19:00. Next to Opéra Garnier at 11 rue Scribe, Mo: Opéra, tel. 01 42 66 62 06.

▲▲**Jacquemart-André Museum (Musée Jacquemart-André)**—This thoroughly enjoyable museum showcases the lavish home of a wealthy, art-loving, 19th-century Parisian couple. After wandering the grand boulevards, you now get inside for an intimate look at the lifestyles of the Parisian rich and fabulous. Edouard André and his wife Nélie Jacquemart—who had no children—spent their lives and fortunes designing, building, and then decorating a sumptuous mansion. What makes this visit so rewarding is the fine audioguide tour (in English, free with admission). The place is strewn with paintings by Rembrandt, Botticelli, Uccello, Mantegna, Bellini, Boucher, and Fragonard—enough to make a painting gallery famous. Plan on spending an hour with the excellent audioguide.

Access: AE, AI, Level 2—Moderately Accessible. Only the ground floor is accessible.

Cost, Hours, Location: €9, not covered by Museum Pass, daily 10:00–18:00, elegant café, at 158 boulevard Haussmann, Mo: Miromesnil or St Philippe de Roule, tel. 01 45 62 11 59, www.musee-jacquemart -andre.com/jandre.

Petit Palais (and its Musée des Beaux-Arts)—This free museum recently reopened after renovation. You'll find a broad collection of paintings and sculpture from the 1600s to the 1900s. To some, it feels like a museum of second-choice art, as the more famous museums in Paris have better collections from the same periods. Others find a few diamonds in the rough from Monet, Renoir, Boudin, and others; some interesting Art Nouveau pieces; and a smattering of works from Dutch, Italian, and Flemish Renaissance artists.

Access: AE, AI, AT, Level 1—Fully Accessible. They have guards who take wheelchair users through the Palais, and also have parking reserved for people with disabilities.

Cost, Hours, Location: Free, Tue–Sun 10:00–17:40, closed Mon, across from Grand Palais, avenue Winston Churchill, just west of place de la Concorde, tel. 01 40 05 56 78.

Grand Palais—This grand exhibition hall, built for the 1900 World's Fair, is busy with generally worthwhile temporary exhibits. Get details on the current schedule from TIs or in *Pariscope*.

Access: AE, AI, AT, Level 1—Fully Accessible.

Cost, Hours, Location: €10.50, €9 after 13:00, not covered by Museum Pass, open Mon and Thu–Sun 10:00–20:00, Wed 10:00–20:00, closed Tue, avenue Churchill, Mo: Rond Point or Champs-Elysées.

▲**La Défense and La Grande Arche**—On the outskirts of Paris, the centerpiece of Paris' ambitious skyscraper complex (La Défense) is the Grande Arche. Inaugurated in 1989 on the 200th anniversary of the French Revolution, it was dedicated to human rights and brotherhood. The place is big—38 floors holding offices for 30,000 people on more than 200 acres. Notre-Dame Cathedral could fit under its arch. The complex at La Défense is an interesting study in 1960s land-use planning. More than 150,000 workers commute here daily, directing lots of business and

development away from downtown and allowing central Paris to retain its more elegant feel. This makes sense to most Parisians, regardless of whatever else they feel about this controversial complex.

For an interesting visit, take the Métro to the La Défense stop, explore La Grande Arche (take the accessible elevator to the top for great city views and displays on the arch's construction), then roll or stroll among the glass buildings to the Esplanade de la Défense Métro station, and return home from there. After enjoying the elegance of downtown Paris' historic, glorious monuments, it's clear that man can build bigger, but not more beautiful.

Access: AE, AI, AL, AT, Level 1—Fully Accessible. A combination of elevators, ramps, and stairlifts makes the Grande Arche fully accessible to wheelchair users. Don't be shy to ask the staff for assistance (operating stairlifts, finding the accessible route, etc.).

Cost, Hours, Location: La Grande Arche elevator-€7.50, kids-€6, family deals, not covered by Museum Pass, daily 10:00–19:00, July–Aug until 20:00, RER or Mo: La Défense, follow signs to *La Grande Arche*, tel. 01 49 07 27 57. The entry price includes art exhibits and a film on the Arche's construction.

Northeast Paris: Marais Neighborhood and More

The Marais neighborhood extends along the Right Bank of the Seine from the Pompidou Center to the Bastille. It contains more pre-Revolutionary lanes and buildings than anywhere else in town and is more atmospheric than touristy. It's medieval Paris. This is how much of the city looked until the mid-1800s, when Napoleon III had Baron Haussmann blast out the narrow streets to construct broad boulevards (wide enough for the guns and ranks of the army, too wide for revolutionary barricades), thus creating modern Paris. Originally a swamp *(marais)* during the reign of Henry IV, this area became the hometown of the French aristocracy. In the 17th century, big shots built their private mansions *(hôtels)*, close to Henry IV's place des Vosges. When exploring the Marais, stick to the west–east axis formed by rue Sainte-Croix de la Bretonnerie, rue des Rosiers (the heart of Paris' Jewish community), and rue St. Antoine. On Sunday afternoons, this trendy area pulses with shoppers and café crowds.

Northeast Paris: Marais Neighborhood and More

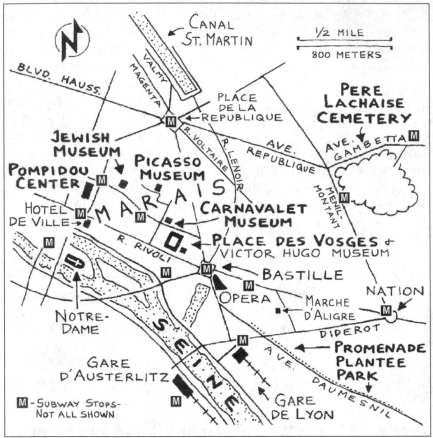

▲**Place des Vosges**—Study the architecture in this grand square: nine pavilions per side. Some of the brickwork is real, some is fake. If you are able, go to the center, where Louis XIII sits on a horse surrounded by locals enjoying their community park. Children frolic in the sandbox, lovers warm benches, and pigeons guard their fountains, while trees shade this retreat from the glare of the big city. Henry IV built this centerpiece of the Marais in 1605. As hoped, this turned the Marais into Paris' most exclusive neighborhood. As the nobility flocked to Versailles in a later age, this too was a magnet for the rich and powerful of France.

With the Revolution, the aristocratic elegance of this quarter became working-class, filled with gritty shops, artisans, immigrants, and Jews. **Victor Hugo** lived at #6, and you can visit his house (**AE, AI, AT,** Level 1—Fully Accessible; free, Tue–Sun 10:00–18:00, last entry 17:40, closed Mon, 6 place des Vosges, tel. 01 42 72 10 16). Leave the place des Vosges through the doorway at southwest corner of the square (near the three-star Michelin restaurant, l'Ambrosie) and pass through the elegant **Hôtel de Sully** (great example of a Marais mansion) to rue St. Antoine.

Access: The park is Level 2—Moderately Accessible. The sidewalks around place des Voges are at street level, but to get into the courtyard at the square's center, you'll have to negotiate three stairs down, then another three back up (no railing).

▲▲**Pompidou Center (Centre Pompidou)**—Europe's greatest collection of far-out modern art is housed in the Musée National d'Art Moderne, on the fourth and fifth floors of this colorful exhibition hall. (Note that

if you're here during the 2006 renovation, the collection may be condensed on either the fourth or fifth floor.) The building is "exoskeletal" (like Notre-Dame or a crab), with its functional parts—the pipes, heating ducts, and escalator—on the outside, and the meaty art inside. It's the epitome of modern architecture, where "form follows function." Once ahead of its time, the 20th-century art displayed in this museum has been waiting for the world to catch up with it. The 20th century—accelerated by technology and fragmented by war—was exciting and chaotic, and this art reflects the turbulence of that century of change. In this free-flowing and airy museum (with great views over Paris), you'll come face to face with works by Matisse, Picasso, Chagall, Dalí, Warhol, Kandinsky, Max Ernst, Jackson Pollock, and many more. And after so many Madonnas-and-Children, a piano smashed to bits and glued to the wall is refreshing

The Pompidou Center and its square are lively, with lots of people, street theater, and activity inside and out—a perpetual street fair. Kids of any age enjoy the fun, colorful fountain called *Homage to Stravinsky*, next to the Pompidou Center. If you need a light meal or snack, try the places lining the Stravinsky fountain. Don't miss the free exhibits on the ground floor of the Center. If you are able, ride the escalator for a great city view from the top (ticket or Museum Pass required), and consider the good mezzanine-level café.

Marais Sights

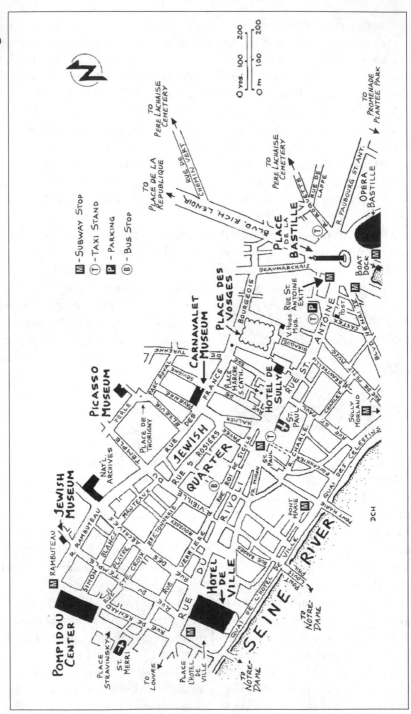

Access: AE, AI, AL, AT, Level 1—Fully Accessible. The vast entry ramp has bumpy cobblestones, but if you like modern art, it's worth the trip to reach the fully accessible interior.

Cost, Hours, Location: €7, free first Sun of month, covered by Museum Pass, Wed–Mon 11:00–21:00, closed Tue, Mo: Rambuteau, tel. 01 44 78 12 33, www.centrepompidou.fr.

▲▲**Jewish Art and History Museum (Musée d'Art et Histoire du Judaïsme)**—This fascinating museum is located in a beautifully restored Marais mansion and tells the story of Judaism throughout Europe, from the Roman destruction of Jerusalem to the theft of famous artworks during World War II.

The museum illustrates the cultural unity maintained by this continually dispersed population. You'll learn about the history of Jewish traditions, from bar mitzvahs to menorahs, and see the exquisite traditional costumes and objects around which daily life revolved. Don't miss the explanation of "the Dreyfus affair," a major event in early 1900s French politics. You'll also see photographs of and paintings by famous Jewish artists, including Chagall, Modigliani, and Soutine. A small but moving section is devoted to the deportation of Jews from Paris.

Helpful, free audioguides and many English explanations make this an enjoyable history lesson (red numbers on small signs indicate the number you should press on your audioguide). Move along at your own speed.

Access: AE, AI, AL, AT, ♥, Level 1—Fully Accessible.

Cost, Hours, Location: €7, includes audioguide, not covered by Museum Pass, Mon–Fri 11:00–18:00, Sun 10:00–18:00, closed Sat, 71 rue du Temple, Mo: Rambuteau or Hôtel de Ville a few blocks farther away, tel. 01 53 01 86 60, www.mahj.org.

▲▲**Picasso Museum (Musée Picasso)**—Tucked into a corner of the Marais and worth ▲▲▲ if you're a Picasso fan, this museum contains the world's largest collection of Picasso's paintings, sculptures, sketches, and ceramics, and includes his small collection of Impressionist art. The art is well-displayed in a fine old mansion with a peaceful garden café. The room-by-room English introductions help make sense of Picasso's work—from the Toulouse-Lautrec-like portraits at the beginning of his career to his gray-brown Cubist period to his return-to-childhood, Salvador Dalí–like finish. The well-done €3 English guidebook helps Picassophiles appreciate the context of his art and learn more about his interesting life. Most will be happy reading the posted English explanations while moving at a steady pace through the museum—the ground and first floors satisfied my curiosity.

Access: AE, AI, AL, Level 1—Fully Accessible. Leaving rue Thorigny, wheelchair users will need to cover 100 feet of bumpy cobblestones to reach the museum.

Cost, Hours, Location: €5.50, free first Sun of month, covered by Museum Pass, April–Sept Wed–Mon 9:30–18:00, Oct–March Wed–Mon 9:30–17:30, last entry 45 min before closing, closed Tue, 5 rue de Thorigny, Mo: St. Paul or Chemin Vert, tel. 01 42 71 25 21, www.musee -picasso.fr.

▲▲**Carnavalet Museum (Musée Carnavalet)**—The tumultuous history of Paris is well-portrayed in this museum, offering a good overview of everything from Louis XIV period rooms, to Napoleon, to the belle époque. Unfortunately, accessibility is difficult, and explanations are in French only—though many displays are fairly self-explanatory.

The Carnavalet, which opened in 1880, is housed in two Marais mansions connected by a corridor. The first half of the museum (pre-Revolution) dates from a period when people generally accepted the notion that some were born to rule, and most were born to be ruled. This section is difficult to follow (rooms numbered out of order, no English descriptions, and sections closed due to understaffing) so see it quickly, then concentrate your energy on the Revolution and beyond.

The Revolution is the museum's highlight. Fascinating exhibits cover this bloody period of French history, when atrocious acts were committed in the name of government "by, for, and of the people." The exhibits take you from events that led up to the Revolution, to the storming of the 100-foot-high walls of the Bastille, to the royal beheadings, and through the reigns of terror that followed. They then trace the rise and fall of Napoleon, and end with the Paris Commune uprisings.

Access: Level 4—Not Accessible (packed with stairs, no elevator).

Cost, Hours, Location: Free, Tue–Sun 10:00–18:00, closed Mon; avoid lunchtime (12:00–14:00), when many rooms close; 23 rue de Sévigné, Mo: St. Paul, tel. 01 44 59 58 58.

▲**Promenade Plantée Park**—This two-mile-long, narrow garden walk on a viaduct was once used for train tracks and is now a joy. Part of the park is elevated. At times, you'll walk along the street until you pick up the next segment. The shops below the viaduct's arches (a creative use of once wasted urban space) make for entertaining window-shopping.

Access: Level 4—Not Accessible. With many stairs up and down, this is inaccessible to all but the most energetic slow walkers.

Cost, Hours, Location: Free, opens Mon–Fri at 8:00, Sat–Sun at 9:00, closes at sunset. It runs from place de la Bastille (Mo: Bastille) along avenue Daumesnil to Saint-Mandé (Mo: Michel Bizot). From place de la Bastille (follow "Sortie Opéra" or "Sortie rue de Lyon" from Bastille Métro station), go down rue de Lyon with the Opera immediately on your left. Find the steps up the red brick wall a block after the Opera.

▲**Père Lachaise Cemetery (Cimetière du Père Lachaise)**—Littered with the tombstones of many of the city's most illustrious dead, this is your best one-stop look at the fascinating, romantic world of "permanent Parisians." More like a small city, the cemetery is confusing, but maps will direct you to the graves of Frédéric Chopin, Molière, Edith Piaf, Oscar Wilde, Gertrude Stein, Jim Morrison, Héloïse and Abélard, and more (helpful €2 maps sold at flower stores near either entry).

Access: Level 3—Minimally Accessible. With lots of steps and cobbled, uneven terrain, the cemetery is best left to energetic slow walkers.

Cost, Hours, Location: Free, Mon–Sat 8:00–18:00, Sun 9:00–18:00, actually closes at dusk. It's down rue Père Lachaise from Mo: Gambetta, or across the street from the Père Lachaise Métro stop (also reachable via bus #69).

North Paris: Montmartre

Explore Paris' highest hilltop (420 feet) for a different perspective on the City of Light. Trace the footsteps of the people who've lived here—monks stomping grapes (1200s), farmers grinding grain in windmills (1600s), dust-coated gypsum miners (1700s), Parisian liberals (1800s), modernist painters (1900s), and all the struggling artists, poets, dreamers, and drunkards who came here for cheap rent, untaxed booze, rustic landscapes, and cabaret nightlife. With vineyards, wheat fields, windmills, animals, and a village tempo of life, it was the perfect escape from grimy Paris.

▲▲**Sacré-Cœur** The five-domed, Roman-Byzantine basilica of Sacré-Cœur took 44 years to build (1875–1919). It stands on a foundation of 83 pillars sunk 130 feet deep, necessary because the ground beneath was honeycombed with gypsum mines.

The exterior is laced with gypsum, which whitens with age.

Access: Level 4—Not Accessible. Wheelchair users and others with limited mobility will probably want to skip the church interior. If you do go, take a taxi to the foot of the church steps. From there, you'll have to climb 26 steps with no railing to reach the entry. Once you're inside, it's all on one level.

Cost, Hours, and Location: Free, daily 7:00–23:00. Non-disabled travelers can pay €5 to climb 260 feet up the tight and claustrophobic spiral stairs to the top of the dome (Level 4—Not Accessible; June–Sept daily 9:00–19:00, Oct–May daily 10:00-18:00).

Getting There: A taxi to the top of the hill saves time and avoids sweat (tell the driver to take you to the foot of the church steps). Non-disabled travelers and slow walkers can take the Métro to the Anvers stop (1 Métro ticket buys your way up the funicular and avoids all but the last 26 stairs) or the closer but less scenic Abbesses stop.

Nearby: One block from the church, the **place du Tertre** was the haunt of Henri de Toulouse-Lautrec and the original bohemians. Today, it's mobbed with tourists and unoriginal bohemians, but it's still fun (go early in the morning to beat the crowds).

Pigalle—Paris' red-light district, the infamous "Pig Alley," is at the foot of butte Montmartre. *Ooh la la*. It's more shocking than dangerous. Roll or stroll from place Pigalle to place Blanche, teasing desperate barkers and fast-talking temptresses. In bars, a €150 bottle of cheap champagne comes with a friend. Stick to the bigger streets, hang on to your wallet, and exercise good judgment. Cancan can cost a fortune, as can con artists in topless bars. After dark, countless tour buses line the streets, reminding us that tour guides make big bucks by bringing their groups to touristy nightclubs like the famous Moulin Rouge (Mo: Pigalle or Abbesses).

Museum of Erotic Art (Musée de l'Erotisme)—Paris' sexy museum has five floors of risqué displays—mostly paintings and drawings—ranging from artistic to erotic to disgusting, with a few circa-1920 porn videos and a fascinating history of local brothels tossed in. It's in the center of the Pigalle red-light district.

Access: AE, AI, AT, Level 1—Fully Accessible.

Cost, Hours, Location: €7, definitely not covered by Museum Pass, daily 10:00–2:00 in the morning, 72 boulevard de Clichy, Mo: Blanche.

Disappointments de Paris

Here are a few negatives to help you manage your limited time:

La Madeleine is a big, neoclassical church with a postcard facade and a postbox interior.

The **Bastille** is Paris' most famous non-sight. The square is there, but confused tourists look everywhere and can't find the famous prison of Revolutionary fame. The building's gone, and the square is good only as a jumping-off point for Promenade Plantée Park (see page 228).

Finally, much of the **Latin Quarter** is a frail shadow of its once bohemian self. The blocks nearest the river (across from Notre-Dame) are more Tunisian, Greek, and Woolworth's than old-time Paris. The neighborhood merits a wander, but you're better off focusing on the area around boulevard St. Germain and rue de Buci, and on the streets around the Maubert-Mutualité Métro stop.

Palace of Versailles

Every king's dream, Versailles was the residence of the French king and the cultural heartbeat of Europe for about 100 years—until the Revolution

of 1789 ended the notion that God deputized some people to rule for Him on Earth. Louis XIV spent half a year's income of Europe's richest country turning his dad's hunting lodge into a palace fit for a divine monarch. Louis XV and Louis XVI spent much of the 18th century gilding Louis XIV's lily. In 1837, about 50 years after the royal family was evicted, King Louis Philippe opened the palace as a museum. Europe's next best palaces are Versailles wannabes.

Palace Access: AE, AI, AL, AT, Level 1—Fully Accessible. For arrival by train or car from Paris, see page 239. From the palace entrance gate, proceed over cobblestones toward the palace (the building with the clock, facing the gate), which was Louis XIV's original hunting lodge. Continue toward the clock until you crest the gradual rise (which used to have steps, but has recently been made wheelchair-accessible). At the top of the rise is the only fully accessible entry, Entrance H (on your right). Consider using the nearby adapted toilet (see below) before entering. When you're ready to enter the palace, ring the bell at Entrance H. A wheelchair user (and a companion) may enter the palace free. Loaner wheelchairs are available. Once inside, an accessible lift will take you to the main floor. Wheelchair users have access only to this main level—but that's where the most interesting sights are anyway (described under "Palace," below). Accessibility details on the rest of the Versailles grounds are described below.

Accessible Toilet: The accessible toilet (€0.50) is near Entrance C, which is just opposite Entrance H. To reach this fully adapted toilet, go into the Entrance C tunnel and follow signs.

Cost: There are several different parts of the palace, each with a

Versailles

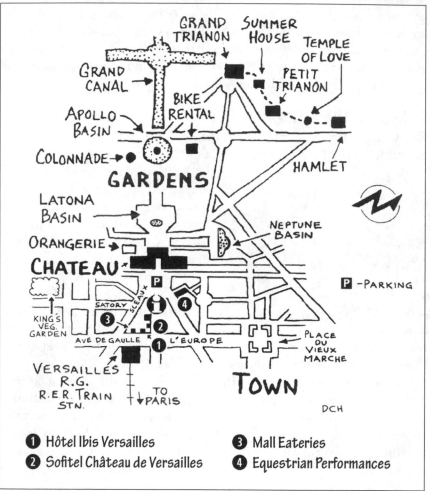

1. Hôtel Ibis Versailles
2. Sofitel Château de Versailles
3. Mall Eateries
4. Equestrian Performances

separate admission. The **State Apartments** are free for a wheelchair user and companion; otherwise €7.50 (€5.50 after 15:30, under 18 free, covered by Paris Museum Pass).

The **gardens** are free, except on weekends April–Sept, when the fountains blast and the price shoots up to €6 (see "Fountain Spectacles," below).

Entering the **Grand and Petit Trianon Palaces** costs €5 together (free for a wheelchair user and companion; covered by Paris Museum Pass).

There are several other, lesser sights: the **King's Private Apartments** (costs €4.50 for audioguide, or visit with guided tour, see "Guided Tours,"

> ## Versailles Renovation—2006 to 2010
>
> The château will be undergoing a massive reorganization to better accommodate its hordes of visitors in the next few years. Rather than the various entries and tours, one grand and user-friendly entry will eventually allow all visitors to enter and flow freely through everything in the palace and grounds for one simple (but higher) price. The palace attic, currently unused, will become a vast 19th-century French history museum. A path across the giant cobbles will enable people who use wheelchairs more comfortable access. And there will be many more toilets. The first step in this vision: Starting in 2006, the gardens are free (except during the fountain spectacles on spring and summer weekends).

below), the sumptuous **Opera House** (only by guided tour, see below), and the **Mesdames Apartments** (exclusively covered by One-Day Pass, see below).

A **One-Day Pass** covers your entrance to just about everything, gives you cut-the-line privileges, and provides audioguides throughout your visit. If you're seeing everything (and don't have a Paris Museum Pass), this can be a money-saver. The pass gives you priority access to the State Apartments, the King's Private Apartments, Mesdames Apartments, both Trianon Palaces, the shuttle train around the gardens, and Les Grand Eaux Musicales (see "Fountain Spectacles," below; note that these run only on summer weekends). If you buy this pass in Paris, it covers your train ride to and from Paris (€21, sold at Paris train stations, RER stations that serve Versailles, and at FNAC department stores). The same pass (without transportation) is sold for €20 at the palace.

Guided Tours: The in-depth guided tours of Versailles are not wheelchair-accessible (there are stairs and other barriers along the route). Slow walkers and non-disabled travelers may want to consider these tours (€5/60 min, €7/90 min, €9/2 hrs; note that you have to pay the €7.50 entry fee for the State Apartments separately from any tour). To take a guided tour, make reservations immediately upon arrival, as tours can sell out by 13:00 (first tours generally begin at 10:00; last tours usually depart at 15:00, but as late as 16:00). The tours can be long, but those with an appetite for the palace history enjoy them. Even if you decide not to pay for the tour up front, keep your ticket as proof you've paid for the palace entry—in case you decide to take a guided tour after you've wandered through Versailles by yourself.

Touring Versailles from A to M

Note that all of this information is subject to change over the next several years. But in all likelihood, the following is what you *should* find at Versailles:

Entrance A to State Apartments (without Pass): If you don't have a Paris Museum Pass or One-Day Pass, and you want to tour the palace on your own (with €4.50 audioguide), join the line at Entrance A. Enter the palace and take a one-way wander through the State Apartments from the King's Wing, through the Hall of Mirrors, and out via the Queen's and Nobles' Wing.

Entrance B-2 to State Apartments (for Passholders): This entrance is for people with a Paris Museum Pass or One-Day Pass who want to tour the palace on their own (with €4.50 audioguide). Note that those taking a guided tour can enter the State Apartments without a wait through this entrance.

Entrance C to King's Private Apartments (without One-Day Pass): If you lack a One-Day Pass, enter here to tour Louis XIV's private bedroom, other rooms, and the Hall of Mirrors, with the help of a dry but informative audioguide (€4.50 admission includes audioguide, not covered by Paris Museum Pass). The Sun King's bedroom and Hall of Mirrors are part of the State Apartments tour, so the King's Private Apartments offer nothing really different to the casual visitor than what you'll see on the main State Apartments tour.

Entrance C-2 to King's Private Apartments (for One-Day Passholders): Same as C, but for visitors with a One-Day Pass.

Entrance D to King's Private Apartments and Opera (with a Guided Tour): This is the place to book a guided tour (see page 233), and where you enter when it's time for your tour to begin. You'll visit the King's Private Apartments (Louis XV, Louis XVI, and Marie-Antoinette), the chapel, and the Opera.

Entrance H: If you use a wheelchair, you'll enter the château through here (described in detail under "Palace Access" on page 231).

Entrance M to Mesdames Apartments (for One-Day Passholders): This exhibit gives a look at the private apartments of the eight daughters of King Louis XV (exclusively for visitors with the One-Day Pass, includes 30-min audioguide). It's Versailles' least interesting sight, as the rooms are quite barren, there's little about their lives to actually see, and the commentary is mostly about the paintings hanging on the walls.

Versailles Entrances

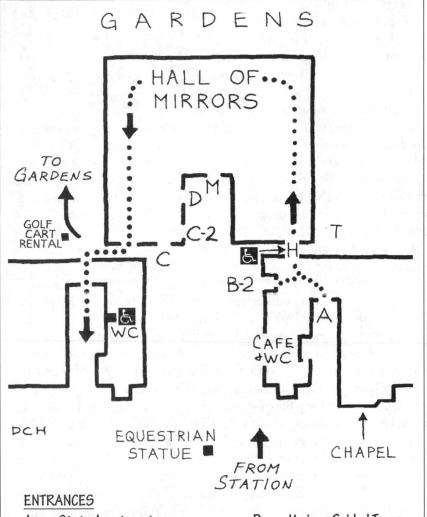

ENTRANCES

A   = State Apartments

B-2 = Museum Passholders' Entrance

C   = King's Private Apartments
      (with Audioguide)

C-2 = Passholders' Entrance
      for King's Private Apartments

D   = Various Guided Tours

H   = Disabled Entrance

T   = Tram

••• = Self-Guided Tour Route

Hours: The **palace** is open April–Oct Tue–Sun 9:00–18:30, Nov–March Tue–Sun 9:00–17:30, closed Mon. Last entry is 30 minutes before closing. The **Grand and Petit Trianon Palaces** open at noon. The **gardens** are open daily from 7:00 (8:00 in winter) to sunset (as late as 21:30 or as early as 17:30).

In summer, Versailles is especially crowded between 10:00 and 13:00, and all day Tue and Sun. Remember, the peasant mobs gave Marie-Antoinette a pain in the neck, too, so relax and let them eat cake. For fewer crowds, go early or late: Either arrive by 9:00 (when the palace opens, touring the palace first, then the gardens) or after 15:30 (you'll get a reduced entry ticket, but note that the last guided tours of the day generally depart at 15:00, though sometimes as late as 16:00). If you arrive midday, see the gardens first and the palace later, at 15:00. The gardens and palace are great late. On one of my visits, I was the only tourist in the Hall of Mirrors at 18:00...even on a Tuesday.

Information: A helpful TI (**AE, AI,** Level 1—Fully Accessible) is just past the Sofitel hotel between the RER station and the palace (April–Sept daily 9:00–19:00, Oct–March daily 9:00–18:00, tel. 01 39 24 88 88, www.chateauversailles.fr). You'll also find information booths inside the château (at Entrances A and B-2) and, during peak season, kiosks scattered around the courtyard. The useful *Versailles Orientation Guide* brochure explains your sightseeing options.

Palace: To tour the palace on your own, join the line at entrance A if you need to pay admission. Those with a Paris Museum Pass or One-Day Pass are allowed in through entrance B-2 without a wait. Wheelchair riders use Entrance H. (For the complete procedure for wheelchair users, see "Palace Access," above. For more entry options, see "Touring Versailles from A to M" sidebar.) Enter the palace and take a one-way roll or stroll through the State Apartments from the King's Wing, through the Hall

of Mirrors, and out via the Queen's and Nobles' Wing.

The Hall of Mirrors was the ultimate hall of the day—250 feet long, with 17 arched mirrors matching 17 windows with royal garden views, 24 gilded candelabra, eight busts of Roman emperors, and eight classical-style statues (7 are ancient originals). The ceiling is decorated with stories of Louis' triumphs. Imagine this place filled with silk gowns and powdered wigs, lit by thousands of candles. The mirrors—a luxury at the time—were a reflection of an era when aristocrats felt good about their looks and their fortunes. In another age altogether, this was the room in which the Treaty of Versailles was signed, ending World War I.

Before leaving at the end, work your way clockwise around the **Hall of Battles,** the long room filled with the great battles of France murals. If you don't have *Rick Steves' Paris,* the guidebook called *The Châteaux, The Gardens, and Trianon* gives a room-by-room rundown.

Getting Around the Gardens: It's a leisurely and lengthy roll or stroll from the palace, down to the canal, past the two Trianon palaces to the Hamlet.

The fast-looking, slow-moving **tram** for tired tourists leaves from behind the château (north side) and serves the Grand Canal and the Trianon palaces. It's designed for walkers, and is not wheelchair accessible (Level 3—Minimally Accessible). You can get on and off as you like (€5, free with One-Day Pass, 4/hr, 4 stops but not the Hamlet, commentary is nearly worthless). The accessible golf carts, described below, are better for people who use wheelchairs.

Gardens Access: The gardens are wheelchair-accessible (**AE, AI,** Level 1—Fully Accessible)—wheelchair riders can use the ramps (also used by tourist train and horse-drawn buggies) to access the dirt and small-stone pathways. The Grand Trianon is accessible, but the Petit Trianon is only minimally so. Parts of the grounds, such as the Hamlet, are accessed via a rough path that may be challenging for wheelchair users. There are several restaurants (most of them moderately accessible) and toilets (only one is accessible) sprinkled throughout the garden. The wheelchair-accessible toilet is located near the entrance of the Grand Trianon (see below).

Accessible Golf Carts: There are no accessible taxis in Versailles, but there are golf carts for use on the palace grounds (€28/hr). Three of the golf carts are adapted to be accessible (hold up to 4 people plus 1 wheelchair). These carts can effectively travel over 80 percent the immense grounds outside the palace. You can rent them at the Orangerie side of the palace (go through Entrance C tunnel and turn right).

Palace Gardens: The gardens offer a world of royal amusements. Outside the palace is *l'orangerie.* Louis, the only person who could grow oranges in Paris, had a mobile orange grove that could be wheeled in and out of his greenhouses according to the weather. A promenade leads from the palace to the Grand Canal, an artificial lake that, in Louis'

day, was a mini-sea with nine ships, including a 32-cannon warship. France's royalty used to float up and down the canal in Venetian gondolas.

While Louis cleverly used palace life at Versailles to "domesticate" his nobility, turning otherwise meddlesome nobles into groveling socialites, all this pomp and ceremony hampered the royal family as well. For an escape from the public life at Versailles, they built more intimate palaces as retreats in their garden. Before the Revolution, there was plenty of space to retreat—the grounds were enclosed by a 25-mile-long fence.

The beautifully restored **Grand Trianon Palace** (**AE, AI,** Level 1—Fully Accessible) is as sumptuous as the main palace, but much smaller. With its pastel-pink colonnade and more human scale, this is a place you'd like to call home. The nearby **Petit Trianon** (**AE, AI+A,** Level 3—Minimally Accessible), which has a fine neoclassical exterior and an interior that can be skipped, was Marie-Antoinette's favorite residence (see "Cost" and "Hours," above).

You can almost see princesses bobbing gaily in the branches as you move through the enchanting forest, past the white marble temple of love (1778) to the queen's fake-peasant **Hamlet** (*le Hameau;* interior not tourable, exterior visitable only via a gravelly, sandy path that may be difficult for wheelchair users). Palace life really got to Marie-Antoinette. Sort of a back-to-basics queen, she retreated further and further from her blue-blooded reality. Her happiest days were spent at the Hamlet, under a bonnet, tending her perfumed sheep and her manicured gardens in a thatch-happy wonderland.

Fountain Spectacles: On spring and summer weekends, classical music fills the king's backyard, and the garden's fountains are in full squirt (April–Sept Sat–Sun 10:30–12:00 & 15:00–16:30, finale 16:50–17:00). On these "spray days," the gardens cost €6 (not covered by Paris Museum Pass, ask for a map of fountains). Louis had his engineers literally reroute a river to fuel these fountains. Even by today's standards, they are impressive. Pick up the helpful *Les Grandes Eaux Musicales* brochure at any information booth. Also ask about the various impressive evening spectacles (Sat in July–Aug).

Equestrian Performances: The Equestrian Performance Academy (Academie du Spectacle Equestre) has brought the art of horseback riding back to Versailles. You can watch its rigorous training sessions every morning except Mon and Fri (€7, Tue and Fri–Sun at 10:00 and 11:00).

The weekend spectacle (Sat and Sun at 14:30, €15, 75 min) features the same students parading their stuff to music without instructor interruptions. The stables (Grande Ecurie)—where you can buy tickets—are across the square from the château, next to the Poste (tel. 01 39 02 07 14, www.acadequestre.fr).

Cafés: The cafeteria and WCs are next to Entrance A (stairs make them Level 4—Not Accessible). You'll find a sandwich kiosk and a decent restaurant (**AE+A, AI,** Level 2—Moderately Accessible) at the canal in the garden. For more recommendations, see "Eating in Versailles," below. A handy McDonald's is immediately across from the train station (fully accessible toilet without crowds).

Getting There: From downtown Paris, take the RER-C train from any of these RER stops: Gare d'Austerlitz, St. Michel, Musée d'Orsay, Invalides, Pont de l'Alma, and Champ de Mars (€6 round-trip, covered by railpass—show pass at SNCF ticket window and get a *contremarque de passage*, which you'll keep until you exit the station, 30 min one-way). If you use a wheelchair, the Invalides station offers the best access (arrive at the station early and ask for assistance at the ticket counter—they will prepare an elevator for your use). Any train whose name starts with a V (e.g., "Vick") goes to Versailles; don't board other trains. Get off at the last stop (Versailles R.G., or "Rive Gauche"—not Versailles C.H., which is farther from the palace), and exit through the turnstiles by inserting your ticket. If you use a wheelchair, tell them that you'll need a ramp to get of the train once at Versailles, so they can call ahead and make arrangements. Once you arrive, leave the train using this ramp and find the ramp that leads outside (on the right side of the station as you leave the platform). This ramp deposits you onto avenue du Général de Gaulle. (Across the street is a McDonald's with a fully accessible toilet, as well as other restaurants—described below.) From this train station, it's about a third of a mile to the palace: By wheelchair or by foot, turn right as you leave the station and go to the first intersection, where you'll turn left down avenue de Paris. Follow this accessible boulevard directly to the palace.

When returning to Paris from Versailles, look through the windows past the turnstiles for the departure board. Any train leaving Versailles serves all downtown Paris RER stops on the C line (they're marked on the schedule as stopping at *"toutes les gares jusqu'à Austerlitz,"* meaning "all stations up to Austerlitz").

Taxis for the 30-minute ride between Versailles and Paris cost about €30 one-way (like all Paris taxis, most require you to make a transfer into the car so the driver can fold your wheelchair and place it in the trunk; for a fully wheelchair accessible minibus option that costs more, see page 189).

To reach Versailles from Paris by **car,** get on the *périphérique* freeway that circles Paris, and take the toll-free A13 autoroute toward Rouen. Follow signs into Versailles, then look for *château* signs and park in the huge pay lot in front of the palace (7 spaces are reserved for visitors with limited mobility). The drive takes about 30 minutes one-way.

Town of Versailles: After the palace closes and the tourists go, the prosperous, wholesome town of Versailles feels a long way from Paris. The central market thrives on place du Marché on Sunday, Tuesday, and Friday until 13:00. Across the street from the RER station is a cluster of restaurants, shops, Internet cafés, and hotels (described below). Consider the wisdom of picking up or dropping your rental car in Versailles rather than in Paris. In Versailles, the Hertz and Avis offices are at Gare des Chantiers (Versailles C.H., served by Paris' Montparnasse station).

Sleeping in Versailles: Versailles, with easy, safe parking and accessible, reasonably priced hotels, can be a good overnight stop. Park in the château's main lot while looking for a hotel, or leave your car there overnight (free 19:30–8:00). Get a map of Versailles at your hotel or at the TI. **Hôtel Ibis Versailles (AE, AI, AL, AR, AB, ♥,** Level 1—Fully Accessible) offers fair value and modern comfort, with 85 air-conditioned rooms, but no character. Packed with young people and business travelers, this hotel features an accessible restaurant and coffee bar. Reserve ahead for one of its three adapted rooms, which have roll-in showers (Db-€60 Fri–Sun, or €90 Mon–Thu, extra bed-€10, breakfast-€6.50, across from RER station, 3 blocks from the palace at 4 avenue du Général de Gaulle, tel. 01 39 53 03 30, fax 01 39 50 06 31, h1409@accor-hotels .com). **Sofitel Château de Versailles (AE, AI, AL, AR, AB+A,** Level 1—Fully Accessible) has a great location near shops and restaurants and just two blocks from the palace. It has three adapted rooms with suitable bathrooms (Db-€320–390, 2 bis avenue de Paris, tel. 01 39 07 46 46, h1300@accor-hotels.com).

Eating in Versailles: All of these eateries are fully accessible (**AE, AI, AT,** Level 1). You'll find them in a little accessible mall on avenue du Général de Gaulle, next to McDonald's and across from the train station: **A la Coiffe Bretonne** is your best bet for crêpes in a friendly, cozy, countryside setting (daily 12:00–14:30 & 19:00–22:30, tel. 01 30 21 78 22). **Class' Croute** offers sandwiches, salads, and desserts (daily 10:00–18:00, tel. 01 39 07 26 56). **Chez César Les Manages** is a cozy sit-down pizzeria (daily 12:00-24:00, tel. 01 39 53 02 29). To surf the Web nearby, try the fully accessible **Internet@ (AE, AI, AT,** Level 1; €4/3hrs, daily 9:00–20:00, tel. 01 39 53 30 30).

SHOPPING

Even staunch anti-shoppers may be tempted to partake in chic Paris. Exploring the elegant and outrageous boutiques provides a break from the heavy halls of the Louvre, and, if you approach it right, a little cultural enlightenment. Here are some tips for avoiding *faux pas* and making the most of the experience.

French Etiquette: Before you enter a Parisian store, remember the following points.

- In small stores, always greet the clerk by saying "*Bonjour,*" plus the appropriate title (*Madame, Mademoiselle,* or *Monsieur*). When leaving, say, *"Au revoir, Madame/Mademoiselle/Monsieur."*
- The customer is not always right. In fact, figure the clerk is doing you a favor by waiting on you.
- Except in department stores, it's not normal for the customer to handle clothing. Ask first.
- Observe French shoppers. Then imitate.

Department Stores: Like cafés, department stores were invented here (surprisingly, not in America). Parisian department stores, monuments to a more relaxed and elegant era, begin with their spectacular perfume sections. Helpful information desks are usually nearby (pick up the handy store floor plan in English). Most stores have a good selection of souvenirs and toys at fair prices and reasonable restaurants; some have great view terraces. Choose from these great Parisian department stores: Galeries Lafayette (**AE, AI, AL, AT,** Level 1—Fully Accessible; behind old Opéra Garnier, Mo: Opéra), Printemps (**AE, AI, AL, AT,** Level 1—Fully Accessible; next-door to Galeries Lafayette), and Bon Marché (**AE, AI, AL, AT,** Level 1—Fully Accessible; Mo: Sèvres-Babylone).

Boutiques: I enjoy window-shopping, pausing at cafés, and observing the rhythm of neighborhood life. While the shops are more intimate, sales clerks are more formal—mind your manners.

Here are four very different areas to explore. Streets and sidewalks are accessible, but some of the specific shops are not. If a place isn't accessible, just savor the window-shopping (or, as the French say, "window-licking").

A roll or stroll from Sèvres-Babylone to St. Sulpice allows you to sample smart, classic clothing boutiques while enjoying one of Paris' prettier neighborhoods—for sustenance along the way, there's La Maison du Chocolat at 19 rue de Sèvres, selling handmade chocolates in exquisitely wrapped boxes.

The ritzy streets connecting place de la Madeleine and place Vendôme form a miracle mile of gourmet food shops, jewelry stores, four-star hotels, perfumeries, and exclusive clothing boutiques. Fauchon (Level 4—Not Accessible), on place de la Madeleine, is a bastion of over-the-top food products, hawking €7,000 bottles of Cognac (who buys this stuff?). Hédiard (**AE, AI, AT, ♥,** Level 1—Fully Accessible), across the square from Fauchon at #21, is an older, more appealing, and accessible gourmet food shop. Next door, La Maison des Truffes sells black mushrooms for about €180 a pound, and white truffles from Italy for €2,500 a pound.

For more eclectic, avant-garde stores, peruse the artsy shops between the Pompidou Center and place des Vosges in the Marais (along rue Ste. Croix de la Bretonnerie and rue des Rosiers).

For a contemporary, more casual, and less frenetic shopping experience, and to see Paris' latest urban renewal project, visit Bercy Village, a once thriving wine warehouse district that has been transformed into an outdoor shopping mall (Mo: Cour St. Emilion).

Flea Markets: Paris hosts several sprawling weekend flea markets (*marché aux puces,* mar-shay oh poos; literally translated, since *puce* is French for flea). While these markets are often moderately accessible, the crowds and tight aisles can make them unappealing to wheelchair users. These oversized garage sales date back to the Middle Ages, when middlemen would sell old, flea-infested clothes and discarded possessions of the wealthy at bargain prices to eager peasants. Today, some travelers find them claustrophobic, crowded, monster versions of those back home, though others find their French diamonds-in-the-rough and return happy.

The Puces St. Ouen (poos sahn-wahn) is the biggest and oldest of them all, with more than 2,000 vendors selling everything from flamingos to faucets (Sat 9:00–18:00, Sun 10:00–18:00, Mon 11:00–17:00, closed Tue–Fri, pretty dead the first 2 weeks of Aug, Mo: Porte de Clingancourt, tel. 01 58 61 22 90, www.st-ouen-tourisme.com and www.parispuces.com).

Street Markets: Several traffic-free street markets overflow with flowers, produce, fish vendors, and butchers, illustrating how most Parisians shopped before there were supermarkets and department stores. While some areas of these markets might be inaccessible, wheelchair users can generally find their way around them well enough. Good market streets include the rue Cler (Mo: Ecole Militaire), rue Montorgueil (Mo: Etienne Marcel), rue Mouffetard (Mo: Cardinal Lemoine or Censier-Daubenton), and rue Daguerre (Mo: Denfert-Rochereau). Browse these markets to collect a classy picnic (open daily except Sun afternoons and Mon, also closed for lunch 13:00–15:00).

Souvenir Shops: Avoid souvenir carts in front of famous monuments. Prices and selection are better in shops and department stores. The riverfront stalls near Notre-Dame sell a variety of used books, magazines, and tourist paraphernalia in the most romantic setting.

Whether you indulge in a new wardrobe, an artsy poster, or just one luscious pastry, you'll find that a shopping excursion provides a priceless slice of Parisian life.

NIGHTLIFE

Paris is brilliant after dark. Save energy from your day's sightseeing and get out at night. There's nothing like experiencing the City of Light when it's lit up. If a **Seine River cruise** sounds appealing, check out "Tours," on page 196.

Pariscope magazine (see "Tourist Information," page 182), offers a complete weekly listing of music, cinema, theater, opera, and other special events. *Paris Voice* newspaper, in English, has a monthly review of Paris entertainment (available at any English-language bookstore, French-American establishments, or the American Church, www.parisvoice.com).

Music

Classical Concerts—For classical music on any night, consult *Pariscope* magazine; the "Musique" section under "Concerts Classiques" lists concerts (both free and for a fee). Look for posters at tourist-oriented churches. From March through November, several churches regularly host concerts, including St. Sulpice (**AE, AI, AT,** Level 1—Fully Accessible, described on page 217), St. Germain-des-Prés (**AE+A, AI,** Level 2—Moderately Accessible, four gentle steps to get in the front door), and Sainte-Chapelle (Level 4—Not Accessible). Look also for daytime concerts in parks, such as the Luxembourg Garden (**AE, AI,** Level 1—Fully Accessible). Even the Galeries Lafayette department store offers concerts (**AE, AI, AL, AT,** Level 1—Fully Accessible). Many concerts are free *(entrée libre)*, such as the Sunday atelier concert sponsored by the American Church (Level 4—Not Accessible; Sept–May at 17:00 or 18:00 but not every week, 65 quai d'Orsay, Mo: Invalides, RER: Pont de l'Alma, tel. 01 40 62 05 00).

Opera—Paris is home to two well-respected opera venues. The Opéra Bastille (**AE, AI, AL,** Level 1—Fully Accessible) is the massive modern opera house that dominates place de la Bastille. Come here for state-of-the-art special effects and modern interpretations of classic ballets and operas. In the spirit of this everyman's opera, unsold seats are available at a big discount to seniors and students 15 minutes before the show (Mo: Bastille, tel. 01 43 43 96 96). The Opéra Garnier (**AE, AI, AL,** Level 1—Fully Accessible), Paris' first opera house, hosts opera and ballet performances. Come here for less expensive tickets and grand belle époque decor (ramp entry on rue Scribe and special seats accessible by lift for wheelchair users; Mo: Opéra, tel. 01 44 73 13 99). For tickets, call 01 44 73 13 00 (wheelchair users call 01 40 01 18 50), go to the opera ticket offices (open 11:00–18:00), or—best—reserve on the Web at www.opera-de-paris.fr (for both opera houses).

After-Dark Bus Tours

Several companies offer evening tours of Paris. I've described a reliable one below. These trips are sold through your hotel (brochures in lobby) or directly at the offices listed below. You save no money by buying direct.

Paris Illumination Tours (**AE+A,** Level 2—Moderately Accessible, must be able to step up into the bus), run by Paris Vision, connect all the great illuminated sights of Paris with a 100-minute bus tour in 12 languages. The double-decker buses have huge windows, but the most desirable front seats are reserved for customers who've bought tickets for the overrated Moulin Rouge. Left-side seats are marginally better. Visibility is fine in the rain.

You'll board with a United Nations of tourists, get a set of headphones, dial up your language, and listen to a tape-recorded spiel (which is interesting, but includes an annoyingly bright TV screen and a pitch for the other, more expensive excursions). Uninspired as it is, the ride provides an entertaining first-night overview of the city at its floodlit and scenic best. Bring your city map to stay oriented as you go. You're always on the bus, but the driver slows for photos at viewpoints (adults-€24, kids under 11 ride free, departures 19:00–22:00 depending on time of year, usually April–Oct only, reserve 1 day in advance, departs from Paris Vision office at 214 rue de Rivoli, across the street from Mo: Tuileries, tel. 01 42 60 30 01, fax 01 42 86 95 36, www.parisvision.com).

SLEEPING

I've recommended hotels in various areas of Paris. Each area has its own characteristics and charms (which I've described). Reserve ahead for Paris—the sooner, the better.

Conventions clog Paris in September (worst), October, May, and June (very tough). In August, when Paris is quiet, some hotels offer lower rates to fill their rooms (if you're planning to visit Paris in the summer, the extra expense of an air-conditioned room can be money well spent). For advice on booking rooms, see "Making Reservations" in this book's Introduction.

Old, characteristic, budget Parisian hotels have always been cramped. Retrofitted with elevators, toilets, and private showers (as most are today), they are even more cramped. Even three-star hotel rooms are small and often not worth the extra expense in Paris. Some hotels include the hotel tax (*taxe du séjour*, about €1 per person per day), though most will add this to your bill.

Recommended hotels have an elevator, unless otherwise noted. Quad rooms usually have two double beds. Because rooms with double beds and showers are cheaper than rooms with twin beds and baths, room prices vary within each hotel.

Continental breakfasts run about €6–9, buffet breakfasts (baked goods, cereal, yogurt, and fruit) cost about €8–14. Café or picnic breakfasts are cheaper, but hotels usually give unlimited coffee.

Get advice from your hotel for safe parking (consider long-term

---

Sleep Code

(€1 = about $1.20, country code: 33)
S = Single, **D** = Double/Twin, **T** = Triple, **Q** = Quad, **b** = bathroom, **s** = shower only, ***** = French hotel rating system (0–4 stars). Unless otherwise noted, credit cards are accepted and English is spoken (in fact, hotels with 2 or more stars are required to have an English-speaking staff).

parking at either airport—Orly is closer—and a taxi in). Garages are plentiful (€20–25/day, with special rates through some hotels). Meters are free in August. Self-serve launderettes are common; ask your hotelier for the nearest one (*"Où est un laverie automatique?"*, ooh ay uh lah-vay-ree auto-mah-teek).

Rue Cler
(7th *arrondissement*, Mo: Ecole Militaire, La Tour-Maubourg, or Invalides)
Lined with open-air produce stands six days a week, rue Cler is a safe, tidy, village-like pedestrian street. It's so French that when I step out of my hotel in the morning, I feel like I must have been a poodle in a previous life. How such coziness lodged itself between the high-powered government district and the wealthy Eiffel Tower and Invalides areas, I'll never know. This is a neighborhood of wide, tree-lined boulevards, stately apartment buildings, and lots of Americans. The American Church, American Library, American University, and many of my readers call this area home. People with disabilities will find a warm welcome and more ❤'s per square block than anywhere else in Paris. The neighborhood streets are accessible for people using wheelchairs. Many of the stores are fully accessible, while others may have an entry step.

Hotels here are relatively spacious and a good value, considering the elegance of the neighborhood and the higher prices of the more cramped hotels in other central areas. For sightseeing, you're very close to the Eiffel Tower, Napoleon's Tomb, the Seine River, and the Orsay and Rodin museums. The fully accessible Invalides Métro/RER station (Level 1, has elevator) is also nearby.

Become a local at a rue Cler café for breakfast, or join the afternoon crowd for *une bière pression* (a draft beer). On rue Cler, you can eat and browse your way through a street full of pastry shops, delis, cheese shops, and colorful outdoor produce stalls. Afternoon *boules* (outdoor bowling) on the Esplanade des Invalides is a relaxing spectator sport (look for the dirt area to the upper right as you face Les Invalides; see sidebar on page 249). The manicured gardens behind the golden dome of Napoleon's Tomb are free, peaceful, and filled with flowers (at southwest corner of grounds, close at about 19:00). A fully accessible esplanade leads you through the grounds.

While hardly a happening nightlife spot, rue Cler offers many low-impact after-dark activities. Take an evening roll or stroll above the river through the parkway between pont de l'Alma and pont des Invalides. For an after-dinner cruise on the Seine, it's a short roll or stroll to the river and the Bateaux-Mouches (see page 196). Or go into Champ de Mars park to admire the glowing Eiffel Tower. For more ideas on Paris after hours, see "Nightlife" on page 243.

Tourist Information: Your neighborhood TI is at the Eiffel Tower (**AE, AI,** Level 1—Fully Accessible; May–Sept daily 11:00–18:42, closed Oct–April, all-Paris TI tel. 08 92 68 30 00).

American Church: The American Church and Franco-American Center (Level 4—Not Accessible, fifteen 6" steps to enter) is the community center for Americans living in Paris. They offer interdenominational worship services (every Sun at 11:00) and occasional concerts (most Sun at 17:00 or 18:00 Sept–May—but not every week), and distribute the useful *Paris Voice* and *France-U.S.A. Contacts* (reception open Mon–Sat 9:30–13:00 & 14:00–22:30, Sun 9:00–14:00 & 15:00–19:00, 65 quai d'Orsay, Mo: Invalides, tel. 01 40 62 05 00, www.acparis.org).

Services: There's a **post office** (**AE, AI,** Level 1—Fully Accessible) at the end of rue Cler on avenue de la Motte-Picquet, and a handy **SNCF train office** at 78 rue St. Dominique (**AE, AI,** Level 1—Fully Accessible; Mon–Sat 8:30–19:30, closed Sun).

Laundry: Laveris Eclat (**AE+A, AI,** Level 2—Moderately Accessible) is a squeaky clean, modern, and roomy spot with one 3" entry step (daily 7:00–22:00, 3 rue Augereau).

Shopping: For groceries, two nearby locations of Le Marché Franprix (109 avenue de la Bourdonnais and 9 rue du Champ de Mars) are both Level 1—Fully Accessible. **Rue St. Dominique** is the area's boutique-browsing street.

Internet Access: Two Internet cafés compete in this neighborhood: **Com Avenue** (**AE, AI,** Level 1—Fully Accessible) is best (€5/hr, shareable and multi-use accounts, Mon–Sat 10:00–20:00, closed Sun, 24 rue du Champ de Mars); **Cyber World Café** (**AE+A, AI,** Level 2—Moderately Accessible, one 8" doorstep) is more expensive and less accessible, but open later (Mon–Sat 12:00–22:00, Sun 12:00–20:00, 20 rue de l'Exposition, tel. 01 53 59 96 54).

In the Heart of Rue Cler

Many of my readers stay in the rue Cler neighborhood. If you want to disappear into Paris, choose a hotel elsewhere.

Level 1—Fully Accessible

Hôtel Prince** (**AE, AI, AL, AR, AB, ❤**), across avenue Bosquet from the Ecole Militaire Métro stop, has a spartan lobby and good rooms at very reasonable rates, considering they're air-conditioned (Sb–€70,

Rue Cler Hotels

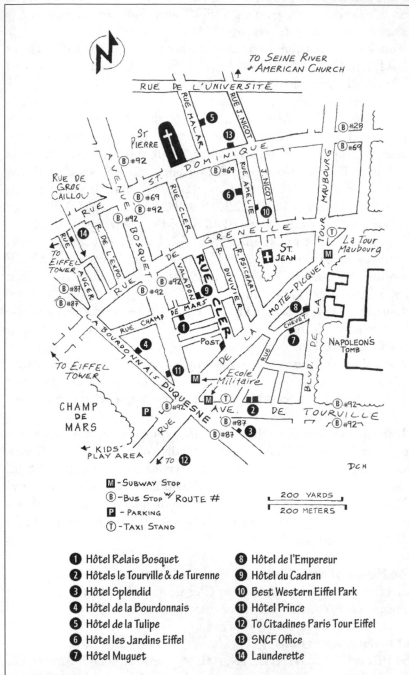

M – SUBWAY STOP
B – BUS STOP ʷ/ ROUTE #
P – PARKING
T – TAXI STAND

200 YARDS
200 METERS

DCH

❶ Hôtel Relais Bosquet
❷ Hôtels le Tourville & de Turenne
❸ Hôtel Splendid
❹ Hôtel de la Bourdonnais
❺ Hôtel de la Tulipe
❻ Hôtel les Jardins Eiffel
❼ Hôtel Muguet

❽ Hôtel de l'Empereur
❾ Hôtel du Cadran
❿ Best Western Eiffel Park
⓫ Hôtel Prince
⓬ To Citadines Paris Tour Eiffel
⓭ SNCF Office
⓮ Launderette

The Rules of *Boules*

Throughout Paris—and particularly on Les Invalides' big "front lawn," near the rue Cler neighborhood—you'll see citizens playing *boules*.

Each player starts with three iron balls, with the object of getting them close to the target, a small wooden ball called a *cochonnet*. The first player tosses the *cochonnet* about 30 feet, then throws the first of his iron balls near the target. The next player takes a turn. As soon as a player's ball is closest, it's the other guy's turn. Once all balls have been thrown, the score is tallied—the player with the closest ball gets one point for each ball closer to the target than his opponent's. The loser gets zero. Games are generally to 15 points.

A regulation *boules* field is 10 feet by 43 feet, but the game is played everywhere—just scratch a throwing circle in the sand, toss the *cochonnet*, and you're off. Strategists can try to knock the opponent's balls out of position, knock the *cochonnet* itself out of position, or guard their best ball with the other two.

Db with shower-€89, Db with tub-€107, Tb-€115, 66 avenue Bosquet, tel. 01 47 05 40 90, fax 01 47 53 06 62, www.hotel-paris-prince.com). In accessible rooms, the bathroom is fully adapted with bars, including the tub.

Level 2—Moderately Accessible
Hôtel Relais Bosquet*** (**AE+A, AI, AR, AB+A**) is modern, spacious, and a bit upscale, with snazzy, air-conditioned rooms, electric darkness blinds, and big beds. Gerard and his friendly staff are politely formal (standard Db-€150, spacious Db-€170, ask about occasional promotional rates and off-season discounts, claim free Rick Steves breakfast at time of booking, extra bed-€20, family suites, free Internet in lobby, parking-€14, 19 rue du Champ de Mars, tel. 01 47 05 25 45, fax 01 45 55 08 24, www.relaisbosquet.com, hotel@relaisbosquet.com). The entryway has one 6" step. There is one large ground floor room that is suitable for a wheelchair user (large entry and bathroom, but no grab bars for toilet or bath).

Hôtel du Cadran*** (**AE+A, AI, AR+A**), while perfectly located and with a nice lobby, lacks charm in its tight, narrow, and way-overpriced rooms (Db-€170-180, air-con, 10 rue du Champ de Mars, tel. 01 40 62 67 00, fax 01 40 62 67 13, www.hotelducadran.com). There is one 6" entry step and a ground-floor room designated for wheelchair users (but it has a narrow entryway and lacks a wheelchair-accessible bathroom).

Near Rue Cler

The following listings are within a few blocks of rue Cler. The first listing is on the other side of the Champ de Mars park, near Métro stop La Motte-Picquet-Grenelle; the rest are near Métro stop Ecole Militaire or RER: Pont de l'Alma.

Level 1—Fully Accessible

Citadines Paris Tour Eiffel*** (AE, AI, AR, AB, AL) is an apartment-hotel offering two adapted rooms in the sophisticated Grenelle district close to cafés, brasseries, and antique shops (Db-€152, 132 boulevard de Grenelle, Mo: La Motte-Picquet-Grenelle, tel. 01 53 95 60 00, www.citadines.com). The Citadines chain has 12 different apartment-hotel locations in Paris, each with at least one fully adapted room. For details, check www.citadines.com or call 01 41 05 79 05.

Level 2—Moderately Accessible

Hôtel de la Tulipe*** (AE+A, AI+A, AR, AB+A), three blocks from rue Cler toward the river, is unique. The 20 smallish but artistically decorated rooms—each one different—come with little, stylish bathrooms and surround a seductive wood-beamed lounge and a peaceful, leafy courtyard (Db-€140, Tb-€160, 2-room suite for up to 5 people-€250, no elevator or air-con, 33 rue Malar, tel. 01 45 51 67 21, fax 01 47 53 96 37, www.paris-hotel-tulipe.com, friendly Bernhard behind the desk). There is one 2" entry step. One more interior 4" step leads to a large, open courtyard-access room that has worked for wheelchair users with assistance in the past (large bathroom is suitable, but not adapted).

Hôtel de la Bourdonnais*** (AE, AI, AL, AR+A, AB+A, ❤) is a *très* Parisian place, mixing Old World elegance with professional service, comfortable and generous public spaces, and mostly spacious, traditionally decorated rooms (Sb-€125, Db-€155, Tb-€175, Qb-€195, air-con, Internet in lobby, 111 avenue de la Bourdonnais, tel. 01 47 05 45 42, fax 01 45 55 75 54, www.hotellabourdonnais.fr, hlb@hotellabourdonnais.fr). The staff is welcoming, and the entry and elevator are fully accessible. There are no specially adapted wheelchair-accessible rooms or bathrooms, but the doors are wide and the rooms are large.

Hôtel de Turenne** (AE, AI, AL) is simple and well-located, with the cheapest air-conditioned rooms I found. Even though the halls are depressing, the lobby is smoky, and the rooms could use some work, the price is right. There are five truly single rooms and several connecting rooms good for families (one 2" entry step, accessible elevator but no accessible rooms; Sb-€64, Db-€74–86, Tb-€104, extra bed-€10, 20

avenue de Tourville, tel. 01 47 05 99 92, fax 01 45 56 06 04, hotel.turenne
.paris7@wanadoo.fr).

Hôtel Splendid*** (AE+A, AI, AR, AB+A, ♥) is Art Deco modern, professional, and worth your while if you land one of its three suites with great Eiffel Tower views. Sixth-floor rooms have small terraces and sideways tower views. All of the rooms seem a bit pricey, as they are not air-conditioned (Db-€170, Db with balcony and view-€180, Db suite-€230, ask about occasional promotional rates, 29 avenue de Tourville, tel. 01 45 51 24 77, fax 01 44 18 94 60, splendid@club-internet.fr). This hotel has hosted wheelchair users in the past and welcomes persons with disabilities. There's one 1" entry step and two large rooms for wheelchair users (grab bars by the toilet, but tub is not accessible).

Hôtel le Tourville**** (AE, AI, AL, AR, AB+A) is the classiest and most expensive of my rue Cler listings. It's surprisingly intimate for its four stars—from its designer lobby and vaulted breakfast area to its pretty but small pastel rooms (fully accessible except for the shower; small standard Db-€170, superior Db-€220, Db with private terrace-€240, junior suite for 3-4 people-€310–330, air-con, 16 avenue de Tourville, tel. 01 47 05 62 62, fax 01 47 05 43 90, www.hoteltourville.com, hotel@tourville.com).

Near La Tour-Maubourg Métro Stop
The next four listings are within two blocks of the intersection of avenue de la Motte-Picquet and boulevard de la Tour-Maubourg.

Level 1—Fully Accessible
Hôtel les Jardins Eiffel*** (AE, AI, AL, AR, AB, ♥), on a quiet street, feels like a modern motel, but earns its three stars with professional service, its own parking garage (€21/day), and a spacious lobby. The 80 rooms—some with private balconies (ask for a room *avec petit balcon*)— are comfortable, if unimaginative (Sb-€136, Db-€157, extra bed-€30 or free for a child up to 10, check online for occasional deals, air-con, Internet in lobby, 8 rue Amélie, tel. 01 47 05 46 21, fax 01 45 55 28 08, www.hoteljardinseiffel.com, paris@hoteljardinseiffel.com). Wheelchair users can avoid the single 2" entry step and access the hotel's elevator in the garage. The hotel has two wheelchair-accessible rooms (including adapted toilets and bathtubs with grab bars; they will place bench in tub). They host many wheelchair-using guests and are very welcoming.

Level 2—Moderately Accessible
Hôtel Muguet** (AE+A, AI, AR, ♥), a peaceful, stylish, and immaculate refuge, gives you three-star comfort for a two-star price. This

delightful place offers 43 tasteful, air-conditioned rooms, a greenhouse lounge, and a small garden courtyard. The hands-on owner, Catherine, gives her guests a restful and secure home in Paris (Sb in a double room-€95, Db with one big bed-€110, twin Db-€125, big Db with view and balcony-€165, Tb-€160, 11 rue Chevert, tel. 01 47 05 05 93, fax 01 45 50 25 37, www.hotelmuguet.com, muguet@wanadoo.fr). There are two 8" steps at the entry and no specially adapted rooms. Three large rooms are designated for wheelchair users (but lack fully accessible bathrooms).

Hôtel de l'Empereur** **(AE, AI, AL, AB+A)** lacks intimacy, but it's roomy and a fair value. Its 38 pleasant rooms come with real wood furniture and all the comforts except air-conditioning. Streetside rooms have views, but some noise; fifth-floor rooms have small balconies and Napoleonic views (Db-€90, Tb-€120, Qb-€140, 2 rue Chevert, tel. 01 45 55 88 02, fax 01 45 51 88 54, www.hotelempereur.com, contact@hotelempereur.com). The entry and elevator are accessible, and the bathrooms are suitable, but there are no adapted rooms. Even so, the hotel has accommodated wheelchair users in the past.

Best Western Eiffel Park*** **(AE, AI, AL, AR, AB+A)** is a dead-quiet, relatively modern concrete business hotel with all the comforts, a friendly staff, 36 pleasant if unexceptional rooms, and a rooftop terrace. (Db-€170–185, check online for promotional rates, 17 bis rue Amélie, tel. 01 45 55 10 01, fax 01 47 05 28, 68, www.eiffelpark.com, reservation@eiffelpark.com). By Paris standards, this place is about as accessible as it gets. The only less than fully accessible feature is the big bathroom (suitable, but not adapted).

In the Marais, near the Pompidou Center
(4th *arrondissement*)

Those interested in a more Soho/Greenwich Village locale should make the Marais their Parisian home. Not long ago, it was a forgotten Parisian backwater, but now the Marais is one of Paris' most popular residential, tourist, and shopping areas. This is jumbled, medieval Paris at its finest, where classy stone mansions sit alongside trendy bars, antique shops, and fashion-conscious boutiques. The streets are a fascinating parade of artists, students, tourists, immigrants, and babies in strollers munching baguettes. The Marais is also known as a hub of the Parisian gay and lesbian scene. This area is *sans* doubt livelier (and louder) than the rue Cler area.

In the Marais, you have these sights close at hand: Picasso Museum, Carnavalet Museum, Victor Hugo's House, the Jewish Art and History Museum, and the Pompidou Center. You're also near Paris' two

Marais Hotels and Restaurants

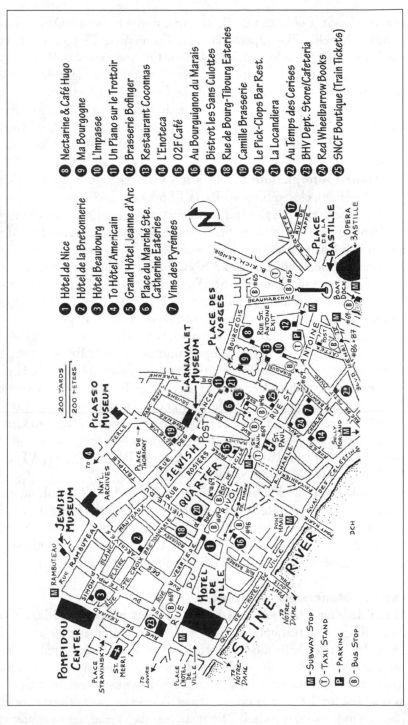

1. Hôtel de Nice
2. Hôtel de la Bretonnerie
3. Hôtel Beaubourg
4. To Hôtel Americain
5. Grand Hôtel Jeanne d'Arc
6. Place du Marché Ste. Catherine Eateries
7. Vins des Pyrénées
8. Nectarine & Café Hugo
9. Ma Bourgogne
10. L'Impasse
11. Un Piano sur le Trottoir
12. Brasserie Bofinger
13. Restaurant Coconnas
14. L'Enoteca
15. O2F Café
16. Au Bourguignon du Marais
17. Bistrot les Sans Culottes
18. Rue de Bourg-Tibourg Eateries
19. Camille Brasserie
20. Le Pick-Clops Bar Rest.
21. La Locandiera
22. Au Temps des Cerises
23. BHV Dept. Store/Cafeteria
24. Red Wheelbarrow Books
25. SNCF Boutique (Train Tickets)

M – Subway Stop
T – Taxi Stand
P – Parking
B – Bus Stop

islands (Ile St. Louis and Ile de la Cité), home to Notre-Dame and the Sainte-Chapelle. The Opéra Bastille, Promenade Plantée park, place des Vosges (Paris' oldest square), Jewish Quarter (rue des Rosiers), and nightlife-packed rue de Lappe are also close by. (For sight descriptions, see "Northeast Paris," page 223; for the Opéra, see page 244.)

The Marais runs from the Pompidou Center to the Bastille; my recommended hotels are closer to the Pompidou Center. The Hôtel de Ville Métro stop works well for all of these hotels, unless a closer stop is noted.

Tourist Information: The nearest TI is in the Gare de Lyon (Mon–Sat 8:00–18:00, closed Sun, all-Paris TI tel. 08 92 68 30 00).

Services: Most banks and other services are on the main drag, rue de Rivoli, which becomes rue St. Antoine. Accessible Marais **post offices** are on rue Castex and on the corner of rue Pavée and rue des Francs Bourgeois. There's an accessible **SNCF Boutique** where you can take care of all train needs on rue St. Antoine at rue de Turenne (Mon–Sat 8:30–20:00, closed Sun). A quieter SNCF Boutique lies nearer the Gare de Lyon at 5 rue de Lyon (Mon–Sat 8:30–18:00, closed Sun).

Markets: The Marais has two good, accessible open-air markets: the sprawling **Marché de la Bastille,** around place de la Bastille (Thu and Sun until 12:30); and the more intimate, untouristy **Marché de la place d'Aligre** (daily 9:00–12:00, cross place de la Bastille and go about 10 blocks down rue du Faubourg St. Antoine, turn right at rue de Cotte to place d'Aligre; or, easier, take Métro line 8 from Bastille toward Créteil-Préfecture to the Ledru-Rollin stop and continue a few blocks southeast from there). For your Parisian "Sears," find the **BHV (AE, AI, AT,** Level 1—Fully Accessible) next to Hôtel de Ville.

Bookstore: The Marais is home to the friendliest English-language bookstore in Paris, **Red Wheelbarrow (AE+A, AI, ♥,** Level 2—Moderately Accessible; daily 10:00–19:00, 22 rue St. Paul, Mo: St. Paul, tel. 01 42 77 42 17). Abigail and Penelope sell most of my guidebooks and carry a great collection of other books about Paris and France.

Level 2—Moderately Accessible

Hôtel de Nice** (AE+A, AI+A, AL, AR+A, ♥)**, on the Marais' busy main drag, is a turquoise-and-rose, "Marie-Antoinette does tie-dye" place. Its narrow halls are littered with paintings and covered with carpets, and its 23 non-air-conditioned rooms are filled with thoughtful touches and include tight bathrooms. Twin rooms, which cost the same as doubles, are larger and on the street side—but have effective double-paned windows (narrow halls, tight spaces, stairs lead to lovely breakfast room; Sb-€74, Db-€105, Tb-€128, Qb-€140, extra bed-€20, 42 bis rue de Rivoli, tel. 01 42 78 55 29, fax 01 42 78 36 07, www.hoteldenice.com, contact@hoteldenice.com).

Hôtel de la Bretonnerie* (AE, AI, AL, AR, AB+A, ♥)**, three blocks from the Hôtel de Ville, makes a fine Marais home. It has a big, welcoming lobby, classy decor, and tastefully appointed rooms with an antique, open-beam warmth (one large suitable room has large marble-floored bathroom, one small step up to toilet with enough space for a wheelchair to go up step, but no grab bars; perfectly good standard "classic" Db-€110, bigger "charming" Db-€145, Db suite-€180, Tb-€170, Tb suite-€205, Qb suite-€235, no air-con, between rue Vieille du Temple and rue des Archives at 22 rue Ste. Croix de la Bretonnerie, tel. 01 48 87 77 63, fax 01 42 77 26 78, www.bretonnerie.com, hotel@bretonnerie .com).

Hôtel Beaubourg* (AE+A, AI, AL, AR, ♥)** is a fine three-star value on a quiet street in the shadow of the Pompidou Center. Its 28 rooms are wood-beam comfy and air-conditioned, and the inviting lounge is warm and pleasant (two entry steps, breakfast room in inaccessible basement but free room service; standard Db-€105, bigger twin Db-€120, 11 rue Simon Le Franc, Mo: Rambuteau, tel. 01 42 74 34 24, fax 01 42 78 68 11, www.hotelbeaubourg.com, htlbeaubourg@hotellerie.net).

Hôtel Americain (AE, AI, AL, AR-A, AB+A)** has two suitable rooms that are very small (Db-€60–70, breakfast-€5, closer to place de la République than to the heart of the Marais, 72 rue Charlot, tel. 01 48 87 58 92, www.paris-hotel-americain.com).

Grand Hôtel Jeanne d'Arc (AE, AI, AR, AB+A)**, a lovely and well-tended hotel with thoughtfully appointed rooms, is ideally located for (and very popular with) connoisseurs of the Marais. It's a fine value and worth booking way ahead. Sixth-floor rooms have views, and corner rooms are wonderfully bright in the City of Light, though no rooms are air-conditioned. Rooms on the street can be noisy until the bars close (one suitable ground-floor room offers decent access, Sb-€60–86, Db-€86, larger twin Db-€100, Tb-€120, good Qb-€150, 3 rue de Jarente, Mo: St. Paul, tel. 01 48 87 62 11, fax 01 48 87 37 31, information @hoteljeannedarc.com).

Luxembourg Garden Area (St. Sulpice to Panthéon)
(6th *arrondissement*)
This neighborhood revolves around Paris' loveliest park and adds quick access to the city's best shopping streets and grandest café-hopping. Sleeping in the Luxembourg area offers a true Left Bank experience,

Hotels and Restaurants near St. Sulpice and the Odéon Theater

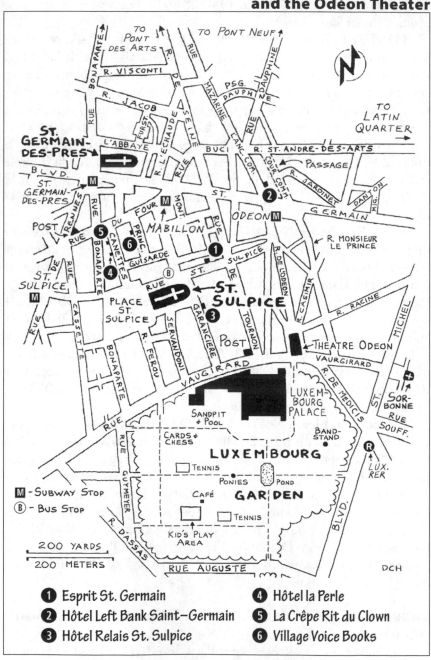

1. Esprit St. Germain
2. Hôtel Left Bank Saint–Germain
3. Hôtel Relais St. Sulpice
4. Hôtel la Perle
5. La Crêpe Rit du Clown
6. Village Voice Books

without a hint of the low-end commotion of the nearby Latin Quarter tourist ghetto. The Luxembourg Garden, boulevard St. Germain, Cluny Museum, and Latin Quarter are all at your doorstep. Here you get the best of both worlds: youthful Left Bank energy and the classy trappings that surround the monumental Panthéon and St. Sulpice Church. The nearest **TI** is across the river in Gare de Lyon (Mon–Sat 8:00–18:00, closed Sun, all-Paris TI tel. 08 92 68 30 00).

The first five hotels are all within a block of St. Sulpice Church, and two blocks from the famous boulevard St. Germain (Mo: St. Sulpice). This is nirvana for boutique-minded shoppers—and you'll pay extra for the location. Métro stops St. Sulpice and Mabillon are equally close. The last hotel (Port-Royal-Hôtel) is away from the Seine and other tourists in an appealing work-a-day area on the edge of the 13th *arrondissement*.

Level 1—Fully Accessible

Esprit St. Germain**** (AE, AI, AL, AB, AR), with plush surroundings and services, is the place for a splurge extraordinaire (Db-€260, 22 rue St. Sulpice, tel. 01 53 10 55 55, www.espritsaintgermain.com).

Citadines Saint-Germain-des-Prés*** (AE, AI, AL, AR, AB) is situated on the River Seine, opposite Notre-Dame. Nearby are many restaurants, art galleries, cafés, RER and bus lines, as well as two beautiful outdoor gardens (Db-€190–205, 53 ter, quai des Grands Augustins, tel. 01 44 07 70 00, www.citadines.com, stgermain@citadines.com).

Hôtel la Perle*** (AE, AI, AL, AR, AB) is a pricey pearl in the thick of the lively rue des Canettes, a block off place St. Sulpice. At this snappy, modern, business-class hotel, sliding glass doors open onto the traffic-free street and a fun lobby built around a central bar and atrium greets you (two fully adapted rooms, one with a roll-in shower; standard Db-€173, bigger Db-€195, luxury Db-€235, air-con, 14 rue des Canettes, tel. 01 43 29 10 10, fax 01 43 34 51 04, www.hotellaperle.com, booking@hotellaperle.com). Right outside your door are several accessible restaurants, including La Crêpe Rit du Clown (€3–8 crêpes and salads, 6 rue des Canettes), as well as pizza and French fare.

Level 2—Moderately Accessible

Hôtel Left Bank Saint-Germain*** (AE+A, AI, AR, AB+A, ♥), a Best Western, offers Old World, wood-paneled, exposed-beam charm, Oriental carpets, and a chandeliered salon (one 2" entry step, one huge convenient ground-floor room, bathroom has grab bars but unadapted tub; Db-€210–252, cheaper promotional rates often available, 9 rue de l'Ancienne-Comedie, tel. 01 43 54 01 70, www.bestwestern-leftbank.com).

Hôtel Relais St. Sulpice*** (AE, AI, AL, AR, AB+A, ♥),** on the small street just behind St. Sulpice Church, feels like a cozy bar, with a melt-in-your-chair lounge and 26 carefully designed, air-conditioned rooms, most of which surround a leafy glass atrium (two ground-floor rooms have large, mostly adapted bathrooms with unadapted tubs; Db-€170–205 depending on size, most Db-€170–180, sauna free for guests, 3 rue Garancière, tel. 01 46 33 99 00, fax 01 46 33 00 10, www .relais-saint-sulpice.com, relaisstsulpice@wanadoo.fr).

Port-Royal-Hôtel* (AE+A, AI, AR, AB+A) has only one star, but don't let that fool you. This 46-room place is polished bottom to top and has been well-run by the same proud family for 67 years. You could eat off the floors of its spotless, comfy rooms, two of which are on the main floor for easy roll-in (S-€39-51, D-€51, big hall showers-€2.50, Db-€77-87 depending on size, Tb-€89, cash only, requires cash deposit, on busy boulevard de Port-Royal at #8, Mo: Les Gobelins, tel. 01 43 31 70 06, fax 01 43 31 33 67, portroyalhotel@wanadoo.fr).

Near Canal St. Martin
(10th and 11th *arrondissements*, Mo: République, Oberkampf)
This up-and-coming neighborhood is just north of the Marais, between place de la République and Canal St. Martin. It feels real and reminds me of how many other neighborhoods looked 20 years ago. This area is the least touristy of those I list, and its hotels and restaurants tend to be great values (for restaurant suggestions, see page 264; for nighttime fun, head over to rue Oberkampf and join the crowd). This neighborhood is less polished and more remote—but if you can put up with some rough edges and don't mind using taxis or public transportation for all of your sightseeing, you'll save plenty.

The murky canal is the central feature of this unpretentious area, with pleasing walkways, arching footbridges, and occasional boats plying its water. A flowery parkway covers the canal where it goes underground toward place de la Bastille. The parkway plays host to an open-air market on Tuesdays and Fridays until 14:00. When the weather agrees, the entire neighborhood seems to descend on the canal in late afternoon, filling the cafés, parkway, and benches. This neighborhood is convenient to the Nord and Est train stations, as well as to the Pompidou Center and the place des Vosges in the Marais.

Level 2—Moderately Accessible
Hôtel de la République** (AE+A, AI, AR, AB+A) is a well-run establishment a block toward the canal from place de la République. Rooms

are sufficiently comfortable, with good natural light, showers instead of baths, and small balconies on the fifth floor (Sb-€50–61, Db-€60, Tb-€70–81, 31 rue Albert Thomas, Mo: République, tel. 01 42 39 19 03, fax 01 42 39 22 66, www.republiquehotel.com). An inviting wheelchair sits in the front entrance (which has one 3" entry step). There is a fairly tight ground-floor room that's suitable but not adapted, with a small bathroom.

Holiday Inn Paris République*** (AE, AI, AR, AL, AB+A) is a hip splurge on a happening street that's a bustling gathering place for tea and conversation. Two accessible restaurants punctuate the sprawling lobby (four roomy, accessible studios have adapted toilet and suitable bathtub; Db-€150, can be much higher during conventions, 10 place de la République, tel. 01 43 14 43 50, www.paris-republique.holiday-inn.com).

Elsewhere in Central Paris

These fully accessible accommodations are scattered around the city center.

Level 1—Fully Accessible

Novotel Les Halles (AE, AI, AL, AR, AB) is a well-located, clean, modern, upscale chain hotel with six adapted rooms near the Louvre (Db-€195, check online for discounts, 8 place Marguerite de Navarre, tel. 01 42 21 31 31, www.accorhotels.com, h0785@accor.com).

Hôtel Pavillon Louvre Rivoli (AE, AI, AL, AR, AB) is clean, upscale, and handy to the pulse of the city (one fully adapted room, Db-€200, 7 rue Jean Lantier, tel. 01 42 33 45 32).

Hôtel Ibis Gare du Nord La Fayette (AE, AI, AL, AR, AB) is a basic, clean, and predictable chain hotel handy to the accessible Nord train station for RER and Thalys trains (three fully equipped and adapted rooms, Db-€95, 122 rue La Fayette, tel. 01 45 23 27 27).

EATING

The Parisian eating scene is kept at a rolling boil. Entire books (and lives) are dedicated to the subject. Paris is France's wine and cuisine melting pot. While it lacks a style of its own (only French onion soup is truly Parisian), it draws from the best of France. Paris could hold a gourmet's Olympics and import nothing.

Parisians eat long and well. Relaxed lunches, three-hour dinners, and endless hours of sitting in outdoor cafés are the norm. Local cafés, cuisine, and wines become a highlight of any Parisian adventure—sightseeing for your palate. Even if the rest of you is sleeping in a cheap hotel, let your taste buds travel first-class in Paris. (They can go coach in London.)

You can eat well without going broke, but choose carefully—you're just as likely to blow a small fortune on a mediocre meal as you are to dine wonderfully for €20. By following the suggestions offered below, you'll have a better dining experience.

My recommendations are centered predominantly near the recommended hotels in the rue Cler and Marais neighborhoods; you can come home exhausted after a busy day of sightseeing and have a good selection of restaurants right around the corner. And evening is a fine time to explore these delightful neighborhoods. I've provided accessibility information for each place. Unless otherwise noted (by **AT** or **AT+A**), these restaurants do *not* have accessible toilets.

Tipping

Virtually all cafés and restaurants include a service charge in the bill (usually 15 percent, referred to as *service compris* or *prix net*), but it's polite to round up for a drink or meal well-served. This bonus tip is usually about 5 percent of the bill (e.g., if your bill is €19, leave €20). In the rare instance that service is not included (the menu states *service non compris*), tip 15 percent. When you hand your payment plus a tip to your waiter, you can say, "*C'est bon*" (say bohn), meaning, "It's good." If you order your food at a counter, don't tip.

Breakfast

Petit déjeuner (puh-tee day-zhuh-nay) is typically *café au lait,* hot chocolate, or tea; a roll with butter and marmalade; and a croissant—though more hotels are starting to provide breakfast buffets with fruit, cereal, yogurt, and cheese (usually for a few extra euros, and well worth it). While breakfasts are available at your hotel (about €8–14), they're cheaper at corner cafés (but no coffee refills; see also "Café Culture," below). It's fine to buy a croissant or roll at a bakery and eat it with your cup of coffee at a café. Better still, some bakeries offer worthwhile breakfast deals with juice, croissant, and coffee or tea for about €3 (consider the chain of bakeries called La Brioche Dorée). If the urge for an egg in the morning gets the best of you, drop into a café and order *une omelette* or *oeufs sur le plat* (fried eggs). You could also buy or bring from home plastic bowls and spoons, buy a box of cereal and a small box of milk, and eat in your room before heading out for coffee.

Picnics and Snacks

Great for lunch or dinner, Parisian picnics can be first-class affairs and adventures in high cuisine. Be daring. Try the smelly cheeses, ugly pâtés, sissy quiches, and minuscule (usually drinkable) yogurts. Local shopkeepers are accustomed to selling small quantities of produce. Try the tasty salads to go and ask for *une fourchette en plastique* (a plastic fork).

Gather supplies early for a picnic lunch; you'll probably visit several small stores to assemble a complete meal, and many close at noon. Look for a *boulangerie* (bakery), a *crémerie* or *fromagerie* (cheeses), a *charcuterie* (deli items, meats, and pâtés), an *épicerie* or *magasin d'alimentation* (small grocery store with veggies, drinks, and so on), and a *pâtisserie* (delicious pastries). For fine picnic shopping, check out the street market recommendations in the Shopping chapter. While wine is taboo in public places in the United States, it's *pas de problème* in France.

Supermarchés offer less color and cost, more efficiency, and adequate quality. Department stores often have supermarkets in the basement, along with top-floor cafeterias offering not really cheap but low-risk, low-stress, what-you-see-is-what-you-get meals. For a quick meal to go, look for food stands and bakeries selling takeout sandwiches and drinks. For an affordable meal, try a *crêperie* or café.

In stores, unrefrigerated soft drinks and beer are half the price of cold drinks. Milk and boxed fruit juice are the most inexpensive drinks. Avoid buying drinks to go at streetside stands; you'll find them far cheaper in a shop. Try to keep a water bottle with you. Water quenches your thirst better and cheaper than anything you'll find in a store or café. I drink tap water in Paris and use that to refill my bottle. You'll pass many fountains on Paris streets with good water (but if it says *non potable*, it's not drinkable).

For good lunch picnic sites, consider these suggestions. The Palais Royal (across the place du Palais Royal from the Louvre) is a good spot for a peaceful, royal picnic, as is the little triangular Henry IV park on the west tip of Ile de la Cité. The pedestrian pont des Arts bridge, across from the Louvre, has great views and plentiful benches, as does the Champ de Mars park below the Eiffel Tower. For great people-watching, try the Pompidou Center (by the *Homage to Stravinsky* fountains), the elegant place des Vosges (closes at dusk), the gardens behind Les Invalides and surrounding the Rodin Museum, and the Tuileries and Luxembourg Gardens.

Café Culture

French cafés (or *brasseries*) provide budget-friendly meals and a relief from museum and church overload. Feel free to order only a bowl of soup and a salad or *plat* (main course) for lunch or dinner at a café.

Cafés generally open by 7:00, but closing hours vary. Unlike restaurants, which open only for lunch and dinner, meals are served throughout the day at most cafés—making them the best option for a late lunch or an early dinner.

It's easier for the novice to feel comfortable when you know the system. Check the price list first, which by law must be posted prominently. You'll see two sets of prices; you'll pay more for the same drink if you're seated at a table *(salle)* than if you're seated at the bar or counter *(comptoir)*. At large cafés, outside tables are most expensive, and prices can rise after 22:00.

Your waiter probably won't overwhelm you with friendliness. Notice how hard they work. They almost never stop. Cozying up to clients (French or foreign) is probably the last thing on their minds.

Standard Menu Items: *Croque monsieur* (grilled ham and cheese sandwich) and *croque madame* (*monsieur* with a fried egg on top) are generally served day and night. Sandwiches are least expensive but plain—and much better—at the *boulangerie* (bakery). To get more than a piece of ham *(jambon)* on a baguette, order a sandwich *jambon crudité*, which means garnished with veggies. Omelettes come lonely on a plate with a basket of bread. The daily special—*plat du jour* (plah dew zhoor), or just *plat*—is your fast, hearty hot plate for €10–16. Regardless of what you order, bread is free; to get more, just hold up your bread basket and ask, *"Encore, s'il vous plaît."*

Salads: I order salads for lunch and for lighter dinners. They're typically large—one is perfect for lunch or a light dinner, or split between two people as a first course. Among the classics are *salade niçoise* (neeswaz), a specialty from Nice that typically includes green salad topped with green beans, boiled potatoes (sometimes rice), tomatoes (sometimes corn), anchovies, olives, hard-boiled eggs, and lots of tuna; *salade au chèvre chaud,* a mixed green salad topped with warm goat cheese and toasted bread croutons; and *salade composée,* "composed" of any number of ingredients, such as *lardons* (bacon), *comte* (a Swiss-style cheese), *roquefort* (blue cheese), *œuf* (egg), *noix* (walnuts), *jambon* (ham, generally

Coffee and Tea Lingo

By law, the waiter must give you a glass of tap water with your coffee or tea if you request it; ask for *"un verre d'eau, s'il vous plaît"* (uhn vayr doh, see voo play).

Coffee

French	Pronounced	English
un express	uhn nex-press	shot of espresso
une noisette	oon nwah-zeht	espresso with a shot of milk
café au lait	kah-fay oh lay	coffee with lots of milk
un grand crème	uhn grahn krehm	just like café au lait, large size
un petit crème	uhn puh-tee krehm	just like café au lait, small size
un grand café noir	uhn grahn kah-fay nwahr	cup of black coffee, closest to American-style
un décaffiné	uhn day-kah-fee-nay	decaf—can modify any of the above drinks

Tea

French	Pronounced	English
un thé nature	uhn tay nah-tour	plain tea
un thé au lait	uhn tay oh lay	tea with milk
un thé citron	uhn tay see-trohn	tea with lemon
une infusion	oon an-few-see-yohn	herbal tea

thinly sliced), *saumon fumé* (smoked salmon), and the highly suspect *gesiers* (chicken livers). To get salad dressing on the side, order *la sauce à part* (lah sohs ah par).

Wine and Beer: House wine at the bar is cheap (about €3 per glass, cheapest by the pitcher—*pichet*, pee-shay), and the local beer is cheaper on tap (*une pression;* oon pres-yohn) than in the bottle (*bouteille;* boo-teh-ee). France's best beer is Alsatian; try Kronenbourg or the heavier Pelfort (even heavier is the Belgian beer Leffe). *Une panaché* (oon pan-a-shay) is a refreshing French shandy (7-Up and beer). For a fun, bright, nonalcoholic drink of 7-Up with mint syrup, order *un diablo menthe* (uhn dee-ah-bloh mahnt). Kids love the local lemonade (*citron pressé;* see-trohn preh-say, you'll need to add sugar) and the flavored syrups mixed with bottled water (*sirops à l'eau;* see-roh ah loh). The ice cubes melted after the last Yankee tour group left.

Restaurants

Choose restaurants filled with locals, not places with big neon signs boasting *We Speak English*. Consider your hotelier's opinion. If a restaurant doesn't post its prices outside, move along.

Restaurants open for dinner around 19:00, and small local favorites get crowded after 21:00. To minimize smoke and crowds, go early (around 19:30). Beware: Many restaurants close Sunday and Monday.

If a restaurant serves lunch, it generally begins at 11:30 and goes until 14:00, with last orders taken at about 13:30. If you're hungry when restaurants are closed (late afternoon), go to a café; most serve all day.

If you ask for the *menu* (muh-noo) at a restaurant, you won't get a list of dishes; you'll get a fixed-price meal. *Menus* (also called *formules*), which offer three or four courses, are generally a good value if you're hungry: You get your choice of soup, appetizer, or salad; your choice of three or four main courses with vegetables; plus a cheese course and/or a choice of desserts. Service is included (*service compris* or *prix net*), but wine and other drinks are generally extra. Restaurants that offer a *menu* for lunch often charge about €5 more for the same *menu* at dinner.

Ask for *la carte* if you want to see a menu and order à la carte like the locals do. Request the waiter's help in deciphering the French. Go with his or her recommendations and anything *de la maison* (of the house), as long as it's not an organ meat *(tripes, rognons, andouillette)*. Galloping gourmets should bring a menu translator; the *Marling Menu Master* is good. The *Rick Steves' French Phrase Book*, with a Menu Decoder, works well for most travelers. The wines are often listed in a separate *carte des vins*.

In France, an *entrée* is the appetizer. *Le plat* or *le plat du jour* (plate of the day) is the main course with vegetables (usually €10–16). If all you want is a salad, find a café instead.

Parisians are willing to pay for bottled water with their meal (*eau minérale;* oh mee-nay-rahl) because they prefer the taste over tap water. If you prefer a free pitcher of tap water, ask for *une carafe d'eau* (oon kah-rahf doh). Otherwise, you may unwittingly buy bottled water. To get inexpensive wine at a restaurant, order table wine in a pitcher (*un pichet;* uhn pee-shay), rather than a bottle (though finer restaurants usually offer only bottles of wine). If all you want is a glass of wine, ask for *un verre de vin* (uhn vehr duh van). A half carafe of wine is *un demi-pichet* (uhn duh-mee pee-shay), a quarter carafe (ideal for one) is *un quart* (uhn kar).

To get a waiter's attention, simply say, *"S'il vous plaît"* (see voo play)—please.

In the Rue Cler Neighborhood

The rue Cler neighborhood caters to its residents. Its eateries, while not destination places, have an intimate charm. My favorites are small mom-and-pop eateries that love to serve traditional French food at good prices to a local clientele. You'll generally find great dinner *menus* for €20–30 and *plats du jour* for around €12–16. Eat early with tourists or late with locals. Unless otherwise noted, all of these restaurants are nearest the Ecole Militaire Métro stop.

Closer to Ecole Militaire, Between Rue de la Motte Picquet and Rue de Grenelle

Café de l'Esplanade (AE+A, AI, Level 2—Moderately Accessible, 2" entry step with wide door, wheelchair users are seated close to door) is your opportunity to be surrounded by chic, yet older and sophisticated Parisians enjoying top-notch traditional cuisine as foreplay. There's not a tourist in sight. It has a sprawling floor plan: Half its tables (with well-stuffed chairs) fill a plush, living-room-like interior, and the other half are lined up outside under its elegant awning facing the grand Esplanade des Invalides in front of Napoleon's Tomb. Dress competitively, as this is *the* place to be seen in the 7th *arrondissement* (€20 *plats du jour*, €45 plus wine for dinner, open daily, reserve ahead—especially if you want a curbside table, non-smoking room in the back, 52 rue Fabert, Mo: La Tour-Maubourg, tel. 01 47 05 38 80). This is the only actual business on the entire esplanade that stretches all the way to the Champs-Elysées.

Léo le Lion (AE+A, AI, ♥, Level 2—Moderately Accessible, one 3" entry step)—small, softly lit, and traditional, with velvet booths—is well-respected by locals for both fish and meat. The plush interior feels like a marionette theater (€20 *plats*, closed Sun, 23 rue Duvivier, tel. 01 45 51 41 77).

Le Florimond (AE+A, AI, Level 2—Moderately Accessible) is ideal for a special occasion. The ambience, while spacious and quiet, is also intimate and welcoming. Locals come for classic French cuisine with elegant indoor or breezy streetside seating. Friendly English-speaking Laurent—with his playful ties changing daily—will take good care of you (€32 *menu*, closed Sun, good and reasonable wine selection and explosively tasty stuffed cabbage, reservations smart, non-smoking, 19 avenue de la Motte Picquet, tel. 01 45 55 40 38).

Rue Cler Restaurants

DCH

Ⓜ –Subway Stop

200 YARDS
200 METERS

❶ Café du Marché & Tribeca Rest.
❷ Café de Mars
❸ Café le Bosquet
❹ Léo le Lion
❺ L'Affriolé & L'Ami Jean
❻ Au Petit Tonneau
❼ Brasserie Thoumieux
❽ Le P'tit Troquet &
   La Casa di Sergio
❾ Restaurant la Serre
❿ La Fontaine de Mars
⓫ La Gourmandine
⓬ Chez Agnès

⓭ Le Florimond
⓮ Café de l'Esplanade
⓯ La Terrasse du 7ème
⓰ Ulysée en Gaule
⓱ Real McCoy
⓲ Pourjauran Bakery
⓳ Petite Brasserie PTT
⓴ Café la Roussillon
㉑ Le Petit Niçois
㉒ To Altitude 95
㉓ Lenôtre Deli
㉔ Late-Night Groceries (2)

Thoumieux (AE, AI, ♥, Level 2—Moderately Accessible), the neighborhood's classy, traditional Parisian brasserie, is a popular local institution. It's big and white-tablecloth dressy, with formal, no-nonsense waiters. As the owner is from southwest France, much of the menu is as well (€15 lunch *menu*, 3-course €33 dinner *menu* includes wine, open daily, 79 rue St. Dominique, Mo: La Tour-Maubourg, tel. 01 47 05 49 75). They open at 18:30, and head waiter Pascal advises making a reservation if arriving after 20:00.

La Terrasse du 7ème (AE+A, AI, Level 2—Moderately Accessible) is a sprawling, happening café with classic outdoor seating and a living-room-like interior with comfy love seats. Located on a corner, it overlooks a grand and busy intersection with a constant parade of people marching by. A meal here is like dinner theater—and the show is slice-of-life Paris (no fixed-price *menu*, great *salade niçoise*, open daily until 2:00 in the morning, at Ecole Militaire Métro stop, tel. 01 45 55 00 02).

Le Petit Niçois (literally, "The Little Nice"; **AE, AI,** Level 2—Moderately Accessible) feels *très* Mediterranean, from its warm colors to its menu selections. This is where rue Cler natives go for their southern seafood fix (€24 *menu*, open daily, 10 rue Amélie, tel. 01 45 51 83 65).

Café du Marché (AE+A, AI, ♥, Level 2—Moderately Accessible, one 3" entry step) boasts the best seats, coffee, and prices on rue Cler. The owner's philosophy: Brasserie on speed—crank out great food at great prices to trendy locals and savvy tourists. It's high-energy, with waiters who barely have time to smile...*très* Parisian. This place is ideal if you want a light lunch or dinner (good, hearty €10 salads) or a more substantial but simple meal (filling €11 *plats du jour*, listed on chalkboard; open Mon–Sat 11:00–23:00, Sun 11:00–17:00, for dinner arrive before 19:30—it's packed at 21:00, can be smoky, at the corner of rue Cler and rue du Champ de Mars, at 38 rue Cler, tel. 01 47 05 51 27). Their new **Tribeca Restaurant (AE, AI, AT,** Level 1—Fully Accessible), next door, offers similar value but more space, a calmer ambience, an accessible toilet, more patient service, and a menu focusing on pizza and Italian cuisine.

Ulysée en Gaule (AE, AI, Level 2—Moderately Accessible), in a prime location right on rue Cler, offers good, cheap, front-row seats for the people-watching fun. The Ulysée family—Stephanos, Chrysa, and their English-speaking son Vassilis—seem to make friends with all who drop by for a bite. The family loves to serve Greek dishes, and their excellent crêpes (to go or sit down for €2 extra) are your cheapest rue Cler hot meal (daily 8:00–22:30, 28 rue Cler, tel. 01 47 05 61 82).

Petite Brasserie PTT (AE+A, AI, Level 2—Moderately Accessible, one 5" entry step) is a classic time-warp, popular with postal workers and offering traditional café fare at reasonable prices next to the PTT (post office) on rue Cler. They offer a great *deux pour douze* breakfast deal for Rick Steves readers: two American breakfasts (normally €8 each) for €12 total (closed Sun, opposite 53 rue Cler).

Café le Bosquet (AE, AI, ♥, Level 2—Moderately Accessible, entry and main floor are fully accessible) is a vintage Parisian brasserie with dressy waiters and a classic interior or sidewalk tables on a busy street. Come here for a bowl of French onion soup, a salad, or a three-course *menu* (€18), and mix it up with waiters Daniel, Nina, and Antoine (closed Sun, many choices—including vegetarian options—from a fun menu, the house red wine is plenty good, reservations smart on weekends, corner of rue du Champ de Mars and avenue Bosquet, at 46 avenue Bosquet, tel. 01 45 51 38 13). This place has regular wheelchair-using customers.

Between Rue Grenelle and the River

Altitude 95 (AE, AI, AL, AT, Level 1—Fully Accessible) is in the Eiffel Tower, 95 meters (about 300 feet) above the ground (€21–31 lunches, €50 dinners, dinner seatings nightly at 19:00 and 21:00, reserve well ahead for a view table; before you ascend to dine, drop by the booth between the north/*nord* and east/*est* pillars to buy your Eiffel Tower ticket and pick up a pass that enables you to skip the line; Mo: Bir-Hakeim or Trocadéro, RER: Champ de Mars-Tour Eiffel, tel. 01 45 55 20 04, fax 01 47 05 94 40).

L'Affriolé (AE+A, AI, ♥, Level 2—Moderately Accessible, one 4" entry step) is a small, trendy eatery where you'll compete with young professionals to get a table. Entering this elegant but rollicking dining hall, you immediately feel you're eating at a restaurant well-deserving of its rave reviews. Menu selections change daily, and the wine list is extensive, with some good bargains (€35 *menu*, closed Sun–Mon, 17 rue Malar, Mo: La Tour-Maubourg, tel. 01 44 18 31 33). The staff has welcomed wheelchair users through the years.

Au Petit Tonneau (AE+A, AI, ♥, Level 2—Moderately Accessible, one 4" entry step) is a souvenir of old Paris. Fun-loving owner-chef Madame Boyer prepares everything herself, wearing her tall chef's hat like a crown as she rules from her family-style kitchen. The small, plain dining room doesn't look like it's changed in the 25 years she's been in charge. Her steaks and lamb are excellent (€28 for 2 courses, €35 3-course *menu*, open daily, can get smoky—come early, 20 rue Surcouf, Mo: La Tour-Maubourg, tel. 01 47 05 09 01).

La Fontaine de Mars (AE+A, AI, ♥, Level 2—Moderately Accessible, one 3" entry step) is a longtime favorite for locals, charmingly situated on a classic, tiny Parisian street and jumbled square. It's a happening scene, with tables jammed together for the serious business of good eating. Reserve in advance to get a table on the accessible ground floor—which is better anyway, to enjoy the fun street-level ambience (€25 *plats*, open nightly, where rue de l'Exposition and rue St. Dominique meet, at 129 rue St. Dominique, tel. 01 47 05 46 44).

Le P'tit Troquet (AE+A, AI, ♥, Level 2—Moderately Accessible, one 3" entry step), a petite eatery taking you back to the Paris of the 1920s, is gracefully and earnestly run by Dominique. She's particularly proud of her *foie gras* and lamb. The delicious, three-course €29.50 *menu* comes with fun, traditional choices. Its delicate charm and gourmet flair make this a favorite of connoisseurs (closed Sun, reservations smart, 28 rue de l'Exposition, tel. 01 47 05 80 39).

La Casa di Sergio (AE+A, AI, ♥, Level 2—Moderately Accessible) serves gourmet Italian cuisine family-style. Only Sergio could make me enthusiastic about Italian food in Paris. Sergio, a people-loving Sicilian, says he's waited his entire life to open a restaurant like this. Eating here involves a little trust...just sit down and let Sergio spoil you (€27–32 *menus*, open nightly from 18:30, 20 rue de l'Exposition, tel. 01 45 51 37 71). Sergio may be moving to a larger, nearby location soon—but he's worth seeking out (ask at your hotel). The current location has one 6" doorstep and a small entryway, but Sergio has been known to take the door off the hinges to allow a wheelchair user into his restaurant—you will feel welcome.

Chez Agnès (AE+A, AI, ♥, Level 2—Moderately Accessible, one 6" entry step), the smallest of my recommended Paris restaurants, is not for everyone. It's tiny, flowery, family-style, and filled with kisses on the cheek. Eccentric but sincere Agnès (a French-Tahitian Roseanne Barr) does it all—cooking in her minuscule kitchen and serving, too. Agnès, who cooks "French with an exotic twist" and clearly loves her work, makes children feel right at home. Don't come for a quick dinner (€23 *menu*, closed Mon, 1 rue Augereau, tel. 01 45 51 06 04).

Café de Mars (AE, AI, Level 2—Moderately Accessible) is an indoor/outdoor sidewalk café with spiffy French service and a varied local menu at reasonable prices. Watch the local shoppers, businesspeople, and university students bustling by (€5–12 dishes, Tue–Sun 12:00–14:30 & 19:00–23:00, closed Mon, 11 rue Augereau, tel. 01 45 55 76 99).

La Gourmandine (AE, AI, Level 2—Moderately Accessible) serves up the hearty country food of Normandy with charming, traditional, low-beamed-cozy, elegant atmosphere (€7–16 dishes, Mon–Fri 12:00–14:30 & 19:00–23:30, Sat 19:00–23:30 only, closed Sun, 28 rue Surcouf, tel. 01 45 51 61 49).

L'Ami Jean (AE+A, AI, Level 2—Moderately Accessible) offers excellent Basque specialties at fair prices. The chef has made his reputation on the quality of his cuisine, not on the dark, simple decor. Arrive by 19:30 or call ahead—by 20:00, there's a line out the door of people waiting to join the shared tables and lively commotion of happy eaters (€15 for a plate of mixed Basque tapas, €28 *menu*, closed Sun–Mon, 27 rue Malar, Mo: La Tour-Maubourg, tel. 01 47 05 86 89).

Restaurant la Serre (AE+A, AI, ♥, Level 2—Moderately Accessible, one 7" entry step) is reasonably priced and worth considering (€11–15 *plats*, good onion soup and duck specialties, closed Sun–Mon, 29 rue de l'Exposition, tel. 01 45 55 20 96, Margot).

Picnicking in Rue Cler

The rue Cler is a moveable feast that gives "fast food" a good name. The entire street is clogged with connoisseurs of good eating. Only the health-food store goes unnoticed. A festival of food, the street is lined with people whose lives seem to be devoted to their specialty: polished produce, rotisserie chicken, crêpes, or cheese.

For a magical picnic dinner at the Eiffel Tower, assemble it in no fewer than five shops on rue Cler. Then lounge on the best grass in Paris, with the dogs, Frisbees, a floodlit tower, and a cool breeze in the parc du Champ de Mars.

Asian delis (generically called *Traiteur Asie*, most of them accessible) provide tasty, low-stress, low-price take-out treats (€6 dinner plates, the one on rue Cler near rue du Champ de Mars has tables). **Ulysée en Gaule (AE, AI,** Level 2—Moderately Accessible), the Greek restaurant on rue Cler across from Grand Hôtel Lévêque, sells take-away crêpes (described above). The elegant **Lenotre** *charcuterie* **(AE, AI,** Level 1—Fully Accessible) offers mouthwatering meals to go (open daily until 23:00, at Ecole Militaire Métro stop). **Real McCoy (AE+A, AI,** Level 2—Moderately Accessible)** is a little shop selling American food and sandwiches (one 2" entry step; closed Sun, 194 rue de Grenelle). There are small **late-night groceries (AE, AI,** Level 1—Fully Accessible) at 186 and 197 rue de Grenelle (open nightly until midnight).

Breakfast in Rue Cler

Hotel breakfasts, while convenient, are generally not a good value. For a great rue Cler start to your day, drop by the **Petite Brasserie PTT**

(**AE+A, AI,** Level 2—Moderately Accessible, one 5" entry step), where managers Jerome and Eric promise Rick Steves readers a *deux pour douze* breakfast special (2 "American" breakfasts—juice, coffee, croissant, ham, and eggs—for €12; described above). **Café la Roussillon (AE+A, AI,** Level 2—Moderately Accessible, one 4" entry step) serves a good American-style breakfast for €9 (open daily, at corner of rue de Grenelle and rue Cler, tel. 01 45 51 47 53). To eat breakfast while watching Paris go to work, stop by **La Terrasse du 7ème (AE+A, AI,** Level 2—Moderately Accessible; described above). The **Pourjauran** bakery (**AE, AI,** Level 1—Fully Accessible), offering great baguettes, hasn't changed in 70 years (20 rue Jean Nicot).

In the Marais Neighborhood

The trendy Marais is filled with locals enjoying good food in colorful and atmospheric eateries. The scene is competitive and changes all the time. I've listed an assortment of eateries—all handy to recommended hotels—that offer good food at reasonable prices, plus a memorable experience. For maximum ambience, go to the place des Vosges or place du Marché Ste. Catherine (several restaurants listed below on each of these squares).

Dining on Romantic Place des Vosges

On and near this square, which offers Old World Marais elegance, you'll find five very different eateries. Roll or stroll around the entire arcade—fun art galleries alternate with enticing restaurants. Choose the restaurant that best fits your mood and budget; each one has perfect arcade seating and provides big space-heaters to make outdoor dining during colder months an option. Also consider a drink or desert on the square at Café Hugo or Nectarine after eating elsewhere. The place des Vosges is near the St. Paul and Bastille Métro stations.

Restaurant Coconnas (AE, AI, AT+A, ♥, Level 2—Moderately Accessible) is the dressiest option, with classic French cuisine, refined ambience, black-suited waiters, and artfully presented gourmet dishes (€30 *plats*, €15 entrées and deserts, closed Mon, on the river side of the square at #2, tel. 01 42 78 58 16).

Ma Bourgogne (AE, AI, Level 2—Moderately Accessible) is a classic old eatery where you'll sit under arcades in a whirlpool of Frenchness, as bowtied and black-aproned waiters serve you traditional Burgundian specialties: steak, *coq au vin*, lots of French fries, escargot, and great red wine. Service at this institution comes with food but few smiles (€32 *menu*, open daily, dinner reservations smart, cash only, at northwest corner at #19, tel. 01 42 78 44 64).

Nectarine (AE+A, AI, Level 2—Moderately Accessible, one 4" entry step, accessible street dining with heaters) is small and demure— with a wicker, pastel, and feminine ambience. This peaceful teahouse serves healthy €10 salads, quiches, and €12 *plats du jour* both day and night. Its fun menu lets you mix and match omelets and crêpes. Its huge deserts are splittable, and dropping by here late for sweets and a drink is a peaceful way to end your day (open daily, at #16, tel. 01 42 77 23 78).

Café Hugo (AE, AI, AT+A, ♥, Level 2—Moderately Accessible, wheelchair-friendly, with accessible street dining), named for the square's most famous resident, is best for drinks only, as the cuisine does not live up to its setting (open daily, at #22).

At **Un Piano sur le Trottoir** (literally, "A Piano on the Sidewalk"; AE, AI, Level 2—Moderately Accessible), you'll enter through the red door into the last century. An antique piano greets you at the entry of this beautifully restored French dollhouse. The exquisite French menu makes it a good place for a special night on the town (*menus* for €15, €19, or €24; à la carte dishes for €8–27; Tue–Fri 19:00–23:00, Sat 12:00–15:00 & 19:00–23:00, Sun 12:00–15:00, closed Mon, 7 rue de Francs Bourgeois, tel. 01 42 77 91 91).

Near the Bastille

To reach these restaurants, use the Bastille Métro stop.

Brasserie Bofinger (AE, AI, Level 2—Moderately Accessible), an institution for over a century, is famous for fish and traditional cuisine with Alsatian flair. You're surrounded by brisk, black-and-white-attired waiters. The sprawling interior features elaborately decorated rooms reminiscent of the Roaring Twenties. Eating under the grand 1919 *coupole* is a memorable treat (as is using the "historic" 1919 WC downstairs). Check out the boys shucking and stacking seafood platters out front before you enter. Their €33 three-course *menu*, while not top cuisine, includes wine and is a good value. The kids' menu makes this restaurant family-friendly (accessible door to right of main entrance, open daily and nightly, reservations smart, mostly non-smoking, 5 rue de la Bastille, don't be confused by the lesser "Petite" Bofinger across the street, tel. 01 42 72 87 82).

L'Impasse (AE+A, AI, Level 2—Moderately Accessible, one 4" entry step), a relaxed bistro on a quiet alley, serves an enthusiastically French three-course *menu* for €28. Françoise, a former dancer and artist, runs the place *con brio* (closed Sun, 4 impasse de Guéménée, tel. 01 42 72 08 45). Françoise promises anyone with this book a free glass of *byrrh*—it's pronounced "beer," but it's a French port-like drink.

Bistrot les Sans Culottes (AE, AI, Level 2—Moderately Accessible), a zinc-bar classic on lively rue de Lappe, serves traditional French cuisine with a proper respect for fine wine (€24 3-course *menu*, closed Mon, 27 rue de Lappe, tel. 01 48 05 42 92). Stay out past your bedtime. Eat here. Then join the rue de Lappe party.

Au Temps des Cerises (AE+A, AI, Level 2—Moderately Accessible, one 4" entry step) is a *très* local wine bar. While they serve lunch plates, it's better for an early dinner or a pre-dinner glass of wine. "Dinner" will be limited to bread, dry sausage, cheese, and wine served by goateed Yves and his wife, Michele. A mixed plate of cheese (€3.50), meat (€3.50), and a carafe of good wine (€3–6) surrounded by the intimate and woody Old World ambience can be a good light meal (Mon–Fri until 20:00, closed Sat–Sun, at rue du Petit-Musc and rue de la Cerisaie).

Vins des Pyrénées (AE+A, AI, Level 2—Moderately Accessible, one 4" entry step) is younger and livelier, with fun ambience, inexpensive meals, some smoke, and a reasonable wine list (open daily, 25 rue Beautreillis, tel. 01 42 72 64 94).

In the Heart of the Marais
These are closest to the St. Paul Métro stop.

On place du Marché Ste. Catherine: This small, romantic square, just off rue St. Antoine, is an international food festival cloaked in extremely Parisian, leafy-square ambience. On a balmy evening, this is clearly a neighborhood favorite, with five popular restaurants offering €20-30 meals. Most of the restaurants here are accessible, but lack accessible toilets (**AE, AI,** Level 2—Moderately Accessible). Survey the square, and you'll find a popular French bistro (Le Marché) and inviting eateries serving Italian, Korean, Russian, and Greek. You'll eat under the trees, surrounded by a futuristic-in-1800 planned residential quarter.

L'Enoteca (AE+A, AI, Level 2—Moderately Accessible, one 2" entry step) is a high-spirited, half-timbered wine bar–restaurant serving reasonably priced Italian cuisine (no pizza) with a tempting *antipasti* bar. It's a relaxed, open setting with busy, blue-aproned waiters serving two floors of local eaters (€10 pastas, €15 *plats*, open daily, across from L'Excuse at rue St. Paul and rue Charles V, 25 rue Charles V, tel. 01 42 78 91 44).

Camille (AE, AI, Level 2—Moderately Accessible), a traditional corner brasserie, is a neighborhood favorite with great indoor and sidewalk seating. White-aproned waiters serve €10 salads and very French *plats du jour* (from €16) to a down-to-earth but sophisticated clientele (open daily, 24 rue des Francs Bourgeois at corner of rue Elzévir, tel. 01 42 72 20 50).

Le Pick-Clops Bar Restaurant (AE, AI, Level 2—Moderately Accessible) is a happy peanuts-and-lots-of-cocktails diner with bright neon, loud colors and a garish local crowd. It's perfect for immersing yourself in today's Marais world—a little boisterous, a little edgy, a little gay, fun-loving, easygoing...and no tourists. Sit inside, on old-fashioned diner stools, or streetside to watch the constant Marais parade. The name means "Steal the Cigarettes"—but you'll pay €10 for your big salad (daily 7:00–24:00, 16 rue Vieille du Temple, tel. 01 40 29 02 18).

O2F (AE, AI, Level 2—Moderately Accessible) is a simple, casual café with youthful, fun atmosphere and a mostly gay clientele (€16–24 *menus*, Mon–Sat 11:00–2:00 in the morning, closed Sun, off rue de Rivoli at St. Paul Métro, 4 rue du Roi de Sicile, tel. 01 42 72 75 75).

La Locandiera (AE, AI, Level 2—Moderately Accessible) is a small coffee, breakfast, and ice-cream bar with great prices (€5–8 dishes, Mon–Fri 8:00–18:00, Sat–Sun 9:00–17:30, indoor and outdoor seating, 27 rue de Turenne, tel. 01 40 27 93 10).

Dining Closer to Hôtel de Ville

These eateries, near the Pompidou Center, appear on the map on page 253. To reach them, use the Hôtel de Ville Métro stop.

Au Bourguignon du Marais (AE+A, AI, Level 2—Moderately Accessible, challenging entry) is a small wine bar–bistro south of rue de Rivoli. Wine-lovers won't want to miss it. Gentle, English-speaking Jacques offers excellent Burgundy wines that blend well with his fine, though limited, selection of *plats du jour*. The escargots are the best I've had, and the dessert was...*délicieux* (allow €35–45 with wine, closed Sat–Sun, call by 19:00 to reserve, 52 rue Francois Miron, tel. 01 48 87 15 40).

A Happening Marais Square: **Rue de Bourg-Tibourg** (just off rue de Rivoli), busy with a fun assortment of popular eateries under its bushy trees, is worth surveying. **Le Fou d'En Face** (only outdoor tables are accessible) specializes in wine and *pot-au-feu* (beef stew–€19). The lively and cheap **Restaurante Sant Antonio (AE, AI,** Level 2—Moderately Accessible) serves up pizza, salads, and Italian. **Feria Café (AE, AI,** Level 2—Moderately Accessible) offers a traditional French menu.

BHV Department Store's (AE, AI, AL, AT, Level 1—Fully Accessible) fifth-floor cafeteria provides full accessibility, nice views, an escape from the busy streets below, and no-brainer, point-and-shoot cafeteria cuisine (Mon–Sat 11:30–18:00, closed Sun, at intersection of rue du Temple and rue de la Verrerie, 1 block from Hôtel de Ville). The store also has accessible changing rooms, if you're in the mood for a little shopping.

Ile St. Louis

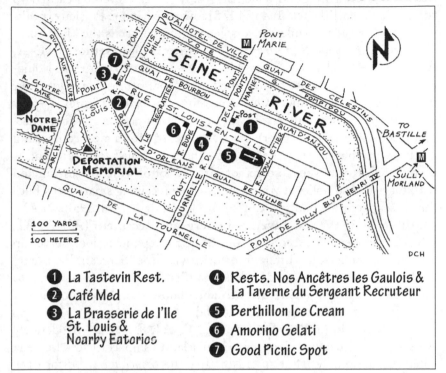

1 La Tastevin Rest.
2 Café Med
3 La Brasserie de l'Ile St. Louis & Nearby Eateries
4 Rests. Nos Ancêtres les Gaulois & La Taverne du Sergeant Recruteur
5 Berthillon Ice Cream
6 Amorino Gelati
7 Good Picnic Spot

Ile St. Louis

The Ile St. Louis is a romantic and peaceful neighborhood to window-shop for plenty of promising dinner possibilities. Cruise the island's main street for a variety of options, from cozy *crêperies* to Italian eateries (intimate pizzerias and upscale) to typical brasseries (a few with fine outdoor seating facing the bridge to Ile de la Cité). After dinner, sample Paris' best sorbet and roll or stroll across to the Ile de la Cité to see an illuminated Notre-Dame, or enjoy a scenic drink on the deck of a floating café moored under the Notre-Dame's right transept. All of these listings line the island's main drag, the rue St. Louis-en-l'Ile (see map above; to get here, use the Pont Marie Métro stop). Consider skipping dessert to enjoy a roll or stroll licking the best ice cream in Paris (described under "Ice-Cream Dessert," below).

Le Tastevin (AE, AI, Level 2—Moderately Accessible) is an eight-table, mother-and-son-run restaurant serving top-notch traditional French cuisine with white-tablecloth, candlelit, gourmet elegance under heavy wooden beams. The *menus* start with three courses at about €30 and offer plenty of classic choices that change with the season to ensure freshness (open daily, good wine list, reserve for late-evening eating, 46 rue St. Louis-en-l'Ile, tel. 01 43 54 17 31; owner Madame Puisieux speaks just enough English, while her son, Jean-Philippe, tends the kitchen).

Medieval Theme Restaurants: Nos Ancêtres les Gaulois (AE+A, AI, Level 2—Moderately Accessible, one 8" entry step) on rue St. Louis-en-l'Ile is famous for its rowdy, medieval-cellar atmosphere. Ideal for barbarians—as the name ("Our Ancestors the Gauls") implies—they serve all-you-can-eat buffets with straw baskets of raw veggies (cut whatever you like with your dagger), massive plates of pâté, a meat course, and all the wine you can stomach for €35. The food is just food; burping is encouraged. If you want to eat a lot, drink a lot of wine, be surrounded with tourists, and holler at your friends while receiving smart-aleck buccaneer service, this food fest can be fun (open daily from 19:00, at #39, tel. 01 46 33 66 07). **La Taverne du Sergeant Recruteur (AE+A, AI,** Level 2—Moderately Accessible, one 8" entry step), next door, serves up the same formula with a different historic twist: The "Sergeant Recruiter" used to get young Parisians drunk and stuffed here, then sign them into the army. You might swing by both and choose the..."ambience" is not quite the right word...that fits your mood.

La Brasserie de l'Ile St. Louis (AE, AI, Level 2—Moderately Accessible) is situated at the prow of the island's ship as it faces Ile de la Cité, offering purely Alsatian cuisine (try the *choucroute garni* for €17), served in Franco-Germanic ambience with no-nonsense brasserie service. This is your perfect balmy-evening perch for watching the Ile St. Louis promenade—or, if it's chilly, the interior is plenty characteristic for a memorable night out (closed Wed, no reservations, 55 quai de Bourbon, tel. 01 43 54 02 59). In the little square adjacent to La Brasserie de l'Ile St Louis, you'll find three charming little spots serving a perfect variety of French goodies inside or on the sidewalk: **Le Flore-en-l'Ile (AE, AI,** Level 2—Moderately Accessible) serves tea, pastries, ice cream and light lunches; **Terrasse Chauffee (AE, AI,** Level 2—Moderately Accessible) serves breakfast, lunch, and dinner French comfort food (including a €16 *menu*); and **The St. Regis (AE, AI,** Level 2—Moderately Accessible) also serves breakfast, lunch, and dinner with crêpes and light meals, plus an €18 *menu*. All three eateries are on the corner of rue Jean du Bellay and rue St. Louis-en-l'Ile.

Café Med (AE+A, AI, Level 2—Moderately Accessible, two 6" entry steps), near Notre-Dame at #77, is best for inexpensive salads, crêpes, and light €12 *menus* in a tight but cheery setting (limited wine list, open daily, tel. 01 43 29 73 17, charming Eva). There's a similar *crêperie* just across the street.

Riverside Picnic

On sunny lunchtimes and balmy evenings, the *quai* on the Left Bank side of Ile St. Louis is lined with locals who have more class than money, spreading out tablecloths and even lighting candles for elegant picnics. Otherwise, it's a great place for people-watching. The *quai* is accessible via the long ramp of Quai d'Orléans, visible from the pont St. Louis.

Ice-Cream Dessert

Half the people strolling Ile St. Louis are licking an ice cream cone, because this is the home of *les glaces Berthillon*. The original **Berthillon** shop (**AE+A, AI+A,** Level 2—Moderately Accessible, one 4" entry doorstep and one interior 4" step), at 31 rue St. Louis-en-l'Ile, is marked by the line of salivating customers (closed Mon-Tue). It's so popular that the wealthy people who can afford to live on this fancy island complain about the congestion it causes. For a less famous but at least as tasty treat, the homemade Italian gelato a block away at **Amorino Gelati** (**AE+A, AI+A,** Level 2—Moderately Accessible) is giving Berthillon competition (no line, bigger portions, easier to see what you want, and they offer little tastes—Berthillon doesn't need to, 47 rue St. Louis-en-l'Ile, tel. 01 44 07 48 08). Having some of each is not a bad thing.

TRANSPORTATION CONNECTIONS

Trains

Paris is Europe's rail hub, with six major train stations, each serving different regions: Gare de l'Est (eastbound trains), Gare du Nord (northern France and Europe), Gare St. Lazare (northwestern France), Gare d'Austerlitz (southwestern France and Europe), Gare de Lyon (southeastern France and Italy), and Gare Montparnasse (northwestern France and TGV service to France's southwest). Any train station has schedule information, can make reservations, and sell tickets for any destination. Buying tickets is handier from an SNCF neighborhood office—including those at Louvre, Invalides, Orsay, Versailles, and airports—or at your neighborhood travel agency. It's worth the small fee. Look for *SNCF* signs in their window that indicate they sell train tickets.

Schedules change by season, weekday, and weekend. Verify train schedules shown in this book (to study ahead on the Web, check Germany's excellent all-Europe Web site, http://bahn.hafas.de/bin/query.exe/en). The nationwide information line for train schedules and reservations is tel. 3635. Dial this four-digit number, then press "3" for reservations or ticket purchase when you get the message (you may get sent to a French-only phone tree as SNCF tries to automate its services; if so, hang up and ask your hotelier for help). Press 321 for Eurostar information, or 322 for Thalys. This incredibly helpful, time-saving service costs €0.34 per minute from anywhere in France (ask for an English-speaking agent and hope for the best, allow 5 min per call). The time and energy you save easily justifies the telephone torture, particularly when making seat reservations (note that phoned reservations must be picked up at least 30 min prior to departure).

All six train stations have banks or change offices, ATMs, information desks, telephones, cafés, newsstands, and clever pickpockets. Because of security concerns, not all have baggage check, though those with this service are identified below.

Métro and RER trains, as well as buses and taxis, are well-marked at every station. When arriving by Métro, follow signs for *Grandes Lignes-SNCF* to find the main tracks.

Each station offers two types of rail service: long distance to other cities, called *Grandes Lignes* (major lines); and suburban service to outlying areas, called *banlieue* or RER. Both *banlieue* and RER trains serve outlying areas and the airports; the only difference is that *banlieue* lines are operated by SNCF (France's train system, called Transilien) and RER lines are operated by RATP (Paris' Métro and bus system). You may also see ticket windows identified as *Ile de France*. This is for Transilien (SNCF) trains serving destinations outside Paris in the Ile de France region (usually no longer than an hour from Paris).

Paris train stations can be intimidating, but if you slow down, avoid peak times, take a deep breath, and ask for help, you'll find them manageable and efficient. Bring a pad of paper for clear communication at ticket/info windows. All stations have helpful *accueil* (information) booths; the bigger stations have roving helpers, usually in red vests. They're capable of answering rail questions more quickly than the information or ticket windows.

Access: Most of Paris' train stations are generally accessible, though each station has areas that a wheelchair user can't access. Most platforms can be reached by wheelchair, but sometimes the wheelchair user will be assisted by staff. Most stations have accessible toilets and elevators. When you arrive at any station, ask an attendant for assistance, or report to the *accueil* (information) booth.

SNCF, the French rail company, has a telephone number with detailed recorded information about accessibility for every station in France (tel. 08 00 15 47 53). The catch: it's all in French. In a pinch, recruit a hotelier or another friendly local to call for you.

Below, we've listed specific access information only for the Gare du Nord station, which you'll use to connect to most destinations in this book (e.g., London, Amsterdam, Bruges, and the Rhine via Köln).

Station Overview

Here's an overview of Paris' major train stations. Métro and RER trains, as well as buses and taxis, are well-marked at every station. When arriving by Métro, follow signs for *Grandes Lignes*-SNCF to find the main tracks.

Gare du Nord

This vast station serves cities in northern France and international destinations north of Paris, including Copenhagen, Amsterdam (see "To Brussels and Amsterdam by Thalys Train," below), and the Eurostar to London (see "To London by Eurostar Train," below).

Arrive early to allow time to navigate this station. If you arrive by Métro, follow *Grandes Lignes* signs (main lines) and keep going up until you reach the tracks at street level. *Grandes Lignes* depart from tracks 3-21, suburban *(banlieue)* lines from tracks 30–36, and RER trains depart from tracks 37–44 (tracks 41–44 are 1 floor below). Glass train information booths *(accueil)* are scattered throughout the station, and information-helpers circulate (all rail staff are required to speak English).

The tourist information kiosk opposite track 16 is a hotel reservation service for Accor chain hotels (they also have free Paris maps). Information booths for the **Thalys** (high-speed trains to Brussels and Amsterdam) are opposite track 8. All non-Eurostar ticket sales are opposite tracks 3–8. Passengers departing on **Eurostar** (London via Chunnel) must buy tickets and check in on the second level, opposite track 6. (Note: Britain's time zone is one hour earlier; times listed on Eurostar tickets are local times—Parisian time for departing Paris and the British time you'll arrive in London.)

Access: AE, AI, AT, Level 2—Moderately Accessible. Some parts of the station are accessible only by escalator, not elevator. Wheelchair users can find an accessible toilet alongside track 3 (push button near door to be let in). Another accessible toilet is located near track 36. The platforms are at street level, so elevators are not needed to leave the station. There are accessible elevators to the lower level, where car rentals and the Métro are located. As you go toward the exit with the taxi stand, you'll find the elevators located just inside the doorway on the right-hand side (go to floor "-1").

Paris Train Stations

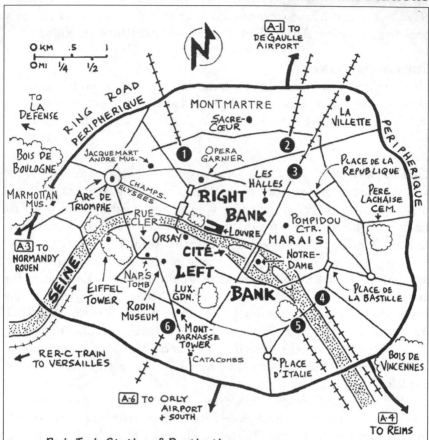

Paris Train Stations & Destinations

1 Gare St. Lazare: To Normandy (also Vernon/Giverny)

2 Gare du Nord: To London, Brussels, Amsterdam & N. France
(also Charles de Gaulle Airport, Chantilly & Auvers-sur-Oise)

3 Gare l'Est: To E. France, S. Germany, Switzerland & Austria

4 Gare de Lyon: To Italy & SE France
(also Fontainebleau, Melun/Vaux-le-Vicomte & Disneyland)

5 Gare d'Austerlitz: To SW France, Loire Valley & Spain

6 Gare Montparnasse: To SW France, Loire Valley,
Normandy & Brittany (also Chartres & Mont St. Michel)

Key Destinations Served by Gare du Nord *Grandes Lignes:*
Brussels (12/day, 1.5 hrs, see "To Brussels and Amsterdam by Thalys Train," page 284), **Bruges** (18/day, 2 hrs, change in Brussels, one direct), **Amsterdam** (5/day direct on fast Thalys train, 4 hrs; more with a transfer in Brussels, 5 hrs. For details, see "To Brussels and Amsterdam by Thalys Train," page 284), **Copenhagen** (1/day, 16 hrs, two night trains), **Koblenz** (6/day, 5 hrs, change in Köln), and **London** Eurostar via Chunnel (17/day, 3 hrs, tel. 08 36 35 35 39, see "To London by Eurostar Train," page 284).

By *Banlieue/*RER Lines: **Chantilly-Gouvieux** (hrly, fewer on weekends, 35 min), **Charles de Gaulle Airport** (2/hr, 30 min, runs 5:30–23:00, track 4), **Auvers-sur-Oise** (2/hr, 1 hr, transfer at Pontoise or St Ouen).

Gare Montparnasse

This big and modern station covers three floors, serves lower Normandy and Brittany, and offers TGV service to the Loire Valley and southwestern France, as well as suburban service to Chartres. At street level, you'll find a bank, *banlieue* trains serving Chartres (you can also reach the *banlieue* trains from the second level), and ticket windows for Ile de France trains in the center, just past the escalators.

Most services are provided on the second (top) level, where the *Grandes Lignes* arrive and depart. Ticket windows and an information booth are to the far left (with your back to glass exterior). *Banlieue* trains depart from tracks 10–19. The main rail information office is opposite track 15. Taxis and car rentals are to the far left as you leave the tracks. Air France buses to Orly and Charles de Gaulle Airports stop in front of the station, down the escalators and outside.

Key Destinations Served by Gare Montparnasse: Chartres (20/day, 1 hr, *banlieue* lines), **Pontorson/Mont St. Michel** (5/day, 4.5 hrs, via Rennes, then take bus from Pontorson; or take train to Pontorson via Caen, then bus from Pontorson), **Dinan** (7/day, 4 hrs, change in Rennes and Dol), **Bordeaux** (14/day, 3.5 hrs), **Sarlat** (5/day, 6 hrs, change in Bordeaux, Libourne, or Souillac), **Toulouse** (11/day, 5 hrs, most require change, usually in Bordeaux), **Albi** (7/day, 6–7.5 hrs, change in Toulouse, also night train), **Carcassonne** (8/day, 6.5 hrs, most require changes in Toulouse and Bordeaux, direct trains take 10 hrs), and **Tours** (14/day, 1 hr).

Gare de Lyon

This huge and bewildering station offers TGV and regular service to southeastern France, Italy, and other international destinations (for more trains to Italy, see "Gare de Bercy," below). Frequent *banlieue* trains serve Melun (near Vaux-le-Vicomte) and Fontainebleau (some depart from the main *Grandes Lignes* level, more frequent departures are from one level down, follow RER-D signs, and ask at any *accueil* or ticket window where the next departure leaves from). Don't leave this station without relaxing in Le Train Bleu Restaurant lounge, up the stairs opposite track G.

Grande Ligne trains arrive and depart from one level, but are divided into two areas (tracks A–N and 5–23). They are connected by the long platform along tracks A and 5, and by the hallway adjacent to track A and opposite track 9. This hallway has all the services, including ticket windows, ticket information, banks, and shops (including Virgin Records/ Books). *Banlieue* ticket windows are just inside the hall adjacent to track A *(billets Ile de France)*. *Grandes Lignes* and *banlieue* lines share the same tracks. A tourist office (Mon–Sat 8:00–18:00, closed Sun) and a train information office are both opposite track L. From the RER or Métro, follow signs for *Grandes Lignes Arrivées* and take the escalator up to reach the platforms. Train information booths *(accueil)* are opposite tracks A and 11 and downstairs. Baggage check (daily 6:45–22:45) is down the stairs opposite track 13 (keep straight off the escalator then turn left). Taxi stands are well-signed in front of the station at and one floor below.

Air France buses to Montparnasse (easy transfer to Orly Airport) and direct to Charles de Gaulle Airport stop outside the station's main entrance (opposite tracks A to L, roll or stroll across the parking lot—the stop is opposite the Café Europeen; €12, 2/hr, normally at :15 and :45 after the hour).

Key Destinations Served by Gare de Lyon: Vaux-le-Vicomte (train to Melun, hrly, 30 min), **Fontainebleau** (nearly hrly, 45 min), **Beaune** (12/day, 2.5 hrs, most require change in Dijon), **Dijon** (15/day, 1.5 hrs), **Chamonix** (9/day, 9 hrs, change in Lyon and St. Gervais; 1 night train), **Annecy** (14/day, 4–7 hrs), **Lyon** (16/day, 2.5 hrs), **Avignon** (9/day in 2.5 hrs, 6/day in 4 hrs with change), **Arles** (14/day, 5 hrs, most with change in Marseille, Avignon, or Nîmes), **Nice** (14/day, 5.5–7 hrs, many with change in Marseille), **Venice** (3/day, 3/night, 11–15 hrs, most require changes), **Rome** (2/day, 5/night, 15–18 hrs, most require changes), and **Bern** (9/day, 5–11 hrs, most require changes, night train).

Gare de Bercy

This smaller station handles some night train service to Italy during renovation work at the Gare de Lyon (Mo: Bercy, one stop east of Gare de Lyon on line #14).

Gare de l'Est

This single-floor station (with underground Métro), which serves eastern France and international destinations east of Paris, is in the midst of a renovation to accommodate new TGV service to Reims and Strasbourg. Expect changes from this description: Train information booths are at tracks 1 and 26; the info booth at track 18 is for Transilien trains serving suburban areas; ticket windows are in the big hall opposite track 8; luggage storage *(consigne)* is through the hall opposite track 12; and Métro access is opposite track 18.

Key Destinations Served by Gare de l'Est: Note that by 2007, many of these trip times will be much shorter, thanks to new TGV train service—**Colmar** (12/day, 5.5 hrs, change in Strasbourg, Dijon, or Mulhouse), **Strasbourg** (14/day, 4.5 hrs, many require changes), **Reims** (12/day, 1.5 hrs), **Verdun** (5/day, 3 hrs, change in Metz or Chalon), **Munich** (5/day, 9 hrs, some require changes, night train), **Vienna** (7/day, 13–18 hrs, most require changes, night train), **Zürich** (10/day, 7 hrs, most require changes, night train), and **Prague** (2/day, 14 hrs, night train).

Gare St. Lazare

This relatively small station serves upper Normandy, including Rouen and Giverny. All trains arrive and depart one floor above street level. Follow signs to *Grandes Lignes* from the Métro to reach the tracks. Ticket windows are in the first hall at departure level. *Grandes Lignes* (main lines) depart from tracks 17-27; *banlieue* (suburban) trains depart from 1–16. The train information office *(accueil)* is opposite track 15. There's a post office (PTT) along track 27, and WCs are opposite track 19. There is no baggage check. You'll find many shops and services one floor below the departure level.

Key Destinations Served by Gare St. Lazare: Giverny (train to Vernon, 5/day, 45 min then bus or taxi 10 min to Giverny), **Rouen** (15/day, 75 min), **Honfleur** (6/day, 3 hrs, via Lisieux, then bus), **Bayeux** (9/day, 2.5 hrs, some with change in Caen), and **Caen** (12/day, 2 hrs).

Gare d'Austerlitz

This small station provides non-TGV service to the Loire Valley, southwestern France, and Spain. All tracks are at street level. The information booth is opposite track 17, and all ticket sales are in the hall opposite track 10. Baggage check, WCs, and car rental are near track 27, along the side of the station, opposite track 21. To get to the Métro, you must go outside to either side of the station.

Key Destinations Served by Gare d'Austerlitz: Amboise (8/day in 2 hrs, 12/day in 1.5 hrs with change in Tours' St. Pierre-des-Corps), Cahors (7/day, 5–7 hrs, most with changes), Barcelona (1/day, 9 hrs, change in Montpellier, night trains), Madrid (2 night trains only, 13–16 hrs), and Lisbon (1/day, 24 hrs).

To Brussels and Amsterdam by Thalys Train

The pricey Thalys train has the monopoly on the rail route (for a cheaper option, try the Eurolines bus; see below). Without a railpass, you'll pay about €80–100 second class for the Paris–Amsterdam train (compared to €45 by bus) or about €60–80 second class for the Paris–Brussels train (compared to €25 by bus). Even with a railpass, you need to pay for train reservations (second class-$13, first class-$26). Wheelchair users and one companion get discounted first-class fares with minimal restrictions. Anyone should book at least a day ahead, as seats are limited (toll tel. 08 25 84 25 97).

Access: AE+A, AI, AT, Level 2—Moderately Accessible. Wheelchair users can pay for second class on Thalys trains, but reserve first-class accessible seats at no additional charge. Wheelchair users should alert Thalys at the time of booking that they will need assistance, then arrive 30 minutes before departure so Thalys staff can prepare for boarding with ramps. On Thalys trains, only first class is accessible, with designated spaces for wheelchairs. Train cars 1, 11, and 21 have a seat with a mobile base to make transfers easier. These three cars also have accessible toilets.

To London by Eurostar Train

The fastest, most accessible, and most convenient way to get to London is by rail—through the "Chunnel." For information on this option, see page 53.

Airports
Charles de Gaulle Airport

Paris' primary airport has two main terminals, T-1 and T-2, and two lesser terminals, T-3 and T-9. Most flights from the United States serve T-1 or T-2. Due to ongoing construction at T-1, it's impossible to predict which airlines will serve this terminal—call ahead or check their Web site (tel. 01 48 62 22 80, www.adp.fr). Terminals are connected every few minutes by a free *navette* (shuttle bus; AE, AI, Level 2—Moderately Accessible), though a new train zips travelers between the terminals effortlessly. The RER (Paris suburban train, connecting to Métro) stops at T-2 and

T-3, and the TGV (tay-zhay-vay, stands for *train à grande vitesse*—high-speed, long-distance train) station is at T-2. There is no baggage storage at the airport. Beware of pickpockets on *navettes* between terminals, and especially on RER trains. Do not take an unauthorized taxi from the men greeting you on arrival. Official taxi stands are well-signed. For the latest information on either of Paris' airports, check www.adp.fr.

General Airport Access: AE, AI, AL, AT+A, Level 2—Moderately Accessible. Although Charles de Gaulle airport has basic accessibility features, wheelchair users have reported that this can be a challenging place to navigate. The TI's *Passager à Mobilité Reduite* guide lists the accessibility of the airport and its hotels and restaurants.

Terminal 1 (T-1): This circular terminal has one main entry and covers three floors—arrival (*arrivées*, top floor), departure (*départs*, one floor down) and shops/boutiques (basement level). For information on getting to Paris, see "Transportation between Charles de Gaulle Airport and Paris," below.

Arrival Level: You'll find a variety of services at the gates listed below. Expect changes to this information as airport construction proceeds. Blue signs will verfiy the gates listed below.

- Gate 36: Called "Meeting Point" *(Point de Rencontre)*, this gate has an information counter with English-speaking staff, a café, and an ATM. Ask here for directions to Disneyland shuttle (€14, daily 7:30–21:00).
- Gate 2: Outside are Air France buses to Paris and Orly Airport (see below).
- Gate 10: Outside are Roissy-Buses to Paris (buy tickets from driver); upstairs is access to car rental.
- Gate 16: A bank with lousy rates for currency exchange.
- Gate 18: Taxis outside.
- Gate 20: Shuttle buses *(navettes,* **AE, AI,** Level 2—Moderately Accessible)* for Terminal 2 and the RER trains to Paris. Take the elevator down to level (*niveau*) 2, then go outside (line #1 serves T-2 including the TGV station; line #2 goes directly to the RER station). A new intra-airport train also shuttles riders between the various terminals.

Departure Level (*niveau* 3): This is limited to flight check-in, though you will find ADP information desks here. Those departing from T-1 will find restaurants, a PTT (post office), a pharmacy, boutiques, and a handy grocery store one floor below the ticketing desks (*niveau* 2 on the elevator).

Access for Terminal 1: AE, AI, AL, AT, Level 1—Fully Accessible, but the toilets and elevators can be hard to find. If you'll be taking the train to Paris, check in with the RER-SNCF information booth to prepare for your journey—they will show you to the elevator. For general assistance for persons with reduced mobility, call 01 48 62 28 24.

Terminal 2 (T-2): This long, horseshoe-shaped terminal is dominated by Air France and divided into several subterminals (or halls), each identified by a letter. You can walk or roll from one hall to the other. Halls are connected to the RER, the TGV station, and T-1 every five minutes with free *navette* shuttle buses (**AE, AI,** Level 2—Moderately Accessible; line #5 runs to T-1).

The RER and TGV stations are below the Sheraton Hotel (access by *navettes* or on foot). Stops for *navettes*, Air France buses, and Roissy Buses are all well-marked and near each hall (see "Transportation between Charles de Gaulle Airport and Paris," below). ADP information desks are located near Gate 5 in each hall. Car-rental offices, post offices, pharmacies, and ATMs *(point d'argent)* are also well-signed.

Access for Terminal 2: AE, AI, AL, AT+A, Level 2—Moderately Accessible. While the interior of the terminal is fully accessible, not all toilet areas are accessible. If using the train to get into Paris, check in with the RER-SNCF information booth to prepare for your journey. For general assistance for persons with reduced mobility, call 01 48 62 59 00.

Transportation between Charles de Gaulle Airport and Paris: Three efficient public-transportation routes, taxis, and airport shuttle vans link the airport's terminals with central Paris. All are well-marked, and stops are centrally located at all terminals. The most accessible route downtown is via taxi or with an airport shuttle.

Taxis with luggage will run about €50 with bags, more if traffic is bad. You can request a minibus with a ramp for accessibility, which costs more than a normal taxi. (For details, see page 189.)

Airport shuttles offer transportation between either of Paris' airports and your hotel, and (since they have more space than cabs) are good for single travelers or families of four or more. Airport pickup must be booked ahead and can be slow given unpredictable arrival times of international flights (plan on a 30-minute wait at the airport; taxis are easier for getting into Paris). Standard airport shuttles (**AE+A,** Level 2—Moderately Accessible) cost about €20–30 for one person, €30-40 for two, and €40-52 for three. A fully accessible van, adapted for wheelchair users, is more expensive (**AE, AI,** Level 1, €130 for wheelchair user plus up to 5 other passengers, reserve a week in advance, available through Golden Air—see below). Some offer deals if you do a round trip, and most are more expensive at night (20:00–6:00). Be clear on where and how you are to meet your driver.

Golden Air is the most reliable of the many shuttles (from Paris to Charles de Gaulle: €27 for one person, €17 per person for two; from Charles de Gaulle to Paris: €35 for one person, €20 per person for two; tel. 01 34 10 12 92, fax 01 34 10 93 89, www.paris-airport-shuttle-limousine .com, goldenair@goldenair.net).

Sleeping at or near Charles de Gaulle Airport: **Hôtel Ibis**** **(AE, AI, AL, AT, AR, AB,** Level 1—Fully Accessible), outside the RER Roissy Rail station at T-3 (the first RER stop coming from Paris), offers standard and predictable accommodations (Db-€80–90, near *navette* stop, free shuttle bus to all terminals, tel. 01 49 19 19 19, fax 01 49 19 19 21, h1404@accor.com). **Novotel***** **(AE, AI, AL, AT, AR, AB,** Level 1— Fully Accessible) is next door and the next step up (weekend Db-€135, weekday Db-€160, tel. 01 49 19 27 27, fax 01 49 19 27 99, www.novotel .com).

Orly Airport

This airport feels small. It's good for rental-car pickup and drop-off, as it's closer to Paris and far easier to navigate than Charles de Gaulle Airport.

Orly has two terminals: Sud (south) and Ouest (west). Air France flights arrive at Ouest, and all others use Sud. At the Sud terminal, you'll exit the baggage claim (near Gate H) and see signs directing you to city transportation, car rental, and so on. Turn left to enter the main terminal area, and you'll find exchange offices with bad rates, an American Express office, an ATM, the ADP (*Espace Tourisme*, a quasi-tourist office that offers free city maps and basic sightseeing information, open until 24:00), and an SNCF rail desk (next to ADP, daily 7:45–12:00 & 13:00–20:00, sells train tickets and even Eurailpasses). Downstairs is a sandwich bar, WCs, a bank (same bad rates), a newsstand (buy a phone card), and a post office. Car-rental offices are located in the parking lot in front of the terminal opposite Gate C. For flight info on any airline serving Orly, call 01 49 75 15 15. For information on either of Paris' airports, visit www.adp.fr.

Transportation between Orly Airport and Paris: Several efficient public-transportation routes, taxis, and a couple of airport shuttle services link Orly with central Paris. Wheelchair users will find taxis and minibuses to be the most convenient option. The gate locations listed below apply to Orly Sud, but the same transportation services are available from both terminals.

Air France buses (outside Gate K) run to Montparnasse train station (with many Métro lines) and to Invalides Métro stop (€8 one-way, €12 round-trip, 4/hr, 40 min to Invalides). These buses are handy for those staying in or near the rue Cler neighborhood (from Invalides bus stop, take the Métro to La Tour Maubourg or Ecole Militaire to reach recommended hotels; see also "RER trains," below). Air France buses also run to Charles de Gaulle Airport (€16, 2/hr, 80 min). Remember that to continue on the Métro, you'll need to buy a separate ticket (for ticket types and prices, see "Getting Around Paris," page 187).

Jetbus (outside Gate H, €5.50, 4/hr) is the quickest way to the Paris subway and the best way to the Marais neighborhood. Take Jetbus to the Villejuif Louis Aragon Métro stop. To reach the Marais neighborhood, take the Métro to the Sully Morland stop.

The **Orlybus** (outside Gate H, €6, 3/hr) takes you to the Denfert-Rochereau RER-B line and the Métro, offering subway access to central Paris, including the Latin Quarter and Notre-Dame Cathedral, as well as the Gare du Nord train station.

These two routes provide access to Paris via **RER trains:** an ADP shuttle (Orly Rail bus) takes you to RER-C (Pont d'Orly stop), with connections to Gare d'Austerlitz, St. Michel/Notre-Dame, Musée d'Orsay, Invalides, and Pont de l'Alma stations and is handy for some Rue Cler hotels (outside Gate G, 4/hr, €5.50). **Orlyval trains** take you to the Antony stop on RER-B (serving Luxembourg, Châtelet-Les Halles, St. Michel, and Gare du Nord stations in central Paris, €9, includes RER ticket).

Taxis are to the far right as you leave the terminal, at Gate M. Allow €25–35 with bags for a taxi into central Paris.

Airport shuttles are good for single travelers or families of four or more, but better from Paris to the airport (see "Charles de Gaulle Airport," above, for a company to contact; from Orly, figure about €23/1 person, €30/2 people, less for larger groups and kids).

Sleeping near Orly Airport: Two chain hotels, owned by the same company, are your best option near Orly. **Hôtel Ibis**** (AE, AI, AL, AT, AR, AB, Level 1—Fully Accessible) is reasonable, basic, and close by (Db-€65, tel. 01 56 70 50 60, fax 01 56 70 50 70, h1413@accor.com). **Hôtel Mercure***** (AE, AI, AL, AR, AB, Level 1—Fully Accessible) provides more comfort for a higher price (Db-€130–160, tel. 01 49 75 15 50, fax 01 49 75 15 51, h1246@accor-hotels.com). Both have free shuttles to the terminal.

Beauvais Airport

Budget airlines such as Ryanair use Beauvais Airport, offering dirt-cheap airfares, but leaving you 50 miles north of Paris. Still, this small airport has direct buses to Paris (see below). It's ideal for drivers who want to rent a car here and head to Normandy or north to Belgium. The airport is basic (the terminal for departing passengers and baggage claim is under a tent, and waiting areas are crowded and have few services), but it's being improved as it deals with an increasing number of passengers (airport tel. 08 92 68 20 66, www.aeroportbeauvais.com; Ryanair tel. 08 92 68 20 73, www.ryanair.com).

Transportation between Beauvais Airport and Paris: Buses depart from the airport 20 minutes after flights arrive, taking you to Porte Maillot, which has a Métro and RER stop on the west edge of Paris (bus costs €13, takes 90 min). Buses depart Paris for Beauvais Airport three hours before scheduled flight departures (catch bus at Porte Maillot in parking lot on boulevard Pershing next to Hôtel Concorde-Lafayette). Bus tickets must be booked 24 hours in advance; call Beauvais Airport for details or buy tickets on their Web site (see contact info above).

Taxis run from Beauvais Airport to Paris: €120 to central Paris, €130 to Orly Airport, and €110 to Charles de Gaulle Airport. Taxis to Beauvais' train station or city center cost €11. **Trains** connect Beauvais and Paris Gare du Nord (20/day, 80 min).

HISTORIC PARIS
ROLL OR STROLL

From Notre-Dame to the Pont Neuf

Paris has been the cultural capital of Europe for centuries. We'll start where it did, on Ile de la Cité, with a foray onto the Left Bank, on a tour that laces together 80 generations of history: from Celtic fishing village to Roman city, bustling medieval capital, birthplace of the Revolution, bohemian haunt of the 1920s café scene, and the working world of modern Paris.

Allow four hours to do justice to this three-mile tour. If the distance seems too long, break it into pieces to make it more manageable. Stops along this tour have varying degrees of accessibility (as noted). Skip those portions that do not suit your mobility level, and move on to the next stop.

THE TOUR BEGINS

• *Start at Notre-Dame Cathedral on the island in the River Seine, the physical and historic bull's-eye of your Paris map. To get there, take a taxi or ride the Métro to Cité, Hôtel de Ville, or St. Michel and roll or stroll to the big square facing the cathedral.*

NOTRE-DAME

• *On the square in front of the cathedral, get far enough back to take in the whole facade. Look at the circular window in the center.*

For centuries, the main figure in the Christian pantheon has been Mary, the mother of Jesus. Catholics petition her in times of trouble to gain comfort, and to ask her to convince God to be compassionate with

Historic Paris Roll or Stroll

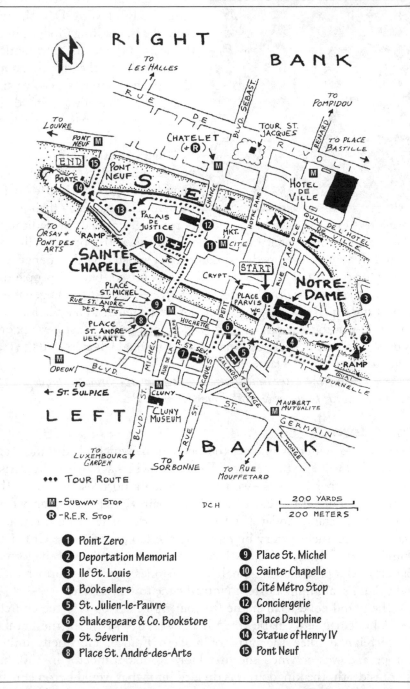

••• TOUR ROUTE

M - SUBWAY STOP

R - R.E.R. STOP

DCH

1 Point Zero
2 Deportation Memorial
3 Ile St. Louis
4 Booksellers
5 St. Julien-le-Pauvre
6 Shakespeare & Co. Bookstore
7 St. Séverin
8 Place St. André-des-Arts
9 Place St. Michel
10 Sainte-Chapelle
11 Cité Métro Stop
12 Conciergerie
13 Place Dauphine
14 Statue of Henry IV
15 Pont Neuf

them. The church is dedicated to "Our Lady" (Notre-Dame), and there she is, cradling God, right in the heart of the facade, surrounded by the halo of the rose window. Though the church is massive and imposing, it has always stood for the grace and compassion of Mary, the "mother of God."

Imagine the faith of the people who built this cathedral. They broke ground in 1163 with the hope that someday their great-great-great-great-great-great grandchildren might attend the dedication Mass two centuries later, in 1345. Look up the 200-foot-tall bell towers and imagine a tiny medieval community mustering the money and energy for construction. Master masons supervised, but the people did much of the grunt work themselves for free—hauling the huge stones from distant quarries, digging a 30-foot-deep trench to lay the foundation, and treading like rats on a wheel designed to lift the stones up, one by one. This kind of backbreaking, arduous manual labor created the real hunchbacks of Notre-Dame.

• *Move toward the cathedral, and view it from the bronze plaque on the ground (30 yards from the central doorway) marked...*

Point Zero

You're at the center of France, the point from which all distances are measured. It was also the center of Paris 2,300 years ago, when the Parisii tribe fished where the east–west river crossed a north–south road. The Romans conquered the Parisii and built their Temple of Jupiter where Notre-Dame stands today (52 B.C.). When Rome fell, the Germanic Franks sealed their victory by replacing the temple with the Christian church of St. Etienne in the sixth century. See the outlines of the former church in the pavement (in smaller gray stones), showing former walls and columns, angling out from Notre-Dame to Point Zero.

The grand equestrian statue (to your right, as you face the church) is of Charlemagne ("Charles the Great," 742–814), King of the Franks, whose reign marked the birth of modern France. He briefly united Europe and was crowned the first Holy Roman Emperor in 800, but after his death, the kingdom was divided into what would become modern France and Germany. (There are clean, but not accessible, toilets

Paris Through History

250 b.c. Small fishing village of the Parisii, a Celtic tribe.

52 b.c. Julius Caesar conquers the Parisii capital of Lutetia (near Paris), and the Romans replace it with a new capital on the Left Bank.

a.d. 497 Rome falls to the Germanic Franks. King Clovis (482–511) converts to Christianity and makes Paris his capital.

885–886 Paris gets wasted in siege by Viking Norsemen = Normans.

1163 Notre-Dame cornerstone laid.

c. 1250 Paris is a bustling commercial city with a university and new construction, such as Sainte-Chapelle and Notre-Dame.

c. 1600 King Henry IV beautifies Paris with buildings, roads, bridges, and squares.

c. 1700 Louis XIV makes Versailles his capital, while Parisians grumble.

1789 Paris is the heart of France's Revolution, which condemns thousands to the guillotine.

1804 Napoléon Bonaparte crowns himself emperor in a ceremony at Notre-Dame.

1830 & 1848 Parisians take to the streets again in revolutions, fighting the return of royalty.

c. 1860 Napoleon's nephew, Napoleon III, builds Paris' wide boulevards.

1889 The centennial of the Revolution is celebrated with the Eiffel Tower. Paris enjoys wealth and middle-class prosperity in the belle époque (beautiful age).

1920s After the draining Great War, Paris is a cheap place to live, attracting expatriates like Ernest Hemingway.

1940–1944 Occupied Paris spends the war years under gray skies and gray Nazi uniforms.

2006 You arrive in Paris to make history.

in front of the church near Charlemagne's statue—down twenty-five 7" steps.)

Before renovation 150 years ago, this square was much smaller, a characteristic medieval shambles facing a rundown church, surrounded by winding streets and higgledy-piggledy buildings. (Yellowed bricks in the pavement show the medieval street plan and even identify some of the buildings.) The church's huge bell towers rose above this tangle of smaller buildings, inspiring Victor Hugo's story of a deformed bell-ringer who could look down on all of Paris.

Looking two-thirds of the way up Notre-Dame's left tower, those with binoculars or good eyes can find Paris' most photographed gargoyle. Propped on his elbows on the balcony rail, he watches all the tourists in line.

• *Much of Paris' history is right underneath you. Some may consider visiting it in the...*

Archaeological Crypt

Access: Level 4—Not Accessible. There are fourteen 6" steps down to the entryway. The inside is mostly level.

Cost and Hours: €3.50, covered by Museum Pass, Tue–Sun 10:00–18:00, closed Mon.

The Sight: Two thousand years of dirt and debris have raised the city's altitude. In the Crypt (entrance 100 yards in front of Notre-Dame's entrance), you can see cellars and foundations from many layers of Paris: a Roman building with central heating; a wall that didn't keep the Franks out; the main medieval road that once led grandly up the square to Notre-Dame; and even (wow) a 19th-century sewer.

• *Now turn your attention to the church facade. Look at the left doorway and, to the left of the door, find the statue with his head in his hands.*

Notre-Dame Facade
St. Denis

When Christianity began making converts in Roman Paris, the bishop of Paris (St. Denis) was beheaded as a warning to those forsaking the Roman gods. But those early Christians were hard to keep down. St. Denis got up, tucked his head under his arm, headed north, paused at a fountain to

Notre-Dame Facade

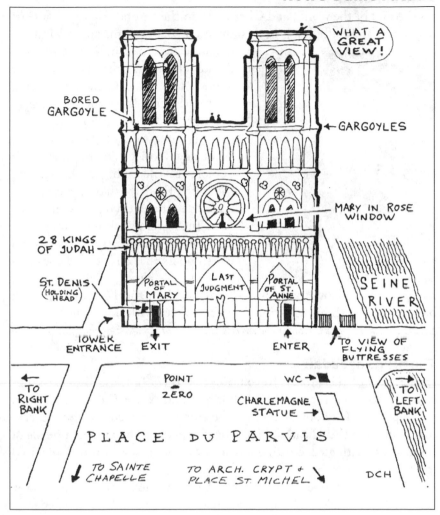

wash it off, and continued until he found just the right place to meet his maker. The Parisians were convinced by this miracle, Christianity gained ground, and a church soon replaced the pagan temple.

• *Above the central doorway, you'll find scenes from the Last Judgment.*

Central Portal

It's the end of the world, and Christ sits on the throne of judgment (just under the arches, holding both hands up). Below him, an angel and a

demon weigh souls in the balance; the demon cheats by pressing down. The good people stand to the left, gazing up to heaven. The naughty ones to the right are chained up and led off to a six-hour tour of the Louvre on a hot day. Notice the crazy, sculpted demons to the right, at the base of the arch. Find the flaming cauldron with the sinner diving into it head-first. The lower panel shows Judgment Day, as angels with trumpets remind worshippers that all social classes will be judged—clergy, nobility, army, and peasants. Below that, Jesus stands between the 12 apostles—each barefoot and with his ID symbol (such as Peter with his keys).

• *Move back 10 yards. Above the arches is a row of 28 statues, known as...*

The Kings of Judah

In the days of the French Revolution (1789–1799), these Biblical kings were mistaken for the hated French kings, and Notre-Dame represented the oppressive Catholic hierarchy. The citizens stormed the church, crying, "Off with their heads!" Plop, they lopped off the crowned heads of these kings with glee, creating a row of St. Denises that wasn't repaired for decades.

But the story doesn't end there. A schoolteacher who lived nearby collected the heads and buried them in his backyard for safekeeping. There they slept until 1977, when they were accidentally unearthed. Today, you can stare into the eyes of the original kings in the Cluny Museum, a few blocks away.

• *Enter the church and find a spot where you can view the long, high central aisle. (Be careful: Pickpockets attend church here religiously.)*

Notre-Dame Interior

Access: AE, AI+A, Level 2—Moderately Accessible. The entryway and three-fourths of the main floor are wheelchair-accessible. There are three 6" steps to enter the area of the Mass and the treasury.

Cost and Hours: Entry to the church is free; it's open daily 7:45–19:00;

treasury-€2.50 (not covered by Museum Pass), daily 9:30–17:30; Sunday Mass at 8:30, 10:00 (Gregorian), 11:30 (international), and 12:45. Tel. 01 42 34 56 10, www.cathedraledeparis.com.

Nave
Remove your metaphorical hat and become a simple bareheaded peasant, entering the dim medieval light of the church. Take a minute to let your pupils dilate, then take in the subtle, mysterious light show that God beams through the stained-glass windows. Follow the slender columns up 10 stories to the praying-hands arches of the ceiling, and contemplate the heavens. Let's say it's dedication day for this great stone wonder. The priest intones the words of the Mass that echo through the hall: *"Terribilis est locus iste"*—"This place is *terribilis*," meaning awe-inspiring or even terrifying. It's a huge, dark, earthly cavern lit with an unearthly light.

This is Gothic. Taller and filled with light, this was a major improvement over the earlier Romanesque style. Gothic architects needed only a few structural columns, topped by crisscrossing pointed arches to support the weight of the roof. This let them build higher than ever, freeing up the walls for windows.

Notre-Dame is designed in the shape of a cross, with the altar placed where the crossbeam intersects. The church can hold up to 10,000 faithful. And it's probably buzzing with visitors now, just as it was 800 years ago. The quiet, deserted churches we see elsewhere are in stark contrast to the busy, center-of-life places they were in the Middle Ages.
• *Approach the main altar.*

Altar
This marks the place where Mass is said and the bread and wine of Communion are blessed and distributed. In olden days, there were no chairs. This was the holy spot for Romans, Christians...and even atheists. When the Revolutionaries stormed the church, they gutted it and turned it into a "Temple of Reason." A woman dressed like the Statue of Liberty held court at the altar as a symbol of the divinity of Man. France today, while nominally Catholic, remains aloof from Vatican dogmatism. Instead of traditional wooden confessional booths, notice the open, glass-walled room (right aisle) where modern sinners seek counseling as much as forgiveness.

Right Transept (and Beyond)
A statue of Joan of Arc (Jeanne d'Arc, 1412–1431), dressed in armor and praying, honors the French teenager who rallied French soldiers to try to

drive English invaders from Paris, before being burned at the stake for claiming to hear heavenly voices. Almost immediately, Parisians rallied to condemn Joan's execution, and finally, in 1909, here in Notre-Dame, the former "witch" was beatified.

Join the statue in gazing up to the blue-and-purple, rose-shaped window—with teeny green Mary and baby Jesus in the center—the only one of the three windows still with its original medieval glass.

A large painting back down to your right shows portly Thomas Aquinas (1225–1274) teaching, while his students drink from the fountain of knowledge. This Italian monk did undergrad and master's work at the multicultural University of Paris, then taught there for several years while writing his theological works. His "scholasticism" used Aristotle's logic to examine the Christian universe, aiming to fuse faith and reason.

Just past the altar are the walls of the choir, where more intimate services can be held in this spacious building. Peeking inside, behind the altar, you'll see a fine 17th-century *pietà* flanked by two kneeling kings: Louis XIII and Louis XIV. The south walls of the choir have Gothic carvings (restored in the 19th century) showing scenes from the life of Christ after his Resurrection. Notice the niches below these carvings—they mark the tombs of centuries of archbishops. Surrounding the choir are chapels, each dedicated to a particular saint and funded by a particular guild. The faithful can pause at their favorite, light a candle as an offering, and meditate in the cool light of the stained glass. (The nearby treasury, containing lavish robes and golden reliquaries, lacks English explanations and probably isn't worth the €2.50 entry fee.)

• *Amble around the ambulatory, spill back outside, and make a slow U-turn left. Enter the park through the iron gates along the riverside.*

Notre-Dame Side View

Along the side of the church, you'll notice the flying buttresses. These 50-foot stone "beams" that stick out of the church were the key to the complex Gothic architecture. The pointed arches we saw inside caused the weight of the roof to push outward rather than downward. The "flying" buttresses support the roof by pushing back inward. Gothic architects were masters at playing architectural forces against each other to build loftier and loftier churches, with walls opened up for stained-glass windows.

Picture Quasimodo limping around along the railed balcony at the base of the roof among the gargoyles.  These grotesque beasts sticking out from pillars and buttresses represent souls caught between heaven and earth. They also function as rainspouts (from the same French root as "gargle") when there are no evil spirits to battle.

The neo-Gothic 300-foot spire is a product of the 1860 reconstruction of the dilapidated old church. Victor Hugo's book *The Hunchback of Notre-Dame* (1831) inspired a young architecture student named Eugène-Emmanuel Viollet-le-Duc to dedicate his career to a major renovation in Gothic style. Find Viollet-le-Duc himself at the base of the spire among the green apostles and evangelists (visible as you approach the back end of the church). The apostles look outward, blessing the city, while the architect (at top) looks up the spire, marveling at his fine work.

• *Behind Notre-Dame, cross the street and go through the accessible iron gate into the park at the tip of the island. Enjoy the sights from this little park. When you're ready to leave the park, go out the same gate and proceed on the sidewalk left of the fence that defines the park. Follow this sidewalk to the corner and cross the street at the curb cut by the light. To reach our next stop, turn right and go past the steps to reach the accessible ramp just beyond.*

Deportation Memorial (Mémorial de la Déportation)

Access: AE, AI, Level 2—Moderately Accessible. Use the accessible ramped entrance just past the steps. Once inside, the gardens are accessible, but the actual memorial chambers are not.

Cost and Hours: Free, daily April–Sept 10:00–12:00 & 14:00–19:00, Oct–March 10:00–12:00 & 14:00–17:00.

The Sight: This memorial to the 200,000 French victims of the Nazi concentration camps (1940–1945) draws you into their experience. France was quickly overrun by Nazi Germany, and Paris spent the war years under Nazi occupation. Jews and dissidents were rounded up and deported—many never returned.

As you enter, the city around you disappears. Surrounded by walls, you have become a prisoner. Your only freedom is your view of the sky and the tiny glimpse of the river below. Enter the dark, single-file chamber up ahead. Inside, the circular plaque in the floor reads, "They went to the end of the earth and did not return."

The hallway stretching in front of you is lined with 200,000 lighted

crystals, one for each French citizen who died. Flickering at the far end is the eternal flame of hope. The tomb of the unknown deportee lies at your feet. Above, the inscription reads, "Dedicated to the living memory of the 200,000 French deportees sleeping in the night and the fog, exterminated in the Nazi concentration camps." The side rooms are filled with triangles—reminiscent of the identification patches inmates were forced to wear—each bearing the name of a concentration camp. Above the exit as you leave is the message you'll find at all Nazi sites: "Forgive, but never forget."

Ile St. Louis

Back on street level, look across the river to the Ile St. Louis. If the Ile de la Cité is a tug laden with the history of Paris, it's towing this classy little residential dinghy laden only with high-rent apartments, boutiques, characteristic restaurants, and famous sorbet shops.

This island wasn't developed until much later than the Ile de la Cité (17th century). What was a swampy mess is now harmonious Parisian architecture and one of Paris' most exclusive neighborhoods. Its uppity residents complain that the local ice cream shop—Berthillon—draws crowds until late into the night (**AE+A, AI+A,** Level 2—Moderately Accessible, one 4" entry doorstep and one interior 4" step; 31 rue St. Louis-en-l'Ile).

On the Left Bank (on your right), at the foot of the bridge across from Ile St. Louis, you'll find one of Paris' most exclusive restaurants, La Tour d'Argent. Because the top floor has floor-to-ceiling windows, your evening meal comes with glittering views—and a golden price (allow €200 minimum, though you get a free photo of yourself dining elegantly with Notre-Dame floodlit in the background).

• *To visit Ile St. Louis now, backtrack to the intersection and cross the little bridge. Otherwise, to continue to the Left Bank, cross the Pont Arch bridge from the tip of Ile de la Cité turn right. Proceed along the river, toward the front end of Notre-Dame. For those who are able, stairs detour down to the riverbank, a fine place to picnic. You can also reach this riverbank by ramp: If you look a half block upriver, you'll see a long ramp that drops down to the riverbank... but beware of rising tides that can "dampen" your ability to get back on the ramp. This side view of the church from across the river is one of Europe's great sights and best from river level.*

LEFT BANK

The Rive Gauche, or the Left Bank of the Seine—"left" if you were floating downstream—still has many of the twisting lanes and narrow buildings of medieval times. The Right Bank is

more modern and business-oriented, with wide boulevards and stressed Parisians in suits. Here along the riverbank, the "big business" is secondhand books, displayed in the green metal stalls on the parapet. These literary entrepreneurs pride themselves on their easygoing business style. With flexible hours and virtually no overhead, they run their businesses as they have since medieval times. For more information, see *"Les Bouquinistes* (Riverside Vendors)" sidebar.

• *Though this is an old neighborhood, they've done a fine job of updating it with curb cuts—so access should be straightforward. When you reach the bridge (pont au Double) that crosses over in front of Notre-Dame, veer to the left across the street to a small park (place Viviani; fill your water bottle from fountain on left). You'll find the small rough-stone church of St. Julien-le-Pauvre just after the square and pass Paris' oldest inhabitant—an acacia tree nicknamed Robinier, after the guy who planted it in 1602—that may once have shaded the Sun King.*

Medieval Paris (1000–1400)

Picture Paris in 1250, when the church of St. Julien-le-Pauvre was still new. Notre-Dame was nearly done (so they thought), Sainte-Chapelle had just opened, the university was expanding human knowledge, and Paris was fast becoming a prosperous industrial and commercial center. The area around the church gives you some of the medieval feel. Looking along nearby rue Galande, you'll see a few old houses leaning every which way. (La Guillotine Pub at #52 sports an authentic guillotine from 1792 on its wall.) In medieval days, people were piled on top of each other, building at all angles, as they scrambled for this prime real estate near the main commercial artery of the day—the Seine. The smell of fish competed with the smell of neighbors in this knot of humanity.

Narrow dirt (or mud) streets sloped from here down into the mucky Seine, until modern quays and embankments cleaned that up.

• *Return to the river and turn left on rue de la Bûcherie. At #37, drop into the...*

Les Bouquinistes (Riverside Vendors)

The used-book sellers *(bouquinistes)* you see along the Seine around Notre-Dame are a Parisian fixture. It seems they've been here forever—at least since the mid-1500s, when shops and stalls lined most of the bridges in Paris. In 1557, they were labeled as thieves for selling forbidden Protestant pamphlets during the Wars of Religion (Parisians were staunchly Catholic).

The term *bouquinistes* (boo-keen-eest) probably comes from the Dutch word *boeckin*, meaning "small book." First using wheelbarrows to transport and sell their goods, these hardy entrepreneurs eventually fastened trays with thin leather straps to the parapets of the bridges. After the Revolution, business boomed when entire libraries were seized from nobles or clergymen and landed on the banks of the Seine. In 1891, *bouquinistes* received permission to permanently attach their boxes to the quaysides. Today, the waiting list is eight years long to become one of Paris' 250 *bouquinistes*.

Each *bouquiniste* is given four boxes (*boîtes*—each 6 feet long, 14 inches high, and 2.5 feet deep), and rent is paid only for the stone on which the boxes rest (less than €100 per year). The most coveted spots are awarded based on seniority. Maintenance costs, including the required *vert* wagon paint (the green color of old train cars), is paid by the *bouquinistes*. With little overhead, prices are usually cheaper than in most shops. While these days tourists buy magnets and coasters more than vintage books, officially the city allows no more than one box of souvenirs for every three boxes of books.

Bouquinistes must be open at least four days a week. Wednesdays are best (when school is out), and warm, dry days are golden (notice that every item is wrapped in protective plastic). And yes, they do leave everything inside when they lock up at night; metal bars and padlocks keep things safe.

Shakespeare and Company Bookstore

Access: AE, AI, Level 2—Moderately Accessible.

Cost and Hours: Free, daily 12:00–24:00.

The Sight: In addition to hosting butchers and fishmongers, the Left Bank has been home to scholars, philosophers, and poets since medieval times. This funky bookstore—a reincarnation of the original shop from the 1920s—has picked up the literary torch. Sylvia Beach, an American with a passion for free thinking, opened Shakespeare and

Company for the post-WWI Lost Generation, who came to Paris to find themselves. American writers flocked here for the cheap rent, fleeing the uptight, Prohibition-era United States. Beach's bookstore was famous as a meeting place of Paris' literary expatriate elite. Ernest Hemingway borrowed books from here regularly. James Joyce struggled to find a publisher for his now classic novel *Ulysses*—until Sylvia Beach published it. George Bernard Shaw, Gertrude Stein, and Ezra Pound also got their English fix here.

Today, the bookstore carries on that literary tradition. Struggling writers are given free accommodations upstairs in tiny rooms with views of Notre-Dame. Downstairs, travelers enjoy a great selection of used English books. Pick up the *Paris Voice* newspaper and say hi to owner George (thriving at 90 years old) and his daughter...Sylvia.

Notice the green water fountain (1900) in front of the bookstore, one

of the many in Paris donated by the English philanthropist Sir Richard Wallace. The hooks below the caryatids once held metal mugs for drinking the water.

• *Continue to the rue du Petit-Pont (which becomes rue St. Jacques). This bustling north-south boulevard was the Romans' busiest boulevard 2,000 years ago, with chariots racing in and out of the city. (Roman-iacs can view remains from the 3rd-century baths, along with a fine medieval collection, at the nearby Cluny Museum, near the corner of boulevards St. Michel and St. Germain; Level 3—Minimally Accessible; for details, see page 215.)*

Moving away from the river for one block, turn right at the Gothic church of St. Séverin and enter the Latin Quarter.

St. Séverin

Don't ask me why, but it took a century longer to build this church than Notre-Dame. This is flamboyant, or "flame-like," Gothic, and you can see the short, prickly spires meant to make

this building flicker in the eyes of the faithful. The church gives us a close-up look at gargoyles. This weird, winged species of flying mammal, now extinct, used to swoop down on unwary peasants, occasionally carrying off small children in their beaks. Today, they're most impressive in thunderstorms, when they vomit rain.

• *At #22 rue St. Séverin, you'll find the skinniest house in Paris, two windows wide. Rue St. Séverin leads right through...*

The Latin Quarter

While it may look more like the Greek Quarter today (cheap gyros abound), this area is the Latin Quarter, named for the language you'd have heard on these streets if you were here in the Middle Ages. The University of Paris (founded 1215), one of the leading educational institutions of medieval Europe, was (and still is) nearby.

A thousand years ago, the "crude" or vernacular local languages were sophisticated enough to communicate basic human needs, but if you wanted to get philosophical, the language of choice was Latin. The class of educated elite of medieval Europe transcended nations and borders. From Sicily to Sweden, they spoke and corresponded in Latin. Now the most Latin thing about this area is the beat you may hear coming from some of the subterranean jazz clubs.

Along rue St. Séverin, you can still see the shadow of the medieval sewer system. The street slopes into a central channel of bricks. In the days before plumbing and toilets, when people still went to the river or neighborhood wells for their water, flushing meant throwing it out the window. At certain times of day, maids on the fourth floor would holler, *"Garde de l'eau!"* ("Watch out for the water!") and heave it into the streets, where it would eventually wash down into the Seine.

As you wander, remember that before Napoleon III commissioned Baron Haussmann to modernize the city with grand boulevards (19th century), Paris was just like this—a medieval tangle. The ethnic feel of this area is nothing new—it's been a melting pot and university district for almost 800 years.

• *Keep wandering straight and you'll come to...*

Boulevard St. Michel

Busy boulevard St. Michel (or "boul' Miche") is famous as the main artery for Paris' café and artsy scene, culminating a block away (to the left), where it intersects boulevard St. Germain. Although nowadays you're more likely to find pantyhose at 30 percent off, there are still many cafés, boutiques, and bohemian haunts nearby.

The Sorbonne—the University of Paris' humanities department—is also close, if you want to make a detour, though entry is not allowed for visitors. (Turn left on boulevard St. Michel and go two blocks south. Gaze at the dome from the place de la Sorbonne courtyard. The buildings are off-limits to tourists). Originally founded as a theological school, the Sorbonne began attracting more students and famous professors—such as St. Thomas Aquinas and Peter Abélard—as its prestige grew. By the time the school expanded to include other subjects, it had a reputation for bold, new ideas. Nonconformity is a tradition here, and Paris remains a world center for new intellectual trends.

• *Cross boulevard St. Michel. Just ahead is...*

Place St. André-des-Arts

This tree-filled square is lined with cafés. In Paris, most serious thinking goes on in cafés. For centuries, these have been social watering holes, where you can get a warm place to sit and stimulating conversation for the price of a cup of coffee. Every great French writer—from Voltaire and Jean-Jacques Rousseau to Jean-Paul Sartre and Jacques Derrida—had a favorite haunt.

Paris honors its writers. If you visit the Panthéon—a few blocks up boulevard St. Michel and to the left—you will find French writers (Voltaire, Victor Hugo, Emile Zola, and Rousseau), inventors (Louis Braille), and scientists (including Marie and Pierre Curie) buried in a setting usually reserved for warriors and politicians. (Unfortunately, the Panthéon is Level 4—Not Accessible.)

• *Adjoining this square toward the river is the triangular place St. Michel, with a Métro stop and a statue of St. Michael killing a devil. Note: If you were to continue west along rue St. André-des-Arts, you'd find more Left Bank action.*

Place St. Michel

You're in the traditional core of the Left Bank's artsy, liberal, hippie, bohemian district of poets, philosophers, and winos. Nearby, you'll find international eateries, far-out bookshops, street singers, pale girls in black berets, jazz clubs, and—these days—tourists. Small cinemas show avant-garde films, almost always in the *version originale* (v.o.). For colorful wandering and café-sitting, afternoons and evenings are best. In the morning, it feels sleepy. The Latin Quarter stays up late and sleeps in.

In less commercial times, place St. Michel was a gathering point for the city's malcontents and misfits. In 1830, 1848, and again in 1871, the citizens took the streets from the government troops, set up barricades

Les Miz–style, and fought against royalist oppression. In World War II, the locals rose up against their Nazi oppressors (read the plaques under the dragons at the foot of the St. Michel fountain).

And in the spring of 1968, a time of social upheaval all over the world, young students battled riot batons and tear gas, took over the square, and declared it an independent state. Factory workers followed their call to arms and went on strike, toppling the de Gaulle government and forcing change. Eventually, the students were pacified, the university was reformed, and the Latin Quarter's original cobblestones were replaced with pavement, so future scholars could never again use the streets as weapons.

• *From place St. Michel, look across the river and find the spire of the Sainte-Chapelle church, with its weathervane angel nearby. Cross the river on pont St. Michel and continue north along the boulevard du Palais. On your left, you'll see the doorway to the Sainte-Chapelle. You'll need to pass through a metal detector to get into the Sainte-Chapelle complex. This is more than a tourist attraction—you're entering the courtyard of France's Supreme Court (to the right of Sainte-Chapelle). Once past security, you'll find restrooms ahead on the left (these are not accessible, but there are wheelchair-accessible toilets near the Palace of Justice entrance, with one 4" curb to negotiate and a long ramp with no railing). The line into the church may be long (but with a Museum Pass, you can bypass this line.)*

After going through the security area and the cobblestone pathway, find the wheelchair-accessible entryway ramp (listed as the exit). Enter the humble ground floor of...

SAINTE-CHAPELLE

Access: Ground floor only—**AE, AI, AT+A,** Level 2—Moderately Accessible. Unfortunately, the upstairs chapel can be reached only by climbing a narrow spiral staircase (Level 4—Not accessible, though slow walkers will find it's worth the climb).

Cost and Hours: Free for wheelchair users, otherwise €7, €10.50 combo-ticket also includes Conciergerie, covered by Museum Pass, open

Sainte-Chapelle

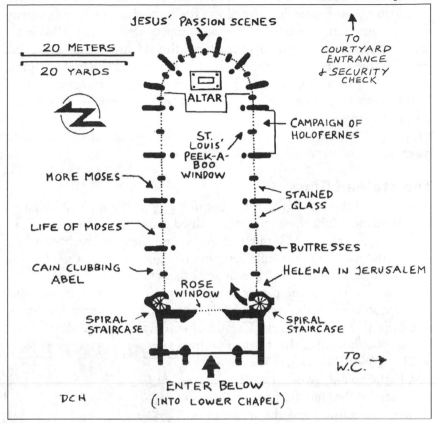

JESUS' PASSION SCENES

TO COURTYARD ENTRANCE & SECURITY CHECK

20 METERS

20 YARDS

ALTAR

CAMPAIGN OF HOLOFERNES

ST. LOUIS' PEEK-A-BOO WINDOW

MORE MOSES

STAINED GLASS

LIFE OF MOSES

BUTTRESSES

CAIN CLUBBING ABEL

HELENA IN JERUSALEM

ROSE WINDOW

SPIRAL STAIRCASE

SPIRAL STAIRCASE

TO W.C.

ENTER BELOW (INTO LOWER CHAPEL)

DCH

March–Oct daily 9:30–18:00, Nov–Feb daily 9:00–17:00, last entry 30 min before closing.

The Sight: Sainte-Chapelle, the triumph of Gothic church architecture, is a cathedral of glass like no other. It was built in 1248 for King Louis IX (the only French king who is now a saint) to house the supposed Crown of Thorns. Its architectural harmony is due to the fact that it was completed under the direction of one architect and in only five years—unheard of in Gothic times. Recall that Notre-Dame took over 200 years.

While the inside is beautiful, the exterior is basically structural. The muscular buttresses hold up the stone roof, so that the walls are essentially for stained glass. The lacy spire is

neo-Gothic—added in the 19th century. Inside, the layout clearly shows an *ancien régime* approach to worship. The low-ceilinged basement was for staff and more common folks—worshipping under a sky filled with painted fleurs-de-lis, a symbol of the king. Royal Christians worshipped upstairs. The paint job, a 19th-century restoration, helps you imagine how grand this small, painted, jeweled chapel was. (Imagine Notre-Dame painted like this....) Each capital is playfully carved with a different plant's leaves.

• *If you are able, climb the spiral staircase to the Haute Chapelle. Leave the rough stone of the earth and move into the light.*

The Stained Glass

Fiat lux. "Let there be light." From the first page of the Bible, it's clear—light is divine. Light shines through stained glass like God's grace shining down to earth, and Gothic architects used their new technology to turn dark stone buildings into lanterns of light. For me, the glory of Gothic shines brighter here than in any other church.

There are 15 separate panels of stained glass, with more than 1,100 different scenes, mostly from the Bible. These cover the entire Christian history of the world, from the Creation in Genesis (first window on the left, as you face the altar), to the coming of Christ (over the altar), to the end of the world (the round, "rose"-shaped window at the rear of the church). Each individual scene is interesting, and the whole effect is overwhelming. Allow yourself a few minutes to bask in the glow of the colored light before tackling the window descrip-

tions below, then remember to keep referring to the map to find the windows.

• *Working clockwise from the entrance, here are some scenes worth a look. (Note: The sun lights up different windows at different times of day. Overcast days give the most even light. On bright, sunny days, some sections are glorious, while others look like a sheet of lead.)*

Genesis—Cain Clubbing Abel (first window on the left—always dark because of a building butted up against it): On the bottom level in the third circle from left, we see God create the round earth and hold it up. On the next level up, we catch glimpses of naked Adam and Eve. On the third level (far right circle), Cain, in red, clubs his brother Abel, creating murder.

Life of Moses (second window, the bottom row of diamond panels):

Stained Glass Supreme

Craftsmen made glass—which is, essentially, melted sand—using this recipe:

- Melt one part sand with two parts wood ash.
- Mix in rusty metals to get different colors—iron makes red, cobalt makes blue, copper green, manganese purple, cadmium yellow.
- Blow glass into a cylinder shape, cut lengthwise, and lay flat.
- Cut into pieces with an iron tool, or by heating and cooling a select spot to make it crack.
- Fit pieces together to form a figure, using strips of lead to hold in place.
- Place masterpiece so high on a wall that no one can read it.

The first panel shows baby Moses in a basket, placed by his sister in the squiggly brown river. Next, he's found by the pharaoh's daughter. Then, he grows up. And finally, he's a man, a prince of Egypt on his royal throne.

More Moses (third window, in middle and upper sections): You'll see various scenes of Moses, the guy with the bright yellow horns—the result of a medieval mistranslation of the Hebrew word for "rays of light," or halo.

Jesus' Passion Scenes (over the altar): These scenes from Jesus' arrest and crucifixion were the backdrop for the Crown of Thorns, which originally was displayed on the altar. Position yourself a few feet back from the altar to look through the canopy to find Jesus in yellow shorts, carrying his cross (5th frame up from right bottom). A little below that, see Jesus being whipped (left) and—the key scene in this relic chapel—Jesus in purple, being fitted with the painful Crown of Thorns (right). Finally (as high as you can see), Jesus on the cross is speared by a soldier (trust me).

Campaign of Holofernes: On the bottom row are four scenes of colorful knights (refer to map to get reoriented). The second circle from the left is a battle scene (the campaign of Holofernes), showing three soldiers with swords slaughtering three men. The background is blue. The men have different-colored clothes—red, blue, green, mauve, and white. Notice some of the details. You can see the folds in the robes, the hair, and facial features. Look at the victim in the center—his head is splotched with blood. Details like the folds in the robes (see the victim in white, lower left) came either by scratching on the glass or by baking on paint. It was a painstaking process of finding just the right colors, fitting them together to make a scene...and then multiplying by 1,100.

Helena in Jerusalem (first window on the right wall by entrance): This window tells the story of how Christ's Crown of Thorns found its way from Jerusalem to Constantinople to this chapel. Start in the lower left corner, where the Roman emperor Constantine (in blue, on his throne) waves goodbye to his Christian mom, Helena. She arrives at the gate of Jerusalem (next panel to the right). Her men (in the two-part medallion above Jerusalem) dig through ruins and find Christ's (tiny) cross and other relics. She returns to Constantinople with a stash of holy relics, including the Crown of Thorns. Nine hundred years later, French Crusader knights (the next double medallion above) invade the Holy Land and visit Constantinople. Finally, King Louis IX, dressed in blue (in the panel up one and to the right of the last one) returns to France with the sacred relic.

Rose Window (above entrance): It's Judgment Day, with a tiny Christ in the center of the chaos and miracles. This window is 200 years newer then the rest, from the Flamboyant period. Facing west and the sunset, it's best late in the day.

If you can't read much into the individual windows, you're not alone. (For some tutoring, a little book with color photos is on sale downstairs with the postcards.)

Altar

The altar was raised up high to better display the relic around which this chapel was built—the Crown of Thorns. This was the crown put on Jesus when the Romans were torturing and humiliating him before his execution. Notice the staircase: Access was limited to the priest and the king,  who wore the keys to the shrine around his neck. Also see that there is no high profile image of Jesus anywhere—this chapel was all about the Crown.

King Louis IX, convinced he'd found the real McCoy, paid £135,000 for the Crown, £100,000 for the gem-studded shrine to display it in (destroyed in the French Revolution), and a mere £40,000 to build Sainte-Chapelle to house it. Today, the supposed Crown of Thorns is kept in the Notre-Dame Treasury (and shown only on

Sainte-Chapelle Area

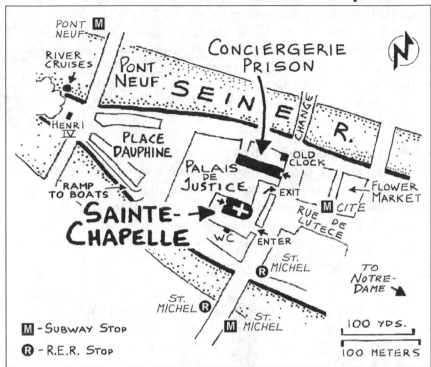

the 1st Friday of the month and during Easter).

Lay your camera on the ground and shoot the ceiling. Those pure and simple ribs growing out of the slender columns are the essence of Gothic structure.

• *Exit Sainte-Chapelle. Back outside, as you go around the church exterior, look down to see the foundation and notice how much Paris has risen in the 750 years since the Sainte-Chapelle was built. Next door to Sainte-Chapelle is the...*

Palais de Justice

You're in a huge complex of buildings that has housed the local government since ancient Roman times. It was the site of the original Gothic palace of the early kings of France. The only surviving medieval parts are Sainte-Chapelle and the Conciergerie prison.

Most of the site is now covered by the giant Palais de Justice, built in 1776, home of the French Supreme Court. The motto *Liberté, Egalité, Fraternité* over the doors is a reminder that this was also the headquarters of the Revolutionary government. Here, they doled out justice, condemning many to imprisonment in the Conciergerie downstairs or to the guillotine.

• *Now pass through the big iron gate to the noisy boulevard du Palais. Cross the street to the wide pedestrian-only rue de Lutèce and go about halfway down.*

Cité "Metropolitain" Stop

Of the 141 original, early-20th-century subway entrances, this is one of only a few survivors—now preserved as a national art treasure. (New York's Museum of Modern Art even exhibits one.) It marks Paris at its peak in 1900—on the cutting edge of modernism, but with an eye to

beauty. The curvy, plantlike ironwork is a textbook example of Art Nouveau, the style that rebelled against the erector-set squareness of the Industrial Age. In Paris, only the stations at Abbesses and Porte Dauphine survive with their canopies.

The flower and plant market on place Louis Lépine is a pleasant detour. On Sundays, this square is all aflutter with a busy bird market. And across the way is the Prefecture de Police, where Inspector Clouseau of *Pink Panther* fame used to work, and where the local resistance fighters took the first building from the Nazis in August of 1944, leading to the Allied liberation of Paris a week later.

• *Pause here to admire the view. Sainte-Chapelle is a pearl in an ugly architectural oyster. Double back to the Palais de Justice, turn right and—if you are able—enter the Conciergerie (entrance on boulevard du Palais). Though pretty barren inside, the Conciergerie echoes with history and is free with the Museum Pass. If you are unable to enter the Conciergerie, simply skip down to "Place Dauphine," below*

Conciergerie

Access: Level 4—Not Accessible. Visitors must negotiate a flight of stairs to get into the courtyard and lobby of the Conciergerie.

Cost and Hours: €7, €10.50 combo-ticket with Sainte-Chapelle, covered by Museum Pass, April–Sept daily 9:30–18:00, Oct–March daily 10:00–17:00, last entry 30 min before closing.

The Sight: Positioned next to the courthouse, the Conciergerie was the gloomy prison famous as the last stop for 2,780 victims of the guillotine, including France's last Old Regime queen, Marie-Antoinette. Before then, kings had used the building to torture and execute failed assassins. (One of its towers along the river was called "the babbler," named for the pain-induced sounds that leaked from it.) When the Revolution (1789) toppled the king, the building kept its same function, but without torture. The progressive Revolutionaries proudly unveiled a modern and more humane way to execute people—the guillotine.

Inside, pick up a free map and breeze through. See the spacious, low-ceilinged Hall of Men-at-Arms (Room 2), with four large fireplaces, used as a guard room. This big room gives a feel for the grandeur of the Great Hall (upstairs, not open to visitors) where the Revolutionary tribunals grilled scared prisoners on their political correctness. The raised area at the far end of the room (Room 4, today's bookstore) was notorious as the walkway of the executioner, who was known affectionately as "Monsieur de Paris."

Upstairs is the Prisoners' Gallery, a hall where the condemned milled about, waiting for the open-air cart (tumbrel) to pull up outside to carry them to the guillotine on place de la Concorde. Some reconstructed cells show how the poor slept on straw, while the wealthy got a cot.

Up a few more steps is a memorial room with the names of the 2,780 citizens condemned to death by the guillotine. In alphabetical order, find: Georges Danton (prominent revolutionary who was later condemned for being insufficiently liberal, a nasty crime), Charlotte Corday (a noblewoman who snuck into the bathroom of the revolutionary writer,

Jean-Paul Marat, and stabbed him while he bathed), Anne-Elizabeth Capet (whose crime was being "sister of the tyrant"), Louis XVI ("called Capet: last king of France"), Marie-Antoinette, and—oh the irony—Maximilien de Robespierre, the head of the Revolution, the man who sent so many to the guillotine, and who was eventually toppled, humiliated, imprisoned here, and beheaded.

Back downstairs, arrows lead through a small museum (with a guillotine blade) to a chapel that was the actual cell of Marie-Antoinette. The chapel was made by Louis

XVIII, the brother of beheaded Louis XVI and the first king back on the throne after the restoration (in 1815, once Napoleon was booted). The paintings show Marie-Antoinette in her cell and receiving the Last Sacrament on the night before her beheading. The walls drip with silver embroidered tears.

The tour continues outside in the courtyard, where women prisoners were allowed a little fresh air (notice the original spikes still guarding from above). In the corner a door leads to a re-creation of Marie-Antoinette's Cell (Room 12). Imagine the Queen spending her last days—separated from her 10-year-old son, and now widowed because the King had already been executed. Mannequins, period furniture, and the real cell wallpaper set the scene. The guard stands modestly behind a screen while the queen psyches herself up with a crucifix. In the glass display case, see her actual crucifix, napkin, and small water pitcher. On October 16, 1793, the queen walked the corridor, stepped onto the cart, and was slowly carried to place de la Concorde, where she had a date with "Monsieur de Paris." A video in the next room gives a taste of prison life during the Reign of Terror.

• *Back outside, turn left on boulevard du Palais and head toward the river (north). On the corner is the city's oldest public clock. The mechanism of the present clock is from 1334, and even though the case is Baroque, it keeps on ticking.*

Turn left onto quai de l'Horloge and continue west along the river, past the round medieval tower called "the babbler." The bridge up ahead is the pont Neuf, where we'll end this tour. At the first corner, veer left into a sleepy triangular square called...

Place Dauphine

It's amazing to find such coziness in the heart of Paris. This city of two million is still a city of neighborhoods, a collection of villages. The French Supreme Court building looms behind like a giant marble gavel. Enjoy the village-Paris feeling in the park. You may see lawyers on their lunch break playing *boules* (see sidebar on page 249).

• *Continue through place Dauphine. As you pop out the other end, you're face to face with a...*

Statue of Henry IV

Henry IV (1553–1610) is not as famous as his grandson, Louis XIV, but Henry helped make Paris what it is today—a European capital of elegant buildings and quiet squares. He built the place Dauphine (behind you), the pont Neuf (to the right), residences (to the left, down rue Dauphine), the Louvre's long Grand Gallery (downriver on the right), and the tree-filled square Vert-Galant (directly behind the statue, on the tip of the island). The square is one of Paris' makeout spots; its name comes from Henry's own nickname, the Green Knight, as Henry was a notorious ladies' man. The park is a great place to relax, looking out over the concrete prow of this boat-shaped island.

• *From the statue, turn right onto the old bridge. Pause at the little nook half-way across.*

Pont Neuf

The pont Neuf, or "new bridge," is Paris' oldest standing bridge (built 1578–1607). Its 12 arches span the widest part of the river. Unlike other bridges, this one never had houses or buildings growing on it. The turrets were originally for vendors and street entertainers. In the days of Henry IV, who promised his peasants "a chicken in every pot every Sunday," this would have been a lively scene. From the bridge, look downstream (west) to see the next bridge, the pedestrian-only pont des Arts. Ahead on the Right Bank is the long Louvre Museum. Beyond that, on the Left Bank is the Orsay. And what's that tall black tower in the distance?

The Seine

Our tour ends where Paris began—on the Seine River. From Dijon to the English Channel, the Seine meanders 500 miles, cutting through the center of Paris. The river is shallow and slow within the city, but still dangerous enough to require steep stone embankments (built 1910) to prevent occasional floods.

In summer, the roads that run along the river are replaced with acres of sand, as well as beach chairs and tanned locals, creating a beach called Paris Plage. The success of the Paris Plage event has motivated some city officials to propose the permanent removal of vehicles from those fast lanes—turning this into riverside parks instead.

Any time of year, you'll see tourist boats and the commercial barges that carry 20 percent of Paris' transported goods. And on the banks, sportsmen today cast into the waters once fished by Paris' original Celtic inhabitants.

• *We're done. You can take a boat tour that leaves from near the base of pont Neuf on the island side (Vedettes du Pont Neuf, **AE, AI**, Level 1—Fully Accessible; €10, tip requested, departs hourly on the hour, 2/hr after dark, has live guide with explanations in French and English). To reach the boats via an accessible ramp, traverse some cobblestones one block upriver (east) of the bridge on the south side of the island. The ramp will lead you along the riverfront and under the Pont Neuf to the boat dock.*

CHAMPS-ELYSEES ROLL OR STROLL

From the Arc de Triomphe to the Tuileries Gardens

Don't leave Paris without experiencing the avenue des Champs-Elysées (shahnz ay-lee-zay). This is Paris at its most Parisian: monumental sidewalks, stylish shops, grand cafés, and glimmering showrooms. This tour covers about three miles. If that seems like too much for you, break it down into several different outings (taxis roll down the Champs-Elysées frequently and Métro stops are located every 3 blocks). Take your time and enjoy. It's a great roll or stroll day or night.

The tour begins at the top of the Champs-Elysées, across a huge traffic circle from the famous Arc de Triomphe. Note that getting to the arch itself, and access within the arch, are extremely challenging for travelers with limited mobility. I suggest simply viewing the arch from across the street (described below).

If you are able, and you wish to visit the arch, here's the information: The arch is connected to the top of the Champs-Elysées via an underground walkway (twenty-five 6" steps down and thirty 6" steps back up). To reach this passageway, take the Métro to the not-accessible Charles de Gaulle Etoile station and follow *sortie #1, Champs-Elysées/Arc de Triomphe* signs. You can take an elevator only partway up the inside of the arch, to a museum with some city views. To reach the best views at the very top, you must climb the last 46 stairs. For more, see the listing on page 219.

THE TOUR BEGINS

The Arc de Triomphe

• *View this famous Paris landmark from the top of the Champs-Elysées.*

Construction on this 165-foot-high arch was begun in 1809 to honor Napoleon's soldiers, who, in spite of being vastly outnumbered by the

Austrians, scored a remarkable victory at the battle of Austerlitz. Patterned after the ceremonial arches of ancient Roman conquerors (but more than twice the size), it celebrates Napoleon as emperor of a "New Rome." On the arch's massive left pillar, a relief sculpture shows a toga-clad Napoleon posing confidently, while an awestruck Paris—crowned by her city walls—kneels at his imperial feet. Napoleon died prior to the Arc's completion, but it was finished in time for his 1840 funeral procession to pass underneath, carrying his remains (19 years dead) from exile in St. Helena to Paris.

On the right pillar is the Arc's most famous relief, *La Marseillaise* (*Le Départ des Volontaires de 1792*, by François Rude). Lady Liberty—looking like an ugly reincarnation of Joan of Arc—screams, "Freedom is this way!" and points the direction with a sword. The soldiers below her are tired, naked, and stumbling, but she rallies them to carry on the fight against oppression.

Today, the Arc de Triomphe is dedicated to the glory of all French armies. Directly under the arch are lists of French victories since the Revolution—19th century on the arch, 20th century in the pavement. On the columns are lists of generals (with a line under the names of those who died in battle). Nearby is the Tomb of the Unknown Soldier (from World War I). Every day at 18:30 since just after World War I, the flame has been rekindled and new flowers set in place.

Like its Roman ancestors, this arch has served as a parade gateway for triumphal armies (French or foe) and important ceremonies. From 1940 to 1944, a large swastika flew from

Champs-Elysées Roll or Stroll

1. Arc de Triomphe
2. Underground Walkway
3. Dresdner Bank Building
4. McDonald's & Peugeot
5. Mercedes-Benz & Lido
6. Fouquet's Café-Rest.
7. Ladurée Tea Salon
8. Thomas Jefferson Plaque & Club Med
9. Arcades des Champs-Elysées, Sephora & English Pharmacy
10. Renault
11. Virgin Music, Disney, Gap & Quiksilver
12. De Gaulle Statue
13. Obelisk of Luxor
14. Hôtel Crillon
15. Pont de la Concorde
16. U.S. Embassy
17. U.S. Consulate
18. W. H. Smith Books

here as Nazis goose-stepped down the Champs-Elysées. In August 1944, Charles de Gaulle led Allied troops under this arch as they celebrated liberation. Today, national parades start and end here with one minute of silence.

• *Surrounding the arch is a swirling...*

Traffic Circle

The 12 boulevards that radiate from the Arc de Triomphe (forming an *étoile*, or star) were part of Baron Haussmann's master plan for Paris: the creation of a series of major boulevards, intersecting at diagonals with monuments (such as the Arc de Triomphe) as centerpieces of those intersections.

His plan did not anticipate the automobile—obvious when you watch the traffic scene. But see how smoothly it really functions. Cars entering the circle have the right of way (the only roundabout in France with this rule); those in the circle must yield. Still, there are plenty of accidents, often caused by tourists oblivious to the rules. Tired of disputes, insurance companies split the fault and damages of any Arc de Triomphe accident 50/50. The trick is to make a parabola—get to the center ASAP, and then begin working your way out two avenues before you want to exit.

• *We'll start our tour down the Champs-Elysées at the Charles de Gaulle-Etoile Métro stop, on the north (sunnier) side of the street. Look straight down the Champs-Elysées to the Tuileries Garden at the far end.*

The Champs-Elysées

You're at the top of one of the world's grandest and most celebrated streets, home to big business, celebrity cafés, glitzy nightclubs, high-fashion shopping, and international people-watching.

In 1667, Louis XIV opened the first section of the street as a short extension of the Tuileries Garden. This date is a considered the birth of Paris as a grand city. The Champs-Elysées soon became *the* place to cruise in your carriage. (It still is today—traffic can be jammed up even at midnight.) One hundred years later, the café scene arrived.

From the 1920s until the 1960s, this boulevard was pure elegance. Parisians actually dressed up to come here. It was mainly residences, rich hotels, and cafés. Then, in 1963, the government pumped up the neighborhood's commercial metabolism by bringing in the RER (commuter train). Suburbanites had easy access, and bam—there went the neighborhood.

• *Start your descent, pausing at the first tiny street you cross, rue de Tilsitt. This street is part of a shadow ring road—an option for drivers who'd like to avoid the chaos of the arch, complete with stoplights.*

A half-block down rue de Tilsitt is the Dresdner Bank building's entry (**AE, AI,** Level 2—Moderately Accessible, one 2" entry step). It's one of the few survivors of a dozen uniformly U-shaped buildings in Haussman's original 1853 grand design. Peek into the foyer for a glimpse of 19th-century Champs-Elysées classiness.

Back on the main drag, look across to the other side of the Champs-Elysées at the big, gray, concrete-and-glass "Publicis" building. Ugh. In the 1960s, venerable old buildings (similar to the Dresdner Bank building) were leveled to make way for new commercial operations like Publicis. Then, in 1985, a law prohibited the demolition of the old building fronts that gave the boulevard a uniform grace. Today, many modern businesses hide behind preserved facades.

The coming of McDonald's—farther down on the left at #140 (**AE, AI, AT,** Level 1—Fully Accessible)—was a shock to the boulevard. At first, it was only allowed to have white arches painted on the window. Today, it spills out legally onto the sidewalk—provided it offers café-quality chairs and flower boxes—and dining *chez MacDo* has become typically Parisian. A €3 Big Mac here buys an hour of people-watching. (There's an adapted toilet inside).

The *nouveau* Champs-Elysées, revitalized in 1994, has new benches and lamps, broader sidewalks, and a fleet of green-suited workers armed with high-tech pooper-scoopers. Blink away the modern elements, and it's not hard to imagine the boulevard pre-1963, with only the finest structures lining both sides all the way to the palace gardens.

Glitz

Fancy car dealerships include Peugeot, at #136 (**AE+A, AI,** Level 2—Moderately Accessible, three 6" entry steps; showing off its futuristic concept cars next to the classic models), and Mercedes-Benz, a block down at #118 (**AE+A, AI,** Level 2—Moderately Accessible, one 8" entry step). In the 19th century, this was an area for horse stables; today, it's the district of garages, limo companies, and car dealerships. If you're serious about selling cars in France, you must have a showroom on the Champs-Elysées.

Next to Mercedes is the famous Lido, Paris' largest cabaret (and a multiplex cinema). Go inside, if you are able (**AE+A, AI,** Level 2—Moderately Accessible, two 6" entry steps). Check out the perky photos, R-rated videos, and shocking prices. Paris still offers the kind of burlesque-type spectacles combining music, comedy, and scantily clad women performed here since the 19th century. Moviegoing on the Champs-Elysées is also popular, with theaters showing the very latest releases. Check to see if there are films you recognize, then look for the showings *(séances)*. A "v.o." *(version originale)* next to the time indicates the film will be in its original language.

• *Now cross the boulevard. Look up at the Arc de Triomphe with its rooftop bristling with tourists. Notice the architecture—old and elegant, new, and new-behind-old facades.*

Café Culture

Fouquet's café-restaurant (**AE+A, AI,** Level 2—Moderately Accessible, one 3" entry step), under the red awning at #99, is a popular spot among French celebrities, serving the most expensive shot of espresso I've found in downtown Paris (€4.80). Opened in 1899 as a coachman's bistro, Fouquet's gained fame as the hangout of France's WWI biplane fighter pilots—those who weren't shot down by Germany's infamous "Red Baron." It also served as James Joyce's dining room. Since the early 1900s, Fouquet's has been a favorite of French actors and actresses. The golden plaques by the entrance honor winners of France's Oscar-like film awards, the Césars—see plaques for Gérard Depardieu, Catherine Deneuve, Roman Polanski, Juliette Binoche, and many famous Americans (but not Jerry Lewis). Recent winners are posted inside. While the hushed interior is at once classy and intimidating, it's a grand experience if you dare (the outdoor setting is also great, and more relaxed). Fouquet's was recently saved from foreign purchase and eventual destruction when the government declared it a historic monument.

Ladurée (**AE, AI, AL,** Level 2—Moderately Accessible, accessible entry on left side; 2 blocks downhill at #75, with green-and-purple awning) is a classic 19th-century tea salon/restaurant/*pâtisserie*. Its interior is right out of the 1860s. Wander in...you can even peek into the cozy rooms on the upper level. A coffee here is *très élégant* (only €3.30). The bakery sells traditional macaroons, cute little cakes, and gift-wrapped finger sandwiches to go (your choice of 4 mini-macaroons for €6).

• *Cross back to the lively (north) side of the street.*

At #92 (opposite Ladurée), a wall plaque marks the place Thomas Jefferson lived (with his 14-year-old slave, Sally Hemings) while minister to France (1785–1789). He replaced the popular Benjamin Franklin, but quickly made his own mark, extolling the virtues of America's Revolution to a country approaching its own.

Club Med (#88), with its travel ads to sunny destinations, is a reminder of the French commitment to the vacation. Since 1936, the French, by law, have enjoyed five weeks of paid vacation (and every Catholic holiday invented). In the swinging "60s, Club Med made hedonism accessible to the middle-class French masses.

French Shopping

Go into the Arcades des Champs-Elysées mall (**AE, AI,** Level 2— Moderately Accessible; it's at #76—don't confuse it with the unappealing Galerie des Champs-Elysées, next door to Club Med). With its fancy lamps, mosaic floors, glass skylight, and classical columns, it captures faint echoes of the *années folles*—the "crazy years," as the roaring '20s were called in France. Architecture buffs can observe how flowery Art Nouveau became simpler, more geometrical Art Deco. Down the street at #74, Galerie du Claridge (**AE, AI,** Level 2—Moderately Accessible) is a fine example of an old facade—with an ironwork awning, balconies, *putti*, and sculpted fantasy faces—fronting a new building.

Take your nose sightseeing at #72; glide down Sephora's ramp into a vast hall of cosmetics and perfumes (**AE, AI, AL,** Level 2—Moderately Accessible, elevator to left of entry; Mon–Sat 10:00–24:00, Sun 11:00–24:00). Grab a disposable white strip from a lovely clerk, spritz it with a sample, and sniff. The store is thoughtfully laid out: The entry hall (on the right) is lined with the new products—all open and ready (with sniff strips) to sample. In the main showroom, women's perfumes line the right wall and men's line the left wall—organized alphabetically by company, from Armani to Versace. The mesmerizing music, carefully chosen just for Sephora, actually made me crave cosmetics. At the rear of the store, you can have your face made over and your nails fixed like new. You can also get the advice of a "skin consultant."

At the corner of rue la Boétie, the English pharmacy (**AE+A, AI,** Level 2—Moderately Accessible, one 3" entry step) is open until midnight, and map-lovers can detour one block down this street to shop at Espace IGN (Institut Géographique National; **AE, AI,** Level 2—Moderately Accessible), France's version of the National Geographic Society.

International Shopping

A block farther down at #54, the Virgin Megastore (**AE+A, AI,** Level 2—Moderately Accessible, one 5" entry step) sells a world of music. Nearby, the Disney, Gap, and Quiksilver stores are reminders of global economics—the French seem to love these places as much as Americans do.

Rond-Point and Beyond

At the Rond-Point des Champs-Elysées, the shopping ends and the fully accessible park begins. This round, leafy traffic circle is always colorful, lined with flowers or seasonal decorations (thousands of pumpkins at Halloween, hundreds of decorated trees at Christmas).

A long block past the Rond-Point, at Avenue de Marigny, look to the other side of the Champs-Elysées to find a new statue of Charles de Gaulle—ramrod straight and striding out as he did the day Paris was liberated in 1944. Charles stands in front of the glass-and-steel-domed Grand and Petit Palais exhibition halls (**AE, AI,** Level 2—Moderately Accessible; entrances accessible, ticket agent can assist), built for the 1900 World's Fair. Today, these examples of the "can-do" spirit of the early 20th century are museums. Impressive temporary exhibits fill the huge Grand Palais (on right, €10.50, €9 after 13:00, not covered by Museum Pass; get details on current exhibitions from TIs or in *Pariscope*). The Petit Palais (left side; **AE, AI, AT,** Level 1—Fully Accessible), recently reopened after a long renovation, houses a permanent collection of 19th-century paintings by Eugène Delacroix, Paul Cézanne, Claude Monet, Camille Pissarro, and other masters.

Beyond the two palaces, the pont Alexandre III leads over the Seine to the golden dome of Les Invalides. This exquisite bridge, spiked with golden statues and ironwork lamps, was built to celebrate a turn-of-the-20th-century treaty between France and Russia. Like the Grand and Petit Palais, it's a fine example of belle époque exuberance.

Les Invalides was built by Louis XIV as a veterans' hospital for his battle-weary troops (see page 213). The esplanade leading up to Les Invalides—possibly the largest patch of grass in Paris—gives soccer balls and Frisbees a rare-in-Paris welcome.

Return to the sunny side of the street. From here, it's a straight shot down the last stretch of the Champs-Elysées. The plane trees (a kind of sycamore with peeling bark that does well in big-city pollution) are reminiscent of the big push Napoleon III made, planting 600,000 trees to green up the city.

• *View the 21-acre place de la Concorde from the obelisk in the center.*

Place de la Concorde

During the Revolution, this was the place de la Révolution. Many of the 2,780 beheaded during the Revolution lost their bodies here during the Reign of Terror. The guillotine sat on this square. A bronze plaque in the ground in front of the obelisk memorializes the place where Louis XVI, Marie-Antoinette, Georges Danton, Charlotte Corday, and Maximilien de Robespierre, among many others, were made "a foot shorter on top." Three people worked the guillotine: One managed the blade, one held the blood bucket, and one caught the head, raising it high to the roaring crowd.

The 3,300-year-old, 72-foot, 220-ton, red granite, hieroglyph-inscribed obelisk of Luxor now forms the centerpiece of place de la Concorde. Here—on the spot where Louis XVI was beheaded—his brother (Charles X) honored the executed with this obelisk. (Charles became king when the monarchy was restored after Napoleon.) It was carted here from Egypt in the 1830s. The gold pictures on the pedestal tell the story of its incredible two-year journey: Pulled down from the entrance to Ramses II's Temple of Amon in

Luxor; encased in wood; loaded onto a boat built to navigate both shallow rivers and open seas; floated down the Nile, across the Mediterranean, along the Atlantic coast, and up the Seine; and unloaded here, where it was reerected in 1836. Its glittering gold-leaf cap is a recent addition (1998), replacing the original stolen 2,500 years ago.

The obelisk also forms a center point along a line locals call the "royal perspective." You can hang a lot of history along this straight line (Louvre–obelisk–Arc de Triomphe–Grande Arche de la Défense). The Louvre symbolizes the old regime (divine right rule by kings and queens). The obelisk and place de la Concorde symbolize the people's revolution (cutting off the king's head). The Arc de Triomphe calls to mind the triumph of nationalism (victorious armies carrying national flags under the arch). And the huge modern arch in the distance, surrounded by the headquarters of multinational corporations, heralds a future in which business entities are more powerful than nations.

Across the river (south) stands the building where the French National Assembly meets (similar to our Congress). On the north side of place de la Concorde is Hôtel Crillon, Paris' most exclusive hotel. It's the left one of two twin buildings that guard the entrance to rue Royale (which leads to the Greek-style Church of the Madeleine). This hotel is so fancy that one of its belle époque rooms is displayed in New York's Metropolitan museum. Eleven years before the king lost his head on this square, Louis XVI met with Benjamin Franklin in this hotel to sign a treaty recognizing the United States as an independent country. (Today's low-profile, heavily fortified American Embassy is located next door.)

For a memorable splurge, consider high tea at the accessible Crillon.

And from the base of the Champs-Elysées, the beautiful Tuileries Garden leads through the iron gates to the Louvre (with a non-accessible public WC just inside on the right). Relax next to the pond, or find one of the cafés in the gardens.

Nearby

Your guided tour is over. From here, you can go: to the closest Métro stop (Concorde), north to a fancy shopping area (near place de la Madeleine), into the park toward the Louvre, or across the river toward the Orsay Museum (read on).

If you go to the river, you'll cross a freeway underpass similar to the one at the pont de l'Alma, three bridges downstream, where Princess Diana lost her life in a 1997 car accident. The pont de la Concorde, built of stones from the Bastille prison (which was demolished by the Revolution in 1789), symbolizes that, with good government, *concorde* (harmony) can come from chaos. Position yourself mid-bridge and gaze upriver (east). If you use a clock as a compass, the Impressionist art museum L'Orangerie hides behind the trees at 10 o'clock, and the tall building with the skinny chimneys at 11 o'clock is the architectural caboose of the sprawling Louvre palace. The thin spire of Sainte-Chapelle is dead center at 12 o'clock, with the twin towers of Notre-Dame to its right. The Orsay Museum is closer on the right, connected with the Tuileries Garden by a sleek pedestrian bridge (the next bridge upriver).

BELGIUM

BELGIUM

Belgium falls through the cracks. It's nestled between Germany, France, and Britain, and it's famous for waffles, sprouts, and endive—no wonder many travelers don't even consider a stop here. But many who do visit remark that Belgium is one of Europe's best-kept secrets. There are tourists—but not as many as the country's charms merit.

Ten million Belgians are packed into a country only a little bigger than Maryland. At 830 people per square mile, it's the second most densely populated country in Europe (after the Netherlands). This population concentration, coupled with a dense and well-lit rail and road system, causes Belgium to shine at night when viewed from space, a phenomenon NASA astronauts call the "Belgian Window."

It's here in Belgium that Europe comes together: Where Romance languages meet Germanic languages, where Catholics meet Protestants, and where the new Europe is growing, sprouting from the seed planted 40 years ago by the Benelux union. Because of Belgium's international importance as the capital of the European Union, more than 25 percent of its residents are foreigners. Belgium flies the flag of Europe more vigorously than any other place on the continent.

The country is split between the French-speaking Walloons in the south and the Dutch-speaking Flemish people (60 percent of the population) in the north. Talk to locals to learn how deep the cultural rift is. Belgium's capital, Brussels, while mostly French-speaking, is officially bilingual. The country also has a small minority of German-speaking people.

With all this diversity, English bridges the gap—it's almost universally spoken in Belgium, especially in the Flemish half (Dutch-speaking,

---

How Big, How Many, How Much

- 12,000 square miles (a little larger than Maryland)
- 10 million people (830 per square mile)
- €1 = about $1.20

Belgium

including Bruges). But if you want to win points, learn a couple of key Dutch words: "hello" is *hallo* (hol-LOH), "please" is *alstublieft* (AHL-stoo-bleeft), and "thank you" is *dank u wel* (dahnk yoo vehl). For language help in French-speaking Belgium (including Brussels), see page 176, and the "French Survival Phrases" near the end of this book.

Belgians brag that they eat as much as the Germans and as well as the French. They are among the world's leading beer consumers and carnivores. And yes, they really do eat waffles here. While Americans think of "Belgian" waffles for breakfast, the Belgians (who don't eat waffles or pancakes for breakfast) think of *wafels* as Liège-style (dense, sweet, eaten plain, and heated up) and Brussels-style (lighter, often with powdered sugar or whipped cream and fruit, served in teahouses only in the afternoons 14:00–18:00). You'll see waffles sold at restaurants and take-away stands.

Bruges is the best first bite of Belgium. It's a wonderfully preserved medieval Flemish gem that expertly nurtures the tourist industry, bringing the town a prosperity it hasn't enjoyed since 500 years ago, when—as one of the largest cities in the world—it helped lead northern Europe out of the Middle Ages.

ACCESSIBILITY IN BELGIUM

Access for people with disabilities is generally good in Belgium, particularly in public spaces, though English-language publications and English-speaking organizations are in short supply.

The **Belgium Tourist Office** will provide information to help you plan your visit (220 E. 42nd St. #3402, New York, NY 10017, tel. 212/758-8130, fax 212/355-7675, www.visitbelgium.com, info@visitbelgium.com).

BRUGES

(Brugge)

With Renoir canals, pointy, gilded architecture, vivid time-tunnel art, and stay-awhile cafés, Bruges is a heavyweight sightseeing destination, as well as a joy. Where else can you roll or stroll along a canal, munch mussels and wash them down with the world's best beer, savor heavenly chocolate, and see Flemish Primitives and a Michelangelo, all within 300 yards of a bell tower that jingles every 15 minutes? And there's no language barrier.

The town is Brugge (BROO-ghah) in Flemish, and Bruges (broozh) in French and English. Its name comes from the Viking word for wharf. Right from the start, Bruges was a trading center. In the 11th century, the city grew wealthy on the cloth trade.

By the 14th century, Bruges' population was 35,000, as large as London's. As the middleman in sea trade between northern and southern Europe, it was one of the biggest cities in the world and an economic powerhouse. In addition, Bruges had become the most important cloth market in northern Europe.

In the 15th century, while England and France were slogging it out in the Hundred Years' War, Bruges was the favored residence of the powerful Dukes of Burgundy—and at peace. Commerce and the arts boomed. The artists Jan van Eyck and Hans Memling had studios here.

But by the 16th century, the harbor had silted up and the economy had collapsed. The Burgundian court left, Belgium became a minor Hapsburg possession, and Bruges' Golden Age abruptly ended. For generations, Bruges was known as a mysterious and dead city. In the 19th century, a new port, Zeebrugge, brought renewed vitality to the area. And in the 20th century, tourists discovered the town.

Accessibility Levels

This book rates sights, hotels, and restaurants using four levels:

Level 1—Fully Accessible: A Level 1 building is completely barrier-free. Entryways, elevators, and other facilities are specifically adapted to accommodate a person using a wheelchair. If there's a bathroom, it has wide doors and an adapted toilet and sink. Where applicable, the bathing facilities are also fully adapted (including such features as bath boards, grab bars, or a roll-in, no-rim shower). Fully adapted hotel rooms often have an alarm system with pull cords for emergencies.

Level 2—Moderately Accessible: A Level 2 building is suitable for, but not specifically adapted to accommodate, a person using a wheelchair. This level will generally work for a wheelchair user who can make transfers and take a few steps. A person who is permanently in a wheelchair may require some assistance here (either from a companion or from staff).

Level 3—Minimally Accessible: A Level 3 building is satisfactory for people who have minimal mobility difficulties (that is, people who usually do not use a wheelchair, but take more time to do things than a non-disabled person). This building may have some steps and a few other barriers—but not too many. Level 3 buildings are best suited to slow walkers; wheelchair users will require substantial assistance here.

Level 4—Not Accessible: Unfortunately, some places in this book are simply not accessible to people with limited mobility. This means that barriers such as staircases, tight interiors and facilities (elevators, bathrooms, etc.), or other impediments interfere with passage for travelers with disabilities. Buildings in this category might include a church tower that has several flights of steep stairs, or a museum interior that has many levels with lots of steps and no elevator.

For a complete listing of the Accessibility Codes used in this chapter, please see pages 6–7.

Today, Bruges prospers because of tourism: It's a uniquely well-preserved Gothic city and a handy gateway to Europe. It's no secret, but even with the crowds, it's the kind of city where you don't mind being a tourist.

Accessibility in Bruges

Bruges is an Easy Access city, far more accessible than Paris, Amsterdam, or Frankfurt. In Bruges, however, cobblestone is the state rock; if you're sightseeing in a wheelchair, you might want to sit on a pillow to absorb the shock of the rock. Luckily, there's often a smooth sidewalk in the middle, so you can wheel your way through the cobbles. While keeping its medieval charm intact, the town manages to open its arms to people at all levels of mobility.

In Bruges, if a hotel has 20 or more rooms, one room has to be designated as accessible. Some hoteliers go to great lengths to adapt their room, while others are merely suitable for a person in a wheelchair. Nevertheless, persons needing Level 1 accessibility can easily find accommodations. The pricier the hotel, the better chance of finding an adapted room; still, I found some fully accessible rooms in less expensive places (see listings on page 348).

Belgian trains and Bruges' city buses are generally accessible. Tours in Bruges are less accessible: Bus tours have Level 1 and Level 2 accessibility (depending on the coach). Boat tours, which require going down steps to the dock, range from Level 3—Minimally Accessible to Level 4—Not Accessible.

Many of Bruges' top sights are at least partly accessible to travelers with limited mobility. Fully accessible (Level 1) sights include Market and Burg squares; most of the Church of Our Lady and the Memling Museum; the lower chapel of the Basilica of the Holy Blood; the Renaissance Hall; and the Bell Tower's Exhibition Hall (but not the top of the tower). The Groeninge Museum, Town Hall Gothic Room, and Begijnhof are moderately accessible (Level 2). Only a handful of sights—such as the top of the Bell Tower, the Gruuthuse Museum, and De Halve Maan Brewery Tour—are not accessible.

Bruges' ultimate sight—the town itself—is open to all. And the best way to enjoy that is to get lost on the back streets, away from the lace shops and ice-cream stands.

ORIENTATION

The tourist's Bruges—and you'll be sharing it—is less than one square mile, contained within a canal (the former moat). Nearly everything of interest and importance is within a convenient cobbled swath between the train station and Market Square (less than a mile apart). Many of my quiet, charming recommended accommodations lie just beyond Market Square.

If You Need Medical Help

Start with your hotel staff. They are accustomed to handling medical problems. Here are other resources to try: To contact a doctor, call 050/391-528 (during the day), 050/364-030 (at night, 20:00–8:00 in the morning), or 050/813-899 (on weekends). To summon an ambulance, call 100. For a Red Cross ambulance, call 050/320-727.

Two hospitals in Bruges offer 24-hour emergency care: Algemeen Ziekenhuis Sint-Jan Te Brugge (Ruddershave 10, tel. 050/452-111) and Algemeen Ziekenhuis Sint-Lucas (St.-Lucaslaan 29, tel. 050/369-111).

Pharmacies *(apotheek)* are marked with a green cross. Every pharmacy displays a list of 24-hour pharmacies that are nearby.

For medical supplies, try Thuiszorg Winkel in the city center (closed Sun, Oude Burg 23, tel. 050/440-352, thuiszorgwinkel.brugge@cm.be).

Tourist Information

The main TI, about a half-mile from the train station, is fully accessible (**AE, AI, AT** just outside the front door, Level 1). Called **In&Uit** (literally, "In and Out") it's in the big, red concert hall on the square called 't Zand (daily 10:00–18:00, Thu until 20:00, 't Zand 34, tel. 050/448-686, www.brugge.be). The other TI is at the train station (**AE, AI,** Level 1—Fully Accessible; generally Tue–Sat 10:00–13:00 & 14:00–17:00, closed Sun–Mon).

The TIs sell a great €1 Bruges visitors guide with a map and listings of all of the sights and services. A separate publication, *The Brugge Accommodation Guide*, lists all of Bruges' hotels, pensions, B&Bs, hostels, and campgrounds with coded icons that tell about accessibility, amenities, and prices (free at TIs). And you can pick up a monthly English-language program called *events@brugge*. The TIs have information on train schedules and on the many tours available (see "Tours," below). Many hotels give out free maps with more detail than the map the TIs sell.

Arrival in Bruges

By Train: Coming in by train, you'll see the square bell tower that marks the main square. Upon arrival, stop by the station TI (described above). The station lacks ATMs, but has lockers (€2-3.50, daily 6:00–24:00).

Access: AE, AI, AL, AT, Level 1—Fully Accessible. However, only platforms 5–10 are accessible by elevator. A fully adapted toilet is near the train information booth (attendant with key on duty at baggage room daily 7:00–19:00).

Getting to the Center: The best way to get to the town center is by bus (**AE, AI, AL,** Level 1—Fully Accessible). All buses have transfer lifts for wheelchairs. Ask at the train station which bus will take you to your hotel; you can pay the €1 fare on the bus, or buy your ticket beforehand from the machine outside the train station door (just to the left as you exit the station). Buses #1, #3, #4, #6, #8, #11, #13, and #16 go directly to Market Square. Buses #4 and #8 continue to the northeast part of town to the windmills.

The **taxi** fare from the train station to most hotels is around €6. For details on taxis, see "Getting Around Bruges," below.

To **roll or stroll** to the town center, note that it's a mile along cobble-stone sidewalks (some curb cuts have 2" steps). Cross the busy street and canal in front of the station, head up Oostmeers, and turn right on Zwidzandstraat.

By Car: Park at the train station for just €2.50 per day and take the bus into town. There are pricier underground parking garages at the square called 't Zand and around town (€10/day, all of them well-marked). Paid parking on the street in Bruges is limited to four hours. Driving in town is very complicated because of the one-way system.

Helpful Hints

Market Days: Bruges hosts markets on Wednesday morning (Market Square) and Saturday morning ('t Zand). On Saturday and Sunday, a flea market hops along Dijver in front of the Groeninge Museum.

Shopping: Shops are open from 9:00 to 18:00, and a little later on Friday. Grocery stores are usually closed on Sunday. The main shopping street, Steenstraat, stretches from Market Square to the square called 't Zand. The Hema department store (**AE, AI, AT,** Level 1—Fully Accessible) is at Steenstraat 73 (Mon–Sat 9:00–18:00, closed Sun).

Money: Although there are no ATMs at the train station, there are plenty in town. An accessible ATM is near Market Square at Steenstraat 40 and at the bank on the south end of 't Zand (across square from TI). These ATMs are moderately accessible: at the post office (Markt 5), Fortis Bank (three branches: Simon Stevins Plein 3, Hoogstraat 23, and Vlamingstraat 78), and KBC (Steenstraat 38).

Internet Access: The relaxing **Coffee Link** (**AE+A, AI+A, AT,** Level 2—Moderately Accessible, one 2" entry step, one 4" step up to computers), with mellow music and pleasant art, is centrally located in a medieval mall across from the Church of Our Lady (€3/30 min, 16 terminals surrounded by sweet temptations, daily 10:00–18:00 in summer, Mariastraat 38, tel. 050/349-973, well-run by Staf). You

---

Museum Tips

Admission prices are steep, but they include great audioguides—so plan to spend some time and really get into it. For information on all the museums, call 050/448-711 or visit www.brugge.be.

Combo-Tickets: The TIs and participating museums sell a museum combo-ticket (any 5 museums for €15, unlimited validity period). Since the Groeninge and Memling museums cost €8 each, art-lovers will save money with this pass. If you use this combo-ticket, you don't need to wait in any lines—simply go directly to the turnstile, get your ticket punched, and head in.

Blue Monday: In Bruges, nearly all museums are open Tuesday through Sunday year-round from 9:30 to 17:00 and are closed on Monday. If you're in Bruges on a Monday, the following attractions are still open: Church of Our Lady, Begijnhof, De Halve Maan Brewery Tour, Basilica of the Holy Blood, Town Hall's Gothic Room, and chocolate shops and museum. You can also join a boat, bus, or walking/wheeling tour.

---

can also get wired at **Happyrom** (**AE, AI,** Level 2—Moderately Accessible; Ezelstraat 8) and the nearby **Snuffel Backpacker Hostel** (**AE, AI,** Level 2—Moderately Accessible; Ezelstraat 47).

Post Office: It's on Market Square near the bell tower (Level 3—Minimally Accessible; Mon–Fri 9:00–18:00, Sat 9:30–12:30, closed Sun, tel. 050/331-411). There are no ramps, since the P.O. is part of a monument (four 8" entry steps).

Laundry: Bruges has two accessible self-service launderettes, each within a few blocks of Market Square. **Mister Wash** (**AE, AI,** Level 2—Moderately Accessible) is at St. Jakobsstraat (tel. 050/336-622), and **Automatisch Wassalon Belfort** (**AE, AI,** Level 2—Moderately Accessible) is at Ezelstraat 51 (tel. 050/354-177).

Best Town View: The best view without a climb is from the rooftop terrace of Bruges' concert hall, the Concertgebouw (**AE, AI, AL,** Level 2—Moderately Accessible). This seven-story building, built in 2002, is the city's only modern high-rise (daily 11:00–23:00, free accessible elevator, on edge of old town on 't Zand, also houses the TI).

Getting Around Bruges

Bruges is nicely compact, but you may want to take a bus or taxi between the train station and the city center (especially with heavy luggage).

By Bus: All city buses are Level 1—Fully Accessible (**AE, AI, AL**), with transfer lifts for wheelchair users. A €1 bus ticket is good for an hour; an all-day pass costs €3. Nearly all city buses go directly from the train station to Market Square and fan out from there. They then return to Market Square and back to the station. Note that buses returning to the station from the center leave from the library bus stop, a block off Market Square on nearby Kuiperstraat (every 5 min).

By Taxi: Standard taxis are only moderately accessible (**AE+A,** Level 2, wheelchair user must be able to transfer into the taxi, driver is willing to assist you and to place wheelchair in trunk). For standard taxis, you'll find taxi stands at the station and on Market Square. If you need a fully adapted minivan taxi (**AE, AI,** Level 1—Fully Accessible), you can call one of two different companies: tel. 050/334-444 or tel. 050/384-660.

TOURS

Of Bruges

Bruges by Boat—The most relaxing and scenic (though not informative or accessible) way to see this city of canals is by boat, with the captain narrating. (Always let them know you speak English to ensure you'll understand the spiel.) Several companies offer basically the same 30-minute tour (€5.70, 4/hr, daily 10:00–17:00). Boats leave from all over town. Stael Boats has fewer steps than the others (€5.70, at Oude Sint Janshospitaal, Katelijnestraat 4, tel. 050/330-041).

Access: Level 3—Minimally Accessible, with steps down onto the dock, and more onto the boat (you can't take a wheelchair onto the boat). The staff at Stael will assist with boarding.

City Minibus Tour—Leaving Market Square every hour, City Tour Bruges gives a rolling overview of the town in an 18-seat, two-skylight minibus with dial-a-language headsets and video support (€11.50, 50 min, 10:00–20:00 in summer, until 18:00 in spring, until 17:00 in fall, less in winter, tel. 050/355-024, www.citytour.be). The narration, while clear, is slow-moving and a bit boring. But the tour is a lazy

Bruges

1 Concert Hall & TI
2 Dumon Chocolate & Bus to Station
3 De Halve Maan Brewery Tour
4 The Chocolate Line
5 Sweertvaegher Chocolate
6 Stael Boat Tours
7 City Minibus Tours
8 Coffee Link Internet Café
9 Choco-Story: The Chocolate Museum
10 Da Vinci Ice Cream
11 Hotel Karos

way to cruise past virtually every sight in Bruges.

Access: Their newer buses offer decent accessibility (**AE, AI+A,** Level 2—Moderately Accessible): You can roll directly on board, but then you'll have to transfer to a seat and stow your wheelchair in the back of the bus. Wheelchair users will want to call ahead to schedule a tour on one of these newer buses. On the older buses, travelers must be able to climb the three steps into and out of the bus (**AE+A, AI+A,** Level 2—Moderately Accessible).

Walking/Wheeling Tour—Local guides lead small groups through the core of town (€5, €12 for a family, 2 hrs, July–Aug daily, mid-May–June and Sept Sat–Sun only, no tours Oct–mid-May, depart from TI on 't Zand at 14:30—just drop in a few minutes early). Though earnest, the tours are heavy on history and given in two languages, so they may be less than peppy. Still, to propel you beyond the pretty gables and canal swans of Bruges, they're good medicine.

Access: Wheelchair users have been part of these tours for years. The guides will adjust the tour to accommodate you. To sign up, contact the VFG office (02/515-0261, info@vfg.be, www.vfg.be).

Horse-and-Buggy Tour—The buggies around town are ready to take you for a clip-clop tour (€30, 35 min, price is per carriage, not per person). When divided among four or five people, this can be a good value.

Access: AE+A, Level 2—Moderately Accessible. Wheelchair users must be able to climb into the carriage. The driver will fold and store the chair.

From Bruges

Daytours—Tour guide Frank loves leading small groups on a fascinating "Flanders Fields Battlefield" day trip. This tour is like Quasimodo's (listed below), but more accessible and more expensive. The differences: seven travelers on a minibus, rather than a big busload; pickup from any hotel or B&B (because the small bus is allowed in the town center); an included restaurant lunch, rather than a picnic; and a little more serious lecturing and a stricter focus on World War I. For instance, you actually visit the In Flanders Fields Museum in Ieper (Ypres in French). Tours cost €59 (Wed–Sun 9:00–17:00, no tours Mon–Tue, call 050/346-060 or toll-free 0800-99133 to reserve).

Access: AE+A, Level 2—Moderately Accessible. Wheelchair users need to be able to get on and off the bus. Frank will be happy to assist. Some of the sights (cemeteries and trenches) may be a challenge, and travelers with limited mobility will have to decide whether to engage in that part of the tour.

Bruges at a Glance

▲▲▲**Groeninge Museum** Top-notch collection of mainly Flemish art. **Hours:** Tue–Sun 9:30–17:00, closed Mon. **Access:** Level 1—Fully Accessible.

▲▲**Bell Tower** Overlooking Market Square, with 366 steps to a town view and a carillon close-up. **Hours:** Daily 9:30–17:00. **Access:** The Bell Tower is Level 4—Not Accessible, but the Exhibition Hall is Level 1—Fully Accessible.

▲▲**Burg Square** Historic square with sights and impressive architecture. **Hours:** Always open. **Access:** Level 1—Fully Accessible.

▲▲**Church of Our Lady** Tombs and church art, including Michelangelo's *Madonna and Child*. **Hours:** Mon–Fri 9:30–16:50, Sat 9:30–15:50, Sun 13:30–16:50 only. **Access:** Level 2—Moderately Accessible.

▲▲**Memling Museum/St. John's Hospital** Art by the greatest of the Flemish Primitives. **Hours:** Tue–Sun 9:30–17:00, closed Mon. **Access:** Level 1—Fully Accessible.

▲▲**Begijnhof** Benedictine nuns' peaceful courtyard and Beguine's House museum. **Hours:** Courtyard always open, museum open daily 10:00–12:00 & 13:45–17:00, shorter hours off-season. **Access:** Level 2—Moderately Accessible.

▲▲**De Halve Maan Brewery Tour** Fun and handy tour includes beer. **Hours:** Daily on the hour 11:00–16:00, Oct–March at 11:00 and 15:00 only. **Access:** Level 4—Not Accessible.

Quasimodo Countryside Tours—If the above tour is full, adventurous slow walkers could consider a similar but more physically demanding package offered by Quasimodo Countryside Tours (**AE+A,** Level 2—Moderately Accessible; they're happy to assist you). There are two different all-day, English-only bus tours through the rarely visited Flemish countryside.

The "In Flanders Fields" tour concentrates on World War I battlefields, trenches, memorials, and poppy-splattered fields (April–Oct Tue–Sun 9:15–17:00; Nov–March Sun, Tue, and Thu only).

▲**Market Square** Main square that is the modern heart of the city, with carillon bell tower (described above). **Hours:** Always open. **Access:** Mostly Level 1—Fully Accessible.

▲**Basilica of the Holy Blood** Romanesque and Gothic church housing a relic of the blood of Christ. **Hours:** April–Sept Thu–Tue 9:30–11:45 & 14:00–17:45, Wed 9:30–11:45 only; Oct–March Thu–Tue 10:00–11:45 & 14:00–15:45, Wed 10:00-11:45 only. **Access:** The Lower Chapel is Level 2—Moderately Accessible; the Upper Chapel and adjacent Treasury are Level 4—Not Accessible.

▲**Town Hall** Beautifully restored Gothic Room from 1400, plus a Renaissance Hall. **Hours:** Gothic Room—daily 9:30–17:00; Renaissance Hall—Tue–Sun 9:30–12:30 & 13:30–16:30, closed Mon. **Access:** Gothic Room is Level 2—Moderately Accessible; Renaissance Hall is Level 1—Fully Accessible.

▲**Gruuthuse Museum** 15th-century mansion displaying an eclectic collection that includes furniture, tapestries, and lots more. **Hours:** Tue–Sun 9:30–17:00, closed Mon. **Access:** Level 3—Minimally Accessible.

▲**Chocolate** Sample Bruges' specialty: Try Dumon, The Chocolate Line, Sweertvaegher, and on and on. **Hours:** Shops generally open 10:00–18:00. **Access:** Most shops are Level 2—Moderately Accessible.

Choco-Story: The Chocolate Museum Learn the whole delicious story of Belgium's favorite treat. **Hours:** Daily 10:00–17:00. **Access:** Level 2—Moderately Accessible.

The other tour, "Triple Treat," focuses on Flanders' medieval past and rich culture, with tastes of chocolate, waffles, and beer (Mon, Wed, and Fri 9:15–17:00). Be ready for lots of walking.

Tours cost €50, or €40 if you're under 26 (includes a picnic lunch, 30-seat, non-smoking bus, reserve by calling tel. 050/370-470 or toll-free tel. 0800-97525, www.quasimodo.be). After making a few big-hotel pickups, the buses leave town at 9:15 from the Park Hotel on 't Zand.

Bus and Boat Tour—The Sightseeing Line offers a bus trip to Damme and a boat ride back. The bus and boat are fully accessible (**AE**); go on a good-weather day, because the accessible part of the boat is not covered

(€16.50, April–Sept daily at 14:00, 2 hrs, leaves from the post office at Market Square, tel. 050/355-024).

SIGHTS

These sights are listed in order from Market Square to Burg Square to the cluster of museums around the Church of our Lady to the Begijnhof (less than a quarter-mile from beginning to end). For a self-guided tour and more information on each sight, see the Bruges City Roll or Stroll, page 363.

▲**Market Square (Markt)**—Ringed by a bank, the post office, lots of restaurant terraces, great old gabled buildings, and the iconic bell tower, this

is the modern heart of the city (most city buses run from near here to the train station—library bus stop, a block down Kuiperstraat). Under the bell tower are two great Belgian french-fry stands, a quadrilingual Braille description of the old town, and a metal model of the tower. In Bruges' heyday as a trading center, a canal came right up to this square.

Geldmuntstraat, just off the square, is a delightful street with many fun and practical shops and eateries.

Access: Most of the square is fully accessible (Level 1), but the cobblestone streets (with 2" curbs) vary in degree of roughness. Geldmuntstraat (**AE+A,** Level 2—Moderately Accessible) has 4" curbs, with curb cuts down to one or two inches. Some stores have wheelchair-accessible entryways, others have entry steps.

▲▲**Bell Tower (Belfort)**—Most of this bell tower has presided over Market Square since 1300, serenading passersby with carillon music. The octagonal lantern was added in 1486, making it 290 feet high—that's 366 steps. If you can manage the steps, the view is worth the climb.

Access: The Bell Tower is Level 4—Not Accessible; the Exhibition Hall is **AE, AI, AL, AT,** Level 1—Fully Accessible. While the Bell Tower requires a long, steep climb, you can reach the Exhibition Hall on the second floor by elevator (in the courtyard, down the hallway toward the toilet). The toilet off the courtyard is wheelchair-accessible (€0.30, ask attendant for key).

Cost and Hours: €5, daily 9:30–17:00, last entry 45 min before closing.

Evening Carillon Concerts: The tiny courtyard behind the bell tower has a few benches where people can enjoy the free carillon concerts (generally Mon, Wed, and Sat at 21:00 in the summer, schedule posted on the wall).

▲▲**Burg Square**—This opulent square is Bruges' civic center, historically the birthplace of Bruges and the site of the 9th-century castle of the first Count of Flanders. Today, the easily accessed square is the scene of outdoor concerts and surrounded by six centuries of architecture.

▲**Basilica of the Holy Blood**—Originally the Chapel of Saint Basil, this church is famous for its relic of the blood of Christ, which, according to tradition, was brought to Bruges in 1150 after the Second Crusade. The lower chapel is dark and solid—a fine example of Romanesque style. The upper chapel (separate entrance, up the stairs) is decorated Gothic. An interesting museum is next to the upper chapel.

Access: The Lower Chapel is **AE, AI,** Level 2—Moderately Accessible; the Upper Chapel and adjacent Treasury are Level 4—Not Accessible (up thirty-seven 7" steps).

Cost, Hours, Location: Museum entry-€1.50; April–Sept Thu–Tue 9:30–11:45 & 14:00–17:45, Wed 9:30–11:45 only; Oct–March Thu–Tue 10:00–11:45 & 14:00–15:45, Wed 10:00–11:45 only; Burg Square, tel. 050/336-792, www.holyblood.org.

▲**Town Hall's Gothic Room**—Your ticket gives you a room full of Bruges history, in the form of old town maps and paintings and a grand, beautifully restored "Gothic Hall" from 1400. Its painted and carved wooden ceiling features hanging arches. Trace the story of Bruges via the series of late-19th-century wall murals. See Bruges City Roll or Stroll, page 369.

Access: AE, AI, AL+A, Level 2—Moderately Accessible. The Gothic Room is upstairs and accessible by elevator.

Cost, Hours, Location: €2.50, includes audioguide and admission to Renaissance Hall, daily 9:30–17:00, Burg 12.

Renaissance Hall (Brugse Vrije)—This is just one ornate room with an impressive Renaissance chimney. Underwhelming to most, the hall is a hit with heraldry fans. See Bruges City Roll or Stroll, page 372.

Access: AE, AI, AT, Level 1—Fully Accessible.

Cost, Hours, Location: €2.50, includes audioguide and admission to Town Hall's Gothic Room, Tue-Sun 9:30-12:30 & 13:30-16:30, closed Mon, entry in corner of square at Burg 11a.

▲▲▲**Groeninge Museum**—This museum houses a world-class collection of mostly Flemish art, from Memling to Magritte. While there's plenty of worthwhile modern art, the highlights are the vivid and pristine Flemish Primitives. ("Primitive" here means before the Renaissance.) Flemish art is shaped by its love of detail, its merchant patrons' egos, and the power of the Church. Lose yourself in the halls of Groeninge: Gaze across 15th-century canals, into the eyes of reassuring Marys, and through town squares littered with leotards, lace, and lopped-off heads.

Access: AE, AI, AT, Level 1—Fully Accessible. The museum's entrance has steps, but if you go past the entry to Groeninge (a little alley-like street), you can enter the museum with no barriers. Inside, there's a unisex adapted toilet in the men's restroom.

Cost, Hours, Location: €8, includes audioguide, Tue–Sun 9:30–17:00, closed Mon, Dijver 12, tel. 050/448-751.

▲**Gruuthuse Museum**—Once a wealthy brewer's home, this 15th-century mansion is a sprawling smattering of everything from medieval bedpans to a guillotine.

Access: Level 3—Minimally Accessible. There are six 6" steps at the entry, and the building includes many levels accessible only by steps, sometimes winding and narrow.

Cost, Hours, Location: €6, includes audioguide and entry to apse in Church of Our Lady, Tue–Sun 9:30–17:00, closed Mon, Dijver 17.

▲▲**Church of Our Lady**—The church stands as a memorial to the power and wealth of Bruges in its heyday. A delicate *Madonna and Child* by Michelangelo is near the apse (to the right if you're facing the altar). It's said to be the only Michelangelo statue to leave Italy in his lifetime (thanks to the wealth generated by Bruges' cloth trade). If you like tombs and church art, pay to wander through the apse.

Access: AE, AI, Level 2—Moderately Accessible. The church is wheelchair-accessible, with the exception of a small room (up two 8" steps) at the end of the apse. The nearest accessible toilet is across the street at the Visitors Center of the Memling Museum (see below).

Cost, Hours, Location: Michelangelo viewing is free, art-filled apse costs €2.50, covered by €6 Gruuthuse admission, Mon–Fri 9:30–16:50, Sat 9:30–15:50, Sun 13:30–16:50 only, Mariastraat.

▲▲**Memling Museum/St. John's Hospital (Sint Janshospitaal)**—The former monastery/hospital complex has two entrances—one is to a welcoming visitors center (free), the other to the Memling Museum. The Memling Museum, in the monastery's former church, was once a medieval hospital and now contains six much-loved paintings by the greatest of the Flemish Primitives, Hans Memling. His *Mystical Wedding of St.*

Catherine triptych is a highlight, as is the miniature gilded oak shrine to St. Ursula.

Access: AE, AI, AL, AT, Level 1—Fully Accessible with the exception of a corner room (two 8" steps). You'll find an elevator (on the right side of the inside entry) and an accessible unisex toilet (€0.30, located in men's room at visitors center). Loaner wheelchairs are available.

Cost, Hours, Location: €8 includes fine audioguide, Tue–Sun 9:30–17:00, closed Mon, across the street from the Church of Our Lady, Mariastraat 38.

▲▲**Begijnhof**—Inhabited by Benedictine nuns, the Begijnhof courtyard almost makes you want to don a habit and fold your hands as you wander under its wispy trees and whisper past its frugal little homes. For a good slice of Begijnhof life, visit the simple museum, the Beguine's House.

Access: AE+A, AI+A, Level 2—Moderately Accessible. The cobblestones in the Begijnhof are heavy and rough, making for a bone-jarring wheelchair ride. The museum has one 4" entry step, one 4" step to visit the kitchen, one 8" step to the courtyard, and two 7" steps to see the sleeping quarters.

Museum Cost and Hours: €2, daily 10:00–12:00 & 13:45–17:00, shorter hours off-season, courtyard always open, English explanations, Beguine's House is left of entry gate.

Minnewater—Just south of the Begijnhof is Minnewater, an idyllic world of flower boxes, canals, and swans.

Almshouses—Returning from the Begijnhof back to the town center, you might detour along Nieuwe Gentweg to visit one of about 20 almshouses in the city. At #8, go through the door marked *Godshuis de Meulenaere 1613* into the peaceful courtyard (free). This was a medieval form of housing for the poor. The rich would pay for someone's tiny room here in return for lots of prayers.

Access: AE+A, AI, Level 2—Moderately Accessible. There are two 6" steps at the almshouse entry.

Bruges Experiences:
Beer, Chocolate, Lace, and Biking

▲**Chocolate Shops**—Bruggians are connoisseurs of fine chocolate. You'll be tempted by chocolate-filled display windows all over town. While Godiva is the best big-factory/high-price/high-quality brand, there are plenty of smaller, family-run places in Bruges that offer exquisite handmade chocolates. Each of the following chocolatiers is proud of its creative varieties. They're all are generous with samples and welcome you to pick any five or six chocolates to assemble a 100-gram assortment.

Dumon: Perhaps Bruges' smoothest and creamiest chocolates are at Dumon (**AE+A,** Level 2—Moderately Accessible; €1.75/100 grams). Madam Dumon and her children (Stefaan and Christophe) make their top-notch chocolate daily and sell it fresh just off Market Square (Thu–Tue 10:00–18:00, closed Wed, old chocolate molds on display in basement, Eiermarkt 6, tel. 050/346-282). Their *ganache,* a dark, creamy combo, wows chocoholics. The

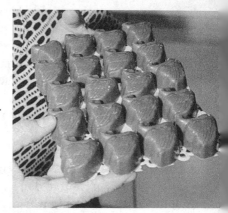

Dumons don't provide English labels because they believe it's best to describe their chocolates in person—and they do it with an evangelical fervor. If you're using a wheelchair, roll up to the window to the left of the entrance and they'll serve you samples there.

The Chocolate Line: Locals and tourists alike flock to The Chocolate Line (**AE+A, AI,** Level 2—Moderately Accessible, wooden ramp available to cover the 8" step—ask; €3.40/100 grams) to taste the *gastronomique* varieties concocted by Dominique Person—the mad scientist of chocolate. His unique creations include Havana cigar (marinated in rum, cognac, and Cuban tobacco leaves—so therefore technically illegal in the United States), lemongrass, lavender, ginger (shaped like a Buddha), saffron curry, spicy chili, and a Moroccan mint that will take you to Marrakech. My fave: the sheets of chocolate with crunchy roasted cocoa beans. Coming soon: a Pop Rocks/cola chocolate. The kitchen—busy whipping up 80 varieties—is on display in the back. Enjoy the window display, renewed monthly (daily 9:30–18:00, between Church of Our Lady and Market Square at Simon Stevinplein 19, tel. 050/341-090).

Sweertvaegher: This smaller place, near Burg Square, features top-quality chocolate (**AE+A, AI,** Level 2—Moderately Accessible, one 4" entry step; €2.65/100 grams) that's darker rather than sweeter, made with fresh ingredients and no preservatives (Tue–Sat 9:30–18:00, closed Sun-Mon, Philipstockstraat 29, tel. 050/338-367).

Choco-Story: The Chocolate Museum—This museum, rated ▲ for chocoholics, explains why, in the ancient Mexican world of the Mayas and the Aztecs, chocolate was considered the drink of the gods, and cocoa beans were used as a means of payment. With lots of actual artifacts well-described in English, the museum fills you in on the production of truffles, chocolates, hollow figures, and bars of chocolate. Then you'll view a delicious little video (8 min long, repeats continuously, alternating

Flemish, French, and then English—peek into the theater before entering the top room to time it right). Your finale is in the "demonstration room," where—after a 10-minute cooking lesson—you get a taste.

Access: AE, AI, Level 2—Moderately Accessible.

Cost, Hours, Location: €6, daily 10:00–17:00, where Wijnzakstraat meets Sint Jansstraat at Sint Jansplein, near Market Square, tel. 050/612-237, www.choco-story.be. Notice how chocolaty the fine building looks from across the street.

▲▲**De Halve Maan Brewery Tour**—Belgians are also Europe's beer connoisseurs. This fun, handy tour is a great way to pay your respects. "The Brugse Zot" is the last beer actually brewed in Bruges. While the tour won't work for wheelchair users, energetic beer-loving slow walkers could manage. The happy gang at this working family brewery gives entertaining and informative 45-minute, three-language tours (often by friendly Inge, tour includes a beer, great rooftop panorama).

Their bistro, where you'll be given your included beer, serves quick, hearty lunch plates. You can eat indoors with the smell of hops, or outdoors with the smell of hops. This is a great place to wait for your tour or to linger afterward. For more on beer, see page 358.

Access: Level 4—Not Accessible, lots of very steep steps with no elevator.

Cost, Hours, Location: €4.50, daily on the hour 11:00–16:00, Oct–March at 11:00 and 15:00 only, 1 block past church and canal, take a right down skinny Stoofstraat to #26 on Walplein, tel. 050/332-697, www.halvemaan.be.

Windmills and Lace by the Moat—At the northeast end of town are four windmills strung along a pleasant grassy setting on the "big moat" canal.

Windmill: The St. Janshuismolen windmill is open, but the ramps to the base of the windmills are steep and rugged, and the windmills themselves are not accessible (€2, May–Sept daily 9:30–12:30 & 13:30–17:00, closed Oct–April, at the end of Carmersstraat, between Kruispoort and Dampoort, on Bruges side of the moat).

Lace: To actually see lace being made, drop by the nearby **Lace Center** (**AE, AI,** Level 2—Moderately Accessible, one 2" entry step), where ladies toss bobbins madly while their eyes go bad (€2.50 includes afternoon demo and small lace museum, as well as adjacent Jeruzalem Church, Mon–Fri 10:00–12:00 & 14:00–18:00, Sat until 17:00, closed Sun, Peperstraat 3, tel. 050/330-072).

The **Folklore Museum (AE+A, AI,** Level 2—Moderately Accessible) in the same neighborhood, is cute but forgettable (€3, Tue–Sun 9:30–17:00, closed Mon, Balstraat 43, tel. 050/448-764-044).

SLEEPING

Bruges is a great place to sleep, with Gothic spires out your window,

no traffic noise, and the cheerily out-of-tune carillon heralding each new day at 8:00 sharp. (Thankfully, the bell tower is silent from 22:00 to 8:00.)

Most Bruges accommodations are located between the train station and the old center, with the most distant (and best) being a few blocks to the north and east of Market Square. Bruges is most crowded Friday and Saturday evenings Easter through October, with July and August weekends being worst. Many hotels charge a bit more on Friday and Saturday, and won't let you stay just one night if it's a Saturday.

Hotels
Level 1—Fully Accessible
Karos Hotel (AE, AI, AL, AR, AB), a block and a half from the TI on 't Zand, is Old World, warm, and welcoming (Db-€70–110, spacious room and bath with roll-in shower, includes breakfast, Hoefijzerlaan 37, tel. 050/341-448).

The adjacent **Novotel** and **Ibis** hotels **(AE, AI, AL, AR, AB)**, closer to the center of town, have three accessible rooms apiece. The Ibis, in a former 15th-century convent, has an entrance ramp and has been updated completely inside and out for accessibility (Db-€69–89, elevator, parking,

Bruges Hotels

1. Hotel Adornes
2. Hotel Patritius
3. Het Gheestelic Hof
4. To Hotels Egmond, Novotel & Ibis
5. To Hotel Groeninghe
6. Hotel Botaniek
7. Hotel Cordoeanier
8. To Debruyne B&B
9. Absoluut Verhulst B&B

Sleep Code

(€1 = about $1.20, country code: 32)
S = Single, **D** = Double/Twin, **T** = Triple, **Q** = Quad, **b** = bathroom, **s** = shower only. Everyone speaks English. Unless otherwise noted, credit cards are accepted and breakfast is included.

Katelijnestraat 65A, tel. 050/337-575, fax 050/336-419, www.hotels -belgium.com/brugge/ibis.htm). The Novotel, in a new, Scandinavian-style building, is also completely accessible (Db-€114–121, elevator, pool, accessible restaurant, parking-€9, Katelijnestraat 65B, tel. 050/337-533, fax 050/336-556, www.novotel.com, h1033@accor.com).

Level 2—Moderately Accessible
Hotel Adornes (AE, AI, AL, AR, AB+A, ❤) is small and classy—a great value. This 17th-century canalside house has 20 rooms with full, modern bathrooms, free parking (reserve in advance), and a cellar lounge (accessible by lift) with games and videos (Db-€90–120 depending on size, singles take a double for nearly the same cost, Tb-€135, Qb-€145, elevator, near Carmersstraat at St. Annarei 26, tel. 050/341-336, fax 050/342-085, www.adornes.be, info@adornes.be, Nathalie runs the family business). The hotel is accessible by wheelchair through the courtyard in back. One large ground-floor room works for guests using wheelchairs. While the toilet and bathtub are not specially adapted, the bathroom is large enough to maneuver a wheelchair.

Hotel Patritius (AE, AI, AL, AR, AB+A), family-run and centrally located, is a grand, circa-1830, neoclassical mansion with 16 stately rooms, a plush lounge and chandeliered breakfast room, and a courtyard garden. This is the best value in its price range (Db-€80-105 depending on size, Tb-€140, about €10 more Fri–Sat, non-smoking, free parking, Riddersstraat 11, tel. 050/338-454, fax 050/339-634, www.hotelpatritius .be, info@hotelpatritius.be, Garrett and Elvi Spaey). There is an elevator accessed outside the hotel and one suitable room with an accessible toilet (but bathtub is not accessible). This unit sleeps four and includes a second room that allows privacy for a companion.

Het Gheestelic Hof (AE+A, AI, AR, AB, one 8" entry step) is centrally located, with cozy, well-appointed, and well-equipped rooms. The adapted room on the main floor contains a roll-in shower (Db-€60–95, includes breakfast served in its four-star sister across the street, Heilige-Geeststraat 2, tel. 050/342-594).

Hotel Egmond (AE+A, AI, AR, AB) is a creaky mansion quietly located in the middle of the idyllic Minnewater. Its eight 18th-century rooms are plain, with small modern baths shoehorned in, and the guests-only garden is just waiting for a tea party. This hotel is right for romantics who want to be in the countryside, but still just outside town (Sb-€92, small twin Db-€112, larger Db-€120–130, Tb-€150, cash only, Minnewater 15, tel. 050/341-445, fax 050/342-940, www.egmond.be, info@egmond.be).

Hotel Groeninghe (AE+A, AI, AR, AB+A) has eight charming, Old World rooms in a good location close to 't Zand. It's run by friendly Laurence (Sb €70, Db €85, Tb €110, no elevator, Korte Vulderstraat 29, tel. 050/343-255, fax 050/340-769, www.hotelgroeninghe.be, hotelgroeninghe@pandora.be).

Level 3—Minimally Accessible
Hotel Botaniek (AE+A, AI, AL, AR+A, AB+A, three 8" entry steps), quietly located a block from pleasant Astrid Park, rents nine rooms (Db-€98, Tb-€106, Qb-€115, more for 1-night stays, less for longer stays, elevator, Waalsestraat 23, tel. 050/341-424, fax 050/345-939, www.botaniek.be, info@botaniek.be).

Hotel Cordoeanier (AE+A, AI, AR, AB+A, three 7" entry steps), a family-run hotel, rents 22 bright, simple, modern rooms on a quiet street two blocks off Market Square. It's the best cheap hotel in town (Sb-€59, Db-€65, Tb-€75, Qb-€88, Quint/b-€101, €5 extra on Fri-Sat, Cordoeanierstraat 16-18, tel. 050/339-051, fax 050/346-111, www.cordoeanier.be, info@cordoeanier.be, Kris, Veerle, Guy, and family). Their "holiday house" across the street sleeps up to 10 for €250 a night (includes a kitchen; cheaper for longer stays). The hotel has two ground-floor rooms with wheelchair-accessible toilets, but not baths.

Bed-and-Breakfasts
B&Bs, run by people who enjoy their work, offer fine value but limited accessibility. They typically have rooms on upper floors reachable only by steep staircases. While none would be suitable for wheelchair users, the two listings below have relatively few stairs and are satisfactory for slow walkers. Parking is generally easy on the street (pay 9:00–19:00, free overnight).

Level 3—Minimally Accessible

Debruyne B&B (AE+A, AI, AR+A, AB+A, ♥), run by Marie-Rose and her architect husband, Ronny, offers artsy, original decor (check out the elephant-sized white doors—Ronny's design) and genuine warmth. If Gothic is getting old, this is refreshingly modern (Sb-€55, Db-€60, Tb-€80, 1-night stays pay €10 more, cash only, non-smoking, free Internet in lobby, north of Market Square, 2 blocks from the little church at Lange Raamstraat 18, tel. 050/347-606, fax 050/340-285, www.bedandbreakfastbruges.com, marie.debruyne@advalvas.be). Two of the rooms are on the ground floor, but can be reached only by climbing steps. Marie-Rose has hosted wheelchair users before and is willing to help guests tackle the nine 5" steps to the breakfast room and also to serve meals in the guest's room. The bathrooms are suitable but not adapted.

Absoluut Verhulst (AE, AI+A, AR, AB+A) is a great, modern-feeling B&B in a 400-year-old house, run by friendly Frieda and Benno. It presents a challenge even for slow walkers, but if you have your heart set on staying at a B&B, this one has fewer stairs than most (Sb-€50, Db-€75, huge and lofty suite-€95 for 2, €115 for 3, and €140 for 4, 1-night stays pay €10 more, cash only, east of Market Square at Verbrand Nieuwland 1, tel. & fax 050/334-515, www.b-bverhulst.com, b-b.verhulst@pandora.be).

EATING

Belgium is where France meets the North, and you'll find a good mix of both Flemish and French influences in Bruges and Brussels. We've included accessibility information for each place. Unless otherwise noted (by **AT** or **AT+A**), these restaurants do *not* have accessible toilets.

Belgian Specialties

These dishes are popular throughout Belgium.
Moules: Mussels are served everywhere, either cooked plain *(nature)*, with white wine *(vin blanc)*, with shallots or onions *(marinière)*, or in a tomato sauce *(provençale)*. You get a big-enough-for-two bucket and a pile of fries. Go local by using one empty shell to tweeze out the rest of the *moules*. When the mollusks are

in season, from about mid-July through April, you'll get the big Dutch mussels. Locals take a break in May and June, when only the puny Danish kind is available.

Frites: Belgian fries (*Vlaamse frites,* or Flemish fries) taste so good because they're deep-fried twice—once to cook, and once to brown. The natives eat them with mayonnaise, not ketchup.

Flemish Specialties

These specialties are traditional to Bruges.

Carbonnade: Rich beef stew flavored with onions and beer.

Chou rouge à la flamande: Red cabbage with onions and prunes.

Flamiche: Cheese pie with onions.

Flemish asparagus: White asparagus (fresh in springtime) in cream sauce.

Lapin à la flamande: Marinated rabbit braised in onions and prunes.

Soupe à la bière: Beer soup.

Stoemp: Mashed potatoes and vegetables.

Waterzooi: Creamy meat stew (chicken, eel, or fish).

...à la flamande: Anything cooked in the local Flemish style.

Brussels Specialties

You can find these specialties in Bruges, though they're technically "native" to Brussels (which tends toward French cuisine).

Anguilles au vert: Eel in green herb sauce.

Caricoles: Sea snails. Very local, seasonal, and hard to find, these are usually sold hot by street vendors.

Cheeses: Remoudou and Djotte de Nivelles are made locally.

Choux de Bruxelles: Brussels sprouts (in cream sauce).

Crevettes: Shrimp, often served as croquettes (minced and stuffed in breaded, deep-fried rolls).

Croque Monsieur: Grilled ham-and-cheese sandwich.

Endive: Typical Belgian vegetable (also called *chicorée* or *chicon*) served as a side dish.

Filet Américain: Beware—for some reason, steak tartare (raw) is called "American."

Tartine de fromage blanc: Open-face cream-cheese sandwich, often enjoyed with a cherry Kriek beer.

...à la brabançonne: Anything cooked in the local Brabant (Brussels) style, such as *faisant* (pheasant) *à la brabançonne.*

Desserts and Snacks

Gaufres: Waffles, sold hot in small shops.
Dame blanche: Hot-fudge sundae.
Spekuloos: Spicy gingerbread biscuits served with coffee.
Pralines: Filled Belgian chocolates.
Pistolets: Round croissants.
Cramique: Currant roll.
Craquelin: Currant roll with sugar sprinkles.

Tipping

It generally isn't necessary to tip in restaurants (15 percent service is usually already included in the menu price). Still, feel free to tip about 5 percent if the service is good. In bars, you can round up to the next euro ("keep the change") if you get table service, rather than order at the bar.

Restaurants in Bruges

Bruges' specialties include mussels cooked a variety of ways (one order can feed two), fish dishes, grilled meats, and french fries. Don't eat before 19:30 unless you like eating alone. Tax and service are always included in your bill. While tap water comes with a smile in Holland, France, and Germany, it's not the case in Belgium, where you'll either pay for water, enjoy the beer, or go thirsty.

You'll find plenty of affordable, touristy restaurants on floodlit squares and along dreamy canals. Bruges feeds 3.5 million tourists a year, and most are seduced by a high-profile location. These can be fine experiences for the magical setting and views, but the quality of food and service is low. I wouldn't blame you for eating at one of these places, but I won't recommend any. I prefer the candle-cool bistros that flicker on back streets. Here are my favorites:

At **Terrastje** (**AE, AI,** Level 2—Moderately Accessible), an accessible ramp leads you to this chicken-soup-for-the-soul, pub-like bistro. A remarkable selection of Belgian beers and fresh peasant food, cranked up a notch by English Ian and Dutch Patricia, make this place resonate with good cheer (€3–7 tapas, €6–13 meals, Fri–Tue 10:30–23:30, closed Wed–Thu, across the canal from Hotel Adornes, Genthof 45, tel. 050/330-919).

The Flemish Pot (**AE, AI, AT,** ♥, Level 1—Fully Accessible; a.k.a. "The Little Pancake House") is a hardworking eatery serving up traditional peasant-style Flemish dishes. They crank out pancake meals (savory and sweet) and homemade *wafels* for lunch. Then, at 18:00, enthusiastic chefs Mario and Rik stow their waffle irons and pull out a

Bruges Restaurants

1 Rock Fort & Barsalon Tapas Bar
2 Rest. Chez Olivier
3 Rest. de Koetse
4 To Bistro de Bekoring
5 To Tom's Diner
6 Bistro in den Wittenkop
7 The Flemish Pot
8 Lotus Vegetarian Restaurant
9 The Hobbit
10 't Brugs Beertje
11 De Garre

12 Terrastje
13 L'Estaminet
14 Herberg Vlissinghe
15 Market Square Frituur
16 Pickles Frituur
17 Pili Pili Rest.
18 Restaurant Hennon
19 De Torre Tea Room & Rest.
20 To Bistro Kok au Vin
21 Delhaize-Proxy Supermarket
   & Da Vinci Ice Cream

traditional menu of vintage Flemish plates (€25 dinner *menu*, Fri–Wed 12:00–22:00, closed Thu, family-friendly, just off Geldmuntstraat at Helmstraat 3, tel. 050/340-086).

Rock Fort (AE+A, AI, Level 2—Moderately Accessible, staff can help with the two 2" entry steps) is a chic, eight-table spot with a modern, fresh coziness and a high-powered respect for good food. Two young chefs, Peter Laloo and Hermes Vanliefde, give their French cuisine a creative and gourmet twist. Reservations are required for dinner, but not lunch. This place is a winner (€11 Mon–Fri lunch special with coffee, beautifully presented €15–20 dinner plates, open Mon–Fri 12:00–14:30 & 18:30–23:00, closed Sat–Sun, great pastas and salads, Langestraat 15, tel. 050/334-113). They also run the Barsalon restaurant next door.

Barsalon Tapas Bar (AE+A, AI, Level 2—Moderately Accessible), more than a tapas bar, is the brainchild of Peter Laloo from Rock Fort (listed above), allowing him to spread his creative cooking energy. This long, skinny slice of L.A. buzzes late into the evening with Bruges' beautiful people. Choose between the long bar, comfy stools, and bigger tables in back. Come early for fewer crowds. The playful menu comes with €6 "tapas" dishes taking you from Spain to Japan (3 selections fill 2 hungry travelers) and more elaborate €14 plates—and don't overlook their daily "suggestions" board, with some special wines by the glass and a "teaser" sampler plate of desserts. Barsalon shares the same kitchen, hours, and dressy local clientele as the adjacent Rock Fort.

Bistro Kok au Vin (AE, AI, Level 2—Moderately Accessible) is a modern-intimate-bistro. Chef Jurgen and his wife Britt have a creative, fresh take on local fare (€5–20, Fri–Tue 12:00–14:30 and 18:30–23:00, closed Wed–Thu, Ezelstraat 19, tel. 050/339-521).

Restaurant Chez Olivier (AE, AI, ♥, Level 2—Moderately Accessible, barrier-free entry, wheelchair-using regulars), with 10 classy, white-tablecloth tables, is considered the best fancy French cuisine splurge in town. While delicate Anne serves, her French husband, Olivier, is busy cooking up whatever he found freshest that day. While you can order à la carte, it's wise to go with the recommended daily *menu* (€34 for 3-course lunch, €45 for 3-course dinner, €55 for 4-course dinner, wine adds €15–20, Mon–Wed and Fri–Sat 12:00–13:30 & 19:00–21:30, closed Sun and Thu, reserve for dinner, Meestraat 9, tel. 050/333-659).

De Torre (AE, AI, Level 2—Moderately Accessible), a tearoom and restaurant, has a fresh interior and a scenic, shady, canalside terrace. I'd eat here only to be along a canal (€10 3-course lunch, €22–35 dinner *menu*s, Thu–Mon 10:00–22:00, closed Tue–Wed, Langestraat 8, tel. 050/342-946).

Pili Pili (AE+A, AI, Level 2—Moderately Accessible, one 3" entry step) is a mod and inviting pasta place, where Reinout and Tom prepare and serve 10 different pastas and great salads at very reasonable prices. The place is clean, low-key, and brimming with quality (€9 lunch plate with wine, €12.50 pasta and wine dinner, Thu–Tue 12:00–14:30 & 18:00–22:30, closed Sun afternoon and Wed, Hoogstraat 17, tel. 050/491-149).

Restaurant de Koetse (AE+A, AI, AT+A, ♥, Level 2—Moderately Accessible, popular with wheelchair users, one 2" entry step) is a good bet for central, affordable, quality, local-style food. The feeling is traditional, yet fun and kid-friendly. The cuisine is Belgian and French, with a stress on grilled meat, seafood, and mussels (€27 3-course meals, €20 plates include vegetables and a salad, Fri–Wed 12:00–15:00 & 18:00–22:00, closed Thu, non-smoking section, Oude Burg 31, tel. 050/337-680). The suitable toilet has enough room to maneuver a wheelchair, but there are no grab bars.

Bistro de Bekoring (AE+A, AI, ♥, Level 2—Moderately Accessible, one 8" step down at entry)—cute, candlelit, and Gothic—fills two alms-houses with people thankful for good food. Rotund and friendly Chef Roland and his wife, Gerda, love to tempt people—as the name of their bistro implies. They serve traditional Flemish food (especially eel and beer-soaked stew) from a small menu to people who like holding hands as they dine (€12 weekday lunch, €32 dinners, Wed–Sat from 12:00 and from 18:30, closed Sun–Tue, out past the Begijnhof at Arsenaalstraat 53, tel. 050/344-157).

Bistro in den Wittenkop (AE, AI, Level 2—Moderately Accessible), very Flemish, is a cluttered, laid-back, old-time place specializing in local favorites. While Lieve cooks, his wife Daniel serves in a cool-and-jazzy, candlelit Flemish ambience (€16–20 main courses, Tue–Sat 12:00–14:00 & 18:00–21:30, closed Sun–Mon, terrace in back, Sint Jakobsstraat 14, tel. 050/332-059).

Lotus Vegetarian Restaurant (AE+A, AI, Level 2—Moderately Accessible, one 4" entry step) serves serious lunch plates (€9 *plat du jour* offered daily), salads, and homemade chocolate cake in a smoke-free, bustling, and upscale setting without a trace of tie-dye (Mon–Sat 11:45–14:00, closed Sun, just off north of Burg at Wapenmakersstraat 5, tel. 050/331-078).

The Hobbit (AE+A, AI, ♥, Level 2—Moderately Accessible, staff can help with the one 4" entry step), featuring an entertaining menu, is always busy with happy eaters. For a swinging deal, try the all-you-can-eat spareribs with salad for €13. It's nothing fancy, just good, basic food in a fun, traditional grill house (daily 18:00–24:00, family-friendly, Kemelstraat 8-10, tel. 050/335-520).

Belgian Beers

Belgium has about 120 different varieties of beer and 580 different brands, more than any other country...and the locals take their beers as seriously as the French regard their wines. Even small café menus include six to eight varieties. Connoisseurs and novices alike can be confused by the many choices, and casual drinkers probably won't like every kind offered, since some varieties don't even taste like beer. Belgian beer is generally yeastier and higher in alcohol than beers in other countries.

In Belgium, certain beers are paired with certain dishes. To bring out their flavor, different beers are served at cold, cool, or room temperature, and each has its own distinctive glass. Whether wide-mouthed, tall, and fluted, with or without a stem, the glass is meant to highlight the beer's qualities. One of my favorite Belgian beer experiences is drinking a Kwak beer in its traditional tall glass. The glass, which widens at the base, stands in a wooden holder, and you pick the whole apparatus up—frame and glass—and drink. As you near the end, the beer in the wide bottom comes out at you quickly, with a "Kwak! Kwak! Kwak!"

To get a draft beer in Bruges, where Flemish is the dominant language, ask for *een pintje* (a pint, pronounced "ayn pinch-ya"). Cheers is *proost* or *gezondheid* in Flemish. The colorful cardboard coasters make nice free souvenirs.

Here's a breakdown of types of beer, with some common brand names you'll find either on tap or in bottles. (Some beers require a second fermentation in the bottle, so they're only available in bottles.) This list is just a start, and you'll find many beers that don't fall into these neat categories. For encyclopedic information on Belgian beers, visit www.belgianstyle.com or www.beerhunter.com.

Ales (Blonde/Red/Amber/Brown): Ales are easily recognized by their color. Try a blonde or golden ale (Leffe Blonde, Duvel, Kwak), a rare and bitter sour red (Rodenbach), an amber (Palm, De Koninck), or a brown (Leffe Bruin).

Lagers: These are the light, sparkling, Budweiser-type beers. Popular brands include Jupiler, Stella-Artois, and Maes.

Lambics: Perhaps the most unusual and least beer-like, *lambics* are stored for years in wooden casks, fermenting from wild yeasts that occur naturally in the air. Tasting more like a dry and bitter cider or champagne, pure *lambic* is often blended with fruits or herbs to improve the taste. Homebrewed *lambics*—such as *gueuze, faro, lambic doux,* and *lambic blanche*—are on tap in old cafés. Only *gueuze,* a blend of aged and young ale, is sold commercially in bottles. Some brand names include Cantillon, Lindemans, and Mort-Subite (literally, "Sudden Death").

Fruit *lambics* include those made with cherries *(kriek)*, raspberries *(frambozen)*, peaches *(peche)*, or blackcurrants *(casis)*. The result for each is a tart beer, similar to a dry pink champagne. People who don't usually enjoy beer tend to like these fruit-flavored varieties.

White (Witte): Based on wheat instead of hops, these milky-yellow summertime beers are often served with a lemon slice. White beer, similar to a Hefeweizen in the United States, is often flavored with spices like orange peel or coriander. Hoegaarden or Dentergems are names to look for.

Trappist Beers: For centuries, between their vespers and matins, Trappist monks have been brewing heavily fermented, malty beers. Three typical Trappist beers (from the Westmalle monastery) are *Trippel,* with a blonde color, served cold with a frothy head; *Dubbel,* which is dark, sweet, and served cool; and *Single,* made especially by the monks for the monks, and considered a fair trade for a life of celibacy. Other Trappist monasteries include Rochefort, Chimay, Westvleteren, and Orval.

Strong Beers: The potent brands include Duvel (meaning "devil," because of its high octane, camouflaged by a pale color), Verboten Vrucht (literally, "Forbidden Fruit," with Adam and Eve on the label), and the not-for-the-fainthearted brands of Judas, Satan, and Lucifer. Gouden Carolus is considered the strongest beer in Belgium, and Delerium Tremens speaks for itself.

Tom's Diner (AE, AI, Level 2—Moderately Accessible), a "bistro eetcafé," glows with a love of food in a quiet, cobbled residential area just outside the center. Young chef Tom gives traditional dishes a delightful modern twist, and your meal comes gorgeously presented, "high food" style. The "diner" comes with Creedence Clearwater soft rock, rusty 1960s kitsch knickknacks under 16th-century beams, and friendly and helpful service (hearty yet delicate €15 plates, Thu–Mon 18:00–24:00, closed Tue–Wed, reserve on weekends, north of Market Square near Sint-Gilliskerk at West-Gistelhof 23, tel. 050/333-382).

Bars Offering Light Meals, Beer, and Ambience

Stop into one of the city's atmospheric bars for a light meal or a drink with great Bruges ambience.

The 't Brugs Beertje (AE+A, AI+A, ♥, Level 2—Moderately Accessible, welcoming but crowded, with tight spaces and a 2" entry step) is the place for a huge selection of Belgian beers. While any pub or restaurant carries the basic beers, you'll find a selection of more than 300 types, including brews to suit any season here. They serve only two light meals: pâté or a traditional cheese plate (5 cheeses, bread, and salad for €9, Thu–Tue 16:00–24:00, closed Wed, Kemelstraat 5, tel. 050/339-616, run by fun-loving manager Daisy).

De Garre (AE+A, AI, Level 3—Minimally Accessible, six 8" entry steps) is another good place to gain an appreciation of the Belgian beer culture. Rather than a noisy pub scene, it has a dressy, sit-down-and-focus-on-your-friend-and-the-fine-beer vibe. Don't come here expecting to eat anything more than grilled cheese sandwiches...this is for beer and camaraderie (great beer selection, daily 12:00–24:00, off Breidelstraat between Burg and Markt, on tiny Garre alley, tel. 050/341-029). Access here is a challenge, but worth the effort. Since the restaurant is part of a monument, no architectural changes are permitted.

L'Estaminet (AE+A, AI, AT+A, Level 2—Moderately Accessible, staff can help with the one 4" entry step, suitable toilet accessed by another 4" step) is a youthful, brown-café-feeling, jazz-filled eatery. Almost intimidating in its lack of tourists, it's popular with local students who come for the Tolkien-chic ambience and hearty €7 spaghetti and good salads. It has more beer than wine, a super characteristic interior, and a relaxed patio facing the peaceful Astrid Park under an all-weather canopy (Tue–Sun 11:30–24:00, closed Mon, Park 5, tel. 050/330-916).

Herberg Vlissinghe (AE+A, AI, Level 3—Minimally Accessible, 6 entry steps) is the oldest pub in town (1515), where Bruno keeps things simple and laid-back, serving just hot snacks (lasagna and grilled cheese sandwiches), but great beer in the best old-time tavern atmosphere in town. This must have been the Dutch Masters' rec room. The garden outside comes with a boules court—free for guests to watch or play (Wed–Sun from 11:00 on, closed Mon–Tue, Blekersstraat 2, tel. 050/343-737).

Fries, Fast Food, and Picnics

Local french fries *(frites)* are a treat. Proud and traditional *frituurs* serve tubs of fries and various local-style shish kebabs. Belgians dip their *frites* in mayonnaise, but ketchup is there for the Yankees (along with spicier sauces). For a quick, cheap, and scenic meal, hit a *frituur* and sit on the steps or benches overlooking Market Square (convenience benches are about 50 yards past the post office).

Market Square Frituur (AE, AI, Level 1—Fully Accessible) are twin take-away french fries carts on the Market Square at the base of

the bell tower (daily 10:00–24:00).

Pickles Frituur (AE+A, AI, Level 2—Moderately Accessible, one 8" entry step), a block off Market Square, is handy for sit-down fries. Its forte is greasy, fast, deep-fried Flemish corn dogs. The "menu 2" comes with three traditional gut bombs: shrimp, chicken, and "spicy gypsie" (daily 11:30–24:00, at the corner of Geldmuntstraat and Sint Jakobstraat, tel. 050/337-957).

Delhaize-Proxy Supermarket (AE, AI, Level 2—Moderately Accessible) is ideal for picnics (push-button produce pricer lets you buy as little as one mushroom, Mon–Sat 9:00–19:00, closed Sun, 3 blocks off the Market Square on Geldmuntstraat). For midnight munchies, you'll find Indian-run corner grocery stores.

Belgian Waffles and Ice Cream

While Americans think of "Belgian" waffles for breakfast, the Belgians (who don't eat waffles or pancakes for breakfast) think of *wafels* as Liège-style (dense, sweet, eaten plain, and heated up) and Brussels-style (lighter, often with powdered sugar or whipped cream and strawberries, served in teahouses only in the afternoon 14:00–18:00). You'll see waffles sold at restaurants and take-away stands.

For good Liège-style *wafels* (€2), stop by **Restaurant Hennon (AE, AI,** Level 2—Moderately Accessible). Their waffles and other dishes are made with fresh ingredients (€2.50–6 plates, Tue–Sun 9:00–18:30, closed Mon, between Market Square and Burg at Breidelstraat 16). You can also try the **Flemish Pot** (**AE, AI, AT, ❤**, Level 1—Fully Accessible, listed above).

Da Vinci Ice Cream (**AE, AI,** Level 1—Fully Accessible), the local favorite for good homemade ice cream, has creative flavors and a great, fun ambience. As you approach, you'll see a line of happy lickers. Before ordering, ask to sample the Ferrero Rocher (chocolate, nuts, and crunchy cookie) and Bacio Bianco—rice with white chocolate (daily 10:00–24:00, Geldmuntstraat 34, run by Sylvia from Austria).

TRANSPORTATION CONNECTIONS

At the Bruges train station, check in at the ticket counter at least 15 minutes before departure to arrange for assistance along the way and at your destination. To use the accessible toilet, ask for the key at the baggage claim. They can also set up a ramp for you, or provide other help boarding.

From Brussels, an hour away by train, all of Europe is at your fingertips. The Brussels Midi/Zuid train station is accessible to people using wheelchairs, and the Brussels Central and Nord stations have recently been retrofitted to improve accessibility. The bathrooms are independently operated and are accessible.

From Bruges by Train to: Brussels (2/hr, usually at :31 and :57, 1 hr, €10), **Ghent** (2/hr, 40 min), **Ostende** (3/hr, 15 min), **Köln** (6/day, 3.5 hrs), **Paris** (hrly via Brussels, 2.5 hrs, railpass-holders must pay supplement—ask at station), **Amsterdam** (hrly, 3.5 hrs, transfer in Antwerp or Brussels), **Amsterdam's Schiphol Airport** (hrly, 3.5 hrs, transfer in Antwerp or Brussels, €35). Train info: tel. 050/302-424.

Trains from London: Bruges is an ideal "Welcome to Europe" stop after London. Take the Eurostar train from London to Brussels (9/day, 2.75 hrs), then transfer, backtracking to Bruges (2/hr, 1 hr, entire trip is covered by same Eurostar ticket; see Eurostar details on page 158).

BRUGES CITY ROLL OR STROLL

This tour—which takes you from Market Square to the Burg to the cluster of museums around the Church of Our Lady (the Groeninge, Gruuthuse, and Memling)—shows you the best of Bruges in a day.

If the route (2/3 mile) seems too long to cover in a day, break it up into manageable pieces. Skip the portions or museums that don't suit your mobility level, and simply move on to the next stop. Wheelchair users can use the bike lanes—just be alert to the many bicycle riders sharing the paths.

THE TOUR BEGINS

Market Square (Markt)

Access: Most of the square is fully accessible (Level 1), but the cobblestone streets (with 2" curbs) vary in degree of roughness.

The pleasant, shop-lined street just off the square, Geldmuntstraat (**AE+A**, Level 2—Moderately Accessible), has 4" curbs, with curb cuts down to one or two inches. Some stores have entries that are wheelchair-accessible; others have steps.

The Sight: Ringed by a bank, the post office, lots of restaurant terraces, great old gabled buildings, and the bell tower, this is the modern heart of the city. And, in Bruges' heyday as a trading city, this was also the center. The "typical" old buildings here were rebuilt in the 19th century in an exaggerated neo-Gothic style (Bruges is often called "more Gothic than Gothic"). This pre-Martin Luther style was a political statement for this Catholic town.

Formerly, a canal came right up to this square. Imagine boats moored where the post office stands today. In the 1300s, farmers shipped their cotton, wool, flax, and hemp to the port at Bruges. Before loading it onto outgoing boats, the industrious locals would spin, weave, and dye it into a finished product.

By 1400, the economy was shifting away from textiles and toward more refined goods, such as high-fashion items, tapestry, chairs, jewelry, and paper—a new invention (replacing parchment) that was made in Flanders with cotton that was shredded, soaked, and pressed.

The square is adorned with **flags,** including the red-white-and-blue lion flag of Bruges, the black-yellow-and-red flag of Belgium, and the blue-with-circle-of-yellow-stars flag of the European Union.

The **statue** depicts two friends, Jan Breidel and Pieter de Coninc, clutching sword and shield and looking toward France during their 1302 people's uprising against the French king. The rebels identified potential French spies by demanding they repeat two words—*schild en vriend* (shield and friend)—that only Flemish locals (or foreigners with phlegm) could pronounce. They won Flanders its freedom. Cleverly using hooks to pull knights from their horses, they scored the medieval world's first victory of foot soldiers over horsed knights, and of common people over nobility. The French knights, thinking that fighting these Flemish peasants would be a cakewalk, had worn their dress uniforms. The peasants had a field day afterward scavenging all the golden spurs from the fallen soldiers after the Battle of the Golden Spurs (1302).

Geldmuntstraat, a block west of the square, has fun shops and eateries. Steenstraat is the main shopping street and is packed with people. Notice the Café-Brasserie Craenenburg (Level 4—Not Accessible) on Market Square, at #18. Originally the house where Maximilian of Austria was imprisoned in 1488, it's been a café since 1905.

Bell Tower (Belfort)

Access: The Bell Tower is Level 4—Not Accessible; the Exhibition Hall is **AE, AI, AL, AT,** Level 1—Fully Accessible. While the Bell Tower requires a long, steep climb (366 steps), you can reach the Exhibition Hall on the second floor by elevator (in the courtyard, down the hallway toward the toilet).

Bruges City Roll or Stroll

1. Market Square
2. Bell Tower
3. Burg Square
4. Basilica of the Holy Blood
5. Town Hall
6. Renaissance Hall
7. Crowne Plaza Hotel
8. Blinde Ezelstraat
9. Fish Market
10. Huidevettersplein
11. Postcard Canal View
12. Groeninge Museum
13. Gruuthuse Museum
14. Church of Our Lady
15. Memling Museum
16. Begijnhof
17. Minnewater

Cost and Hours: €5, daily 9:30–17:00, last entry 45 min before closing.

The Sight: Most of this bell tower has stood over Market Square since 1300. The octagonal lantern was added in 1486, making it 290 feet high. The tower combines medieval crenellations, pointed Gothic arches, round Roman arches, flamboyant spires, and even a few small flying buttresses (two-thirds of the way up).

Try some french fries from either stand at the bottom of the tower (both are fully accessible). Look for the small metal model of the tower and the Braille description of the old town. Enter the courtyard. At the base of the bell tower, find the posted schedule of free carillon concerts (with photos of carillonneur at keyboard; normally Mon, Wed, and Sat at 21:00, sit in courtyard—a great experience). This courtyard also has an accessible toilet (€0.30, ask attendant for key).

If you can handle the 366 steps, consider climbing the tower (€5, no wheelchair access). Just before you reach the top, peek into the carillon room. The 47 bells can be played mechanically with the giant barrel and movable tabs (as they are on each quarter hour), or with a manual keyboard (as they are during concerts). The carillonneur uses his fists and feet, rather than fingers. Be there on the quarter hour, when things ring. It's *bellissimo* at the top of the hour.

Atop the tower, survey the town. On the horizon, you can see the towns along the North Sea coast.

• *Leaving the bell tower, turn right (east) onto pedestrian-only Breidelstraat. Thread yourself through the lace and waffles to...*

Burg Square

This opulent square is Bruges' historical birthplace, political center, and religious heart. Today it's the scene of outdoor concerts and local festivals.

Pan the square to see six centuries of architecture. Starting with the view of the bell tower above the rooftops, sweep counterclockwise 360

degrees. You'll go from Romanesque (the interior of the fancy, gray-brick **Basilica of the Holy Blood** in the corner), to the pointed Gothic arches and prickly steeples of the white sandstone **Town Hall,** to the well-proportioned Renaissance windows of the **Old Recorder's House** (next door, under the gilded statues), to the elaborate 17th-century Baroque of the **Provost's House** (past the park behind you). The **park** at the back of the square is the site of a cathedral that was demolished during the French Revolutionary period. Today, the foundation is open to the public in the **Crowne Plaza Hotel** basement (described below).

• *Complete your spin and go to the small, fancy, gray-and-gold building in the corner of the Burg Square.*

Basilica of the Holy Blood

Access: The Lower Chapel is **AE, AI,** Level 2—Moderately Accessible; the Upper Chapel and adjacent Treasury are Level 4—Not Accessible (up thirty-seven 7" steps).

Cost and Hours: Museum entry-€1.50; April–Sept Thu–Tue 9:30–11:45 & 14:00–17:45, Wed 9:30–11:45 only; Oct–March Thu–Tue 10:00–11:45 & 14:00–15:45, Wed 10:00–11:45 only; tel. 050/336-792, www.holyblood.org.

The Sight: The gleaming gold knights and ladies on the church's gray facade remind us that the double-decker church was built (c. 1150) by a brave Crusader to house the drops of Christ's blood he brought back from Jerusalem.

Lower Chapel: Enter the lower chapel through the door labeled *Basiliek*. Inside, the stark and dim decor reeks of the medieval piety that drove crusading Christian Europeans to persecute Muslims. With heavy columns and round arches, the style

The Legend of the Holy Blood

Several drops of Christ's blood, washed from his lifeless body by Joseph of Arimathea, were preserved in a crystal phial in Jerusalem. In 1150, the patriarch of Jerusalem gave the blood to a Flemish soldier, Derrick of Alsace, as thanks for rescuing his city from the Muslims during the Second Crusade. Derrick (also called Dedric or Thierry) returned home and donated it to the city. The old, dried blood suddenly turned to liquid, a miracle repeated every Friday for the next two centuries, and verified by thousands of pilgrims from around Europe who flocked here to adore it. The blood dried up for good in 1325.

Every year on Ascension Day (usually falls in May), Bruges' bankers, housewives, and waffle vendors put on old-time costumes for the parading of the phial through the city. Crusader knights re-enact the bringing of the relic, Joseph of Arimathea washes Christ's body, and ladies in medieval costume with hair tied up in horn-like hairnets come out to wave flags, while many Bruges citizens just take the day off.

is pure Romanesque. The annex along the right aisle displays somber statues of Christ being tortured and entombed, plus a 12th-century relief panel over a doorway showing St. Basil (a 4th-century scholarly monk) being baptized by a double-jointed priest, and a man-sized Dove of the Holy Spirit.

• *Leave the Lower Chapel and go outside. If you need to avoid stairs, head directly to the Town Hall (see listing below). Otherwise, take the staircase to reach the...*

Upper Chapel: After being gutted by Napoleon's secular-humanist crusaders in 1797, the upper chapel's original Romanesque decor

was redone in a neo-Gothic style. The nave is colorful, with a curved wooden ceiling, painted walls, and stained-glass windows of the dukes who ruled Flanders, along with their duchesses.

The painting at the main altar tells how the Holy Blood got here. Derrick of Alsace, having helped defend Jerusalem *(Hierosolyma)* and Bethlehem *(Bethlema)* from Muslim incursions in the Second Crusade, kneels (left) before the grateful Christian patriarch of Jerusalem, who rewards him with the relic. Derrick returns home (right) and kneels before Bruges' bishop to give him the phial of blood.

The relic itself—some red stuff preserved inside a clear, six-inch tube of rock crystal—is kept in the adjoining room (through the 3 arches). It's in the tall, silver tabernacle on the altar. (Each Friday—and increasingly on other days, too—the tabernacle's doors will be open, so you can actually see the phial of blood.) On holy days, the relic is shifted across the room, and displayed on the throne under the canopy.

The Treasury (next to Upper Chapel): For €1.50, you can see the impressive gold-and-silver, gem-studded, hexagonal reliquary (c. 1600, left wall) that the phial of blood is paraded around in on feast days. The phial is placed in the "casket" at the bottom of the four-foot structure. On the wall, flanking the shrine, are paintings of kneeling residents who, for centuries, have tended the shrine and organized the pageantry as part of the 31-member Brotherhood of the Holy Blood. Elsewhere in the room are the Brothers' ceremonial necklaces, clothes, chalices, and so on.

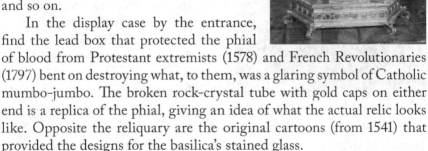

In the display case by the entrance, find the lead box that protected the phial of blood from Protestant extremists (1578) and French Revolutionaries (1797) bent on destroying what, to them, was a glaring symbol of Catholic mumbo-jumbo. The broken rock-crystal tube with gold caps on either end is a replica of the phial, giving an idea of what the actual relic looks like. Opposite the reliquary are the original cartoons (from 1541) that provided the designs for the basilica's stained glass.

Town Hall (Stadhuis)

Access: AE, AI, AL+A, Level 2—Moderately Accessible. The Gothic Room is upstairs and accessible by elevator.

Cost and Hours: Entrance Hall-free, Gothic Room-€2.50, includes audioguide and entry to Renaissance Hall, daily 9:30–17:00.

The Sight: Built around 1400, when Bruges was a thriving bastion of capitalism with a population of 35,000, this building served as a model for town halls elsewhere, including Brussels. The white sandstone facade is studded with statues of knights, nobles, and saints with prickly Gothic steeples over their heads. A colorful double band of cities' coats of arms includes those of Bruges (Brugghe) and Dunquerke. (Back then, Bruges' jurisdiction included many towns in present-day France.) The building is still the Town Hall, and it's not unusual to see couples arriving here to get married.

Entrance Hall: The ground-level lobby (free, closed Mon) leads to a picture gallery with scenes from Belgium's history, from the Spanish king to the arrival of Napoleon, shown meeting the mayor here at the Town Hall in 1803.

• *Take the elevator up to the...*

Gothic Room: Some of modern democracy's roots lie in this ornate room, where, for centuries, the city council met to discuss the town's affairs (€2.50 entry includes audioguide and Renaissance Hall). In

1464, one of Europe's first parliaments, the Estates General of the Low Countries, convened here. The fireplace at the far end bears a proclamation from 1305, which says, "All the artisans, laborers...and citizens of Bruges are free—all of them" (provided they pay their taxes).

The elaborately carved and painted wooden ceiling (a reconstruction from 1800) features Gothic-style tracery in gold, red, and black. Five dangling arches ("pendentives") hang down the center, now adorned with modern floodlights. Notice the New Testament themes carved into the circular medallions that decorate the points where the arches meet.

The **wall murals** are late-19th-century Romantic paintings depicting episodes in the city's history. Start with the biggest painting along the left wall, and work clockwise, following the numbers found on the walls:

1. Hip, hip, hooray! Everyone cheers, flags wave, trumpets blare, and dogs bark, as Bruges' knights, dressed in gold with black Flemish lions, return triumphant after driving out French oppressors and winning Flanders' independence. The Battle of the Golden Spurs (1302) is remembered every July 11.

2. Bruges' high-water mark came perhaps at this elaborate ceremony, when Philip the Good of Burgundy (seated, in black) assembled his court here in Bruges and solemnly founded the knightly Order of the Golden Fleece (1429).

3. The Crusader knight, Derrick of Alsace, returns from the Holy Land and kneels at the entrance of St. Basil's Chapel to present the relic of Christ's Holy Blood (c. 1150).

4. A nun carries a basket of bread in this scene from St. John's Hospital.

5. A town leader stands at the podium and hands a sealed document to a German businessman, renewing the Hanseatic League's business license. Membership in this club of trading cities was a key to Bruges' prosperity.

6. As peasants cheer, a messenger of the local duke proclaims the town's right to self-government (1190).

7. The mayor visits a Bruges painting studio to shake the hand of Jan van Eyck, the great Flemish Primitive painter (1433). Jan's wife, Margareta, is there, too. In the 1400s, Bruges rivaled Florence and Venice as Europe's cultural capital. See the town in the distance, out van Eyck's window.

8. Skip it.

9. City fathers grab a ceremonial trowel from a pillow to lay the fancy cornerstone of the Town Hall (1376). Bruges' familiar towers stand in the background.

10. Skip it.

11. It's a typical market day at the Halls (the courtyard behind the bell tower). Arabs mingle with Germans in fur-lined coats and beards in a market where they sell everything from armor to lemons.

12. A bishop blesses a new canal (1404) as ships sail right by the city. This was Bruges in its heyday, before the silting of the harbor. At the far

right, the two bearded men with moustaches are the brothers who painted these murals.

In the adjoining room, old paintings and maps show how little the city has changed over the centuries. Map #8 (on the right wall) shows in exquisite detail the city as it looked in 1562. (The map is oriented with south on top.) Find the bell tower, the Church of Our

Lady, and Burg Square, which back then was bounded on the north by a cathedral. Notice the canal (on the west) leading from the North Sea right to Market Square. A moat circled the city with its gates, unfinished wall, and 28 windmills (4 of which survive today). The mills pumped water to the town's fountains, made paper, ground grain, and functioned as the motor of the Middle Ages. Most locals own a copy of this map that shows how their neighborhood looked 400 years ago.

• *Back on the square, leaving the Town Hall, turn right and go to the corner.*

Renaissance Hall (Brugse Vrije)

Access: AE, AI, AT, Level 1—Fully Accessible.

Cost and Hours: €2.50, includes audioguide and admission to Town Hall's Gothic Room, Tue–Sun 9:30–12:30 & 13:30–16:30, closed Mon.

The Sight: This elaborately decorated room has a grand Renaissance chimney carved from oak by Bruges' Renaissance man, Lancelot Blondeel, in 1531. If you're into heraldry, the symbolism makes this room worth a five-minute stop. If you're not, you'll wonder where the rest of the museum is.

The centerpiece of the incredible carving is the Holy Roman Emperor Charles V. The hometown duke, on the far left, is related to Charles V. By making the connection to the Holy Roman Emperor clear, this carved family tree of Bruges' nobility helped substantiate their power. Notice the closely guarded family jewels. And check out the expressive little cherubs.

Crowne Plaza Hotel

Access: AE, AI, AL, AT, Level 1—Fully Accessible. Wheelchair access is through the De Linde restaurant, which is connected to the hotel. Once inside, you can reach the ruins by elevator.

The Sight: One of the city's newest buildings (1992) sits atop the ruins of the town's oldest structures. Around 900, when Viking ships regularly docked here to rape and pillage, Baldwin Iron Arm built a fort *(castrum)* to protect his Flemish people. In 950, the fort was converted into St. Donatian's Church, which became one of the city's largest.

Ask politely at the hotel's reception desk to see the archaeological site—ruins of the fort and the church—in the basement. If there's no conference, they'll let you take the elevator down and have a peek.

In the basement of the modern hotel are conference rooms lined with old stone walls and display cases of objects found in the ruins of earlier structures. On the immediate left hangs a document announcing the *Vente de Materiaux* (sale of material). When Napoleon destroyed the church in the early 1800s, its bricks were auctioned off. A local builder bought them at auction, and now the pieces of the old cathedral are embedded in other buildings throughout Bruges.

See oak pilings once driven into this former peat bog to support the fort and shore up its moat. Paintings show the immensity of the church that replaced it. The curved stone walls are from the foundations of the ambulatory around the church altar.

Excavators found a town water hole—a bonanza for archaeologists—turning up the refuse of a thousand years of habitation: pottery, animal skulls, rosary beads, dice, coins, keys, thimbles, pipes, spoons, and Delftware.

Don't miss the 14th-century painted sarcophagi—painted quickly for burial, with the crucifixion on the west ends and the Virgin and Child on the east.

• *Back on Burg Square, roll or stroll south under the Goldfinger family down the alleyway called...*

Blinde Ezelstraat

Midway down on the left side (about a foot above the ground), see an original iron hinge from the city's south gate, back when the city was ringed by a moat and closed up at 22:00. On the right wall higher up, a black patch shows just how grimy the city had become before a 1960s cleaning. Despite the cleaning and a few fanciful reconstructions, the city looks today much as it did in centuries past.

The name "Blinde Ezelstraat" means "Blind Donkey Street." In medieval times, the donkeys, carrying fish from the North Sea on their backs, were stopped here so that their owners could put blinders on them. Otherwise, the donkeys wouldn't cross the water between the old city and the fish market.

• *Cross the bridge over what was the 13th-century city moat. On your left are the arcades of the...*

Fish Market (Vismarkt)

The North Sea is just 12 miles away, and the fresh catch is sold here (Tue–Sat 6:00–13:00). Once a thriving market, today it's mostly full of souvenirs...and the big catch is the tourists.

• *Take an immediate right (west), entering a courtyard called...*

Huidevettersplein

This tiny, picturesque, restaurant-filled square was originally the head-quarters of the town's skinners and tanners. On the facade of the Hotel Duc de Bourgogne, six old relief panels show scenes from the leather tanners—once a leading Bruges industry. First, they tan the hides in a bath of acid; then, with tongs, they pull it out to dry; then they beat it to make it soft; and finally, they scrape and clean it to make it ready for sale.

• *Continue a few yards to Rozenhoedkaai street, where you can look back to your right and get a great...*

Postcard Canal View

The bell tower reflected in a quiet canal lined with old houses—the essence of Bruges. Seeing buildings rising straight from the water makes you understand why this was the Venice of the North. Can you see the bell tower's tilt? It leans about four feet. The tilt has been carefully monitored since 1740, but no change has been detected.

Looking left (west) down the Dijver canal (past a flea market on weekends) looms the huge spire of the Church of Our Lady, the tallest brick spire in the Low Countries. Between you and the church is the Europa College (a postgraduate institution for training future "Eurocrats" about the laws, economics, and politics of the European Union) and two fine museums.

• *Two blocks away on Dijver street is the...*

Groeninge Museum

Access: AE, AI, AT, Level 1—Fully Accessible. The museum's entrance has steps, but if you go past the entry to Groeninge (a little alley-like street), you can enter the museum with no barriers. Inside, there's a unisex adapted toilet in the men's restroom.

Cost and Hours: €8, includes audioguide, Tue–Sun 9:30–17:00, closed Mon, tel. 050/448-751.

The Sight: This sumptuous collection of paintings takes you from 1400 to 1945. While the museum has plenty of worthwhile modern art, the highlights are its vivid and pristine Flemish Primitives. ("Primitive" here means before the Renaissance.) Flemish art is shaped by its love of detail, its merchant patrons' egos, and the power of the Church. Lose yourself in the halls of Groeninge: Gaze across 15th-century canals, into the eyes of reassuring Marys, and through town squares littered with leotards, lace, and lopped-off heads.

• *Next door is the...*

Gruuthuse Museum

Access: Level 3—Minimally Accessible. There are six 6" steps at the entry, and the building includes many levels accessible only by steps, sometimes winding and narrow.

Cost and Hours: €6, includes audioguide and entry to apse in Church of Our Lady, Tue–Sun 9:30–17:00, closed Mon.

The Sight: This 15th-century mansion of a wealthy Bruges merchant displays period furniture, tapestries, coins, and musical instruments. Nowhere in the city do you get such an intimate look at the materialistic revolution of Bruges' glory days.

With the help of the excellent and included audioguide, browse through rooms of secular objects that are both functional and beautiful. Here are some highlights:

On the left, in the first room (or **Great Hall**), the big fireplace, oak table, and tapestries attest to the wealth of Louis Gruuthuse, who got rich providing a special herb used to spice up beer.

Tapestries like the ones you see here were a famous Flemish export product, made in local factories out of raw wool imported from England and silk from the Orient (via Italy). Both beautiful and useful (as insulation), they adorned many homes and palaces throughout Europe.

These **four tapestries** (of 9 originals) tell a worldly story of youthful lust that upsets our stereotypes about supposed medieval piousness. The first tapestry, the *Soup-Eating Lady* (on the left), shows a shepherd girl with a bowl of soup in her lap. The horny shepherd lad cuts a slice of bread (foreplay in medieval symbolism) and saucily asks (read the archaic French cartoon bubbles) if he can "dip into the goodies in her lap," if you catch my drift. On the right, a woman brazenly strips off her socks to dangle her feet in water, while another woman lifts her dress to pee.

The next tapestry (moving clockwise), called *The Dance*, shows couples freely dancing together under the apple tree of temptation. *The Wedding Parade* (opposite wall) shows where all this wantonness leads— marriage. Music plays, the table is set, and the meat's on the BBQ as the bride and groom enter...reluctantly. The bride smiles, but she's closely escorted by two men, while the scared groom (center) gulps nervously.

From here, the next stop is *Old Age* (smaller tapestry), and the aged shepherd is tangled in a wolf trap. "Alas," reads the French caption, "he was once so lively, but marriage caught him, and now he's trapped in its net."

In Room 2, see the **Bust of Charles V** (on top of an oak chest) and ponder the series of marriages that made Charles (1500–1558), the grandson of a Flemish girl, the powerful ruler of most of Europe, including Bruges. Mary of Burgundy (and Flanders) married powerful Maximilian I of Austria. Their son Philip married Juana, the daughter of Ferdinand and Isabel of Spain, and when little Charles was born to them, he inherited all his grandparents' lands, and more. Charles' son, Philip II (see his bust opposite), a devout Catholic, brought persecution and war to the Protestant Low Countries.

• *If you are able, continue to the rest of the museum: Facing Philip, climb the stairs on the left to the third floor, pass through Room 10, and cross the open mezzanine. In the far left corner of Room 16, find a chapel.*

The Gruuthuse mansion abuts the Church of Our Lady and has a convenient little **chapel** with a window overlooking the interior of the huge church. In their private box seats above the choir, the family could attend services without leaving home. From the balcony, you can look down on two reclining gold statues in the church, marking the tombs of Charles the Bold and his daughter, Mary of Burgundy (the grandmother of powerful Charles V).

The last room (ground floor, directly below) deals with old-time justice. In 1796, the enlightened city of Bruges chose the new-fangled **guillotine** as its humane form of execution. This 346-pound model was tested on sheep before being bloodied twice by executions on the Market Square. Also see the branding irons, a small workbench for slicing off evildoers' members, and posts used to chain up criminals for public humiliation.

Leaving the museum, contemplate the mountain of bricks that towers 400 feet above, as it has for 600 years. You're heading for that church.

• *Return to the main street, then go left to Mariastraat and the church.*

If you're on foot, take the interesting back way to the church (includes six 6" steps over rough cobblestone): At the Arentshuis Museum entrance, duck under the arch at #16 and into a quiet courtyard. Veer right and cross a tiny 19th-century bridge. From the bridge, look up at the corner of the Gruuthuse mansion, where there's a teeny-tiny window, a toll-keeper's lookout. The bridge gives you a close-up look at Our Lady's big buttresses and round apse. The church entrance is around the front.

Church of Our Lady

Access: AE, AI, Level 2—Moderately Accessible. The church is wheel-chair-accessible, with the exception of a small room (up two 8" steps) at the end of the apse. The nearest accessible toilet is across the street at the Visitors Center of the Memling Museum (see below).

Cost and Hours: Michelangelo viewing is free, art-filled apse costs €2.50, covered by €6 Gruuthuse admission, Mon–Fri 9:30–16:50, Sat 9:30–15:50, Sun 13:30–16:50 only.

The Sight: This church stands as a memorial to the power and wealth of Bruges in its heyday.

A delicate *Madonna and Child* by **Michelangelo** (1504) is near the apse (to the right as you enter), somewhat overwhelmed by the ornate Baroque niche it sits in. It's said to be the only Michelangelo statue to leave Italy in his lifetime, bought in Tuscany by a wealthy Bruges businessman, who's buried beneath it.

As Michelangelo chipped away at the masterpiece of his youth, *David,* he took breaks by carving this (1504). Mary, slightly smaller than life-size, sits, while young Jesus stands in front of her. Their expressions are mirror images—serene, but a bit melancholy, with downcast eyes, as though pondering the young child's dangerous future. Though they're

lost in thought, their hands instinctively link, tenderly. The white Carrara marble is highly polished, something Michelangelo only did when he was certain he'd gotten it right.

If you like tombs and church art, pay €2.50 to wander through the apse (also covered by €6 Gruuthuse admission). The highlight is the reclining statues marking the tombs of the last local rulers of Bruges, Mary of Burgundy, and her father, Charles the Bold. The dog and lion at their feet are symbols of fidelity and courage.

In 1482, when 25-year-old Mary of Burgundy tumbled from a horse and died, she left behind a toddler son and a husband who was heir to the Holy Roman Empire. Beside her lies her father, Charles the Bold, who also died prematurely, in war. Their twin deaths meant Bruges belonged to Austria, and would soon be swallowed up by the empire and ruled from afar by Hapsburgs—who didn't understand or care about its problems. Trade routes shifted, and goods soon flowed through Antwerp, then Amsterdam, as Bruges' North Sea port silted up. After these developments, Bruges began four centuries of economic decline. The city was eventually mothballed, and later discovered by modern-day tourists to be remarkably well-pickled—which explains its modern-day affluence.

The balcony to the left of the main altar is part of the Gruuthuse mansion next door, providing the noble family with prime seats for Mass.

Excavations in 1979 turned up fascinating grave paintings on the tombs below and near the altar. Dating from the 13th century, these show Mary represented as Queen of Heaven (on a throne, carrying a crown and scepter) and Mother of God (with the baby Jesus on her lap). Since Mary is in charge of advocating with Jesus for your salvation, she's a good person to have painted on the wall of your tomb. Tombs also show lots of angels—generally patron saints of the dead person—swinging thuribles (incense burners).

• *Just across Mariastraat from the church entrance is the entry to the St. John's Hospital's Visitors Center (**AE, AI, AT**, Level 1—Fully Accessible; good Internet café and an accessible toilet for €0.30). The entrance to the Memling Museum, which fills that hospital's church, is 20 yards south on Mariastraat.*

Memling Museum

Access: AE, AI, AL, AT, Level 1—Fully Accessible, with the exception of a corner room (two 8" steps). You'll find an elevator (on the right side of the inside entry) and an accessible unisex toilet (€0.30, located in men's room at the St. John's Hospital's Visitors Center, described above). Loaner wheelchairs are available.

Cost and Hours: €8 includes fine audioguide, Tue–Sun 9:30–17:00, closed Mon.

The Sight: This medieval hospital contains some much-loved paintings by the greatest of the Flemish Primitives, Hans Memling. His *Mystical Wedding of St. Catherine* triptych deserves a close look. Catherine and her "mystical groom," the baby Jesus, are flanked by a headless John the Baptist and a pensive John the Evangelist. The chairs are there so you can study it. If you know the Book of Revelation, you'll understand St. John's wild and intricate vision. The St. Ursula Shrine, an ornate little mini-church in the same room, is filled with impressive detail.

• *Continue south about 150 yards on Mariastraat. Turn right on Walstraat, which leads into the pleasant square called Walplein. From here, the lacy cuteness of Bruges crescendos as you approach the...*

Begijnhof

Access: AE-A, AI-A, Level 2—Moderately Accessible. The cobblestones in the Begijnhof are heavy and rough, making for a bone-jarring wheelchair ride. The museum has one 4" entry step, one 4" step to visit the kitchen, one 8" step to the courtyard, and two 7" steps to see the sleeping quarters.

Cost and Hours: The courtyard is free and always open. The museum costs €2, open daily 10:00–12:00 & 13:45–17:00, shorter hours off-season, English explanations, Beguine's House is left of entry gate.

The Sight: The peaceful courtyard is lined with small buildings. The simple museum to the left of the entry gate gives you a sense of *beguine*

life.

Begijnhofs (pronounced gutturally: buh-HHHINE-hof) were built to house women of the lay order, called Beguines, who spent their lives in piety and service without having to take the same vows a nun would. For military and other reasons, there were more women than men in the medieval

Low Countries. The order of Beguines offered women (often single or widowed) a dignified place to live and work. When the order died out, many Begijnhofs were taken over by towns for subsidized housing. Today single religious women live in the small homes. Benedictine nuns live in a building nearby.

In the church, the rope that dangles from the ceiling is yanked by a nun around 17:15 to announce a sung vespers service.

• *Exiting opposite the way you entered, you'll hook left (over some big, rough cobbles) and see a lake with silver swans...*

Minnewater

Just south of the Begijnhof is Minnewater (literally, "Water of Love"), a peaceful, lake-filled park with canals and swans. This was once far from quaint—a busy harbor where small boats shuttled cargo from the big, ocean-going ships into town. From this point, the cargo was transferred again to flat-bottomed boats that went through the town's canals to their respective warehouses and Market Square.

When locals see these swans, they remember the 15th-century mayor—famous for his long neck—who collaborated with the Austrians. The townsfolk beheaded him as a traitor. The Austrians warned them that similarly long-necked swans would inhabit the place to forever remind them of this murder. And they do.

• *You're a .3-mile roll or stroll from the train station (where you can catch a bus or taxi to Market Square), or a .7-mile roll or stroll from Market Square—take your pick.*

THE NETHERLANDS

THE NETHERLANDS

Holland: Windmills, wooden shoes, tulips, cheese, and great artists. In its 17th-century glory days, tiny Holland was a world power—politically, economically, and culturally—with more great artists per square mile than any other country.

Today, the Netherlands is Europe's most densely populated country and also one of its wealthiest and best organized. A generation ago, Belgium, the Netherlands, and Luxembourg created the nucleus of a united Europe when they joined to form the Benelux Economic Union.

Efficiency is a Dutch custom. The average income is higher than in the United States. Though only 8 percent of the labor force is made up of farmers, 70 percent of the land is cultivated, and you'll travel through vast fields of barley, wheat, sugar beets, potatoes, and flowers.

"Holland" is just a nickname for the Netherlands. North Holland and South Holland are the largest of the 12 provinces that make up the Netherlands. The word Netherlands means "lowlands," and the country is so named because half of it is below sea level, reclaimed from the sea (or rivers). That's why the locals say, "God made the Earth, but the Dutch made Holland." Modern technology and plenty of Dutch elbow grease have turned much of the sea into fertile farmland. Though a new, 12th province—Flevoland, near Amsterdam—has been drained, dried, and populated in the last 100 years, Dutch reclamation projects are essentially finished.

The Dutch pride themselves on their frankness, and they like to split the bill. Traditionally, Dutch cities have been open-minded, loose,

---

How Big, How Many, How Much

- 13,000 square miles (a little larger than Maryland)
- 16.4 million people (1,250 people per square mile; 15 times the population density of the U.S.)
- €1 = about $1.20

The Netherlands

and liberal (to attract sailors in the days of Henry Hudson). And today, Amsterdam is the capital of alternative lifestyles—a city where nothing's illegal, as long as nobody gets hurt. From marijuana to prostitution, you can get it all—legally—in the Netherlands.

But contrary to nervous Americans' expectations, Holland is safe. The buzzword here is "social control," meaning that neighborhood security comes not from iron shutters, heavily armed cops, and gated communities, but from neighbors looking out for each other. Everyone knows everyone in this tight-knit neighborhood. If Magrit doesn't buy bread for two days, the baker asks around. Unlike in many big cities, there's no chance that anyone here could lie dead in his house unnoticed for weeks. Video surveillance cameras watch prostitutes, while prostitutes survey the streets, buzzing for help if they spot trouble. Watch the men who watch the women who watch out for their neighbors across the street who watch the flower shop on the corner—"social control."

You'll find almost no language barrier anywhere in the Netherlands, as all well-educated folks, nearly all young people, and the majority of people in the tourist trade speak English. Still, take a few minutes to learn some polite Dutch pleasantries. Just like in Flemish-speaking Belgium, "Hello" is *hallo* (hol-LOH), "please" is *alstublieft* (AHL-stoo-bleeft), and "thank you" is *dank u wel* (dahnk yoo vehl).

In the Netherlands, you'll find basic Dutch fare, with plenty of cheese and bread. For some variety, try ethnic specialties from the country's former colonies such as Indonesia and Surinam. For dessert, sample a gooey, super-sweet *stroopwafel* (syrup waffle) or a dessert pancake *(pannenkoeken)*.

Amsterdam is Holland's highlight. While the freewheeling capital does have a quiet side, travelers who prefer small towns can sleep in nearby Haarlem (see page 464) and side-trip into the big city.

ACCESSIBILITY IN THE NETHERLANDS

Due to a strong commitment to equal rights, access for people with disabilities is generally good in the Netherlands.

The **Netherlands Board of Tourism** offers helpful resources. The Web site offers some accessibility information for people with disabilities, including a searchable database of hotels and other attractions (355 Lexington Ave., 19th floor, New York, NY 10017, tel. 212/557-3500, fax 212/370-9507, www.holland.com, information@holland.com).

Transportation

The Dutch Rail company publishes a leaflet called *Rail Travel for the Disabled*, available at larger Amsterdam stations.

To rent an adapted car or minivan, contact **Budget** (tel. 0800-023-8238) or **KAV Autoverhuur** (tel. 020/311-9811, www.kav.nl).

Organizations

The **National Association for the Handicapped** is available to answer questions about accessibility in Holland (Mon–Fri 9:30–13:00, closed Sat–Sun, tel. 020/291-6600).

Mobility International Netherlands provides information on international tours and exchanges for people with disabilities (Heidestein 7, Driebergen, tel. 034/382-1795, fax 034/381-6776, jaberend@worldonline.nl).

The Haarlem-based **Stichting Recreatie Gehandicapten** organizes travel in Holland for people with limited mobility (Boedapeststraat 25, tel. 023/536-8409, www.srg-vakanties.nl).

AMSTERDAM

Amsterdam is a progressive way of life housed in Europe's most 17th-century city. Physically, it's built upon millions of pilings. But more than that, it's built on good living, cozy cafés, great art, street-corner jazz, stately history, and a spirit of live-and-let-live. It has 737,000 people and almost as many bikes. It also has more canals than Venice...and about as many tourists.

During its Golden Age in the 1600s, Amsterdam was the world's richest city, an international sea-trading port, and the cradle of capitalism. Wealthy, democratic burghers built a planned city of canals lined with trees and townhouses topped with fancy gables. Immigrants, Jews, outcasts, and political rebels were drawn here by its tolerant atmosphere,

while painters such as young Rembrandt captured that atmosphere on canvas.

The Dutch are unique. They may be the world's most handsome people—tall, healthy, with good posture—and the most open, honest, and refreshingly blunt. They like to laugh. As connoisseurs of world culture, they appreciate Rembrandt paintings, Indonesian food, and the latest French film—but with an unsnooty, blue-jeans attitude.

Approach Amsterdam as an ethnologist observing a strange culture. Roll or stroll through any neighborhood and see things that are commonplace here, but rarely found elsewhere. Carillons chime quaintly in neighborhoods selling sex, as young professionals smoke pot with impunity next to old ladies in bonnets selling flowers. Observe the neighborhood's "social control," where an elderly man feels safe in his home knowing he's being watched by the prostitutes next door.

Be warned: Amsterdam, a bold experiment in freedom, may box your Puritan ears. Take it all in, then pause to watch the sunset—at 10:00 P.M. during summer—and see the Golden Age reflected in a quiet canal.

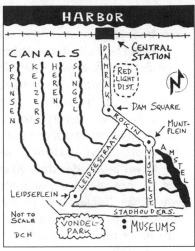

Accessibility in Amsterdam

For travelers with limited mobility, Amsterdam is both challenging and rewarding. While locals have a friendly attitude toward people with disabilities, they also have great respect for the historical nature of their beautiful (and largely non-accessible) canalside buildings. The city has strict rules about making adaptations to monumental structures—useful for historical preservation, not so helpful for accessibility. The good news is that attitudes regarding accessibility are slowly improving.

The streets and sidewalks of Amsterdam have a certain freedom of movement: thousands of bikes mingling and merging with cars and pedestrians. Wheelchair users here are smart to adapt to the chaos—maneuvering their way through the streets, across trolley tracks, along the pink bike-only paths, and on the sidewalks. Stay alert and keep a steady line as you make your way through this bustling city.

Many Amsterdam sights are fully accessible to travelers with limited mobility (Level 1): Van Gogh Museum, Heineken Brewery, Anne Frank House Museum (but not the house interior), Royal Palace, New Church, Begijnhof, Amsterdam History Museum (except the carillon loft), Stedelijk Museum CS, the museum at Rembrandt's House (but not the house itself), Dutch Theater, Dutch Resistance Museum, Red Light District, and the Old Church.

Other sights are only moderately accessible (Level 2): Rijksmuseum, Amsterdam Film Museum, Houseboat Museum, Westerkerk (except for the tower), *Holland Experience* 3-D movie, Gassan Diamonds tour, Hermitage Amsterdam Museum, De Hortus Botanical Garden, Jewish

Accessibility Levels

This book rates sights, hotels, and restaurants using four levels:

Level 1—Fully Accessible: A Level 1 building is completely barrier-free. Entryways, elevators, and other facilities are specifically adapted to accommodate a person using a wheelchair. If there's a bathroom, it has wide doors and an adapted toilet and sink. Where applicable, the bathing facilities are also fully adapted (including such features as bath boards, grab bars, or a roll-in, no-rim shower). Fully adapted hotel rooms often have an alarm system with pull cords for emergencies.

Level 2—Moderately Accessible: A Level 2 building is suitable for, but not specifically adapted to accommodate, a person using a wheelchair. This level will generally work for a wheelchair user who can make transfers and take a few steps. A person who is permanently in a wheelchair may require some assistance here (either from a companion or from staff).

Level 3—Minimally Accessible: A Level 3 building is satisfactory for people who have minimal mobility difficulties (that is, people who usually do not use a wheelchair, but take more time to do things than a non-disabled person). This building may have some steps and a few other barriers—but not too many. Level 3 buildings are best suited to slow walkers; wheelchair users will require substantial assistance here.

Level 4—Not Accessible: Unfortunately, some places in this book are simply not accessible to people with limited mobility. This means that barriers such as staircases, tight interiors and facilities (elevators, bathrooms, etc.), or other impediments interfere with passage for travelers with disabilities. Buildings in this category might include a church tower that has several flights of steep stairs, or a museum interior that has many levels with lots of steps and no elevator.

For a complete listing of the Accessibility Codes used in this chapter, please see pages 6–7.

History Museum, sex museums, and Hash, Marijuana, and Hemp Museum.

Unfortunately, these Amsterdam sights are not accessible to travelers with limited mobility (Level 3 or 4): the interior of the Anne Frank House, the loft at the Amsterdam History Museum, Rembrandt's House, and Amstelkring Museum.

ORIENTATION

(area code: 020)

Amsterdam's Central Train Station, on the north edge of the city, is your starting point (TI and trams fanning out to all points). Damrak is the main north–south street axis, connecting Central Station with Dam Square (people-watching and hangout center) and its Royal Palace. From this spine, the city spreads out like a fan, with 90 islands, hundreds of bridges, and a series of concentric canals—named Herengracht (Gentleman's Canal), Keizersgracht (Emperor's Canal), and Prinsengracht (Prince's Canal)—that were laid out in the 17th century, Holland's Golden Age. Amsterdam's major sights are near Dam Square.

To the east of Damrak is the oldest part of the city (today's Red Light District), and to the west is the newer part, where you'll find the Anne Frank House and the Jordaan neighborhood. Museums and Leidseplein nightlife cluster at the southern edge of the city center.

Tourist Information

There are four VVV offices. "VVV," pronounced "vay vay vay," is Dutch for "TI," a tourist information office. These are inside of Central Station at track 2b (**AE, AI,** Level 2—Moderately Accessible, wheelchair-accessible elevator, press outside button to get staff's attention; Mon–Sat 8:00–20:00, Sun 9:00–17:00), in front of Central Station (**AE, AI,** Level 2—Moderately Accessible; daily 9:00-17:00, most crowded), on Leidsestraat (**AE+A, AI,** Level 2—Moderately Accessible, one 4" entry step; daily 9:00–19:00, less crowded), and at the airport (**AE, AI,** Level 2—Moderately Accessible; daily 7:00–22:00).

Avoid Amsterdam's crowded, inefficient tourist offices if you can. For €0.60 a minute, you can save yourself a trip by calling the TI toll line at 0900-400-4040 (Mon–Fri 9:00–17:00). If you're staying in nearby Haarlem, ask your Amsterdam questions and pick up the brochures at the helpful, friendly, and rarely crowded Haarlem TI (see page 464).

At any Amsterdam TI, ask for the extremely helpful *Amsterdam Accessibility Guide* (sometimes you have to ask more than one person to find it, but it's there). This resource provides information about levels of accessibility at hotels, restaurants, museums, theaters, cinemas, and other attractions around the city. You'll also find all the details on getting around Amsterdam if you have a disability—including renting a modified car, requesting a wheelchair-accessible taxi, finding accessible parking, and getting assistance at train stations and airports. For more information, call 020/577-7955.

Amsterdam

Also at the TI, consider buying a city map (€2) and any of the self-guided tour brochures (€1.50 each, including *Discovery Tour Through the Center*, *The Former Jewish Quarter*, and *Walks Through Jordaan*; these aren't designed for wheelchair users, but they contain interesting information). For entertainment, pick up the *Day by Day* calendar (€1.75), call the Last Minute Ticket Shop (tickets for theater, classical music, and major rock shows, tel. 0900-0191, www.lastminuteticketshop.nl), and check out this chapter's "Nightlife" section (page 423).

Don't use the TI or a booking service to find a room; you'll pay €5 per person and your host loses 13 percent—meaning you'll likely be charged a higher rate. The phone system is easy, everyone speaks English, and the listings in this book are a better value than the potluck booking you'd get from the TI.

I amsterdam **Card:** At many Amsterdam museums, a wheelchair user pays for entry, but his or her companion enters for free. If you're doing lots of sightseeing in a limited amount of time, consider buying an *I amsterdam* Card. This card includes free entry to most city sights, discounts on other sights and attractions, two free canal boat tours, and unlimited use of the trams, buses, and metro (€33/24 hrs, €43/48 hrs, €53/72 hrs, sold at TIs, www.iamsterdamcard.com). The pass covers most major Amsterdam museums, including the Van Gogh and the Rijksmuseum (but not the Anne Frank House). This is only worthwhile for very busy sightseers. For example, if you visit the Van Gogh Museum, the Rijksmuseum, and the Amsterdam History Museum, plus take a canal boat tour—all in one day—this pass will save you a little money (€2.50). While they are sold at the TI, avoid the line by buying it at the adjacent GVB transit office (across from the station).

Tourist Information Online: Try www.visitamsterdam.nl (Amsterdam Tourism Board), www.amsterdam.nl (City of Amsterdam), and www.holland.com (Netherlands Board of Tourism).

Arrival in Amsterdam

By Train: Amsterdam swings, and the hinge that connects it to the world is its perfectly central Central Station. Expect a chaotic construction zone—the station is being renovated through 2010. The international ticket office should be at track 2, and luggage lockers are at the far east end of the building (from €5.70/24 hrs, daily 7:00–23:00, ID required).

Go out the door of the station, and you're in the heart of the city. Just in front are trams ready to take you anywhere in town. Straight ahead is Damrak street, leading to Dam Square. With your back to the entrance of the station, the TI and GVB public-transit offices are just ahead and

Dutch Landmarks

Dam (pronounced dahm)	Amsterdam's main square
Damrak (DAHM-rock)	Main street between Central Station and Dam Square
Spui (spow, rhymes with cow)	Both a street and square
Rokin (roh-KEEN)	Street connecting Dam Square and Spui
Kalverstraat (KAL-ver-strot)	Pedestrian street
Leidseplein (LIDE-zuh-pline)	Lively square
Jordaan (yor-DAHN)	Neighborhood in southwest Amsterdam
Museumplein (myoo-ZAY-um-pline)	Square with Rijks and Van Gogh museums
gracht (khrockt, guttural)	canal
straat (straht)	street
plein (pline)	public square
huis (house)	house
kerk (kerk)	church

to your left. And on your right is a vast, multistory bike garage.

Access: AE, AI, AL, AT, Level 1—Fully Accessible. All train platforms have wheelchair-accessible elevators (except platform 15). There is a wheelchair-accessible toilet (€0.35) in the Balcon Restaurant, located on platform 2.

Contact the Disability Service Line in advance if you'll be arriving by train and want help making arrangements for assistance, including getting to a taxi to your destination (tel. 030/235-7822, daily 7:00–23:00, call at least 3 hours ahead). This service is available at larger stations throughout the Netherlands.

By Plane: For details on getting from Schiphol Airport into downtown Amsterdam, see page 441.

Helpful Hints

Theft Alert: Tourists are considered green and rich, and the city has more than its share of hungry thieves—especially on trams and at the many hostels. Wear your money belt.

Street Smarts: Most canals are lined by streets with the same name. When moving around town, beware of the silent transportation—trams and bicycles. Slow walkers shouldn't walk on tram tracks or

If You Need Medical Help

Your hotel is the best first point of contact. But if you need to get help on your own, Amsterdam's main hospital is the Academic Medical Center (Meibergdreef 9, tel. 020/566-9111). Also consider the Onze-Lieve-Vrouwe Gasthuis (Eerste Oosterparkstraat 179, tel. 020/599-9111). Most hospitals have clinics for emergencies.

In an emergency (to summon an ambulance, the police, or the fire department), dial 112 (operators speak English). Other useful emergency phone numbers include the Crisis Help Line (tel. 020/675-7575) and the Central Medical Service (24-hour emergency and dental service, tel. 020/592-3434).

A convenient pharmacy in the city center is Dam Apotheek (Damstraat 2, tel. 020/624-4331). The emergency pharmacy number is 020/212-1568.

To reach the Netherlands Disabled Assistance, dial 030/291-7822 (daily 7:00–23:00).

---

pink bicycle paths, but wheelchair users will find that bike paths are sometimes the only way to go.

Accessible Toilets: Your best bets for wheelchair-accessible toilets are modern **restaurants** (for example, just about any McDonald's, or near the restaurant inside the Krasnapolsky Grand Hotel at Dam Square 9) or major **museums** (including the Anne Frank House, Van Gogh Museum, Rijksmuseum, and many more—as listed below).

Wheelchair Rental: Try Beumer de Jong (book in advance, Haarlem-mermeerstraat 47-53, tel. 020/615-7188, www.beumer-de-jong.nl). For more options, see www.welzorg.nl.

Shop Hours: Most shops are open Tuesday through Saturday 10:00–18:00, and Sunday and Monday 12:00–18:00. Some shops stay open later (21:00) on Thursdays. Supermarkets are generally open Monday through Saturday 8:00–20:00, and closed on Sundays.

Internet Access: It's easy at cafés all over town. Two huge **easyInternet-cafés** offer hundreds of terminals with fast, cheap (€2.50/hr) access: there's one a block in front of the train station at Damrak 33 (**AE, AI,** Level 2—Moderately Accessible; daily 10:00–20:00) and another between Mint Tower and Rembrandtplein at Reguliersbreestraat 22 (**AE, AI,** Level 2—Moderately Accessible; daily 9:00–21:00). "Coffeeshops," which sell marijuana, usually also offer Internet access—letting you surf the Net with a special bravado.

English Bookstore: For fiction and guidebooks—including mine—try the **American Book Center** (**AE, AI, AL,** Level 2—Moderately Accessible) at Kalverstraat 125 (Mon–Sat 10:00–20:00, Sun 11:00–18:30) or the huge and helpful **Scheltema** (**AE, AI,** Level 2—Moderately Accessible), near the Leidsestraat at Koningsplein 20 (included in Amsterdam City Roll or Stroll—see page 443, store open Mon–Sat 10:00–18:00, Thu until 21:00, Sun 12:00–18:00; lots of English novels, guidebooks, and maps).

Maps: The free and cheap tourist maps can be confusing. Consider paying a bit more (around €2) for a top-notch map. I like the *Carto Studio Centrumkaart Amsterdam* or, better yet, the *Amsterdam: Go Where the Locals Go* map by Amsterdam Anything.

Queen's Day: On Queen's Day, April 30, Amsterdam turns into a gigantic garage sale/street market.

Getting Around Amsterdam

The longest roll or stroll a tourist would take is from the station to the Rijksmuseum (about 1.5 miles). Watch out for silent but potentially dangerous bikes and trams.

To cover distances more quickly, you have several other options. Many trams are fully accessible. If your destination is not on an accessible tram route, and you use a wheelchair, take a taxi instead.

By Tram, Bus, and Metro

Trams #2 and #5 travel the north–south axis from Central Station to Dam Square to Leidseplein to Museumplein. Tram #14 goes east–west (Westerkerk–Dam Square–Muntplein–Waterlooplein–Plantage). If you get lost in Amsterdam, 10 of the city's 17 trams take you back to Central Station. The metro (underground train) is used mostly for commuting to the suburbs, but it does connect Central Station with some sights east of Damrak (Nieuwmarkt–Waterlooplein–Weesperplein).

Access: The newest **trams,** with low central doors, are fully adapted (**AE, AI,** Level 1—Fully Accessible; look for the low-to-the ground section in the middle of the train for easy boarding). There are also several older, inaccessible trams in service (**AE+A, AI+A,** Level 2—Moderately

Daily Reminder

The biggest Amsterdam sights—the Rijksmuseum, the Van Gogh Museum, and the Anne Frank House—are open daily year-round. The city's naughty sights, as you might expect, stay open late every day (Erotic Museum until 24:00, Damrak Sex Museum until 23:30, and the Hash, Marijuana, and Hemp Museum until 22:00).

Sunday: These sights have limited, afternoon-only hours today: the Amstelkring Museum (13:00–17:00), New Church (13:00-18:00), and the Old Church (13:00–17:00). The Westerkerk church and tower are closed, and the Waterlooplein flea market is shut down.

Monday: These are closed today: the Heineken Brewery and Houseboat Museum (also closed Tue–Thu Nov–Feb).

Tuesday–Thursday: All recommended sights are open.

Friday: These are open late—the Rijksmuseum and Van Gogh Museum (both until 22:00), plus Rembrandt's House (until 21:00).

Saturday: All recommended sights are open.

Accessible, entry steps and very narrow aisles, and also often a post at the entry). The adapted trams run sporadically on all lines except #6. Since they stagger accessible and inaccessible trams on the same route, you may have to wait for an accessible tram to come along.

Amsterdam's **buses** are built low to the ground, but they have no ramps. These low buses are a challenge for someone who uses a wheelchair, but they can work if you are able take a few steps.

As for the **metro,** some—but not all—stops on the handy Nieuwemarkt–Waterlooplein–Weesplein line are wheelchair-accessible (virtually level entrances, access provided by a lift or a ramp). Ask about access on your specific route at the GVB transit information office (in front of train station) or ticket-seller before purchasing your ticket.

Tickets and Passes: The helpful GVB public transit information office (**AE, AI,** Level 1—Fully Accessible) is in front of the train station (next to TI, daily 8:00–21:00). Its free, multilingual *Public Transport Amsterdam Tourist Guide* includes a transit map and explains ticket options and tram connections to all the sights. In keeping with the Dutch mission to automate life, they'll tack on a €0.50 penalty if you buy your transit tickets from a human ticket-seller, rather than from a machine.

You have various ticket options:

- **Individual tickets** cost €1.60 and give you an hour on the buses, trams, and metro system (pay as you board on trams and buses; for the metro, buy tickets from machines).

- The **24-hour** (€6.30), **48-hour** (€10), or **72-hour** (€13) **tickets** give you unlimited transportation on Amsterdam's (and the Netherlands') public transit network. Buy them at the GVB public-transit office (all versions available) or as you board (24-hr version only, costs €0.50 extra).
- **Strip tickets** *(strippenkaart)*, cheaper than individual tickets, are good on buses, trams, and the metro in Amsterdam and anywhere in the Netherlands. The further you go, the more strips you'll use: Any downtown ride in Amsterdam costs two strips (good for 1 hr of transfers). A card with 15 strips costs €6.50 (you can share them with your partner). Shorter strip tickets (2, 3, and 8 strips) are sold on some buses and trams, but the per-strip cost is about double. It's cheapest to buy the 15-strip tickets at the GVB public-transit office, machines at the train station, bookstores, post offices, airport, or tobacco shops throughout the country. You can also buy them (for a little more) directly from the driver.

  Armed with your *strippenkaart*, board the tram (you may have to press a button to open the doors) and have your strip ticket stamped by a conductor/driver or a machine. For the machine, fold over the number of strips you need (2 for rides in central Amsterdam), stick that end in the slot, and it will stamp the time. To transfer (good for 1 hr), just show the conductor/driver your stamped *strippenkaart*.
- If you need assistance traveling on public transport, your companion is eligible for a free **Public Transport Escort Pass** that covers them on all local journeys (call 030/235-4661, open Mon–Fri 9:00–12:00).
- Along with its sightseeing perks, the *I amsterdam* **Card** offers unlimited use of the tram, bus, and metro for its duration (1, 2, or 3 days, see above).

By Taxi

Amsterdam's non-adapted taxis are expensive (€3.50 drop, €2 per kilometer). You can wave them down, find a rare taxi stand, or call one (tel. 020/677-7777). While taxis are often not a good value, they can save time, energy, and frustration if you're unsure of your route.

Access: On standard taxis (described above; **AE+A,** Level 2— Moderately Accessible), the driver will assist the wheelchair user and place the folded wheelchair in the trunk.

Three companies offer fully accessible minivan taxis with ramps (**AE, AI,** Level 1—Fully Accessible). They charge more than standard taxis (a flat rate of €36/hr). Call an hour before you need the taxi: **Boonstra** (tel. 020/613-4134), **Connexxion Taxi Services** (tel. 020/606-2200 or 020/609-0103), and **Lagerberg Taxi** (tel. 020/647-4700).

Bike Taxis: You'll also see bike taxis, particularly near Dam Square and Leidseplein. Negotiate a rate for the trip before you board (no meter) and they'll wheel you wherever you want to go. While these probably won't work for wheelchair users, slow walkers who can climb into the taxi might find them useful (30 min-€10, no surcharge for baggage or extra weight, sample fare from Leidseplein to Anne Frank House: about €6).

By Boat

Several companies do "hop-on, hop-off" boat tours with several stops to shuttle tourists between sights, but none is fully wheelchair-accessible. **Canal Bus** (all-day ticket-€16), with three steps to the boat, offers better access than **Museum Boat** (€14), with several steps to the dock and then more to the boat (both boats: about hourly, daily 10:00–17:00). The sales booths in front of the Central Station (and the boats) offer handy, free brochures with museum times and admission prices. These boats are designed as transportation, but for wheelchair riders and slow walkers, taxis and trams are more accessible and convenient. If you want a boat experience, the easier option is a nonstop tour, which gives more information, covers more distance, and costs less (see "Tours," below).

By Car

Forget it—all you'll find are frustrating one-way streets, terrible parking, and meter maids with a passion for booting cars wrongly parked.

TOURS

▲▲**Canal Boat Tours**—These long, low, tourist-laden boats leave continually from several docks around the town for a relaxing one-hour, nonstop introduction to the city (with recorded, uninspiring headphone commentary). Two companies offer fully accessible boats:

Rederij Noord-Zuid (AE, AI, AL, Level 1—Fully Accessible), across from the Casino at Leidseplein, has four adapted boats that work for people who use wheelchairs (call 2 days ahead to get schedule for accessible boats; €9, covered by *I amsterdam* Card during the day but not in evening, April–Oct daily 10:00–18:00, Nov–March daily 10:00–17:00, tel. 020/679-1370, www.canal-cruises.nl).

Lovers Cruises (AE, AI, AL, Level 1—Fully Accessible) operates one fully accessible boat called the *Ganneslovers* (call ahead to check schedule for accessible boat and reserve; €8.50, departs from in front of Central

Amsterdam at a Glance

▲▲▲**Rijksmuseum** Best collection anywhere of the Dutch Masters: Rembrandt, Hals, Vermeer, and Steen. **Hours:** Daily 9:00–18:00. **Access:** Level 2—Moderately Accessible.

▲▲▲**Van Gogh Museum** 200 paintings by the angst-ridden artist. **Hours:** Daily 10:00–18:00, Fri until 22:00. **Access:** Level 1—Fully Accessible.

▲▲▲**Anne Frank House** Young Anne's hideaway during the Nazi occupation. **Hours:** April–Aug daily 9:00–21:00, Sept–March 9:00–19:00. **Access:** The house is Level 4—Not Accessible; the adjacent museum is Level 1—Fully Accessible.

▲▲**Dutch Resistance Museum** History of the Dutch struggle against the Nazis. **Hours:** Tue–Fri 10:00–17:00, Sat–Mon 12:00–17:00. **Access:** Level 1—Fully Accessible.

▲▲**Amstelkring Museum** Catholic church hidden in the attic of a 17th-century merchant's house. **Hours:** Mon–Sat 10:00–17:00, Sun 13:00–17:00. **Access:** Level 4—Not Accessible.

▲▲**Red Light District** Women on the job at the world's oldest profession. **Hours:** Best between noon and night—avoid late night. **Access:** Level 1—Fully Accessible.

▲**Heineken Brewery** Best beer tour in Europe. **Hours:** Tue–Sun 10:00–18:00, closed Mon. **Access:** Level 1—Fully Accessible.

Station by the Ibis Hotel at Prinshendrik Kade 25–27, tel. 020/530-1090, www.lovers.nl). No fishing is allowed—but bring your camera. Some prefer to cruise at night, when the bridges are illuminated.

Private Guide—**Ab Walet** is a likeable, hardworking, and knowledgeable local guide who enjoys personalizing tours for Americans interested in knowing his city better. He specializes in history and architecture and exudes a passion for Amsterdam. He can also take you to nearby towns (wheelchair riders and slow walkers welcome, €40/2 hrs, €80/4 hrs, for small groups of up to 4 people, tel. 020/671-2588, mobile 06-2069-7882, abwalet@yahoo.com). Ab says that his favorite clients are elderly folks

▲**Begijnhof** Quiet courtyard lined with picturesque houses. **Hours:** Daily 8:00–17:00. **Access:** Level 1—Fully Accessible.

▲**Amsterdam History Museum** Shows city's growth from fishing village to trading capital to today, including some Rembrandts and a playable carillon. **Hours:** Mon–Fri 10:00–17:00, Sat–Sun 11:00–17:00. **Access:** Level 1—Fully Accessible, except loft with carillon, which is Level 4—Not Accessible.

▲**Rembrandt's House** The master's reconstructed house, displaying his etchings. **Hours:** Sat–Thu 10:00–17:00, Fri 10:00–21:00. **Access:** The house itself is Level 4—Not Accessible, but the attached museum is Level 1—Fully Accessible.

▲**Diamonds** Tours at shops throughout the city, most notably Gassan near Rembrandt's House. **Hours:** Generally daily 9:00–17:00. **Access:** Level 2—Moderately Accessible.

▲**Hermitage Amsterdam Museum** Russia's Tsarist treasures on loan from St. Petersburg **Hours:** Daily 10:00–17:00. **Access:** Level 2—Moderately Accessible.

▲**Dutch Theater** Moving memorial in former Jewish detention center. **Hours:** Daily 11:00–16:00. **Access:** Level 1—Fully Accessible.

▲**Hash, Marijuana, and Hemp Museum** All the dope, from history and science to memorabilia. **Hours:** Daily 11:00–22:00. **Access:** Level 2—Moderately Accessible.

who just enjoy taking their time seeing the sights.

Red Light District Tours—You have two walking/wheeling tour options for seeing Amsterdam's most infamous neighborhood with a guide. For either company, call ahead to explain your mobility level (Randy Roy's offers better access).

Randy Roy's Red Light Tours consists of one ex-pat American woman, Kimberly. She lived in the Red Light District for years, and she gives fun, casual, yet informative 90-minute tours through this fascinating and eye-popping neighborhood. While the actual information is light, you'll explore various porn and drug shops and have an expert along to answer your questions (€12.50 includes a drink in a colorful bar at the end, nightly at 20:00, occasional Fri and Sat 22:00 tours, meet in front of Victoria Hotel—in front of the station, mobile 06-4185-3288, call her to confirm).

Zoom Amsterdam Citywalk starts at a café in the Tower of Tears (located across from Central Station, to the southwest). This building is not accessible—if you can climb the eight entry steps, you'll do fine on the rest of the tour. You'll listen to an initial 30-minute spiel about the history of the city. Then hit the streets for another two hours to find out the complicated story behind the Red Light District, including some fascinating, locals-only info (such as the scams that unscrupulous bar owners use on the many young male Brits who flock here). If you're curious about the area but would rather explore with a group, Zoom Amsterdam is a good way to go (€12.50, daily at 17:00; book ahead at VVV, through hotel, or by calling 020/623-6302; www.zoomamsterdam.com).

SIGHTS

One of Amsterdam's delights is that it has perhaps more small specialty museums than any other city its size. From houseboats to sex, cannabis to costumes, you can find a museum to suit your interests. Note that most museums require baggage check (usually free, often in coin-op lockers where you get your coin back).

The following sights are arranged by neighborhood for handy sightseeing.

Southwest Amsterdam

▲▲▲**Rijksmuseum**—Built to house the nation's great art, the Rijksmuseum owns several thousand paintings, including an incomparable collection of Dutch masters: Rembrandt, Vermeer, Hals, and Steen. The museum has made it easy for you to focus on the highlights, because that's all that is on display while most of the building undergoes several years of renovation (due to reopen in summer 2008). Wander through the Rijksmuseum's Philips Wing for a wonderful, concentrated dose of 17th-century Dutch masterpieces.

Southwest Amsterdam

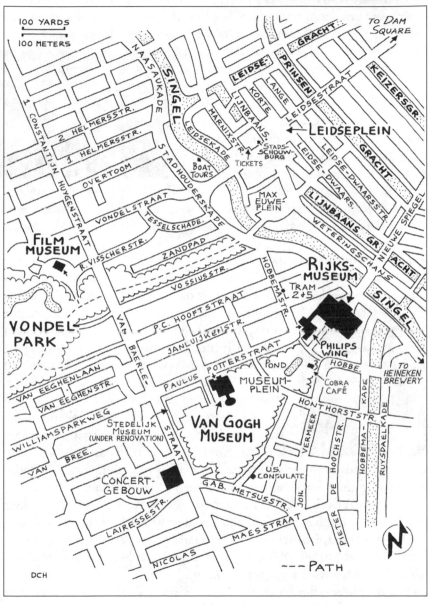

100 YARDS
100 METERS

TO DAM SQUARE

GRACHT
PRINSEN
KEIZERSGR.
LEIDSE·GRACHT
LEIDSEPLEIN
NAASAUKADE
SINGEL
CONSTANTIJN HUYGENSTRAAT
2 HELMERSSTR.
1 HELMERSSTR.
OVERTOOM
STADHOUDERSKADE
LEIDSEKADE
HARNIXSTR.
JNBAANS
KORTE
ANGE
LEIDSESTRAAT
STADS-SCHOUW-BURG
TICKETS
BOAT TOURS
MAX EUWE-PLEIN
LEIDSE·DWAARSSTR.
LIJNBAANS GR.
NIEUWE SPIEGEL
ACHT.
WETERINGSCHANS
SINGEL
FILM MUSEUM
VONDELSTRAAT
TESSELSCHADE
R. VISSCHERSTR.
ZANDPAD
VOSSIUSSTR.
VAN
VONDEL PARK
BAERLE
P.C. HOOFTSTRAAT
JANLUIJKENSTR.
POTTERSTRAAT
HOBBEMASTR.
RIJKS-MUSEUM
TRAM L 2 & 5
PHILIPS WING
HOBBE
COBRA CAFÉ
TO HEINEKEN BREWERY
KADE
POND
MUSEUM-PLEIN
VAN EEGHENLAAN
VAN EEGHENSTR.
WILLIAMSPARKWEG
STEDELIJK MUSEUM (UNDER RENOVATION)
PAULUS
VAN GOGH MUSEUM
HONTHORSTSTR.
VERMEER
DE HOOCHSTR.
HOBBEMA-
RUYSDAELKADE
VAN BREE.
CONCERT-GEBOUW
STRAAT
GAB. METSUSSTR.
U.S. CONSULATE
JOH.
PIETER
LAIRESSESTR.
MAESSTRAAT
NICOLAS
--- PATH

N

DCH

Access: AE+A, AI, AT, Level 2—Moderately Accessible. Wheelchair users can cut to the head of the line. Ask at the entry for assistance in finding the accessible entrance (which may change during renovation). Interior lifts provide access to all floors. A wheelchair-accessible toilet is located in the basement on the "A" entry side. Loaner wheelchairs are available.

Cost, Hours, Location: €10, covered by *I amsterdam* Card, audioguide-€4, daily 9:00–18:00, Friday until 22:00, tram #2 or #5 from train station to Hobbemastraat, tel. 020/674-7047, www.rijksmuseum.com. The Philips Wing entrance is near the corner of Hobbemastraat and Jan Luijkenstraat on the south side of the Rijks—the part of the huge building nearest the Van Gogh Museum.

▲▲▲**Van Gogh Museum**—Near the Rijksmuseum, this remarkable museum showcases works by the troubled Dutch artist whose art

seemed to mirror his life. Vincent, who killed himself in 1890 at age 37, is best known for sunny, Impressionist canvases that vibrate and pulse with life. The museum's 200 paintings, a taste of the artist's work and life, were owned by Theo, Vincent's younger, art-dealer brother. Highlights include *Sunflowers*, *The Bedroom*, *The Potato Eaters*, and many brooding self-portraits. The third floor shows works that influenced Vincent, from Monet and Pissarro to Gauguin, Cézanne, and Toulouse-Lautrec. The worthwhile audioguide includes insightful commentaries and quotes from Vincent himself.

Access: AE, AI, AT, AL, Level 1—Fully Accessible. Wheelchair users can cut to the head of the line. Loaner wheelchairs are available.

Cost, Hours, Location: €10, covered by *I amsterdam* Card, audioguide-€4, daily 10:00–18:00, Fri until 22:00, Paulus Potterstraat 7, tel. 020/570-5200, www.vangoghmuseum.nl).

▲**Museumplein**—Bordered by the Rijks, Van Gogh, and the Concertgebouw (classical music hall), this square is interesting even to art-haters. Amsterdam's best acoustics are found underneath the Rijksmuseum, where street musicians perform everything from chamber music to Mongolian throat singing. Mimes, human statues, and crafts' booths dot the square. Skateboarders careen across a concrete tube, while locals enjoy a park bench or a coffee at the Cobra Café.

Van Gogh Museum

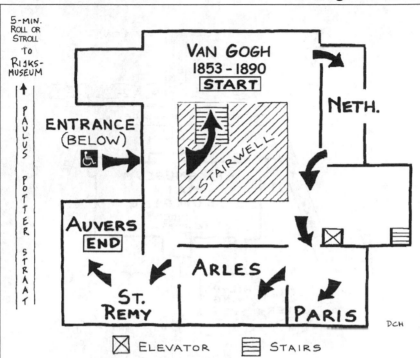

NETHERLANDS
The Potato Eaters
The Old Church Tower at Nuenen
Still Life with Bible

ARLES
The Yellow House
Sunflowers
The Bedroom
Gauguin's Chair
The Sower

PARIS
Self-Portrait as an Artist
Self-Portrait with Straw Hat
Red Cabbages and Onions
Self-Portrait with Gray Felt Hat

ST. REMY / AUVERS-sur-OISE
Pietà
The Fall of the Leaves
Wheatfield with a Reaper
The Sheaf-Binder
Branches of an Almond Tree in Blossom
Wheatfield with Crows

Museumplein

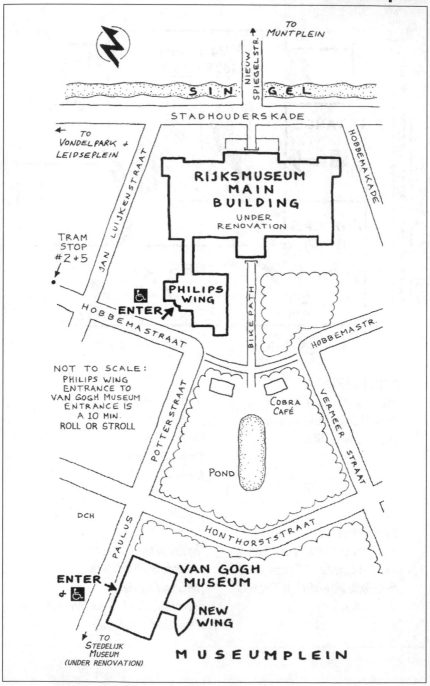

Access: Level 1—The square is fully accessible and has adapted toilets.

▲**Heineken Brewery**—The leading Dutch beer is no longer brewed here, but this old brewery now welcomes visitors to a slick and entertaining beer-appreciation experience. It's the most enjoyable brewery tour I've encountered in Europe. You'll learn as much as you want, marvel at the huge vats and towering ceilings, see videos, and go on rides. "What's it like to be a Heineken bottle and be filled with one of the best beers in the world? Try it for yourself." An important section recognizes a budding problem of our age, vital to people as well as to beer: this planet's scarcity of clean water. With globalization, corporations are well on their way to owning the world's water supplies.

Access: AE, AI, AL, AT, Level 1—Fully Accessible.

Cost, Hours, Location: €10 for self-guided, 75-minute tour and 3 beers or soft drinks; must be over age 18, Tue–Sun 10:00–18:00, last entry 17:00, closed Mon, tram #16 or #24 to Heinekenplein, close to Rijksmuseum, tel. 020/523-9666.

▲**Leidseplein**—Brimming with cafés, this people-watching mecca is an impromptu stage for street artists, accordionists, jugglers, and unicyclists. Sunny afternoons are liveliest. The Boom Chicago theater fronts this square (see page 425). Roll or stroll nearby Lange Leidsedwarsstraat (1 block north) for a taste-bud tour of ethnic eateries, from Greek to Indonesian.

Access: Level 1—Fully Accessible. The sidewalks in this area are all wheelchair-accessible. You'll also find the accessible Rederij Noord-Zuid canal boat tour (see "Tours," above).

▲▲**Vondelpark**—This huge and lively city park is popular with the

Dutch—families with little kids, romantic couples, strolling seniors, and hippies sharing blankets and beers. It's a favored venue for free summer concerts. On a sunny afternoon, it's a hedonistic scene that seems to say, "Parents...relax."

Access: Level 1—Fully Accessible. Wheelchair users can travel on the bikeway or on the two dirt paths on either side of the bikeway.

Amsterdam Film Museum—This is actually not a museum, but a movie theater. In its three 80-seat theaters, it shows several films a day, from small foreign productions to 70-mm classics drawn from its massive archives.

Access: AE+A, AI+A, Level 2—Moderately Accessible. Wheelchair users will find barriers both at the entry and inside the building.

Cost, Hours, Location: €8, always in the original language, often English subtitles, Vondelpark 3, tel. 020/589-1400, www.filmmuseum .nl.

Rembrandtplein and Tuschinski Theater—One of the city's premier nightlife spots is the leafy **Rembrandtplein** (the artist's modest statue stands here) and the adjoining Thorbeckeplein. Several late-night dance clubs (such as IT, a half-block east down Amstelstraat) keep the area lively into the wee hours. Utrechtsestraat is lined with upscale shops and restaurants.

The **Tuschinski Theater,** a movie palace from the 1920s (a half block from Rembrandtplein down Reguliersbreestraat) glitters inside and out.

Still a working theater, it's a delightful old place to see first-run movies. The exterior is an interesting hybrid of styles, forcing the round peg of Art Nouveau into the square hole of Art Deco. The stone-and-tile facade features stripped down, functional Art Deco squares and rectangles, but is ornamented with Art Nouveau elements—Tiffany-style windows, garlands, curvy iron lamps, Egyptian pharaohs, and exotic gold lettering over the door. Inside (lobby is free), the sumptuous decor features red carpets, nymphs on the walls, and semi-abstract designs. Watch the ceiling morph (Reguliersbreestraat 26–28).

Access: AE+A, AI, Level 3—Minimally Accessible, four 7" entry steps.

Houseboat Museum (Woonbootmuseum)—In the 1930s, modern cargo ships came into widespread use—making small, sail-powered cargo boats obsolete. In danger of extinction, these little vessels found new life as houseboats lining the canals of Amsterdam. Today, 2,500 such boats—their cargo holds turned into classy, comfortable living rooms—are called home by locals. For a peek into this *gezellig* (cozy) world, visit this tiny museum. Captain Vincent enjoys showing visitors around the houseboat, which feels lived-in because, until 1997, it was.

Access: AE+A, AI, Level 2—Moderately Accessible. The staff will assist you getting in the small entry. Once inside, it's barrier-free.

Central Amsterdam

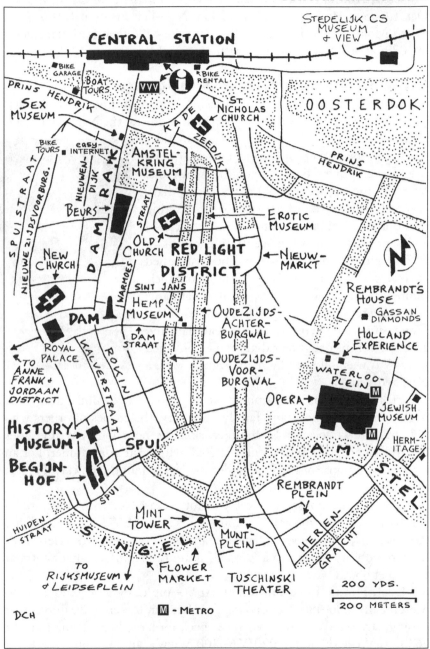

Cost, Hours, Location: €3, covered by *I amsterdam* Card, March–Oct Tue–Sun 11:00–17:00, closed Mon; Nov–Feb Fri–Sun 11:00–17:00, closed Mon-Thu; on Prinsengracht, opposite #296 facing Elandsgracht, tel. 020/427-0750, www.houseboatmuseum.nl.

Central Amsterdam, near Dam Square

▲▲▲**Anne Frank House**—A pilgrimage for many, this house offers a fascinating look at the hideaway of young Anne during the Nazi occupation of the Netherlands. Anne, her parents, an older sister, and four others spent just over two years in a "Secret Annex" behind her father's business. While in hiding, 13-year-old Anne kept a diary chronicling her extraordinary experience. Acting on a tip, the Nazis arrested them in August 1944 and sent the group to concentration camps in Poland and Germany. Anne and her sister died of typhus in March 1945, only weeks before their camp was liberated. Of the eight inhabitants of the Secret Annex, only Anne's father, Otto Frank, survived. He returned to Amsterdam and arranged for his daughter's diary to be published in 1947. It was followed by many translations, a play, and a movie.

Pick up the English pamphlet at the door. The exhibit offers thorough coverage of the Frank family, the diary, the stories of others who hid, and the Holocaust. In summer, skip the hour-long daytime lines by arriving after 18:00 (last entry is 20:30) and visit after dinner. For an interesting glimpse of Holland under the Nazis, rent the powerful movie *Soldier of Orange* before you leave home.

Access: The house is Level 4—Not Accessible, with many stairs and tight hallways; the adjacent museum is **AE, AI, AT,** Level 1—Fully Accessible. In the museum, wheelchair users and other travelers with limited mobility can watch a "virtual" tour of the house. Ask for entry at the ticket booth.

Cost, Hours, Location: €7.50, April–Aug daily 9:00–21:00, Sept–March daily 9:00–19:00, closed for Yom Kippur, last entry 30 min before closing, strict and required baggage check for large bags, Prinsengracht 267, near Westerkerk, tel. 020/556-7100, www.annefrank.org.

Westerkerk—Near the Anne Frank House, this landmark church has a barren interior, Rembrandt's body buried somewhere under the pews, and Amsterdam's tallest steeple.

Access: AE, AI, Level 2—Moderately Accessible. The church tower, which doesn't have an elevator, is Level 4—Not Accessible.

Cost and Hours: Free, generally open April–Sept Mon–Sat 10:00–15:00, closed Sun.

Royal Palace (Koninklijk Huis)—The palace, which will be closed for renovation through 2008, is right on Dam Square. It was built as a lavish City Hall for Amsterdam, when the country was a proud new republic and Amsterdam was the richest city on the planet—awash in profit from trade. When constructed in 1648, this building was one of Europe's finest, with a sumptuous interior. Today, it's the official (but not actual) residence of the queen (tel. 020/620-4060, www.koninklijkhuis.nl).

Access: AE, AI, AL, AT, Level 1—Fully Accessible.

New Church (Nieuwe Kerk)—Barely newer than the "Old" Church (located in the Red Light District), this 15th-century church has an intentionally dull interior, after the decoration was removed by 16th-century iconoclastic Protestants seeking to unclutter their communion with God. This is where many Dutch royal weddings and all coronations take place, and it hosts temporary exhibits.

Access: AE, AI, AT, Level 1—Fully Accessible. The associated restaurant (to the right) is also fully accessible and has adapted toilets.

Cost, Hours, Location: While there's a steep €8 entrance fee to see the various exhibitions (covered by *I amsterdam* Card), anyone can pop in free for a look at the vast interior (Mon–Sat 10:00–18:00, Sun 13:00–18:00, on Dam Square, tel. 020/638-6909, www.nieuwekerk.nl; also see page 448).

▲Begijnhof—Entering this tiny, idyllic courtyard in the city center, you escape into the charm of old Amsterdam. Notice house #34, a 500-year-old wooden structure (rare, since repeated fires taught city fathers a trick called brick). Peek into the hidden Catholic church, dating from the time when post-Reformation Dutch Catholics couldn't worship in public. It's opposite the English Reformed church, where the Pilgrims worshipped while waiting for their voyage to the New World (marked by a plaque near the door). Be considerate of the people who live around the courtyard.

Access: AE, AI, Level 1—Fully Accessible. The entrance on the east side of the courtyard has no steps. The courtyard has fully accessible pathways. The hidden Catholic church (**AE+A, AI,** Level 2—Moderately Accessible) has large doors and two 2" steps, one on either side of the landing.

Cost, Hours, Location: Free, daily 8:00–17:00, on Begijnensteeg lane, just off Kalverstraat between #130 and #132, pick up flier at office near entrance; for more details, see page 454.

▲**Amsterdam History Museum (Amsterdams Historisch Museum)**— Follow the city's growth from fishing village to world trader to hippie haven. Housed in a 500-year-old former orphanage, this creative and hardworking museum features Rembrandt's paintings, fine English descriptions, and a carillon loft. The loft comes with push-button recordings of the town bell tower's greatest hits, and a self-serve carillon "keyboard" that lets you ring a few bells yourself.

Access: Museum is **AE, AI, AT,** Level 1—Fully Accessible. The loft is Level 4—Not Accessible. The museum has wheelchair-accessible elevators (that do not go to the loft) and an adapted toilet (near the fully accessible David and Goliath café). Loaner wheelchairs are available.

Cost, Hours, Location: €6.50, covered by *I amsterdam* Card, Mon–Fri 10:00–17:00, Sat–Sun 11:00–17:00, pleasant restaurant, next to Begijnhof, Kalverstraat 92, tel. 020/523-1822, www.ahm.nl. The museum's free pedestrian corridor—lined with old-time group portraits—is a powerful teaser.

Southeast Amsterdam

To reach these sights from the train station, take tram #9 or #14 (both Level 1—Fully Accessible). All of these sights are close to each other and can easily be connected into an interesting roll or stroll. Several of the sights in southeast Amsterdam cluster near the large square, Waterlooplein, dominated by the modern opera house. Most sights are covered by the *I amsterdam* Card.

For an orientation, survey the neighborhood from the accessible, lamp-lined Blauwbrug ("Blue Bridge")—a modest, modern version of Paris' Pont Alexandre III. The bridge crosses the Amstel River. From this point, the river is channeled to form the city's canals.

Pan clockwise. The big, curved modern facade belongs to the new opera house (commonly called the "Stopera," after a public outcry wanting to stop its construction). Behind the Stopera are these sights (not visible from here, but described below): the Waterlooplein flea market, Rembrandt's House, *Holland Experience,* and Gassan Diamonds. To the right of the Stopera are the twin gray steeples of the Moses and Aaron Church, which sits roughly in the center of the former Jewish Quarter.

Several Jewish sights cluster to the right of the Moses and Aaron Church: the Jewish Historical Museum, the Portuguese Synagogue, and the dockworker memorial. Just east of those is the De Hortus Botanical Garden.

The modern drawbridge in the foreground, though not famous, is

Southeast Amsterdam

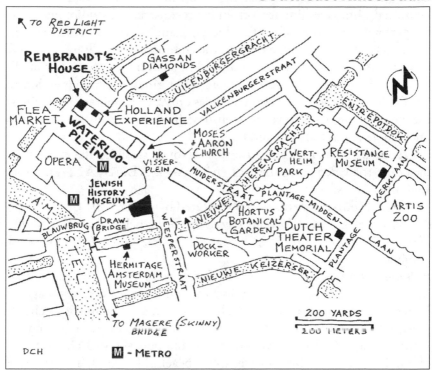

photogenic. Beyond that is the Hermitage Amsterdam Museum (see below). Crossing the Amstel upstream is one of the city's romantic spots, the Magere Brug ("Skinny Bridge").

Waterlooplein Flea Market—For more than a hundred years, the Jewish Quarter flea market has raged daily except Sunday behind the Rembrandt House. The long, narrow park is filled with stalls selling cheap clothes, hippie stuff, old records, tourist knickknacks, and garage-sale junk. (The flea market is right at the Waterlooplein metro station.)

Access: Level 1—Fully Accessible.

▲**Rembrandt's House (Rembrandthuis Museum)**—A middle-aged Rembrandt lived here after his wife's death, as his popularity and wealth dwindled down to obscurity and bankruptcy (1639–1658). If you are able, tour the place this way: See the 10-minute introductory video (Dutch and English showings alternate); explore Rembrandt's reconstructed house (filled with exactly what his bankruptcy inventory of 1656 said he owned); imagine him at work in his reconstructed studio; marvel at his personal collection of exotic objects, many of which he included in paintings; ask the printer to explain the etching process (drawing in soft wax on a metal plate that's then dipped in acid, inked up, and printed); then, for the finale, enjoy several rooms of original Rembrandt etchings. While the permanent collection includes only two Rembrandt paintings, the etchings are marvelous and well-described. I came away wanting to know more about the man and his art.

Access: The house itself is Level 4—Not Accessible. The museum—including the video and gallery of etchings—is **AE, AI, AL, AT,** Level 1—Fully Accessible.

Cost, Hours, Location: €7.50, covered by *I amsterdam* Card, €13.50 combo-ticket includes *Holland Experience*—see below, Sat–Thu 10:00–17:00, Fri 10:00–21:00, Jodenbreestraat 4, tel. 020/520-0400, www.rembrandthuis.nl.

Holland Experience—Bragging "Experience Holland in 30 minutes," this 3-D movie takes you traveling through an idealized montage of Dutch clichés. There are no words, but lots of images. While it's a cheesy presentation (and the schedule, with showings only every couple hours, is frustrating), the *Experience* is relaxing, and puts you in a Dutch frame of mind. The men's urinal is a trip to the beach. Plan for it. There's also a goofy chance to pose in a fake Red Light District window.

Access: AE, AI, Level 2—Moderately Accessible.

Cost, Hours, Location: €8.50, €13.50 combo-ticket includes Rembrandt's House, daily 10:00–18:00, several shows a day, alternating in 2006 with a Rembrandt video, adjacent to Rembrandt's House at Jodenbreestraat 8, tel. 020/422-2233, www.holland-experience.nl.

▲**Diamonds**—Many shops in the "city of diamonds" offer tours. These tours come with two parts: a chance to see experts behind magnifying glasses polishing the facets of precious diamonds, followed by a visit to an intimate sales room to see (and perhaps buy) a mighty shiny yet very tiny souvenir.

The handy and professional **Gassan Diamonds** facility fills a huge warehouse a block from Rembrandt's House. A visit here puts you in the big-tour-group fray (notice how each tour group has a color-coded sticker, so they know which guide gets the commission on what they buy). You'll get a sticker, join a tour to see a polisher at work, and hear a general explanation of the process (free, 15 min). Then you'll have an opportunity to have color and clarity described and illustrated with diamonds ranging in value from $100 to $30,000. Before or after, you can have a free cup of coffee in the waiting room across the parking lot.

Access: AE+A, AI, AL, AT+A, Level 2—Moderately Accessible. There's one 6" entry step and an accessible restaurant.

Cost, Hours, Location: Daily 9:00–17:00, Nieuwe Uilenburgerstraat 173, tel. 020/622-5333, www.gassandiamonds.com.

▲**Hermitage Amsterdam Museum**—The famous Hermitage Museum in St. Petersburg, Russia, loans art to Amsterdam for display in the Amstelhof, a 17th-century former nursing home on the Amstel River. The exhibit changes twice a year. For the latest, ask at the TI or check www.hermitage.nl.

Why all this Russian-owned art in Amsterdam? The Hermitage collection in St. Petersburg is so vast that they can only show about 5 percent of it at any one time. Therefore, the Hermitage is establishing satellite collections around the world. The one here in Amsterdam is the biggest, and will be growing considerably as the museum takes over more of the Amstelhof. By law, the great Russian collection can only be out of the country for six months at a time, so the collection will always be rotating. Curators in Amsterdam make a point to display art that complements—rather than just repeats—what the city's other museums show so well.

Access: AE+A, AI, Level 2—Moderately Accessible. The staff will assist you with the three entry steps.

Cost, Hours, Location: €6, covered by *I amsterdam* Card, daily 10:00–17:00, Nieuwe Herengracht 14, tram #4 to Rembrandtplein or #9 to Waterlooplein, tel. 020/531-8751, www.hermitage.nl.

De Hortus Botanical Garden—This is a unique oasis of tranquility within the city (no mobile phones are allowed, because "our collection of plants is a precious community—treat it with respect"). One of the oldest botanical gardens in the world, it dates from 1638, when medicinal herbs were grown here. Today, among its 6,000 different kinds of plants—most of which were collected by the Dutch East India Company in the 17th and 18th centuries—you'll find medicinal herbs, cacti, several greenhouses (one with a fluttery butterfly house—a hit with kids), and a tropical palm house. Much of it is described in English: "A Dutch merchant snuck a coffee plant out of Ethiopia, which ended up in this garden in 1706. This first coffee plant in Europe was the literal granddaddy of the coffee cultures of Brazil—long the world's biggest coffee producer."

Jews in Amsterdam

In 1940, one in ten Amsterdammers was Jewish, and most lived in the neighborhood behind Waterlooplein. Jewish traders had long been welcome in a city that cared more about business than religion. In the late 1500s, many Sephardic Jews from Spain and Portugal immigrated, fleeing persecution. (The philosopher Baruch Spinoza's ancestors were among them.) In the 1630s, Yiddish-speaking Eastern European Jews (Ashkenazi) poured in. By 1700, the Jewish Quarter was a bustling, exotic, multicultural world, with more people speaking Portuguese, German, and Yiddish than Dutch.

Jews were not first-class citizens. They needed the city's permission to settle there, and they couldn't hold public office (but then, neither could Catholics under Calvinist rule). Still, the Jewish Quarter was not a ghetto (enforced segregation), there were no special taxes, and cosmopolitan Amsterdam was well-acquainted with all types of beliefs and customs.

In 1796, Jews were given full citizenship. In exchange, they were required to learn the Dutch language and submit to the city's legal system…and the Jewish culture began assimilating into the Dutch.

In 1940, Nazi Germany occupied the Netherlands. On February 22, 1941, the Nazis began rounding up Jews—herding hundreds of them to Jonas Daniel Meyerplein to be shipped to extermination camps in Eastern Europe. The citizens responded with a general strike that shut down the entire city, a heroic gesture honored today with a statue of a striking dockworker on Jonas Daniel Meyerplein. Despite the strike, the roundups continued. By war's end, more than 100,000 of the city's 130,000 Jews had died.

Today, about 25,000 Jews live in Amsterdam, and the Jewish Quarter has blended in with the modern city.

Access: AE, AI+A, AT, Level 2—Moderately Accessible. Loaner wheelchairs are available. While the "Museum Maps" rate the garden as wheelchair-accessible, the stone path makes it a challenge, especially in the spots where the stones are at their deepest. They do have a wheelchair-accessible toilet.

Cost, Hours, Location: €6, covered by *I amsterdam* Card, Mon–Fri 9:00–17:00, Sat–Sun 10:00–17:00, until 16:00 in winter, Plantage Middenlaan 2A, tel. 020/625-9021, www.hortus-botanicus.nl.

Jewish Historical Museum (Joods Historisch Museum)—Four historic buildings have been joined by steel and glass to make one modern complex that tells the story of Amsterdam's Jews through the centuries, while serving as a good introduction to Judaism in general. There are several sections ("Jews in Amsterdam," children's museum, temporary exhibits), but the highlight is the Great Synagogue, restored in 1981.

Sit in the high-ceilinged synagogue, surrounded by religious objects, and imagine it in its prime (1671–1943). The hall would be full for a service—men downstairs, women above in the gallery. On the east wall (the symbolic direction of Jerusalem) is the ark, where they keep the scrolls of the Torah (the Jewish scriptures, which include the first 5 books of the Christian bible). The rabbi and other men, wearing thigh-length prayer shawls, would approach the ark and carry the Torah to the raised platform in the center of the room. After unwrapping it from its drapery and silver cap, one would use a *yad* (ceremonial pointer) to follow along while singing the text aloud.

Video displays around the room explain Jewish customs, from birth (circumcision) to puberty (the bar/bat mitzvah, celebrating the entry into adulthood) to marriage—culminating in the groom stomping on a glass while everyone shouts, "Mazel tov!"

Access: AE+A, AI, AT, Level 2—Moderately Accessible. Wheelchair users enter through a side door; ring the bell to gain entrance. The museum has accessible toilets.

Cost, Hours, Location: €6.50, covered by *I amsterdam* Card, daily 11:00–17:00, free audioguide but displays all have English explanations, good kosher café, Jonas Daniel Meijerplein 2, tel. 020/626-9945, www .jhm.nl.

▲**Dutch Theater (Hollandsche Schouwburg)**—Once a lively theater in the Jewish neighborhood, and today a moving memorial, this building was used as an assembly hall for local Jews destined for Nazi concentration camps. On the wall, 6,700 family names pay tribute to the 104,000 Jews deported and killed by the Nazis. Some 70,000 victims spent time here, awaiting transfer to concentration camps. Upstairs is a small history exhibit with photos and memorabilia of some victims, putting a human face on the staggering numbers. Press the buttons on a model of the neighborhood to see round-up spots from the Nazi occupation. The ruined theater actually offers little to see but plenty to think about. Back on the ground floor, notice the hopeful messages that visiting school groups attach to the wooden tulips.

Access: AE, AI, AT, AL, Level 1—Fully Accessible. Enter to the left of the main door (ring bell to gain entry). Loaner wheelchairs are available.

Cost, Hours, Location: Free, daily 11:00–16:00, Plantage

Middenlaan 24, tel. 020/626-9945, www.hollandscheschouwburg.nl.

▲▲**Dutch Resistance Museum (Verzetsmuseum)**—This is an impressive look at how the Dutch resisted their Nazi occupiers from 1940 to 1945. You'll see propaganda movie clips, study forged ID cards under a magnifying glass, and read about ingenious and courageous efforts—big and small—to hide local Jews from the Germans and undermine the Nazi regime.

The first dozen displays set the stage, showing peaceful, upright Dutch people of the 1930s, living oblivious to the rise of fascism. Then— bam—it's May 1940 and the Germans invade the Netherlands, pummel Rotterdam, send Queen Wilhelmina into exile, and—in four short days of fighting—hammer home the message that resistance is futile. The Germans install local Dutch Nazis in power (the "NSB"), led by Anton Mussert.

Next, in the corner of the exhibition area, push a button to see photos of the event that first mobilized organized resistance. In February 1941, Nazis started rounding up Jews from the neighborhood, killing nine protesters. Amsterdammers responded by shutting down the trams, schools, and businesses in a massive two-day strike. (The next display makes it clear that this brave action still did little to save 100,000 Jews from extermination.)

Turning the corner into the main room, you'll see numerous exhibits on Nazi rule and the many ways the Dutch resisted it: schoolkids telling "Kraut jokes," vandals turning Nazi V-for-Victory posters into W-for-Wilhelmina, preachers giving pointed sermons, printers distributing underground newspapers (such as *Het Parool*, which became a major daily paper), counterfeiters forging documents, and ordinary people hiding radios under floorboards and Jews inside closets. As the war progressed, the armed Dutch Resistance became bolder and more violent, killing German occupiers and Dutch collaborators. In September 1944, the Allies liberated Antwerp, and the Netherlands started celebrating... too soon. The Nazis dug in and punished the country by cutting off rations, plunging West Holland into the "Hunger Winter" of 1944–1945, in which 20,000 died. Finally, springtime came. The Allies liberated the country, and at war's end, Nazi helmets were turned into bedpans.

Besides the history lesson, this thought-provoking exhibit examines the moral dilemmas of life under oppressive rule. Is it right to give money to poor people if the charity is run by Nazis? Should I quit my government job when the Nazis take control, or stay on to do what good I can? If I disagree with my government, is it okay to lie? To vandalize? To kill?

Access: AE, AI, AT, Level 1—Fully Accessible. If you need a loaner wheelchair, call ahead to reserve one.

Cost, Hours, Location: €5, covered by *I amsterdam* Card, Tue–Fri 10:00–17:00, Sat–Mon 12:00–17:00, well-described in English, no flash photos, tram #9 from station, Plantage Kerklaan 61, tel. 020/620-2535, www.verzetsmuseum.org. The recommended Restaurant Plancius is adjacent to the museum (see page 439) and Amsterdam's famous zoo is just across the street.

Northeast Amsterdam

Stedelijk Museum CS—The modern art museum, temporarily located on the second and third floors of the towering post office building, features art that would normally be displayed at the main Stedelijk Museum building (near the Rijksmuseum), but it's under renovation until 2008. The fun, far-out, refreshing collection consists of post-1945 experimental and conceptual art. The Stedelijk's famous masterpieces (works by Picasso, Chagall, Cézanne, Kandinsky, and Mondrian) will not be on display until the museum moves back into its regular home (which is also Level 1—Fully Accessible).

Access: AE, AI, AL, AT, Level 1—Fully Accessible.

Cost, Hours, Location: €9, covered by *I amsterdam* Card, daily 10:00–18:00, just east of Central Station—to the left as you exit—look for *Post CS* tower at Oosterdokskade 5, tel. 020/573-2911, www.stedelijk.nl.

Best Amsterdam Viewpoint: Along with the Westerkerk's tower, the best viewpoint of the city is from the 11th floor of the Post building (near the train station, which temporarily houses the Stedelijk Museum). Café 11 is a trendy nightspot that doubles as an eatery during the day. Ride the fully accessible elevator to the 11th floor to see the view for free.

Red Light District

▲▲Amstelkring Museum (Our Lord in the Attic)—While Amsterdam has long been known for its tolerant attitudes, 16th-century politics forced Dutch Catholics to worship discreetly. Near the train station in the Red Light District, you'll find a fascinating hidden Catholic church filling the attic of three 17th-century merchants' houses. Don't miss the silver collection and other exhibits of daily life from 300 years ago.

Access: Level 4—Not Accessible. The many stairs leading to this attic make it accessible only to energetic slow walkers.

Cost, Hours, Location: €7, covered by *I amsterdam* Card, Mon–Sat 10:00–17:00, Sun and holidays 13:00–17:00, closed Jan 1

and April 30, Oudezijds Voorburgwal 40, tel. 020/624-6604, www
.museumamstelkring.nl.

▲▲**Red Light District**—Europe's most touristed ladies of the night tease
and tempt, as they have for centuries here, in 450 display-case windows
around Oudezijds Achterburgwal and Oudezijds Voorburgwal, surrounding the Old Church (Oude Kerk, see below). Drunks and drug-
gies make the streets uncomfortable late at night, after the gawking tour
groups leave (around 23:00), but it's a
fascinating roll or stroll between noon
and nightfall.

The neighborhood, one of Amsterdam's oldest, has had prostitutes since
1200. Prostitution is entirely legal here,
and the prostitutes are generally entrepreneurs, renting space and running
their own businesses. Popular prostitutes
net around €500 a day (S&F, €25–50),
fill out tax returns, and even pay union dues.

Access: The Red Light District neighborhood is fully accessible.

Sex Museums—Amsterdam has two sex museums: one in the Red Light
District, and another a block in front of the train station on Damrak.
While visiting one can be called sightseeing, visiting both is hard to
explain. Here's a comparison:

The **Erotic Museum** (**AE, AI,** Level 2—Moderately Accessible) in
the Red Light District is less offensive. Its five floors rely heavily on
badly dressed dummies of prostitutes in various acts. It also has a lot of
uninspired paintings, videos, phone sex, old photos, and sculpture (€5,
daily 11:00–24:00, along the canal at Oudezijds Achterburgwal 54, tel.
020/624-7303).

The **Damrak Sex Museum** goes farther, telling the story of por-
nography from Roman times through 1960. Every sexual deviation is
revealed in various displays, and the nude and pornographic art is a cut
above that of the other sex museum. Also interesting are the early French
pornographic photos and memorabilia from Europe, India, and Asia.
You'll find a Marilyn Monroe tribute and some S&M displays, too. The
museum's first floor is moderately accessible (**AE, AI**), but the upper
level is not (€2.50, daily 10:00–23:30, Damrak 18, a block in front of
station).

Old Church (Oude Kerk)—This 14th-century landmark—the needle
around which the Red Light District spins—has served as a reassuring welcome-home symbol to sailors, a refuge to the downtrodden, an

ideological battlefield of the Counter-Reformation, and today, a tourist sight with a dull interior.

Access: AE, AI, AT, Level 1—Fully Accessible. There is an adapted toilet; ask at the reception desk.

Cost, Hours, Location: €4, covered by *I amsterdam* Card, Mon–Sat 11:00–17:00, Sun 13:00–17:00, www.oudekerk.nl.

▲**Hash, Marijuana, and Hemp Museum**—This is a collection of dope facts, history, science, and memorabilia. While small, it has a shocking finale: the high-tech grow room, in which dozens of varieties of marijuana are cultivated in optimal hydroponic (among other) environments.

Some plants stand five feet tall and shine under the intense grow lamps. The view is actually through glass walls into the neighboring Sensi Seed Bank Grow Shop, which sells carefully cultivated seeds and all the gear needed to grow them (Seed Bank may move 50 yards north in 2006).

Access: AE, AI, Level 2—Moderately Accessible.

Cost, Hours, Location: €5.70, daily 11:00–22:00, Oudezijds Achterburgwal 148, tel. 020/623-5961, www.hashmuseum.com.

The **Cannabis College,** "dedicated to ending the global war against the cannabis plant through public education," is a half-block away at #124.

Access: Level 3—Minimally Accessible. There are seven 8" entry steps and no accessible toilets.

Cost, Hours, Information: Free, daily 11:00–19:00, tel. 020/423-4420, www.cannabiscollege.com.

SMOKING

Tobacco

A third of Dutch people smoke tobacco. You don't have to like it, but expect it—in restaurants, bars, bus stops, almost everywhere. Holland has a long tradition as a smoking culture, being among the first to import the tobacco plant from the New World. Tobacco shops such as the House of Hajenius glorify the habit. Smoking seems to be part of an overall diet and regimen that—no denying it—makes the Dutch people among the healthiest in the world. Tanned, trim, firm, 60-something Dutch people sip their beer, take a drag, and ask me why Americans murder themselves with Big Macs.

Still, their version of the Surgeon General is finally waking up to the drug's many potential health problems. Since 2002, warning stickers bigger than America's are required on cigarette packs, and some of them are almost comically blunt, such as: "Smoking will make you impotent... and then you die." (The warnings prompted gag stickers like, "If you can read this, you're healthy enough," and "Life can kill you.")

Smoking was recently prohibited on trains. It's unclear how much this will be obeyed or enforced.

Marijuana (a.k.a. Cannabis)

Amsterdam, Europe's counterculture mecca, thinks the concept of a "victimless crime" is a contradiction in terms. Heroin and cocaine are strictly illegal in the Netherlands, and the police stringently enforce laws prohibiting their sale and use. But, while hard drugs are definitely out, marijuana causes about as much excitement as a bottle of beer. If tourists call an ambulance after smoking too much pot, medics just say, "Drink something sweet and wait it out."

Throughout the Netherlands, you'll see "coffeeshops"—pubs selling marijuana. The minimum age for purchase is 18. Coffeeshops can sell up

to five grams of marijuana per person per day. Locals buy marijuana by asking, "Can I see the cannabis menu?" The menu looks like the inventory of a drug bust. Display cases show various joints or baggies for sale.

The Dutch usually include a little tobacco in their pre-rolled joints (though a few coffeeshops sell joints of pure marijuana). To avoid the tobacco, smokers roll their own (cigarette papers are free with the purchase, dispensed like toothpicks) or borrow a pipe or bong. Baggies of marijuana usually cost €10–15, and a smaller amount means better quality. As long as you're a paying customer (e.g., buy a cup of coffee), you can pop into any coffeeshop and light up, even if you didn't buy your pot there.

Pot should never be bought on the street in Amsterdam. Well-established coffeeshops are considered much safer. Coffeeshop owners have an interest in keeping their trade safe and healthy. They warn Americans—unused to the strength of the local stuff—to try a lighter leaf. In fact, they are generally very patient in explaining the varieties available.

Several forms of the cannabis plant are sold. Locals smoke more hashish (the sap of the cannabis plant) than the leaf of the plant (which they call "marijuana" or "grass"). White varieties (called "White Widow" or "Amsterdam White") are popular, featuring marijuana with white, fiber-like strands.

So, what am I? Pro-marijuana? Let's put it this way: I agree with the Dutch people, who remind me that a society either has to allow alternative lifestyles...or build more prisons. Last year alone, more than 700,000 Americans were arrested for marijuana use; only Russia incarcerates more of its citizens. The Dutch are not necessarily pro-marijuana, but they do believe that a prohibition on marijuana would cause more problems than it solves. Statistics support the Dutch belief that their system  works. They have fewer hard drug problems than other countries. And they believe America's policy—like so many other touchy issues in the news lately—is based on electoral politics, rather than rationality.

To learn more about marijuana, drop by Amsterdam's Cannabis College or the Hash, Marijuana, and Hemp Museum. To see where cannabis growers buy their seeds, stop by the Sensi Seed Bank Store. These three places are located on Oudezijds Achterburgwal street (see page 419). Back home, if you'd like to support an outfit dedicated to taking the crime out of pot, read up on the National Organization for the Reform of Marijuana Laws (www.norml.org).

Coffeeshops

Most of downtown Amsterdam's coffeeshops feel grungy and foreboding to anyone over 30. The neighborhood places (and those in small towns around the countryside) are much more inviting to people without piercings, tattoos, and favorite techno artists. I've listed a few places with a more pub-like ambience for Americans wanting to go local, but within reason. For locations, see the map on page 434.

Paradox (AE, AI, Level 2—Moderately Accessible, one accessible table on same level as entry) is the most *gezellig* (cozy) coffeeshop I found—a mellow, graceful place. The managers, Ludo and Jan, are patient with descriptions and happy to explain all your options. This is a rare coffeeshop that serves light meals. The juice is fresh, the music is easy, and the neighborhood is charming. Colorful murals with bright blue skies are all over the walls, creating a fresh and open feeling (loaner bongs, games, daily 10:00–20:00, 2 blocks from Anne Frank House at Eerste Bloemdwarsstraat 2, tel. 020/623-5639, www.paradoxamsterdam .demon.nl).

The Grey Area (AE+A, Level 2—Moderately Accessible, two 10" entry steps, narrow door) is a cool, welcoming, and smoky hole-in-the-wall appreciated among local aficionados as winner of Amsterdam's Cannabis Cup awards. Judging by the proud autographed photos on the

wall, many famous Americans have dropped in. You're welcome to just nurse a bottomless cup of coffee (open Tue–Sun high noon to 20:00, closed Mon, between Dam Square and Anne Frank House at Oude Leliestraat 2, tel. 020/420-4301, www.greyarea.nl, run by 2 friendly Americans, Steven and Jon—who know the value of a bottomless cup of coffee).

Coffee Shop Relax (AE+A, AI, Level 2—Moderately Accessible, two 5" entry steps) is simply the neighborhood pub serving a different drug. It's relaxed and has a helpful staff and homey atmosphere, with plants, couches, and bar seating. The great, straightforward menu chalked onto the board details what it has to offer (daily 10:00–24:00, a bit out of the way, but a pleasant Jordaan wander to Binnen Orangestraat 9).

Siberie Coffeeshop (AE, AI, ♥, Level 2—Moderately Accessible, lots of room) is central, but feels cozy, with a friendly canalside ambience (daily 11:00–23:00, Internet access, helpful staff, fun English menu that explains the personality of each item, Brouwersgracht 11, www.siberie .net).

La Tertulia (AE, AI, ♥, Level 2—Moderately Accessible, one wheelchair-accessible table near entry door) is a sweet little mother-and-daughter-run place with pastel decor and a cheery terrarium ambience (Tue–Sat 11:00–19:00, closed Sun–Mon, sandwiches, brownies, games, Prinsengracht 312, www.coffeeshopamsterdam.com).

The Bulldog (Level 3—Minimally Accessible) is the high-profile, leading touristy chain of coffeeshops. These establishments are young but welcoming, with reliable selections. They're pretty comfortable for green tourists wanting to just hang out for a while. The flagship branch, in a former police station right on Leidseplein, is very handy, offering fun outdoor seating where you can watch the world skateboard by (daily 9:00–1:00 in the morning, Leidseplein 17, tel. 020/625-6278, www.bulldog.nl). They opened up their first café (on the canal near the Old Church in the Red Light District) in 1975.

Rookies (AE, AI, Level 2— Moderately Accessible), a block east of Leidseplein along "Restaurant Row," is one of the rare coffeeshops that sells individual, pre-rolled, decent-quality joints of pure marijuana—with no tobacco (€5.50, daily 10:00–1:00 in the morning, Fri-Sat until 3:00 in the morning, Korte Leidsedwarsstraat 14).

The Dampkring (AE, AI, Level 2—Moderately Accessible) is one of very few coffeeshops that also serve alcohol. It's a high-profile and busy place, filled with a young clientele, but the owners still take the time to explain what they offer. Scenes from the movie *Ocean's Twelve* were filmed here (daily 11:00–1:00 in the morning, close to Spui at Handboogstraat 29).

Smartshops

These business establishments (one is listed on page 459) sell "natural" drugs that are legal. Many are harmless nutritional supplements, but they also sell hallucinogenic mushrooms, stimulants similar to Ecstasy, and strange drug cocktails rolled into joints. It's all perfectly legal, but if you've never taken drugs recreationally, don't start here.

NIGHTLIFE

Amsterdam hotels serve breakfast until 11:00 because so many people—

visitors and locals—live for nighttime in Amsterdam.

On summer evenings, people flock to the main squares for drinks at outdoor tables. Leidseplein is the glitziest, surrounded by theaters, restaurants, and nightclubs. The slightly quieter Rembrandtplein (with adjoining Thorbeckeplein) is the center of gay discos. Spui features a full city block of bars. And Nieuwmarkt, on the east edge of the Red Light District, is a bit rough, but is probably the most local.

The Red Light District (particularly Oudezijds Achterburgwal) is less sleazy at night and almost carnival-like, as the neon comes on and the streets fill with Japanese tour groups.

Information

Boom! and *Uitkrant* are two free publications (available at TIs and many bars) that list festivals and performances of theater, film, dance, cabaret, and live rock, pop, jazz, and classical music. The irreverent *Boom!*, which has the best lowdown on the youth and nightlife scene, is packed with practical tips and countercultural insights (includes €3 discount on the Boom Chicago R-rated comedy theater act described below). *Uitkrant* is in Dutch, but it's just a calendar of events, and anyone can figure out the name of the event and its date, time, and location.

There's also *What's On in Amsterdam, Time Out Amsterdam,* the Thursday edition of many Dutch papers, and the *International Herald Tribune*'s special Netherlands inserts (all sold at newsstands).

The Last Minute Ticket Shop (**AE, AI,** Level 2—Moderately Accessible) at Stadsschouwburg Theater (Leidseplein 26, tel. 0900-0191, www.lastminuteticketshop.nl) is the best one-stop-shopping box office for theater, classical music, and major rock shows. They also sell same-day (after 12:00), half-price tickets to select shows.

Music

You'll find classical music at the Concertgebouw (**AE, AI, AT,** Level 1—Fully Accessible; free 12:30 lunch concerts on Wed, at far south end of Museumplein, tel. 020/671-8345, www.concertgebouw.nl) and at the former Beurs on Damrak (**AE, AI,** Level 2—Moderately Accessible). For opera and dance, try the new opera house on Waterlooplein (**AE, AI,** Level 2—Moderately Accessible; tel. 020/551-8100). In the summer, Vondelpark hosts open-air concerts.

Two rock music (and hip-hop) clubs near Leidseplein are Melkweg (**AE, AI, AL, AT,** Level 1—Fully Accessible; Lijnbaansgracht 234a, tel. 020/531-8181, www.melkweg.nl) and Paradiso (Level 4—Not Accessible; Weteringschans 6, tel. 020/626-4521, www.paradiso.nl). They present big-name acts that you might recognize if you're younger than I am.

The nearby town of Haarlem offers free pipe organ concerts on Tuesdays in summer at its 15th-century church, the Grote Kerk (at 20:15 mid-May–mid Oct, see page 469).

Comedy

Boom Chicago (AE, AI, AT, ♥, Level 1—Fully Accessible), an R-rated comedy improv act, was started 10 years ago by a group of Americans on a graduation tour. They have been entertaining tourists and locals alike ever since. The show is a series of rude, clever, and high-powered improvisational skits offering a raucous look at Dutch culture and local tourism (€18–20, 25 percent discount with *I amsterdam* Card, Sun–Fri at 20:15, Fri also at 23:30, Sat at 19:30 and 22:45, in Leidseplein Theater, Leidseplein 12, tel. 020/423-0101, www.boomchicago.nl). They do various shows: *Best of Boom* (a collection of their greatest hits over the years), as well as new shows for locals and return customers. You'll sit in a 300-seat theater with optional meal and drink service.

Theater

Amsterdam is one of the world centers for experimental live theater (much of it in English). Many theaters cluster around the street called the Nes, which stretches south from Dam Square.

Movies

Catch modern movies in the 1920s setting of the classic Tuschinski Theater (**AE+A, AI,** Level 2—Moderately Accessible, four 7" entry steps; between Muntplein and Rembrandtplein, described on page 406). The Amsterdam Film Museum, which has some evening showings, is also worth checking out (**AE+A, AI+A,** Level 2—Moderately Accessible; Vondelstraat 69, near Vondelpark, tel. 020/589-1400, www.filmmuseum .nl, see page 405). It's not unusual for movies at many cinemas to be sold out—consider buying tickets during the day.

Museums

Several of Amsterdam's museums stay open late. The Anne Frank House is open daily until 21:00 in summmer (April–Aug) and until 19:00 the rest of the year. The Rijksmuseum and Van Gogh Museum are open on Fridays until 22:00. The Hash, Marijuana, and Hemp Museum is open daily until 22:00.

SLEEPING

Greeting a new day overlooking a leafy canalside scene—graceful bridges, historic gables, and bikes clattering on cobbles—is a fun part of experiencing Amsterdam. But Amsterdam is a tough city for budget accommodations, and any room under €140 will have rough edges. Still,

---

Sleep Code

(€1 = about $1.20, country code: 31, area code: 020)
S = Single, **D** = Double/Twin, **T** = Triple, **Q** = Quad, **b** = bathroom,
s = shower only. Nearly everyone speaks English in the Netherlands.
Credit cards are accepted, and prices include breakfast and tax unless
otherwise noted. Where I've listed a range of prices, the actual price
depends on the season.

---

you can sleep well and safely in a great location for €80 per double. I've also listed some fully accessible splurges.

Amsterdam is jammed during convention periods, Queen's Day (usually April 30), and on summer weekends. Many hotels will not take weekend bookings for people staying fewer than three nights.

Parking in Amsterdam is even worse than driving. You'll pay €32 a day to park safely in a garage—which can be blocks from your hotel.

If you'd rather trade big-city action for small-town coziness, consider sleeping in Haarlem, 15 minutes away by train (see page 464).

Near the Train Station
Level 1—Fully Accessible
Hotel Luxer (AE, AI, AL, AR, AB), near Central Station and just around the corner from the Red Light District, is a cozy, modestly modern, English-style hotel. Two of its 47 rooms are adapted (Db-€90–130, Warmoesstraat 11, tel. 020/330-3205, fax 020/330-3206, www.hotelluxer.com, info@hotelluxer.com).

Albus Grand Hotel (AE, AI, AL, AR, AB, ♥) is a modern yet warm and elegant three-star hotel (with four-star amenities) that offers a friendly welcome and excellent value. It's centrally located just off Rembrandt Square near the Flower Market (Db-€135–180, breakfast not included, Vijzelstraat 49, tel. 020/530-6215, fax 020/530-6299, www.albusgrandhotel.com, info@albusgrandhotel.com). There are several adapted rooms for full accessibility.

Swissôtel Amsterdam (AE, AI, AL, AR, AB, ♥) is a centrally located, stylish, modern boutique hotel with 109 rooms—two of them

Amsterdam Hotels

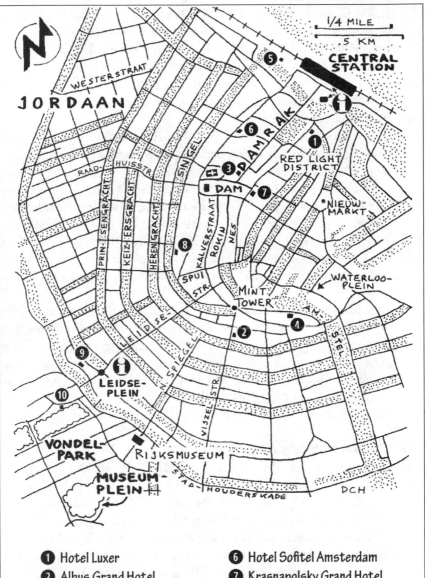

1. Hotel Luxer
2. Albus Grand Hotel
3. Swissôtel Amsterdam & Hotel Amsterdam
4. Best Western Eden Hotel
5. Ibis Amsterdam Hotel
6. Hotel Sofitel Amsterdam
7. Krasnapolsky Grand Hotel
8. NH City Center
9. Hotel Maas
10. Stayokay Vondelpark Hostel

adapted—and a fully accessible restaurant (Db-€125–360, breakfast-€17.50, Damrak 92, tel. 020/522-3344, fax 020/522-3223, http://amsterdam.swissotel.com, ask-us.amsterdam@swissotel.com).

Best Western Eden Hotel (AE, AI, AL, AR, AB) is close to the Flower Market on a canal near Rembrandt Square (Db-€135–180, Amstel 144, tel. 020/530-7888, fax 020/624-2946, res.eden@hotelgroup.com). There is one fully adapted room and five other ground-floor rooms that are suitable for wheelchair users.

Ibis Amsterdam Hotel (AE, AI, AL, AR, AB) is a modern and efficient, 187-room place towering over the station and a multistory bicycle garage. It offers a central location, comfort, and good value, without a hint of charm (Db-€122, Qb-€179, €10 extra Fri–Sat, skip breakfast and save €15 per person, check Web site for deals, book long in advance, air-con, smoke-free floor, Stationsplein 49, tel. 020/638-9999, fax 020/620-0156, www.ibishotel.com, h1556-fo@accor-hotels.com). When business is slow, they often rent rooms to same-day drop-ins for €105. The hotel has one fully adapted room (#701) with an adapted bathroom and shower.

Hotel Sofitel Amsterdam (AE, AI, AL, AR, AB) is an upscale modern chain hotel tastefully set in a restored 17th-century building just off Dam Square. Everything is first-class—including the prices. They have an excellent central location, a restaurant and bar, an adapted room for full accessibility, and all the top-end amenities to make your stay comfortable (Db-€255–305, Nieuwezijds Voorburgwal 67, tel. 020/627-5900, fax 020/623-8932, h1159@accor-hotels.com).

Level 2—Moderately Accessible

Hotel Amsterdam (AE, AI, AL, AR+A, AB+A, ♥), on Dam Square, is large and well-maintained, combining modern comforts with a historic location (Db-€185–210, Damrak 93–94, tel. 020/555-0666, fax 020/620-4716, www.hotelamsterdam.nl, info@hotelamsterdam.nl). Even though the rooms have not been adapted, they are suitable for wheelchair users. The hotel has hosted wheelchair users in the past, and the staff is eager to offer assistance. The hotel also has a fully accessible restaurant.

Between Dam Square and the Anne Frank House
Level 1—Fully Accessible

Krasnapolsky Grand Hotel (AE, AI, AL, AR, AB), not to be confused with the Grand Hotel next door, is over 130 years old, but has been modernized to include one wheelchair-accessible room (flexible rates, Db-€140–200, Dam 9, tel. 020/554-9111, fax 020/622-8607, www.nh-hotels.com, nhkrasnapolsky@nh-hotels.nl). They welcome wheel-chair users, and the staff is ready to assist as needed. The adapted room includes a fully wheelchair-accessible toilet and shower. The hotel also has two wheelchair-accessible restaurants, with an accessible toilet nearby.

Leidseplein Neighborhood

The area around Amsterdam's rip-roaring nightlife center (Leidseplein) is colorful, comfortable, and convenient. These places are within a few blocks of Leidseplein, but in generally quiet and characteristic settings.

Level 1—Fully Accessible

NH City Center (AE, AI, AL, AR, AB) is antique on the outside, fresh and trendy on the inside. The hotel's 289 rooms (one of them fully adapted) put you in the heart of the shopping and close to museum areas (Db-€110–150, Spuistraat 288-292, tel. 020/420-4545, fax 020/430-4300, www.nh-hotels.com, nhcitycentre@nh-hotels.com).

Hotel Maas (AF, AI, AL, AR, AB) is a big, quiet, and stiffly hotelesque place. Though it's on a busy street rather than a canal, it's a handy option (S-€99, D-€95, Db-€145, suite-€205, prices vary with view and room size, extra person-€20, hearty breakfast, elevator; tram #1, #2, or accessible #5 from station; Leidsekade 91, tel. 020/623-3868, fax 020/622-2613, www.hotelmaas.nl, info@hotelmaas.nl). They have a few adapted rooms and are welcoming to wheelchair users.

Stayokay Vondelpark (AE, AI, AL, AR, AB, ♥) is Amsterdam's top hostel (€19.50–27 per bed, D-€68–80, family rooms, higher prices are for March–Oct, non-members pay €2.50 extra, cash only, lots of school groups, 4–20 beds per room, lockers, right on Vondelpark at Zandpad 5, tel. 020/589-8996, fax 020/589-8955, www.stayokay.com). With three adapted rooms (including roll-in showers), this hostel prides itself on its accessibility.

EATING

Traditional Dutch food is basic and hearty, with lots of bread, cheese, soup, and fish. Lunch and dinner are served at American times (roughly 12:00–14:00 and 18:00–21:00).

Dutch treats include cheese, pancakes *(pannenkoeken)*, gin *(jenever)*, light, pilsner-type beer, and "syrup waffles" *(stroopwafel)*.

Experiences you owe your tongue in Holland: trying a raw her-ring at an outdoor herring stand, lingering over coffee in a "brown café," sipping an old *jenever* with a new friend, and consuming an

Indonesian feast—a *rijsttafel*.

Budget Tips: Get a sandwich to go and munch a canalside picnic. Sandwiches *(broodjes)* of delicious cheese on fresh bread are cheap at snack bars, delis, and *broodjes* restaurants. Ethnic fast-food stands abound, offering a variety of meats wrapped in pita bread. Easy to buy at grocery stores, yogurt in the Netherlands (and throughout Northern Europe) is delicious and often drinkable right out of its plastic container.

Types of Eateries

Any place labeled "restaurant" will serve full meals for lunch or dinner. But there are other places to fill the tank.

An *eetcafé* is a simple restaurant serving basic soups, salads, sandwiches, and traditional meat-and-potatoes meals in a generally comfortable but no-nonsense setting.

A *salon de thé* serves tea and coffee, yes, but also croissants, pastries, and sandwiches for a light brunch, lunch, or afternoon snack.

Cafés are all-purpose establishments, serving light meals at mealtimes and coffee, drinks, and snacks the rest of the day and night. *Bruin* cafés ("brown cafés," named for their nicotine-stained walls) are usually a little more bar-like, with dimmer lighting, wood paneling, and more tobacco smoke.

A *proeflokaal* is a bar (with snacks) for tasting wine, spirits, or beer.

Coffeeshop is the code word for an establishment where marijuana is sold and consumed, though most also offer drinks and munchies, too (for details, see "Smoking" on page 419).

There's no shortage of take-out places serving fast food, sandwiches, and all kinds of quick ethnic fare.

No matter what the type of establishment you choose, expect it to be *gezellig*—a much-prized Dutch virtue, meaning an atmosphere of relaxed coziness.

Etiquette and Tipping

The Dutch are easygoing. Pay as you go or pay after? Usually it's your choice. Tip or don't tip? Your call. Wait for table service or order at the bar? Whatever you do, you won't be scolded for your *faux pas*, as you might be in France or Italy. Dutch establishments are *gezellig*. Still, here are some guidelines:

- Tipping is not necessary in restaurants (15 percent service is usually already included in the menu price), but a tip of about 5 percent is a nice reward for good service. In bars, rounding up to the next euro ("keep the change") is appropriate if you get table service, rather than order at the bar.
- When ordering drinks in a café or bar, you can just pay as you go (especially if the bar is crowded), or wait until the end to settle up, as many locals do. If you get table service, take the cue from your waiter.
- Cafés with outdoor tables generally do not charge more if you sit outside (unlike in France or Italy).
- Expect tobacco smoke in any establishment.
- Waiters constantly say *"Alstublieft"* (AHL-stoo-bleeft). It's a catch-all polite word meaning, "please," "here's your order," "enjoy," and "you're welcome." You can respond with a thank you by saying, "Dank u wel" (dahnk oo vehl).

Typical Meals

Breakfast: Breakfasts are big by continental standards—bread, meat, cheese, and maybe an egg or omelet. Hotels generally put out a buffet spread, including juice and cereal.

Lunch: Simple sandwiches are called *broodjes* (most commonly made with cheese and/or ham). An open-face sandwich of ham and cheese topped with two fried eggs is an *uitsmijter* (OUTS-mi-ter). Soup is popular for lunch.

Snacks and Take-out Food: Small stands sell french fries *(frites)* with mayonnaise; raw or marinated herring; falafel (fried chickpea balls in pita bread); *shoarmas* (lamb tucked in pita bread); and *doner kebabs* (Turkish version of a *shoarma*). Delis have deep-fried croquettes *(kroketten)*.

Dinner: It's the biggest meal of the day, consisting of meat or seafood with boiled potatoes, cooked vegetables, and a salad. Hearty stews are served in winter. These days, many people eat more vegetarian fare.

Sweets: Try *poffertjes* (small, sugared doughnuts without holes), *pannenkoeken* (pancakes with fruit and cream), *stroopwafels* (syrup waffles), and *appelgebak* (apple pie).

Local Specialties

Cheeses: Edam (covered with red wax) or Gouda (HOW-dah). Gouda can be young or old: *jong* is mellow, and *oude* is salty, crumbly, and strong, sometimes seasoned with cumin or cloves.

French Fries: Commonly served with mayonnaise (ketchup and curry sauce are often available) on a paper tray or in a newspaper cone. Flemish *(Vlaamse) frites* are made from whole potatoes, not pulp.

Haring **(herring):** Fresh, raw herring, marinated or salted, often served with onions or pickles, sometimes with sour cream, on a thick, soft, white bun.

Hutspot: Hearty meat stew with mashed potatoes, onions, and carrots, especially popular on winter days.

Kroketten **(croquettes):** Log-shaped rolls of meats and vegetables (kind of like corn dogs) breaded and deep-fried, such as *bitterballen* (meatballs), *frikandelen* (sausage), or *vlammetjes* (spring rolls).

Pannenkoeken: Either sweet dessert pancakes or crêpe-like dinner pancakes.

Ethnic Foods

If you're not in the mood for meat and potatoes, sample some of Amsterdam's abundant ethnic offerings.

Indonesian (Indisch): The tastiest "Dutch" food is Indonesian, from the former colony. Find any Indisch restaurant and experience a *rijsttafel* (rice table). With as many as 30 spicy dishes and a big bowl of rice (or noodles), a *rijsttafel* can be split and still fill two hungry tourists. *Nasi rames* is a cheaper, smaller version of a *rijsttafel*. Another popular dish is *bami goreng*—stir-fried noodles served with meat, vegetables, and *rijsttafel* items. *Nasi goreng* is like *bami,* but comes with fried rice. *Saté* is skewered meat, and *gado-gado* consists of steamed vegetables and hard-boiled eggs with peanut sauce. Among the most common sauces are peanut, red chili *(sambal),* and dark soy.

Middle Eastern: Try a *shoarma* (roasted lamb with garlic in pita bread, served with bowls of different sauces), falafel, gyros, or a *doner kebab.*

Surinamese (Surinaamse): Surinamese cuisine is a mix of Caribbean and Indonesian influences, featuring *roti* (spiced chicken wrapped in a tortilla) and rice (white or fried) served with meats in sauces (curry and spices). Why Surinamese food in Amsterdam? In 1667, Holland traded New York City ("New Amsterdam") to Britain in exchange for the small country of Surinam (which borders Guyana on the northeast coast of South America). For the next three centuries, Surinam (renamed Dutch Guyana) was a Dutch colony, which is why it has indigenous Indians,

Creoles, and Indonesian immigrants who all speak Dutch. When Surinam gained independence in 1975, 100,000 Surinamese emigrated to Amsterdam, sparking a rash of Surinamese fast-food outlets.

Drinks

Beer: Order "a beer," and you'll get a *pils,* a light lager/pilsner-type beer in a 10-ounce glass with a thick head leveled off with a stick. (Typical brands are Heineken, Grolsch, Oranjeboom, and Amstel.) A common tap beer is Palm Speciale, an amber ale served in a stemmed, wide-mouth glass. Belgian beers are popular, always available in bottles and sometimes on tap. *Witte* (white) beer is light-colored and summery, sometimes served with a lemon slice (it's like American Hefeweizen, but yeastier).

Jenever: This is Dutch gin made from juniper berries. *Jong* (young) is sharper; *oude* (old) is mellow. Served chilled, *jenever* (yah-NAY-ver) is meant to be chugged with a *pils* chaser (this combination is called a *kopstoot*—head-butt). While cheese gets harder and sharper with age, *jenever* grows smooth and soft. Old *jenever* is best.

Liqueur: You'll find a variety of local fruit brandies and cognacs.

Wine: Dutch people drink a lot of fine wine, but it's almost all imported.

Coffee: The Dutch love their coffee, enjoying many of the same drinks (espresso, cappuccino) served in American or Italian coffee shops. Coffee usually comes with a small spice cookie. A *koffie verkeerd* (fer-KEERT, "coffee wrong") is an espresso with a lot of steamed milk.

Soft Drinks: You'll find the full array.

Orange Juice: Many cafés/bars have a juicer for making fresh-squeezed orange juice.

Water: The Dutch (unlike many Europeans) drink tap water with meals, but many prefer mineral water, still or sparkling (Spa brand is popular).

Restaurants

Of Amsterdam's thousand-plus restaurants, no one knows which are best. I'd pick an area and explore. The rowdy food ghetto thrives around Leidseplein; wander along Leidsedwarsstraat, Restaurant Row. The area around Spui canal and that end of Spuistraat is also trendy and not as noisy. For fewer crowds and more charm, find something in the Jordaan district. Most hoteliers keep a reliable eating list for their neighborhood and know which places keep their travelers happy.

Unless otherwise noted (by **AT** or **AT+A**), these restaurants do *not* have accessible toilets.

Amsterdam Restaurants and Coffeeshops

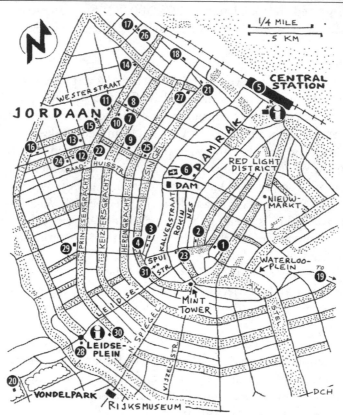

1. Atrium University Cafeteria
2. Restaurant Kapitein Zeppos
3. Restaurant Haesje Claes
4. Rest. Kantjil en de Tijger
5. Stationsrestauratie
6. Brasserie Rest. de Roode Leeuw
7. Café 't Kalfje & Ruhe Delicatessen
8. Café de Klepel
9. Restaurant de Luwte
10. The Pancake Bakery
11. De Bolhoed
12. De Groene Lantaarn
13. Café Restaurant de Reiger
14. Café 't Papeneiland
15. Café 't Smalle
16. Restaurant Vliegende Schotel
17. Catering Small World

18. Toscana Italian Restaurant
19. To Rest. Plancius & Taman Sari Rest.
20. Café Vertigo
21. Stubbe's Haring
22. Wil Ganstraa's Frites
23. New York Pizza

Coffeeshops
24. Paradox
25. The Grey Area
26. Coffee Shop Relax
27. Siberie Coffeeshop
28. The Bulldog
29. La Tertulia
30. Rookies
31. The Dampkring

Near Spui, in the Center

The first four places cluster along the colorful, student-filled Grimburgwal lane, near the intersection of Spui and Rokin (midway between Dam Square and the Mint Tower).

Atrium University Cafeteria (AE, AI, AT, Level 1—Fully Accessible) feeds students and travelers well at great prices. Enjoy the budget eats among all the Amsterdam University students (€6 meals, Mon–Fri 11:00–15:00 & 17:00–19:30, closed Sat–Sun, from Spui, roll or stroll west down Landebrug Steeg past canalside Café 't Gasthuys 3 blocks to Oudezijds Achterburgwal 237, go through arched doorway on the right; tel. 020/525-3999). Once inside, find the Manager's Office and ask to have the gate to the food lines unlocked, and if needed, the key to the adapted toilet.

Restaurant Kapitein Zeppos (AE, AI, Level 2—Moderately Accessible, one 2" entry step, double doors open for easier access), named for an old-time Belgian TV star, serves French-Dutch food in dressy yet unpretentious 1940s ambience. The light lunch specials—soups and sandwiches—cost €5–10. Dinner plates go for around €20 (€30 *menu*, daily 11:00–15:30 & 17:30–23:00, good Belgian beer on tap, just off Grimburgwal at Gebed Zonder End 5, tel. 020/624-2057).

Restaurant Haesje Claes (AE, AI, Level 2—Moderately Accessible) is popular with tour groups for traditional Dutch cooking in the center. It's the Dutch equivalent of TGI Friday's: big, with fast service, edible food, and reasonable prices (€20 *menu*, daily 12:00–22:00, Spuistraat 275, tel. 020/624-9998). The area around it is a huge and festive bar scene. Wheelchair access is through the entrance at Nieuwezijds Voorburgwal 320 or through the door on the side between the buildings. The area around the restaurant is a huge and festive bar scene.

Restaurant Kantjil en de Tijger (AE, AI, Level 2—Moderately Accessible) is a plain yet thriving place, full of happy eaters who know a good value. The food is purely Indonesian; the waiters are happy to explain your many enticing options. Their three *rijsttafels* (traditional "rice tables" with 11 dishes) range €20–30 per person (ask for a description of each). While they are designed for two, there's plenty of food for more. Their mini-*rijsttafel* (*Nasi Rames*—with rice, and *Bami Rames*—with noodles) will fill you memorably for €13 (daily 16:30–22:30, reserve on weekends, mostly indoor with a little outdoor seating, non-smoking section, Spuistraat 291, tel. 020/620-0994).

Kantjil To Go (AE, AI, Level 2—Moderately Accessible) is a tiny take-out bar serving up inexpensive Indonesian fare (€4–6 meals, vegetarian specials, daily 12:00–21:00, storefront at Nieuwezijds Voorburgwal

342, connected through a back hallway to main sit-down restaurant listed directly above, tel. 020/620-3074).

In the Train Station

Stationsrestauratie (**AE, AI, AT,** Level 1—Fully Accessible) is a surprisingly good budget, self-service option inside the station on platform 2 (daily 8:00–20:00). The entire platform 2 is lined with eateries, including the tall, venerable, 1920s-style First Class Grand Café. Many of the restaurants are wheelchair-accessible. There is one adapted toilet (in the Balcon restaurant).

Near Dam Square

Brasserie Restaurant de Roode Leeuw (**AE, AI, AT,** Level 1—Fully Accessible, hotel receptionist has key for accessible toilet) offers a respite from the crush of Damrak. Choose the restaurant in back (finer service and tablecloths, higher prices) or the brasserie in front (casual, simpler menu from same kitchen, better people-watching on the Damrak). Either way, you'll get a menu filled with traditional Dutch food, good service, and the company of plenty of tourists (restaurant: €18–23 entrées, €30 for a 3-course *menu* with lots of intriguing choices; brasserie: €10–13 entrées; daily 12:00–22:00, Damrak 93-94, tel. 020/555-0666).

Near the Anne Frank House and in the Jordaan District

Nearly all of these places are within a few scenic blocks of the Anne Frank House, providing handy lunches and atmospheric dinners in Amsterdam's most characteristic neighborhood. The area is filled with enchanting little restaurants. But be warned that it's especially difficult to find a truly accessible place (with an accessible toilet) here.

Café 't Kalfje (**AE, AI,** Level 2—Moderately Accessible, narrow front door but most wheelchairs can squeak through) is a small, inviting eatery run by knowledgeable and friendly Chef Emiel. Prices won't break the bank, and the diversity of his menu changes with his moods (3-course *menu* for €19.50, entrées for €8–15, daily 18:00–1:00 in the morning, Prinsenstraat 5, tel. 020/626-3370).

Café de Klepel (**AE, AI,** Level 2—Moderately Accessible) is a friendly neighborhood hangout where locals come to read the paper, have a smoke, talk about the weather, and linger over a drink. Only 14 meals a day are lovingly created in Madame's tiny kitchen. Come early if you want to get one of her fine dinners (€9–10 meals, daily 16:00–1:00 in the morning, Prinsenstraat 22, tel. 020/623-8244).

Restaurant de Luwte (**AE+A, AI,** Level 2—Moderately Accessible, one 2" entry step) is a romantic place, on a picturesque street overlooking a canal, with lots of candles, a muted but fresh modern interior, a few cool outdoor canalside tables, and French Mediterranean cuisine (€20 entrées, €32 for a 3-course *menu*, big dinner salads for €16, non-smoking section, daily 18:00–22:00, Leliegracht 26–28, tel. 020/625-8548, Marko). In the daytime (daily 12:00–15:00), a second team of owners is on duty—operating a casual and colorful *eetcafé* serving great food (but only in the tiny bar section of the restaurant). Even during the day, the atmosphere is mellow candlelight, and the price is a fraction of what you pay at night (€5–11 lunches).

The Pancake Bakery (**AE+A, AI,** Level 3—Minimally Accessible, staff will assist with three 7" entry steps) serves good pancakes in a nothing-special, family atmosphere. The menu features a fun selection of ethnic-themed pancakes—including Indonesian, for those who want two experiences in one (€8–12 pancakes, 25 percent discount with *I amsterdam* card, splitting is OK, daily 12:00–21:30, Prinsengracht 191, tel. 020/625-1333).

De Bolhoed (**AE, AI,** Level 2—Moderately Accessible) serves serious vegetarian and vegan food in a colorful setting that Buddha would dig (€15 meals, light lunches, daily 12:00–22:00, serious dinners from 17:00, Prinsengracht 60, tel. 020/626-1803).

De Groene Lantaarn (**AE, AI+A,** Level 3—Minimally Accessible, six 6" steps with railing after entry) is fun for fondue. The menu offers fish, meat, and cheese (Dutch and Swiss) with salad and fruit for €17–25 (Thu–Sun from 18:00, closed Mon–Wed, a few blocks into the Jordaan at Bloemgracht 47, tel. 020/620-2088).

Café Restaurant de Reiger (**AE+A,** Level 3—Minimally Accessible, three 8" entry steps and small doorway) must offer the best cooking of any *eetcafé* in the Jordaan. It's famous for its fresh ingredients and delightful bistro ambience. In addition to an English menu, ask for a translation of the €15–18 daily specials on the chalkboard. The café, which is crowded late and on weekends, takes no reservations, but you're welcome to have a drink at the bar while you wait. While there's a non-smoking section in front, the energy is with the smokers in the back room (they're proud of their fresh fish, glass of house wine-€2.50, veggie options, daily 18:00–22:30, Nieuwe Leliestraat 34, tel. 020/624-7426).

Café 't Papeneiland (**AE+A, AI,** Level 2—Moderately Accessible, staff can assist with the one 7" entry step), a classic brown café with Delft tiles, an evocative old stove, and a stay-awhile perch overlooking a canal with welcoming benches, has been the neighborhood hangout since the 17th century (drinks but no food, overlooking northwest end of Prinsengracht at #2, tel. 020/624-1989). It feels a little exclusive; patrons who come here to drink and chat aren't eager to see it overrun by tourists. The café's name literally means "Papists' Island," since this was once a refuge for Catholics (there used to be an escape tunnel here for priests on the run).

Café 't Smalle (**AE, AI,** Level 2—Moderately Accessible) is extremely charming, with three zones where you can enjoy a light lunch or a drink: canalside, inside around the bar, and up some steep stairs in a quaint little loft. While the café is open daily until midnight, food (salads, soup, and fresh sandwiches) is served only at lunch from 12:00 to 17:00 (plenty of fine Belgian beers on tap and interesting wines by the glass posted, at Egelantiersgracht 12 where it hits Prinsengracht, tel. 020/623-9617).

Restaurant Vliegende Schotel (**AE, AI,** Level 2—Moderately Accessible, special accessible door available upon request) is a folksy, unvarnished little Jordaan eatery decorated with children's crayon art. Its cheap and fun, meatless menu features fish and vegetarian fare. Choose a table (I'd avoid the empty non-smoking section and eat with the regulars), and then order at the counter. Nothing trendy about this place—just locals who like vegetarian food and don't want to cook. Their €8 *Vliegende Schotel* salad is a vegetarian extravaganza (€8–11 entrées, wine by the glass, daily 17:00–23:00, Nieuwe Leliestraat 162, tel. 020/625-2041).

Catering Small World (**AE+A, AI,** Level 2—Moderately Accessible, one 3" entry step) is a cozy sandwich bar with good coffee, the best muffins in town, and only a few seats (€4–10 items, Mon–Sat 10:30–20:00, Sun 12:00–20:00, Binnen Oranjestraat 14).

Ruhe Delicatessen (**AE+A,** Level 2—Moderately Accessible), run for decades by Mr. Ruhe, is the perfect late-night deli for a quick, cheap picnic dinner. The front door is small, but he will come out and take your order if you tap on his window (daily 12:00–22:00, Prinsenstraat 13, tel. 020/626-7438).

Toscana Italian Restaurant (**AE+A, AI,** Level 2—Moderately Accessible) is the Jordaan's favorite place for good, inexpensive Italian, including pizza, in a woody Dutch-beer-hall setting (pizza-€4–8, pastas-€7, daily 16:00–24:00, Haarlemmerstraat 130, tel. 020/622-0353). This is a favorite place for local wheelchair users, and if you need help over the entry step, the staff will assist.

Near the Botanical Garden and Dutch Resistance Museum

Restaurant Plancius (AE, AI, Level 1—Fully Accessible, use door facing museum and sidewalk, accessible toilet in nearby museum), adjacent to the Dutch Resistance Museum, is a mod, handy spot for lunch. Its good indoor and outdoor seating make it popular with the broadcasters from the nearby local TV studios (creative breakfasts, light €4–8 lunches and €15–18 dinners, daily 10:00–22:00, Plantage Kerklaan 61a, tel. 020/330-9469).

Taman Sari Restaurant (AE, AI, Level 2—Moderately Accessible) is the local choice for Indonesian, serving hearty, quality €9.50 dinners and *rijsttafel* dinners for €16–22.50 (daily 17:00–23:00, Plantage Kerklaan 32, tel. 020/623-7130). They will seat a wheelchair user at their table near the front door to avoid steps.

Near Vondelpark

Café Vertigo (AE+A, AI, Level 2—Moderately Accessible, accessible outdoor tables, interior access through Film Museum with staff assistance) offers a fun selection of excellent soups and sandwiches. The service can be slow, but if you grab an outdoor table, you can watch the world spin by (daily 11:00–24:00, beneath Film Museum, Vondelpark 3, tel. 020/612-3021).

Munching Cheap

Traditional fish stands sell €3 herring sandwiches and other salty treats, usually from easy-to-understand photo menus. **Stubbe's Haring** (AE, AI, Level 1—Fully Accessible, just roll up to this little stand at the locks), where the Stubbe family has been selling herring for 100 years, is handy and well-established (Tue–Sat 10:00–18:00, closed Sun–Mon, at the locks where Singel canal arrives at the train station). Grab a sandwich and picnic canalside. There's another accessible herring stand called **Wil Ganstraa's Frites** at the Westerkerk around the corner from the Anne Frank House.

New York Pizza (AE, AI, Level 1—Fully Accessible) serves hearty €2.50 pizza slices that are much loved by local students (same price munched on a stool or to go; at Spui 2 just across from the end of Rokin Canal). Find another accessible New York Pizza at Leidsestraat 23.

TRANSPORTATION CONNECTIONS

Amsterdam's train-information center can require a long wait. Save lots of time by getting train tickets and information in a small-town station (such as Haarlem), at the airport upon arrival, or from a travel agency. Remember, you can use *strippenkaart* on any train that travels within the Netherlands.

You have two options for buying train tickets in the Netherlands: at a ticket window (costs €0.50 extra), or at an automated machine (no extra charge). Some machines have instructions only in Dutch, and you can pay in euros (no credit cards). Frustratingly, the newer machines—which have instructions in English—accept only Dutch debit cards (no cash, Visa, or MasterCard). If you're having trouble, visit the yellow information booth, or enlist the help of any official-looking employees (most wear portable computers with timetables) to help you with train departure times, or to navigate your way through the older, Dutch-only machine menus. If lines are short and frustration levels high, pay the extra €0.50 to buy your ticket at the window.

The easiest way to get train schedules is online. The German Rail site has comprehensive schedules for virtually anywhere in Europe (http://bahn.hafas.de/bin/query.exe/en). Or try the Dutch Rail site (www.ns.nl). For phone information, dial 0900-9292 for local trains or 0900-9296 for international trains (€0.50/min, daily 7:00–24:00, wait through recording and hold...hold...hold...).

From Amsterdam by Train to: Schiphol Airport (6/hr, 20 min, €3.40, have coins to buy from a machine to avoid lines, train usually departs from track 13a), **Haarlem** (6/hr, 15 min, €3.40 one-way, €6 same-day round-trip), **The Hague/Den Haag** (every 10 min, 45 min, may require switch in Leiden to get to main station), **Delft** (every 10 min, 50 min), **Arnhem** (2/hr, 75 min, transfer likely), **Rotterdam** (4/hr, 1 hr), **Brussels** (hrly, 3 hrs, €30–42.50), **Ostende** (hrly, 4 hrs, change in Antwerp), **Copenhagen** (hrly, 15 hrs, requires multiple transfers), **Frankfurt** (hrly, 4-5 hrs, some are direct, others involve transfer in Köln or Duisburg), **Munich** (7/day, 7–8 hrs, transfer in Frankfurt or Düsseldorf), **Bonn** (10/day, 3 hrs, some direct but most transfer in Köln), **Bern** (5/day, 9 hrs, 1 direct but most transfer in Mannheim)

To Paris: 5/day direct on fast Thalys train, 4 hrs; more with a transfer in Brussels, 5 hrs. For details, see "To Brussels and Amsterdam by Thalys Train," page 284.

To Bruges: Hourly, 3.5 hrs, transfer in Brussels or Antwerp's central station; transfer can be timed closely—be alert and check with conductor.

To London: 6–7/day, 6 hrs, with transfer to Eurostar Chunnel train in Brussels, Eurostar discounted with railpass, www.eurostar.com. For details on the Eurostar train, see page 158.

Amsterdam's Schiphol Airport

Schiphol (SKIP-pol) Airport, like most of Holland, is English-speaking, user-friendly, and below sea level.

Access: AE, AI, AL, AT, Level 1—Fully Accessible. Let the airline know in advance what your needs are. The airport offers a service called IHD (International Help for the Disabled) that specializes in assisting travelers with limited mobility. For more information on airport accessibility, call 020/316-1414 or visit www.ihd-schiphol.nl.

Information: Schiphol flight information (tel. 0900-7244-7465) can give you flight times and your airline's Amsterdam phone number for reconfirmation before going home (€0.45/min to climb through its phone tree—or visit www.schiphol.nl). To reach the airlines directly, call: KLM and Northwest, tel. 020/649-9123 or 020/474-7747; Martinair, tel. 020/601-1222; SAS, tel. 0900-746-63727; American Airlines, tel. 06/022-7844; British Air, tel. 023/554-7555; and easyJet, tel. 023/568-4880.

Services: The ABN/AMRO **banks** offer fair rates (in arrivals and lounge area). The GWK **public transit office** is located in Schiphol Plaza. Surf the **Internet** and make phone calls at the Communication Centre on the top level of lounge 2 (daily 6:00–20:00, behind customs—not available once you've left the security checkpoint). Convenient luggage **lockers** are at various points around the terminal—and a big bank of them is on the bottom floor—allowing you to leave your bag at the airport on a lengthy layover (both short-term and long-term lockers).

If you have extra time to kill at Schiphol, check out some **fine art,** actual Dutch Masters by Rembrandt, Vermeer, and others. The Rijksmuseum loans a dozen or so of its minor masterpieces from the Golden Age to the unique airport museum "Rijksmuseum Amsterdam Schiphol," a little art gallery behind the passport check at Holland Boulevard between piers E and F. Yes, this is really true (free, daily 7:00–20:00). To escape the crowds in the airport, follow signs for the *Panorama Terrace* to the third floor, where you'll find a quieter, locals-only cafeteria, a kids' play area, and, a view terrace where you can watch planes come and go while you nurse a coffee.

Transportation Connections: The most accessible way into either Amsterdam or Haarlem from the airport is by **taxi.** For information on calling an accessible taxi in Amsterdam, see page 396. The airport also has easy **train** connections with **Amsterdam** (**AE, AI,** Level 2—Moderately Accessible; every 10 min, 20 min, €3.40) and **Haarlem** (**AE, AI,** Level 2—Moderately Accessible; 4/hr, 40 min, transfer at Amsterdam-Sloterdijk, €4.55).

The airport has a train station of its own. You can validate your Eurailpass and hit the rails immediately, or, to stretch your railpass, buy an inexpensive ticket into Amsterdam today and start the pass later.

From Schiphol Airport by Train to: The Hague/Den Haag (2/hr, 30 min), **Delft** (4/hr, 45 min, transfer in The Hague or Leiden), **Rotterdam** (3/hr, 45 min). International trains to Belgium run every hour: **Brussels** (2.5 hrs), **Bruges** (3.25 hrs, change in Antwerp or Brussels).

Sleeping at Schiphol: Ibis Amsterdam Airport Hotel (**AE, AI, AL, AT, AR, AB,** Level 1—Fully Accessible) is a modern and efficient 644-room place. It offers close proximity to the airport, comfort, and good value (Db-€95–122, book long in advance, air-con, non-smoking rooms, Schipholweg 181, reservation tel. 020/502-5111, reception tel. 020/502-5100, fax 020/657-0199, www.ibishotel.com). This hotel has one wheelchair-accessible room, including an adapted bathroom and shower.

From the Airport to Haarlem: The big #300 **bus** is direct, stopping at Haarlem's train station and near the Market Square (4/hr, 40 min, €5.80—buy ticket from driver, or use 7 strips on your bus card, departs from lane B2 in front of airport). This bus is **AE, AI,** Level 1—Fully Accessible, but can take only one wheelchair user at a time.

From the Airport to Amsterdam: The Connexxion **shuttle bus** takes you to your hotel neighborhood; since there are various routes, ask the attendant which works best for your hotel (2/hr, 20 min, €11 one-way, €17.50 round-trip, one route stops at Westerkerk near Anne Frank House and many recommended hotels, bus to other hotels may cost a couple euros more, departs from lane A7 in front of airport, tel. 020/653-4975, www.airporthotelshuttle.nl). The standard buses are Level 2—Moderately Accessible (**AE+A,** must be able to transfer into bus), but if you reserve in advance, they can provide you with a fully adapted minivan (**AE, AI,** Level 1—Fully Accessible, may cost a few euros extra).

AMSTERDAM CITY ROLL OR STROLL

From the Train Station to the Rijksmuseum

Amsterdam today looks much as it did in its Golden Age, the 1600s. It's a retired sea captain of a city, still in love with life, with a broad outlook and a salty story to tell.

Take this barrier-free Dutch sampler tour from one end of the old center to the other, tasting all that Amsterdam has to offer along the way. It's your best single roll or stroll through Dutch clichés, hidden churches, surprising shops, thriving happy-hour hangouts, and eight centuries of history.

ORIENTATION

The tour starts at the central-as-can-be train station. You'll roll or stroll about three miles, heading down Damrak to Dam Square, continuing south down Kalverstraat to the Mint Tower, then wafting through the Bloemenmarkt (flower market), before continuing south to Leidseplein and swinging left to the Rijksmuseum. To return to Central Station, catch accessible tram #5 or #2 from the southwest corner of the Rijksmuseum.

If this tour proves too much to tackle all at once, consider breaking it up into easy-to-tackle chunks. Along the way, tour the museums that you find interesting and suitable to your level of personal mobility (I've listed accessibility details for each one).

You can find public toilets at fast-food places (generally €0.30, often accessible) and near the entrance to the Amsterdam History Museum (fully accessible). Beware of silent transport—trams and bikes. Stay off the tram tracks. If you're walking, keep off the bike paths and yield to bell-ringing bikers. If you're using a wheelchair, you may have to use these bike paths at times—do your best to avoid bikers.

THE TOUR BEGINS

Central Station

Here where today's train travelers enter the city, sailors of yore disembarked from seagoing ships to be met by street musicians, pickpockets, hotel-runners, and ladies carrying red lanterns. When the station was built (on reclaimed land) at the former harbor mouth, Amsterdam lost some of its harbor feel, but it's still a bustling port of entry.

Central Station, with warm red brick and prickly spires, is the first of several neo-Gothic buildings we'll see from the late 1800s, built during

Amsterdam's economic revival. One of the towers has a clock dial; the other tower's dial is a weathervane. Watch the hand twitch as the wind gusts.

As you emerge from the train station, the first thing you see is a mess. All the construction is for the new cultural center and library (left of station) and subway line (in front of station). The new north–south metro line (scheduled to open in 2011) will complement the existing east–west one. While it sounds like a fine idea, the billion euros being spent on it is considered riddled with corruption. The big, ugly building in the canal directly in front of the train station will eventually be sunk underground and become part of the subway station.

Beyond the construction, the city spreads out before you in a series of concentric canals. Ahead of you stretches the street called Damrak, leading to Dam Square, a half mile away. To the left of Damrak is the city's old *(oude)* side, to the right is the new *(nieuwe)*.

The big church towering above the old side (at about 10 o'clock) is St. Nicholas Church, built in the 1880s when Catholics—after about three centuries of oppression—were finally free to worship in public. The church marks the beginning of the Red Light District. The city's biggest bike garage, a multistory wonder, is on your right (in front of the Ibis Hotel).

• *We'll basically head south from here to the Rijksmuseum. The art museum and the station—designed by the same architect—stand like bookends holding the old town together. Follow the crowds south on Damrak, going along the right side of the street.*

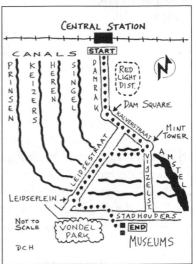

Damrak

You'll pass every Dutch cliché at the tourist shops: wooden shoes, plastic tulips, Heineken fridge magnets, and windmill saltshakers. Listen to a hand-cranked barrel organ. Order french fries (called *Vlaamse frites*, or Flemish fries, since they were invented in the Low Countries) and dip them in mayonnaise, not ketchup. Eating international cuisine (Indonesian *rijsttafel*, Argentine steak, Middle Eastern *shoarma*—pronounced SHWAHR mah) is like going local in cosmopolitan Amsterdam. And you'll find the city's most notorious commodity displayed at the Damrak Sex Museum (1st floor is moderately accessible—**AE, AI**—but upper level is not; see page 418).

The street was once a riverbed, where the Amstel River flowed north into the IJ (pronounced "eye") river behind today's train station. Both rivers then emptied into a vast inlet of the North Sea (the Zuiderzee), making Amsterdam a major seaport. Today, the Amstel is channeled into canals, its former mouth has been covered by Central Station, the North Sea inlet has been diked off to make an inland lake, and 100,000 ships a year reach the open waters by sailing west through the North Sea Canal.

Local landowners are concerned that the tunneling for the new subway line will cause their buildings to settle. The snoopy-looking white cameras mounted on various building corners (such as the Beurs) are monitoring buildings to check for settling.

• *The long brick building with the square clock tower, along the left side of Damrak, is the...*

Stock Exchange (Beurs)

Built with nine million bricks on about 5,000 tree trunks hammered into the marshy soil, the Beurs stands as a symbol of the city's long tradition as a trading town.

Back when "stock" meant whatever could be loaded and unloaded onto a boat, Amsterdammers gathered to trade. Soon, rather than trading goats, chickens, and kegs of beer, they were exchanging slips of paper and "futures" at one of the world's first stock exchanges. Traders needed moneychangers, who needed bankers, who made money by lending money...and Amsterdam of the 1600s became one of the world's first great capitalist cities, loaning money to free-spending kings, dukes, and bishops.

This impressive building, built in 1903 in a geometric, minimal, no-frills style, is one of the world's first "modern" (i.e., 20th-century-style) buildings, emphasizing function over looks. In 1984, the stock exchange moved next door (see the stock prices readout) to the Euronext complex—a joint, if overly optimistic, attempt by France, Belgium, and the Netherlands to compete with the power of Britain's stock exchange. The old Beurs building now hosts concerts and a museum for temporary exhibits.

Amsterdam still thrives as the center of Dutch businesses, such as Heineken, Shell Oil, Philips Electronics, KLM Airlines, and Unilever. Amsterdammers have always had a reputation for putting business above ideological differences, staying neutral while trading with both sides.

• *Damrak opens into...*

Dam Square

The city got its start right here around 1250, when fishermen in this marshy delta settled along the built-up banks of the Amstel River. They blocked the river with a *damme,* and created a small village called "Amstel-damme." Soon the fishermen were trading with German riverboats traveling downstream and with seafaring boats from Stockholm, Hamburg, and London. Dam Square was the center of it all.

The dam on the Amstel divided the *damrak* (meaning "outer harbor"—for sea traffic) from the *rokin* ("inner harbor"—for river traffic).
Land trade routes converged here as well, and a customs house stood here. Today, the Damrak and Rokin (roh-KEEN) are major roads, and the city's palace and major department stores face the square, where mimes, jugglers, and human statues mingle with locals and tourists. This is the historic heart of the city. As the symbolic center of the Netherlands, it's

Amsterdam City Roll or Stroll—First Half

8 Nes Street Theaters
9 De Drie Fleschjes Pub
10 Wynand Fockink Pub
11 Amsterdam Diamond Center
12 De Papegaai Hidden Catholic Church
13 Amsterdam History Museum, Courtyard & Civic Guard Gallery
14 Begijnhof
15 Spui Square
16 Rokin Street
17 Kalvertoren Mall (Viewpoint)
18 Vroom & Dreesman Store
19 Mint Tower
20 Tuschinski Theater
21 Rembrandtplein

1 Damrak Sex Museum
2 Stock Exchange
3 Royal Palace
4 New Church
5 Magna Plaza
6 Sinterklaas Plaque on ABN Amro Bank
7 National Monument

where political demonstrations begin and end.

Pan the square clockwise to see the following: the Royal Palace (the large domed building on the west side), the New Church (Nieuwe Kerk), an ABN Amro bank, Damrak, the proud old De Bijenkorf (literally, "The Beehive") department store, the Krasnapolsky Grand Hotel, the white, phallic obelisk of the National Monument, the Rokin, touristy Madame Tussaud's, and the entrance to pedestrian-only Kalverstraat (look for *Rabobank* sign).

Royal Palace

The name is misleading, since Amsterdam is one of the cradles of modern democracy. For centuries, this was the Town Hall of a self-governing community that prided itself on its independence and thumbed its nose at royalty. The current building, built in 1648, is appropriately classical (like the democratic Greeks), with a triangular pediment featuring— fittingly for Amsterdam—denizens of the sea cavorting with Neptune (with his green copper trident.)

After the city was conquered by the French, Napoleon imposed a monarchy on Holland, making his brother Louis the king of the Netherlands (1808). Louis used the city hall as his "royal palace," giving the building its current name. When Napoleon was defeated, the victorious powers dictated that the Netherlands remain a monarchy, under a noble Dutch family called the House of Orange. If the current Queen Beatrix is in town, this is, technically, her residence (thought it's currently under renovation, and closed to visitors through 2008; when open, it's Level 1—Fully Accessible). Amsterdam is the nominal capital of the Netherlands, but all governing activity—and the Queen's actual permanent home—are in The Hague (a city 30 miles southwest).

New Church (Nieuwe Kerk)

Access: AE, AI, AT, Level 1—Fully Accessible. The associated restaurant (to the right) is also fully accessible and has adapted toilets.

Cost and Hours: €8, covered by *I amsterdam* Card, Mon–Sat 10:00–18:00, Sun 13:00–18:00.

The Sight: The "New" Church is 600 years old (newer than the 700-year-old "Old" Church in the Red Light District). The sundial above the entrance once served as the city's official timepiece.

The church's bare, spacious, well-lit interior (often occupied by temporary art exhibits) looks quite different from the Baroque-encrusted churches found in the rest of Europe. In 1566, clear-eyed Protestant extremists throughout Holland marched into Catholic churches (like this once was), lopped off the heads of holy statues, stripped gold-leaf angels from the walls, urinated on Virgin Marys, and shattered stained-glass windows in a wave of anti-Catholic vandalism.

This iconoclasm (icon-breaking) of 1566 started an 80-year war against Spain and the Hapsburgs, leading finally to Dutch independence in 1648. Catholic churches like this one were converted to the new dominant religion, Calvinist Protestantism (today's Dutch Reformed Church). From then on, Dutch churches downplayed the "graven images" and "idols" of ornate religious art.

From just inside the door, you can get a free look at the 1655 organ (far left end, often encased in its painted wooden cupboard); the stained-glass window (opposite entrance) showing Count William IV giving the city its "XXX" coat of arms; and the window (over entrance) showing the inauguration of Queen Wilhelmina. She grew to become the steadfast center of Dutch Resistance during World War II.

This church is where many of the Netherlands' monarchs are married and all are crowned. In 1980, Queen Beatrix—Wilhelmina's granddaughter—said "I do" in the New Church. When Beatrix dies or retires, her son, Crown Prince Willem Alexander, will parade to the center of the church, sit in front of the golden choir screen, and—with TV lights glaring and flashbulbs popping—be crowned the next sovereign.

• *Looking between the Royal Palace and the New Church, you'll see the fanciful brick facade of the Magna Plaza shopping center. Back in Dam Square, on the wall of the ABN Amro bank, find the colorful little stone plaque of...*

Sinterklaas—St. Nicholas

Jolly old St. Nicholas (Nicolaas in Dutch) is the patron saint of seafarers (see the 3 men in a tub) and of Amsterdam, and is also the model for Sinterklaas—the guy we call Santa Claus. Every year in late November, Holland's Santa Claus arrives by boat near Central Station (from his legendary home in Spain), rides a white horse up Damrak with his servant, Peter (in blackface), and arrives triumphant in this square while thousands of kids cheer.

December 5, the feast day of St. Nicholas, is when the Dutch exchange presents and Sinterklaas leaves goodies in good kids' wooden shoes. (Smart kids maximize capacity by putting out big boots.) Many Dutch

celebrate Christmas on December 25 as well.

Around the corner on Damrak, the bank has an ATM and a chip-loader *(Oplaadpunt)*. The ATM is familiar, but what's that small key-pad next to it? It's for loading up the Dutch cash card—an attempt to eliminate the need for small change. With the keypad, the Dutch trans-fer money from their accounts onto a card with a computer chip. Then they can make purchases at stores by inserting the card into a pay-point, the way Americans buy gas from the pump.

National Monument

The obelisk, which depicts a crucified Christ, men in chains, and howling dogs, was built in 1956 as a WWII memo-rial. Now it's considered a monument for peace.

The Nazis occupied Holland from 1940 to 1945. They deported more than 100,000 Amsterdam Jews, driving many—includ-ing young Anne Frank and her fam-ily—into hiding. Near the end of the war, the "Hunger Winter" of 1944–1945 killed thousands and forced many to survive on tulip bulbs. Today, Dutch people in their 70s—whose growth-spurt years coincided with the Hunger Winter—are easy to identify, because they are uniformly short.

Circling the Square

You're at the center of Amsterdam. A few blocks to the east is the top of the Red Light District. Amsterdam is a world center for experimental theater, and several edgy theaters line the street called the Nes (stretch-ing south from Krasnapolsky Grand Hotel).

Office workers do afternoon happy hours at crowded bars that stock *jenevers* and liqueurs in wooden kegs. De Drie Fleschjes (**AE, AI,** Level 2—Moderately Accessible), a particularly casual pub, is tucked right behind the New Church. The more upscale Wynand Fockink (**AE, AI,** Level 2—Moderately Accessible; 100 yards down the alley along the right side of Hotel Krasnapolsky) serves fruit brandies produced in its adjoining distillery (which you can visit). Though the brew is bottled and distributed all over Holland, what you get here in the home-office bar is some of the best Fockink liqueur in the entire world.

At the Amsterdam Diamond Center (Level 4—Not Accessible; free, Mon–Sat 10:00–18:00, Sun 11:00–18:00, where Rokin street meets Dam Square), see cutters and jewelry-setters handling diamonds, plus some small educational displays and fake versions of big, famous stones. Since the 1500s, the city has been one of the world's diamond capitals. Eighty percent of industrial diamonds (for making drills and such) pass through here, as do many cut and polished jewels, like the Koh-I-Nohr diamond.

• *From Dam Square, head south (at* Rabobank *sign) on...*

Kalverstraat

This pedestrian-only street is lined with many familiar franchise stores and record shops. This has been a shopping street for centuries, and today it's

notorious among locals as *the* place for cheesy, crass materialism. For smaller and more elegant stores, try the adjacent district called De Negen Straatjes (literally, "The Nine Little Streets"), where 190 shops mingle by the canals (about 4 blocks west of Kalverstraat).

• *About 120 yards along (across from the McDonald's) is...*

De Papegaai Hidden Catholic Church (Petrus en Paulus Kerk)

Access: AE+A, AI, Level 2—Moderately Accessible. The wheelchair user can ring a bell to gain entry through the regular door instead of trying to get through the revolving door. The interior of the church is accessible, with flat aisles.

Cost and Hours: Free, daily 10:00–16:00.

The Sight: This Catholic church, while not exactly hidden (you found it), keeps a low profile, even now that Catholicism has been legalized in Amsterdam. In the late 1500s, with Protestants fighting Catholics and

City on a Sandbar

Amsterdam is built on millions of wooden pilings. The city was founded on unstable mud, which sits on stable sand. In the Middle Ages, buildings were made of wood, which rests lightly and easily on mud. But devastating fires repeatedly wiped out entire neighborhoods, so stone became the building material of choice. Stone is fire-resistant, but was too heavy for a mud foundation. For more support, pilings were driven 30 feet through the mud and into the sand. The Royal Palace sits upon 13,000 such pilings—still solid after 350 years. (The wood survives fine if kept wet and out of the air.) Since World War II, concrete, rather than wood, has been used for the pilings, with foundations driven 60 feet deep through the first layer of sand, through more mud, and into a second layer of sand. And today's biggest buildings have foundations sinking as much as 120 feet deep.

the Dutch fighting Spanish invaders, Amsterdam tried to stay neutral, doing business with all parties. Finally, in 1578, Protestant extremists (following the teachings of Reformer John Calvin) took political control of the city. They expelled Catholic leaders and bishops, outlawed the religion, and allied Amsterdam with anti-Spanish forces in an action known to historians as the Alteration.

For the next two centuries, Amsterdam's Catholics were driven underground. Catholicism was illegal but tolerated, as long as it was not practiced in public, but in humble, unadvertised places like this. (The stuffed parrot—*papegaai*—hanging in the nave refers to the house formerly on this site, with a parrot gable stone.)

Today, the church, which asks for a mere "15 minutes for God" *(een kwartier voor God)*, stands as a metaphor for how marginal religion has long been in highly commercial and secular Amsterdam.

• *Farther along (about 75 yards) at #92, where Kalverstraat crosses Wijde Kapel Steeg, look to the right at an archway leading to the...*

Courtyard of the Amsterdam History Museum

Access: Museum is **AE, AI, AT,** Level 1—Fully Accessible. The loft is Level 4—Not Accessible. The museum has wheelchair-accessible elevators (that do not go to the loft) and an adapted toilet (near the fully accessible David and Goliath café). Loaner wheelchairs are available.

Cost, Hours, Location: €6.50, covered by *I amsterdam* Card, Mon–Fri 10:00–17:00, Sat–Sun 11:00–17:00, Kalverstraat 92.

The Sight: On the arch is Amsterdam's coat of arms—a red shield with three Xs and a crown. Not a reference to the city's sex trade, the X-shaped crosses (which appear everywhere in the city) represent the crucifixion of St. Andrew, the patron saint of fishermen, and symbolize heroism, determination, and mercy. The crown dates to 1489, when Maximilian I (the Low Countries' first Hapsburg ruler and later Holy Roman Emperor) paid off a big loan from city bankers and, as thanks for

the cash, gave the city permission to use his prestigious trademark, the Hapsburg crown, atop its shield. The relief above the door (see photo), dated 1581, shows boys around a dove, reminding all who pass that this was an orphanage and asking for charity. Go inside.

The pleasant David & Goliath café (with a shady courtyard; **AE, AI, AT,** Level 1—Fully Accessible) is watched over by a giant statue of Goliath and a knee-high David (from 1650). In the courtyard are the lockers for the orphans' uniforms and an accessible pay toilet.

• *The courtyard leads to another courtyard with the best city history museum in town, the Amsterdam History Museum (access details above; for more information, see page 410). In between the two courtyards (on the left) is a free, glassed-in passageway lined with paintings, called the...*

Civic Guard Gallery (Schuttersgalerij)

In these group portraits from Amsterdam's Golden Age (early 1600s), look into the eyes of the frank, dignified men (and occasionally women) with ruffs and lace collars, who made Amsterdam the most prosperous city in Europe, sending trading ships to distant colonies and pocketing

interest from loans. The weapons they carry are mostly symbolic, since these "Civic Guards," who once protected the town (fighting the Spanish), had become more like fraternal organizations of business bigwigs.

Many paintings look the same in this highly stylized genre. Military companies often sit in two rows. Someone holds the company flag.

Captains wield pikes (axe-like weapons topped with spearhead-shaped tips), lieutenants hold partisans (pikes with sword-like tips), and others wield hatchet-headed halberds or muskets. Later group portraits showed "captains" of industry going about their work, dressed in suits, along with the tools of their trade—ledger books, quill pens, and money.

Everyone looks straight out, and every face is lit perfectly. Each paid for his own portrait and wanted it right. It took masters like Rembrandt and Frans Hals to take the starch out of the collars and compose more natural scenes.

• *The gallery offers a shortcut to the Begijnhof, 75 yards farther south. But if the gallery is closed, backtrack to Kalverstraat, continue south, then turn right on Begijnensteeg. Either route leads to the entrance of the walled courtyard called the...*

Begijnhof

Access: AE, AI, Level 1—Fully Accessible. The entrance on the east side of the courtyard has no steps. The courtyard has fully-accessible pathways. The hidden Catholic church (**AE+A, AI,** Level 2—Moderately Accessible) has large doors and two 2" steps, one on either side of the landing.

Cost, Hours, Location: Free, open daily 8:00–17:00 for "tourist visits" (groups and guided tours). At other times, be quiet and stick to the area near the churches. Don't photograph homes or the residents, and always remember that this is a private residence (on Begijnensteeg lane, just off Kalverstraat between #130 and #132). The English Reformed Church is sometimes open for tourists (free, open about 4 days a week 10:00–14:00 and always for English-speaking worshippers, Sun service at 10:30).

The Sight: This quiet courtyard (pronounced gutturally: buh-HHHINE-hof), lined with houses around a church, has sheltered women since 1346. This was for centuries the home of Beguines—women who removed themselves from the world at large to dedicate their lives to God. It literally was a "woman's island"—a circle of houses facing a peaceful courtyard, surrounded by water.

The Beguines' ranks swelled during the Crusades, when so many men took off, never to return, leaving society with an abundance of

single women. Later, women widowed by the hazards of overseas trade lived out their days as Beguines. Poor and rich women alike turned their backs on materialism and marriage to live here in Christian poverty. While obedient to a mother superior, the lay order of Beguines were not nuns. The Beguines were very popular in their communities for the unpretentious, simple, and Christ-like lives they led. They spent their days deep in prayer and busy with daily tasks—spinning wool, making lace, teaching, and caring for the sick and poor. In quiet seclusion, they inspired each other as well as their neighbors.

In 1578, when Catholicism was outlawed, the Dutch Reformed Church (and the city) took over many Catholic charities like this place. The last Beguine died in 1971, but this Begijnhof still provides subsidized housing to about a hundred needy single women (mostly Catholic seniors and students). The Begijnhof is just one of about 75 *hofjes* (housing projects surrounding courtyards) that dot Amsterdam.

Begin your visit at the statue of one of these charitable sisters. She faces the **wooden house** *(houten huys)* at #34. The city's oldest, it dates from 1477. Originally, the whole city consisted of wooden houses like this one. To the left of the house is a display of carved gable stones that once adorned housefronts and served as street numbers (and still do at #19 and #26, the former mother superior's house). Inside the covered passageway at the south end of the square (near the oldest house), find images of  things forbidden in this all-female enclave—roosters (male), dogs (dirty), and male humans over age three (dangerous).

The brick-faced **English Church** (Engelse Kerk, from 1420) was the Beguine church until 1607, when it became Anglican. The Pilgrims (strict Protestants), fleeing persecution in England, stopped here in tolerant Amsterdam and prayed in this church before the *Mayflower* carried them to religious freedom at Plymouth Rock in America. If the church is open (sporadic hours), go inside to see a stained-glass window of the Pilgrims praying before boarding the *Mayflower* (far end), an old pew they may have sat on (right wall), and a 1763 Bible (on the altar) with lot*f* of old-*f*tyle *ff*'s.

The "hidden" **Catholic Church** (notice the painted-out windows, 2nd and 3rd floors) faces the English Church. Amsterdam's oppressed 17th-century Catholics, who refused to worship as Protestants, must have eagerly awaited the day when, in the 19th century, they were legally allowed to say Mass. Go inside (through the low-profile doorway), pick up an English brochure near the entry, and rap softly on a "marble" column.

Today, Holland is still divided religiously, but without the bitterness. Roughly a third of the population is Catholic, a third Protestant...and a third list themselves as "unchurched."

• *Backtrack to busy Kalverstraat, turn right, and continue south. Pause at the intersection with Spui straat and look to the right.*

Spui and the Rokin

A block to the right is the square called **Spui** (spow, rhymes with "cow"). Lined with cafés and bars, it's one of the city's more popular spots for

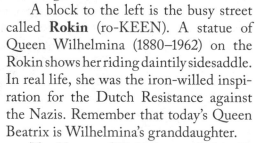

nightlife and sunny afternoon people-watching.

A block to the left is the busy street called **Rokin** (ro-KEEN). A statue of Queen Wilhelmina (1880–1962) on the Rokin shows her riding daintily sidesaddle. In real life, she was the iron-willed inspiration for the Dutch Resistance against the Nazis. Remember that today's Queen Beatrix is Wilhelmina's granddaughter.

The **House of Hajenius,** at Rokin 92 (50 yards left of the canal dock, toward the train station), is a temple of cigars, a "paradise for the connoisseur" showing "175 years of tradition and good taste." To enter this sumptuous Art Nouveau building with painted leather ceilings is to go back to 1910 (**AE+A, AI,** Level 2—Moderately Accessible; free, Tue–Sat 9:30–18:00, Sun 12:00–17:00, Mon 12:00–18:00). One 6" entry step leads to the

accessible ground floor. Don't be shy—the place is as much a free museum for visitors as it is a store for paying customers. The brown-capped canisters are for smelling fine pipe tobacco. Take a whiff. The personal humidifiers (read the explanation) allow locals (famous local names are on the cupboard doors) to call in an order and have their cigars waiting for them at just the right humidity. Look up at the

Amsterdam City Roll or Stroll—Second Half

200 YARDS

200 METERS

FLOWER MARKET
START

SINGEL

MINT TOWER

KEIZERS STRAAT

HERENGRACHT

REGULIERS

PRINSEN

LEIDSE GRACHT

LEIDSEPLEIN

KORTE

MARNIX STRAAT

LEIDSE KADE

LEIDSE DWARSSTRAAT

L.IJN.BAANS

SINGEL GRACHT

VONDEL PARK

HOBBEMASTR.

STAD HOUDERSKADE

P.C. HOOFT

STR.

JAN LUIJKEN

END

RIJKS-MUSEUM

㉑ Flower Market
㉒ Koningsplein
㉓ Metz & Co. (view)
㉔ Smartshop
㉕ The Delft Shop
㉖ Stadsschouwburg
㉗ Last Minute Ticket Shop
㉘ Melkweg
㉙ Boom Chicago Nightclub
㉚ "Restaurant Row"
㉛ Bulldog Café
㉜ Rederij Noord-Zuid
    canal boats
㉝ Max Euweplein
㉞ Paradiso
㉟ Rijksmuseum
㊱ Trams #2 & #5

humidifier pipes pumping moisture into the room. Upstairs in back is a small, free museum (unfortunately, it's not accessible—up eleven narrow 5" steps).

Head back toward the pedestrian street, Kalverstraat, and turn left when you get there. You'll pass various department stores with cafeterias. At the end of Kalverstraat, the **Kalvertoren** shopping complex (**AE, AI, AL,** Level 2—Moderately Accessible) offers a top-floor viewpoint and café. Go straight into the glass atrium and go past the escalators to ride the accessible slanting glass elevator (Mon 11:00–18:30, Tue–Fri 10:00–18:30, Thu until 21:00, Sat 10:00–18:00, Sun 12:00–18:00). Across

Kalverstraat, the **Vroom & Dreesman** department store (at #200) is one of Holland's oldest chains. Inside, La Place (Level 3—Minimally Accessible, has stairs) is a sprawling self-service cafeteria—handy for a quick and healthy lunch (Mon–Sat 10:00–20:00, Thu until 21:00, Sun 12:00–20:00).

• *Continue on Kalverstraat, which dead-ends at the...*

Mint Tower (Munttoren)

This tower, which marked the limit of the medieval walled city, served as one of the original gates (the steeple was added later, in 1620). The city walls were girdled by a moat—the Singel canal. Until about 1500, the area beyond here was nothing but marshy fields and a few farms on reclaimed land.

From the busy intersection at Muntplein, look left (at about 10 o'clock) down Reguliersbreestraat. A long block east of here (where you see trees) is Rembrandtplein, another major center for nightlife. Halfway down the block (past the massive easyInternetcafé—**AE, AI,** Level 2—Moderately Accessible; daily 9:00–21:00, Reguliersbreestraat 33), the twin green domes mark the exotic Tuschinski Theater (**AE+A, AI,** Level 3—Minimally Accessible, four 7" entry steps), where you can see current movies in a sumptuous Art Deco setting (see page 406). In the lobby, stare at the ever-changing ceiling, imagining this place during the Roaring '20s.

• *Just past the Mint Tower, turn right and go west along the south bank of the Singel, which is lined with the greenhouse shops of the...*

Flower Market (Bloemenmarkt)

This busy block of cut flowers, plants, bulbs, seeds, and garden supplies attests to Holland's reputation for growing flowers. Tulips, imported from Turkey in the 1600s, grew well in the sandy soil of the dunes and reclaimed land. By the 1630s, the country was in the grip of a full-blown tulip mania, when a single bulb sold for as much as a house, and fortunes were won and lost. Finally, in 1637, the market plummeted, and the tulip became just one of many beauties in the country's flower arsenal. Today, Holland is a major exporter of flowers. Certain seeds are certified and OK to bring back into the United States (merchants have the details).

• *The long Flower Market ends at the next bridge, where you'll see a square named...*

Koningsplein

Choke down a raw herring—the commodity that first put Amsterdam on the trading map—with locals who flock to this popular outdoor herring stand (one 12" step to reach ordering platform). *Hollandse nieuwe* means the herring are in season.

• *From Koningsplein, we'll turn left, heading straight to Leidseplein. At first, the street southward is just labeled Koningsplein (Scheltema, Amsterdam's leading bookstore, is at Koningsplein 20;* **AE, AI, AL,** *Level 2—Moderately Accessible). Soon, Koningsplein becomes...*

Leidsestraat

Between here and Leidseplein, you'll cross several grand canals, following a street lined with fashion and tourist shops, and crowded with shoppers, tourists, bicycles, and trams. Trams must wait their turn to share a single track as the street narrows.

The once grand, now frumpy **Metz & Co.** department store (**AE, AI, AL,** Level 2—Moderately Accessible; where Leidsestraat crosses Herengracht) offers a rare above-the-rooftops panorama of the city from its fully accessible sixth-floor café.

Looking left down Herengracht, you'll see the **"Golden Curve"** of the canal, lined with grand, classical-style gables.

• *Past the posh stores of Laura Ashley, DKNY, and Lush, find a humble establishment where Leidsestraat crosses the Keizersgracht...*

When Nature Calls Smartshop

Access: AE+A, AI+A, Level 2—Moderately Accessible. Two exterior 3" entry steps, then two more 8" steps after the landing. The rest of the store is very small, packed with display cases.

Hours and Location: Daily 10:00–22:00, Keizersgracht 508.

The Sight: "Smartshops" like this one are clean, well-lighted, fully

professional retail outlets that sell powerful drugs, many of which are illegal in America. Their "natural" drugs include harmless nutrition boosters (royal jelly), harmful but familiar tobacco, herbal versions of popular dance-club drugs (herbal Ecstasy), and powerful psychoactive plants (psilocybin mushrooms). The big item: marijuana seeds.

Prices are clearly marked, with brief descriptions of the drugs, their ingredients, and effects. The knowledgeable salespeople can give more information on their "100 percent natural products that play with the human senses."

Still, my fellow Americans, *caveat emptor!* We've grown used to thinking, "If it's legal, it must be safe. If it's not, I'll sue." While perfectly legal and aboveboard, some of these substances can cause powerful, often unpleasant reactions.

• *Where Leidsestraat crosses the Prinsengracht, just over the bridge on the right (at Prinsengracht 440), you'll find...*

The Delft Shop

Access: Level 4—Not Accessible. But if Delft is your thing, try the accessible shop at Prinsengracht 170, near Leidseplein.

The Sight: The distinctive blue-and-white design characterizes glazed ceramics made in Delft (30 miles southwest of here). Dutch traders learned the technique from the Chinese of the Ming dynasty, and many pieces have an Oriental look. The doodads with arms branching off a trunk are popular "flower pagodas," vases for displaying tulips.

• *Leidsestraat empties into the square called...*

Leidseplein

Filled with outdoor tables under trees, ringed with cafés, theaters, and nightclubs, bustling with tourists, diners, trams, mimes, and fire-eaters, and lit by sun- or lantern-light, Leidseplein is Amsterdam's liveliest square.

Do a 360-degree spin: Leidseplein's south side is bordered by the city's main serious theater, the **Stadsschouwburg** (**AE, AI, AT, Level 1**—Fully Accessible, designated seating for wheelchair users), which dates back to the 17th-century Golden Age (present building from 1890). Tucked into a corner of the theater is the **Last Minute**

Ticket Shop (AE, AI, AT, Level 1—Fully Accessible), which sells tickets to all the shows in town (including half-price, same-day tickets to select shows, Leidseplein 26, tel. 0900-0191). To the right of the Stadsschouwburg, down a lane behind the big theater at Lijnbaansgracht 234a, stands the **Melkweg** (literally, "Milky Way"; AE, AI, AL, AT, Level 1—Fully Accessible). This once revolutionary, now institutional entertainment complex houses all things youth-oriented under one roof; go into the lobby or check out posters plastered on the walls to find out who's playing tonight. On Leidseplein's west side, at #12, is the **Boom Chicago** nightclub theater, presenting English-language spoofs of politics, Amsterdam, and tourists (AE, AI, AT, ♥, Level 1—Fully Accessible, see page 425; pick up their free, informative intro-to-Amsterdam magazine at the door). The neighborhood beyond Häagen-Dazs and Burger King is the **"Restaurant Row,"** featuring countless Thai, Brazilian, Indian, Italian, Indonesian, and even a few Dutch eateries. Next, on the east end of Leidseplein, is the **Bulldog Café and Coffeeshop** (Level 3—Minimally Accessible), the flagship of several café/bar/coffeeshops in town with that name. (Notice the sign above the door: It once housed the police bureau.) A small green-and-white decal in the window indicates that it's a city-licensed "coffeeshop," where marijuana is sold and smoked legally. Nearby are Rederij Noord-Zuid **canal boats,** offering one-hour tours (4 of their 6 boats are AE, AI, Level 1—Fully Accessible, ideally call ahead for schedule of accessible boats; see page 397).

• *From Leidseplein, turn left and head along the taxi stand down the broad, busy, tram-filled boulevard called Kleine-Gartman Plantsoen, which becomes Weteringschans. At the triangular garden filled with iguanas, cross the street and pass under a row of tall, gray, Greek-style columns, entering...*

Max Euweplein

Access: AE, AI, Level 1—Fully Accessible.

The Sight: The Latin inscription above the colonnade—*Homo Sapiens non urinat in ventum*—means "Don't pee into the wind." Pass between the columns and through a passageway to reach a pleasant, accessible interior courtyard with cafés and a large chessboard with knee-high kings. (Max Euwe was a Dutch world champion in chess.)

Canals

Amsterdam's canals tamed the flow of the Amstel River, creating pockets of dry land to build on. The city's 100 canals are about 10 feet deep, crossed by some 1,200 bridges, fringed with 100,000 Dutch elm and lime trees, and bedecked with 2,500 houseboats. A system of locks (back near Central Station) controls the flow outward to (eventually) the North Sea and inward to the Amstel River. The locks are opened periodically to flush out the system.

Some of the boats in the canals look pretty funky by day, but Amsterdam is an unpretentious, anti-status city. When the sun goes down and the lights come on, people cruise the sparkling canals with an on-board hibachi and a bottle of wine, and even scows can become chick magnets.

The square gives you access to the Casino, and just over the small bridge is the entrance to accessible **Vondelpark.**

• *Return to Weteringschans street. Turn right and continue 75 yards east to a squat, red-brick building called...*

Paradiso

Back when rock-and-roll was a religion, this former church staged intimate concerts by big-name acts such as the Rolling Stones. In the late 1960s, when city fathers were trying hard to tolerate hordes of young pot-smokers, this building was redecorated with psychedelic colors and opened up as the first place where marijuana could be smoked—not legally yet, but it was tolerated. Today, the club hosts live bands and DJs and sells pot legally (for current shows, see www.paradiso.nl). Unfortunately, the entry is Level 4—Not Accessible.

• *Continue down Weteringschans to the first bridge, where you'll see the Rijksmuseum across the canal.*

The Rijksmuseum and Beyond

The best visual chronicle of the Golden Age is found in the Rijksmuseum's portraits and slice-of-life scenes (**AE+A, AI, AT,** Level 2—Moderately

Accessible, for access details see page 400; €10, covered by *I amsterdam* Card, daily 9:00–18:00).

On this tour, we've seen landmarks built during the city's late-19th-century revival: Central Station, the Stadsschouwburg, and now the Rijksmuseum. They're all similar, with red-brick and Gothic-style motifs (clock towers, steeples, prickly spires, and stained glass). Petrus Cuypers (1827–1921), who designed the train station and the Rijksmuseum, was extremely influential. Mainly a builder of Catholic churches, he made the Rijksmuseum, with its stained glass windows, a temple to art. The building is currently closed for renovation, with the highlights of the collection beautifully displayed in its Philips Wing (around back, on the right). Next to the Philips Wing, a small, free exhibit describes the exciting renovation project.

Behind the Rijksmuseum are the Museumplein (always entertaining) and the Van Gogh Museum (**AE, AI, AT,** Level 1—Fully Accessible; €9, covered by *I amsterdam* Card, Sat–Thu 10:00–18:00, Fri 10:00–22:00, Paulus Potterstraat 7). The Heineken Brewery museum is a half mile east of the Rijks on Stadhouderskade (**AE, AI, AL, AT,** Level 1—Fully Accessible, €10 for self-guided tour and 3 beers, Tue–Sun 10:00–18:00, last entry 17:00, closed Mon), and the Albert Kuyp street market is a block south of Heineken.

• *The tour is finished. To return to Central Station (or to nearly anyplace along this tour), catch tram #2 or #5 (both accessible) or from the southwest corner of the Rijks.*

HAARLEM

Cute, cozy, authentic, and handy to the airport, Haarlem is a fine home base, giving you small-town warmth overnight, with easy access (15 min by train) to wild and crazy Amsterdam during the day.

Bustling Haarlem gave America's Harlem its name back when New York was New Amsterdam, a Dutch colony. For centuries, Haarlem has been a market town, buzzing with shoppers heading home with fresh bouquets, nowadays by bike.

Enjoy the market on Monday (clothing) or Saturday (general), when the square bustles like a Brueghel painting, with cheese, fish, flowers, and families. Make yourself at home; buy some flowers to brighten your hotel room.

Accessibility in Haarlem

Haarlem is not ideal in terms of accessibility. We've listed only the most accessible hotels and restaurants. The best local resource is the *Holiday Magazine* (see below).

ORIENTATION

(area code: 023)

Tourist Information

Haarlem's TI (**AE, AI,** Level 2—Moderately Accessible), at the train station, is friendlier, more helpful, and less crowded than Amsterdam's. Ask your Amsterdam questions here. They also offer train travel advice and sell tickets for destinations in Holland, Belgium, and Germany

Haarlem of the Golden Age

Parts of Haarlem still look like they did four centuries ago, when the city was a bustling commercial center rivaling Amsterdam. It's easy to imag-

ine local merchants and their wives dressed in black with ruff collars, promenading the Market Square.

Back then, the town was a port on the large Haarlemmer Lake, with the North Sea only about five miles away. As well as being the tulip capital of the country, Haarlem was a manufacturing center, producing wool, silk, lace, damask cloth, furniture, smoking pipes (along with cheap, locally grown tobacco), and mass quantities of beer. Haarlemers were notorious consumers of beer. It was a popular breakfast drink, and the average person drank six pints a day.

In 1585, the city got an influx of wealthy merchants when Spanish troops invaded the culturally rich city of Antwerp, driving Protestants and Jews north. Even when hard-line, moralistic Calvinists dominated Haarlem's politics, the city remained culturally and religiously diverse.

In the 1700s, Haarlem's economy declined, along with that of the Netherlands. In the succeeding centuries, industry—printing, textiles, ship building—once again made the city an economic force.

(April–Sept Mon–Fri 9:00–17:30, Sat 10:00–16:00, closed Sun; Oct–March Mon–Fri 9:30–17:00, Sat 10:00–15:00, closed Sun; tel. 0900-616-1600—€0.50/min, helpful parking brochure). The €1 *Holiday Magazine* has a good accessibility section (free if you buy the fine €2 town map). The TI also sells a €2 self-guided walking-tour map for overachievers. The little yellow computer terminal on the curb outside the TI prints out free maps anytime. (It's fun...just dial the street and hit print. Drivers will also find these terminals stationed at roads coming into town.)

Arrival in Haarlem

By Train: Haarlem's train station has elevators that allow wheelchair users access from the platform to the street level. As you emerge from Haarlem's train station (lockers available), the TI is on your right and the bus station is across the street. Two parallel streets flank the train station (Kruisweg and Jansweg). Head up either street, and you'll reach the town square and church in six wheelchair-accessible blocks (narrow sidewalks and lots of pedestrians). If you need help, ask a local person to point you toward the Grote Markt (Market Square).

By Car: Parking is expensive on the streets (€2.50/hr) and cheaper in several central garages (€1.50/hr). Two main garages let you park overnight for €2 (at the train station and near Die Raeckse Hotel).

By Plane: For details on getting from Schiphol Airport into Haarlem, see page 442.

Helpful Hints

Blue Monday: Most sights are closed on Monday except for the church.

Money: The handy, accessible GWK currency exchange office at the train station offers fair rates (Mon–Fri 8:00–20:00, Sat 9:00–17:00, Sun 10:00–17:00).

Internet Access: Try **Internet Café Amadeus** (in Hotel Amadeus overlooking Market Square, Level 3—Minimally Accessible, steep stairs and no elevator up to lounge, €1.20/15 min) or nearly any **coffeeshop** (if you don't mind marijuana smoke; varying accessibility). Perhaps the cheapest place in town is **Sony Teletechniques (AE+A, AI,** Level 2—Moderately Accessible, one 4" entry step; €2/hr, daily 10:00–24:00, near the train station at Lange Herenstraat 4).

Post Office: It's at Gedempte Oude Gracht 2 (**AE, AI,** Level 1—Fully Accessible; Mon–Fri 9:00–18:00, Sat 10:00–13:30, closed Sun, has ATM).

Laundry: My Beautiful Launderette is handy and cheap (**AE, AI,** Level 2—Moderately Accessible; €6 self-service wash and dry, daily 8:30–20:30, €9 full service available Mon–Fri 9:00–17:00, near Vroom & Dreesmann department store at Boter Markt 20).

Taxi: For a fully accessible minivan taxi (**AE, AI,** Level 1—Fully Accessible, entry ramps), call Otax at 023/512-3456 (best to reserve 1–2 hours in advance).

Local Guide: For a historical look at Haarlem, consider hiring Walter Schelfhout (€75/2 hours, tel. 023/535-5715, schelfhout@dutch.nl). Walter is happy accommodate travelers with limited mobility—contact him in advance to let him know your needs.

Bulb Flower Parade: One Saturday each April, an all-day Bulb Flower Parade of floats, decorated with blossoms instead of crepe paper, wafts through eight towns, including Haarlem. The floats are parked in Haarlem at Gedempte Oude Gracht overnight, when they're illuminated, and through the next day.

SELF-GUIDED ROLL OR STROLL

Welcome to Haarlem's Market Square

Haarlem's market square (Grote Markt, worth ▲▲), where 10 streets converge, is the town's delightful centerpiece...as it has been for 700 years. To enjoy a coffee or beer here, simmering in Dutch good living, is a quint-

essential European experience. In a recent study, the Dutch were found to be the most content people in Europe. In another study, the people of Haarlem were found to be the most content in the Netherlands. Observe. Relax and gaze at the church, appreciating the same scene Dutch artists captured in oil paintings that now hang in museums.

Just a few years ago, trolleys ran through the square, and cars were parked everywhere. But today, it's a wheelchair-accessible people zone, filled with market stalls on Mondays and Saturdays and café tables on other days.

This is a great place to build a picnic with Haarlem finger foods: raw herring, local cheese (Gouda and Edam), a *frikandel* (little corn-dog sausage), french fries with mayonnaise, *stroopwafels* (waffles with syrup), *poffertjes* (little sugar doughnuts), or one of many different ethnic foods (falafel, *shoarma*, Indonesian dishes).

• *Overseeing the square is the...*

L. J. Coster Statue: Forty years before Gutenberg invented movable type, this man carved the letter *A* out of wood, dropped it into some wet sand, and saw the imprint it left. He got the idea of making movable type out of wood (and later, he may have tried using lead). For Haarlemers, that was good enough, and they credit their man, Coster, with inventing modern printing. In the statue, Coster (c. 1370–1440) holds up a block of movable type and points to himself, saying, "I made this." How much Coster did is uncertain, but Gutenberg trumped him by building a printing press, casting type in metal, and pounding out the bible.

• *Coster is facing the...*

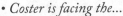

Haarlem

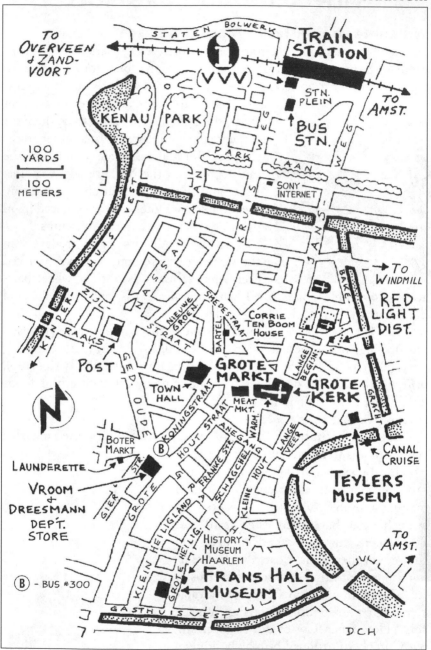

Town Hall: While most of medieval Europe was ruled by kings, dukes, and barons, Haarlem has been largely self-governing since 1425. The town hall—built from a royal hunting lodge in the mid-1200s, then rebuilt after a 1351 fire—has served as Haarlem's town hall since about 1400. The facade dates from 1630. (The entry is wheelchair accessible, with a fully adapted toilet—one of the few in town.)

The town drunk used to hang out on the bench in front of the town hall, where he'd expose himself to newlyweds coming down the stairs. The Dutch, rather than arresting the man, moved the bench.

• *Next to the church is the...*

Meat Market (Vleeshall), 1603: The fine Flemish Renaissance building nearest the cathedral is the old meat hall. It was built by the rich butchers' and leatherworkers' guilds. The meat market was on the ground floor, the leather was upstairs, and the cellar was filled with ice to keep the meat preserved. It's decorated with carved bits of early advertising—sheep and cows for sale. Today, rather than meat, the hall shows off temporary art exhibits (**AE, AI+A,** Level 2—Moderately Accessible, some steps to reach upper level once inside; €5, Tue–Sat 11:00–17:00, closed Sun, tel. 023/511-5775, www.dehallen.com).

SIGHTS

▲**Church (Grote Kerk)**—This 15th-century Gothic church (now Protestant) is worth a look, if only for its Oz-like organ (from 1738, 100 feet high, its 5,000 pipes impressed

both Handel and Mozart). Note how the organ, which fills the west end, seems to steal the show from the altar. Quirky highlights include a replica of Foucault's pendulum, the "Dog-Whipper's Chapel," and a 400-year-old cannonball.

Access: AE+A, AI, Level 2—Moderately Accessible. There is a tall step and a ledge to get in the door, but the interior is accessible.

Cost, Hours, Location: €2, Mon–Sat 10:00–16:00, closed Sun to tourists, tel. 023/553-2040. To enter, find the small *Entrée* sign behind the church at Oude Groenmarkt 23.

Organ Concerts: Consider attending (even part of) a concert to hear Holland's greatest pipe organ (regular free concerts Tue at 20:15 mid-May–mid-Oct, additional concerts Thu at 15:00 July–Aug, concerts nearly nightly at 20:15 during the organ competition in July, confirm schedule at TI or at www.bavo.nl; bring a sweater—the church isn't heated).

▲▲**Frans Hals Museum**—Haarlem is the hometown of Frans Hals, the foremost Dutch portrait painter of the 17th-century Golden Age. This refreshing museum—an almshouse for old men back in 1610—displays many of his greatest paintings, done with his nearly Impressionistic style. You'll see group portraits and take-me-back paintings of old-time Haarlem. Look for the 250-year-old dollhouse on display in a former chapel.

Access: AE, AI, AT, Level 2— Moderately Accessible. Most of the interior is accessible, except for a couple of steps into two rooms and four steps into another room. They have one loaner wheelchair (first come, first served).

Cost, Hours, Location: €7, wheelchair user pays, but companion goes free (only if companion pushes wheelchair), Tue–Sat 11:00–17:00, Sun 12:00–17:00, closed Mon, Groot Heiligland 62, tel. 023/511-5775, www.franshalsmuseum.nl.

History Museum Haarlem—This small museum, across the street from the Frans Hals Museum, offers a glimpse of old Haarlem. Request the English version of the 10-minute video. Study the large-scale model of Haarlem in 1822 (when its fortifications were still intact), and enjoy the "time machine" computer and video display that shows you various aspects of life in Haarlem at different points in history. The adjacent architecture center (free) may be of interest to architects.

Access: AE, AI, AT, Level 1—Fully Accessible.

Cost, Hours, Location: €1, Tue–Sat 12:00–17:00, Sun 13:00–17:00, closed Mon, Groot Heiligland 47, tel. 023/542-2427.

Corrie Ten Boom House—Haarlem is home to Corrie Ten Boom, popularized by *The Hiding Place*, her inspirational book and the movie that followed, about the Ten Boom family's experience protecting Jews from the Nazis. Corrie Ten Boom gives the other half of the Anne Frank story—the point of view of those who risked their lives to hide Dutch Jews during the Nazi occupation (1940–1945).

The clock shop was the Ten Boom family business. The elderly father and his two daughters—Corrie and Betsy, both in their 50s—lived above the store and in the brick building attached in back (along Schoutensteeg alley). Corrie's bedroom was on the top floor at the back. This room was tiny to start with, but the family built a second, secret room (only about a foot deep) at the very back—the hiding place, where they could hide six or seven Jews at a time.

Devoutly religious, the family had a long tradition of tolerance, having for generations hosted prayer meetings here in their home for both Jews and Christians.

The Gestapo, tipped off that the family was harboring Jews, burst into the Ten Boom house. Finding a suspicious number of ration coupons, the Nazis arrested the family, but failed to find the six Jews in the hiding place (who later escaped). Corrie's father and sister died while in prison, but Corrie survived the Ravensbruck concentration camp to tell her story in her memoir.

Access: Level 4—Not Accessible. Unfortunately, since it has many levels and tight hallways, this museum is best left to energetic slow walkers.

Cost, Hours, Location: The Ten Boom House is open for 60-minute English tours; the tours are sometimes mixed with preaching (free, but donation accepted, April–Oct Tue–Sat 10:00–16:00, Nov–March Tue–Sat 11:00 15:00, closed Sun–Mon, 50 yards north of Market Square at Barteljorisstraat 19; the clock-shop people get all wound up if you go inside—wait in the little side street at the door, where hourly tour times are posted; tel. 023/531-0823, www.corrietenboom.com).

▲**Teylers Museum**—Famous as the oldest museum in Holland, Teylers is a time-warp experience, filled with all sorts of fun curios for science buffs: fossils, minerals, primitive electronic gadgetry, and examples of 18th- and 19th-century technology. This place feels like a museum of a museum. They're serious about authenticity here: The presentation is perfectly preserved, right down to the original labels. Since there was no electricity in the olden days, you'll find no electric lighting...if it's dark outside, it's dark inside. The museum's benefactor, Pieter Teyler van der Hulst, was a very wealthy merchant who willed his estate, worth the equivalent of €80 million today, to a foundation whose mission was to "create and maintain a museum to stimulate art and science." (His last euro was spent in 1983, and now it's a national museum.) The museum opened in 1784, six years after Teyler's death. Add your name to the guest book that goes back literally to before Napoleon's visit here. The oval room—a temple of science and learning—is the core of the museum; the painting gallery hangs paintings in the old style. While there are no English descriptions, there is an excellent English audioguide.

Access: AE+A, AI, AT, Level 3—Minimally Accessible. Wheelchair users gain entrance by alerting the staff inside the entry (three 6" steps). Loaner wheelchairs are available.

Cost, Hours, Location: €5.50, Tue–Sat 10:00–17:00, Sun 12:00–17:00, closed Mon, Spaarne 16, tel. 023/531-9010, www.teylersmuseum .nl.

De Adriaan Windmill—Haarlem's old-time windmill welcomes visitors with a short video, little museum, and fine town views.

Access: Level 4—Not Accessible.

Cost, Hours, Location: €2, Wed–Fri 13:00–16:00, Sat–Sun 10:00–16:00, closed Mon–Tue, Papentorenvest 1, tel. 023/545-0259.

Canal Cruise—Making a scenic 50-minute loop through and around Haarlem with a live guide who speaks up to four languages, these little trips by Woltheus Cruises are more relaxing than informative.

Access: One new boat is **AE, AI,** Level 1—Fully Accessible. Call ahead to reserve for this boat.

Cost, Hours, Location: €7, May–Oct daily departures at the top of each hour 12:00–17:00, closed Mon in May and Oct, no tours Nov–April, across canal from Teylers Museum at Spaarne 11a, tel. 023/535-7723, www.woltheuscruises.nl.

Red-Light District—Wander through a little Red-Light District as precious as a Barbie doll—and legal since the 1980s (2 blocks northeast of Market Square, off Lange Begijnestraat, no senior or student discounts). Don't miss the mall marked by the red neon sign reading *t'Steegje* (free, on Begijnesteeg).

Access: Level 1—Fully Accessible.

Amsterdam to Haarlem Train Tour

Since you'll be commuting from Amsterdam to Haarlem, here's a tour to keep you entertained. Departing from Amsterdam, sit on the right side (with your back to Amsterdam, on the top deck if you are able). Everything is on the right unless I say it's on the left.

You're riding the oldest train line in Holland. Across the harbor, behind the Amsterdam station, the tall brown skyscraper is the corporate office of **Royal Dutch Shell Oil.** The Dutch had the first multinational corporation (the United East India Company, back in the 17th century). And today, this international big-business spirit survives with huge companies like Shell, Unilever, and Philips.

Leaving Amsterdam, you'll see the cranes and ships of its **harbor**— sizable, but nothing like the world's biggest in nearby Rotterdam.

On your left, a few minutes out of Amsterdam, find the old **windmill.** In front of it, the little garden plots and cottages are escapes for

The Haarlemmermeer

The land between Haarlem and Amsterdam—where trains speed through, cattle graze, and 747s touch down—was once a lake the size of Washington, D.C.

In the 1500s, a series of high tides and storms caused the IJ River to breach its banks, flooding this sub-sea-level area and turning a bunch of shallow lakes into a single one nearly 15 feet deep, covering 70 square miles. By the 1800s, floods were licking the borders of Haarlem and Amsterdam, and the residents needed to act. First, they dug a ring canal to channel away water (and preserve the lake's shipping business). Then, using steam engines, they pumped the lake dry, turning marshy soil into fertile ground. The Amsterdam–Haarlem train line that soon crossed the former lakebed was the country's first.

big-city people who probably don't even have a balcony.

Coming into the Sloterdijk Station (where trains connect for Amsterdam airport), you'll see huge office buildings, such as Dutch Telecom KPN. These grew up after the station made commuting easy.

Passing through a forest and by some houseboats, you enter a *polder*—reclaimed land. This is part of an ecologically sound farm zone, run without chemicals. Cows, pigs, and chickens run free—they're not raised in cages. The train tracks are on a dike, which provides a solid foundation not susceptible to floods. This way, the transportation system functions right through any calamity. Looking out at the distant dike, remember you're in the most densely populated country in Europe. On the horizon, sleek, modern windmills whirl.

On the right, just after the IKEA building, find a big beige-and-white building. This is the **mint,** where currency is printed (top security, no advertising). This has long been a family business—see the name: Johan Enschede.

As the train slows down, you're passing through the Netherlands' biggest train-car maintenance facility and entering Haarlem. Look left. The domed building is a prison, built in 1901 and still in use. The windmill burned down in 1932 and was rebuilt in 2002.

When you cross the Spaarne River, you'll see the great church spire towering over Haarlem, as it has since medieval times—back when a fortified wall circled the town. Notice the white copy of the same spire capping the smaller church between the prison and the big church. This was the original sandstone steeple that stood atop the big church until structural problems forced them to move it to another church and build a new spire for the big church. Get off the train and enter one of Holland's oldest stations. Art Nouveau decor from 1908 survives all around.

NIGHTLIFE

Haarlem's evening scene is great. The bars around the Grote Kerk and Lange Veerstraat are colorful and lively. You'll find plenty of music. The best show in town: the café scene on Market Square. In good weather, café tables tumble happily out of the bars.

For trendy local crowds, sip a drink at **Café Studio** (ground floor is **AE, AI,** Level 2—Moderately Accessible) on Market Square (daily 12:00–4:00 in the morning, next to Hotel Carillon, tel. 023/531-0033). **Grand Café XO** (**AE, AI, AT,** Level 1—Fully Accessible) is another hip nightspot on the square (daily 10:00–24:00, Grote Markt 8, 023/551-1350). Tourists gawk at the old-fashioned, belt-driven ceiling fans in **Café 1900** (**AE, AI,** Level 2—Moderately Accessible) across from the Corrie Ten Boom House (daily 9:00–24:30, live music Sun night except in July, Barteljorisstraat 10, tel. 023/531-8283).

SLEEPING

Haarlem is most crowded in April and May (particularly Easter weekend, the flower parade, and Queen's Day—usually April 30) and in July and August.

The listed prices include breakfast (unless otherwise noted) and usually include the €1.80-per-person-per-day tourist tax. To avoid this town's louder-than-normal street noises, forgo views for a room in the back. Hotels and the TI have a useful parking brochure.

In Haarlem
Level 1—Fully Accessible
Joops Hotel (**AE+I, AI, AL, AR, AB, ♥**), with 30 comfortable rooms, is located just behind the Grote Kerk church (Db-€85, €95 Fri–Sat, buffet breakfast-€9.50, Internet access in lobby, Oude Groenmarkt 20, tel. 023/532-2008, fax 023/532-9549, www.joopshotel.com, Joops@easynet .nl). Joops' nearby sister hotel, **Hotel Arendshoek** (**AE, AI, AL, AR, AB**), rents studios with kitchenettes for two to four people. They have 29 accessible rooms, each with a small bath (Db-€75, Qb-€120, elevator, contact Joops Hotel). Note that at both hotels, the bathrooms inside the rooms are not accessible. However, there is one shared, adapted bathroom

Haarlem Hotels and Restaurants

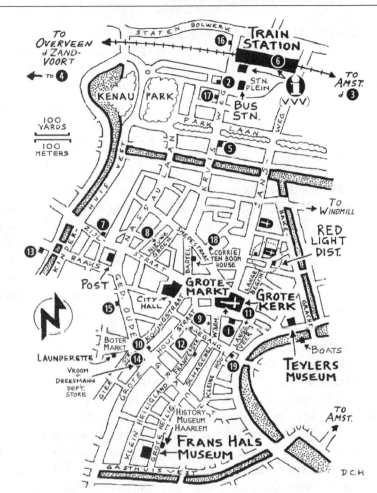

1. Joops Hotel & Hotel Arendshoek
2. Hotel Lion D'Or
3. To Hotel Haarlem Zuid
4. To Stayokay Haarlem Hostel
5. Pannenkoekhuis de Smikkel
6. Stations Café
7. Eko Eet Café
8. Vincent's Eethuis
9. Jacobus Pieck Eetlokaal & Friethuis de Vlaminck
10. Pizzeria-Rist. Venezia
11. La Plume & BastiJan Rest.
12. De Lachende Javaan Rest.
13. De Buren Eetlokaal
14. La Place Cafeteria
15. DekaMarkt Supermarket
16. Albert Heijn Supermarket
17. Willie Wortel Sativa Coffeeshop
18. 'T Theehuis Coffeeshop
19. High Times Coffeeshop

Sleep Code

(€1 = about $1.20, country code: 31, area code: 023)
S = Single, **D** = Double/Twin, **T** = Triple, **Q** = Quad, **b** = bathroom,
s = shower only. Credit cards are accepted unless otherwise noted.
Nearly every Dutch person you'll encounter speaks English.

---

on the hall that can be used by any guest who has limited mobility. To reach the front desk, you'll have to manage one 2" entry step.

Level 2—Moderately Accessible

Hotel Lion D'Or (AE+A, AI, AL, AR, AB+A) is a classy, 34-room business hotel with all the professional comforts and a handy location. Expect a proficient welcome (Db-€135, €95 Fri–Sat, extra bed-€20, air-con, some non-smoking rooms, elevator, across the street from train station at Kruisweg 34, tel. 023/532-1750, fax 023/532-9543, www.goldentulip.com, reservations@hotelliondor.nl). There is a small entry step, and the bathroom is small.

Near Haarlem
Level 1—Fully Accessible

Hotel Haarlem Zuid (AE, AI, AL, AR, AB), with 300 rooms and very American, is sterile, but a good value for drivers. It sits in an industrial zone about a mile from Market Square, on the road to the airport (Db-€80, breakfast-€12, elevator, free parking, laundry service, fitness center-€5, inexpensive hotel restaurant, Toekanweg 2, tel. 023/536-7500, fax 023/536-7980, www.hotelhaarlemzuid.nl, info@hotelhaarlemzuid.valk.nl). The hotel has one fully adapted room for wheelchair users (including a roll-in shower). Bus #300 (**AE, AI,** Level 1—Fully Accessible, can take one wheelchair user at a time) connects the hotel conveniently with the train station, Market Square, and the airport every 10 minutes.

Stayokay Haarlem (AE, AI, AR, AB), completely renovated and with all the youth-hostel comforts, charges €19–25 for beds in four-, six-, and eight-bed dorms. They also rent simple €60 doubles (€2.50 less for members, includes sheets and breakfast, daily 7:30–24:00, Jan Gijzenpad 3, 2 miles from Haarlem station—take bus #2 from station, or a quarter-mile from Santpoort Zuid train station, tel. 023/537-3793, fax 023/537-1176, www.stayokay.com/haarlem, haarlem@stayokay.com). They have one fully adapted ground-floor room with a roll-in shower and four beds.

EATING

For details on eating Dutch, see "Eating" in the Amsterdam chapter, page 429. Unless otherwise noted (by **AT** or **AT+A**), these restaurants do *not* have accessible toilets.

In or near the Train Station
Pancakes for lunch or dinner? **Pannenkoekhuis De Smikkel (AE+A, AI,** Level 2—Moderately Accessible, one 4" entry step) serves a selection of over 50 pancakes for a meal (meat, cheese, etc.) and dessert. The €8 pancakes can fill two (daily 12:00–21:00, Sun from 16:00, 2 blocks in front of station, Kruisweg 57, tel. 023/532-0631).

Enjoy a sandwich or coffee surrounded by trains and 1908 architecture in the **Stations Café (AE, AI,** Level 2—Moderately Accessible; daily 6:30–20:00, between tracks #3 and #6 at the station).

On or near Zijlstraat
Eko Eet Café (AE, AI, Level 2—Moderately Accessible) is great for a cheery, tasty vegetarian meal (€10–15 *menu*s, daily 11:30–21:30, Zijlstraat 39, tel. 023/532-6568).

Vincent's Eethuis (AE+A, AI, Level 2—Moderately Accessible, one 5" entry step, then another 2" step, wide-open interior), the cheapest restaurant in town, offers basic Dutch food and a friendly staff. This former St. Vincent's soup kitchen now feeds more gainfully employed locals than poor (daily plate-€5.50, specials-€8, Mon–Fri 16:30–19:30, closed Sat–Sun, Nieuwe Groenmarkt 22).

Between the Market Square and Frans Hals Museum
Jacobus Pieck Eetlokaal (Level 3—Minimally Accessible, three 6" entry steps, narrow landing, and tight aisles) is popular with locals for its fine-value "global cuisine" and peaceful garden courtyard (plate of the day-€9.50, great €5 sandwiches at lunch, cash only, good salads, Mon 10:00–17:00, Tue–Sat 10:00–22:00, closed Sun, Warmoesstraat 18, behind church, tel. 023/532-6144).

Friethuis de Vlaminck (Level 3—Minimally Accessible) is *the* place for a cone of old-fashioned fresh "Flemish fries." Be creative with their dazzling array of sauces (€2, Tue–Sat until 18:30, closed Sun–Mon, Warmoesstraat 3, behind church).

Pizzeria-Ristorante Venezia (AE+A, AI, Level 2—Moderately Accessible, one 6" entry step), run for 10 years by the same Italian family

Marijuana in Haarlem

Haarlem is a laid-back place for observing the Dutch approach to recreational marijuana. The town is dotted with 16 easygoing coffeeshops, where pot is casually sold and smoked by relaxed, non-criminal types. These coffeeshops are more welcoming than they may feel—bartenders are happy to answer questions from curious Yankee travelers.

If you don't like the smell of pot, avoid places sporting wildly painted walls, plants in the windows, or Rastafarian yellow, red, and green colors.

Willie Wortel Sativa Coffeeshop (**AE+A, AI,** Level 2—Moderately Accessible, one 8" entry step) is one of the best established of the town's coffeeshops (daily 9:00–24:00, in front of train station at Kruisweg 46). The display case–type menu explains what's on sale (€2.50–3.60 joints, €5 baggies, space cakes, no alcohol, only soft drinks and mellow music).

The tiny **'T Theehuis** (**AE, AI,** Level 2—Moderately Accessible), which feels like a hippie teahouse, was Haarlem's first coffeeshop (c. 1984). Along with a friendly staff and a global selection of pot, it has 50 different varieties of tea on the menu (daily 13:00–22:00, a block off Market Square at Smedestraat 25).

High Times (**AE, AI,** Level 2—Moderately Accessible) offers smokers 12 varieties of joints in racks behind the bar (neatly prepacked in trademarked "Joint Packs," €2.50–5, daily 11:00–23:00, Internet access, Lange Veerstraat 47). They make a tobacco-free joint especially for Americans (€4.50).

from Bari, is where to go for pizza or pasta (€8–17 meals, pizza from €7.50, daily 13:00–23:00, facing Vroom & Dreesmann department store at Verwulft 7, 023/531-7753).

La Plume steakhouse (**AE, AI,** Level 2—Moderately Accessible) is noisy, with a happy, local, and carnivorous crowd (€12–18 meals, daily from 17:30, Lange Veerstraat 1, tel. 023/531-3202). The relaxing outdoor seating faces the church and a lively pedestrian mall.

BastiJan (**AE, AI,** Level 2—Moderately Accessible) serves good Mediterranean cuisine in an atmosphere of youthful elegance (€20 meals, 4-course dinner for €25, Tue–Sun from 18:00, closed

Mon, Lange Veerstraat 8, tel. 023/532-6006).

De Lachende Javaan (literally, "The Laughing Javanese"; **AE, AI,** Level 2—Moderately Accessible) serves the best Indonesian food in town in a spacious, classy, and woody dining area. Their €18–22 *rijsttafels* are excellent (Tue–Sun from 17:00, closed Mon, Frankestraat 27, tel. 023/532-8792).

De Buren Eetlokaal (**AE, AI,** Level 2—Moderately Accessible) is a fun, traditional place just outside the center serving good Franco-Dutch food with an old-time ambience to an enthusiastic local crowd (€10–14 meals, Thu–Mon 16:00–22:00, closed Tue–Wed, Brouwersvaart 146, tel. 023/532-7078).

La Place (**AE, AI, AL, AT,** Level 1—Fully Accessible) serves fresh, healthy, budget food with Haarlem's best view. Sit on the top floor or roof garden of the Vroom & Dreesmann department store (Mon 11:00–18:00, Tue–Sat 9:30–18:00, Thu until 21:00, closed Sun except for 1st Sun of month 12:00–17:00, large non-smoking section, Grote Houtstraat 70, on corner of Gedempte Oude Gracht, 023/515-8700). Find the accessible lift at the back corner of the store and take it to the sixth floor.

Picnic shoppers have two good choices (both **AE, AI,** Level 2—Moderately Accessible): the **DekaMarkt supermarket** near Market Square (Mon 11:00–20:00, Tue–Sat 8:30–20:00, Thu until 21:00, closed Sun, Gedempte Oude Gracht 54, between Vroom & Dreesmann department store and post office) or the **Albert Heijn supermarket** near the train station (Mon–Sat 8:00–20:00, closed Sun, Kruisweg 10).

TRANSPORTATION CONNECTIONS

From Haarlem by Train to: Amsterdam (6/hr, 15 min, €3.40 one-way, €6 same-day round-trip), **The Hague** (4/hr, 35 min), **Delft** (2/hr, 40 min), **Rotterdam** (2/hr, 50 min, may require change in Leiden), **Hoorn** (2/hr, 1 hr), **Alkmaar** (2/hr, 45 min), **Brussels** (hrly, 2.75 hrs, transfer in Rotterdam), **Bruges** (1–2/hr, 3.5 hrs, transfer required).

To Schiphol Airport: Your options are **bus #300** (**AE, AI,** Level 1—Fully Accessible, can take one wheelchair user at a time; 4/hr, 40 min, €5.80, departs from Haarlem's train station in "Zuidtangent" lane), **train** (**AE, AI,** Level 2—Moderately Accessible; 4/hr, 40 min, requires a transfer at Amsterdam-Sloterdijk station, €4.90), or **taxi** (for an accessible taxi, call Otax at tel. 023/512-3456).

GERMANY

GERMANY

(Deutschland)

Deutschland is energetic, efficient, and organized. It is Europe's muscle man—both economically and wherever people line up (Germans have a reputation for pushing ahead). Its bustling cities hold 85 percent of its people, and average earnings are among the highest on earth. Ninety-seven percent of the workers get one-month paid vacations, and, during the other 11 months, they create a gross national product that's about one-third of the United States' and growing. Germany has risen from the ashes of World War II to become the world's fifth-largest industrial power, ranking fourth in steel output and nuclear power and third in automobile production. Germany shines culturally, beating out all but two countries in the production of books, Nobel laureates, and professors.

Germany is young by European standards. In 1850, there were 35 independent countries in what is now Germany. In medieval times, there were 350, each with its own weights, measures, coinage, king, and lotto. "Germany" was finally united in 1871 by Otto von Bismarck. Over the next century, it lost two World Wars and was split down the middle during the Cold War.

While its East–West division lasted about 40 years, historically Germany has been divided between north and south. While northern Germany was barbarian, is Protestant, and assaults life aggressively, southern Germany was Roman, is Catholic, and enjoys a more relaxed tempo of life. The American image of Germany is beer-and-pretzel Bavaria (probably because that was "our" sector after the war). This historic north–south division is less pronounced these days, as Germany becomes a more mobile society. The big chore facing Germany today

---

How Big, How Many, How Much

- 138,000 square miles (half the size of Texas)
- 82 million people (four times that of Texas)
- 1 euro (€) = about $1.20

Germany

is integrating the wilted economy of what was East Germany into the powerhouse economy of the West. This monumental task has given the West higher taxes (and second thoughts).

Most Germans in larger towns and the tourist trade speak at least some English. Still, you'll get more smiles by using the German pleasantries. In smaller, nontouristy towns, German is the norm. German—like English, Dutch, Swedish, and Norwegian—is a Germanic language, making it easier on most American ears than Romance languages (such as French and Italian). The most important phrases: "Hello" is *guten Tag* (GOO-tehn tahg), "please" is *bitte* (BIT-teh), and "thank you" is *danke*

(DAHNG-keh). For more, see the "Survival Phrases" near the end of this book (excerpted from *Rick Steves' German Phrase Book*).

For most visitors, the rich pastries, wine, and beer provide the fondest memories of Germanic cuisine. The wine (85 percent white) is  particularly good from the Mosel and Rhine areas. Germany is also a big beer country. The average German, who drinks 40 gallons of beer a year, knows that *dunkles* is dark, *helles* is light, *Flaschenbier* is bottled, and *vom Fass* is on tap. *Pils* is barley-based, *Weize* is wheat-based, and *Malzbier* is the malt beer that children learn with. *Radler* is half beer and half lemon-lime soda. As for treats, gummi bears are local gumdrops, with a cult following (beware of imitations—you must see the word *Gummi*), and Nutella is a chocolate-hazelnut spread that may change your life.

Germany's tourist route today—Rhine, Romantic Road, Bavaria—was yesterday's trade route, connecting its most prosperous medieval cities. Your best first glance at Germany is the Rhine River Valley. We've featured this romantic region in this book, along with two convenient, interesting big cities nearby: Köln, which is directly on the Rhine train line, and Frankfurt, connected by its airport to most anywhere in the world.

ACCESSIBILITY IN GERMANY

Even though the Rhine Valley is hilly and often inaccessible, Germany generally has good access. The western half of the country, bombed during World War II, has been rebuilt into more modern styles that often meet good accessibility standards. Bigger cities such as Frankfurt and Köln are relatively flat and offer decent access.

Under the slogan "Tourism Without Barriers," Germany is offering a wide range of travel packages that include barrier-free accommodation, activities, and services. Germany even celebrated the "Year of the Disabled" in 2003. In German, a wheelchair is called a *Rollstuhl* (roll-shtool).

The **German National Tourist Office** can help you plan your trip (www.cometogermany.com). Contact the nearest office: in New York (122 E. 42nd St. #2000, New York, NY 10168, tel. 800-651-7010 or

212/661-7200, fax 212/661-7174, gntonyc@d-z-t.com), in Illinois (P.O. Box 59594, Chicago, IL 60659, tel. 773/539-6303, fax 773/539-6378, gntoch@aol.com), or in California (501 Santa Monica Blvd. #607, Santa Monica, CA 90401, tel. 310/394-2580, fax 310/260-2923, info@gntolax .com).

Transportation

Facilities at German airports and train stations are usually good. Throughout the German transportation system, symbols provide guidance for those who do not speak the language. In most big cities, subways have at least some accessible stations and trains—ask for a map with access marked.

The **German Rail Company** (Deutsche Bahn) offers free assistance for passengers with limited mobility. You can contact the all-Germany Mobility Service Office (MobilitatsServiceZentrale) at least one day before your trip (Mon–Fri 8:00–20:00, Sat 8:00–14:00, closed Sun, tel. 0180-551-2512). They'll arrange for assistance—such as ramps and lifts— at major train stations along your route (but may not be able to provide assistance at smaller, unmanned stations). On the Web site, you'll find more information about this service, including an online request form you can fill out for a specific journey: www.bahn.de, click on "Internat .Guests," then "Handicapped."

Organizations

The **Federal Association for the Disabled** (Bundesverband Selbsthilfe Körperbehinderter) can answer basic questions on access (Altkrautheimer Strasse 20, Krautheim, tel. 06294/42810, fax 06294/428-179, www.bsk -ev.org).

Bifos helps people with disabilities find resources to assist them during a stay in Germany. They also rent accessible vans (Jordanstrasse 5, Kassel, tel. 0561/728-8540, fax 0561/728-8529, www.bifos.org, bifos @t-online.de).

The **National Tourism Coordination Agency for All** (Nationale Koordinationstelle Tourismus für Alle, a.k.a. "NatKo") runs tours for the disabled (tel. 06131/250-410, fax 06131/214-848, www.natko.de).

RHINE VALLEY

The Rhine Valley is storybook Germany, a fairytale world of legends and robber-baron castles. Cruise the most castle-studded stretch of the romantic Rhine as you listen for the song of the treacherous Loreley. Explore the castle-crowned villages of Bacharach and St. Goar. And for real hands-on castle thrills, roll or stroll through this Rhineland's greatest castle, Rheinfels.

Nearby destinations—Köln and Frankfurt—offer a modern, big-city German experience, and much better accessibility than those quaint Rhine villages. Köln is an urban Jacuzzi that keeps the Rhine churning. It's home to Germany's greatest Gothic cathedral and its best collection of Roman artifacts, a world-class art museum, and a healthy dose of German urban playfulness. And Frankfurt, while not on the Rhine, is the closest major transportation hub. Many Americans stream in to and out of Europe through Frankfurt's huge airport—but consider staying for a while to check out the city's lively square and gaze at its towering skyscrapers.

Accessibility in the Rhine Valley

The Rhine Valley is the least accessible destination covered in this book. Though beautiful and enticing, the Rhine Valley presents wheelchair riders with many barriers: steep hillside villages, lots of stairs and narrow passageways, small train stations with stairs instead of elevators, and unevenly cobbled public spaces. Slow walkers have a few more options.

The big city of Köln offers the best accessibility, from the train station and hotels to its best sights. From there, accessibility goes down as quaintness goes up: Mid-sized Rhine towns like Koblenz have more

Rhine Overview

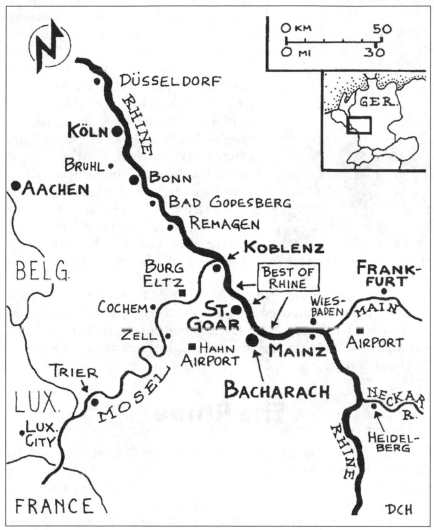

barriers, and Bacharach and St. Goar, the Rhine's most charming villages, have mediocre accessibility (especially train stations). The good news is that travelers of all mobility levels can take advantage of the valley's best experience: a lazy boat cruise down the Rhine (or, even more accessible, a quick zip along the river by train).

For a wheelchair user, the best Rhine experience begins in Köln (a convenient first stop in Germany if you're coming from London, Paris, Bruges, or Amsterdam). From there, take a train along the Rhine to Frankfurt (following the self-guided Rhine Blitz Tour, below).

Frankfurt's international airport is a convenient departure point for returning home. To add more adventure to your trip, break up the Köln-to-Frankfurt journey with a boat cruise along the best part of the Rhine. Slow walkers and more adventurous and mobile wheelchair users may want to spend more time in the Rhine's quaintest villages—Bacharach and St. Goar—and venture by taxi up to St. Goar's Rheinfels Castle. But hotels in Bacharach and St. Goar do not have good accessibility (with a few exceptions); wheelchair users may prefer to stay in Köln or Frankfurt instead, or at the fully accessible INNdependence Hotel in Mainz (managed by the town's disabled community and convenient to Frankfurt's airport).

As you decide which Rhineland activities best suit your abilities, keep in mind that with uneven terrain and lots of stairs, the castles are tough—even for non-disabled travelers. Sometimes it's better to "visit with your eyes," rather than go there in person. To castle or not to castle, the choice is yours.

The Rhine

Ever since Roman times, when this was the empire's northern boundary, the Rhine has been one of the world's busiest shipping rivers. You'll see a steady flow of barges with 1,000–2,000-ton loads. Tourist-packed buses, hot train tracks, and highways line both banks.

Many of the castles were "robber-baron" castles, put there by petty rulers (there were 300 independent little countries in medieval Germany, a region about the size of Montana) to levy tolls on passing river traffic. A robber baron would put his castle on, or even in, the river. Then, often with the help of chains and a tower on the opposite bank, he'd stop each ship and get his toll. There were 10 customs stops in the 60-mile stretch between Mainz and Koblenz alone (no wonder merchants were early proponents of the creation of larger nation-states).

Some castles were built to control and protect settlements, and others were the residences of kings. As times changed, so did the lifestyles of the rich and feudal. Many castles were abandoned for

Accessibility Levels

This book rates sights, hotels, and restaurants using four levels:

Level 1—Fully Accessible: A Level 1 building is completely barrier-free. Entryways, elevators, and other facilities are specifically adapted to accommodate a person using a wheelchair. If there's a bathroom, it has wide doors and an adapted toilet and sink. Where applicable, the bathing facilities are also fully adapted (including such features as bath boards, grab bars, or a roll-in, no-rim shower). Fully adapted hotel rooms often have an alarm system with pull cords for emergencies.

Level 2—Moderately Accessible: A Level 2 building is suitable for, but not specifically adapted to accommodate, a person using a wheelchair. This level will generally work for a wheelchair user who can make transfers and take a few steps. A person who is permanently in a wheelchair may require some assistance here (either from a companion or from staff).

Level 3—Minimally Accessible: A Level 3 building is satisfactory for people who have minimal mobility difficulties (that is, people who usually do not use a wheelchair, but take more time to do things than a non-disabled person). This building may have some steps and a few other barriers—but not too many. Level 3 buildings are best suited to slow walkers; wheelchair users will require substantial assistance here.

Level 4—Not Accessible: Unfortunately, some places in this book are simply not accessible to people with limited mobility. This means that barriers such as staircases, tight interiors and facilities (elevators, bathrooms, etc.), or other impediments interfere with passage for travelers with disabilities. Buildings in this category might include a church tower that has several flights of steep stairs, or a museum interior that has many levels with lots of steps and no elevator.

For a complete listing of the Accessibility Codes used in this chapter, please see pages 6–7.

more comfortable mansions in the towns.

Most Rhine castles date from the 11th, 12th, and 13th centuries. When the pope successfully asserted his power over the German emperor in 1076, local princes ran wild over the rule of their emperor. The castles saw military action in the 1300s and 1400s, as emperors began reasserting their control over Germany's many silly kingdoms.

The castles were also involved in the Reformation wars, in which Europe's Catholic and Protestant dynasties fought it out using a fragmented Germany as their battleground. The Thirty Years' War (1618–1648) devastated Germany. The outcome: Each ruler got the freedom to decide if his people would be Catholic or Protestant, and one-third of Germany was dead. Production of Gummi bears ceased entirely.

The French—who feared a strong Germany and felt the Rhine was the logical border between them and Germany—destroyed most of the castles prophylactically (Louis XIV in the 1680s, the revolutionary army in the 1790s, and Napoleon in 1806). They were often rebuilt in neo-Gothic style in the Romantic age—the late 1800s—and today are enjoyed as restaurants, hotels, hostels, and museums.

These days, the Rhine Valley is in a bit of a rut. After the U.S. military pulled out of the region, tourism took a hit and jobs became scarce. Perhaps, for the tourist industry, there is a silver lining: Hahn Airport, once serving the American military, is now a hub for discount airlines (www.hahn-airport.de). For information on Rhine castles, visit www.burgen-am-rhein.de. For more on the Rhine, visit www.loreleytal.com (heavy on hotels, but has maps, photos, and a little history).

Getting Around the Rhine

While the Rhine flows north from Switzerland to Holland, the scenic stretch from Mainz to Koblenz hoards all the touristic charm. Studded with the crenellated cream of Germany's castles, it bustles with boats, trains, and highway traffic. Have fun exploring with a mix of big steamers, tiny ferries *(Fähre)*, trains, and bikes.

By Boat

While many travelers do the whole trip by boat, the most scenic hour is from St. Goar to Bacharach. If you are able, sit on the top deck with your handy Rhine map-guide (or the kilometer-keyed tour in this chapter) and enjoy the parade of castles, towns, boats, and vineyards.

There are several boat companies, but most travelers sail on the bigger, more expensive, and romantic **Köln-Düsseldorfer (K-D) line** (free with a consecutive-day Eurailpass or with dated Eurail Flexipass, Eurail Selectpass, or German railpass—but it uses up a day of any Flexipass, otherwise about €9 for the 1st hour, then progressively cheaper per hour; the recommended Bacharach–St. Goar trip costs €9 one-way, €11 round-trip;

Rhine Transport Accessibility

The following chart represents the best possible scenario for access, but some boats are more accessible than others (the boats named *Stolzenfels*, *Rüdesheim*, and *Drachenfels* are the least accessible). Call ahead to find out when the most accessible boat will arrive at the town you're interested in.

Town	Train Station	K-D Boat Dock
Köln	Level 1—Fully Accessible.	Level 2—Moderately Accessible, with shore ramps.
Koblenz	Level 2—Moderately Accessible.	Level 2—Moderately Accessible, with shore ramps.
St. Goar	Level 4—Not Accessible; twenty-three 6″ steps lead down to long landing, then another nine 6″ steps down to street.	Level 2—Moderately Accessible, with shore ramps.
Bacharach	Going south to north (Mainz to Koblenz), the train station is Level 4—Not Accessible (twenty-three 6″ steps lead down to long landing, then another twenty-four 6″ steps up to town). But if you're going north to south, the station is Level 1—Fully Accessible.	Level 2—Moderately Accessible, with shore ramps.
Mainz	Level 1—Fully Accessible.	Level 2—Moderately Accessible, with shore ramps.
Frankfurt	Level 1—Fully Accessible.	N/A

Rhine Cruise Schedule

Boats run May through September and on a reduced schedule for parts of April and October; no boats run November through March. These times are based on the 2005 schedule. Check www.euraide.de /ricksteves for updates.

Koblenz	Boppard	St. Goar	Bacharach
	9:00	10:15	11:25
*9:00	*11:00	*12:20	*13:35
11:00	13:00	14:15	15:25
—	—	15:15	16:15
14:00	16:00	17:15	18:25
13:10	11:50	10:55	10:15
14:10	12:50	11:55	11:15
—	13:50	12:55	12:15
18:10	16:50	15:55	15:15
—	16:55	16:15	—
*20:10	*18:50	*17:55	*17:15

*Riding the "Nostalgic Route," you'll take the 1913 steamer Goethe (**AE+A, AI, AT,** Level 2—Moderately Accessible), with working paddle wheel and viewable little-boy-thrilling engine room (departing Koblenz at 9:00 and Bacharach at 17:15).*

half-price Mon and Fri for seniors over 60, tel. 06741/1634 in St. Goar, tel. 06743/1322 in Bacharach, www.k-d.com). Boats run daily in both directions April through October, with no boats off-season. Complete, up-to-date schedules are posted in any station, Rhineland hotel, TI, or at www.euraide.de/ricksteves. Purchase tickets at the dock up to five minutes before departure. (Confirm times at your hotel the night before.) The boat is never full. Romantics will plan to catch the old-time *Goethe* (**AE+A, AI, AT,** Level 2—Moderately Accessible), which sails each direction once a day (see "Rhine Cruise Schedule," above; confirm time locally).

K-D Line Access: AE+A, AI, AL, AT, Level 2—Moderately Accessible. Aside from requiring some assistance boarding (which can be more or less difficult, depending on the river level—lower water means steeper ramps), K-D boats offer very good accessibility. You'll enter by ramp, sometimes with a small gap (staff will assist). Most of the boats have fully accessible interiors, including adapted toilets and elevators. The least accessible boats are named *Stolzenfels*, *Rüdesheim*, and *Drachenfels*—call ahead to be sure you don't wind up on one of these (classified by K-D as non-accessible for boarding, with little accessibility once on board).

The smaller **Bingen-Rüdesheimer line** is slightly cheaper than K-D (railpasses not valid, buy tickets on boat, tel. 06721/14140, www.bingen -ruedesheimer.com), with three two-hour round-trip St. Goar–Bacharach trips daily in summer (about €8.50 one-way, €10.50 round-trip; departing St. Goar at 11:00, 14:10, and 16:10; departing Bacharach at 10:10, 12:00, and 15:00).

Bingen-Rüdesheimer Access: AE+A, AI, AL, AT, Level 2— Moderately Accessible. Bingen-Rüdesheimer boats are wheelchair-accessible, with better access at St. Goar (ramps only, no steps) than at Bacharach (one 7" entry step). The ramp into the boat is steep, but boat staff is willing to help. Some boats have wheelchair-accessible bathrooms, plus ramps or elevators to the top deck. Call ahead for a schedule of the most accessible boats.

By Train

Hourly milk-run trains down the Rhine hit every town: St. Goar–Bacharach, 12 min; Bacharach–Mainz, 60 min; Mainz–Frankfurt, 45 min. Some train schedules list St. Goar but not Bacharach as a stop, but any schedule listing St. Goar also stops at Bacharach. Tiny stations are not staffed—buy tickets at the platform machines (user-friendly, takes paper). Prices are cheap (for example, €2.70 between St. Goar and Bacharach).

Train Access: Trains range from Level 1—Fully Accessible to Level 3—Minimally Accessible. Some trains have wheelchair-accessible cars (including accessible toilets). Sometimes the train floor does not meet the level of the platform, so there can be a gap to get on or off a train. Ask at the station which trains offer the best access. The easiest way to request extra help is to contact the all-Germany Mobility Service Office (MobilitatsServiceZentrale) at least one day before your trip (Mon–Fri 8:00–20:00, Sat 8:00–14:00, closed Sun, tel. 0180-551-2512); they arrange assistance for train travelers, except at small stations such as St. Goar and Bacharach. Or, on the day of travel, you can get the conductor's attention to assist with boarding and let him know your destination to get assistance disembarking.

Station Access: Stations in bigger towns and cities (Köln, Koblenz, Mainz, Frankfurt) are Level 1—Fully Accessible. Wheelchair users who'd like extra help can call the Mobility Service Office (see above) or contact a station attendant. The small, quaint Rhine villages suffer from very poor accessibility at their train stations. In St. Goar (Level 4—Not Accessible), twenty-three 6" steps lead down to a long landing, then it's another nine 6" steps down to the street. Bacharach offers mixed accessibility: If you're coming from the south (i.e., from Mainz or Frankfurt), the train station is Level 4—Not Accessible (twenty-three 6" steps lead down to long landing, then another twenty-four 6" steps up to town). But if you're arriving in Bacharach from the north (i.e., from Koblenz or Köln), the station is Level 1—Fully Accessible. Arriving by boat to these two towns is the far more accessible option.

By Ferry

While there are no bridges between Koblenz and Mainz, you'll see car-and-passenger ferries (usually family-run for generations) about every three miles. Ferries near St. Goar and Bacharach cross the river every 10 minutes daily in the summer from about 6:00 to 20:00, connecting Bingen–Rüdesheim, Lorch–Niederheimbach, Engelsburg–Kaub, and St. Goar–St.Goarshausen (adult-€1, car and driver-€3, pay on the boat). For a fun little jaunt, take a quick round-trip with some time to explore the other side.

SELF-GUIDED TOUR

Der Romantische Rhein Blitz Zug/Schiff Fahrt

One of Europe's great train thrills is zipping along the Rhine enjoying this fast ▲▲▲ tour. Or, even better, do it relaxing on the deck of a Rhine steamer, surrounded by the wonders of this romantic and historic gorge. Here's a quick and easy tour (you can cut in anywhere) that skips the syrupy myths filling normal Rhine guides.

Sit on the left (river) side of the train or boat going south from Koblenz. While nearly all the castles listed are viewed from this side, I'll note the times when you should cross to (or look out) the other side.

You'll notice large black-and-white kilometer markers along the riverbank. I erected these years ago to make this tour easier to follow. They tell the distance from the Rhinefalls, where the Rhine leaves Switzerland and becomes navigable. Now the river-barge pilots have accepted these as navigational aids as well. We're tackling just 36 miles (58 kilometers)

Best of the Rhine

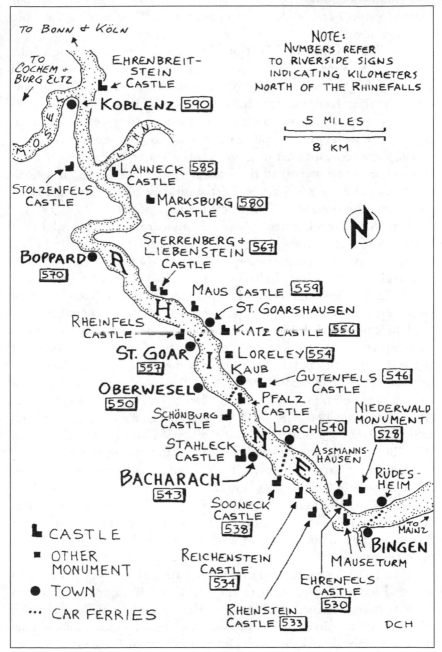

TO BONN & KÖLN

TO COCHEM & BURG ELTZ

EHRENBREIT-STEIN CASTLE

KOBLENZ 590

NOTE:
NUMBERS REFER
TO RIVERSIDE SIGNS
INDICATING KILOMETERS
NORTH OF THE RHINEFALLS

5 MILES
8 KM

N

LAHNECK 585 CASTLE

STOLZENFELS CASTLE

MARKSBURG 580 CASTLE

STERRENBERG & LIEBENSTEIN 567 CASTLE

BOPPARD 570

MAUS CASTLE 559

ST. GOARSHAUSEN

RHEINFELS CASTLE

KATZ CASTLE 556

ST. GOAR 557

LORELEY 554

KAUB

GUTENFELS 546 CASTLE

OBERWESEL 550

PFALZ CASTLE

SCHÖNBURG CASTLE

NIEDERWALD MONUMENT 528

LORCH 540

STAHLECK CASTLE

ASSMANNS-HAUSEN

RÜDES-HEIM

BACHARACH 543

SOONECK CASTLE 538

TO MAINZ

L CASTLE

■ OTHER MONUMENT

● TOWN

··· CAR FERRIES

REICHENSTEIN CASTLE 534

EHRENFELS CASTLE 530

BINGEN

MAUSETURM

RHEINSTEIN CASTLE 533

DCH

of the 820-mile-long (1,320 kilometer) Rhine. Your Rhine Blitz Tour starts at Koblenz and heads upstream to Bingen. If you're going the other direction, it still works. Just hold the book upside down.

Km 590—Koblenz: This Rhine blitz starts with Romantic Rhine thrills—at Koblenz. Koblenz is not a nice city (it was really hit hard in World War II), but its place as the historic *Deutsche Eck* (German corner)—the tip of land where the Mosel joins the Rhine—gives it a certain historic charm. Koblenz, from the Latin for "confluence," has Roman origins. If you choose to spend some time in Koblenz, explore the park, noticing the reconstructed memorial to the kaiser. It's a six-block roll or stroll from the station to the Koblenz boat dock (or catch a taxi). Accommodations for Koblenz are listed on page 522. Across the river, the yellow Ehrenbreitstein Castle now houses a hostel.

Km 585—Burg Lahneck: Above the modern autobahn bridge over the Lahn River, this castle *(Burg)* was built in 1240 to defend local silver mines; the castle was ruined by the French in 1688 and rebuilt in the 1850s in neo-Gothic style. Burg Lahneck faces another Romantic rebuild, the yellow Schloss Stolzenfels (out of view above the train). Note that *Burg* means a defensive fortress, while a *Schloss* is mainly a showy palace.

Km 580—Marksburg: This castle (black and white, with the 3 modern chimneys behind it, just before town of Spay) is the best-looking of all the Rhine castles and the only surviving medieval castle on the Rhine. Because of its commanding position, it was never attacked. It's now open as a museum (unfortunately, it's Level 4—Not Accessible; €4.50, April–Oct daily 10:00–18:00, last tour departs at 17:00; Nov–March daily 11:00–17:00, last tour at 16:00, tel. 02627/206, www.marksburg .de). The three modern smokestacks vent Europe's biggest car-battery recycling plant just up the valley. (If you haven't read the sidebar on river traffic on page 500, now's a good time.)

Km 570—Boppard: Once a Roman town, Boppard has some impressive remains of 4th-century walls. Notice the Roman towers and the substantial chunk of Roman wall near the train station, just above the main square.

If you visit Boppard, head to the fascinating church below the main square. Find the carved Romanesque crazies at the doorway. Inside, to the right of the entrance, you'll see Christian symbols from Roman times. Also notice the painted arches and vaults. Originally most Romanesque churches were painted this way. Down by the river, look for the high-water *(Hochwasser)* marks on the arches from various flood years. (You'll find these flood marks throughout the Rhine and Mosel Valleys.)

Km 567—Burg Sterrenberg and Burg Liebenstein: These are the "Hostile Brothers" castles across from Bad Salzig. Take the wall between the castles (actually designed to improve the defenses of both castles), add two greedy and jealous brothers and a fair maiden, and create your own legend. Burg Liebenstein is now a fun, friendly, and affordable family-run hotel.

Km 560: While you can see nothing from here, a 19th-century lead mine functioned on both sides of the river with a shaft actually tunneling completely under it.

Km 559—Burg Maus: The Maus (mouse) got its name because the next castle was owned by the Katzenelnbogen family. (*Katz* means "cat.") In the 1300s, it was considered a state-of-the-art fortification... until Napoleon had it blown up in 1806 with state-of-the-art explosives. It was rebuilt true to its original plans around 1900. Today, the castle hosts a falconry show.

Km 557—St. Goar and Rheinfels Castle: Look (or cross) to the other side of the train. The pleasant town of St. Goar was named for a 6th-century hometown monk. It originated in Celtic times (really old) as a place where sailors would stop, catch their breath, send home a postcard, and give thanks after surviving the seductive and treacherous Loreley crossing. St. Goar is worth a stop to explore its mighty Rheinfels Castle. (For information, a guided castle tour, and accommodations, see page 508.)

Km 556—Burg Katz: Burg Katz (Katzenelnbogen) faces St. Goar from across the river. Together, Burg Katz (built in 1371) and Rheinfels Castle had a clear view up and down the river, effectively controlling traffic. There was absolutely no duty-free shopping on the medieval Rhine. Katz got Napoleoned in 1806 and rebuilt around 1900.

Today, the castle is under a rich and mysterious ownership. In 1995, a wealthy and eccentric Japanese man bought it for about $4 million. His vision: to make the castle—so close to the Loreley that Japanese tourists are wild about—an exotic escape for his countrymen. But the town wouldn't allow his planned renovation of the historic (and therefore protected) building. Stymied, the frustrated investor just abandoned his plans. Today, Burg Katz sits empty...the Japanese ghost castle.

Below the castle, notice the derelict grape terraces—worked since the eighth century, but abandoned only in the last generation. The Rhine wine is particularly good because the slate absorbs the heat of the sun and stays warm all night, resulting in sweeter grapes. Wine from the flat fields above the Rhine gorge is cheaper and good only as table wine.

The wine from the steep side of the Rhine gorge—harder to grow and harvest—is tastier and more expensive.

About Km 555: A statue of the Loreley, the beautiful-but-deadly nymph (see next listing for legend), combs her hair at the end of a long spit—built to give barges protection from vicious icebergs that until recent years would rage down the river in the winter. The actual Loreley, a cliff (marked by the flags), is just ahead.

Km 554—The Loreley: Steep a big slate rock in centuries of legend and it becomes a tourist attraction, the ultimate Rhinestone. The Loreley (flags on top, name painted near shoreline), rising 450 feet over the narrowest and deepest point of the Rhine, has long been important. It was a holy site in pre-Roman days. The fine echoes here—thought to be ghostly voices—fertilized the legendary soil.

Because of the reefs just upstream (at kilometer 552), many ships never made it to St. Goar. Sailors (after days on the river) blamed their misfortune on a *wunderbares Fräulein* whose long blonde hair almost covered her body. Heinrich Heine's *Song of Loreley* (the *Cliffs Notes* version is on local postcards) tells the story of a count who sent his men to kill or capture this siren after she distracted his horny son, causing him to drown. When the soldiers cornered the nymph in her cave, she called her father (Father Rhine) for help. Huge waves, the likes of which you'll never see today, rose from the river and carried Loreley to safety. And she has never been seen since.

But alas, when the moon shines brightly and the tour buses are parked, a soft, playful Rhine whine can still be heard from the Loreley. As you pass, listen carefully ("Sailors...sailors...over my bounding mane").

Km 552: Killer reefs, marked by red-and-green buoys, are called the "Seven Maidens." Okay, one more goofy legend: The prince of Schönburg Castle (*ober* Oberwesel) had seven spoiled daughters who always dumped men because of their suitors' shortcomings. Fed up, he invited seven of his knights up to the castle and demanded that his daughters each choose one to marry. But they complained that each man had too big a nose, was too fat, too stupid, and so on. The rude and teasing girls escaped into a riverboat. Just downstream, God turned them into the seven rocks that form this reef. While this story probably isn't entirely true, there's a lesson in it for medieval children: Don't be hard-hearted.

Km 550—Oberwesel: Look (or cross) to the other side of the train. Oberwesel was a Celtic town in 400 B.C., then a Roman military station. It now boasts some of the best Roman-wall and medieval-tower remains on the Rhine, and the commanding Schönburg Castle. Notice how many of the train tunnels have entrances designed like medieval turrets—they were actually built in the Romantic 19th century. Turn your attention back to the riverside.

Km 546—Burg Gutenfels and Pfalz Castle, the Classic Rhine View: Burg Gutenfels (see white-painted *Hotel* sign) and the shipshape

Pfalz Castle (built in the river in the 1300s) worked very effectively to tax medieval river traffic. The town of Kaub grew rich as Pfalz raised its chains when boats came and lowered them only when the merchants had paid their duty. Those who didn't pay spent time touring its prison, on a raft at the bottom of its well. In 1504, a pope called for the destruction of Pfalz, but a six-week siege failed. Notice the overhanging outhouse (tiny white room—with faded medieval stains—between two wooden ones). Pfalz is tourable but bare, dull, and not accessible.

In Kaub, on the riverfront directly below the castles, a green statue honors the German general Blücher. He was Napoleon's nemesis. In 1813, as Napoleon fought his way back to Paris after his disastrous Russian campaign, he stopped at Mainz—hoping to fend off the Germans and Russians pursuing him by controlling that strategic bridge. Blücher tricked Napoleon. By building the first major pontoon bridge of its kind here at the Pfalz Castle, he crossed the Rhine and outflanked the French. Two years later, Blücher and Wellington teamed up to defeat Napoleon once and for all at Waterloo.

Km 544—"The Raft Busters": Immediately before Bacharach, at the top of the island, buoys mark a gang of rocks notorious for busting up rafts. The Black Forest is upstream. It was poor, and wood was its best export. Black Foresters would ride log booms down the Rhine to the Ruhr (where their timber fortified coal-mine shafts) or to Holland (where logs were sold to shipbuilders). If they could navigate the sweeping bend just before Bacharach and then survive these "raft busters," they'd come home reckless and likely horny, the German folkloric equivalent of American cowboys after payday.

Km 543—Bacharach and Burg Stahleck: Turn your attention to the other side of the train. Bacharach is a great stop (see details and accommodations below). Some of the Rhine's best wine is from this town, whose name means "altar to Bacchus." Local vintners brag that the medieval Pope Pius II ordered Bacharach wine by the cartload. Perched above the town, the 13th-century Burg Stahleck is now a hostel.

Rhine River Trade and Barge-Watching

The Rhine is great for barge-watching. There's a constant parade of action, and each boat is different. Since ancient times, this has been a highway for trade. Today, the world's biggest port (Rotterdam) waits at the mouth of the river.

Barge workers are almost a subculture. Many own their own ships. The captain (and family) live in the stern. Workers live in the bow. The family car often decorates the bow like a shiny hood ornament. In the Rhine town of Kaub, there was a boarding school for the children of the Rhine merchant marine—but today, it's closed, since most captains are Dutch, Belgian, or Swiss. The flag of the boat's home country flies in the stern (German; Swiss; Dutch—horizontal red, white, and blue; or French—vertical red, white, and blue). Logically, imports go upstream (Japanese cars, coal, and oil) and exports go downstream (German cars, chemicals, and pharmaceuticals). A clever captain manages to ship goods in each direction. Recently, giant Dutch container ships (which transport 5 times the cargo) are driving many of the traditional barges out of business, presenting the German economy with another challenge.

Tugs can push a floating train of up to five barges at once. Upstream it gets steeper and they can push only one at a time. Before modern shipping, horses dragged boats upstream (the faint remains of towpaths survive at points along the river). From 1873 to 1900, they laid a chain

Km 540—Lorch: This pathetic stub of a castle is barely visible from the road. Check out the hillside vineyards. These vineyards once blanketed four times as land as they do today, but modern economics have driven most of them out of business. The vineyards that do survive require government subsidies. Notice the small car ferry (3/hr, 10 min), one of several along the bridgeless stretch between Mainz and Koblenz.

Km 538—Castle Sooneck: Look back to the other side of the train. Built in the 11th century, this castle was twice destroyed by people sick and tired of robber barons.

Km 534—Burg Reichenstein, and **Km 533—Burg Rheinstein:** Keep watching from the other side of the train to see two of the first castles to be rebuilt in the Romantic era. Both are privately owned, tourable, and connected by a pleasant trail.

from Bonn to Bingen, and boats with cogwheels and steam engines hoisted themselves upstream. Today, 265 million tons travel each year along the 530 miles from Basel on the Swiss border to Rotterdam on the Atlantic.

Riverside navigational aids are of vital interest to captains who don't wish to meet the Loreley. Boats pass on the right unless they clearly signal otherwise with a large blue sign. Since downstream ships can't stop or maneuver as freely, upstream boats are expected to do the tricky do-si-do work. Cameras monitor traffic all along and relay warnings of oncoming ships by posting large triangular signals before narrow and  troublesome bends in the river. There may be two or three triangles per signpost, depending upon how many "sectors," or segments, of the river are covered. The lowest triangle indicates the nearest stretch of river. Each triangle tells whether there's a ship in that sector. When the bottom side of a triangle is lit, that sector is empty. When the left side is lit, an oncoming ship is in that sector.

Km 530—Ehrenfels Castle: Opposite Bingerbrück and the Bingen station, you'll see the ghostly Ehrenfels Castle (clobbered by the Swedes in 1636 and by the French in 1689). Since it had no view of the river traffic to the north, the owner built the cute little *Mäuseturm* (mouse tower) on an island (the yellow tower you'll see near the train station today). Rebuilt in the 1800s in neo-Gothic style, it's now used as a Rhine navigation signal station.

Km 528—Niederwald Monument: Across from the Bingen station on a hilltop is the 120-foot-high Niederwald monument, a memorial built with 32 tons of bronze in 1877 to commemorate "the reestablishment of the German Empire." A lift takes tourists to this statue from the famous and extremely touristy wine town of Rüdesheim.

From here, the Romantic Rhine becomes the industrial Rhine, and our tour is over.

Bacharach

Once prosperous from the wine and wood trade, Bacharach (BAHKH-ah-rahkh, with a guttural *kh* sound) is now just a pleasant half-timbered village of a thousand people working hard to keep its tourists happy. For accommodations in Bacharach, see page 518.

Accessibility in Bacharach

Bacharach is a quaint, old, cobbled town—less than ideal for wheelchair users. The train station is Level 1—Fully Accessible if arriving from the north. But if you're coming from the south, it's Level 4—Not Accessible; instead, you can take K-D boat to Bacharach's fully accessible dock. For details on train station and boat accessibility, see "Getting Around the Rhine," page 490. There are three wheelchair-accessible toilets in town: near the K-D boat dock (€0.50), in the courtyard near the Posthof TI office (free), and inside the modern post office (free).

Tourist Information

The TI is on the main street in the Posthof court-yard next to the church (**AE+A, AI, AT,** Level 2—Moderately Accessible, staff is willing to assist wheelchair users; April–Oct Mon–Fri 9:00–17:00, Sat 10:00–14:00, Sun 10:00–14:00; Nov–March Mon–Fri 9:00–12:00, closed Sat–Sun; Internet access–€2/hr, Oberstrasse 45, from train station turn right and go 5 blocks down main street with castle high on your left, tel. 06743/919-303, www.bacharach.de or www.rhein-nahe-touristik.de, Herr Kuhn and his team). The TI stores bags for day-trippers and provides ferry schedules. For accommodations, see "Sleeping," page 518.

Helpful Hints

Shopping: The Jost beer-stein stores carry most everything a shopper could want. The more accessible shop (**AE, AI,** Level 2—Moderately Accessible) is next to the post office at Rosenstrasse 16 (barrier-free entryway and wide aisles; Mon–Sat 8:30–18:00, closed Sun, ships overseas, tel. 06743/1224, www.phil-jost-germany.com). The other branch (Level 3—Minimally Accessible, three 8" steps and an obstructed, narrow entry) is across from the church in the main

Bacharach

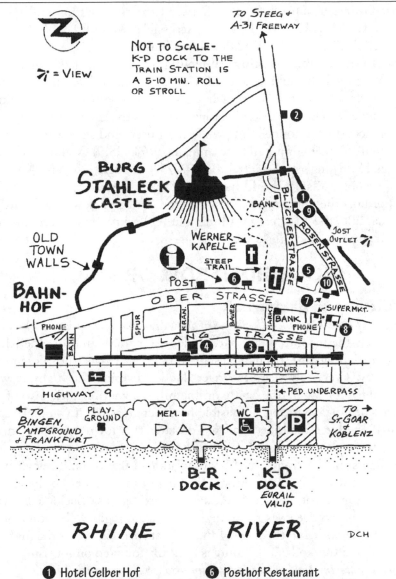

❶ Hotel Gelber Hof		❻ Posthof Restaurant	
❷ Pension Winzerhaus		❼ Altes Haus Restaurant	
❸ Hotel Rhein		❽ Kurpfälzische Münze Rest.	
❹ Hotel/Rest. Kranenturm		❾ Bistro Zur Alte Backstube	
❺ Hotel Altkölnischer Hof		❿ Weingut zum Grüner Baum	

square (same hours as above and also open Sun 10:00–17:00).

Post Office: It's on Oberstrasse between the train station and the TI (**AE, AI, AT,** Level 1—Fully Accessible; Mon–Fri 9:00–12:00 & 15:00–18:00, Sat 9:00–12:00, closed Sun).

Local Guides and Walking/Wheeling Tours: Get acquainted with Bacharach by taking a tour. Charming Herr Rolf Jung, retired headmaster of the Bacharach school, is a superb English-speaking guide who loves sharing his town's story with Americans. Herr Jung is accustomed to including wheelchair users and slow walkers in his tours (€30, 90 min, call to reserve, tel. 06743/1519). Manuela Maddes is Herr Jung's back-up (tel. 06743/2759). If Herr Jung and Manuela are not available, the TI has a list of other English-speaking guides, or take the self-guided roll or stroll, described below. On Saturdays at 11:00, the TI offers a walking tour (€4) primarily in German—but if you ask for English, you'll get it as well.

SELF-GUIDED ROLL OR STROLL

Welcome to Bacharach

• *Start at the Köln-Düsseldorfer ferry dock (next to a fine picnic park).*

View the town from the parking lot—a modern landfill. The Rhine used to lap against Bacharach's town wall, just over the present-day highway. Every few years the river floods, covering the highway with several feet of water. The **castle** on the hill is a youth hostel. Two of the town's original 16 towers are visible from here (up to 5 if you look really hard). The huge roadside wine keg declares this town was built on the wine trade.

Reefs up the river forced boats to unload upriver and reload here. Consequently, Bacharach became the biggest wine trader on the Rhine. A riverfront crane hoisted huge kegs of prestigious "Bacharach" wine (which, in practice, was from anywhere in the region). The tour buses next to the dock and the flags of the biggest spenders along the highway remind you that today's economy is basically founded on tourism.

• *Before entering the town, go upstream through the riverside park.*

This park was laid out in 1910 in the English style. Notice how the trees were planted to frame fine town views, highlighting the most picturesque bits of architecture. Until recently, going onto the grass was *verboten*. The dark, sad-looking monument—its eternal flame long snuffed-out—is a war memorial. The German psyche is permanently scarred with memories of wars. Today, many Germans would rather avoid monuments like this, which revisit the dark periods before Germany became a nation of pacifists. Take a close look at the monument. Each panel honors sons of Bacharach who died for the Kaiser: in 1864 against Russia, in 1870 against France, in 1914 during World War I. The military Maltese Cross—flanked by classic German helmets—comes with a W, for Kaiser Wilhelm.

• *Continue to where the park meets the playground, and then cross the highway to the fortified riverside wall of the Catholic church—decorated with high-water marks recalling various floods.*

Check out the metal ring on the medieval slate wall. Before the 1910 reclamation project, the river extended out to here, and boats would use the ring to tie up. Upstream from here, there's a trailer park, and beyond that there's a campground. In Germany, trailer vacationers and campers are two distinct subcultures. Folks who travel in trailers, like many retirees in the U.S., are a nomadic bunch, hauling around the countryside in their mobile homes and paying about €6 a night to park. Campers, on the other hand, tend to set up camp—complete with comfortable lounge chairs and even TVs—and stay put for weeks, even months. They often come back to the same plot year after year, treating it like their own private estate. These camping devotees have made a science out of relaxing.

• *At the big town map and accessible public toilet (€0.50), take the underpass, ascend on the ramp to the left, continue the short distance farther to the left, then pass under the train tracks through the medieval gate (one out of an original fifteen 14th-century gates). Travel across rough cobblestones for 100 feet and continue to the end of the street (Bauerstrade) over medium-rough cobblestones and an asphalt-paved street to Bacharach's main street, Oberstrasse.*

From here, Oberstrasse goes right to the half-timbered, red-and-white Altes Haus (from 1368, the oldest house in town) and left 400 yards to the train station. To the left (or south) of the church, a golden horn hangs over the old **Posthof** (**AE, AI, AT,** Level 1—Fully Accessible; free accessible toilet at back of courtyard, through middle door, and non-accessible toilet upstairs in smaller courtyard). This courtyard houses the TI and other tourist services. The post horn symbolizes the postal service throughout Europe. In olden days, when the postman blew this, traffic stopped and the mail sped through. This post station dates from 1724, when stagecoaches ran from Köln to Frankfurt and would change horses here, Pony Express–style.

Enter the courtyard—once a carriage house and inn that accommodated Bacharach's first VIP visitors. Notice the fascist eagle (from 1936, on the left as you enter; a swastika once filled its center) and the fine view of the church and a ruined chapel above. The Posthof is on a charming square. Spin around to enjoy the higgledy-piggledy building style.

Two hundred years ago, Bacharach's main drag was the only road along the Rhine. Napoleon widened it to fit his cannon wagons. The steps alongside the church lead to the castle. Return to the church, passing the **Italian Ice Cream** café (**AE+A, AI,** Level 2—Moderately Accessible), where friendly Mimo serves his special invention: Riesling wine-flavored gelato (€0.60 per scoop, opposite Posthof at Oberstrasse 48).

The church marks the town center. If you enter the church (Level 3—Minimally Accessible, eleven 7" entry steps; daily 9:30–18:00, English info on table near door), you'll find Grotesque capitals, brightly painted in medieval style, and a mix of round Romanesque and pointed Gothic arches. Left of the altar, some medieval frescoes survive where an older Romanesque arch was cut by a pointed Gothic one.

• *Continue down Oberstrasse to the **Altes Haus**.*

Notice the 14th-century building style—the first floor is made of stone, while upper floors are half-timbered (in the ornate style common in the Rhine Valley). Some of its windows still look medieval, with small flattened circles as panes (small because that's all that glass-blowing technology of the time would allow), pieced together with molten lead. Frau Weber welcomes visitors to enjoy the fascinating ground floor of her Altes Haus, with its evocative old photos and etchings (consider eating here later—see page 519).

• *Keep going down Oberstrasse to the **old mint** (Münze), marked by a crude coin in its sign.*

Across from the mint, the wine garden of Bastian family is the liveliest place in town after dark (see page 520). Above you in the vineyards stands a lonely white-and-red tower.

At the next street, look right and see the mint tower, painted in the medieval style (illustrating that the Dark Ages weren't really *that* dark), and then turn left. Wander 30 yards up Rosenstrasse to the **well.** Notice the sundial and the wall painting of 1632 Bacharach with its walls intact.

• *If you have limited mobility, end the tour here, skip the next paragraph, and read the rest of the tour for its historical detail. Adventurous slow walkers can continue, climbing the tiny-stepped lane behind the well up into the vineyard and to the tower. The slate steps (four 7" steps to a rough, narrow, uphill path, then eighteen 6"-to-11" steps to another narrow, rough path) lead to a small, extremely steep path through the vineyard that deposits you at a viewpoint atop the stubby remains of the old town wall. If the tower's open, hike to its top floor for the best view.*

A grand medieval town spreads before you. When Frankfurt had 15,000 residents, medieval Bacharach had 4,000. For 300 years (1300– 1600), Bacharach was big, rich, and politically powerful.

From this perch, you can see the chapel ruins and six surviving **city towers.** Visually trace the wall to the castle. The castle was actually the capital of Germany for a couple of years in the 1200s. When Holy Roman Emperor Frederick Barbarossa went away to fight the Crusades, he left his brother (who lived here) in charge of his vast realm. Bacharach was home of one of seven electors who voted for the Holy Roman Emperor in 1275. To protect their own power, these elector-princes did their best to choose the weakest guy on the ballot. The elector from Bacharach helped select a two-bit prince named Rudolf von Hapsburg (from a no-name castle in Switzerland). The underestimated Rudolf brutally silenced the robber barons along the Rhine and established the mightiest dynasty in European history. His family line, the Hapsburgs, ruled much of Central Europe until 1918.

Plagues, fires, and the Thirty Years' War (1618–1648) finally did Bacharach in. The town, with a population of about a thousand, has slumbered for several centuries. Today, the castle houses commoners— 40,000 overnights annually by youth hostelers.

In the mid-19th century, painters such as J. M. W. Turner and writers such as Victor Hugo were charmed by the Rhineland's romantic mix of past glory, present poverty, and rich legend. They put this part of the Rhine on the old Grand Tour map as the "Romantic Rhine." Victor Hugo pondered the ruined 15th-century chapel that you see under the castle. In his 1842 travel book, *Rhein Reise (Rhine Travels),* he wrote, "No doors, no roof or windows, a magnificent skeleton puts its silhouette against the sky. Above it, the ivy-covered castle ruins provide a fitting crown. This is Bacharach, land of fairytales, covered with legends and sagas." If you're enjoying the Romantic Rhine, thank Victor Hugo and company.

• *To get back into town, take the level path away from the river that leads along the once mighty wall up the valley past the next tower. Then cross the street into the parking lot. Pass Pension Malerwinkel on your right, being careful not to damage the old arch with your head. Follow the creek past a delightful little series of half-timbered homes and cheery gardens known as "Painters' Corner" (Malerwinkel). Resist looking into some pervert's peep show (on the right) and continue downhill back to the village center. Nice work.*

St. Goar

St. Goar is a classic Rhine town—its hulk of a castle overlooking a half-timbered shopping street and leafy riverside park busy with sightseeing ships and contented strollers. From the boat dock, the main drag—a pedestrian mall without history—cuts through town before winding up to the castle. Rheinfels Castle, once the mightiest on the Rhine, is the single best Rhineland ruin to explore. Accommodations are listed on page 520.

Accessibility in St. Goar

Like other small Rhine villages, St. Goar suffers from poor accessibility. The main drag is accessible, as is the riverfront pathway. But most shops in town have a few entry steps, and none of the town's three public toilets (one at each end of town, a third up at the castle) is wheelchair-accessible.

Tourist Information

The helpful St. Goar TI (**AE+A, AI,** Level 2—Moderately Accessible, three 7" entry steps), which books rooms and offers a free baggage-check service, is on the pedestrian street, three blocks from the K-D boat dock and train station (Mon–Fri 9:00–12:30 & 13:30–18:00, Sat 10:00–12:00, closed Sun; Oct–April weekdays until 16:30, closed Sat–Sun; from train station, go downhill around church and turn left on Heer Strasse, tel. 06741/383).

Helpful Hints

Picnics: St. Goar's waterfront park is hungry for a picnic. The small Edeka **supermarket** on the main street is great for picnic fixings. You can buy any quantity of produce—just push the photo or number on the scales (**AE, AI,** Level 2—Moderately Accessible; July–Sept Mon–Fri 8:00–18:00, Sat 8:00–13:00, usually closed Sun, shorter hours Oct–June, tel. 06741/380).

Shopping: The friendly and helpful Montag family runs the Hotel Montag (Michael) and three **shops** (steins—Misha, Steiffs—Maria, and cuckoo clocks—Marion), all at the base of the castle hill road. The stein shop (**AE, AI,** Level 2—Moderately Accessible, one of the few stores in town without steps) under the hotel has Rhine guides, fine steins, and copies of this year's *Rick Steves' Germany & Austria* guidebook. All three shops offer 10 percent off any of their souvenirs (including Hummels) for travelers with this book (€5 minimum

St. Goar

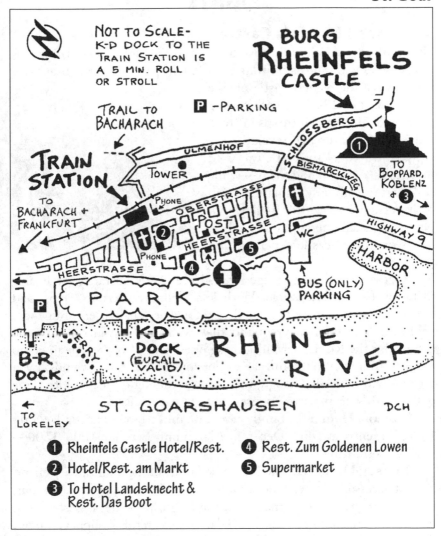

NOT TO SCALE— K-D DOCK TO THE TRAIN STATION IS A 5 MIN. ROLL OR STROLL

P —PARKING

TRAIL TO BACHARACH

BURG **RHEINFELS** CASTLE

SCHLOSSBERG

ULMENHOF

BISMARCKWEG

TRAIN STATION

TOWER

TO BOPPARD, KOBLENZ & ③

TO BACHARACH + FRANKFURT

PHONE

OBERSTRASSE

POST

HEERSTRASSE

HIGHWAY 9

PHONE

HEERSTRASSE

WC

HARBOR

④

⑤

②

❶

P A R K

BUS (ONLY) PARKING

P

FERRY

K-D DOCK (EURAIL VALID)

RHINE RIVER

B-R DOCK

TO LORELEY

ST. GOARSHAUSEN

DCH

❶ Rheinfels Castle Hotel/Rest.
❷ Hotel/Rest. am Markt
❸ To Hotel Landsknecht & Rest. Das Boot
❹ Rest. Zum Goldenen Lowen
❺ Supermarket

purchase). On-the-spot VAT refunds cover about half your shipping costs (if you're not shipping, they'll give you VAT form to claim refund at airport). The Montags' teddy bear store has four 7" entry steps, while the clock shop has five 6" entry steps, with staff willing to assist.

Internet Access: Hotel Montag (Level 4—Not Accessible, stairs with no elevator) has expensive coin-op access (see "Getting to the Castle," page 510; €8/hr, disk-burning service, Heer Strasse 128, tel. 06741/1629).

SIGHTS

St. Goar's Rheinfels Castle

Sitting like a dead pit bull above St. Goar, this mightiest of Rhine castles rumbles with ghosts from its hard-fought past. Burg Rheinfels *was* huge—once the biggest castle on the Rhine (built in 1245). It withstood a siege of 28,000 French troops in 1692. But in 1797, the French revolutionary army destroyed it. The castle was used for ages as a quarry, and today—while still mighty—it's only a small fraction of its original size. This hollow but interesting shell offers your single best hands-on ruined-castle experience on the river.

Access: Accessibility ranges from Level 2—Moderately Accessible to Level 4—Not Accessible. With lots of uneven terrain, steps, and levels, this castle presents a challenge for wheelchair users. But more adventurous wheelchair users and slow walkers will want to visit the castle—for the Rhine view, if nothing else—and, if you're able to go up hills and over uneven terrain, can explore quite a bit of the grounds. Even the most adventurous, though, will likely encounter difficulty with some of the castle's steep, narrow stairs and tight passageways.

Cost and Hours: €4, family card-€10, mid-March–Nov daily 9:00–18:00, last entry at 17:00, Dec–mid-March only Sat–Sun 11:00–17:00—weather permitting.

Tours and Information: The guided tours of the castle are excellent, but not accessible (instead, do what you are able of the self-guided tour, below). The castle map is mediocre; the English booklet is better, with history and illustrations (€2). If it's damp, be careful of slippery stones. An inaccessible WC is in the castle courtyard under the stairs to the restaurant entry. Information: tel. 06741/7753.

Let There Be Light: If you're planning to explore the mine tunnels, bring a flashlight or do it by candlelight (museum sells candles with matches, €0.50).

Getting to the Castle: From St. Goar's boat dock or train station, take a €5 taxi ride (**AE+A,** Level 2—Moderately Accessible; €6 for a minibus, tel. 06741/7011), or the kitschy "tschu-tschu" tourist train (**AE+A,** Level 2—Moderately Accessible, driver will assist wheelchair user in stepping up to seat, then will load folded wheelchair into front of train; €2 one-way, €3 round-trip, 7 min to the top, daily 9:30–18:00 but unreliable, 3/hr, runs from square between station and dock, also stops at Hotel Montag, complete with lusty music, tel. 06741/2030). Slow walkers with stamina could hike up the steep hill up to the castle (dangerous by wheelchair: 18" wide sidewalk, 17 percent grade, short curved section through railroad underpass).

● **Self-Guided Tour:** This tour was designed for non-disabled travelers, though I've provided details so that those with limited mobility who want to give it a try will know what to expect.

From the ticket gate, enter the complex (the 8-foot-wide, 14-foot-tall gate will be opened for wheelchair users). Go straight uphill, over the rough cobblestones and a rutted path. Pass *Grosser Keller* on the left (where this tour ends) and head through an internal gate past the *zu den gedeckten Wehrgängen* sign on the right (where we'll pass later) uphill to the museum in the only finished room of the castle (**AE+A, AI,** Level 2—Moderately Accessible, one 6" entry step through 5-foot-wide wooden door; daily 10:00–12:30 & 13:00–17:30).

❶ **Museum and Castle Model:** The seven-foot-tall carved stone immediately inside the door (marked *Keltische Säule von Pfalzfeld*)—a tombstone from a nearby Celtic grave—is from 400 years before Christ. There were people here long before the Romans...and this castle. Find the old wooden library chair near the tombstone. If you smile sweetly, the man behind the desk may demonstrate—pull the back forward and it becomes stairs for accessing the highest shelves.

The sweeping castle history exhibit in the center of the room is well described in English. The massive fortification was the only Rhineland castle to withstand Louis XIV's assault during the 17th century. At the far end of the room is a model reconstruction of the castle (not the one with the toy soldiers) showing how much bigger it was before French revolutionary troops destroyed it in the 18th century. Study this. Find where you are (hint: Look for the tall tower). This was the living quarters of the original castle, which was only the smallest ring of buildings around the tiny central courtyard (13th century). The ramparts were added in the 14th century. By 1650, the fortress was largely complete. Ever since its destruction by the French in the late 18th century, it's had no military value. While no WWII bombs were wasted on this ruin, it served St. Goar as a quarry for generations. The basement of the museum shows the castle pharmacy and an exhibit of Rhine-region odds and ends, including tools and an 1830 loom. Don't miss the photos of ice-breaking on the Rhine. While once routine, ice-breaking hasn't been necessary here since 1963.

St. Goar's Rheinfels Castle

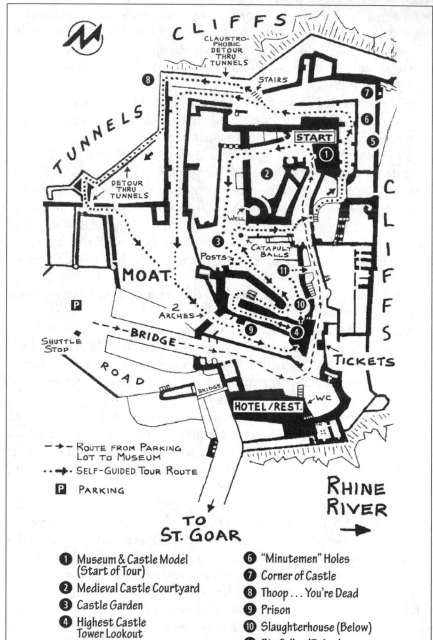

- ─ ▸ ─ ROUTE FROM PARKING LOT TO MUSEUM
- ··· ▸ SELF-GUIDED TOUR ROUTE
- **P** PARKING

RHINE RIVER →

TO ST. GOAR

❶ Museum & Castle Model (Start of Tour)
❷ Medieval Castle Courtyard
❸ Castle Garden
❹ Highest Castle Tower Lookout
❺ Covered Defense Galleries

❻ "Minutemen" Holes
❼ Corner of Castle
❽ Thoop … You're Dead
❾ Prison
❿ Slaughterhouse (Below)
⓫ Big Cellar (Below)

• *Exit the museum and go 30 yards directly out, slightly uphill into the castle courtyard.*

❷ **Medieval Castle Courtyard:** Five hundred years ago, the entire castle circled this courtyard. The place was self-sufficient and ready for a siege with a bakery, pharmacy, herb garden, brewery, well (top of yard), and livestock. During peacetime, 300–600 people lived here; during a siege, there would be as many as 4,000. The walls were plastered and painted white. Bits of the original 13th-century plaster survive.

• *Continue through the courtyard and out Erste Schildmauer, turn left into the next courtyard, and go straight to the two old, wooden, upright posts. Find the pyramid of stone catapult balls on your left.*

❸ **Castle Garden:** Catapult balls like these were too expensive not to recycle—they'd be retrieved after any battle. Across from the balls is a well—essential for any castle during the age of sieging. Look in. Spit. The old posts are for the ceremonial baptizing of new members of the local trading league. While this guild goes back centuries, it's now a social club that fills this court with a huge wine party the third weekend of each September.

• *All but the hardiest of slow walkers will want to call it quits here and head back to the entry gate; otherwise, climb the cobbled path up to the castle's best viewpoint—up where the German flag waves (4 flights of stairs: eleven 8" steps, seventeen 6" steps, sixteen 8" steps, nineteen curving 10" steps).*

❹ **Highest Castle Tower Lookout:** Enjoy a great view of the river, the castle, and the forest. Remember, the fortress once covered five times the land it does today. Notice how the other castles (across the river) don't poke above the top of the Rhine canyon. That would make them easy for invading armies to see.

• *Return to the catapult balls, head down the road, go through the tunnel, veer left through the arch marked* zu den gedeckten Wehrgängen, *go down two flights of stairs (twenty-five 7" steps, then thirteen 6" steps), and turn left into the dark, covered passageway (Covered Defense Galleries). From here, we will begin a rectangular route taking us completely around (counterclockwise) the perimeter of the castle.*

❺ & ❻ **Covered Defense Galleries with "Minutemen" Holes:** Soldiers—the castle's "minutemen"—had a short commute: defensive positions on the outside, home in the holes below on the left. Even though these living quarters were padded with straw, life was unpleasant. A peasant was lucky to live beyond age 45.

• *Continue straight through the dark gallery and to the corner of the castle, where you'll see a white painted arrow at eye level. Stand with your back to the arrow on the wall.*

❼ Corner of Castle: Look up. A three-story, half-timbered building originally rose beyond the highest stone fortification. The two stone tongues near the top just around the corner supported the toilet. (Insert your own joke here.) Turn around and face the wall. The crossbow slits below the white arrow were once steeper. The bigger hole on the riverside was for hot pitch.

• *Follow that white arrow along the outside to the next corner. Midway, you'll pass stairs on the right leading down* zu den Minengängen—*into the mine tunnels (sign on upper left; adventurous non-disabled travelers with flashlights could poke around in the tunnels). Continue on, going level to the corner. At the corner, turn left.*

❽ Thoop...You're Dead: Look ahead at the smartly placed crossbow slit. While you're lying there, notice the stonework. The little round holes were for scaffolds used as they built up. They indicate this stonework is original. Notice also the fine stonework on the chutes. More boiling pitch...now you're toast, too.

• *Continue along the castle wall around the corner. At the grey railing, look up the valley and uphill where the sprawling fort stretched. Below, just outside the wall, is land where attackers would gather. The mine tunnels are under there, waiting to blow up any attackers (read below).*

Continue along the perimeter, turn left, go down five steps and into an open field, and proceed toward the wooden bridge. You may detour here into the passageway (on right) marked 13 Halsgraben. *The "old" wooden bridge is actually modern. Angle left through two arches (before the bridge) and through the rough entry to the* Verliess *(prison) on the left.*

❾ Prison: This is one of six dungeons. You came through an entrance prisoners only dreamed of 400 years ago. They came and went through the little square hole in the ceiling. The holes in the walls supported timbers that thoughtfully gave as many as 15 residents something to sit on to keep them out of the filthy slop that gathered on the floor. Twice a day, they were given bread and water. Some prisoners actually survived longer than two years in here. While the town could torture and execute, the castle only had permission to imprison criminals in these dungeons. Consider this: According to town records, the two men who spent the most time down here—2.5 years each—died within three weeks of regaining their freedom. Perhaps after a diet of bread and water, feasting on meat and wine was simply too much.

• *Continue through the next arch, under the white arrow, then turn left and go 30 yards to the* Schlachthaus.

❿ Slaughterhouse: Any proper castle was prepared to survive a six-month siege. With 4,000 people, that's a lot of provisions. The cattle that lived within the walls were slaughtered in this room. The castle's mortar was congealed here (by packing all the organic waste from the kitchen into kegs and sealing it). Notice the drainage gutters. "Running water" came through from drains built into the walls (to keep the mortar dry and therefore strong...and less smelly).

• *Back outside, climb the modern stairs (nine 8" steps) to the left. A skinny, dark passage (yes, that's the one) leads you into the...*

⓫ Big Cellar: This *Grosser Keller* was a big pantry. When the castle was smaller, this was the original moat—you can see the rough lower parts of the wall. The original floor was 13 feet deeper. The drawbridge rested upon the stone nubs on the left. When the castle expanded, the moat became this cellar. Halfway up the walls on the entrance side of the room, square holes mark spots where timbers made a storage loft, perhaps filled with grain. In the back, an arch leads to the wine cellar (sometimes blocked off) where finer wine was kept. Part of a soldier's pay was wine...table wine. This wine was kept in a single 180,000-liter stone barrel (that's 47,550 gallons), which generally lasted about 18 months.

The count owned the surrounding farmland. Farmers got to keep 20 percent of their production. Later, in more liberal feudal times, the nobility let them keep 40 percent. Today, the German government leaves the workers with 60 percent...and provides a few more services.

• *You're free. Climb out (seventeen 8" steps), turn right, and leave. For coffee on a great view terrace, visit the Rheinfels Castle Hotel, opposite the entrance (WC at base of steps).*

Koblenz

The Rhine and Mosel rivers flow together at a confluence known as "German Corner" (Deutsche Ecke)—home to Koblenz, one of the oldest towns in Germany (which recently celebrated its 2,000th birthday). While not quite matching up to Bacharach and St. Goar for quaintness, Koblenz has its own advantages: It's far more accessible than those smaller Rhine towns, and it's a good place to catch a boat going south to see the best parts of the Rhine. Accommodations in Koblenz are listed on page 522.

Accessibility in Koblenz

The townsfolk are trying to modernize their little city without losing its historic quaintness. Most museums, sights, and churches are accessible to wheelchair users. The free TI map (gives accessibility information for Koblenz's sights see "Tourist Information," below).

For any additional help you need that the TI can't provide, contact **Der Kreis Club Behinderter** (tel. 0261/14447, a short taxi ride from the station at Am Alten Hospital 3a, www.der-kreis-cbf.de).

Immoblien-Center is another excellent resource for people with limited mobility, providing medical help and information on accessibility (**AE, AI, AT, ♥,** Level 1—Fully Accessible; Mon–Fri 9:00–17:00, closed Sat–Sun, Friedrich-Ebert-Ring 53, 1 block from Ibis Hotel, tel. 0261/393-278).

Tourist Information

Koblenz's TI (**AE, AI, ♥,** Level 2—Moderately Accessible) is friendly and helpful (Mon–Fri 9:00–19:00, Sat–Sun 10:00–19:00, until 18:00 Oct–April, closed Sun Nov–March, just south of the station at Bahnhofplatz 7, tel. 0261/303-880). The free TI map shows all the streets in Koblenz that are accessible for wheelchair users, lists Koblenz's 18 most historically significant sights (including accessibility notes), and tells the story of this historic confluence. There's no accessible toilet at the TI, but two are nearby, in or near the train station (see below).

Arrival in Koblenz

The **train station** is Level 2—Moderately Accessible, requiring some assistance to get on and off the trains. Wheelchair users should contact the all-Germany Mobility Service Office (tel. 0180-551-2512; see page 485 for more details) to arrange for a station assistant to set up a ramp for the train and lift. The station has an accessible toilet (near the main entrance, at the lower level—reached by the accessible lift; another accessible toilet is in the adjoining McDonald's). Permanent ramps lead to the street on both the north and south exits of the station. The south ramp takes you to the taxis and the TI.

The **boat dock** (with both Rhine and Mosel boats) is five blocks on Markenbildchenweg Strasse from the station. At the river, you can access a ramp a half-block upstream from the boat dock (to avoid eight 7" steps).

Sleeping and Eating on the Rhine

Sleeping

The Rhine is an easy place for cheap sleeps, but accessible rooms can be hard to come by. In terms of sheer quaintness, Bacharach and St. Goar are the best towns for an overnight stop (10 miles, apart, connected by milk-run trains, riverboats, and a riverside bike path). Slow walkers, and highly mobile wheelchair users traveling with a companion, will want to consider these listings first. Bacharach is a more interesting town, but St. Goar has the famous castle. Parking in Bacharach is simple along the highway next to the tracks (3-hour daytime limit is generally not enforced) or in the boat parking lot. Parking in St. Goar is tighter; ask at your hotel.

Those with limited mobility will find far better options in some of the valley's larger towns (or in big cities like Köln or Frankfurt; see accessible hotel listings later in this chapter). For wheelchair users traveling alone, I've listed some good, accessible options in the towns of Koblenz and Mainz—both of which also have access to the region's best activity, the Rhine boat cruise.

Eating

Germans eat lunch and dinner about when we do. Order house specials whenever possible. Pork, fish, and venison are good, and don't miss the bratwurst and sauerkraut. Potatoes are the standard vegetable, but *Spargel* (giant white asparagus) is a must in season. The bread and pretzels in the basket on your table often cost extra. If you need a break from pork, order the *Salatteller*. Great beers and white wines abound. Go with whatever beer is on tap.

I've included the most accessible restaurants for each place. But unless otherwise noted (by **AT** or **AT+A**), these restaurants do *not* have accessible toilets.

Tipping: Tipping is an issue only at restaurants that have waiters and waitresses. Don't tip if you order your food at a counter. At restaurants with wait staff, the service charge (10–15 percent) is usually listed on the menu and included in your bill. When the service is included, there's no need to tip beyond that, but if you like to tip and you're pleased with the service, you can round up the bill (but not more than five percent). If the service is not included, tip up to 10 percent. Rather than leaving coins on the table, Germans usually pay with paper, saying how much they'd like the bill to be (e.g., for an €8.10 meal, give a €20 bill and say "*Neun Euro*"—9 euros—to get €11 change).

Sleep Code

(€1 = about $1.20)
S = Single, **D** = Double/Twin, **T** = Triple, **Q** = Quad, **b** = bathroom,
s = shower only. All hotels speak some English. Breakfast is included,
and credit cards are accepted unless otherwise noted.

Sleeping in Bacharach
(country code: 49, area code: 06743)
See map on page 503 for locations.

Level 2—Moderately Accessible
Hotel Gelber Hof (AE, AI, AL, AR, AB+A) has been operated by the
Mades family since 1728—a whopping 278 years (Renate and Heiner have
been in charge for the last 38). Inside you'll find a newly renovated entry
and modern, well-cared-for rooms (accessible toilets in hallway—ramp
to sink available upon request; Sb-€65, Db-€70, closed Nov–Easter, one
block from church at 26 Blucherstrasse, tel. 06743/910-100, fax 06743/910-
1050, www.hotel-gelber-hof.com, mades@hotel-gelber-hof.com).

    Pension Winzerhaus (AE+A, AI, AR, AB+A) has 10 simple,
clean, modern rooms in a less-charming location 200 yards up the valley
from the town gate (Sb-€30, Db-€45, Tb-€60, Qb-€65, cash only, free
bikes for guests, non-smoking rooms, some street noise, easy parking,
Blücherstrasse 60, tel. 06743/1294, winzerhaus@compuserve.de).

Level 3—Minimally Accessible
Hotel Rhein (AE+A, AI, AR+A, AB+A), with 14 spacious and comfortable rooms, is classy, well-run, decorated with a modern flair, and
overlooks the river. Since it's right on the train tracks, its river- and
train-side rooms come with four-paned windows and air-conditioning
(Db-€86, cheaper for 2 nights, half-board option, directly inland from
the K-D boat dock at Landstrasse 50, tel. 06743/1243, fax 06743/1413,
info@rhein-hotel-bacharach.de, www.rhein-hotel-bacharach.de). This
place has been in the Stuber family for six generations.

    Hotel Kranenturm (AE+A, AI+A, AR, AB+A), offering castle
ambience without the climb, combines hotel comfort with *Zimmer* coziness right downtown. Run by hardworking Kurt Engel and his intense
but friendly wife, Fatima, this hotel is actually part of the medieval fortification. Its former *Kran* (crane) towers are now round rooms. When

the riverbank was higher, cranes on this tower loaded barrels of wine onto Rhine boats. While just 15 feet from the train tracks, a combination of medieval sturdiness, triple-paned windows, and included earplugs makes the riverside rooms sleepable (Sb-€40–44, Db-€55–62, bigger Db-€58–65, Db in huge tower rooms with castle and river views-€70–80, Tb-€80–95, honeymoon special-€90–105, lower price is for off-season or stays of at least 3 nights in high season, family deals, cash preferred, Rhine views come with ripping train noise, back rooms are quieter, kid-friendly, laundry service-€12.50, Langstrasse 30, tel. 06743/1308, fax 06743/1021, www.kranenturm.com, hotel-kranenturm@t-online.de). Kurt, a good cook, serves €6–18 dinners.

Hotel Altkölnischer Hof (AE+A, AI+A, AR, AB+A), a grand old building near the church, rents 20 rooms with modern furnishings (and some balconies) over an Old World restaurant. Public rooms are old-time elegant (call to reserve larger room for wheelchair access, bathrooms not accessible, staff will place wooden ramp over 2 steps on side entry, small elevator fits wheelchair only if it's folded; Sb €48–70, small or dark Db-€62–65, bright new Db-€72–82, new Db with balcony-€80–105, elevator, closed Nov–March, tel. 06743/1339 or 06743/2186, fax 06743/2793, www.hotel-bacharach-rhein.de, altkoelnischer-hof@t-online.de).

Eating in Bacharach

You can easily find atmospheric restaurants offering inexpensive (€10–15) indoor and outdoor dining.

Posthof Restaurant (AE, AI, AT, Level 1—Fully Accessible) is a historic carriage house—a stopping place for centuries of guests—newly opened as a restaurant. The menu is trendier, with free German tapas (ask), seasonal specials, and local "as organic as possible" produce. You'll sit in a half-timbered cobbled courtyard (€5–15, good salads and veggie dishes, fun kids' play area, daily 11:00 until late, Oberstrasse 45, tel. 06743/599-663).

Altes Haus (AE+A, AI, Level 2—Moderately Accessible), the oldest building in town (see page 506), serves reliably good food in Bacharach's most romantic atmosphere (€9–15, Thu–Tue 12:00–15:30 & 18:00–21:30, closed Wed and Dec–Easter, dead center by the church, tel. 06743/1209). Find the cozy little dining room with photos of the opera singer who sang about Bacharach, adding to its fame. You can enter the restaurant through the large door in front (three 7" steps), or if your wheelchair is less than 22" wide, use the back door (two 7" steps).

Kurpfälzische Münze (AE, AI, AT+A, Level 2—Moderately Accessible) is a popular standby for lunch or a drink on its sunny terrace or in its pubby candlelit interior (€7–21, daily 11:00–22:00, in the old mint, a half-block down from Altes Haus, tel. 06743/1375).

Bistro Zur Alte Backstube (AE, AI, Level 2—Moderately Accessible) is an intimate spot with varied international fare, including exotic Greek and Indonesian dishes and standards such as pub grub and coffee and *kuchen* (€4–7, Tue–Sun 10:00 until late, closed Mon, Blucherstrasse 16, next to Hotel Gelber Hof).

Wine-Tasting: Drop in on entertaining Doris Bastian's **Weingut zum Grüner Baum** wine bar (AE, AI, Level 2—Moderately Accessible). Groups of two to six people pay €13.50 for a wine carousel of 15 glasses— 14 different white wines and one lonely rosé—and a basket of bread. Your mission: Team up with others who have this book to rendezvous here after dinner. Spin the lazy susan, share a common cup, and discuss the taste. Doris insists: "After each wine, you must talk to each other." They offer soup, cold cuts, and good ambience indoors and out (Mon–Wed and Fri from 13:00, Sat–Sun from 12:00, closed Thu and Feb–mid-March, just past Altes Haus, tel. 06743/1208). To make a meal of a carousel, consider their *Kase Teller* (7 different cheeses, including *Spundekase*, the local soft cheese).

Sleeping in and near St. Goar
(country code: 49, area code: 06741)

Level 1—Fully Accessible
Hotel Landsknecht (AE, AI, AL, AR, AB, ❤), with 35 modern rooms, is the only fully accessible hotel in town. It's a newly remodeled, charming place on the banks of the Rhine just downstream from St. Goar. The delightful owner, Martina—the first Rhine Wine Queen—is a wealth of information on wine and accessibility issues (Db-€60–90, closed Jan–Feb, free parking, Aussiedlung Landsknecht 6, tel. 06741/2011, fax 06741/7499, www.hotel-landsknecht.de, info@hotel-landsknecht.de). You have several options for reaching this hotel, which is about a mile north of St. Goar's town center. If you're coming by train, get off at Boppard's train station (which offers much better access than St. Goar's), then call for Taxi Erdmann's accessible service for a ride to the hotel (€7.50, tel. 06741/7738). If you're arriving by boat, get off at St. Goar and follow the accessible riverside path from town to the hotel. Once you get to the hotel, Martina will provide accessible shuttle service to St. Goar.

Level 2—Moderately Accessible
Rheinfels Castle Hotel (AE+A, AI, AL, AR) is the town splurge.

Actually part of the castle but an entirely new building, this luxurious 60-room place is good for those with money and a car (Db-€140-180 depending on river views and balconies, extra adult bed-€37, extra bed for kids aged 7–11—€25, kids under 7 free, elevator, free parking, indoor pool and sauna, dress-up restaurant, Schlossberg 47, tel. 06741/8020, fax 06741/802-802, www.castle-hotel-rheinfels.com, info@burgrheinfels.de). Access to the exterior ramp is available upon request. The rooms are large enough for wheelchair users, but the bathrooms are not. But the staff have hosted wheelchair users in the past, and are willing to assist.

Level 4—Not Accessible
Hotel am Markt, well-run by Herr and Frau Velich, is rustic, with all the modern comforts. It features a hint of antler with a pastel flair, 18 bright rooms (enter through side door, then five 5" steps into hallway and twenty 7.5" steps to hotel rooms, bathroom not wheelchair-accessible), and a good restaurant where the son, Gil, is a fine chef (see "Eating," below). It's a good value and a stone's throw from the boat dock and train station (S-€35, Sb-€43, standard Db-€59, bigger riverview Db-€69, Tb-€82, Qb-€88, March–mid-April and Oct–mid-Nov Db-€50, closed mid-Nov–Feb, Am Markt 1, tel. 06741/1689, fax 06741/1721, www.hotelammarkt1.de, hotel.am.markt@gmx.de). Rental bikes are available to guests (€5/day). They now also rent 10 rooms of equal quality for the same price (also not accessible) in a smaller riverside hotel a block away.

Eating in St. Goar
Das Boot (AE, AI, AT, Level 1—Fully Accessible) is a beached tour boat serving German fare on the banks of the Rhine, halfway between the town square and the Hotel Landsknect (€5–13, April–Nov daily 12:00–22:00, closed Dec–March, tel. 6741/934-488).

Zum Goldenen Lowen (AE, AI, ♥, Level 2—Moderately Accessible) dishes up traditional German food in a cozy, romantic setting overlooking the Rhine (€3–12, open daily, Heerstrasse 82, tel. 06741/1674).

Hotel am Markt (AE+A, AI, Level 2—Moderately Accessible) serves tasty traditional meals with plenty of game and fish (try Chef Gil's specialties—roast wild boar and homemade cheesecake) at fair prices with good atmosphere and service (€5–16 daily specials, March–mid-Nov daily 11:00–21:00, closed mid-Nov–Feb). To enter, use the three 5" steps on the side, travel across the patio, and go up two 7" front entry steps; the staff can assist you during non-peak times.

For your Rhine splurge, ascend to **Rheinfels Castle Hotel (AE+A,**

AI, AL, Level 2—Moderately Accessible) for its incredible view terrace in an elegant setting (€15–20 dinners, daily 18:30–21:15, reserve a table by the window, tel. 06741/8020, see hotel listing above). To enter, go through the parking lot and locked gate—which must be opened by staff—then down the ramp, through hallways, and to the elevator.

Sleeping in Koblenz
(country code: 49, area code: 0261)
Each of these four hotels is fully accessible with adapted rooms, and all are located conveniently close to the station (or within a short taxi trip).

Level 1—Fully Accessible
Ibis Hotel (AE, AI, AL, AR, AB) is an inexpensive, modern chain hotel a short roll or stroll from the train station (4 adapted rooms). This Ibis is particularly warm and inviting, full of activity and social interaction. It's surrounded by shops, markets, restaurants, and beer halls (Db-€49–64, Rizzastrasse 42, tel. 0261/30240, fax 0261/302-4240, www.ibishotel .com).

Cityhotel Kurfürst Balduin (AE, AI, AL, AR, AB) is a centrally located, business-class hotel (Sb-€58, Db-€96, Hohenfelder Strasse 12, tel. 0261/13320, fax 0261/332-100, www.cityhotel-koblenz.de, info@cityhotel-koblenz.de).

Hotel Im Stüffje (AE, AI, AL, AR, AB) is a quaint old-style hotel that has been retrofitted for accessibility (Sb-€60, Db-€80, Tb-€105, Hohenzollernstrasse 5–7, tel. 0261/915-220, fax 0261/915-2244, www .handicap-hotel.de, hotel-im-stueffje@t-online.de).

Hotel Mercure (AE, AI, AL, AR, AB) is a modern 168-room chain hotel near the station (Db-€120, Julius-Wegeler-Strasse 6, tel. 0261/1360, fax 0261/136-1199, www.mercure.de, h2004@accor-hotels .com).

Eating in Koblenz
Schlemmercafe Antik (AE, AI, AT, Level 1—Fully Accessible), adjoining the Ibis Hotel, is a friendly, stylish café serving coffee, champagne, and all the goodies that go with them (€3–10, daily 10:00–20:00, Rizzastrasse 44, tel. 0261/921-5441)

Hotel Im Stüffje Bierstube (AE, AI, AT, Level 1—Fully Accessible) is a beer-and-brats *Bierstube* one block from the Ibis Hotel (€4–8, daily 11:00–22:00, Hohenzollernstrasse 5–7, tel. 0261/915-222).

Kruft Konditorei Café (AE+A, AI, Level 2—Moderately Accessible) is a wonderland of German delicacies, where marzipan

Koblenz

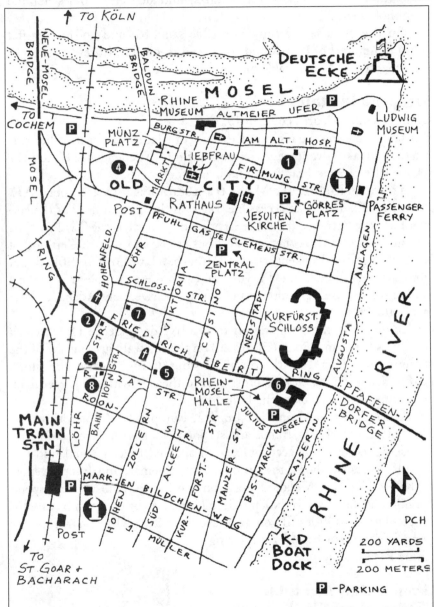

200 YARDS

200 METERS

P – PARKING

1. Der Kreis Club Behinderter (Info)
2. Immoblien-Center (Info)
3. Ibis Hotel & Schlemmercafe Antik
4. Cityhotel Kurfürst Balduin
5. Hotel Im Stüffje & Bierstube
6. Hotel Mercure
7. Kruft Konditorei Café
8. Scheidterhof Imbiss Buffet

fruits, Black Forest cakes, linzer tarts, and delicate cookies abound (Bahnhofstrasse 3).

On Rizzastrasse is a fully accessible salad bar and hot-food buffet called **Scheidterhof Imbiss** and three **picnic-perfect stores:** a bakery, a meat market, and a vegetable market.

Sleeping in Mainz
(country code: 49, area code: 06131)
Consider spending the night in the town of Mainz—if for no other reason than to take advantage of the wonderful INNdependence Hotel. The town is also close to Frankfurt and its airport.

Arrival in Mainz: The Mainz **train station** is fully accessible (**AE, AI, AL, AT**). There's an accessible toilet on the bottom floor of the station near the entrance (take the lift down). To reach the TI, leave the station, go across the courtyard and bus stops, and into the left end of the building (Im Brückenturm am Rathaus, tel. 06131/286-210). To get from the **boat dock** to the TI, you can catch the accessible tram, take a taxi, or roll or stroll up Kaiser Strasse from the riverfront Adenauer-Ufer (a 45-min trek).

To get from the train station to the INNdependence Hotel, catch the accessible tram (#50 or #51, €2.20) on the sidewalk just outside of the station's front door. Take the tram five stops (to the "Pariser Tor" stop), get off facing the busy street, cross over to the side with the soccer field, and roll or stroll a block to the hotel.

Accessibility in Mainz: Mainz is at Europe's forefront with accessibility issues. All buses, trams, and stations, along with all museums and tourist sights, are fully accessible, with adapted toilets. You'll find lots of fully accessible shops, restaurants, bars, cinemas, and Internet spots at the outdoor Fort Malakoff mall, on the Rhine. And you can spend the night at the classy INNdependece Hotel (see below), run by and for people with disabilities. If you are traveling with a wheelchair, consider using Mainz as a base for exploring the Rhine River Valley.

Level 1—Fully Accessible
INNdependence Hotel is fully accessible (**AE, AI, AL, AR, AB, ♥**), run by the Mainz disabled community. These hospitable folks are justifiably proud of their establishment (Sb-€74, Db-€85, Gleiwitzer Strasse 4, tel. 06131/250-5380,

fax 06131/211-451, www.inndependence.de, info@inndependence.de). For directions to the hotel from the station, see "Arrival in Mainz," above.

Ibis Mainz (AE, AI, AL, AR, AB) belongs to the inexpensive, no-frills Ibis hotel chain (some adapted rooms; Db-€89, less off-season, Holzhofstrasse 2, tel. 06131/934-240, fax 06131/234-126, www.ibishotel .com).

TRANSPORTATION CONNECTIONS

For information on train station accessibility, see the "Rhine Transport Accessibility" sidebar on page 491. Milk-run trains stop at all Rhine towns each hour, starting as early as 6:00. Koblenz, Boppard, St. Goar, Bacharach, Bingen, and Mainz are each about 15 minutes apart. From Koblenz to Mainz takes 75 minutes. The St. Goar–Bacharach segment departs at about :20 after the hour in each direction (€2.60, buy tickets from the machine in the unmanned station). To get a faster big train, go to Mainz (for points east and south) or Koblenz (for points north, west, and along Mosel). Train info: tel. 11861 (€0.46/min). Trains connecting Bacharach and St. Goar leave hourly (at about :20 after the hour in each direction, 10 min ride, €2.60 trip, buy tickets from the machine in the unmanned station).

From Mainz by Train to: Bacharach/St. Goar (hrly, 1 hr), **Cochem** (hrly, 2.5 hrs, change in Koblenz), **Köln** (3/hr, 90 min, change in Koblenz), **Frankfurt** (3/hr, 45 min), **Frankfurt Airport** (4/hr, 25 min), **Baden-Baden** (hrly, 1.5 hrs), **Munich** (hrly, 4 hrs).

From Koblenz by Train to: Köln (4/hr, 1 hr), **Frankfurt** (3/hr, 1.5 hrs, 1 change), **Berlin** (2/hr, 5.5 hrs, up to 2 changes), **Cochem** (2/hr, 50 min), **Trier** (2/hr, 2 hrs), **Brussels** (12/day, 4 hrs, change in Köln), **Amsterdam** (12/day, 4.5 hrs, up to 5 changes).

From Frankfurt by Train to: Bacharach (hrly, 1.5 hrs, change in Mainz; first train to Bacharach departs at 6:00, last train at 20:45), **Koblenz** (hrly, 1.5 hrs direct), **Rothenburg** (hrly, 3 hrs, transfers in Würzburg and Steinach), **Würzburg** (hrly, 2 hrs), **Nürnberg** (hrly, 2 hrs), **Munich** (hrly, 4 hrs, 1 change), **Amsterdam** (8/day, 5 hrs, up to 3 changes), **Paris** (9/day, 6.5 hrs, up to 3 changes).

From Bacharach by Train to: Frankfurt Airport (hrly, 1.5 hrs, change in Mainz, first train to Frankfurt airport departs about 5:40, last train 21:30).

Köln

Germany's fourth-largest city, Köln ("Cologne" in English), has a compact, lively center. The Rhine was the northern boundary of the Roman Empire and, 1,700 years ago, Constantine—the first Christian emperor—made Colonia the seat of a bishopric. Five hundred years later, under Charlemagne, Köln became the seat of an archbishopric. With 40,000 people within its walls, it was the largest German city and an important cultural and religious center throughout the Middle Ages. Today, the city is most famous for its toilet water. Eau de Cologne was first made here by an Italian chemist in 1709.

Even though WWII bombs destroyed 95 percent of Köln (population down from 800,000 to 40,000), it has become, after a remarkable recovery, a bustling commercial and cultural center, as well as a fun, colorful, and pleasant-smelling city.

ORIENTATION

(area code: 0221)
Köln's old-town core, bombed out then rebuilt quaint, is traffic-free and includes a park and bike path along the river. From the cathedral/TI/train station, Hohe Strasse leads into the shopping action.

For a quick old-town ramble, roll or stroll down Hohe Strasse and take a left at the city hall *(Rathaus)* to the river (where K-D Rhine cruises start). Enjoy the quaint old town and the waterfront park. The Hohenzollernbrücke, crossing the Rhine at the cathedral, is the busiest railway bridge in the world (30 trains per hour all day long).

Accessibility in Köln
As a big, modern, sophisticated city—but with the feel of a small town—Köln offers much better accessibility than other Rhine destinations in this chapter. The wheelchair user can move freely between the boat dock, train station, hotels, restaurants, and museums. Accessible Köln is a monument to efficient, progressive German thinking.

Tourist Information
Köln's energetic TI (**AE, AI,** Level 2—Moderately Accessible), opposite the church entrance, has a basic €0.20 city map and several brochures (July–Aug Mon–Sat 9:00–22:00, Sun 10:00–18:00; Sept–June Mon–Sat 9:00–21:00, Sun 10:00–18:00; Unter Fettenhennen 19, tel.

Köln

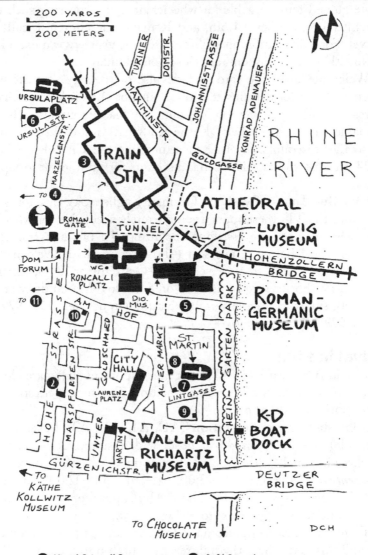

1 Hotel Cristall & Classic Hotel Harmonie
2 Hotel Engelbertz
3 Hotel Ibis Köln am Dom
4 To Residenz am Dom & Maternushaus
5 Sofitel Köln am Dom
6 Café Stovchen
7 Gaffel Haus Restaurant
8 Papa Joe's Klimperkasten Pub
9 Papa Joe's Jazzlokal
10 Früh am Dom Restaurant
11 To Café Canapé im MAK

0221/2213-0400, www.koelntourismus.de). They also offer a range of private guided tours suitable for wheelchair users, covering such topics as architecture, medieval Köln, and Romanesque churches (call TI to reserve). For information on Köln's museums, visit www.museenkoeln. de. Note that most museums are closed on Monday.

WelcomeCard: The card includes use of the city's transit system (which includes local trains to Bonn, but not the slick InterCity and Express trains), a 50 percent discount on major museums (Roman-Germanic Museum, Ludwig, Käthe Kollwitz, and Wallraf-Richartz), and smaller discounts on other museums like the Chocolate Museum (€9/24 hrs, €14/48 hrs, €19/72 hrs; discounts for families or groups of 3 or more).

City Bus Tours: Two-hour German/English city bus tours leave daily from the TI. These tours are moderately accessible for wheelchair users, who may require assistance boarding the bus and transferring from the wheelchair to a bus seat (€14, discount with WelcomeCard, cash only, buy tickets from driver, April–Oct daily at 10:00, 12:30, and 15:00, plus a shorter version at 17:30 on Sat; Nov–March daily at 11:00 and 14:00; smart to reserve summer Saturday tours, tel. 0221/979-2570 or 0221/979-2571).

Arrival in Köln

Köln couldn't be easier to visit—its three important sights are clustered within two blocks of the TI and train station. This super pedestrian zone is a constant carnival of people.

Köln's bustling **train station** (AE, AI, AL, AT, Level 1—Fully Accessible) has everything you need: a drugstore, food court, juice bar, shopping mall with grocery store, pricey WC (€1), travel center (*Reisezentrum,* Mon–Fri 5:30–23:00, Sat–Sun 6:00–22:00), and lockers (€3/24 hrs, accepts coins and €5 and €10 bills, put money in and wait 30 seconds for door to open; next to *Reisezentrum*).

To get to the cathedral from the train station, exit the station's front door and turn left. The cathedral, reaching high into the sky, is directly in front of you, about 100 yards away. The lift up to the cathedral is to the right of the cathedral's steps, in a tower with a big blue "U." Exit right from the lift, and follow the building around to the front.

If you **drive** to Köln, follow signs to *Zentrum,* then continue to the huge, accessible Parkhaus am Dom pay lot under the cathedral (€1.50/hr, €13/day).

Helpful Hints

Internet Access: Via Phone (AE, AI, Level 2—Moderately Accessible) offers Internet access and an inexpensive phone service right near the station (€2.50/hr, daily 9:00–1:00 in the morning, tel. 0221/1399-6200). Heading out of the train station, turn left on Marzellenstrasse; Via Phone is on your right at #3-5.

Ticket Office: To get tickets to concerts, the opera, and the theater, stop by KölnMusik Ticket (**AE, AI,** Level 1—Fully Accessible) next to the Roman-Germanic Museum (Mon–Fri 10:00–19:00, Sat 10:00–16:00, closed Sun, tel. 0221/2040-8160, can book ahead at www.koelnticket.de).

Festival: Köln's Lichter Festival lights up the sky on one Saturday each July, with fireworks, music, and lots of boats on the river (get details from TI or at www.koelner-lichter.de).

SIGHTS

Köln's Cathedral (Dom)

The neo-Gothic Dom—Germany's most exciting church, and easily worth ▲▲▲—looms immediately up from the train station.

Cathedral Access: AE, AI, AL, Level 1—Fully Accessible. As you face the cathedral, the accessible entrance is on the right. There is also an accessible glass lift that takes you halfway up the side of this colossal structure (entrance on side of Dom facing train station). The toilets are difficult to reach, but there is a free, accessible toilet next door in the Ludwig Museum.

Cost and Hours: Free, open daily 6:00–19:30; no tourist visits during church services daily 6:30–10:00 and at 18:30, Sun also at 12:00, 17:00, and 18:30; get schedule at Dom Forum office or www.koelner-dom.de).

Tours: The one-hour English-only tours are reliably excellent; wheelchair users are welcome (€4, Mon–Sat at 10:30 and 14:30, Sun at 14:30, meet inside front door of Dom, tel. 0221/9258-4730). Your tour ticket also gives you free entry to the English-language 20-minute video in the Dom Forum directly following the tour (see "Dom Forum," page 534).

➔ Self-Guided Tour: If you don't take the guided tour, follow this seven-stop route (note that stops 3–7 are closed during confession Mon–Fri 7:45–9:00, Sat 14:00–18:00).

❶ Roman Gate and Cathedral Exterior: The square in front of the cathedral has been a busy civic meeting place since ancient times. A Roman temple stood where the cathedral stands today. The north gate of the Roman city, from A.D. 50, marks the start of Köln's 2,000-year-old main street.

Look for the life-size replica tip of a spire. The real thing is 515 feet above you. The cathedral facade, finished according to the original 13th-century plan, is "neo-Gothic" from the 19th century.

Postcards show the church after the 1945 bombing. The red-brick building—off to your right as you face the church—is the Diocesan Museum. The Roman-Germanic Museum is between that and the cathedral, and the modern-art Ludwig Museum is behind that (all described below).

Go inside the church, to the pews in the center of the nave.

❷ Nave: If you feel small, you're supposed to. The 140-foot-tall ceiling reminds us of our place in the vast scheme of things. Lots of stained glass—enough to cover three football fields—fills the church with light, representing God.

The church was begun in 1248. The choir—the lofty area from the center altar to the far end ahead of you—was finished in 1322. Later, with the discovery of America and routes to the Indies by sea, trade shifted away from inland ports like Köln. Funds dried up, and eventually the building stopped. For 300 years, the finished end of the church was walled off and functioned as a church, while the unfinished torso (where you now sit) waited. For centuries, the symbol of Köln's skyline was a huge crane that sat atop the unfinished west spire.

With the rise of German patriotism in the early 1800s, Köln became a symbol of German unity. And the Prussians—the movers and shakers behind German unity—mistakenly considered Gothic a German style. They initiated a national tax that funded the speedy completion of this gloriously Gothic German church. Seven hundred workers (compared to 100 in the 14th century) finished the church in just 38 years (1842–1880). The great train station was built in the shadow of the cathedral's towering spire.

Köln Cathedral

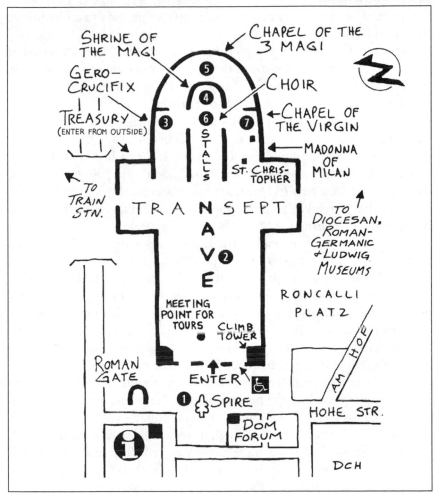

The glass windows in the front of the church are medieval. The glass surrounding you in the nave is not as old, but it's precious nevertheless. The glass on the left is Renaissance. That on the right—a gift from Ludwig I, father of "Mad" King Ludwig of tourist fame—is 19th-century Bavarian.

While 95 percent of Köln was destroyed by WWII bombs, the structure of the cathedral survived fairly well. In anticipation of the bombing, the glass and art treasures were taken to shelters and saved. The new "swallow's nest" organ above you was installed to celebrate the cathedral's 750th birthday in 1998. Relics (mostly skulls) fill cupboards on each side of the nave. The guys in the red robes are cathedral cops, called *Schweizers* (after the Swiss guard at the Vatican); if a service is getting ready to start, they might hustle you out (unless you'd like to stay for the service).

❸ **Gero-Crucifix:** As you go through the gate into the oldest part of the church, look for the mosaic of the ninth-century church on the floor. It shows a saint holding the Carolingian Cathedral, which stood on this spot for several centuries before this one was built.

Ahead of you on the left, the Chapel of the Cross features the oldest surviving monumental crucifix from north of the Alps. Carved in 976 with a sensitivity 300 years ahead of its time, it shows Jesus not suffering and not triumphant—but with eyes closed...dead. He paid the price for our sins. It's quite a two-fer: great art and powerful theology in one. The cathedral has three big pilgrim stops: this crucifix, the Shrine of the Magi, and the *Madonna of Milan* (both coming up).

Continue to the front end of the church, stopping to look at the big golden reliquary in the glass case behind the high altar.

❹ **Shrine of the Magi:** Relics were a big deal in the Middle Ages. Köln's acquisition of the bones of the Three Kings in the 12th century put it on the pilgrimage map and brought in enough money to justify the construction of this magnificent place. By some stretch of medieval Christian logic, these relics also justified the secular power of the local king. This reliquary, made in about 1200, is the biggest and most splendid I've seen. It's seven feet of gilded silver, jewels, and enamel. Old Testament prophets line the bottom, and 12 New Testament apostles—with a wingless angel in the center—line the top.

Inside sit the bones of the Magi...three skulls with golden crowns. So what's the big deal about these three kings of Christmas carol fame? They were the first to recognize Jesus as the savior and the first to come as pilgrims to worship him. They inspired medieval pilgrims and countless pilgrims since. For a thousand years, a theme of this cathedral has been that life is a pilgrimage...a search for God.

❺ **Chapel of the Three Magi:** The center chapel, at the far end, is the oldest. It also features the church's oldest window (center, from 1265). The design is typical: a strip of Old Testament scenes on the left with a theologically and visually parallel strip of New Testament scenes on the right (such as, on bottom panels: to the left, the birth of Eve; to the right, the birth of Mary with her mother Anne on the bed).

Later, glass (which you saw lining the nave) was painted and glazed. This medieval window is actually colored glass, which is assembled like a mosaic. It was very expensive. The size was limited to what pilgrim donations could support. Notice the plain, budget design higher up.

❻ **Choir:** Peek into the center zone between the high altar and the carved wooden central stalls. (You can usually only get inside if you take the tour.) This is surrounded by 13th- and 14th-century art: carved oak stalls, frescoed walls, statues painted as they would have been, and original stained glass high above. Study the fanciful oak carvings. The woman cutting the man's hair is a Samson-and-Delilah warning to the sexist men of the early Church.

❼ **Chapel of the Virgin:** The nearby chapel faces one of the most precious paintings of the important Gothic School of Köln.

The Patron Saints of Köln was painted in 1442 by Stefan Lochner. Notice the photographic realism and believable depth. There are lit-

erally dozens of identifiable herbs in the grassy foreground. During the 19th century, the city fought to have it in the museum. The Church went to court to keep it. The judge ruled that it could stay in the cathedral only as long as a Mass was said before it every day. For more than a hundred years, that happened at 18:30. Now, 21st-century comfort has trumped 19th-century law; in winter, services take place in the warmer Sacraments Chapel instead. (For more on the School of Köln art style, see "Wallraf-Richartz Museum," page 535.)

Overlooking the same chapel, the *Madonna of Milan* sculpture (1290), associated with miracles, was a focus of pilgrims for centuries.

As you head for the exit, find the statue of St. Christopher (with Jesus on his shoulder and the pilgrim's staff). Since 1470, pilgrims and travelers have looked up at him and taken solace in the hope that their patron saint is looking out for them. Go in peace.

More Cathedral Sights

Treasury—The treasury sits outside the cathedral's left transept (when you exit through the front door, turn right and continue right around the building to the gold pillar that reads *Schatzkammer*). The six dim, hushed rooms are housed in the cathedral's 13th-century stone cellar vaults. Spotlights shine on black cases filled with gilded chalices and crosses, medieval reliquaries (bits of chain, bone, cross, and cloth in gold-crusted glass capsules), and plenty of fancy bishop garb: intricately embroidered miters and vestments, rings with fat gemstones, and six-foot gold cro-siers. Displays come with brief English descriptions, but the fine little €4 book sold inside the cathedral shop provides extra information.

Access: AE, AI, AL, Level 1—Fully Accessible.

Cost and Hours: €4, €5 combo-ticket also includes spire, daily 10:00–18:00, last entry 30 min before closing, lockers at entry with €1 coin deposit, tel. 0221/1794-0300.

Dom Forum—This helpful visitors center, across from the entrance of the cathedral, is a good place to take a break. They offer an English-language "multi-vision" video on the history of the church daily at 11:30 and 15:30 (starts slow, but gets a little better, 20 min, €1.50 or included with church tour).

Access: AE, AI, Level 1—Fully Accessible.

Cost and Hours: Free, Mon–Fri 10:00–18:30, Sat 10:00–17:00, Sun 13:00–17:00, plenty of info, welcoming lounge with €0.70 coffee and juice, clean WC downstairs—free but not accessible, tel. 0221/9258-4720, www.domforum.de.

Diocesan Museum—This museum contains some of the cathedral's finest art.

Access: AE+A, AI, Level 2—Moderately Accessible, one 4" entry step with no railing.

Cost and Hours: Free, Fri–Wed 10:00–18:00, closed Thu, brick building to right of Roman Museum, Roncalliplatz 2, tel. 0221/257-7672, www.kolumba.de.

Near the Cathedral

▲▲**Roman-Germanic Museum (Römisch-Germanisches Museum)**— Germany's best Roman museum offers minimal English among its elegant and fascinating display of Roman artifacts: fine glassware, jewelry, and mosaics. The permanent collection is downstairs and upstairs; temporary exhibits are on the ground floor.

Budget travelers can view the museum's prize piece, a fine mosaic floor, free from the front window. Once the dining-room floor of a rich merchant, this is actually its original position (the museum was built around it). It shows scenes from the life of Dionysus...wine and good times, Roman-style. The tall monument over the Dionysus mosaic is the mausoleum of a first-century Roman army officer. Upstairs, you'll see a reassembled, arched original gate to the Roman city with the Roman initials for the town, CCAA, still legible, and incredible glassware that Roman Köln was famous for producing. The gift shop's €0.50 brochure provides too little information, and the €12 book too much (detailed descriptions for this museum and about Roman artifacts displayed in other German cities).

Access: AE, AI, AL, Level 1—Fully Accessible. A free, accessible toilet is at the nearby Ludwig Museum (see below).

Cost, Hours, Location: €4.50, 50 percent discount with WelcomeCard, Tue–Sun 10:00–17:00, closed Mon, Roncalliplatz 4, tel. 0221/2212-4590, www.museenkoeln.de/rgm.

▲▲**Ludwig Museum**—Next door and more enjoyable, this museum—in a slick and modern building—offers a stimulating trip through the art of the last century and American Pop and post-WWII art. Artists include German and Russian expressionists, the Blue Rider school, and Picasso. The floor plan is a mess. Just enjoy the art. The *Agfa History of Photography* exhibit is three rooms with no English; look for the pigeon with the tiny vintage camera strapped to its chest.

Access: AE, AI, AL, AT, Level 1—Fully Accessible.

Cost, Hours, Location: €7.50, often more due to special exhibitions, 50 percent discount with WelcomeCard, Tue–Sun 10:00–18:00, closed Mon, last entry 30 min before closing, must check large bags, exhibits are fairly well described in English; classy but pricey cafeteria—€5–9 salads, pastas, sandwiches, and soups; Bischofsgartenstrasse 1, tel. 0221/2212-6165, www.museum-ludwig.de.

Hohe Strasse—The Roman arch in front of the cathedral reminds us that even in Roman times, this was an important trading street and a main road through Köln. In the Middle Ages, when Köln was a major player in the heavyweight Hanseatic Trading League, two major trading routes crossed here. This high street thrived. Following its complete destruction in World War II, it emerged once again as an active trading street—the first pedestrian shopping mall in Germany. Today, it remains a wonderful place to explore and shop.

Farther from the Cathedral

These museums are several blocks south of the cathedral area.

▲▲**Wallraf-Richartz Museum**—Housed in a cinderblock of a building near the city hall, this minimalist museum features a world-class collection of old masters, from medieval to northern Baroque and Impressionist. You'll see the best collection anywhere of Gothic School of Köln paintings (1300–1550), offering an intimate peek into those times. Included is German, Dutch, Flemish, and French art by masters such as Dürer, Rubens, Rembrandt, Hals, Steen, van Gogh, Renoir, Monet, Munch, and Cézanne.

Access: AE, AI, AL, AT, Level 1—Fully Accessible.

Cost, Hours, Location: €5.80, often more due to special exhibitions, 50 percent discount with WelcomeCard, Tue 10:00–20:00, Wed–Fri

10:00–18:00, Sat–Sun 11:00–18:00, closed Mon, English descriptions and good €2.50 audioguide for permanent exhibit, Martin Strasse 39, tel. 0221/2212-1119, www.museenkoeln.de/wrm.

Imhoff-Stollwerck Chocolate Museum—Chocoholics love this place, cleverly billed as the "MMMuseum." You'll take a well-described-in-

English tour following the origin of the cocoa bean to the finished product. You can see displays on the culture of chocolate and watch treats trundle down the conveyor belt in the functioning chocolate factory, the museum's highlight. The top-floor exhibit of chocolate advertising is fun. Sample sweets from the chocolate fountain, or take some home from the fragrant, choc-full gift shop.

Access: AE, AI, AL, AT, ♥, Level 1—Fully Accessible.

Cost, Hours, Location: €6, discount with WelcomeCard, Tue–Fri 10:00–18:00, Sat–Sun 11:00–19:00, closed Mon, last entry 1 hr before closing, Rheinauhafen 1a, tel. 0221/931-8880, www.schokoladenmuseum .de.

Getting There: The museum is south on the riverfront between Deutzer and Severins bridges. Or take the handy Schoko-Express tourist train from Roncalliplatz (€2 each way, 2/hr, pickup point changes depending on events on the church square—either by TI or by the Ticket Office, confirm location at TI).

Käthe Kollwitz Museum—This contains the largest collection of the artist's powerful expressionist art, welling from her experiences living in Berlin during the tumultuous first half of the last century.

Access: AE, AI, AL, Level 1—Fully Accessible. The entry and store interior are accessible for a person using a wheelchair. The glass elevator is accessible, as is the lift in the museum. You will need to ask the ticket agent for access to the elevator in order to visit the fourth-floor exhibits.

Cost, Hours, Location: €3, 50 percent discount with WelcomeCard, Tue–Fri 10:00–18:00, Sat–Sun 11:00–18:00, closed Mon, Neumarkt 18-24, tel. 0221/227-2899, www.kollwitz.de).

Getting There: From Hohe Strasse, go west on Schildergasse for about 10 minutes; go past Neumarkt Gallerie to Neumarkt Passage, enter Neumarkt Passage, and go to the glass-domed center courtyard.

SLEEPING

Köln is *the* convention town in Germany. Consequently, the town is either jam-packed, with hotels in the €180 range, or empty and hungry. Unless otherwise noted, prices listed are the non-convention weekday rates. You'll find that prices are much higher during conventions, but soft on weekends (always ask) and for slow-time drop-ins. To find out which conventions are in town when you are, visit www.koelnmesse .de. Unlisted smaller conventions can lead to small price increases. Big conventions in nearby Düsseldorf can also fill up rooms and raise rates in Köln. Outside of convention times, the TI can always get you a discounted room in a business-class hotel (for a €3 fee).

Level 1—Fully Accessible

Residenz am Dom (AE, AI, AL, AR, AB), a block and a half from the train station, is a fully accessible dream. It has 44 adapted, spacious, light, and cheery suites with full kitchens and all the amenities. Features include roll-in showers, emergency alarms, four restaurants on the premises, tranquil gardens, physical therapy, sauna, massage, and bank services (rates vary wildly depending on demand, from a low of Db-€80 to a high of Db-€240, An den Dominikanern 6–8, tel. 0221/166-4910, www .residenz-am-dom.de, zeitwohnen@residenz-am-dom.de). The reception desk can help you get theater tickets, find someone to do your laundry, or offer other tips for your stay in Köln.

Classic Hotel Harmonie (AE, AI, AL, AR, AB) is all class, striking a perfect balance between modern and classic. Its 72 rooms include some luxurious "superior" rooms (with hardwoods and swanky bathrooms, including a foot-warming floor) that become affordable on weekends. So *this* is how the other half lives (Sb-€75–95, Db-€115, €20 less on non-convention weekends if you ask, some rooms have train noise so request quiet room, non-smoking rooms, air-con, elevator, Ursulaplatz 13-19, tel. 0221/16570, fax 0221/165-7200, www.classic-hotel-harmonie .de, harmonie@classic-hotels.com).

Sleep Code

(€1 = about $1.20, country code: 49, area code: 0221)
S = Single, **D** = Double/Twin, **T** = Triple, **Q** = Quad, **b** = bathroom, **s** = shower only. Unless otherwise noted, credit cards are accepted, English is spoken, and breakfast is included.

Maternushaus (AE, AI, AL, AR, AB), on a quiet tree-lined street in the center of Köln, is where the pope stays when he's in town. This Catholic guesthouse is a hub of activity; the attentive hotel staff focuses on nurturing community. Two adapted, high-tech rooms include emergency alarm cords, remote light switches, and roll-in showers (Sb-€84, Db-€114, Kardinal-Frings-Strasse 1-3, tel. 0221/163-1208, www.maternushaus.de).

Sofitel Köln am Dom (AE, AI, AL, AR, AB) is a modern, upscale chain hotel offering full accessibility, professionalism, and all the amenities (Db-€170–320 depending on season, just below the Dom on Kurt Hackenberg-Platz, tel. 0221/20630, fax 0221/206-3527, h1306@accor-hotels.com).

Level 2—Moderately Accessible

Hotel Ibis Köln am Dom (AE, AI, AL, AR), a huge budget chain with a 71-room modern hotel right at the train station, offers all the comforts in a tidy, affordable package (no accessible toilets in rooms; Sb-€77, Db-€89; convention rate: Sb-€109, Db-€121; breakfast-€9, non-smoking rooms, air-con, elevator, Hauptbahnhof, entry across from station's *Reisezentrum*, tel. 0221/912-8580, fax 0221/9128-58199, www.ibishotel.com, h0739@accor.com). The hotel's fine restaurant is accessible (with a nearby accessible toilet).

Hotel Engelbertz (AE, AI, AL, AR, AB+A) is a fine, family-run, 40-room place an eight-minute roll or stroll from the station and cathedral at the end of the pedestrian mall (Sb-€52 and Db-€68 if you call to book on same day or day before, Sb-€64 and Db-€85 if you reserve in advance; regular rate Sb-€70 and Db-€100, convention rate Db-€190, elevator, just off Hohe Strasse at Obenmarspforten 1-3, tel. 0221/257-8994, fax 0221/257-8924, www.hotel-engelbertz.de, info@hotel-engelbertz.de). Although the entry, lobby, and rooms are wheelchair-accessible, the bathrooms are not adapted for wheelchair users.

Hotel Cristall (AE, AI, AL, AR, AB+A) is a modern "designer hotel" with 84 cleverly appointed rooms (enjoy the big easel paintings and play human chess on the carpet). The deeply-hued breakfast room and lounge are so hip that German rock stars have photo shoots here (Sb-€72, Db-€95 but drops to €89 on weekends, rack rates can be higher, request quiet room to escape street and train noise, non-smoking rooms, air-con, elevator, Ursulaplatz 9-11, tel. 0221/16300, fax 0221/163-0333, www.hotelcristall.de, info@hotelcristall.de).

EATING

Kölsch is both the dialect spoken here and the city's distinct type of beer (pale, hoppy, and highly fermented). You'll find plenty of places to enjoy both in the streets around Alter Markt (2 blocks off the river, near city hall), as well as along Lintgasse and the waterfront area called the Frankenwerft.

Hotel Ibis am Dom Restaurant (AE, AI, AT, Level 1—Fully Accessible) has an upscale, trendy dining room with a varied menu and a welcoming staff (see hotel listing above; €5–18 entrées, daily 11:00 until late).

Café Canapé im MAK (AE, AI, AL, AT, Level 1—Fully Accessible), with sophisticated locals enjoying light fare, is a good option for a non-*Bräuhaus* lunch (€3–7 meals, Tue–Sun 11:00–17:00, closed Mon, just across Hohe Strasse from the cathedral in Museum of Applied Arts—or Museum für Angewandte Kunst—at An der Rechtschule 1, inside front door and down the stairs, smoky inside, courtyard seating outside, tel. 0221/2212-6721).

Touristy **Früh am Dom** (AE, AI, AT, Level 1—Fully Accessible), closer to the cathedral and train station, offers three floors of drinking and dining options; the main floor is best for wheelchair users (€7–16 meals, daily 8:00–24:00, Am Hof 12–14, tel. 0221/261-3211

Café Stovchen (AE, AI, Level 2—Moderately Accessible) is an intimate and friendly neighborhood *Bierstube*/café with a living room feeling and a spaghetti-and-sauerkraut menu (€4–7 entrées, Mon–Sat 11:00–1:00 in the morning, closed Sun, Ursulakloster 4-6, tel. 0221/131-712).

Winning the atmosphere award are **Papa Joe's Klimperkasten** (AE, AI, Level 2—Moderately Accessible), in a dark pub packed with memorabilia and nightly live jazz (piano only, €4–8 meals, open daily for lunch and dinner, Alter Markt 50-52, tel. 0221/258-2132) and its rowdier sibling, **Papa Joe's Jazzlokal** (AE+A, AI, Level 3—Minimally Accessible; nightly from 20:00, Buttermarkt 37, tel. 0221/257-7931, www.papajoes .de for jazz schedule).

Gaffel Haus (AE+A, AI+A, Level 3—Minimally Accessible) serves good local food (€10 meals, daily until 24:00, near Lintgasse at Alter Markt 20-22, tel. 0221/257-7692). The staff can assist with the one 6" entry step and three more 6" steps up to the tables.

TRANSPORTATION CONNECTIONS

From Köln by Train to: Frankfurt Airport (at least hrly, 1 hr), **Koblenz** (4/hr, 1 hr), **Bacharach** or **St. Goar** (hrly, 1.5 hrs, transfer in Koblenz), **Bonn** (6/hr, 20 min), **Remagen** (2/hr, 30–60 min), **Aachen** (2/hr, 30–60 min), **Cochem** (every 2 hrs direct, 1.75 hrs; more with a transfer in Koblenz, 2 hrs), **Trier** (hrly, 2.75 hrs direct; more with a transfer in Koblenz, 2.75 hrs), **Paris** (7/day, 4 hrs), **Amsterdam** (every 2 hrs direct, 3 hrs; more with a transfer in Utrecht). Train info: tel. 11861 (€0.50/min).

Frankfurt

Frankfurt, the northern terminus of the Romantic Road, offers a good look at today's no-nonsense modern Germany. There's so much more to this country than castles and old cobbled squares.

You might fly into or out of Frankfurt am Main (nicknamed "Mainhattan" by locals because it's on the Main River), or at least pass through. While Frankfurt is Germany's trade and banking capital, leading the country in skyscrapers—mostly bank headquarters—a third of the city is green space. Especially in the area around the train station, you'll notice the fascinating multiethnic flavor of the city. A third of its 650,000 residents carry foreign passports.

Spending even two or three hours in Frankfurt leaves you with some powerful impressions. The city's great sights are 15 minutes from its train station, which is 12 minutes from its airport. For years, Frankfurt was a city to avoid...but today, it has a special energy that makes it worth a look.

Accessibility in Frankfurt

As a modern city (largely destroyed and rebuilt after World War II), Frankfurt offers fair accessibility (not as good as Köln, Mainz, or Koblenz). The city has made an admirable attempt to make streets accessible, but curb cuts are often rough and sidewalks range from smooth to cobbled and bumpy. Some new trams are fully accessible, as are some subway stops. The streets meet each other at every angle imaginable, and getting from point A to point B on foot or in a wheelchair can sometimes be a challenge.

Travelers with disabilities can pick up a guidebook called *Wegweiser—für Menschen mit Behinderungen* (in German only) featuring accessibility information on the city's sights. To purchase while in the U.S., call 011-49-69-2123-5771 or write Berliner Strasse 33–35, 60311 Frankfurt am Main, Deutschland. Another good resource for accessibility information is the Magistrate for Disability (www.frankfurt -handicap.de, friederikeschlegel@stadt-frankfurt.de).

ORIENTATION

(area code: 069)

Tourist Information

Frankfurt has several TIs. The handiest, offering an abundance of bro-

chures and a free hotel-booking service, is inside the train station's main entrance (**AE, AI, AT,** Level 1—Fully Accessible; Mon–Fri 8:00–21:00, Sat–Sun 9:00–18:00, tel. 069/2123-8800, www .frankfurt-tourismus.de). Buy the city/ subway map (the basic €0.50 version is fine—skip the detailed €1 map) and consider the *Frankfurt Welcome* brochure (€0.50). The TI sells the Museum Ticket (€12, valid 2 days, covers 25 museums) and Frankfurt Card (see below), and offers bus tours of the city (see below). You'll find other TIs on Römerberg's square (Mon–Fri 9:30–17:30, Sat–Sun until 16:00), on the pedestrian shopping street Zeil, and at the airport.

The **Frankfurt Card** gives you a transit pass (including connections to and from the airport), 50 percent off all major museums, and 25 percent off the city bus tour, which virtually pays for the pass (€8/1 day, €12/2 days, sold at TI). If you're touring like mad for a day, this card can be worthwhile. Note that most museums are closed Monday and most are open until 20:00 on Wednesday (confirm at any TI).

The basic **city bus tour** (**AE+A,** Level 2—Moderately Accessible) gives a 2.5-hour orientation to Frankfurt, including Römerberg, Goethe House, and (summer only) the Main Tower. Wheelchairs users need to be able to transfer into the bus; wheelchairs are folded and stored under the bus (€25, 25 percent discount with Frankfurt Card, recorded narration, April–Oct daily at 10:00 and 14:00, Nov–March daily at 14:00). The bus picks up at the Römerberg TI first, then 15 minutes later at the Frankfurt train station TI.

Frankfurt

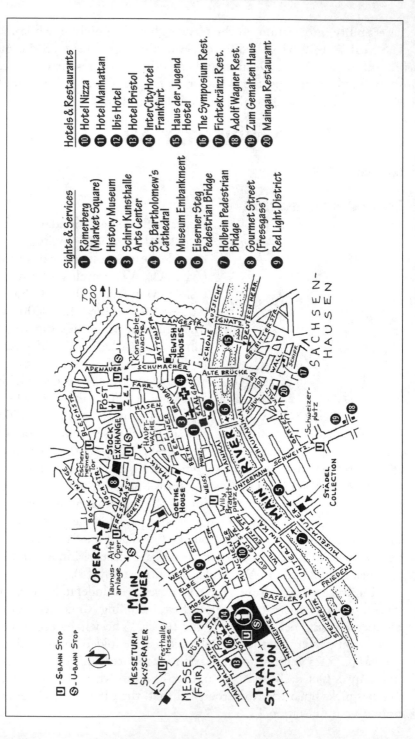

Hotels & Restaurants
- ⑩ Hotel Nizza
- ⑪ Hotel Manhattan
- ⑫ Ibis Hotel
- ⑬ Hotel Bristol
- ⑭ InterCityHotel Frankfurt
- ⑮ Haus der Jugend Hostel
- ⑯ The Symposium Rest.
- ⑰ Fichtekränzi Rest.
- ⑱ Adolf Wagner Rest.
- ⑲ Zum Gemalten Haus
- ⑳ Maingau Restaurant

Sights & Services
- ① Römerberg (Market Square)
- ② History Museum
- ③ Schirn Kunsthalle Arts Center
- ④ St. Bartholomew's Cathedral
- ⑤ Museum Embankment
- ⑥ Eiserner Steg Pedestrian Bridge
- ⑦ Holbein Pedestrian Bridge
- ⑧ Gourmet Street (Fressgass')
- ⑨ Red Light District

U - S-BAHN STOP
S - U-BAHN STOP

Local Guide: Elisabeth Lücke loves her city and shares it very well (€50/hr, reserve in advance, tel. 06196/45787, www.elisabeth-luecke.de, elisabeth.luecke@t-online.de).

Arrival in Frankfurt

By Train: The Frankfurt train station (Hauptbahnhof; **AE, AI, AT,** Level 1—Fully Accessible) bustles with travelers. This is Germany's busiest train station: 350,000 travelers make their way to 25 platforms to catch 1,800 trains every day. While it was big news when it opened in the 1890s, it's a dead-end station, which, with today's high-speed trains, makes it outdated. In fact, the speedy ICE trains are threatening to bypass Frankfurt altogether unless it digs a tunnel to allow for a faster pass-through stop (a costly project is now in the discussion stage).

The TI is in the main hall just inside the front door. Lockers and baggage check (€3/day, daily 6:00–20:00) are in the main hall across from the TI. More lockers are at track 24, across from the post office (Mon–Fri 7:00–19:30, Sat 8:00–16:00, closed Sun, does not accept packages, automatic stamp machine outside). There is one wheelchair-accessible toilet, near track 9 (key available upon request from Railway Information booth behind tracks 12 and 13). Inquire about train tickets in the Reisezentrum across from track 9 (daily 6:00–22:00). Pick up a snack at the fine food court across from tracks 4 and 5. Above the Reisezentrum is a peaceful lounge with a snack bar, clean WCs, telephones, and a children's play area (free entry with ticket or railpass, free coffee and juice in first-class lounge). The station is a five-minute roll or stroll from the convention center (Messe), a three-minute subway ride from the center, or a 12-minute shuttle train from the airport.

By Plane: See "Frankfurt's Airport," page 552.

Getting Around Frankfurt

By Public Transit: Frankfurt's public transit network includes buses, above-ground trams, and a mostly below-ground subway system (U-Bahn and S-Bahn). Some buses, trains, and stations are accessible, while others are not; before taking a trip, confirm that your journey is accessible. (For example, tram #11 from the train station to Römerberg is fully accessible, while the subway trip on that same route is not.) All modes of transport use the same tickets *(Fahrkarten)*, which you can buy at an RMV machine. Find your destination on the chart, key in the number, choose your ticket type, then pay. Choose *Einzelfahrt* for a regular single ticket (€2.10), *Kurzstrecke* for a short ride (€1.60, 3 stops or less), or *Tageskarte* for an all-day pass (€4.90). A one-way ticket to the airport costs €3.35.

By Taxi: A taxi stand is just outside the main entrance of the train station to your left. An average ride to the Römerberg square should cost you €6 (more in slow traffic). To get to the airport from any of my recommended hotels, count on at least €22.

SIGHTS

Römerberg

I've listed these sights in the order of a brief self-guided sightseeing tour around Römerberg, Frankfurt's lively market square. Wheelchair users will encounter few curb cuts, some semi-buried railroad tracks, and many sections of cobblestone sidewalk. There are accessible toilets at the Starbucks on Römerberg and at Kaufhof Department Store at the top end of Römerberg.

Getting There: Römerberg is three-quarters of a mile east of the train station. You have several options for getting there: roll or stroll up Kaiserstrasse; take a taxi (€6); use the fully accessible tram #11 (with low floors for barrier-free boarding); or take a three-minute subway ride (take U-4 or U-5 line 2 stops to Römerberg; unfortunately, this only works for highly mobile slow walkers, since there's an elevator at Römerberg, but not at train station; also, the subway cars aren't accessible, with a post in the middle of the entry door).

• *Our tour begins at the square called...*

▲**Römerberg**—Frankfurt's market square was the birthplace of the city. The town hall *(Römer)* houses the *Kaisersaal,* or Imperial Hall, where Holy Roman Emperors celebrated their coronations. Today, the *Römer* houses the city council and mayor's office. The cute row of half-timbered houses (rebuilt in 1983) opposite the *Römer* is typical of Frankfurt's quaint old center before World War II.

• *Go past the red-and-white church downhill, toward the river to Frankfurt's...*

History Museum (Historisches Museum)—Most won't want to spend time in the actual museum upstairs (accessible by lift—ask attendant; €4, 2 floors of artifacts, paintings, and displays—without a word of English). But the wheelchair-accessible models in the ground-floor annex are fascinating (€1, follow signs to *Altstadtmodelle,* English film and explanations). Study the maps of medieval Frankfurt. The wall

surrounding the city was torn down in the early 1800s to make the ring of parks and lakes you see on your modern map. The long, densely packed row of houses on the eastern end of town was Frankfurt's Jewish ghetto from 1462 to 1796. The five original houses that survive comprise one of the city's two Jewish Museums. (Frankfurt is the birthplace of Anne Frank and the Rothschild banking family.) The big model in the middle of the room shows the town in the 1930s. Across from it, you can see the horror that befell the town in 1940, 1943, and on the "fatal night" of March 23, 1944. This last Allied bombing accomplished its goal of demoralizing the city. Find the facade of the destroyed city hall—where you just were. The film behind this model is a good 15-minute tour of Frankfurt through the ages (ask them to change the language for you—*"Auf Englisch, bitte?"*). At the model of today's Frankfurt, orient yourself, then locate the riverfront (a nice detour with a grassy park and fun Eiserner Steg pedestrian bridge—**AE, AL,** Level 1—Fully Accessible—to the left as you leave this museum), and the long, skinny "pistol" (the Schirn arts exhibition center) pointing at the cathedral—where you're going next.

Access: AE+A, AI, AL, Level 2—Moderately Accessible. To gain entry to the museum, wheelchair users need to press the outside button to notify the staff.

Hours and Location: Tue–Sun 10:00–17:00, Wed until 20:00, Sat 13:00–17:00, closed Mon, Saalgasse 19, tel. 069/2123-5599, www.historisches-museum.frankfurt.de.

• *Leaving the museum, turn right to...*

Saalgasse—Literally called "hall street," this lane of postmodern buildings echoes the higgledy-piggledy buildings that stood here until World War II. In the 1990s, famous architects from around the world were each given a ruined house of the same width and told to design a new building to reflect the building that stood there before the war. As you continue down the street, guess which one is an upside-down half-timbered house with the stars down below.

(Hint: Animals are on the "ground floor.")

Saalgasse leads to some ancient **Roman ruins (AE+A,** Level 2— Moderately Accessible, ramp near church entrance leads to four 6" steps for access to full exhibit) in front of St. Bartholomew's Cathedral. The grid of stubs was the subfloor of a Roman bath (allowing the floor to be heated). The small monument in the middle of the ruins commemorates the 794 meeting of Charlemagne (king of the Franks and first Holy Roman Emperor) with the local bishop—the first official mention of a town called Frankfurt. When

Charlemagne and the Franks fled from the Saxons, a white deer led them to the easiest place to cross the Main—where the Franks could ford the river—hence, Frankfurt. The skyscraper with the yellow emblem in the distance is the tallest office block in Europe (985 feet). Next to it, with the red-and-white antenna, is the Main Tower (open to the public—see below).

St. Bartholomew's Cathedral (Kaiserdom)—Ten Holy Roman Emperors were elected and crowned in this cathedral between 1562 and 1792. The church was destroyed in World War II, rebuilt, and reopened in 1955. Twenty-seven scenes from the life of St. Bartholomew (Bartholomäus, in German) flank the high altar and ring the choir. Everything of value was moved to safety before the bombs came. But the delightful red sandstone chapel of Sleeping Mary (to the left of the high altar), carved and painted in the 15th century, was too big to move—so it was fortified with sandbags. The altarpiece and fine stained glass next to it survived the bombing (**AE, AI,** Level 2—Moderately Accessible; free, Sat–Thu 9:00–12:00 & 14:30–17:00, closed Fri, enter on side opposite river).

• *From the cathedral, it's a short roll or stroll back to Römerberg or to the Zeil, Frankfurt's lively department store-lined pedestrian boulevard. Or you can explore more of Frankfurt's sights, such as the Main Tower.*

Between Römerberg and the Station

▲**Main Tower**—Finished in 2000, this tower houses the Helaba Bank and offers the best public viewpoint from a Frankfurt skyscraper. A 45-second, ear-popping elevator ride—and then 55 steps—takes you to the 55th floor, 650 feet above the city.

Access: The observation deck is Level 4—Not Accessible (must climb 55 steps from elevator to deck). But wheelchair users and other visitors with limited mobility (and companions) will be accompanied to the part of the roof next to the restaurant, just below the observation deck, where you'll enjoy similar views.

Cost, Hours, Location: Free passage to restaurant deck for limited-mobility visitors and their companions, otherwise €4.50 for observation deck, daily 10:00–21:00, Fri–Sat until 23:00, last entry 30 min before closing, enter at Neue Mainzer Strasse 52, near corner of Neue Schlesingerstrasse, tel. 069/365-4777.

۞ Self-Guided Tour: The Main Tower is wheelchair-accessible up to the restaurant level, where a special outdoor viewing deck lets wheelchair users and their companions see the whole city. Slow walkers and non-disabled people can consider taking the final 55 steps to the top of the building, Frankfurt's ultimate viewpoint. If you do venture to the top, here's what you'll see (surveying clockwise, starting with the biggest skyscraper, with the yellow emblem).

1. Commerce Bank Building: Designed by Norman Foster (of Berlin Reichstag and London City Hall fame), the Commerce Bank building was finished in 1997. It's 985 feet high, with nine winter gardens spiraling up its core. Just to the left is Römerberg—the old town center. Look to the right (clockwise).

2. European Central Bank: The blue and gold euro symbol (€) decorates the front yard of the Euro Tower, home of the European Central Bank (a.k.a. "City of the Euro"). Its 1,000 employees administer the all-Europe currency from here. Typical of skyscrapers in the 1970s, it's slim—to allow maximum natural light into all workplaces inside. The euro symbol in the park was unveiled on January 1, 2002, the day the euro went into circulation in the 12 Eurozone countries.

The Museum Embankment lines Schaumainkai (see page 549 for more information) on the far side of the Main River, just beyond the Euro Tower.

3. Airport: The Rhine-Main Airport, in the distance, is the largest employment complex in Germany (62,000 workers). Frankfurt's massive train station dominates the foreground. From the station, the grand Kaiserstrasse cuts through the city to Römerberg.

4. Messe: The Frankfurt fair (Messe), marked by the skyscraper with the pointy top, is a huge convention center—the size of 40 soccer fields. It sprawls behind the skyscraper that looks like a classical column sporting a visor-like capital. (The protruding lip of the capital is heated so that icicles don't form, break off, and impale people on the street below.) Frankfurt's fair originated in 1240, when the emperor promised all participating merchants safe passage (www.messefrankfurt.com). The black twin towers of the Deutsche Bank in the foreground are typical of mid-1980s mirrored architecture.

5. West End and Good Living: The West End—with vast green spaces and the telecommunications tower—is Frankfurt's trendiest residential quarter. The city's "good-living spine" cuts from the West End to the right. Stretching from the classic-looking **Opera House** are broad and people-filled boulevards made to order for eating and shopping. Your skyscraper spin-tour is over. Why don't you go join them?

Opera House, Gourmet Street, and Zeil—From the Opera House to pedestrian boulevards, this is Frankfurt's good-living spine (fully accessible for wheelchair users). The Opera House was finished in 1880 to celebrate high German culture and the newly created nation. When they see both Mozart and Goethe flanking the entrance, all are reminded that this is a house of both music and theater. The original opera house was destroyed in World War II. Over the objections of a mayor nicknamed "Dynamite Rudy," the city rebuilt it in the original style (U-Bahn: Alte Oper). Facing the opera, turn right and go down a restaurant-lined boulevard (Grosse Bockenheimer) nicknamed "Gourmet Street" *(Fressgass)*. (Frankfurt's version of Fifth Avenue, lined with top fashion shops, is the parallel Goethe Strasse.) Gourmet Street leads to Zeil, a lively, tree-lined, festival-of-life pedestrian boulevard and department-store strip.

Across the River

The Schaumainkai riverside promenade (across the river, over Eiserner Steg pedestrian bridge from Römerberg) is great for an evening roll or stroll—or for people-watching on any sunny day. Keep your eyes peeled for nude sunbathers. On Saturdays, the museum strip street is closed off for a sprawling flea market.

Sachsenhausen District and Frankfurt's Culinary Specialties—Rather than beer-garden ambience, Frankfurt offers an apple-wine pub district. The area is moderately accessible, with sometimes bumpy streets. For a traditional eating-and-drinking zone with more than a hundred characteristic apple-wine pubs (and plenty of ethnic and other options), visit cobbled and cozy Sachsenhausen (wander to the east end of Schaumainkai, or from the train station take tram #16 to Schweizerplatz, also see "Eating," page 551). *Apfelwein*, drunk around here since Charlemagne's time 1,200 years ago, became more popular in the 16th century, when local grapes were diseased. It enjoyed another boost two centuries later, when a climate change meant that grapes grew poorly in the area. Apple wine is about the strength of beer (5.5 percent alcohol). It's served spiced and warm in winter, cold in summer. To complement your traditional drink with a traditional meal, order Frankfurt sausage or pork chops and kraut.

Frankfurt's Museum Embankment (Museumsufer)—The Museum Embankment features nine museums lining the Main River along Schaumainkai (mostly west of Eiserner Steg pedestrian bridge). In the 1980s, Frankfurt decided that it wanted to buck its "Bankfurt" and "Krankfurt" (*krank* means "sick") image. It went on a culture kick and devoted 11 percent of the city budget to the arts and culture. The result: Frankfurt has become a city of art. Today, locals and tourists alike enjoy an impressive strip of museums housed in striking buildings. These nine museums (including architecture, film, world cultures, and great European masters—the Städel Collection) and a dozen others are all well described in the TI's *Museumsufer* brochure (covered by €12 Museum Ticket sold at TI and participating museums, good for 2 days, most museums Tue–Sun 10:00–17:00, Wed until 20:00, closed Mon, www.kultur.frankfurt.de).

SLEEPING

Avoid driving or sleeping in Frankfurt, since the city's numerous trade fairs send hotel prices skyrocketing. The busiest months for trade fairs are generally January, March, May, September, and November. July and December have almost none, and the rest of the months fall somewhere in between (an average of 7 days a month). Visit www.messefrankfurt .com (and select "Trade Fairs") for an exact schedule. To sleep at the airport, see "Frankfurt's Airport," below.

Sleep Code

(€1 = about $1.20, country code: 49, area code: 069)
S = Single, **D** = Double/Twin, **T** = Triple, **Q** = Quad, **b** = bathroom, **s** = shower only. Unless otherwise noted, credit cards are accepted, English is spoken, and breakfast is included.

Level 1—Fully Accessible

Nizza (AE, AI, AL, AR, AB) is in a beautiful old building in the city center, with rooms furnished with antiques and artwork. In summer, breakfast is served on the rooftop garden, with good views of the city and skyline (Db-€75–105, Elbestrasse 10, tel. 069/242-5380).

Ibis (AE, AB, AL, AR, AB), well-located between the train station and Römerberg on the riverbank, is a functional and tidy hotel with two fully adapted rooms, a restaurant, snack shop, bar with happy hour, and free Internet access (Db-€59, Speicherstrasse 4, tel. 069/273-030, www.ibishotel.com).

InterCityHotel Frankfurt (AE, AI, AL, AR, AB) has 384 modern rooms (including 1 wheelchair-accessible room with a fully adapted bathroom) and offers four-star amenities (Sb/Db rates vary wildly depending on demand, from €70 to €220, Poststrasse 8, tel. 069/273-910, fax 069/2739-1999, www.intercityhotel.de, frankfurt@intercityhotel.de).

Hostel: The **Haus der Jugend** (AE, AI, AR, AL, AB) is a fine, accessible option for travelers on a budget. It's open to guests of any age (€20–24 per bed in 8- and 10-bed dorms, €24–28 in 3–4 bed dorms, Sb-€39–43, Db-€34–38, higher prices are for guests over age 27, includes daily hostel membership fee, sheets and breakfast, 470 beds, €4.80 for lunch or dinner, Internet access in lobby, laundry, curfew-2:00 in the morning, take bus #46 direction Mühlberg—goes 3/hr from station to Frankenstein Platz, Deutschherrnufer 12, tel. 069/610-0150, fax 069/6100-1599, www.jugendherberge-frankfurt.de, jugendherberge_frankfurt@t-online.de).

Level 2—Moderately Accessible

Hotel Manhattan (AE, AI, AL, AR, AB+A), with 60 sleek, arty rooms, is beautifully located across from the station. An unusual mix of warm and accommodating staff with all the business-class comforts, it's a good splurge on a first or last night in Europe (Db-€90, more during conventions, kids under 12 free, elevator, free Internet access in lobby, Düsseldorfer Strasse 10, tel. 069/269-5970, fax 069/2695-97777, www.manhattan-hotel.com, manhattan-hotel@t-online.de, Herr Rosen). They have one room set aside for wheelchair users, with an accessible toilet but a non-accessible bath/shower.

Hotel Bristol (AE, AI, AL, AR, AB+A) is a swanky new boutique hotel run by Michael Rosen, owner of the Manhattan hotel. The Bristol reflects a new generation of train-station hotels, serving up the most style and flair for your money. The place is young, hip, and modern, from its nod to Pacific Rim architecture to its teak-furnished patio café called Summer Lounge. Thirsty? Have a drink at the 24-hour bar downstairs.

Just two blocks from the station, it's surprisingly quiet (€95, more during conventions, free Internet in lobby, huge breakfast buffet, elevator, Ludwigstrasse 15, tel. 069/242-390, fax 069/251-539, www.bristol-hotel .de, info@bristol-hotel.de).

EATING

Near the Train Station

Everything in the train station, including eateries, shops, and outlets, is accessible. Several good Middle Eastern takeout places are one block from the station, up Taunusstrasse toward the Red Light District.

The Symposium (AE, AI, Level 2—Moderately Accessible), near the train station across from Hotel Bristol, is a New World Mediterranean restaurant, bar, and patio, serving beautifully presented, innovative, fresh cuisine (€5–15 entrées, daily 10:00–24:00, Ludwigstrasse 7, tel. 069/9494-2355).

In Sachsenhausen

The Sachsenhausen District—on the other side of the river, a simple roll or stroll from Schweitzerplatz—abounds with traditional apple-wine pubs (see page 549). All the ones I've listed have both indoor and outdoor seating in a woodsy, rustic setting. Not just for tourists, these characteristic places are popular with Frankfurters, too. If you are craving *Leiterchen* ("ladders," or spare ribs), these are your best bet. Here are two more local specialties, available at most apple-wine bars, for the adventurous to try: Boiled eggs and beef topped with a green sauce of seven herbs *(Grüne Sosse)*, or an aged, cylindrical, ricotta-like cheese served with onions and vinegar, called *Handkäse mit Musik* ("hand cheese with music").

Adolf Wagner (AE, AI, Level 2—Moderately Accessible) is a traditional joint that serves a local constituency. It tends to get a little smoky, so try to score a table in the outside courtyard area (€7–11 entrées, daily 11:00–24:00, Schweizer Strasse 71, tel. 069/612-565).

Fichtekränzi (AE+A, AI, Level 3—Minimally Accessible) offers the typical specialties (and some lighter fare) both in its cozy picnic-table and bench-filled beer hall, and outside under the trees. The staff is friendly and the atmosphere relaxed (€7–12 entrées, daily from 17:00, Wall Strasse 5, tel. 069/612-778).

Zum Gemalten Haus (AE+A, AI, Level 3—Minimally Accessible), named for the wall murals that adorn the facade of the building, serves German cuisine and is deceptively mellow—it's rumored to get a little wild on the weekends (€10–20 entrées, Wed–Sun 10:00–24:00, closed

Mon–Tue, Schweizer Strasse 67, tel. 069/614-559).

Irish pubs and salsa bars clutter the pedestrian zone around Rittergasse and Klappergasse, just north of the Affentor. The cobblestone streets and medieval buildings feel like Epcot Center, rather than historic Frankfurt, but if you're looking for a place to do a pub crawl, this is it.

For a break from traditional German food and pubs, splurge at **Maingau** (**AE+A, AI,** Level 3—Minimally Accessible). Repeatedly hailed as one of the best restaurants in Frankfurt, it boasts an extensive wine list, fancy tasting menus, recommended wine pairings, and an international lineup, including filet of venison and vegetarian options such as thyme-infused risotto. For less of an investment, indulge in a three-course lunch special. Don't be fooled by its modest exterior—this place is elegant inside (€13–20 entrées, tasting *menus*-€13–30 for lunch, €25–46 for dinner, more with wine pairings, Tue–Fri 11:30–15:00 & 17:00–22:30, Sat 18:00–22:30, Sun 11:30–15:00, closed Mon, call for reservations tel. 069/610-752, Schiffer Strasse 38, www.maingau.de).

TRANSPORTATION CONNECTIONS

Frankfurt am Main

From Frankfurt by Train to: Bacharach (hrly, 1.5 hrs, change in Mainz; first train to Bacharach departs at 6:00, last train at 20:45), **Koblenz** (hrly, 1.5 hrs direct), **Köln** (almost hrly, 1.25 hrs direct; more with a transfer at Frankfurt Airport), **Rothenburg** (hrly, 3 hrs, changes in Würzburg and Steinach; the tiny Steinach–Rothenburg train often leaves from track 5, shortly after the Würzburg train arrives), **Würzburg** (hrly, 2 hrs), **Nürnberg** (hrly, 2 hrs), **Munich** (hrly, 4 hrs, 1 change), **Baden-Baden** (2/hr, 1.5 hrs, transfer in Mannheim or Karlsruhe), **Freiburg** (hrly, 2 hrs, change in Mannheim), **Bonn** (hrly, 1.75 hrs direct), **Berlin** (hrly, 6 hrs), **Amsterdam** (every 2 hrs, 4.5 hrs direct, more with a transfer in Utrecht), **London** (6/day, 8 hrs, 3 changes), **Milan** (hrly, 9 hrs, 2 changes), **Paris** (9/day, 6.5 hrs, up to 3 changes), **Bern** (hrly, 4.5 hrs, changes in Mannheim and Basel), **Brussels** (hrly, 5 hrs, change in Köln), **Copenhagen** (6/day, 9 hrs, change in Hamburg), **Vienna** (8/day, 8 hrs, 2 changes). Train info: tel. 11861 (€0.46/min).

Frankfurt's Airport

The airport *(Flughafen)* is user-friendly. There are two separate terminals (know your terminal, call the airline). All trains and subways operate out of Terminal 1 (but taxis serve both). A skyline train connects the two terminals. The airport offers showers (€6), a baggage-check desk (daily 6:00–22:00, €3.50 per bag/day), lockers (€3–5/24 hrs, depending on size), free Internet access (at the *e-lounge* by departures Terminal 1B), ATMs, fair banks with long hours, a grocery store (daily 6:30–21:30, Terminal 1, on level 0 between sectors A and B), a post office, a train station, a business lounge (Europe City Club—€16/4 hrs for anyone with a plane ticket, on departure level, daily 7:00–22:00), easy rental-car pickup, plenty of parking, an information booth, a pharmacy (7:00–21:30, Terminal 1/B), a medical clinic (Terminal 1C), a casino, and even McBeer. McWelcome to Germany. If you're meeting someone, each terminal has a hard-to-miss "meeting point" near where arriving passengers pop out.

Access: Travelers with limited mobility will be transported by electric cart to the baggage claim or the gate. If you're using a gate-checked wheelchair, ask for assistance in order to gain access to the elevator that will take you to the lower level. The toilets located in the arrival halls are accessible; toilets at the baggage-claim area are not. Taxis will take wheelchair users if the baggage and wheelchair will fit in the trunk (**AE+A,** Level 2—Moderately Accessible). For train station access, see "Trains," below.

Airport Info (in English): For flight information, tel. 01805/372-4636 (www.frankfurt-airport.de) or contact the airlines directly during business hours (wait for an announcement in English): Lufthansa—tel. 01803-803-803 or 069/6969-4433, American Airlines—tel. 01803-242-324 or 069/6902-1781, Delta—tel. 01803-337-880 or 069/6902-8751, Northwest/KLM—01805-214-201 or 069/6902-1831. Pick up the free brochure *Your Airport-Assistant* for a map and detailed information on airport services (available at the airport and at most Frankfurt hotels).

Getting to the Airport: The airport is a 12-minute train ride from downtown (€3.30, 4/hr, ride included in €8 Frankfurt Card but not in €4.70 all-day *Tageskarte* transit pass). Figure around €25 for a taxi from any of my recommended hotels.

Trains: The airport has its own train station (Terminal 1). Train travelers can validate railpasses or buy tickets at the airport station. To connect by train to Frankfurt or beyond, check in with the airport's Deutsche Bahn (DB) Information Booth (located in airport's regional train station, Terminal 1, Level O, Booth 316). The DB staff can assist the wheelchair user to the appropriate train platform, and then onto the train. The DB staff will also contact train personnel at train stations for either interim or final destination assistance disembarking. (Smaller, unmanned stations—such as in Bacharach and St. Goar—do not offer this service.)

From Frankfurt Airport by Train to: Köln (at least hrly, 1 hr), **Koblenz** (hrly, 1.25 hrs, more with a transfer in Mainz), **Bacharach** (hrly, 1 hr, change in Mainz; first train to Bacharach departs at 6:00, last train at 21:00), **Rothenburg** (hrly, 3 hrs, with transfers in Würzburg and Steinach), **Würzburg** (2/hr, 2 hrs), **Nürnberg** (hrly, 2 hrs), **Munich** (2/hr, 4 hrs, 1 change), **Baden-Baden** (every 2 hrs, 1.5 hrs direct; more with a transfer in Mainz, 1.5 hrs), and **international destinations** (such as Paris, London, Amsterdam, Vienna, Milan, and many more).

Flying Home from Frankfurt: Some of the trains from the Rhine stop at the airport on their way into Frankfurt (e.g., hrly 90-min rides direct from Bonn; hrly 90-min rides from Bacharach with a change in Mainz; earliest train from Bacharach to Frankfurt leaves about 5:40, last train at 21:30). By car, head toward Frankfurt on the autobahn and follow the little airplane signs to the airport.

Sleeping at Frankfurt Airport: You can sleep at the airport, but you'll pay a premium and miss out on seeing Frankfurt. Considering the ease of the shuttle train from Frankfurt (12 min, 4/hr), I don't advise it. But if you must, the airport **Sheraton (AE, AI, AL, AT, AR, AB,** Level 1—Fully Accessible) has one fully adapted room for wheelchair users (#3081) and a thousand standard, international business-class rooms (rates vary wildly depending on season and conventions, but Db usually around €200–250, about 25 percent discount with major corporate ID—try anything, AAA and senior discounts, kids up to 18 free in the room, includes big breakfast, non-smoking rooms, fitness club, Terminal 1, tel. 069/69770, fax 069/6977-2351, www.sheraton.com/frankfurt, salesfrankfurt@sheraton.com). Most other bedrooms are accessible for wheelchair users, but without adapted bathrooms. The staff can assist wheelchair users in getting between the airport and the hotel.

The **Ibis (AE, AI, AL, AR, AB,** Level 1—Fully Accessible) has cheaper rooms in the same neighborhood, but it isn't as handy and the staff is rude (Db-€80–100, breakfast-€9, includes free accessible airport shuttle, Langer Kornweg 9a-11, Kelsterbach, tel. 06107/9870, fax 06107/987-444, www.ibishotel.com, h2203@accor-hotels.com).

Route Tips for Drivers

Frankfurt to Rothenburg: The three-hour autobahn drive from the airport to Rothenburg is something even a jet-lagged zombie can handle. It's a 75-mile straight shot to Würzburg on A-3; just follow the blue autobahn signs to Würzburg. While you can carry on to Rothenburg by autobahn, for a scenic back-road approach, leave the freeway at the Heidingsfeld-Würzburg exit. If going directly to Rothenburg, follow signs south to

Stuttgart/Ulm/Road 19, then continue to Rothenburg via a scenic slice of the Romantic Road. If stopping at Würzburg, leave the freeway at the Heidingsfeld-Würzburg exit and follow Stadtmitte, then Centrum and Residenz signs from the same freeway exit. From Würzburg, Ulm/Road 19 signs lead to Bad Mergentheim and Rothenburg.

Frankfurt to the Rhine: Driving from Frankfurt to the Rhine or Mosel takes 90 minutes (follow blue autobahn signs from airport, major cities are signposted).

The Rhine to Frankfurt: From St. Goar or Bacharach, follow the river to Bingen, then autobahn signs to Mainz, then Frankfurt, then Messe, and finally the Hauptbahnhof (train station). The Hauptbahnhof garage (€15/day) is under the station near all recommended hotels.

APPENDIX

European National Tourist Offices in the United States

Belgian National Tourist Office: 220 E. 42nd St. #3402, New York, NY 10017, tel. 212/758-8130, fax 212/355-7675, www.visitbelgium.com, info@visitbelgium.com. Hotel and city guides; brochures for ABC lovers—antiques, beer, and chocolates; map of Brussels; information on WWI and WWII battlefields; and a list of Jewish sights.

Visit Britain: 551 Fifth Ave. #701, New York, NY 10176, tel. 800-462-2748, fax 212/986-1188, www.visitbritain.com, travelinfo@visitbritain.org. Free maps of London and Britain. Regional information, garden-tour map, urban cultural-activities brochures.

French Government Tourist Office: 444 Madison Ave., 16th floor, New York, NY 10022, fax 212/838-7855, www.franceguide.com, info.us@franceguide.com. For questions and brochures (on regions, barging, wine country, etc.), call 410/286-8310 or order online. One brochure and the *France Guide* magazine are free; additional brochures are $0.50 each, with a handling fee of $2 per order. Order will arrive in 2–3 weeks; rush delivery is extra.

German National Tourist Office: Maps, Rhine schedules, castles, biking, genealogical information, and city and regional information. Visit www.cometogermany.com and contact the nearest office:

In New York: 122 E. 42nd St. #2000, New York, NY 10168, tel. 800-651-7010 or 212/661-7200, fax 212/661-7174, gntonyc@d-z-t.com.

In Illinois: P.O. Box 59594, Chicago, IL 60659, tel. 773/539-6303, fax 773/539-6378, gntoch@aol.com.

In California: 501 Santa Monica Blvd. #607, Santa Monica, CA

90401, tel. 310/394-2580, fax 310/260-2923, info@gntolax.com.
Netherlands Board of Tourism: 355 Lexington Ave., 19th floor,
New York, NY 10017, tel. 212/557-3500, fax 212/370-9507, www.holland.
com, information@holland.com. They no longer distribute printed material; all information is now available only on the Internet.

U.S. Embassies and Consulates

Belgium: U.S. Embassy at Regentlaan 27 Boulevard du Regent, Brussels
(Mon–Fri 9:00–18:00, closed Sat–Sun; passport services Mon–Fri
13:30–16:30, closed Sat–Sun; tel. 02/508-2111, www.usembassy.be).

Britain: U.S. Embassy at 24 Grosvenor Square, London (Tube:
Bond Street, tel. 020/7499-9000, www.usembassy.org.uk).

France: U.S. Embassy at 2 avenue Gabriel, Paris (to the left as you
face Hôtel Crillon, Mo: Concorde, tel. 01 43 12 22 22). U.S. Consulate
at 2 rue St. Florentin, Paris (Mon–Fri 9:00–13:00, closed Sat–Sun, Mo:
Concorde, tel. 01 43 12 22 22, www.amb-usa.fr).

Germany: U.S. Embassy at Neustädtische Kirchstrasse 4–5, Berlin
(tel. 030/83050). U.S. Consulate at Clayallee 170, Berlin (Mon–Fri
8:30–12:00, closed Sat-Sun, tel. 030/832-9233—Mon–Fri 14:00–16:00
only, www.usembassy.de, consberlin@state.gov).

The Netherlands: U.S. Embassy at Lange Voorhout 102, The Hague
(Mon–Fri 8:15–17:00, closed Sat–Sun, tel. 070/310-2209, www.usemb.nl).
U.S. Consulate at Museumplein 19, Amsterdam (for passport concerns, open
Mon–Fri 8:30–11:30, closed Sat–Sun, tel. 020/575-5309, http://netherlands
.usembassy.gov/consular_visa.html, consularamster@state.gov).

Let's Talk Telephones

To make international calls, you need to break the codes: the international access codes and country codes (see next page). For information
on making local, long-distance, and international calls, see "Telephones"
in this book's introduction.

Country Codes

After you've dialed the international access code (011 if you're calling
from the U.S.A. or Canada; 00 if you're calling from Europe), dial the
code of the country you're calling.

Austria—43
Belgium—32
Britain—44
Canada—1
Croatia—385
Czech Rep.—420
Denmark—45
Estonia—372
Finland—358
France—33
Germany—49
Gibraltar—350
Greece—30
Ireland—353

Italy—39
Morocco—212
Netherlands—31
Norway—47
Poland—48
Portugal—351
Slovakia—421
Slovenia—386
Spain—34
Sweden—46
Switzerland—41
Turkey—90
U.S.A.—1

Numbers and Stumblers

- Europeans write a few of their numbers differently than we do: 1 = 1,
  4 = 4, 7 = 7. Learn the difference or miss your train.
- Europeans write dates as day/month/year (Christmas is 25/12/07).
- Commas are decimal points, and decimals are commas. A dollar and
  a half is 1,50. There are 5.280 feet in a mile.
- When counting with fingers, start with your thumb. If you hold up
  your first finger to request one item, you'll probably get two.
- What we Americans call the second floor of a building is the first
  floor in Europe.
- Europeans keep the left "lane" open for passing on escalators and
  moving sidewalks. Keep to the right.

Metric Conversion (approximate)

1 inch = 25 millimeters	32°F = 0°C
1 foot = 0.3 meter	82°F = about 28°C
1 yard = 0.9 meter	1 ounce = 28 grams
1 mile = 1.6 kilometers	1 kilogram = 2.2 pounds
1 centimeter = 0.4 inch	1 quart = 0.95 liter
1 meter = 39.4 inches	1 square yard = 0.8 square meter
1 kilometer = 0.62 mile	1 acre = 0.4 hectare

European Calling Chart

Just smile and dial, using this key:
AC = Area Code, LN = Local Number.

European Country	Calling long distance within ...	Calling from the U.S.A./ Canada to ...	Calling from a European country to ...
Austria	AC + LN	011 + 43 + AC (without the initial zero) + LN	00 + 43 + AC (without the initial zero) + LN
Belgium	LN	011 + 32 + LN (without initial zero)	00 + 32 + LN (without initial zero)
Britain	AC + LN	011 + 44 + AC (without initial zero) + LN	00 + 44 + AC (without initial zero) + LN
Croatia	AC + LN	011 + 385 + AC (without initial zero) + LN	00 + 385 + AC (without initial zero) + LN
Czech Republic	LN	011 + 420 + LN	00 + 420 + LN
Denmark	LN	011 + 45 + LN	00 + 45 + LN
Finland	AC + LN	011 + 358 + AC (without initial zero) + LN	00 + 358 + AC (without initial zero) + LN
France	LN	011 + 33 + LN (without initial zero)	00 + 33 + LN (without initial zero)
Germany	AC + LN	011 + 49 + AC (without initial zero) + LN	00 + 49 + AC (without initial zero) + LN
Greece	LN	011 + 30 + LN	00 + 30 + LN
Hungary	06 + AC + LN	011 + 36 + AC + LN	00 + 36 + AC + LN
Ireland	AC + LN	011 + 353 + AC (without initial zero) + LN	00 + 353 + AC (without initial zero) + LN
Italy	LN	011 + 39 + LN	00 + 39 + LN

European Country	Calling long distance within ...	Calling from the U.S.A./ Canada to ...	Calling from a European country to ...
Netherlands	AC + LN	011 + 31 + AC (without initial zero) + LN	00 + 31 + AC (without initial zero) + LN
Norway	LN	011 + 47 + LN	00 + 47 + LN
Poland	AC + LN	011 + 48 + AC (without initial zero) + LN	00 + 48 + AC (without initial zero) + LN
Portugal	LN	011 + 351 + LN	00 + 351 + LN
Slovakia	AC + LN	011 + 421 + AC (without initial zero) + LN	00 + 421 + AC (without initial zero) + LN
Slovenia	AC + LN	011 + 386 + AC (without initial zero) + LN	00 + 386 + AC (without initial zero) + LN
Spain	LN	011 + 34 + LN	00 + 34 + LN
Sweden	AC + LN	011 + 46 + AC (without initial zero) + LN	00 + 46 + AC (without initial zero) + LN
Switzerland	LN	011 + 41 + LN (without initial zero)	00 + 41 + LN (without initial zero)
Turkey	AC (if no initial zero is included, add one) + LN	011 + 90 + AC (without initial zero) + LN	00 + 90 + AC (without initial zero) + LN

- The instructions above apply whether you're calling a fixed phone or mobile phone.
- The international access codes (the first numbers you dial when making an international call) are 011 if you're calling from the U.S.A./Canada, or 00 if you're calling from anywhere in Europe.
- To call the U.S.A. or Canada from Europe, dial 00, then 1 (the country code for the U.S.A. and Canada), then the area code and number. In short, 00 + 1 + AC + LN = Hi, Mom!

Climate

Here is a list of average temperatures (first line—average daily low; second line—average daily high; third line—days of no rain).

	J	F	M	A	M	J	J	A	S	O	N	D
BELGIUM • Brussels												
	30°	32°	36°	41°	46°	52°	54°	54°	51°	45°	38°	32°
	40°	44°	51°	58°	65°	72°	73°	72°	69°	60°	48°	42°
	10	11	14	12	15	15	14	13	17	14	10	12
BRITAIN • London												
	36°	36°	38°	42°	47°	53°	56°	56°	52°	46°	42°	38°
	43°	44°	50°	56°	62°	69°	71°	71°	65°	58°	50°	45°
	16	15	20	18	19	19	19	20	17	18	15	16
FRANCE • Paris												
	34°	34°	39°	43°	49°	55°	58°	58°	53°	46°	40°	36°
	43°	45°	54°	60°	68°	73°	76°	75°	70°	60°	50°	44°
	14	14	19	17	19	18	19	18	17	18	15	15
GERMANY • Berlin												
	23°	23°	30°	38°	45°	51°	55°	54°	48°	40°	33°	26°
	35°	38°	48°	56°	64°	70°	74°	73°	67°	56°	44°	36°
	15	12	18	15	16	13	15	15	17	18	15	16
NETHERLANDS • Amsterdam												
	31°	31°	34°	40°	46°	51°	55°	55°	50°	44°	38°	33°
	40°	42°	49°	56°	64°	70°	72°	71°	67°	57°	48°	42°
	9	9	15	14	17	16	14	13	11	11	9	10

Temperature Conversion: Fahrenheit and Celsius

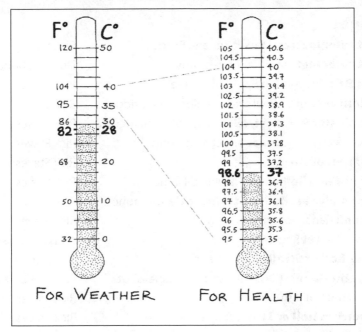

Europe takes its temperature using the Celsius scale, while we opt for Fahrenheit. For weather, remember that 28°C is 82°F—perfect. For health, 37°C is just right.

CREDITS

Images

Front color matter: Market Square, Bruges — Rick Steves

Front color matter: Eiffel Tower, Paris — Dominic Bonuccelli

Great Britain: London Eye Ferris Wheel — Rick Steves

London: View of St. Paul's from Millennium Bridge — Rick Steves

Westminster Roll or Stroll: Houses of Parliament — Rick Steves

France: Anne Steves in a Paris cheese shop — Rick Steves

Paris: The Louvre — Rick Steves

Historic Paris Roll or Stroll: Notre-Dame — Rick Steves

Champs-Elysées Roll or Stroll: Arc de Triomphe — Rick Steves

Belgium: Canal boat ride in Bruges — Rick Steves

Bruges: Market Square — Jennifer Hauseman

Bruges Roll or Stroll: Bruges Canal — Ken Plattner

The Netherlands: Classic Amsterdam canal shot — Rick Steves

Amsterdam: Rijksmuseum — Rick Steves

Amsterdam Roll or Stroll: Amsterdam canal — Rick Steves

Haarlem: Market Square — Rick Steves

Germany: Bacharach — Dominic Bonuccelli

Rhine Valley: Bacharach and the Rhine — Dominic Bonuccelli

Basic French Survival Phrases

English	French	Phonetics
Good day.	**Bonjour.**	bohn-zhoor
Mrs./Mr.	**Madame/Monsieur**	mah-dahm/muhs-yur
Do you speak English?	**Parlez-vous anglais?**	par-lay-voo ahn-glay
Yes./No.	**Oui./Non.**	wee/nohn
I understand.	**Je comprends.**	zhuh kohn-prahn
I don't understand.	**Je ne comprends pas.**	zhuh nun kohn-prahn pah
Please.	**S'il vous plaît.**	see voo play
Thank you.	**Merci.**	mehr-see
I'm sorry.	**Désolé.**	day-zoh-lay
Excuse me.	**Pardon.**	par-dohn
(No) problem.	**(Pas de) problème.**	(pah duh) proh-blehm
It's good.	**C'est bon.**	say bohn
Goodbye.	**Au revoir.**	oh vwahr
one/two	**un/deux**	uhn/duh
three/four	**trois/quatre**	twah/kah-truh
five/six	**cinq/six**	sank/sees
seven/eight	**sept/huit**	seht/weet
nine/ten	**neuf/dix**	nuhf/dees
How much is it?	**Combien?**	kohn-bee-an
Write it?	**Ecrivez?**	ay-kree-vay
Is it free?	**C'est gratuit?**	say grah-twee
Included?	**Inclus?**	an-klew
Where can I buy/find...?	**Où puis-je acheter/ trouver...?**	oo pwee-zhuh ah-shuh-tay/ troo-vay
I'd like/We'd like...	**Je voudrais/ Nous voudrions...**	zhuh voo-dray/ noo voo-dree-ohn
...a room.	**...une chambre.**	ewn shahn-bruh
...the bill.	**...l'addition.**	lah-dee-see-ohn
...a ticket to ___.	**...un billet pour ___.**	uhn bee-yay poor
Is it possible?	**C'est possible?**	say poh-see-bluh
Where is...?	**Où est...?**	oo ay
...the train station	**...la gare**	lah gar
...the bus station	**...la gare routière**	lah gar root-yehr
...tourist information	**...l'office du tourisme**	loh-fees dew too-reez-muh
Where are the toilets?	**Où sont les toilettes?**	oo sohn lay twah-leht
men	**hommes**	ohm
women	**dames**	dahm
left/right	**à gauche/à droite**	ah gohsh/ah dwaht
straight	**tout droit**	too dwah
When does this open/ close?	**Ça ouvre/ferme**	sah oo-vruh/fehrm
At what time?	**À quelle heure?**	ah kehl ur
Just a moment.	**Un moment.**	uhn moh-mahn
now/soon/later	**maintenant/bientôt/ plus tard**	man-tuh-nahn/bee-an-toh/ plew tar
today/tomorrow	**aujourd'hui/demain**	oh-zhoor-dwee/duh-man

When using the phonetics, try to nasalize the n sound.

For more user-friendly French phrases, check out Rick Steves' French Phrase Book and Dictionary or Rick Steves' French, Italian & German Phrase Book and Dictionary.

Basic German Survival Phrases

Good day.	**Guten Tag**.	**goo**-ten tahg
Do you speak English?	**Sprechen Sie Englisch?**	**shprekh**-en zee **eng**-lish
Yes. / No.	**Ja. / Nein.**	yah / nīn
I (don't) understand.	**Ich verstehe (nicht).**	ikh fehr-**shtay**-heh (nikht)
Please.	**Bitte.**	**bit**-teh
Thank you.	**Danke.**	**dahng**-keh
I'm sorry.	**Es tut mir leid.**	es toot meer līt
Excuse me.	**Entschuldigung.**	ent-**shool**-dee-goong
(No) problem.	**(Kein) Problem.**	(kīn) proh-**blaym**
(Very) good.	**(Sehr) gut.**	(zehr) goot
Goodbye.	**Auf Wiedersehen.**	owf **vee**-der-zayn
one / two	**eins / zwei**	īns / tsvī
three / four	**drei / vier**	drī / feer
five / six	**fünf / sechs**	fewnf / zex
seven / eight	**sieben / acht**	zee-ben / ahkht
nine / ten	**neun / zehn**	noyn / tsayn
How much is it?	**Wieviel kostet das?**	**vee**-feel **kos**-tet dahs
Write it?	**Schreiben?**	**shrī**-ben
Is it free?	**Ist es umsonst?**	ist es oom-**zohnst**
Included?	**Inklusive?**	in-kloo-**see**-veh
Where can I	**Wo kann ich**	voh kahn ikh
buy / find...?	**kaufen / finden...?**	**kow**-fen / **fin**-den
I'd like /	**Ich hätte gern /**	ikh **het**-teh gehrn
We'd like...	**Wir hätten gern...**	veer **het**-ten gehrn
...a room.	**...ein Zimmer.**	īn **tsim**-mer
...the bill.	**...die Rechnung.**	dee **rekh**-noong
...a ticket to ___.	**...eine Fahrkarte nach**	ī-neh **far**-kar-teh nahkh
Is it possible?	**Ist es möglich?**	ist es **mur**-glikh
Where is...?	**Wo ist..?**	voh ist
...the train station	**...der Bahnhof**	dehr **bahn**-hohf
...the bus station	**...der Busbahnhof**	dehr **boos**-bahn-hof
...tourist information	**...das Touristen-**	dahs too-ris-ten-
	informationsbüro	in-for-maht-see-
		ohns-bew-roh
...toilet	**...die Toilette**	dee toh-**leh**-teh
men	**herren**	**hehr**-ren
women	**damen**	**dah**-men
left / right	**links / rechts**	links / rekhts
straight	**geradeaus**	geh-rah-deh-**ows**
When is this	**Um wieviel Uhr ist hier**	oom **vee**-feel oor ist heer
open / closed?	**geöffnet /**	geh-**urf**-net /
	geschlossen?	geh-**shlos**-sen
At what time?	**Um wieviel Uhr?**	oom **vee**-feel oor
Just a moment.	**Moment.**	moh-**ment**
now / soon / later	**jetzt / bald / später**	yetzt / bahld / **shpay**-ter
today / tomorrow	**heute / morgen**	**hoy**-teh / **mor**-gen

When using the phonetics, pronounce ī as the long i sound in "light."

Slow Walkers: Faxing Your Hotel Reservation

You can photocopy this form and fax it to the hotel (it's also online at www.ricksteves
.com/reservation).

One-Page Fax

To: _____ @ _____
         hotel   *fax*

From: _____ @_____
            name   *fax*

Today's date: _____ / _____ / _____
           day   *month*   *year*

Dear Hotel _____ ,

My name: _____

Total # of people: _____ Number of rooms: _____

Room(s): Single _____ Double _____ Twin _____ Triple _____Quad _____

With private bathroom _____ Bathroom down the hall _____

# of nights: _____

Arriving: _____ / _____ / _____ My time of arrival (24-hr clock): _____
      day   *month*   *year* (I will telephone if I will be late)

Departing: _____ / _____ / _____
       day   *month*   *year*

I have difficulty walking. I have the following needs:

No stairs _____ Very few stairs _____ Ground floor room _____ Elevator _____

If you have a suitable room available, please reserve it for me. Please fax, mail, or e-mail confirmation of my reservation, along with the type of room reserved and the price. Please also inform me of your cancellation policy. After I hear from you, I will quickly send my credit-card information as a deposit to hold the room. Thank you.

_____
Signature

_____
Name

_____
Address

_____
City   *State*   *Zip Code*   *Country*

_____
E-mail Address

Wheelchair Users: Faxing Your Hotel Reservation

You can photocopy this form and fax it to the hotel (it's also online at www.ricksteves
.com/reservation).

One-Page Fax

To: _____ @ _____
         hotel   *fax*

From: _____ @_____
           name   *fax*

Today's date: _____ / _____ / _____
                      day   *month*   *year*

Dear Hotel _____ ,

I use a wheelchair and would like to stay at your hotel if you have a room that meets my needs.

Total # of people: _____   Number of rooms: _____

Single _____   Double _____   Twin _____   Triple _____   Quad _____

With private bathroom _____   Bathroom down the hall _____

# of nights: _____

Arriving: _____ / _____ / _____   My time of arrival (24-hr clock): _____
               day   *month*   *year*   (I will telephone if I will be late)

Departing: _____ / _____ / _____
                 day   *month*   *year*

My wheelchair measurements are _____ cm (width) and _____ cm (height).

I have the following needs:

_____ No steps at the hotel entrance or to my hotel room

_____ Doorways at hotel entrance and in the hotel room wide enough for my wheelchair

_____ A ground-floor room or an elevator large enough for my wheelchair

_____ An adapted bathroom with these features: _____ low sink, _____ roll-in shower,
_____ grab bars for tub, _____ handheld shower nozzle, _____ grab bars for toilet

If you have a suitable room available, please reserve it for me. Please fax, mail, or e-mail confirmation
of my reservation, along with the type of room reserved and the price. Please also inform me of your
cancellation policy. After I hear from you, I will quickly send my credit-card information as a deposit
to hold the room. Thank you.

_____
Signature

_____
Name

_____
Address

_____
City   **State**   **Zip Code**   **Country**

_____
E-mail Address

INDEX

Start your trip at
www.ricksteves.com

Rick Steves' website is packed with over 3,000 pages of timely travel information. It's also your gateway to getting FREE monthly travel news from Rick — and more!

Free Monthly European Travel News

Fresh articles on Europe's most interesting destinations and happenings. Rick will even send you an e-mail every month (often direct from Europe) with his latest discoveries!

Timely Travel Tips

Rick Steves' best money-and-stress-saving tips on trip planning, packing, transportation, hotels, health, safety, finances, hurdling the language barrier…and more.

Travelers' Graffiti Wall

Candid advice and opinions from thousands of travelers on everything listed above, plus whatever topics are hot at the moment (discount flights, packing tips, scams…you name it).

Rick's Annual Guide to European Railpasses

The clearest, most comprehensive guide to the confusing array of railpass options out there, and how to choo-choose the railpass that best fits your itinerary and budget. Then you can order your railpass (and get a bunch of great freebies) online from us!

Great Gear at the Rick Steves Travel Store

Enjoy bargains on Rick's guidebooks, planning maps and TV series DVDs—and on his custom-designed carry-on bags, wheeled bags, day bags and light-packing accessories.

Rick Steves Tours

Every year more than 6,000 lucky travelers explore Europe on a Rick Steves tour. Learn more about our 30 different one-to-three-week itineraries, read uncensored feedback from our tour alums, and sign up for your dream trip online!

Rick on Radio and TV

Read the scripts and run clips from public television's "Rick Steves' Europe" and public radio's "Travel with Rick Steves."

Respect for Your Privacy

Ordering online from us is secure. When you buy something from us, join a tour, or subscribe to Rick's free monthly travel news e-mails, we promise to never share your name, information, or e-mail address with anyone else. You won't be spammed!

Have fun raising your Travel I.Q. at
www.ricksteves.com

Travel smart...carry on!

The latest generation of Rick Steves' carry-on travel bags is easily the best—benefiting from two decades of on-the-road attention to what really matters: maximum quality and strength; practical, flexible features; and no unnecessary frills. You won't find a better value anywhere!

Convertible, expandable, and carry-on-size:
Rick Steves' Back Door Bag $99

This is the same bag that Rick Steves lives out of for three months every summer. It's made of rugged water-resistant 1000 denier Cordura nylon, and best of all, it converts easily from a smart-looking suitcase to a handy back-pack with comfortably-curved shoulder straps and a padded waistbelt.

This roomy, versatile 9" x 21" x 14" bag has a large 2600 cubic-inch main compartment, plus three outside pockets (small, medium and huge) that are perfect for often-used items. And the cinch-tight compression straps will keep your load compact and close to your back—not sagging like a sack of potatoes.

Wishing you had even more room to bring home souvenirs? Pull open the full-perimeter expando-zipper and its capacity jumps from 2600 to 3000 cubic inches. When you want to use it as a suitcase or check it as luggage (required when "expanded"), the straps and belt hide away in a zippered compartment in the back.

Attention travelers under 5'4" tall: This bag also comes in an inch-shorter version, for a compact-friendlier fit between the waistbelt and shoulder straps.

Convenient, expandable, and carry-on-size:
Rick Steves' Wheeled Bag $129

At 9" x 21" x 14" our sturdy Rick Steves' Wheeled Bag is rucksack-soft in front, but the rest is lined with a hard ABS-lexan shell to give maximum protection to your belongings. We've spared no expense on moving parts, splurging on an extra-long button-release handle and big, tough inline skate wheels for easy rolling on rough surfaces.

Wishing you had even more room to bring home souvenirs? Pull open the full-perimeter expando-zipper and its capacity jumps from 2600 to 3000 cubic inches.

Rick Steves' Wheeled Bag has exactly the same three-outside-pocket configuration as our Back Door Bag, plus a handy "add-a-bag" strap and full lining.

Our Back Door Bags and Wheeled Bags come in black, navy, blue spruce, evergreen and merlot.

For great deals on a wide selection of travel goodies, begin your next trip at the Rick Steves Travel Store!

Visit the Rick Steves Travel Store at
www.ricksteves.com

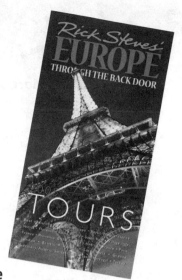

Rick Steves

More *Savvy.* More *Surprising.* More *Fun.*

COUNTRY GUIDES 2006

England
France
Germany & Austria
Great Britain
Ireland
Italy
Portugal
Scandinavia
Spain
Switzerland

CITY GUIDES 2006

Amsterdam, Bruges & Brussels
Florence & Tuscany
London
Paris
Prague & The Czech Republic
Provence & The French Riviera
Rome
Venice

BEST OF GUIDES

Best of Eastern Europe
Best of Europe

As the #1 authority on European travel, Rick gives you inside information on what to visit, where to stay, and how to get there—economically and hassle-free.

www.ricksteves.com

PHRASE BOOKS & DICTIONARIES

French
French, Italian & German
German
Italian
Portuguese
Spanish

MORE EUROPE FROM RICK STEVES

Easy Access Europe
Europe 101
Europe Through the Back Door
Postcards from Europe

RICK STEVES' EUROPE DVDs

All 43 Shows 2000-2005
Britain
Eastern Europe
France & Benelux
Germany, The Swiss Alps & Travel
Skills
Ireland
Italy
Spain & Portugal

PLANNING MAPS

Britain & Ireland
Europe
France
Germany, Austria & Switzerland
Italy
Spain & Portugal

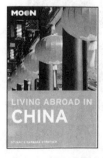

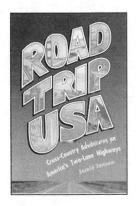

For a complete listing of Rick Steves' books, see page 13.
Avalon Travel Publishing
1400 65th Street, Suite 250
Emeryville, CA 94608

For the latest on Rick Steves' lectures, guidebooks, tours, public radio show, and public television series, contact Europe Through the Back Door, Box 2009, Edmonds, WA 98020, tel. 425/771-8303, fax 425/771-0833, www.ricksteves.com, or rick@ricksteves .com.

ISBN (10): 1-56691-999-1
ISBN (13): 978-1-56691-999-9
ISSN: 1549-1811

Europe Through the Back Door Editors: Cameron Hewitt, Kevin Yip,
   Jennifer Hauseman
ETBD Managing Editor: Risa Laib
Avalon Travel Publishing and Series Manager: Patrick Collins
Avalon Travel Publishing Editor: Madhu Prasher
Copy Editor: Mia Lipman
Indexer: Stephen Callahan
Research Assistance: Carol Fisher
Production & Typesetting: Patrick David Barber, Holly McGuire
Cover Design: Kari Gim, Laura Mazer
Maps and Graphics: David C. Hoerlein, Lauren Mills, Laura VanDeventer
Photography: Rick Steves, Ken Plattner, Gene Openshaw, Cameron Hewitt, Bruce
   VanDeventer
Front Matter Color Photos: Bruges Square, Bruges ©Rick Steves; Eiffel Tower, Paris
   ©Dominic Bonuccelli
Cover Photo: front image, Flower Market in Brussels ©Novastock/FOLIO, Inc.; back
   image, Michelangelo's *Slaves*, Louvre, Paris ©Rick Steves
Distributed to the book trade by Publishers Group West, Berkeley, California